A
STUDY
IN
COURAGE

A
STUDY
IN
COURAGE

The Story of
Jan and Catharina Wübbena
and Their Ten Children

Edited by
D. W. & B. B. HENDRICKS

PUBLISHED BY B&D PRESS

Hershey, Pennsylvania

Published by B&D Press
Burton and Dawn Hendricks
56 Brownstone Drive
Hershey, Pennsylvania 17033-2501
(717) 534-2962
Produced by B. Williams & Associates
1009 West Main Street
Durham, North Carolina 27701
(919) 956-9111

Manufactured in the U.S.A.

First edition, first printing

Library of Congress Cataloging in Publication Data:
A study in courage : the story of Jan and Catharina Wübbena
and their ten children /
[compiled by Burton Hendricks, Dawn Wubbena Hendricks]. — 1st ed.
p.   cm.
Includes index.
ISBN 0-9650662-0-7 (lib. bdg.)
1. German Americans—Biography. 2. Wübbena family. 3. Wübbena,
Jan Janssen, 1845–1907—Family. 4. Wübbena, Catharina Jungjohann,
1855–1894—Family. I. Hendricks, Burton B. 1923– .
II. Hendricks, Dawn Wubbena, 1926– .
E184.G3S84   1996   96-1745
939'.2'08931073 — dc20   CIP

*This book is dedicated
to the memory of
Jan and Catharina Wübbena,
for the courage and character
they exhibited in their struggle
to succeed in this new world.*

CONTENTS

LIST OF MAPS

ACKNOWLEDGMENTS

A large number of persons worked on this book. Probably some should be mentioned by name. Lois Dick was the person that undertook to get the Wubbena cousins interested, motivated, and started. Catherine Wubbena, assisted by her dedicated helper Carol Yops, was a mainstay in research and writing. She authored more pages of the book than anyone else; reestablished a link with Germany; worked with patience to uncover the details of Jan's naturalization in supposedly lost records in the vaults of the Arenac County Court House; helped collect the family photographs; and so on. Bill and Marie Wubbena were responsible for assembling the family tree. Bill also was the person who went to the National Archives and searched until he located the records for the 1886 trip of the steamship *Trave* which brought the young family to the United States. Pastor Günter Fassbender of Tergast and our newly-found cousin, Jan Jungjohann of Moormerland (both towns in Ostfriesland, Germany), supplied a gratifyingly large amount of information regarding our Frisian heritage.

Lastly, we would like to express our special appreciation to: Professor James Scott for his translation of Jan's sea log, farm journal, and steersman certificate; Joe Hawk for the preliminary draft of the Standish maps; Bill Gray of A&M Drafting for the maps and the diagrams of the Old World family tree; Erin Willder for her fine editorial work; and Barbara Williams and her entire staff for putting it all together.

The identified authorship of the various writings indicate many others who also helped. In most cases each person whose name appears was assisted by at least one other person that remains anonymous merely because we felt that if we were to try to start naming all who helped we would inadvertently leave others out.

A Note of Thanks

This book would not have been published without the impetus of Burton B. Hendricks. Burt is the husband of Dawn Eleanor Wubbena (daughter of the youngest of the "Original Ten," William).

Burt and his brother Charles have produced an extensive and comprehensive Hendricks family book involving oral history as well as research in Europe. That project convinced Burt that family history is both precious and perishable. For many months he urged us to begin work on a Wubbena family book. When we did not, he undertook the effort himself.

The casual reader of this book cannot grasp the hundreds of hours Burt has devoted to it, including all of the typing. Moreover, he and Dawn have totally financed its publication.

We are unable to express our thanks in sufficient force—Burt has preserved our heritage.

William L. Wubbena, Jr.

PREFACE

by Catherine Wubbena

This book is written with the intent that there will be a record of what might otherwise be forgotten. The strength of character of the immigrants as they arrived here, bringing the richness of generations of culture, was reflected in their reactions to the conditions they faced. Jan and Catharina Wübbena refused to consider the lands they left behind a vanished world. Instead they maintained here the Old World skills and abilities, and the tradition of family stability and cohesiveness, and blended these values with the newness and freshness of what they deemed to be the best in their new way of life. The stories of their lives could be read in their faces. In their later years the wrinkles and crinkles around their blue eyes and the sets of their mouths with lines of tenderness and stern purpose spoke volumes of their self-reliance.

How much did the ten children inherit from their parents? Except for the first four, the children hardly knew their mother. Yet each spoke of her with tenderness. Their father served as a vivid example of sturdy perseverance in the face of hardships, of an unshakable faith in the value of an education, and of the wonderful strength that comes from the bonds of family.

We, the authors of this book, are descendants of those ten children.* Much of who and what we are was shaped by them and their parents. Are we too late to set down in writing something of what they knew and felt? We

---

*As of June 21, 1995, there were 198 living descendants of Jan and Catharina Wübbena living in twenty-eight states and five foreign countries. The largest concentrations lived in the states of Michigan (72), Texas (16), California (13), Virginia (10) and Pennsylvania (8).

hope not. We all need to carry with us their courage and strength if we are to retain the values and the greatness that they could see in this new land. Memories have flooded our minds as we have tried to recapture and put into words what our ancestors bequeathed to us. We are filled with awe as we sort out our memories and realize how many are worth recording and saving.

May God's blessing and guidance be with those of us who feel committed to uphold our ancestors' values. We're all one family! As the hymn writer tells us, "We praise Him for all that is past, and trust Him for all that's to come."

INTRODUCTION

FAMILY UNITY, MUTUAL SUPPORT, LOVE

An Introduction
by William L. Wubbena, Jr.

The offspring of Jan Janssen and Catharina Jungjohann Wübbena were remarkable in many ways. Theirs was a special family whose great strength was manifested by unmatched unity and mutual support. Their love for one another was total, and that support was a constant— sometimes subtle, sometimes open, sometimes requested. My father, William, was the youngest of those ten children and quite possibly the biggest beneficiary of that support. He spoke of the family history in a worshipful way and adored each of his nine siblings.

It is surprising that the family survived at all. That the family survived *intact* is amazing, a testimony to the character and tenacity of each member, but *especially* of the eldest children—those who came from Germany. They took over when tragedy struck: Aunt Talka became "mother" at twelve. Uncle John did not marry until his younger brothers and sisters were in their teens and no longer depended upon him as the de facto "father."

John's and Talka's sacrifices were wonderful and were never forgotten by the other children. To my father, Talka and John were saints; the others contributed much as well and he felt they too were very close to sainthood. One need only consider that Catharina died when my father was three weeks old. Jan died when he was thirteen. The ten children scratched to survive as an immigrant family, first without a mother and then without parents. They attempted to farm without any real knowledge of farming. They got by, in quiet desperation, simply through united effort. There were no gaps. The older ones, working away from home, sent money. While he was alive, Jan kept the working children informed of the family's needs and the appreciation for their contributions. Later, as "father," John took control. They were ten, but together they had the strength of many times more.

We can assume, no doubt, that these ten received a full dose of Teutonic discipline: Jan was a naval person; Catharina was a traditional *Hausfrau*. This needs no elaboration; the children knew right and wrong, good and evil, and were taught to adhere to the right and to seek the good—period.

If discipline was a source of strength, it was buttressed by religious faith. God was the ultimate determinant. The early years held intense, active worship and mandatory attendance at Gospel Hall meetings. Spiritually, then, the twigs were all bent properly. On their own, some, mostly the girls, continued in their demonstrative worship. Scripture threaded their conversation, easily and sincerely, along with praises for and reference to our Savior. Others, like my father and John, eschewed religious ritual but retained a deep and abiding faith. They remembered the Sabbath, and prayer remained a powerful force in their lives.

But discipline plus faith in God did not alone equate to family unity and mutual support. The other ingredient was love. Their love for one another reached beyond mere affection or fondness; it was devotion to the individual and respect for the person; it was total. Every memory of every incident is touched by the love of this miraculous group of people—this family. The second and third generations relate multiple examples of this love in the accounts about each of the ten (see Part Five).

No analysis can truly explain this unity and mutual support. We cannot reconstruct it; we can reflect on it and we can understand it. On the farm they labored for a common goal; they sacrificed for the greater need. Later they watched over one another and helped in every possible way. Note that once, when my father was very young, he lost his job, and Uncle Harry wrote to Uncle John to tip him off that Bill had played around (to Harry's and Fred's displeasure) and "blew it." We can only imagine what John had to say when Dad arrived back at John's farm to stay with him and Aunt Laura for a while, but whatever he said must have worked.

They all knew where the others were and what they were doing. There were no unanswered questions, no doubts—they *knew*! This unity and mutual, loving support lasted a lifetime and beyond. An immigrant family, against fierce odds, made its way and prospered. Not one member ever received welfare or relief from local, state, or federal agencies. Not one member ever ran afoul of the law. All members are remembered in their communities with respect and admiration. They stayed in touch, however distant they lived, and continued their support and love over the years.

The "chain letter" was an outgrowth of this phenomenon. It kept everyone in constant touch. That institution still continues today, with their children now keeping in touch in this same mode. [See page 617 for a description of how the chain letter operated.]

In 1946, the family held a reunion in Standish. It was the last time all ten were to be together. They formed an "Alumni Association" to institutionalize the group—a step that speaks volumes. They were, by that time, spread coast-to-coast and they seemed driven to reassert continued unity.

Also speaking volumes at that reunion were remarks by my father, who described the family ethos. We will repeat those remarks now to underline how that love, unity, and mutual support defined their relationships with each other. Of special note is the poem at the end of his remarks, which tells us to strive for perfection, yet to be content with the best that is in us. That poem has been recited in graduation speeches by two succeeding generations. It could be a family credo.

Remarks by W. L. Wubbena, Sr.
13 August 1946
at Standish, Michigan

Mr. Toastmaster, Officers and Members of the Family Reunion Committee, Members of the Wubbena Clan, and Friends.

It is, indeed, an exceptional honor to have the privilege of being called up to answer the able and well-delivered address of welcome just received. I was overwhelmed with pride when, a few weeks ago, a letter was received which contained a request that I make a speech. Yes, a speech! As you know, a speech is something like a child—it is easy to conceive but hard to deliver and, John, circumstances prevented me from preparing one. In fact, I wouldn't know how to begin. Should I say, "Mr. Master of Ceremonies, Members of the blue-blooded, thoroughbred original ten"—then bring in the 'sprouts' and the off shoots until all individuals are encompassed, and what categories should be used? No, a speech is out of the question, and it is hoped you will be content with a few extemporaneous remarks. These remarks are based on personal impressions only, and may or may not be in harmony with the prevalent opinions of the rest of the tribe. It is not intended that any animosity, antagonism or resentment be aroused and too much importance should not be attached to anything said. With this understanding I can proceed.

Since my last attendance at a family reunion, the tribe has increased. The many here present bear witness to that fact. I understand that in addition to my own family there are many here who haven't come yet. Some of the new members were acquired by marriage, birth, adoption and other means. Now, while these members are not thoroughbreds like the original ten, they are in fact Wubbenas and therefore rank. We would remind them, however, that while they rank, we the original ten are the rankest.

The original ten can be divided into two groups—the older group and the younger group. The older group, say, from Harry on up, might be termed the family sacrificers, and the younger group might be termed the family beneficiaries. The older they were the more sacrifices were made and the younger they were the more benefits were received. I happen to be the youngest. In a world following capitalism, socialism, communism, anarchism and so on, these ten practiced what may be called 'familism.' That is to say, all efforts were devoted to the welfare of the family. All surplus over and above an individual's barest necessities was used to keep the helpless younger ones. Actual cash or currency was obtained by 'working out' procedure. This 'working out' meant working away from home, on other farms, in lumber camps, saw and heading mills, factories, stores and offices. I recall that the first 'working out' money earned by my oldest sister, Talka, was used to buy a jacket for me. Even the older members of the younger group contributed to those still younger. For instance, my education at Ferris Institute could not have been finished to the extent necessary to hold a job as a railroad telegrapher without financial assistance from my brother, Fred.

The material benefits were meager, but the best to be afforded. It is recalled that I was around six years of age when I wore my first suit of real underwear. But, while the material benefits were scanty, we were greatly blessed with the high ideals and principles that the older ones inherited from our dear father. Of course, Mother must have entered into this character-building at some time, some way, some place, some how, but unfortunately, I do not recall her. The older ones assumed the role of parents and followed the ancient precept that, "If God Almighty should present you with a son, it is natural to rejoice, but at the same time you should tremble at the responsibility he imposes upon you. Be unto this child the image of Divinity. Command his respect until five years of age. Until ten years be his master, until twenty be his father, and until death be his friend. Think to give him good morals and principles, rather than elegant manners, that he may owe you a shining interior rather than a polished exterior, and make him a good man rather than a clever man." We were told that, "Sow a thought and reap an act, sow an act and reap a habit, sow a habit and reap a character, sow a character and reap a destiny."

Unfortunately, we were not able to develop our natural talents and follow our natural inclinations. Being victims of circumstances, we merely drifted but did the best we could with the work at hand, following the words of the poet who once said,

"If you can't be a pine on the top of the hill,
     Be a scrub in the valley, but be
The best little scrub on the side of the hill, and
     Be a bush if you can't be a tree.
If you can't be a bush, be a bit of the grass,
     Some highway to happier make, and
If you can't be a muskie, why just be a bass,
     But be the liveliest bass in the lake.
We can't all be captains, we have to have crew,
     there's something for all of us here.
There's big work to do, and there's lesser to do,
     And the work we must do is the near,
So, if you can't be a highway, just be a trail
     If you can't be a sun be a star.
It isn't by size that you win or you fail,
     Just be the best at whatever you are."

and so we merely drifted. And while none of us have made the national headlines, we take a certain amount of pride in the fact that not one of these parentless ten ever saw the inside of a jail, prison or penitentiary as a convicted inmate. On the contrary, the name of Wubbena is highly respected in every community in which one of them has ever resided. We intend to keep that record.

Although none of us have attained eminence I believe I can speak for the other members of the younger group, when I say to the Older Group, "We are proud to be your product, and we are doing our utmost to merit the sacrifices you made for us, and we are exerting every effort to make you equally proud of your handiwork." And I believe I have the concurrence of the other visitors—those vultures who come here and take advantage of these elaborate arrangements—when I say to the officers and members of the Reunion Committee, "You did a tremendous job and we are deeply indebted to you. It's a wonderful privilege to be here, and we are extremely happy to be present. Thank you very, very much."

VITAL STATISTICS OF JAN AND CATHARINA WÜBBENA AND THEIR TEN CHILDREN

Summary Compiled by Catherine Wubbena

Name, Birth Date, & Birth Place	Date & Cause of Death	Spouse & Marriage Date
Parents:		
Jan Janssen Wübbena 10 April 1845 Tergast, Germany	28 May 1907 Congestive Heart Failure & (?) Pneumonia	Catharina Jungjohann 7 December 1873
Catharina Jungjohann 31 March 1855 Neermoor, Germany	23 January 1894 Childbed Fever (Puerperal Sepsis)	Jan Janssen Wübbena 7 December 1873
Children:		
1. John 18 April 1874 Neermoor, Germany	6 July 1954 Myocardial Infarction	Laura Mary Wyatt 14 March 1911
2. Charles 8 October 1875 Neermoor, Germany	15 November 1956 Cancer & Heart Failure	Myrtle Rose Duncan 12 January 1897
3. Henry 4 November 1878 Neermoor, Germany	29 September 1962 Myocardial Infarction	Martha Link 14 June 1911
4. Talka 16 August 1881 Neermoor, Germany	20 February 1951 Cerebral Vascular Accident (Stroke) &/or Heart Attack	Not Married

6

Name, Birth Date, & Birth Place	Date & Cause of Death	Spouse & Marriage Date
5. Minnie 8 March 1887 Standish, Michigan	1 April 1974 Congestive Heart Failure	Louis W. Gabler 8 July 1913
6. Harry 8 June 1888 Standish, Michigan	6 June 1947 Cirrhosis of the Liver	Lenore Stralow 7 October 1913
7. Emma 28 September 1890 Standish, Michigan	15 August 1959 Cancer & Hypertension	George J. Flutur 24 December 1921
8. Fred 17 November 1891 Standish, Michigan	31 May 1982 Pulmonary Fibrosis with Respiratory Failure	Mildred Whyte 17 June 1925
9. Ella 26 January 1893 Standish, Michigan	28 July 1983 Cerebral Vascular Accident (Stroke)	George J. Flutur 15 October 1960
10. William 5 January 1894 Standish, Michigan	7 February 1967 Myocardial Infarction	Maude Martin 7 July 1922

Comment: It appears that various aspects of cardiovascular disease contributed to the death of almost every member of the family. All were sensitive, impulsive people, quick to respond to any situation. This neuro-vascular aspect of their constitution was apparently a genetic part of their makeup.

The one to marry first, and at a young age, was Charles who married at age 22. Harry was 25, Minn was 26, Bill was 28, Emma was 31, Henry was 33, Fred was 34, John was 37, and Ella was 67. I think it can be said that, with the possible exception of Charles, not one was swept off his or her feet at an early age.

THE ORIGINS OF JAN WÜBBENA AND CATHARINA JUNGJOHANN WÜBBENA

by Dawn W. Hendricks

Jan and Catharina came from Ostfriesland (East Friesland) which lies at the extreme northwest corner of Lower Saxony in northwest Germany [see Map G-1]. It is a flat, low-lying land, parts of which were being reclaimed from the sea and swampland during those decades of the 1800s before and after the birth of Jan and Catharina. In some senses at that time Friesland was the frontier of Germany; colonists were being brought in as the land was reclaimed.

The Friesians are an ancient people, the forebears of both the Dutch and the Germans of Ostfriesland. The Friesian language was a Germanic language quite similar to German and Dutch, though in some ways a little closer to English than either. At one time Friesland extended from what is now Bruges, Belgium, to the Weser River in Germany. The Friesians were never conquered in the sense that the other Germanic tribes finally submitted to the Roman Empire.

Only a few of the East Friesians took part in the great German tribal migrations of the second and first centuries before Christ. Instead they managed to isolate themselves from the influences to the south, where Germany was dominated first by the Romans and later by the Franks. They continued to maintain their home territory over the following centuries, thus preserving their culture, religion, and language.

Finally in 785 A.D. Friesland surrendered to King Charles the Great (Charlemagne), thus becoming a part of the Holy Roman Empire. The country was permitted to keep its own identity, being under the control of the king himself with no earl or baron ruling over them, contrary to what was customary in other parts of Germany.

These Free Friesians were left ungoverned by outsiders, with the King exercising little control over them, in substantial part due to the area in which they lived. Their land was bordered on the south by large, impenetrable forests and dangerous morasses, while the unpredictable Weser River on the east made entry on that side adventurous. The sea was to the north, and only sailors from the area knew their way through the mud flats. The Friesians were left alone in splendid isolation, which allowed them to maintain their old Friesian language and tribal organization in a semi-democratic federation.

Eventually Ostfriesland was raised to the level of a county of the Holy Roman Empire in 1454, and became a duchy in 1654. It passed to Prussia in 1744 and, after various transfers during the French revolutionary wars, was attached to Hanover in 1815. It became a Prussian province in 1866 and a German province in 1871.*

Until the Middle Ages the Friesian language was spoken throughout much of the original area of Friesland, though it was driven back toward the smaller area of Ostfriesland. The language survives today only with a few scholars, plus a few words that are in general use, such as the motto of the Friesian counts, *Eala Frya Fresena*, meaning "Always a free Friesian country."

Of course, the language survived in old names, too, though the original meaning is generally lost. The old family name "Wübbena" was once quite common in Ostfriesland, though it is not clear if the several families share an ultimate common ancestor. It was probably originally "Wibbe," of meaning unknown today. The "ena" in the old Friesian language is something like a title of nobility. In High German the noble title is "von" while in Low German it is "van," but in Friesian it is "ena."

Jan was born on April 10, 1845 in Tergast, a hamlet located a few kilometers north of Leer, and about 15 kilometers east-northeast of the Dutch border [see Map G-2]. His father was Jannes Freerks Wübbena and his mother was Taalke Janssen Reuvezaad. Jannes Freerks Wübbena and his father, Freerk Janssen Wübbena, were what is known as *Warfsluden*. That is, they leased a farm and lived from it.

Ed. Note: This sequence probably explains why Jan taught his children that they were Prussians. It may also explain why Jan's patriotism to his German fatherland was not as important to him as keeping his sons from serving in coming wars. The wars under Bismarck had cost many lives, and more wars could be expected. There had been so many changes in government that it was natural not to feel intense patriotism for Bismarck's Germany. An interesting contrast: Jan's children were always very proud that the two youngest sons and one daughter served their new country in World War I.

Jannes Freerk's mother and father both died in 1838, about two years before the first child of Jannes Freerk and Taalke Janssen Reuvezaad was born on October 27, 1840. That child, Jan Janssen, died on March 6, 1844. On April 10, 1845 their second and last child was born and given the same name—Jan Janssen. It is this Jan who married Catharina and emigrated to the United States.

The family tree of Jannes Freerks can be traced back in the records of the Tergast Evangelical Reformed Church for many generations. One of his ancestors, Johannes Wübbena, was pastor of the church from 1711 to 1734.*

Taalke Janssen Reuvezaad, Jan's mother, was born in Tergast. Her father, Jan Hinrichs Reuvezaad, was a master weaver who had been born in Midwolde in the Netherlands. That town is directly west of Tergast about fifteen kilometers inside the Dutch border in the Friesian part of Holland. In all likelihood he was Dutch-Friesian. Taalke Janssen's mother was a local girl from Tergast whose family lines can be traced back in that region for several generations.

Catharina Jungjohann was born March 31, 1855. Her father, Carl Friederich Jungjohann, who was born in the town of Uslar in the Ruhr, came to Neermoor on foot from Unna near Frankfurt in the mid-1850s, a distance of about 250 miles, when the railroad from the Port of Emden to the Ruhr was being built. He learned that a position was opening up as a train crossing guard in Neermoor. He applied for the job and was accepted. This meant that he lived with his family outside the village of Neermoor beside the railroad track in a well-built house with a large garden, pigs, chickens, and other farm animals. His position made him a respected member of the upper-middle class of those days.

Catharina's mother was Catharina Klemme. She and Carl had three children (one girl and two boys) of whom young Catharina was the oldest. When she was six her mother died and, after exactly one year, her father married Hindertje Buss who had been a maid in their home and had nursed Catharina's mother in her final illness. Hindertje undertook to raise his children by his first marriage. A year later, the first of the four children of this second marriage was born. Thus Engelke was eight years younger than Catharina.

So the children of both marriages grew up together. Gesine, the youngest,

---

Ed. Note: This pastor is also the common ancestor of Jan and Mensen Harm Wübbena, whose four sons emigrated to the United States in the second half of the nineteenth century and settled in the Midwest. See Appendix C for information regarding that "tribe" of American Wubbenas.

was born in 1875, two years after Catharina had married Jan Wubbena. Gesine spent her life with the Salvation Army in Berlin, dying at age fifty of heart trouble.

Engelke was a tailor in Neermoor until he died in 1927. His wife, Lukke, kept in touch with some of Jan's children into the late 1940s. In 1956 William visited his aunt, as did William's children, Bill and myself.

By the time Jan had been born the land was one of farms, canals, dikes, and windmills. Jan's German-born children later described such characteristics of their homeland as they related childhood memories to younger generations. It was quite natural in that setting for Jan to take up a seafaring career. Having seen other opportunities in his travels, it was then quite natural for him to consider emigrating to far-away shores to try to improve his loved ones' lot in life. His motive may have been primarily to protect his sons from military duty, or to try to improve their economic future, or other things. We really don't know. It was probably a combination of motives, as is true for most important decisions we humans make. All we know for sure is that they came.*

Ed. Note: See Appendix B for exchange of several letters between Dawn W. Hendricks and Günter O. Fassbender, Pastor of the Evangelical Reformed Church of Tergast, which amplify much of the material put forth above.

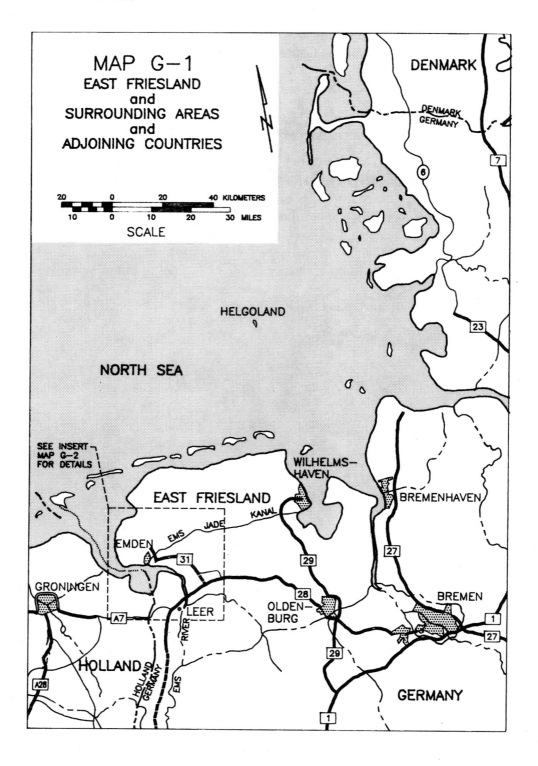

MAP G-1
EAST FRIESLAND
and
SURROUNDING AREAS
and
ADJOINING COUNTRIES

20   0   20   40 KILOMETERS
10   0   10   20   30 MILES
SCALE

DENMARK

DENMARK
GERMANY

6

7

23

HELGOLAND

NORTH SEA

SEE INSERT
MAP G-2
FOR DETAILS

EAST FRIESLAND

WILHELMS-
HAVEN

BREMENHAVEN

KANAL

EMS   JADE

EMDEN

31

29

27

GRONINGEN

A7   LEER

RIVER

OLDEN-
BURG

28

BREMEN

1

29

27

HOLLAND

HOLLAND
GERMANY

EMS

A28

GERMANY

1

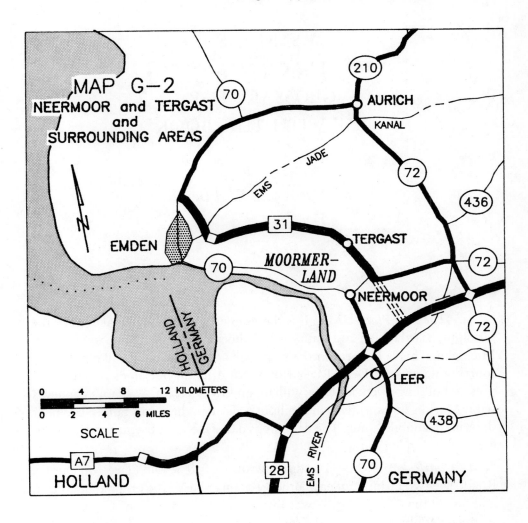

MAP G—2
NEERMOOR and TERGAST
and
SURROUNDING AREAS

A STANDISH
PLACE NAME
GLOSSARY FOR
USE WITH THIS BOOK

by Catherine Wubbena

1. *"The Old Place"* (Map I) is the term used by the Original Ten for the farm purchased by Jan and Catharina Wübbena when they came to Standish, Michigan. This is located on the south side of Johnsfield Road about one-fourth mile west of Deep River Road. No original buildings remain. The present buildings were built by William and Eve Ingram. William's nephew's wife (Marion Ingram) lives in the house; her daughter and family live next door in the mobile home. The daughter's name is Karen Irwin, and the property is listed in her name.

2. *Charles' farm* (Map I) is directly south of "The Old Place" on Dupres Road. The two farms abut each other. Tenants abused the original buildings, and finally the original house was burned down by an arsonist. Shirley and Jeannette Wubbena bought the farm and built a new house. Since Shirley's death in 1972, Jeannette continued to own the property and live in the house until her death in 1995.

3. *Henry's Farm* (Map I), located at the southwest corner of Johnsfield and Deep River Roads, is directly east of the "Old Place." The two properties abut each other. After Henry relinquished ownership, the farm was owned by the Holevar family. The property has since been divided and Red (Leon) Treichel now owns the greater share of it.

4. *The Johnsfield School building* (Map I) was located about a mile west of "The Old Place" on the south side of Johnsfield Road. The old wood building, which was built in 1894, burned down (cause unknown) in 1922 and was replaced by a new brick building. In 1944 many country schools abandoned the "old system" and consolidated with nearby city schools. After fifty years of existing as an entity, Johnsfield School District became a part of

the Standish School District. The brick building stood for several years after 1944, then was sold to Guy Shoe. He tore down the building and sold the bricks to Tony Zygiel. Catherine Wubbena bought the school bell; it now hangs by the back porch of her home. The site of the old school is now a parking lot next to the Lincoln Township Hall.

5. *John's farm* (Map I), located at 4406 South Melita Road, is about two miles south of M-61, which is approximately three miles from his father's place. Eighty acres were purchased by John in 1902. The huge white pines had been lumbered off the property, leaving stumps and new growth of elm, maple, ash, and cedar. The property was acquired by Catherine Wubbena in 1972 following the death of her mother, Laura Wubbena. The family organ, which John purchased through a mail-order catalog, is in the hall upstairs. The Johnsfield School bell hangs from posts next to the back porch. The two barns that John built still stand. The tillable acreage is rented and farmed by Lawrence Morley and his sons Ivan and Tim. When I-75 was built, sixteen acres were taken for that highway.

6. *The Ernst and Louise Krause farm* (Map II) is located on M-61, two miles west of Melita Road. The property is on the southeast corner of Eight Mile Road and M-61. Mr. and Mrs. Krause kept young Fred for several months after Catharina Wübbena died. They loved him and wanted to adopt him, but Jan would have never allowed it. The farm is now owned by Virgil and Betty Kraatz.

7. Across from the Krause farm, on the southwest corner of Eight Mile Road and M-61, was located the *County Line Cheese Factory* (Map II). Jan refers to this in his *Tage Buch* (Journal), and in one place states that he was elected to the Management Board of the small factory.

8. *Glover Switch* (Map II) was a district on M-61, two or three miles west of the Krause farm. When the pine trees were being logged in this area, narrow gauge railroads were established. The steam engines angled through the woods, powered by chunks of wood with some coal, pulling cars loaded with logs. There was a switch here where more than one set of rails met; a switch had to be "thrown" to prevent a collision, and to force one of the trains to proceed in the direction desired. However, the economical method of transporting logs was to let rivers move the logs.*

---

*This was accomplished by dumping logs down a bank called a rollway into a river. Sometimes as logs moved downriver they became jammed into huge masses, usually because one or more logs became snagged on the river bottom or river bank. Men became quite skilled at jumping from log to log, pushing and rolling the logs with cant hooks to release the jam. The rivers used in this area of Michigan were the Pine and Rifle Rivers.

9. About two miles north of Glover Switch was ***Moore's Junction*** (Map II), which was near Moore's Junction and Adams Roads. This also was a point where smaller logging train lines merged, though it accommodated somewhat larger trains. In Moore's Junction there was a two-room school, post office, store, and Grange Hall. In 1889 Joe Price was the postmaster. The post office was discontinued in 1907. Some years before John bought his farm in 1902, these little logging trains were transporting logs out of his woods to collecting points three or four miles northwest of what was to become his property. As John cleared his land of stumps and new growth, he also had to pick up some of the remnants of these railroads.

10. Entering Standish from the west on M-61, or Cedar Avenue, you find the location where the ***Congregational Church*** (Map III) stood at the southwest corner of Court Street and Cedar Avenue. (*Note:* Cedar Avenue is called Pine River Road east of Standish and M-61 west of Standish. In other words, M-61 terminates in the center of Standish.) The church building was replaced with two homes many years ago. Ministers of this congregation (one was a Mr. Barnes) were great friends of Talka, Minnie, and their father. Talka helped with the housework and church secretarial work there.

11. To reach what used to be the ***Mill Pond*** (Map III), turn off M-61 onto Court Street and go north as far as the street extends. What used to be the Middle Branch of the Pine River is now just a creek. The bridge that once spanned it has long been gone. It was washed away and never replaced. Located around the Mill Pond were lumber mills and stave mills, some of which belonged to Mr. James Norn. The train tracks still exist on the east side of this formerly busy area, with infrequent trains still running on them. The property is now owned by the Forward Corporation.

12. The ***Julius Perlberg brick factory*** (Map III) was located at the southwest corner of the junction of Court Street and Wheeler Road. The Perlbergs were one of the families who kept baby Bill when Catharina died. Mr. Perlberg's grandson, Ed Perlberg, resides in Standish and owns the local newspaper, the *Arenac County Independent*.

13. To reach the ***Charles Wubbena home*** (Map III) proceed east on Cedar Avenue through town until you see the elementary school building on your left. Watch for Almont Street, which extends from Cedar to the south. Their home was the house on the southeast corner of Almont and Cedar.

14. The fourth house west of Charles' home is the ***house built by Andries (Buddy) and Grace Strauss*** (Map III). Grace was the second of Charles' seven daughters. This house is on the southeast corner of Cass and Cedar.

15. The *Gospel Hall* (Map III) was located on the northeast corner of Main Street (US 23) and Beaver Street. This was the site of the Gospel Hall Assembly of which Jan and his daughters became faithful members.

16. A *War Memorial* (Map III) is located on the lawn of the County Building, which is on Grove Street two blocks north of Cedar Avenue. Names of several Wubbenas are listed here for service in World War I and World War II.

17. *Woodmere Cemetery* (Map III) is on US 23. From the County Building continue north on Grove Street to US 23. Turn right onto US 23 and go about one-fourth mile. The Catholic cemetery is on the right. Go a few rods* farther and the Woodmere is on the left. Enter at the main entrance and proceed straight ahead. The Wubbena plot is about thirteen rods from the entrance, on the left side of the road.

18. The *Daley home* (Map II) was located about one-half mile north of Sterling. Old M-76 bifurcates at this point; M-70 is the arm that branches to the right and M-76 continues on up to West Branch. The Daley home was on M-76 just at the point of bifurcation. The Daleys kept twelve-month-old Ella for several months after her mother died. A year or two after Ella was given back to her father, they named their new-born baby daughter Ella as evidence of their love for Ella Wubbena. The two Ellas maintained a friendship for many years by visiting and writing letters to each other.

19. The *Worth School* (Map I) was formerly located on the northeast corner of South Huron Road (M-13) and Worth Road. The building was moved west on Worth Road approximately one-fourth mile from the corner. It is now used for auto repair work and is owned by Richard Shoultes. It retains the form of the school building. Emma taught here for nine consecutive years (1908–1917) and was much beloved in that community. Worth Road is located two miles south of John's farm. Take Melita Road south two miles, turn left onto Worth Road.

20. The *Hoobler farm* (Map I) can be reached by going east on Worth Road, crossing Arenac State Road, and turning left on Sturman Road. The farm was located on the left side of Sturman Road at the point where White's Beach Road goes east and straight on to Saginaw Bay. Saganing Creek crosses the road in this area. Just north of the creek was Hoobler's farm. The Hooblers kept John, Charles, and Henry for several months just a few months after the boys arrived from Germany. Mr. and Mrs. Hoobler were

---

*A rod measures 16½ feet.

educated people, so Jan asked them to teach the boys English, reading, and writing. The boys did farm work for Mr. Hoobler daytimes and did lessons around the table evenings.

21.   Located just south of the Hoobler farm, across the Saganing Creek, were an ***Indian church and cemetery*** (Map I), which exist to this day. The village of Saganing was about one mile east of the Detroit and Mackinaw Railroad. At one time a stave mill and shingle mill were located here, as well as a school, post office, and store. Ed Chamberlain was postmaster here in 1877. A few Indian families still live in the area, but most of them have moved. With willows along the creek, this must have been a picturesque area.

22.   ***White's Beach*** (Map I) is located at the end of White's Beach Road on Saginaw Bay. In past years this was a favorite swimming spot for the young people who went there after working hot days on the farm.

23.   ***Timber Island*** (Map I) is no more. That site is now occupied by the Beardsley Fishery. To reach this spot go east on Palmer Road to where it terminates at the Bay. The original swimming and picnic sites have been replaced by boat docks on the north side of Palmer Road, and by huge trees and vines on the south side. When the Original Ten held their reunion in 1921, this is where George Flutur was ducked by his soon-to-be brothers-in-law who were trying to make him acquiesce to letting his soon-to-be wife Emma "handle the pocketbook."

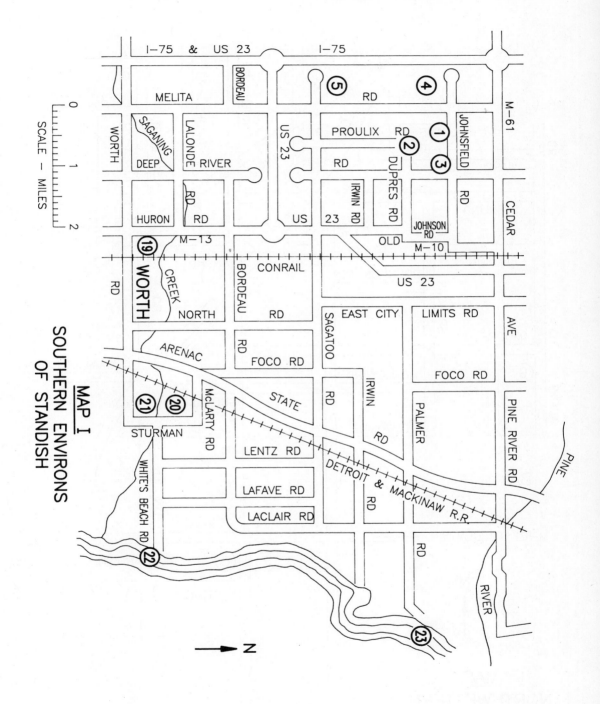

SOUTHERN ENVIRONS
OF STANDISH

MAP I

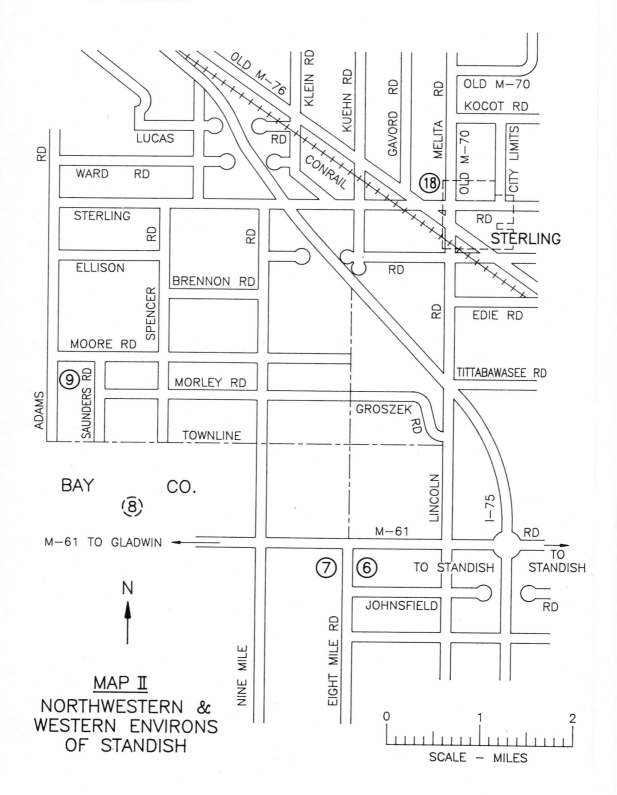

MAP II
NORTHWESTERN &
WESTERN ENVIRONS
OF STANDISH

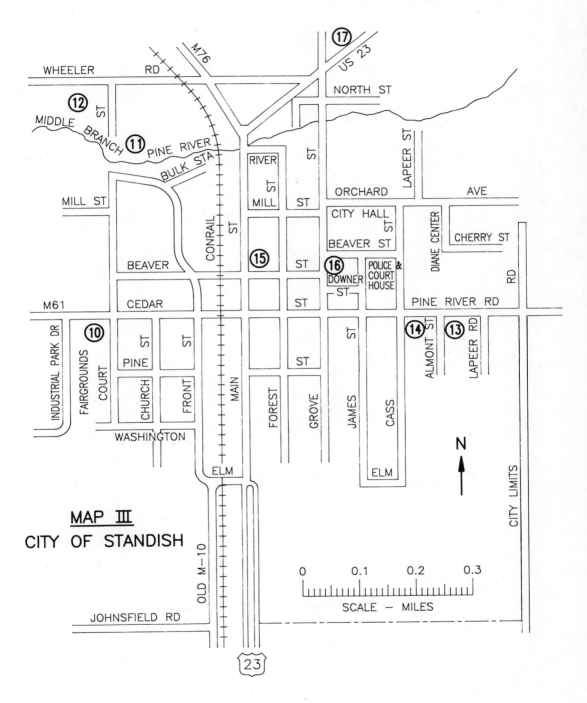

MAP III
CITY OF STANDISH

Part One

JAN
AND
CATHARINA—
THEIR STORY

JAN JANSSEN WÜBBENA (1845–1907) AND CATHARINA JUNGJOHANN WÜBBENA (1855–1894)

I am Catherine Wubbena, daughter of John Wubbena, oldest son of Jan and Catharina Wübbena.

Our county, Arenac County, celebrated its centennial in 1983. My dad used to reminisce a lot about those early days, and I'm pleased that he did. In the Book of James it says, "For what is your life? It is a vapour that appeareth for a little time, and then vanisheth away." The younger generations don't realize, until they grow older, how much every little action and reaction, word and attitude contribute to the woof and warp of a community, and to the characters of those who must carry on as the older generation passes. I had been thinking a lot about this a few years ago, as anecdotes were being collected from old-timers, and I realized just how favorably and appreciatively the sons and daughters of Jan and Catharina Wübbena are remembered. So I shall try to put on paper some of the things I can remember.

Jan and Catharina were married and lived in Neermoor, Germany. This is in northwestern Germany near Bremen. Jan was a sailor for the German Merchant Marine, and was a steersman by the time he left that work to move to America. As a sailor he visited many parts of the world and so was able to study the features of countries to which he considered moving. He gave most serious consideration to Argentina, Texas, and Iowa. For several years, when he returned from each voyage he and Catharina would count their money and acknowledge that there was not yet enough to finance a move. Then he would go back to the ship for another trip. The impetus for leaving Germany was the law that conscripted all fourteen-year-old boys into Kaiser Wilhelm's army. The eldest son, John, was growing up fast.

By 1886 they felt they could make the move. A piece of paper that has survived from his diary tells of how before leaving Germany they placed an ad in a newspaper. The notice indicated that on June 3, 1886, at 1 P.M. there would be an auction sale of the following items: a wardrobe for clothes, hutch with glass doors, commode, wall clock, Singer sewing machine (almost new), mirror with frame, three tables, six chairs, a stove with pipes, articles for knitting, flowers with flower boxes, hand harmonica, two pairs of porcelain roosters, books, knickknacks of porcelain, etc. I cannot locate the record of the income derived from the sale.

On July 9, 1886, Jan, Catharina, and their four children (John, Charles, Henry, and Taalke) sailed from Bremerhaven for New York, steerage class, on the steamship *Trave*, with the intention of settling in Iowa. They entered the United States via Castle Garden on July 16, 1886. Castle Garden is located at the foot of Manhattan Island and has been restored to its 1812 appearance. It is known as Castle Clinton National Monument, a name derived from the fort that once stood there.* Ellis Island did not become the immigration entrance point until 1892. In November 1992, in order to learn more about the Wübbena family's passage, Bill Wubbena, Jr., visited the research section of the National Archives in Washington, D.C. Parts of the report he made as a result of his search are included at the end of this writing.

At the time of the passage my dad, John, was twelve years old. Charles was eleven, Henry was seven, and Taalke was four. As they got off the boat with $400, a real estate salesman was there enticing the "foreigners" to go to Michigan where "berries grew wild by the roadside and were free for the picking, and there was plenty of work in lumber camps and mills." So their destination was changed from Iowa to Michigan. They bought forty acres, sight unseen, about two miles outside the village of Standish, Michigan [see map in Introduction]. This was land from which the timber had been cut, but the stumps remained. Upon arrival they found some abandoned lumber camp buildings on their property. These quarters were tolerable for summer living, but with the arrival of winter the family was subjected to some pretty rough times.

The property was on what is now called Johnsfield Road, one-fourth mile west of Deep River Road. The property was purchased under a land contract for the sum of $240. A record of those years shows that their mortgage payments ranged from $15 to $40; the amount apparently depended on what was available at the time. Standish Manufacturing Co. held title until April 21, 1894, when the amount due for the land was finally paid in full and the deed was conveyed.

Ed. Note: The location is also known as The Battery.

Since Grandma (Catharina) had died on January 23, 1894, she did not live to see the acquisition of the deed. This would have been a thrilling event for her. The lack of her presence must have been a real regret to Grandpa and the older boys who had all worked so hard to pay off the debt. This property is now owned by Karen Irwin, a descendant of William Ingram's family. William Ingram was the husband of Eva Wubbena (Charles' daughter).

Back in Germany the children had been taught to hate the French people. Hundreds of years of wars between Germany, France, and neighboring countries incited this attitude. A few days after arriving in Michigan my dad, John, after scouting around their territory, rushed to his parents, saying, "We've got to get out of here—there are French people to the west of us, and some more over to the east!" As it turned out these very French people helped them survive during those first months in a wild and cold Michigan. And thus they had their first lesson in what the "melting-pot America" was all about.

The French family living next to them was the Proulx family, Edward Peter and his wife Ida, née Demo. Their children played an influential part in the Americanization of the Wubbena children as they all grew up together. Many activities included the children of both families. The Proulx children were: Malora (Mrs. Neil Kiley), Rosie (Mrs. Dave Demo), Fedelia (Mrs. John Cardinal), and son Peter. Mentioned most often was Feedell (their pronunciation), who was the youngest daughter, apparently sweet-natured and much loved by the Wubbenas.

Another neighborhood family was the Thoms family. The sons, Erie and Bill, were close to Fred and Bill Wubbena; they worked in the community together and also played Halloween pranks together. In later years when Bill visited his brother John, he made an effort to call on Erie, who lived and farmed in the Johnsfield area. Bill Wubbena and Erie had shared some common experiences together in Germany in World War I and had developed especially close bonds. Bill Thoms became a barber. In John's last years, when he had to spend time in the local hospital (which happened on three separate occasions) Bill Thoms went to his hospital bedside, trimmed his hair, and gave him a shave as needed. John felt like a prince!

In addition to his desire to have his family "Americanized," Grandpa (Jan) was strongly committed to supporting the workings of the government of his new land. It was on August 3, 1886, only three weeks after his arrival in Standish, that Jan appeared at the County Court House and made "application and declared intention" of becoming a U.S. citizen.

On July 11, 1892 he was finally granted citizenship after he had met the requirement of residing five continual years in the United States. Recorded at the end of this chapter is a verbatim copy of the page in the Arenac County

Circuit Court Naturalization Journal. On that day he must have walked home from town, his face shining with joy, with his precious papers in hand. Both he and Catharina must have been very proud!

Grandpa worked in the Standish lumber mill six days a week, from 7 A.M. to 6 P.M. Then every evening until far into the night he cleared his land of stumps and tried to raise food for his growing family. On the barn he painted the word "EBENEZER" in large letters. This Old Testament word means, "Hitherto hath the Lord helped us." He started and ended every letter he wrote with the words *Gott mit uns* (God with us).

At first he took his family to the closest Lutheran church, which was five miles away in Sterling. Every Sunday morning the family walked the five miles up the railroad tracks to the church, and sometimes even returned again for the evening service. Later, after Catharina's death, the family attended church in Standish at the Gospel Hall.

| |

By 1894 there were ten children. Grandma died on January 23, 1894, of "childbed fever." This was three weeks after Uncle Bill was born. She was only thirty-nine years old. She was often lonesome and cried for relatives and friends back in Germany, and she endured hardships and deprivations, all for the sake of giving their children a life in the wonderful U.S.A. At the time of her death friends took the three littlest children into their homes—newborn Bill to one place, Ella to another, Fred to another.

On her deathbed Catharina asked her oldest son, John, to: (1) never drink alcohol; and (2) take care of the little ones until they were grown; she knew the latter would be too big a job for her husband alone. Taalke was twelve at that point, and so she, with the help of John, kept house and took care of the others. Once a week Grandpa visited each home where a child was being kept. At the time he did this he was also working the long, hard hours at the sawmill. His traveling was usually done on foot. Their horse, Prince, had been acquired after they had lived in Michigan for three or four years. But to use Prince to pull a buggy for Grandpa's Sunday visiting would have been too much of a burden; the horse was used all week for farmwork and deserved a day of rest.

To the best of their abilities, John, Charles, and Henry contributed to the family upkeep wherever a job could be found. At one point Grandpa set up an arrangement that lasted several months whereby these three boys lived with the family of a well-educated man, Mr. Samuel Hoobler, on a farm in the district of Saganing.

The Book of the Register of Deeds reports that this farm was purchased in 1883 by Mr. Hoobler, who came from New York State [see maps in Introduction]. It was located on what is now called State Road at its juncture with McLarty Road. The Saganing Creek runs through the property. With the willow trees along its banks, it must have been a picturesque sight then, and still is now. Chippewa Indians lived close by, wanting to be near Saginaw Bay where they could trap for furs and fish. Indians still live in that same area. The little Indian church with cemetery that was there then is still active and under the care of the Standish Methodist Church [see maps in Introduction].

Mr. and Mrs. Hoobler taught the Wubbena boys reading, writing, and arithmetic along with their own children; lessons took place around the table evenings after the boys had done farm work for Mr. Hoobler all day. Mrs. Hoobler was Mr. Worth's daughter. Mr. Worth was an early Arenac County pioneer for whom a school, road, and district were named. The Hooblers' own children became noted doctors and educators in Michigan and New York.

The boys learned not only the basics, but assimilated some of the graces of refined living from these wonderful people. They especially enjoyed the music as Mrs. Hoobler played the organ, Mr. Hoobler played the violin, and all sang.

This arrangement was in effect for several months. The boys then were needed back at home where they could get jobs in town and bring in paychecks to add to the total family income.

This experience at the Hooblers', the boys' limited schooling in Germany, and their short stay in the Standish schools were all the formal education these three ever had. Yet they all seemed to be rather well-schooled. The remainder of their education for life was obtained by being observant and using every opportunity to learn. Grandpa firmly believed in education and lamented his inability to send his three oldest sons to school. But I'm sure we who remember them noted that those three boys spoke perfect English without an accent. Their grammar and spelling were very good, too.

Grandpa encouraged his younger children to go to school. Because his children and the neighbors' children had to walk to Standish, he instigated the movement to form a school district in their own home area. Property located two miles west of the Wubbena farm was purchased from a Mr. Charles Nehls, Sr., and a large, wood-frame, one-room school was built. After two or three years of existence, the school harbored as many as ninety-six pupils in that one room!

Grandpa was appointed Director of the school board, a position he held for many years. It was he who chose the name, Johnsfield, for the school. He at first considered using the name of their village in Germany, Neermoor. After further thought, it was decided that Johnsfield would be better, and so the school and the surrounding district were renamed. Some years later, when roads were being named, the road on which the school and the old Wubbena farm were located was named Johnsfield Road.

Aunt Emma is listed in the school attendance record as being four years old when in the chart class (kindergarten). Grandpa lived to see Aunt Minnie become a teacher. Emma and Ella taught in local country schools also, but that was after their father's death. When the rural schools were being consolidated I bought the old school bell and it now hangs here on our farm.

Years ago, whenever we drove into town on M-61 we would note the plate riveted to the bridge that spanned the middle branch of the Pine River. This bridge was built in the early 1900s. Located near the Gammon home, which later became the property of Joe Martin, it was about one-half mile east of South Melita Road. On the plate, along with two or three other names, was the name Jan J. Wubbena. His name on the bridge indicated that he had been on the Lincoln Township Board. I think he was the Township Clerk at that time. This was further evidence of his sense of responsibility for his community. It was also additional proof of the "thrill" he felt to be able to have a voice in the affairs of the United States, a voice not permitted in his native Germany. When Harry was born, the first boy to be born in this country, Grandpa looked down at him with pride and said, "Just think! He can become President of the United States!"

Grandma wanted Harry to be baptized in a German Reformed church — the denomination to which they had belonged in Germany. The nearest congregation was in Bay City. With some penny-pinching she managed the railroad fare to and from Bay City, taking baby Harry in her arms. Safely back home she was aglow as she told of the train conductor's courtesy and kindness. In Germany a man in a comparable position would have been haughty and arrogant, and would have let a mother struggle as best she could to get herself and her baby on and off the train.

All of the children had to help with housework and farm work. My dad, John, was in charge when Grandpa was away. When he wanted a job to be done fast he asked Emma to do it. When he wanted a job done well (albeit slowly, very slowly) he asked Ella to do it. Charles married Aunt Myrtie (Myrtle Duncan) in 1897, and Henry became affiliated with the phone company about 1902 (though he was working away from home for a few years before that), so both Charles and Henry were gone a large part of the time that the other children were growing up.

My dad, John, bought some land about two miles, as the crow flies, from his father's farm and spent all of his spare time clearing out trees and stumps on his own place. This property is located on South Melita Road, two miles south of M-61 in Section 17 of Lincoln Township; this is where I still live today.

In summer months the family's cows were pastured on John's farm and had to be brought back to the old farm every evening to be milked night and morning. Then they had to be driven back to pasture each morning. It was usually Willie's job (Bill was called Willie then) to take the cattle back and forth. He would sometimes be gone two to three hours; then it was discovered that, as he picked his way through the woods, he was practicing "throwing his voice," much to the amusement of the two or three farm families in the vicinity. In later years, as we were growing up, we were always delighted when Uncle Bill demonstrated his skill as a ventriloquist.

| |

Several months after coming to Michigan, Grandpa decided to treat Grandma to a drink (probably beer) so they entered one of the saloons in Standish. As they seated themselves, the patrons became quiet. The saloon-keeper came over to them and said, "Mr. Wübbena, in this country women do not come into saloons." Stung, Grandpa said, "If this saloon is not good enough for my wife, neither is it good enough for me." And that was the last time he ever entered a saloon.

After Catharina died Talka, as housekeeper and substitute mother, felt the burden of making the food go as far as possible. (The old pictures show that they were all very skinny little kids.) The rule was that each of them could have only one slice of bread per meal, but they could eat all the potatoes they wanted. Grandpa and the daughters liked company and often hospitably asked people to come to their house. One evening a preacher was there for supper. Fred thought it would be his chance to get an extra slice of bread without Talka daring to reprimand him. He reached out to take a second slice but sharp Talka gave him a hard rap across the knuckles and said, "Fred, you know you're supposed to use the fork!" So poor little Fred got the message even though the advice was socially incorrect!

The ten children had a great love of music and loved to sing "parts." Each could play several kinds of instruments and were delighted when they could get their hands on someone's accordion or mouth organ, or even an organ. It was a great red-letter day when the mail-order organ my dad bought for the family was brought home on the horse-drawn wagon. That organ was the center of many a social gathering in their home. The old organ is now situated upstairs here in this house where I live on South Melita Road. Sometimes we wheeze out a tune on it—it's still in pretty good shape.

The eyes of the old timers light up when the Wubbenas are mentioned. Three characteristics are always attributed to them: their love of singing, their generosity with their scarce worldly goods, and their love of fun. So, in all their poverty and hardships, they lived more fully than do many folks. They got the very best out of what they had and what they worked for.

I have many other memories of what I was told. For example, while living in Germany the three boys learned to skate on the canals and dikes almost as soon as they could walk. While their father was away from home on voyages, their mother had to be the stern disciplinarian. Charles was stubborn and refused to cry when Mother delivered a licking. One day Catharina heard John tell Charles, "You should cry right away, then she'll not whip you so hard." Thereafter John's early crying did not prevent his getting a more severe punishment.

Catharina was skilled in needlework and did much knitting. She even sewed tailored jackets and trousers, not only for her own family, but for sale to others. My father was proud of his mother's ability to do the following simultaneously: knit, read a book perched within eyesight, rock the baby in the cradle with her toe, and sing to the baby.

Their home in Germany was made of brick. It lacked a garden and yard, but had flower boxes. Next door lived two maiden ladies who had gooseberry and currant bushes. These berries were a great temptation to the fruit-hungry boys. When they could stand it no longer they would sneak in and eat a few. The sharp-eyed ladies would always report them to their mother. At times the boys would help these two women care for their two cows, which were kept some distance from the village. Every morning and every evening they walked out to the cows, milked them, and carried the milk back to the ladies' home. The boys were a big help to the ladies and were rewarded with some milk for their family.

Another example of their mother's diligence in overseeing her sons' behavior: when the boys went to the store to get syrup it was necessary to take an empty little pail with them which served as the syrup container. As the boys walked back home they would stick their fingers in the syrup and have a few "licks" as they walked along. If the dipping was done too close to home, the indentations would be still in evidence when they reached their mother's alert eye. They learned to do their "dipping" early on their return trip.

My father remembered some of the foods that his mother had prepared. He would ask my mother to fix them for him. I remember he asked for fried dough bread; dumplings made from bread dough and served with syrup; milk and cinnamon; caraway seeds served on many things, even cottage cheese with sugar and cream; cinnamon in boiled coffee; and raisins or currants in puddings and rolls. Grandma liked tea as a beverage, though it was costly enough to be a luxury. Another precious memory my father had concerning his mother was the watch fob and short watch chain she had made for him from her own hair while they were still living in Germany. Her hair was a very dark brown. The braiding was done with four or five plaits, rather than the three we know now. It is very tight, fine braiding and very smooth and neat. There are some gold circles binding some parts of it. With time it seemed to have been lost but has been located just recently.

Taalke, the baby sister who was only four years old when the family came to America, was a frail little girl. Their mother coaxed her appetite by giving her extra tid-bits, goodies, and special sweets. The envious boys would make deals with their sister behind their mother's back, and thus Taalke did not get the nutrients her mother thought she was getting.

In the old German family Bible this oldest daughter's name is recorded as Taalke. Since the letter "e" is pronounced as short "a" in English, and since we Americans are prone to eliminate unnecessary letters, her name became spelled Talka. For some unknown reason, her brothers and sisters often called her Talch. I learned from my father that Grandpa Jan's mother's name was Taalke Janssen Reuvezaad (Reuvezaad is translated as turnip-seed).*

| | |

The warm, relaxed childhood enjoyment they had known in Germany was in contrast to their lifestyle in America. Harsh changes and hardships were encountered in order to obtain the bare necessities for daily living.

My father, John, was in the eighth grade when the family left Germany. In the Standish school he was placed in the fourth grade. He attended school for four months until his parents needed his help to contribute to the family income. He split firewood and helped his father deliver it to people in town. When they could spare their garden produce from their own table, that was also sold to families in town. Soon he had a job in the shingle mill. I do not know what a thirteen-year-old boy did in a shingle mill. Whatever it was, it helped to buy clothing for his brothers and sisters. At the same time they were undergoing these difficulties, Grandpa saw to it that they learned to speak and write the English language. He also insisted that they retain their ability to speak and write German.

Having been educated and trained to be a sailor, Grandpa was not a

---

Ed. Note: Dr. James Scott, professor of German at Lebanon Valley College and the translator of Jan's sea log and farm journal, feels that the name Reuvezaad is not German. He believes it is Dutch, and in origin probably meant the seed of a root crop that was raised as cattle feed and not as a vegetable for table consumption. He said that this type of turnip is no longer used extensively as cattle feed because its nutritional content is not as good as other available crops. In any event, since Jan's maternal grandfather, Jan Hinrichs Reuvezaad, was born in Midwolde in the northern (i.e., Friesian) part of Holland, this explanation is quite consistent with his place of birth. (See article on origins.)

farmer. He learned from his neighbors, but never achieved the necessary knowledge and skill to be a successful crop producer. Most of the family income came from the work he and his sons did at the stave mill and lumber mills in Standish.

An essay written by Clara Hamilton indicates the respect that the community felt for Grandpa Jan. Her father's farm abutted John's on the west side. She and her brother Frank were pupils in the early days of the Johnsfield School, and both later taught there.* As a requirement for an English course at the University of Michigan, Clara wrote an essay titled, "The Best Educated Person I Know." This appears to have been written about 1920, and the person she described was our grandfather, Jan. It is an interesting description of him.

Excerpts of thoughts from this paper can be summarized as follows: To look at results is the only fair way to estimate the success of our undertakings. Through studying with his children, he gained the equivalent of a high school education, although he never enrolled in high school. Through his self-sacrificing efforts his children received training and education that have made them self-supporting and a credit to their communities. These children have become a farmer, a mail carrier, an installer of telephones, school teachers, nurses, an accountant, and a telegraph operator. A kind man, he was always interested in community works and contributed to the development of his neighborhood. He had been mellowed by the hardships and sorrows of his life, as well as by the support and love of a wife whose influence remained after her early death.

| |

After a few years, a new house was built on the farm property. By this time the older boys had left home to get work, taking jobs wherever they were available. The girls and younger boys lived in the new house with Jan until he died and for a few years thereafter.

This new, larger house was built of wood in the typical farmhouse style of architecture. There was a large front porch. I do not recall ever having been inside this house. I remember that Dad's sisters, when they came back to Standish to visit, wanted to be driven past the old home and shed tears as they rode along in the horse-drawn wagon.

After the daughters had moved out, about 1914, the house sat empty.

---

*Frank taught from about 1900 to 1902 [see picture of Jan with pupils and Frank inside the school building], and Clara taught there from about 1906 to 1908. Clara later became Mrs. Gus Kitzman.

Henry and Charles took care of the taxes, and Charles took care of renting it to some family now and then. Eventually it was bought from the family by Eva Wubbena Ingram and her husband William Ingram. They tore the house down and replaced it with a small house which has been inhabited for many years by relatives of William Ingram. The barn stood for several more years, but it, too, was eventually torn down.

The bulk of the lumber property and work in Standish was owned by James Norn. He was a sharp businessman, knowledgeable in lumber and its products. He had come from Scotland with his wife, Isabella, bringing her sister and brother with them. The sister, Elizabeth Milne, was always called Lizzie. She was the bookkeeper for all the Norn Enterprizes. The brother, who was called Alex, was handicapped.

Mr. Norn was a zealous worker for the Lord and encouraged his employees to become born-again Christians. They all attended the Gospel Hall, which under his financial support and missionary fervor grew in size of attendance. Mr. Norn would give his personal attention to those of his employees who got saved and subsequently became active in the Gospel Assembly. The building was in Standish on the northeast corner of what is now Main Street and Beaver Street.

The Assembly that met in the Gospel Hall derived from what is still known as the Plymouth Brethren in England and Scotland. Immigrants from those countries that settled in Canada and the United States continued to practice their religion in their new communities. They grouped together in Assemblies and met in buildings called Gospel Halls.

These companies of believers did not recognize denominational boundaries or sectarian limitations. They met regularly to study the scriptures. On the Lord's Day (Sunday) they sat in a circle around the Lord's Table. There was no ritual or stated order of service; any of the brethren present, as led by the Spirit, prayed and offered praise, gave out a hymn, and read or ministered a few verses of scripture. The elements on the table were a whole loaf of bread and a goblet of wine. The loaf was broken just prior to being passed to symbolize the wholeness of the Lord's body until broken on the cross; it was then passed from one to another around the circle. A prayer of thanks for Christ's blood was offered and then the cup was passed.

The distinction between "clergy" and "laity" was not recognized; no man was called Reverend or Father. They did not ask for or accept any money from the unsaved. They believed the Christian's life should be one of devotedness to Christ, and of separation from the way of the world.

After Catharina's death Jan and his daughters became faithful members, though none of the sons did so formally. Grandpa Jan found comfort in following the Spirit as he prayed, offered praise, read the Word, and gave out a hymn. He spent time daily studying the scriptures with his family. He and his daughters felt in their individual souls what they referred to as "the wonderful works of God"; neighbors and friends told of hearing them in their home singing hymns as they worked.

Gradually the members of this Standish group died or moved to the cities to work in factories. After Mr. Norn died, his wife and his sister-in-law, Lizzie Milne, continued to support the congregation. But now, since their deaths, and because of the passing of time, no vestige of the building remains. The Christian Assembly continues in other cities and states.

Jan died in his home on May 27, 1907, at the age of sixty-two. I have never heard anyone state a diagnosis of the cause of his death, but I imagine it was closely related to congestive heart failure. He had become very round-shouldered (a physical trait seen in some of his sons, and even his grandsons) even before he was fifty years old. Hard work and a loyalty to what he felt was his duty, regardless of how tired he was, surely contributed to the appearance of old age at a relatively young age.

In late May of that year his daughters, all of whom were living with him, could see his condition deteriorating. They sent a telegram to John and Harry, who were working near Wolverine, Michigan, asking them to come home at once. John said to Harry, "We'll wait until morning to go. You know how excited the girls get." When they reached home by train the next day they found their father had gone. My dad always sadly regretted his not being there when his dad died, both for his father's sake, and for his sisters' need of a strong shoulder.

| |

Back in Germany when Grandpa proposed to Grandma she blushingly said, "I'll have to think about it." So he left on his next sea voyage with the promise that she would give him her answer upon his return about four months hence. When he arrived back his first question was, "What's your answer?" And she, not wanting to appear to be an easy catch, replied, "My answer to what?" This so angered him that he went out, slamming the door behind him. She immediately started crying, apparently rather noisily. He was listening outside, and so he came back in and asked her what she was crying about. She said, "You know." And so the proposal was accepted. And now all of you who have their blood in your veins know how Jan Janssen Wübbena and Catharina Carolina Louise Jungjohann came to be your forebears.

Stories Told by My Father,
Henry Wubbena, Regarding His Childhood
by Florence Wubbena Neubauer

They lived in a well-constructed brick home with dirt floors, so hardened with usage they could be swept with a broom. The home was above average for the time. Their food supply was ample and fruits such as apples and plums were preserved by the drying process.

They loved nature and grew flowers in every available spot. In the spring they had pink and white peonies and white, purple, and lavender lilacs. Later in the year they had roses, geraniums and petunias which lasted until late fall.

They loved birds and learned a poem that meant, "Don't kill the birds, the pretty birds that fly from pole to pole." They also sang a song about a bird sitting on a foot. My parents sang the song to us when we were children. Our friends in Germany teach their children the same song today.

One time when the boys were playing around the church, John and Henry played a trick on Charles and locked him in the bell tower. Soon they began playing with other things and forgot about him. When they came to dinner, Grandma asked where Charles was. The boys suddenly remembered. When they went to release him, they found him holding a bird that he had accidentally squeezed to death from fright. "Now you even made me kill my bird," he sobbed.

They crossed the ocean by steamship with quarters on the lower deck. Grandpa knew some of the sailors who allowed him to show his children the workings of the ship. On clear nights he took them on deck and pointed out the different planets that had guided him on prior journeys.

As the children grew in that spartan environment in Standish they created their own entertainment without adult organization or supervision. Charades and "Victim" were their favorites. One time, while playing charades, Uncle Charles stumped the group by merely standing in front of them. He explained he was a sunflower. He was a son, and everyone knew he was a flower.

[The victim game was a somewhat elaborate village "morality" game, brought from the Old World and enthusiastically played by the Original Ten and their friends in their growing up years. It was then carried over into many of their homes and again played by them and their families.

The game required at least six players—victim, lawyer, judge, punisher (sheriff?), citizen who perpetrated the crime, and at least one other citizen. If more persons played, then more citizen roles were assigned and the game became even more complex and interesting. Citizen roles were occupations of the society in which they lived (e.g., miller, blacksmith, farmer #1, farmer #2, mayor, banker, preacher, teacher, constable, etc.).

The roles of the players were assumed publicly. Then slips were drawn by the citizens. One of the slips identified who the perpetrator of the crime was to be. Obviously, the criminal kept his identity as a lawbreaker to himself, and the game began.

The victim, represented by the lawyer, appeared before the judge, and declared that he had been harmed in some way (e.g., assault in the dark, robbery, haystack burned, horse stolen, or whatever). The judge examined him, determined the details of the crime at some length, and then asked him who he thought did it. The victim looked at the citizens in attendance, determined who he thought had the slip designating that person as perpetrator, and named him as the offender. If the victim was right in his accusation the judge assessed punishment to the perpetrator (maybe, run around the house ten times) and the punisher saw the sentence was carried out. If, however, the victim was wrong the judge assessed punishment against the victim for his wrongful accusation. In either case, the game ended, slips were again drawn to determine the roles, and the game started again.

The game acted out the concepts that: (1) crime would be punished; (2) wrongful accusations could have adverse consequences and one should be careful; and (3) justice isn't always free to the victim, in the sense that if one seeks retribution through the courts it may not all turn out well. All of the Original Ten set high standards of right and wrong in their lives, were quite careful to be good neighbors, and rarely made accusations lightly.]

Jan J. Wubbena's Naturalization Record
As Shown in the
Circuit Court Naturalization Journal No. 1 of Arenac County

Naturalization Record
State of Michigan   **In the Circuit**
County of Arenac   **Court for Said County**

At a general term of the Circuit Court for the County of Arenac and the State of Michigan, continued and held at the Court House in the Village of Standish in said County on the 11th day of July A.D. 1892.

Present, Honorable George P. Cobb, Circuit Judge. The Court having opened for business in due form. In the matter of the application of Jan J. Wubbena an alien, to become a citizen of the United States.

Jan J. Wubbena, of Lincoln Township, Michigan, a native of Germany, having made application on the 3d day of August, the year one thousand eight hundred and eighty-six, did declare, on his oath, before the clerk of the Circuit Court for the County of Arenac, in the State of Michigan, that it was his bona fide intention to become a citizen of the United States, and to renounce all allegiance and fidelity to any foreign Prince, Potentate, State or Sovereignty, and particularly the Emperor of Germany of whom he was then a subject; and the said Jan J. Wubbena, having also made due proof, to the satisfaction of said court, that he has resided within the United States for the continual term of five years, and within the State of Michigan one year and upwards, and during that time he has behaved as a man of good moral character, attached to the principles of the Constitution of the United States, and well disposed to the good order and happiness of the same; and that the said Jan J. Wubbena has never borne any hereditary title, nor has been of any of the orders of nobility in the kingdom or state from which he came; and the said Jan J. Wubbena, having solemnly declared on his oath, in open Court, that he would support the Constitution of the United States, and that he did absolutely and entirely renounce and abjure all allegiance and fidelity to any foreign Prince, Potentate, State or Sovereignty, and particularly the Emperor of Germany, of whom he was then a subject.

Therefore, it is ordered and adjudged, by the Court now here, that the said Jan J. Wubbena be and he is hereby admitted a citizen of the United States.

Signed, George P. Cobb, Circuit Judge

GERMAN REICH
CERTIFICATE OF COMPETENCE
AS A
SAILOR IN EUROPEAN WATERS

The former seaman, Jan Janssen Wübbena, born in Tergast the 10th of April 1845 residing in Neermoor, who, following his acceptance as a steersman for international voyages, having completed the required number of days at sea and as sole steersman, according to Sections 11 and 3 of the Regulations for Demonstration of Competence as high seas sailor and steersman on the high seas on German Trading ships of 25 September 1869 (Federal Statute p. 660) is hereby authorized to work as sailor on the high seas and high seas steersman for German trading ships i.e. sailing ships carrying under 250 tons (@ 1000 Kilograms) and steamships of every size between European ports and ports in the Mediterranean Sea, the Black Sea, and the Sea of Azov.

Aurich, January 26th, 1878.

Royal Prussian Governor's Office

Jaressewski

Deutsches Reich.

Zeugniss
über die Befähigung
zum
Schiffer auf Europäischer Fahrt.

Dem bisherigen *Matrosen Jan Janssen Wübbena,*

geboren zu *Tergast* , den *10* ten *April* 18*45*,

wohnhaft in *Neermoor* ,

welcher nach seiner Zulassung als Steuermann auf grosser Fahrt die vorschriftsmässige Fahr-
zeit zur See und als Einzelsteuermann zurückgelegt hat, wird hierdurch auf Grund der §§. 11
und 3 der Vorschriften über den Nachweis der Befähigung als Seeschiffer und Seesteuermann
auf Deutschen Kauffahrteischiffen vom 25sten September 1869 (Bundes-Gesetzblatt Seite 660)
die Befugniss beigelegt, Deutsche Kauffahrteischiffe, und zwar Segelschiffe unter 250 Tonnen
(zu 1000 Kilogramm) Tragfähigkeit und Dampfschiffe jeder Grösse zwischen Europäischen Häfen
und Häfen des Mittelländischen, Schwarzen und Azowschen Meeres zu führen.

Aurich , den *26* ten *Januar* 18*78*.

Königlich-Preussische Landdrostei.

Nº *1016.*

Formular F.

Two letters from Jan Wübbena to his son Harry, transcribed verbatim as he wrote them in English. At this point we do not know where Harry was or what kind of work he was involved in at the time these letters were written.

Johnsfield, August 12, 1905

My dear son Hinrich: God be with us:

Having read the letter which you sent to Taalke, I feel glad you are content in your line of business. Also that you sent the ten dollars. We have been very busy lately and today we have drawn the last of the oats; that is together with timothy and clover hay forty-three loads of rough fodder. Henry was home Saturday. Sunday night he and Charles took the team "Prince and John" with them. Henry was looking nicely and found everything to satisfaction. John has helped us faithfully to cut and reap the crops; so we have a great reason to be thankful when we consider our worthlessness to receive all blessings. My dear son don't forget to study the word of God; "this world and its pursuits will perish, its beauty fadeth like a flower, the brightest scheme this earth can cherish is but the pastime of an hour; each heart may seek and love its own, my goal is Christ and Christ alone." With him the Father bestows on us everything what is needed; content to be is one of the greatest gifts.

Mr. Kroske enlarges our school, will be done by next Monday noon with the carpenter work; Andrew the plasterer from Standish will do the plastering and Burkhardt the painting. Mr. Barness visited us last Thursday, he was very satisfied with the place where he is working; he sends you his best regards and so does Newall, and if I feel to run away I know where to find a home. Mrs. Timrick was here also, she was sorry that she did not find you and Henry home. One of her daughters Grete was with her; they stayed for about two hours. She was mourning of course over the loss of her husband, but otherwise she was well content; she told with all satisfaction of her children and of Mr. Dubke and of the crops and all her work and doings. "Jack," the crow has left us, I have not seen him since yesterday morning, so I conclude that he went off with all the progress of speech, he intended to make. It does not seem as if anyone is sorry about his departure — so I dost not fret either. You know that little girl, Ina Stone, she is with us now for more than a week; the little girl seems to like it here. I am glad to know that you hold to the church; hold fast to the word of God and continue in the things which you have learned, and have been assured of knowing of whom you have learned them, and that from a child you have known the holy scriptures, which

are able to make you mine unto salvation through faith which is in Christ
Jesus, 2 Tim. 5:14,15.

Committing you in the care of God Almighty, I close sending
love and best regards to Henry and Charles,
as your loving father,
Jan Wübbena

Answer soon again

Johnsfield, September 12, 1905

My dear son Harry:

God be with us:

Received your letter with the ten dollars, with which I am very much
pleased; the Lord will pay you back in some way or another; I paid nine
dollars on debts today to Michigan Cooperage Co. and our debts altogether have come down to 165 dollars. So you can in some measure imagine how the money was spent. Minnie started teaching today a week ago;
she was home over Sunday, she likes the office first rate. Emma goes to
school in Standish again and Ella here in the district. Clara Hamilton is
teacher here. The school is nice and lots of room there is now; there were
63 children today. Freddie and Willie are with me home; we have been
cutting corn; it will not become ripe; half of it is cut I suppose. Taalke
works for Chamberlain again and John on his own place. Four yearlings
we have sold, which brought somewhat 58 dollars. We intend to butcher
the old cow "Blossom" tomorrow, and we intend to butcher a pig for
conference.* I wish you could be here that time. It will begin with a

---

*Ed. Note: The conference referred to here was an annual gathering of the members
of Assemblies who came by train, most of them from Michigan, but from the other
states and Canada also. Meals were served in the hall, beds were provided by the citizens of Standish, gratis. The Opera House, a large building located next to the Hall,
was rented in order to have auditorium space for those attending the meetings.

The conference lasted from Thursday evening through the following Sunday
evening and featured daily meetings held morning, afternooon, and evening. Speakers were usually men whom the Spirit moved to bring a message. There was always
much singing, a capella, and a beautiful blending of voices of men, women, and children of all ages. Many a courtship and ensuing marriage came out of every conference. The Standish Conference was considered to be one of the better conferences;
the city folks liked the farm atmosphere, many having come originally from a farm
or small town; the preachers seemed to be more fervently imbued with the warmth
and love of their message, and the overall tone was one of blessing and unity.

prayer meeting next Thursday evening; what preachers will come I don't know, but one by the name of Erskine from Alger will come; Minnie knows him. I wish you could be here them few days. I saw Gossett yesterday; he saw you Saturday he said, but he was in an awful hurry, just he let me know that he had seen you well. Charles was home Sunday for a short while. He brought "Prince" home and took "Topsy" back again. "Prince," the faithful horse, had eaten a little too much oats and so he went away from Charles a couple of times and they had to get rid of him somehow; Henry writes in his letter that they could not do anything with him. John had him yesterday and today on his place. So you know all the important news about home; other news about courtships and connections I will leave to sis Taalke and Carl and the rest. Now, my dear son, I will close reminding you again of not to neglect to pray and to read the precious word of God; indeed, the proper use of it convinces one that it is "quick and powerful and sharper than any two-edged sword, piercing even to the dividing asunder of soul and spirit and of the joints and marrow and is a discerner of the thoughts and intents of the heart; and this is my comfort in affliction; for thy word has quickened me," says the psalmist Psalm 119:50.

Best regards and love from all, especially from your loving and rejoicing father, rejoicing in your behavior.

I sign with love as a father.

Wübbena

Walter Cuttle is married in Detroit, came home today with his mistress; Taalke has seen them.

Report of Search of National Archives Research Section by William L. Wubbena, Jr.

In November 1992 I visited the National Archives Research Section in Washington, D.C. I was assigned a microfilm reading machine and was shown where to find passenger lists on reels of microfilm which are catalogued by month, year, and port of entry. I found two reels for the month of July, 1886, for the Port of New York. The passenger lists are actually manifests submitted by the vessel to customs officials. My reaction was to marvel at the volume of immigrants from *everywhere*—thousands of immigrants! Some came as families and some came alone. They represented myriad crafts and trades.

It caused me to pause and consider the overall magnitude of this influx and how there was a separate story for each one of them—their struggles and hardships, what made them come, and how it all turned out for them and their descendants.

Finally I found it! It was the steamship *Trave*, of about 2,900 tons, arriving New York from Bremen on July 16, 1886. Her master was Captain W. Willigored. The ship departed Bremen on July 7th, which made for an amazingly fast trip (in 1954 my troopship required nine days to go from New Jersey to Bremerhaven).

One of the pages looked like this:

	Name	Age	Sex	Occupation	Native of
250 -					
1 -					
2 -					
3 -					
4 -					
5 -					
6 -	Jan Wubbena	41	M	Farmer	US
7 -	Cath "	31	F		US
8 -	Johs "	14 ¼	M		US
9 -	Carl "	6	M		US
260 -	Friedr "	7	M		US
1 -	Henrietta "	5	F		US

There are mistakes in this listing, which after a lot of thought and soul-searching, I blame on the recorder. The erroneous ages of John and Charles are not troublesome, but the occupation "farmer" and the entry of "Native of US" for the entire family bothered me. Grandfather was too meticulous and precise to be part of such misinformation—just look at his navigation work and the records and accounts he kept as a seaman and, later, on the farm. Maybe Grandfather told the recorder that he *intended* to become a citizen and a farmer. One can only imagine the tumult of hundreds of people milling about, with hundreds more waiting. Ships were stacked up in the harbor. (Ellis Island did not exist in 1886.) Immigrants were processed in an overcrowded, inadequate facility in lower Manhattan called Castle Garden. (Ellis Island was created later to handle a capacity of 5,000 immigrants a day!) We can certainly understand how a harried Castle Garden staff confronted by all this confusion on July 16, 1886, perhaps late in the day, would allow a small group wearing tags marked "US" to pass through.

(From the Arenac County Independent, *May 30, 1907)*

JAN WUBBENA DEAD

It was a sad surprise Thursday morning to his friends and neighbors when the news spread rapidly around that Mr. Wubbena had passed away of heart trouble. Everything that medical skill could do had been done but the hand of death was stronger and our friend had to succumb to it. He was a sincere Christian man, being especially noted for his honesty and highly respected by all who knew him. He has held several township offices and the school with which he was connected since its origin was closed for two days on account of his death. Death was not a horror to Mr. Wubbena for he was prepared to go.

He leaves a family of ten children, six boys and four girls and a host of friends to mourn his loss for they have lost a good friend, kind neighbor and a good citizen.

The funeral services were held at the Gospel Hall on Saturday afternoon, Mr. Kay of Saginaw conducting the services. The floral offerings were very large, and the crowd of sympathizing neighbors and friends was immense, the hall not being nearly large enough to hold a great many as the sidewalk outside was lined with friends who realized that one whom they respected and loved had gone from their midst.

Jan Wubbena was born April 10, 1845, in Tergast, Germany, died May 28, 1907, at his home in Standish. Mr. Wubbena was orphaned at an early age. Altho very well educated in several different languages, he received his education through his own efforts, graduating from high school in Leer, Germany, after which he was married to Catharina Jungjohann.

He had travelled all over the world, leading a sailor's life for many years, after which he moved to his home in Standish so as to be with his family, where they have resided twenty-one years, he being one of our early pioneers.

The death of his wife in 1894 was a terrible stroke, as it left him with a family of ten small children, the youngest of which was only three weeks old and the oldest daughter 12 years of age, who took upon herself the household duties. He was an ideal father, the welfare and education of his children being his chief aim and he has succeeded.

MEMORIES OF OUR PAST:
A CONVERSATION OF
HENRY, FRED, AND
ELLA WUBBENA IN 1961

Transcribed by Lois Wubbena Dick,
Daughter of Henry Wubbena

Bernice Van Kleek, Henry's oldest daughter, knew that Uncle Fred, Aunt Mildred, and Aunt Ella were planning to visit Henry in October, 1961. She arranged to have a tape recorder available to record some of the conversation during their visit. Henry was 82 years old, Fred almost 70, and Ella 68 at that time. The tape was made on October 2, 1961. What follows is as close to a transcription as possible, in order to best reflect their personalities, manner of speaking, and interaction with each other.

It must be remembered that a tape recorder was a fairly new instrument at that time, a device unfamiliar to the older generation. From what was said and how it was said, it is obvious that the three took the recording very seriously and wanted everything they said to be authentic.

Fred apparently was in charge of the recording. Fred's starting words on the tape were, "Testing with Eve and William Ingram. When that flashes, that is talking. This is a test. Hope everything is working. This is a get-together. Eve and William [Eve is Charles' oldest daughter] took Fred and Ella to the "famous" residence of Henry and Martha Wubbena [typical of Fred's flattery] at 1113 Borton Avenue, Essexville, Michigan."

| |

Fred and Mildred Wubbena had travelled by train from Seattle, Washington to Elgin, Illinois. Jesse Whyte, Mildred's sister, drove them and Ella from Elgin to Michigan. It had been over a year since Fred had visited Henry. This day they were reminiscing about their parents and their childhood days.

The four older children of Jan and Catharina Wübbena—John, Charles,

Henry and Talka—were born in Neermoor, Germany [see Map G-2]. This is where Jan and Catharina were raised. Their father's parents were Jan J. Wübbena and Taalke Janssen Reuvezaad.

Their grandfather died when Jan, their father, was very young. Jan was too young to be drafted into military service as was required of all young men in Germany. When their grandmother was left a widow her only son, Jan, was her only means of support. He was a sailor by vocation and sailed to all parts of the world.

Henry was asked if he knew anything about his mother's background. He recalled that his mother's father's name was Carl Frederick Jungjohann, born in Neermoor. Her mother's name was Catharine Elizabeth Caroline Klemm. They had four sons: Engelke, Gerhardt, Wilhelm and Karl; and two daughters named Catharina Louise Caroline and Tante [Aunt] Gesina. Gesina was a nurse.

Jan and Catharina's four children were growing up and their father wanted them to come to America, a free country. Jan's mother lived with them. After she passed away their father made definite plans to come to America because John, the oldest son, was coming of military age. If they had not come when they did, the government would not have allowed John to leave the country.

The Jan Wübbena family came to America in 1886. Jan had made plans to settle in Iowa where friends from Germany had settled. But when they landed in New York there were several realtors who met immigrants as they came from abroad. An agent from Cross and Dyer Land Co., the owners of the lumber company, gave a flowery description of the area in Michigan and so the family decided to move to Standish instead of Iowa [see maps in Introduction].

Jan bought forty acres of land from Cross and Dyer. It was an empty lumber camp, so the buildings on it gave them a roof over their heads. The forty acres of land cost $240.00, with $5.00 down and payments of $5.00 per month. The price was reasonable to entice people to settle there.

Six children were born after they came to Standish: Minnie, Harry, Emma, Fred, Ella and William, making a family of ten children. Later, a two-story house was built on the forty acres.

In Germany they had lived in a brick house and were comfortable. Henry told his family that there had been dirt floors in their home in Germany. They had tied straw together and used this to sweep the floors. The home was paid for, but they did not own any other property. They sold their home to have the money to come to America.

When they arrived in America, they went directly to Castle Garden—a landing place for immigrants coming from the Old Country to New York.

They had their papers cleared there and then went to a hotel—in English "The Lutheran Pilgrim's Home."

Ella did not remember her mother and asked about her. Henry said that she was a nice woman and very attractive. She had long, dark brown hair, and wore it in braids around her head. Their father took some of her hair that had been cut with him on one of his trips to a foreign country and had it made into earrings and brooches that were beautiful. Hopefully, some of the offspring have some of the things that he had made up for her.

Their father was away sailing and did not come home very often. Henry remembered hearing from him when he was in South America bringing back a load of cattle or cowhides to another country to be made up into leather, etc.

Their father did no sailing after coming to America. When they moved onto the land in Standish, he worked in a sawmill that was operated by the same company that sold him the land. He piled and handled the lumber. This was difficult for him as he was not used to that kind of work. The family got along pretty well, but he still had the Iowa fever.

Their mother liked the country in Standish. She grew a nice garden, bought a cow, had their own milk, and got along fine. As the family grew older, John and Charles (the two older boys) got jobs in the sawmill also. Their mother was comfortable, they were getting along fine and she did not want to move to Iowa. But their father decided to go to Iowa, where he had friends (relatives?) from Germany. He went to Iowa and worked on a newspaper.

Fred asked if their father had any education and, if so, why he did not work where he could apply his education. Henry said that jobs were scarce at that time, especially in Michigan, and that he was fortunate to get a job as a lumber piler. But he did have an education and was very good in mathematics and was very clever with his figures. He surprised his older children after they became school teachers, and his grandchildren after they were educated, with his knowledge. "He matched wits with them." Their father could read, write, and speak seven different languages.

When they lived in Germany they were members of the Reformed Church. When they came to this country they affiliated themselves with the Lutheran Church. They went there for years. Later they went to the Christian Gospel Hall. We were told that each child had his own Bible. In the evening the family sat around the table and read from the Bible—by candlelight in the winter months.

Since Jan and family were among the first pioneers, it was up to him to lay out the land, as a sailor might be expected to do. He used the North Star as a guide and years later when surveyors came to subdivide the land, they found that their father's measurements were quite accurate.

It wasn't long before Jan organized a school district. A school board was elected and he was chosen director of the board, a position he held until his death in 1907. Because of his interest in community affairs, the school district surrounding the school for several miles was named for him by the residents of the area. The name Johnstown was suggested but their father thought that was too elaborate; he suggested Johnsfield, the name that area still carries.

Ella asked Henry what he remembered about the schools in Germany. Henry said that they went to school every day of the year except Sunday and they had no summer vacations. Their mother taught "practical classes" in her home: knitting and sewing. Talka could knit mittens and stockings when she was four years old.

Ella commented that their mother must have been very busy with the four children and teaching classes. Henry said that she was busy but had a very cheerful disposition. She would sometimes get depressed when their father was away sailing and she was there with the children alone, but she was happy with her children and garden. When their father was in Iowa (after they came to Michigan) she had the children there alone. Father sent money he earned in Iowa, and as they grew older the two older boys got jobs in the mill and contributed, so they got along pretty well. They got more cattle and this was right in her line so she was quite satisfied and cheerful.

The comment was made that usually in a large family the children did a lot of arguing and scrapping. Fred asked how their mother handled this. Henry said that their mother kept them in line pretty well. When their father spoke they jumped and moved immediately. Their mother was not as stern as their father. They all got along pretty good. Everyone was busy making a living and there was no time for arguing. As the children grew older and worked out they helped financially. They were able to get more cattle and were fairly prosperous for those days.

When their father was on the school board, he would sometimes go to the schoolhouse and teach a lesson in mathematics. Then whenever he had the floor he would immediately suggest that the whole school sing. Ella told of the time the teacher had an entertainment when he was there. The singing did not seem to please him as it was not loud enough. So he mentioned each of his own children by name and said, "Freddie, Ellie, Villie, vy don't you sing?" Well, they did the best they could, but that is the way he reprimanded them in front of the whole class. They were so embarrassed.

The teacher spoke up and said, "Mr. Wubbena, the children had worked very hard and had just finished examinations and had not practised for this entertainment."

"All right, Mam, that's all right, Mam." He was so kind about it after the teacher explained it, and made up for his reprimand later.

Ella told how the older boys were so good to the younger children, and would often bring them little candies or treats that they didn't have at home. She told about the time Henry brought home a beautiful hair ribbon from West Branch. Hank added that this was in later years, and then gave his version of the story. He was working for the telephone company and had come home for the weekend. For entertainment he would get the younger children wrestling. He said that Ella was the strongest. She would throw Emma, Minnie, and even Freddie and Bill—she could handle them all. On one occasion the prize for the winner was to be a belt. Before Henry left to go back to West Branch on Sunday evening on the train, Ella told Henry that she did not need a belt, but wished that he would get her a nice, broad hair ribbon. Hank said, "All right, how long a ribbon do you want?" He thought she wanted two yards to make the ribbon.

"OK. Will it cost more than the belt would?" asked Henry.

"No, it won't cost too much," Ella replied.

The next Monday evening after Hank went back to West Branch, he went to the store and got the ribbon. The belt was to be fifty cents. Come to find out, the ribbon was sixty-five cents. So Ella stung him for fifteen cents there. So he packed the ribbon in a box he got at the store, and included a note telling his sisters and brothers how they had stung him for fifteen cents. When he went to mail the box the next day and asked how much the postage was, he was asked if there was any writing in the box. He said, "Yes." So he had to send the box first class and it would be six cents, where he had figured it would be two cents. So that evening he wrote another letter and mailed it separately telling them how he had been stung for postage and everything else, and from then on the wrestling would be over, and that he was not buying any more prizes.

Ella asked about the boat trip to America. Henry said they came from Germany on the *Trave*, a steamer that was modern for those times. The steamer belonged to the North German Lloyd (name of the steamship company). Their father, being a sailor, knew the ropes pretty well, and had a few privileges on the boat that other travellers didn't have. He was able to take the children through the kitchens and show them other things of interest on the boat.

They were third-class passengers. The first-class passengers were above them and would throw oranges and "stuff" down to the kids just to see them grabble after them. The first- and second-class decks had dances and an orchestra playing, but there was nothing like that on the deck they were on. Everyone got sea sick—there was no getting around it—but it wasn't too bad. Every room (cabin) on the boat was occupied.

In the morning the crew would come on their deck with a big cart with a big tub of oatmeal and condensed milk. Passengers came out of their cabins with their dishes, and dished up a few scoops of oatmeal with the milk. That was their breakfast. The food was very plain.

The family travelled from Neermoor by train to Bremen. They stayed there for two days, and then got on a small slow boat on the Weser River that took them to the North Sea where they boarded their steamer, the *Trave*. From there they got on the ocean for the trip to America. Some ships took up to six weeks to come across, but the *Trave* was one of the fastest and most modern at that time (1886) and they came across in nine days. Henry could not remember the day they left Germany or when they arrived in New York. But it was July 23, 1886, that they arrived in Standish. The company they had bought the land from met them at the train with a team of horses and a wagon. They loaded their belongings—bedding, feather beds in big boxes, and everything they had—and took them to the camp.

The four children ran behind the wagon that was loaded with their belongings. There were raspberries growing wild along the log roads. There had been raspberries in Germany, but you were fined if you ever touched one. It was quite a treat for the kids to run behind the wagon and pick the raspberries that were as free as water. They appreciated that very much.

Their mother had this garden instinct and had brought some beans from Germany. She planted the beans on their land in Standish after they arrived on July 23 and they had green beans out of their garden before the frost that year. That was wonderful for then and would be even now.

In the fall they went to school in Standish as there was no school in Johnsfield then. A neighbor, Mr. Demund, took Taalke (age five) and Henry (age seven) to school in Standish. It was quite an experience, too. Of course, they could not speak English, so the other kids had a pretty good time with them.

In Germany they had been taught not to throw stones at the birds. In the Standish school they learned a poem: *Don't kill the birds, the pretty birds, / That sing about the door.*

The Wubbena children studied that poem and talked about it and figured out that "Don't kill the birds" meant, "Don't throw stones at the birds." In school some of the kids who sat behind them would make up little paper wads and throw them at the Wubbena children when the teacher was not looking. Henry raised his hand. When the teacher asked what he wanted, Henry said, "All the boys after me are all the time killing me," thinking that throwing was killing.

There was a big fellow, Richard White, who used to pick on them. John Wubbena and Richard got into a fight at recess. After recess the teacher called both boys on the platform to be questioned and criticized.

TEACHER: "John, did you start the fight?"

JOHN: "No."

TEACHER: "Richard, did you start the fight?"

RICHARD: "No."

TEACHER: "Who started the fight?" No answer. "John, did you hit Richard first?"

JOHN: "I don't understand."

The teacher pretended that John hit Richard first and said, "Did you hit Richard first?'

JOHN: "No."

Then, the teacher pretended that Richard hit John first and said, "Richard, did you hit first?"

Henry, who was sitting in his seat and wondering why John couldn't seem to understand, replied loudly, "Yes!"

John and Richard got a spanking—and their hands were slapped with a ruler.

Fred inquired what the facilities were at the school. Henry replied that they had had regular individual seats.

They only went to that school in Standish for one year. Then a school was started in their own district, Johnsfield, and they went there. Their dad was a director at the school district. Their teacher was Mary Martin. They hired her and paid her $12.00 per month. She was a grand teacher and, looking back, she had a lot to put up with.

Benches were built out of planks and that is where they had their school. But Henry, looking back, felt that they had as good a training as anywhere else. They studied geography, reading, writing, and arithmetic, and were taught thoroughly. They did have singing but there was no football or basketball. Four times a year they had spelling matches and that was the only competition they had.

FRED: "Hank, you used to have a voice like a canary. I would like to hear you. I lost my voice crying for bread when I was a baby."

HANK: "Yes, you had a lot of reason to. I may have sung like a canary, but I'm more like a crow now."

Ella told Henry that he used to sing a song their mother used to sing and agreed to sing it with him. Ella told Fred that he learned bass at that school, but Fred did not know that hymn, so did not join in. Henry and Ella sang it.

Hymn Ella and Henry sang:

I. In evil long I took the light unawed by shame or fear
Til a new object met my sight and stopped my wild career.

Chorus:

> Ah, the Lamb, the bleeding Lamb, the Lamb upon Calvary
> The Lamb that was slain and liveth again to intercede for
> > me.

II. I saw one hanging on a tree in agony and blood
> Who shaked his languid eyes on me as near the cross I stood.

III. My conscience felt and ah my guilt and plunged me in despair
> I saw my sin His blood had spilt and helped to nail him
> > there.

IV. A second look He gave which said, "I freely all forgive."
> "This blood is for thy ransomed fate, I die that thou mayst
> > live."

Fred asked how they learned to sing. They took lessons from Professor Claus in Johnsfield. They received thirteen lessons for $1.00.

Ella said that she did not remember their mother at all. Fred asked what Hank remembered about their mother's illness, etc. Mother died at age thirty-nine and looked young for her age. Their youngest brother William was (Henry thought) eighteen days old. She was buried at Sterling, five miles north of Standish, because there was no cemetery in Standish at that time. When their father died, the children bought a lot in the Standish cemetery and moved their mother to Standish where she was buried with their father. Later Talka and John were buried there also.

When their mother died Talka, the oldest girl, was twelve years old. Billy, the eighteen-day-old baby, was placed with the Lutheran preacher who had held their mother's funeral service. Ella went to Daleys. Ella remembered that Father would visit Bill one Sunday and then her the next.

Fred stayed at Earnest and Louise Krause's. Fred was a cute little fellow with curly hair. The Krauses wanted to adopt Fred but Jan wanted to keep the family together. [The Krause farm was located on the southeast corner of what became known as M-61 and Eight Mile Road [see maps in Introduction]. When the Krauses took Fred, Earnest must have been thirty-eight years old and his wife, Louise, thirty-one. Earnest died in 1916 and sometime later his widow re-married.]

One Sunday their father couldn't come and see Ella, so there were two to three weeks when Ella did not see her father. When he came the next time Ella had forgotten him, so he never missed another Sunday after that. He probably had to walk five miles to visit the children. Neither Ella nor Fred could remember those days, just remembered what was told them.

Hank stayed at home and worked in the stave mill. He lost his finger in 1894, the same year that their mother died. He still had the finger bandaged when she passed away.

Fred asked how long the younger children stayed with families. Harry stayed at Caldwell's and they wanted to adopt him also. Later Fred stayed at Spooners' and the Spooners had a girl by the name of Arlettus. After Mr. Spooner passed away, Mrs. Spooner tried to hook their father, Jan, thinking he would be a good husband, but he sidestepped and did not take the bait for some reason or another.

Then Bill was put with the family of Julius Perlberg, who had a soap factory and brickyard in Standish.* Their dad gave the Perlbergs a cow for keeping Bill for a year.

The reminiscing went back to their father's going to Iowa. He was in Iowa only sixteen months. When he came back to Standish he worked in the lumber mill again. At the same time they were clearing more land on the farm, they started farming, raised crops, got more cows and a couple of pigs, etc., and did fairly well. The older boys were working in the mill—Hank in the stave and heading mill.

Hank said their father was not too successful at farming. It was not the best land or location for farming. It was all timberland, so there were stumps—pine stumps, logs, and debris to clean up. He continued working in the mill while clearing the land.

The forty acres was not a large farm, so they did not have enough crops to sell or to market. The forty acres was all they could work with the equipment and material they had, but they raised enough hay and oats for their cows and horses and enough corn for their pigs. But they had to work away from the farm to earn enough money to live.

On the farm they drove the cows to Gammon's Creek to drink. They arranged with Mr. Demo and Ralph Demo to dig a well. The agreement was $50.00 water or no pay. They struck water. Many years later, in 1961, William Ingram, who then owned the farm, said that the well was still going strong after fifty years.

Fred said that their father was a "well-witcher." He would take a willow stick and run around until the stick bent. Hank said that he did not have that much faith in that.

Their father died May 28, 1907. He had been a widower for thirteen years. Looking back, Henry thought that he died of cancer, and that he had suffered for years. But the cause of death was given as pneumonia.

Ed. Note: Catherine recalls that the brickyard the Julius Perlberg family owned was located at the north end of Court Street (See maps in Introduction). At that time there was a bridge which crossed the creek by the mill. This creek was the middle branch of the Pine River. The bridge was eventually washed away, and never replaced. The brickyard buildings gradually deteriorated. Now there is no hint of such a business ever having been there.

Ella remembered when their father died. It was eight o'clock in the morning. Hank (Henry) had left for work about two hours earlier, after staying up with him all night. Hank was working for the telephone company at the time and happened to be working in Standish. Harry and John were working in the lumber-woods at Dewards out of Frederic, about one hundred miles from Standish. A telegram told them of their father's death. They received it while way back in the woods, and came home on the next afternoon train. Fred went to tell Henry, who was on top of a pole working. He came down and the two brothers "drove" home.

James Kay preached the funeral sermon. Two of the songs that were sung were, "Time Is Earnest Passing By" and "Forever with the Lord."

Their father had many friends. The Gospel Hall (where the funeral was held) was packed and people were standing outside, quite a ways back. Many stores in Standish and the school in Johnsfield (of which he had been director) were closed for the funeral.

The scripture that Mr. Kay gave was from Ecclesiastes (7:2): "It is better to go to a house of mourning than to a house of feasting." It appeared the whole of Standish and Johnsfield was mourning.

After the funeral the family went home. Talka, aged twenty-five and John, aged thirty-three, took the reins of leadership. Talka took over the housekeeping and John the management of the farm, and both took care of the younger children. They did this for a year or two. Then John went back to camp and worked in the woods, and came home at intervals to check on how things were going.

Fred said that Talka deserved a lot of credit for keeping the family together. She was a strong disciplinarian, very fair—fair above reproach. She was the type of person that would whip first and talk after. Fred felt that he had many whippings he did not deserve but also did many capers for which he should have had a spanking, so he believed he had come out about even.

Ella remembered so many nice things Talka did for them. She knitted their stockings and mittens, saw that they were clothed, and patched their clothes—sometimes patches upon patches.

Fred asked Henry to sing his favorite hymn, "When My Life's Work Is Ended." Henry said that he would make an attempt and then added that this hymn was written by Fanny Crosby.

"When My Life Work Is Ended"

When my life work is ended and I cross the swelling tide
   When the bright and glorious morning I shall see.
I shall know my Redeemer when I reach the other side
   And His smile will be the first to welcome me.

Chorus:
I shall know Him, I shall Know Him
    As redeemed by His side I shall stand
I shall know Him, I shall know Him
    By the print of the nails in His hand.

Part Two

THE RECORDS
OF
JAN WÜBBENA

TRANSLATIONS OF
JAN WÜBBENA'S
SEA LOG AND
FARM JOURNAL

Introductory Comments by
Dawn W. Hendricks

The following pages set forth a translation of Jan's sea log and farm journal. The sea log is a journal kept by Jan during a voyage in 1882. Missing from the farm journal are the first twenty-five pages. A glossary of terms relating to the farm journal, prepared by Catherine Wubbena, has been appended thereto in order to make the document more understandable.

Also in existence is Jan's workbook for the study of celestial navigation. This has not been translated or included because the content consists only of 118 pages of neatly done solutions to celestial navigation problems. One interesting aspect of this book: there is a marginal notation in red written by someone other than Jan wherein he was roundly castigated for the inadequacy of his solution. This did not happen again. Although there were a few other places where his work was corrected or commented upon with marginal comments in red, most of the other problems apparently were accepted without comment.

All of these writings were done neatly in black ink with minimal corrections or writeovers. In some cases pages are missing, in other cases parts of pages have been torn out. In a few cases there are writings on them in English by someone other than Jan, all of which appear to have no significance other than that someone needed some paper to write upon. Some of these extraneous writings appear on the blank pages and some on the pages where Jan had written. But for the greater part, Jan's writings that do still exist are intact and legible.

These records were written in German script, sometimes called "Gothic," a cursive hand peculiar to Germany. The letters are more angular and several are formed so differently that they are unrecognizable to readers of Roman script. Until fifty years ago German schools taught both styles of handwriting, using the German script for German words and Roman script for foreign words. Educated Germans were able to read both styles of writing with equal ease. That is not true today! It was under Adolph Hitler that training in the German script was terminated and children began learning to read and write only in Roman script. Today special seminars are needed to train German scholars to "decode" the old German script.

Fortunately, we were put in touch with Dr. James Scott, Professor of German at Lebanon Valley College, who had the required expertise in the old German script. He kindly undertook the translation of the sea log, the farm journal, and the steersman's certificate, and we are indebted to him.

| |

It is interesting to look at the creation of the sea log in relation to other events in Jan's life; such examination may also shed light on his possible motivations to come to America.

1. The red notations by the instructor in his 8" by 13-½" navigation studies workbook were dated from March 11 to June 24, 1872. Apparently Jan did these problems while attending a course, either on ship or ashore. He was twenty-seven at that point.

2. Jan and Catharina were married on December 7, 1873. He was twenty-eight and she was eighteen.

3. Their first child (John) was born on April 18, 1874, with Charles following on October 8, 1875, Henry on November 4, 1878, and Taalke on August 16, 1881.

4. Jan received his steersman certificate on January 26, 1878. This was a little over 5 ½ years after he finished his course in navigation and a little over 4 years after they were married. Jan was thirty-three at this point. Had he been serving an apprenticeship as a steersman in these interim years? We don't know.

5. The sea log which we have is for a round-trip from Hamburg to Lagos* during the period starting January 6, 1882 and ending on July 5 of that year. He was thirty-seven at this point. We know that he was serving as a steersman at this point [see April 5 entry].

This round-trip voyage took place about four years after he was granted his steersman certificate. We don't know what capacity he was filling on voy-

---

Ed. Note: Lagos was a British colony on the west coast of Africa at this time. Eventually it was merged into what is now Nigeria and today is the country's capital.

ages in the interim, but the log seems to reflect that by this time he was fully experienced and competent in his job.

The ship was powered by wind. It was small. We can see this both from the cargo list and from a roster of the crew (and monthly pay in Reichsmarks) as follows: steersman (Jan, 75 Rmk); cook (48 Rmk); 2 sailors (45 Rmk each); steward (33 Rmk); and cabin boy (5 Rmk) [see January 26 entry].

Apparently there was a captain in charge [see April 14 entry]. Strangely, there is but this one reference to him and no entries by him. This seems to suggest that this sea log was a private journal kept by Jan and not an official ship's log.

It should be noted that while not under sail they observed Easter and Good Friday and each Sabbath, and he made notes to that effect. Apparently the rule was that no work was done on these days, except that there was an exception based upon necessity [see January 29 entry].

6. By 1886 his mother (who lived with them) had died. At this point Jan was forty-one and Catharina thirty-one. On June 3 they sold their household goods by auction and on July 9 sailed from Bremerhaven for the United States.

From these facts it seems that when Jan was courting Catharina he was a young man who had ambitions to get ahead and was working toward them. By the mid-eighties when Jan was about forty he had made progress, but it was apparent that his career was not on a fast track. Considering what we know about his determination and capacity for hard work as later exhibited in the United States, was he satisfied with his progress? One could surmise that he probably was not. Was the fact that he was forty at that time relevant? Did some men have a mid-life crisis at age forty in those days as they do now?

It is conventional wisdom of our family that Jan and Catharina came to the United States so that their sons could escape service in the Kaiser's army. This wisdom apparently is founded on solid fact, because we know that those of their offspring that were born in Germany (i.e., the oldest) all said that this was so. But we humans often do things for more than one reason. It is interesting to speculate to what extent their movement to the United States was also motivated by career frustration on the part of Jan. We will never know.

Aspects of the farm journal are interesting, too. As indicated above, the first twenty-five pages are missing. The 273 pages we do have are dated from July 16, 1899, to the end of June 1904, with the last 5½ months of 1899 taking up fifteen pages. We can reasonably assume that the journal was probably started at some point between July 1898 and January 1899.

Was another journal kept before this one? This journal was started at least five years after Catharina died. The years from their arrival in Standish to her death had been years of intense strain in getting established, while the years immediately after her death had been years of desperately trying to hold the family together. It was only as the children grew older that Jan's life became easier. Surmise what you like. My personal belief is that it is more likely that this was the first farm journal that Jan had kept.

We don't know if he started a new journal after this volume was filled. They were working on their new house in the summer of 1904 (e.g., see June 2 and June 31 [*sic*] entries) and undoubtedly were very busy. Jan was 59 and would be dead in two years and eleven months.

Henry felt that his father had suffered from cancer for years before he died [see page 55]. Catherine records that he died of congestive heart failure and possibly pneumonia [see page 6]. Jan notes in the Wednesday, April 6, 1904, entry: "Overcast and Wet. Went to bed in the forenoon." Again, on Sunday, April 24 of that year: "Good weather. Kept the Sabbath. Spent the whole day in bed. Rain in the morning; good weather in the afternoon."

So did he start a new journal, which has been lost? Or was he too busy? Or was he simply worn out by this point and without the strength to do it? We will never know.

Various intriguing aspects of their daily lives and of Jan's personality stand out in the journal. Examples: on May 1, 1904, he noted that Johannes (John) departed without saying good-bye to him. On Tuesday, March 1 of that year, he wrote to Mr. Kitzman explaining that their daughters had broken a school windowpane, that the replacement had cost eighty cents, and that he had installed it, and asking if Mr. Kitzman would like to share in the expense of the pane to the extent of forty cents. On Tuesday, January 12, 1904: "I want to note that my fall on the 31st of December has made it so that I cannot do any work with my right arm. I sorted potatoes."

From the start to the finish of the journal Jan's deep devotion and gratitude to God is apparent. There are a great number of references to keeping the Sabbath, just as in the sea log, as well as many comments expressing gratitude to God. There are many scriptural citations. The last daily journal entry ends with the following notation: "This book is full. It was begun in God's name and it ends in His name. Praise be to Him and thanks!"

Finally, a comment regarding the language in which the farm journal was written. At the start the journal was entirely in German, with two exceptions: (1) apparently when he knew the English word and did not feel comfortable with the German equivalent he used the English word; and (2) when he was recording correspondence addressed to him or written by him, he carefully set it down in the English language in which it was written.

One could anticipate that by the end of the five years covered by the entries, he might be using more English words in his journal. The interesting thing is that he was not! He could write English with a fair degree of ease when he wanted to, as when writing to his sons, and he had insisted that his children become totally Americanized. And yet he continued to keep his records in his mother tongue.

It should be noted that frequent reference to the glossary (page 305) while reading the farm journal will substantially increase one's understanding of the entries.

TRANSLATION OF JAN WÜBBENA'S SEA LOG

Description of the Manuscript

The Log written by Jan Wübbena is a slim folio volume bound in brown, leather-grain paper boards of the time (nineteenth century). This translator numbered the existing leaves and parts of leaves in pencil in the upper right hand corner; these folio numbers appear in square brackets along the left margin of the translation. A letter "r" signifies the recto, or right, side of a leaf; a letter "v" stands for the verso, or left, side. The book consists of six signatures sewn into the binding as follows [dashes indicate missing leaves; x's indicate incomplete leaves; leaves 7 and 60 have broken free of the binding].

```
24 ——————————|—————————— 25
23 ——————————|—————————— 26
22 ——————————|—————————— 27        Signature 3
21 ——————————|—————————— 28
20 ——————————|—————————— 29


35 ——————————|—————————— 36
34 ——————————|—————————— 37
(33) - - - - - - - -|—————————— 38        Signature 4
(32) - - - - - - - -|—————————— 39
(31) - - - - - - - -|—————————— 40
30 ——————————|—————————— 41


46 ——————————|—————————— 47
45 ——————————|—————————— 48
44 ——————————|—————————— 49        Signature 5
43 ——————————|—————————— 50
42 ——————————|—————————— 51


56 ——————————|—————————— 57
55 ——————————|- - - - - - - -58
54 ——————————|—————————— 59        Signature 6
53 ——————————|——————— 60
52 ——————————|————— end paper
```

The Log records two voyages of the *Lützburg*. The first, from Hamburg to Lagos,
began on January 6, 1882, and ended March 26 of the same year [leaves 1–12].
The second, from Lagos to Falmouth, began April 6, 1882, and ended three
months later on July 2 [leaves 13–24]. Leaf 25^r is blank and serves to divide the
record of the two voyages from the rest of the journal. Leaves 25^v–60 contain
nautical observations, notes, and calculations made underway to determine the
ship's position. Mr. Wübbena appears to have begun these notes generally at the
back of the Log and to have worked toward the front.

[1ʳ]   Log written on board the ship *Lützburg* out of Norden.

1882	On the 6th of January I came aboard the ship *Lützburg*. The ship lay in port in Hamburg beside the *Duc Alben*. In the evening I signed on. I was hired on as a steersman at the rate of 75 Reichsmark per month.
Jan. 7	On Saturday cleaned the hold and made preparations to go into dry dock.
Jan. 8	Kept the Sabbath.
Jan. 9	The steamer was hauled up into dry dock. With the help of the carpenters we came aboard. The ship was then gone over and repaired under expert supervision. The work was completed on Jan. 14. We returned the same day to the harbor and got ready to take on a load of mixed cargo with which we were to sail to Lagos. The ship was seaworthy.
Jan. 17	We began to load the same day and worked continuously to load the following cargo:

Date	Shipper	Mark	No.	Freight	
Jan. 17	J.C. Müller & Sons	E	1/3	130	boards
				68	scrapers [*Scheben?*]
	F.P.D. Rupke			3	*Liverpooler* with iron bands
		B	1/2	2	*Liverpooler* with bottoms
				25	Bundles of iron bands
Jan. 18	Podlech			91	scrapers
				91	Bundles of iron
				9	barrels with bottoms
Jan. 19	Joh. Wichmann			1600	Sacks of salt
Jan. 20	J. Rüdiger Naeff			1400	Sacks of Salt
Jan. 21	J.C. Müller & Son			40	Boards
Jan. 22				Kept the Sabbath	
Jan. 23	C.G. Welling & Co.			2	Balls machine thread
	Jansen & Schmulinsky	J&S	19	1	crate
			20/22	3	iron plates
			23	1	bundle iron rods
	J.H. Helmers	I	37	1	crate
[1ᵛ]	J.H. Helmers	PN	20	1	crate

		DI	19	1 crate
	F.W.Aden			25 rush baskets
	Witt & Busch	BT	6540	1 crate
		PS	7203/12	10 crates
		JSG	9945/7	3 crates
		MW	6125/6	2 crates
		EB	3537	1 barrel
		WK	61/85	25 crates
		DI	584/8	5 crates
		FM	1/5	5 crates
Jan. 24		CF	2368/72	5 crates
	Schulte &	S&S	1/2	2 crates
	Schemmann		3/6	4 rolls of tarpaper
			7/9	3 barrels
	Otto Tietz	AT	1/25	25 cases of beer
	Janssen &			
	Schmilinsky	J&S	24/21	4 pieces of iron
	Green &	G&S	813	1 barrel of oil

Date	Shipper	Mark	No.	Freight
Jan. 24	Saermann		814	1 barrel of oil
			815	1 barrel of oil
	U. Pätzel Heirs	I	21/24	4 barrels
		PN	11/12	2 barrels
		DI	11/12	2 barrels
	F. J. Aehrens	I	28/29	2 crates
		PN	15	1 crate
		DI	15	1 crate
	E. Stelzig	I	50	1 crate
		I	27/27½	2 crates
		I	51/63	9 barrels
		PN	14	1 crate
	F.M.Fett & Co.	I	28/32	5 hams
		I	33/36	2 sausages
		PN	15/16	2 hams
		PN	17/19	3 sausages
		DI	15	1 ham
[2ʳ]		DI	16/18	3 sausages
	F.U. Müller	I	12/13	2 crates
	& Co.	PN	5	1 crate
		DI	5	1 crate

	Shipper	Mark	No.	Freight
		I	14	1 barrel
		PN	6	1 barrel
		DI	6	1 barrel
	F.G. Voigt	PN	23	1 crate
		DI	27	1 crate
		DI	21	1 barrel
	Witt & Busch	WB	127	1 crate
		HW		1 crate
		PNP		1 crate
		WB		1 crate
		CCS		1 crate
		FK		1 crate
		AH	29	1 crate
		M&G	203	1 crate
				1 sail
				1 packet
				13 strainers
	Rodenburg Bros.	HE	1/3	3 barrels
	Wm. Rufer	I	46/49	4 sacks
		I	50	1 sack
	Wilh. Riechus	I	44	1 crate
		PN	24	1 crate
		DI	28	1 crate
	Otto Fortmann	PN	13	1 crate
		I	25	1 crate
		DI	13	1 crate
	F.A.C. Deller	DI	20/21	2 crates
		I	38/39	3 crates
		PN	21/22	2 crates
	Alex Brandes	I	18/20	3 crates
		PN	9/10	2 crates
[2ᵛ]		DI	9/10	2 crates
	Oberdörffer &	I	15/17	3 crates
	Linkeisen	PN	7/8	2 crates
Date	**Shipper**	**Mark**	**No.**	**Freight**
		DI	7/8	2 crates
	Carl Matscheng	I	44/47	4 crates
		DI	26/27	2 crates
		DI	24/25	2 barrels
	F. Heveke	S&B	1	1 crate

Jan. 25	C.W. Herwig		1500	demijohns
	Witt & Busch	W&B	50	crates
Jan. 26	F.P.D.Rupke		25	scrapers
			16	barrels
		K&I	1	barrel
			12	bundles of iron bands
			44	scrapers; this was the load.

The cargo was stowed aboard by packers. During this time we had almost continuously foggy weather and a westerly wind. On the 18th the cabinboy Alphons Wein from Nauen came on board, the cook Weert Vogelsang from Gaudrsche on the 25th of January and the two sailors Weert Miller and Simon Büscher from Warsingsfehn and the sailor August Schäffer on the 26th of January. The crew was mustered on the 25th, to wit: the steersman J. Wübbena at a monthly wage of 75 Rmk., the cook 48 Rmk., the two sailors at 45 Rmk. each, the Steward at 33 Rmk. and the Cabinboy at 5 Rmk. The sailors closed the hatches with tarred, three-ply bat-

Jan. 27   tening and got everything ready to sail. On January 28 a pilot came on board during the day.

Jan. 28   Under his direction we cast off. A steamer took us in tow and brought us down the Elbe. At three o'clock in the afternoon we dropped anchor in the port of Glückstadt. The ship drew 11' at the bow and 11' at the stern.

Jan. 29   Kept the Sabbath. Wind from the west and foggy. The hatches were sealed. The following night

Jan. 30   The wind shifted to blow from the east bringing clearing. At daybreak we raised anchor and began to sail down the Elbe in a stiff breeze which grew stronger as we sailed. At about 2 o'clock P.M. we passed the pilot's station [3ʳ] and dropped the pilot. At about 2 P.M. we passed the outermost banks of the Elbe. We continued to sail with angled sails, an east wind, a stiff breeze, along the coast. At about 5 o'clock P.M. we sighted the Weser

light p. 5' at a distance of 10 km. We sighted the
Nordaney beacon SE p. 6' at a distance of 16 km.
The sky was clear; the hatches were sealed. We continued to steer along the coast and saw the Borkum
light; the east wind was blowing a stiff breeze. At
11:30 sighted the light at Borkum Reef and passed
the same at 12:30 in the morning.

Jan. 31   We sighted and passed the beacons at Terschelling,
and Vlieland. The wind continued from the east, a
stiff breeze. We ran full sails, sighted the Texel
beacon and shot the sun at noon which showed out
location to be 53° 0' north latitude and 4° 18'east
longitude. Nice weather. The wind from the east
blowing a stiff breeze, the hatches were closed.

Jan. 31/ Feb. 1	Bell	St.Cs.	Wind	Dist.	Var.	Ac.	Cs.	D.	Notes
N	8	S5½W	SE	0	1¾	S3	¾W	30	Stiff breeze,
A	8							30	full.
E	8							30	
L	8								
M	8								
V	8								

Continued to steer, sighted the Galloper light and
passed the same at 3:00 A.M., the wind SE, lt. breeze,
S.d. [?]. Sighted the North Foreland light at 5:00
A.M. WSW *p.b.i.Ger* [?], at 8:00 passed the North Land
Head light and then set course for the Gullstream
light. The Wind SE, a fresh breeze. Passed the
Gullstream light at 11:00 A.M. Continued at the helm,
passed South Foreland at 2:00 P.M. and then set course
into the Channel. Beautiful weather, the wind SE,
favorable breeze.

Sailed onward. sighted at 6:00 P.M. the Dungeness
light at 3 km.. Set course for Beachy Head, the wind
SE, breeze fair. Sighted and passed Beachy Head.
Wind and weather beginning to become less favorable.
Sighted Beachy Head at 2:30 P.M. as it disappeared off
the horizon.

Feb. 1/2	Bell	St.Cs.	Wind	Dist.	Var.	Ac.	Cs.	D.	Notes
N	8								
A	8								
E	8								
L	8⁵3	S7°hW	StW	o	1¼W	S5¾W		5	breeze fair
M	8							11	calm, overcast
V	8		none						no rudder

[3ᵛ] [Each side of the following eight leaves shows the ship's progress for three days on the above chart. The following is a translation of just the **"Notes"** part of these entries. There are several abbreviations which this translator does not understand; they appear in italics. Tr.]

Feb. 2/3 Breeze fair. Hatches closed.
Lively breeze, beautiful weather *S. d.*
Fresh, bright. *S. d.*

Lat. 50° 2' W.   Long. 2° 28' W.

Feb. 3/4 Sighted the Start Point light at 4:00 A.M. disappeared beyond the horizon.
A fresh breeze, beautiful weather. *S. d.*
Sailed on, the Lizard light in sight. A stiff breeze.
Lizard light at 2:00 P.M. off the NE.
Beautiful weather, set sails out of the north-west.
The same.

Lat. 49° 15' N.   Long. 6° 22' W.

Feb. 4/5 Winds changeable. Sails set for the north-west. *S. d.*
The same
Nice weather

Lat. 48° 1' N.   Long. 8° 15' W.

[4ʳ]
Feb. 5/6 Breeze fair, clouding up. *S. d.*
Irregular wind, overcast. *S. d.*
Stiff breeze, overcast. *S. d.*

Lat. 46° 38' N.   Long. 10° 36' W.

Feb. 6/7   Stiff breeze, overcast. *S. d.*
                High waves, heavy seas. *S. d.*
                Winds increasing, furled gaffsail and staysail
                furled flying jib and topgallant
                Overcast

                Lat. 44° 36' N.   Long. 12° 51' W.

Feb. 7/8   Stiff breeze, sky overcast
                Clearing toward evening.
                Furled jib sail.
                Overcast.

                Lat. 44° 25' N.   Long. 14° 32' W.

[4v]
Feb. 8/9   Strong winds. Seas rising.
                Upper topsail and top staysail furled.
                Threatening, overcast sky,
                Calmed down toward end of the watch. high seas.
                Overcast, rainy.

                Lat. 44°, 38' N.   Long. 16° 7' W.

Feb. 9/10   Light breeze, high waves out of the north-west.
                Light breeze, set full sail
                Stiff, irregular breeze, high seas.

                Lat. 42° 56' N.   Long. 16° 27' W.

Feb. 10/11   Wind picking up. Furled the light sails, upper
                topsail, top staysail.
                Wind gathering strength. Reefed the foresail and
                mainsail. High, heavy seas. The ship tossed around.
                Wind and seas continued to rise. Furled the foresail
                and decksweeper. all sails furled
                except for the closely reefed mainsail, lower top-
                sail and topmast staysail.
                Waves often breaking over the ship.
                Occasional large *handiger* waves from the north-west.

                Furled the reefed sweeper. *handiger.*

                Lat. 41° 24' N.   Long. 15° 43' W.

[5ʳ]
Feb. 11/12   Storm abating. In the evening set all sails.
              Large waves running north-west.
              Irregular breeze, high seas.
              Overcast.
              Lat. 39° 28' N.   Long. 17° 38' W.

Feb. 12/13   Good weather. Large waves.
              Scant breeze. Overcast.
              Scant breeze. Large waves
              Lively breeze. Sea running high.
              Lat. 38° 22' 5" N.   Long. 16° 23' 0" West

Feb. 13/14   Scarcely any wind. Beautiful weather.
              A lively breeze picked up.
              Breeze became irregular.
              Lat. 36° 30' 0" N.   Long. 16° 48" 0' W.

[5ᵛ]
Feb. 14/15   Fresh breeze, cloudy sky.
              Lat. 34° 2.7' N.   Long. 17° 8' W.

Feb. 15/16   A stiff breeze.
              Caught sight of Madeira after dark. Stiff breeze.
              Stiff breeze blowing. Cloudy.
              Lat. 31° 26' 7" N.   Long. 17° 28' W.

Feb. 16/17   A fresh breeze.
              Sighted the Isle of Palma at 8:00 in the morning.
              Lat. 28° 49' 8" N.   Long. 17° 55' W.

[6ʳ]
Feb. 17/18   Calm, gentle. Still—unbroken.
              Irregular. Cloudy
              Gentle breeze.
              Lat. 27° 55' 8" N.   Long. 18° 40'0 W.

Feb. 18/19   Beautiful weather. Hardly a breeze
              Gentle breeze
              Fresh wind.

              Lat. 26° 18.8' N.   Long. 18° 55'

Feb. 19/20   A fresh breeze.
              Stiff breeze

              Lat. 23° 17' 0" N.   Long. 18° 55.0'

                                                          21st day of the voyage
[6ᵛ]
Feb. 20/21   A fresh breeze. Nice weather.

              Lat. 21° 9' 0" N.   Long. 18° 55'West

Feb. 21/22   A fresh breeze. Beautiful day.

              Lat. 18° 31' N.   Long. 18° 55' W.

Feb. 22/23   Calm, no wind, broken
              Regular, evenly blowing lively breeze
              Bright stars
              Beautiful weather

              Lat. 16° 17' N.   Long. 18° 55' W.

[7ʳ]
Feb. 23/24   A lively breeze.
              Breeze slackened off
              A fresh breeze.

              Lat. 14° 0' N.   Long. 18° 55' W.

Feb. 24/25   A light breeze. Beautiful weather. Hot.

              Lat. 12° 11.2' N.   Long. 18° 39' W.

Feb. 25/26   Calm, clear day.
              Light breeze, clear.
              Fresh breeze, clear.

              Lat. 10° 22' 4" N.   Long. 18° 25' W.

27th day of the voyage

[7ᵛ]

Feb. 26/27   A beautiful day.

                Lat. 8° 49' N.   Long. 17° 45' W.

Feb. 27/28   Calm, clear sky.

                Lat. 8° 4' N.   Long. 17° 10' W.

Feb. 28/
Mar. 1   Moderate, nice weather
                Still, nice.

                Lat. 7° 28' 4" N.   Long. 16° 4' W.

[8ʳ]

Mar. 1/2   Slight breeze
                No wind. Storm brewing, oppressive
                hot.

                [no position given]

Mar. 2/3   Slight breeze
                No wind, very hot

                Lat. 6° 38' N.   Long. 16° 0' W.

Mar. 3/4   Moderate and slight breezes

                Lat. 6° 6.2' N.   Long. 15° 10' W.

[8ᵛ]

Mar. 4/5   Hot weather, threatening

                Lat. 6° 6.2' N.   Long. 15° 10' W.

Mar. 5/6   No wind. threatening skies

                [no position given]

Mar. 6/7   Changeable winds, threatening storm
                Slight breeze to no wind
                Moderate breeze
                Calm
                Storm threatening

                Lat. 5° 18' N.   Long. 14° 40' W.

[9^r]

Mar. 7/8   Strong storm gusts with heavy rains; filled the water
            casks. Skies cleared about 8:00.
            Set full sail.
            Lat. 4° 26' N.   Long. 14° 40' W.

Mar. 8/9   No wind. Threatening storm
            [no position given]

Mar. 9/10   Slight breeze
            Distant lightning
            Lat. 4° 26' N.   Long. 13° 51' W.

[9^v]

Mar. 10/11 No wind. Clear skies, hot
            Threatening storm
            [no position given]

                                                        40 Days at sea

Mar. 11/12 Slight breeze, hot.
            4° 19.6' N.   Long. 13° 6' W.

Mar. 12/13 Clear, moderate breeze
            [no position given]

[10^r]

Mar. 13/14 Threatening storm.
            [no position given]

Mar. 14/15 Clear, moderate breeze.
            Lat. 3° 44' N.   Long. 11° 17' W.

Mar. 15/16 No wind. Bright and hot.
            [no position given]

                                                        45 days at sea

[10^v]

Mar. 16/17 Wind from the south. Hot, clear.
            Bright, moderate breeze
            Lat. 3° 54' N.   Long. 10° 12' W.

46 days at sea

Mar. 17/18   Wind from the south. Moderate breeze, hot
Remained so all day.

Lat. 3° 54.9' N.   Long. 9° 0' W.

Mar. 18/19   Wind from the southwest.
Moderate breeze.
Storm threatening
Slight to moderate breeze

Lat. 3° 39' N.   Long. 7° 44' W.

Mar. 19/20   Wind from the southwest.
Moderate breeze.
Storm threatening
Clear, moderate breeze.

Lat. 3° 39.9' N.   Long. 7° 44' W.

[11ʳ]

Mar. 20/21   Southwesterly wind.
Moderate breeze, hot.
Overcast

Lat. 3° 21.4' N.   Long. 6° 42' W.

Mar. 21/22   Wind from the west. Moderate breeze
Storm gusts with rain
Stormy
Clearing
Clear

Lat. 3° 34' N.   Long. 5° 38' W.

Mar. 22/23   Southwesterly wind. Clear, overcast

Lat. 3° 34' N.   Long. 4° 28' W.

51 days at sea

[11ᵛ]

Mar. 23/24   Southwesterly wind. Slight breeze, clear sky
Clear weather

Lat. 3° 52.7' N.   Long. 3° 19' W.

Mar. 24/25   Wind from the southwest. Clear. Moderate breeze.
             Lat. 4° 23.3' N   Long. 2° 5' W.

Mar. 25/26   Southwesterly wind. Moderate breeze, clear sky
             Very hot.
             Clear
             Storm threatening
             Clearing
             Lat. 5° 57.9' N.   Long. 1° 11' W.

Mar. 26   Clearing. At 2:00 P.M. caught sight of the coast.
             Measured 30 fathoms, continued steering, slight
             breeze; at 8:00 P.M. set course along the coast;
             steered NE by N and continued to measure the depth
             regularly; measured 10 fathoms at 8:10 P.M.;—the
             wind died out as night
Mar. 27   fell; at dawn we saw Lagos, breeze continued slight
             and calm, around noon a breeze came up out of the
             southwest, I steered in the direction of Lagos and
             dropped anchor outside the har-
Mar. 29   bor about 3:00 P.M. Fine, clear weather. We lay
             at anchor until the afternoon of the 29th when a
             steamer towed us into the harbor at Lagos. The next
             morning we tied up to one of the docks there and
             then began to unload the cargo, which was in good
             condition. The job was
Apr. 5   completed by April 5.
             Praise be to God!
                  J. Wübbena, Steersman

Apr. 3   Monday, April 3, the Consul of the German Reich sent
             two men needing assistance on board. These were Mr.
             Claassen, a carpenter from Rostock and Mr. Michel-
             sen, a sailmaker from Christiania. They had been
             aboard the ship "Elise" from Elsfleth which has been
             lost. We were to return them to Europe.
             [The remaining third of the page has been cut away.]

[12ᵛ]
1882   Log written on board the *Lützburg* during the voyage
            from Lagos to Falmouth (as ordered).

            After the cargo had been unloaded, the hold
            cleaned and the ship carefully inspected both
            inside and out, we prepared the hold for taking on
            new cargo. We put down the underlayment and cov-
            ered it with mats. Everything was done most care-
            fully in preparation for taking on a load of palm
            kernels. The ship was tight and in seaworthy condition.

Apr. 6 Th.   Began *eine Parthie* [a game of cards? Tr.]
Apr. 7   Observed Good Friday
Apr. 8 Sat.   Again began *eine Parthie*.
Apr. 9 & 10   Celebrated Easter
Apr. 11 Tu.   Carried out my duties aboard ship.
Apr. 12 & 13   Began another *Parthie*. We lay at anchor in the
               river.
Apr. 14 Fr.   Carried out my duties aboard ship. On the 11th
               the two men the Imperial Consul had sent aboard
               became sick. A doctor examined them on the 13th
               and on the 14th the captain sent them to a hospi-
               tal on orders from the Consul.
Apr. 15 & 16   Carried out my duties on board ship and kept the
               Sabbath.
Apr. 17 Mon.   Picked up the two castaways at the hospital on
               orders of. . . . [The remainder of the page is
               cut away. Tr.]

[13ʳ]
Apr. 20/21   Breeze from SW. At 8:00 we were 12 km NNW of the
               Lagos wharf. A lively breeze.
               Breeze died down.
               The hatches are open.

               Lat. 5° 45.9' N.   Long. 3° 25' E.

                                                        1 day at sea

Apr. 21/22   Very light breeze from SW W. clear sky.
               Very hot. The two sick men were given quinine in wine.
               Lovely weather

1882   Log written on board the *Lützburg* during the voyage
            from Lagos to Falmouth (as ordered).

            Light breeze, calm sea.
            Lat. 5° 2' N.   Long. 4° 9' E.

Apr. 22/23 A fresh breeze from SW W, hot.
            Storm brewing. Carefully closed and sealed the hatches.
            Lat. 4° 3' N.   Long. 4° 49' E.

[13ᵛ]
Apr. 23/24 No wind. Nice weather. Hatches open.
            [no position given]

                                                                4 days at sea

Apr. 24/25 Lively breeze shifting from W. to S.
            Choppy seas.
            Nice weather, the sea calmer.
            Lat. 3° 38.1' N.   Long. 5° E.

Apr. 25/26 Light breeze from WSW.
            Beautiful day
            Seemed stormy, closed the hatches.
            Remained so.

[14ʳ]
Apr. 26/27 Stormy, heavy rains
            Wind turning south
            Clearing, hatches opened
            Nice.
            Lat. 1° 37.3' N.   Long. 4° 52' E.

Apr. 27/28 No wind. Nice weather
            [no position given]

Apr. 28/29 Nice weather. choppy seas
            Seas calmer
            Lat. 1° 18' N.   Long. 3° 54' E.

                                                                9 days at sea

1882   Log written on board the *Lützburg* during the voyage
from Lagos to Falmouth (as ordered).

[14ᵛ]
Apr. 29/30   No wind.

[no position given]

10 days at sea

Apr. 30/
May 1   Thunderstorm, heavy rains. Hatches carefully
sealed
Rough sea
Nice weather, hatches open

Lat. 0° 5.9' N.   Long. 2° 56.6' E.

May 1/2   A moderate breeze
Closed the hatches during the night
A fresh breeze

Lat. 0° 10' N.   Long. 1° 36.6' W.

[15ʳ]
May 2/3   Fresh breeze, heavy seas.
Breeze died down
wind picked up, opened the hatches.
Stiff breeze.

Lat. 0° 27.9' N.   Long. 0° 11.4' W.

May 3/4   Stiff breeze, heavy seas. Hatches opened.

Lat. 0° 44' S.   Long. 2° 20' W.

May 4/5   Stiff breeze, heavy seas, large waves.
Hatches open.

Lat. 0° 52' S.   Long. 4° 27' W.

[15ᵛ]
May 5/6   Fair, cloudy
Hatches closed during the night.
Opened during the day.
Fresh Passat breeze

1882   Log written on board the *Lützburg* during the voyage
        from Lagos to Falmouth (as ordered).

The sailmaker (passenger) reported himself sick.
Medicine.

Lat. 0° 52.1' S.   Long. 6° 27.1' W.

May 6/7   Scattered small rain showers. Hatches sealed
           Stiff breeze
           Set the lee sail.

Lat. 0° 52.1' S.   Long. 8° 42.1' W.

May 7/8   Fresh breeze
           Continued all day

Lat. 0° 52.1' S.   Long. 11° 2' W.

                                        21 days at sea

[16ʳ]
May 8/9   Wind from WSE. Large waves.
           Seas quieter, nice weather

Lat. 0° 28.2 S.   Long. 13° 2.1' W.

May 9/10   Moderate breeze
           Beautiful weather
           Wind dying down.

Lat. 0° 2.2' N.   Long. 14° 37.6' W.

May 10/11 Light breeze.
           Lively.
           Stormy weather.

Lat. 0° 26.6' N.   Long. 15° 35.6' W.

[16ᵛ]
May 11/12 Light breeze
           Lively

Lat. 0° 17.5' N.   Long. 15° 41.6' W.

May 12/13 Fair weather, cloudy

Lat. 2° 50' N.   Long. 16° 11.6' W.

1882   Log written on board the *Lützburg* during the voyage
         from Lagos to Falmouth (as ordered).

May 13/14   Gusty
             Furled the lee sail
             Wind dropped off
             Sighted two ships coming the opposite way.
             Lat. 3° 28.8' N.   Long. 16° 26.6' W.

[17ʳ]
May 14/15   Heavy rain at noon. Ship did not answer the helm.
             [no position given]

May 17/18   Moderate breeze. Sky cleared off around noon.
             Lat. 4° 29.8' N.   Long. 17° 16.6' W.

May 18/19   Thunderstorm. Very choppy sea. Rain.
             Dry weather. Clearing.
             Changeable winds
             Very rough sea.
             Lat. 5° 2.8' N.   Long. 18° 6.6'W.

[17ᵛ]
May 19/20   Strong Breeze
             Furled the jib.
             Choppy sea, overcast sky
             The ship pitched in the rough water and had waves
             breaking over it.
             Lat. 6° 7.2' N.   Long. 18° 54.6' W.

                                              30 days at sea

May 20/21   Very choppy sea. Jib furled
             The ship pitched and rolled heavily and had the sea
             break over it.
             Lat. 7° 28.7' N.   Long. 19° 52.6' W.

May 21/22   A fresh breeze, cloudy.
             Lat. 10° 4' N.   Long. 20° 44.6' W.

1882   Log written on board the *Lützburg* during the voyage
            from Lagos to Falmouth (as ordered).

[18ʳ]
May 22/23   A fresh breeze
             Lat. 11° 15.8' N.   Long. 21° 50.6' W.

May 23/24   A fresh breeze
             Hatches open during the day.
             Lat. 12° 29.6' N.   Long. 22° 53.6' W.

May 24/25   A fresh breeze
             Hatches open during the day.
             Lat. 13° 48.4' N.   Long. 24° 1.6' W.

                                                    35 days at sea

[18ᵛ]
May 25/26   A strong breeze
             Gaff topsail furled
             Jib furled
             In the evening set the jib and opened the hatches.
             Lat. 15° 8.8' N.   Long. 25° 9.6' W.

                                                    36 days at sea

May 26/27   A stiff breeze.
             Lat. 16° 23' N.   Long. 26° 14.6' W.

May 27/28   A very stiff breeze.
             Furled the light sails, closed the hatches.
             Opened the hatches
             Lat. 17° 50.9' N.   Long. 27° 12.6' W.

[19ʳ]
May 28/29   A stiff breeze. Hatches sealed because of waves break-
             ing over the ship.
             Lat. 19° 20.5' N.   Long. 28° 7.6' W.

May 29/30   Stiff breeze. Clear sky. Choppy sea.
             Lat. 20° 51' N.   Long. 28° 44.6' W.

1882   Log written on board the *Lützburg* during the voyage
          from Lagos to Falmouth (as ordered).

May 30/31   Stiff breeze. Choppy sea.
            Set the jib sail. Opened the hatches
            Lat. 23° 0.3' N.   Long. 29° 22.6' W.

[19ᵛ]
May 31/
June 1   Set all sails. Redistributed the cargo below
            deck. Closed the hatches toward evening.
            A moderate breeze blowing.
            Opened the hatches.
            Lat. 24° 12.3' N.   Long. 30° 15.6' W.

                                             42 days at sea

June 1/2   A moderate breeze. Carefully sealed the hatches with
            triple tarps.
            Fair weather, cloudy.
            Lat. 25° 46.8' N.   Long. 31° 3.6' W.

June 2/3   Light wind. Beautiful weather. Calm sea. Remained so
            all day.
            Lat. 26° 42.9' N.   Long. 31° 40.6' W.

[20ʳ]
June 3/4   Light winds. Calm sea.
            Ship does not answer the helm.
            Lat. 28° 1.5' N.   Long. 31° 25.6' W.

June 5/6   Moderate
            Lively
            Lat. 28° 50' N.   Long. 31° 10.6' W.

June 6/7   Light winds to no wind.
            Lat. 29° 37.5' N.   Long. 31° 17.6' W.

                                             48 days at sea

1882   Log written on board the *Lützburg* during the voyage
              from Lagos to Falmouth (as ordered).

[20ᵛ]
June 7/8   Fair weather, light winds.

              Lat. 30° 38' N.   Long. 31° 36' W.

                                                          49 days at sea

June 8/9   Light winds, cloudy
              Moderate wind.
              Lively breeze

              Lat. 31° 28.5' N.   Long. 31° 3.1' W.

June 9/10   Moderate winds, cloudy.
              Fresh breeze.
              Lively breeze.

              Lat. 32° 38.5' N.   Long. 30° 59.1' W.

[21ʳ]
June 10/11   Fine weather, fresh breeze.
              Overcast sky.

              Lat. 34° 12' N.   Long. 30° 59.1' W.

June 11/12   Fresh breeze. Cloudy
              Changeable winds.

              Lat. 35° 40.4' N.   Long. 31° 7.1' W.

June 12/13   A stiff breeze, sky overcast.
              Fresh breeze.

              Lat. 37° 18.9' N.   Long. 31° 19.1' W.

[21ᵛ]
June 13/14   Overcast sky. Light winds.
              Moderate winds.

              Lat. 38° 14' N.   Long. 31° 19' W.

                                                          55 days at sea

June 14/15   Moderate wind.

              Lat. 39° 7.9' N.   Long. 30° 18.1' W.

1882   Log written on board the *Lützburg* during the voyage
                from Lagos to Falmouth (as ordered).

June 15/16   Lively wind. Overcast.
               Clear.
               Lat. 40° 43.8' N.   Long. 30° 13' W.

[22ʳ]
June 16/17   Beautiful weather. Bright.
               Lat. 41° 57' N.   Long. 29° 22.1 W.

June 17/18   Light winds, cloudy.
               Lat. 42° 29.6' N.   Long. 27° 42.1' W.

June 18/19   Moderate winds, cloudy.
               Lively winds.
               Lat. 43° 21.8' N.   Long. 25° 55.1' W.

                                                    60 days at sea.

[22ᵛ]
June 19/20   Fresh breeze. Set the leesail.
               Overcast sky.
               Foggy and rainy weather.
               The German bark TDGR from Mobile to Bordeaux.
               Clearing
               Lat. 44° 17.2' N.   Long. 24° 1.1' W.

June 20/21   Moderate wind. Foggy.
               Took down the lower leesail.
               Lat. 44° 44.8' N.   Long. 22° 4.1 W.

June 21/22   Irregular wind with patches of fog.
               Clearing.
               Lat. 45° 19' N.   Long. 20° 21.1' W.

[23ʳ]
June 22/23   Very light breeze, irregular.
               Lively breeze.
               Fresh breeze.
               Lat. 45° 41.5' N.   Long. 18° 8' W.

| 1882 | Log written on board the *Lützburg* during the voyage from Lagos to Falmouth (as ordered). |

June 23/24   Stiff breeze, heavy seas.
Furled the jib
Reefed the mainsail
Eve. set full sail
Lat. 46° 36' N.   Long. 14° 58' W.

June 24/25   Strong breeze, gusty.
Fore-and-aft sails furled, mainsail reefed
Lat. 47° 21' N.   Long. 11° 27' W.

[23ᵛ]
June 25/26   Winds began to die back. Little by little set
full sail.
Wind less strong, seas calmer
Lat. 47° 53.3' N.   Long. 8° 25' W.

                                                                67 days at sea.

June 26/27   Light wind. Toward evening a fresh breeze with
rain.
Stiff breeze, foggy.
Wind died down, heavy rain.
At 9:00 it cleared up.
Lat. 48° 41.5' N.   Long. 5° 31' W.

June 27/28   Moderate winds. Overcast sky
Unable to touch bottom with a 100 fathom line
Strong wind. Overcast.
Light wind, rain. Measured 90 fathoms at 8 bells.
No wind, rain.
Lat. 49° 5.6' N.   Long. 4° 26' W.

[24ʳ]
June 28/29   Light winds, foggy
At 8:00 measured 85 fathoms
Rain and fog
No wind. Foggy.

1882   Log written on board the *Lützburg* during the voyage
              from Lagos to Falmouth (as ordered).

              Measured 82 fathoms at 8 bells, fog.
              Clearing, cloudy.
              Lat. 49° 23.2' N.   Long. 3° 22' W.

June 29/30   No wind. Cloudy
              Foggy.
              Clearing
              Lat. 49° 23' N.   Long. 3° 22' W.

June 30/
July 1   Light or no wind. Overcast
              Bright
              Overcast
              At 8:00 A.M. took on a pilot from Cutter No. 36.
              Dropped anchor and cleared the chains. Moderate
              breeze.
              Overcast sky.
              Lat. 49° 42.7' N.   Long. 1° 59' W.

                                                            72 days at sea.

[24ᵛ]
July 1/2   Sailed then on with a moderate northwesterly
              breeze. Caught sight of the Scilly Islands to the
              northeast about 2:00 P.M. Beautiful weather.
              About 3:00 P.M. caught sight of Land's End in the
              northeast. Sailed onward. About 8:00 saw the
              light at Walf Rock in the NE. Saw the Lizard
              light and passed Lizard at a distance of 3 km.
              about 8:00 A.M. on July 2. Winds moderate to
              light from the north during the night. Nice
              weather.

July 2, Sun. Set course for Manickeln Bay which we passed about
              5:00 P.M. Light winds from the north or calm.
              Tacked in Falmouth Bay. About 5:00 P.M. a boat
              brought the order to sail to Rotterdam. The boat
              departed following receipt of the order and took
              the pilot back to land as well. A moderate breeze

1882   Log written on board the *Lützburg* during the voyage
from Lagos to Falmouth (as ordered).

was blowing from the north. Continued on then
with the voyage without having cast anchor. Saw
the Eddystone light and passed the same at 5:00
A.M. on July 3 at a

July 3, Mon.   distance of 6 km. Nice weather. A moderate
breeze blowing from the north. Set the leesails
and sailed onward. Changable winds from the
northwest. Passed Mitt. Lt. Point at a distance
of 6 km. Steered east by south with light winds
from the west. Beautiful weather. Saw the Portland light about 10:00 set course with the same
about 12:00 at a distance of 16 km. Light winds
from the southwest, sky overcast. Steered east by
south.

July 4, Tues.   At 4:00 A.M. fixed position on the Portland light
NNW½W before it disappeared from sight. A fresh
breeze blowing. The sky dull. Wind from the
west. Steered onward. Sighted St. Catherine
Point at 7:00 and passed the same at 11:00 A.M.
and set course by the light at 2:00 P.M. NW (20
km). A moderate breeze blowing. Cloudy. Sailed
onward. The wind , light to moderate, blowing to
the south. At a distance of 10 km caught sight of
the Beachy Head light ENE. The wind SSE a fresh
breeze. continued to steer onward.

July 5, Wed.   Passed Beachy Head at 5:00 A.M. at a distance of
10 km. Set course for Dungeness. The wind held
steady blowing a stiff breeze. Caught sight of
Dungeness at 6:00 A.M. and passed it at 11:00 A.M.
Continued to steer on. At 5:00 P.M. caught sight
of Oak Goodwin light disappearing off the horizon
in the NW. The wind blowing WSW a good stiff
breeze. The sky misty. At 7:00 P.M. caught sight
on the North Hinder light and passed the same at
8:00 P.M. Kept a sharp lookout. A forceful
breeze from the WSW. steered . . . [end of the
record. Tr.]

TRANSLATION OF JAN WÜBBENA'S FARM DIARY KEPT IN JOHNSFIELD, ARENAC COUNTY, MICHIGAN

[25]   **July 1899**

Sunday the 16th
Dry. Kept the Sabbath.

Monday the 17th
From M.M.& Co.: rice 0.25, baking powder 0.10, wicks 0.01, total; 0.36; from Marfileus: plaster of paris 0.01, camphor 0.10, total; 0.11. Dry, but the sky always looked as though it would rain. In the morning we had a fairly heavy shower. Dried hay and stacked it. Hauled two loads into the new barn. Praise be to God! May many more of the same follow with God's blessing. N.B. Weaver: whetstone 0.05.

Tuesday the 18th
Nice. Hauled the haystacks home, 3 loads. From M.M.& M. Co. for salt 0.85, matches 0.10; total; 0.95. Earnest Knight for washer & pin: 0.25. Fair & dry.

Wednesday the 19th
Nice. From N.B. Weaver for rope 0.30; Gottenmyer, pork steak, 0.25; M.M.& M. Co., beans 0.30, yeast cakes 0.08, Gold Dust 0.25, soap 0.25, celery 0.05; total; 0.85. Had Ch. Johnson half a day to cut hay with the machine; I cultivated. Heinrich worked in the hay. Credit for milk 8.85, received 1.00 in cash.

Thursday the 20th
Nice. The sky overcast but dry. Raked the hay cut the previous day with Proulx's horsedrawn rake; broke the whippletree in the process, replaced it

93

with a new one to be paid to Earnest Knight. Hauled in two loads of the hay and put the rest up in stacks.

[26]   July, 1899

Friday the 21st
Good Weather. Brought in three loads of hay. From M.M.& M. Co. for potatoes 1.00. Borrowed Duncan's horsedrawn rake then brought in another small load of hay. Heinr. mowed. Paid to Peppel 1.00.

Saturday the 22nd
Good weather. William Caldwell & John Dobson, each with a mowing machine helped out for two hours. From M.M.& M. Co. for tea 0.25, sugar 0.25, total; 0.50. From N.B. Weaver for fatback 0.75. From Gottenmyer for meat products 0.50.

Sunday the 23rd
Very hot. Kept the Sabbath.

Monday the 24th
Very hot. Raked the hay cut Saturday and brought it in: 5 loads. Heinrich also made some.

Tuesday the 25th
In the night there was a thunderstorm with heavy rain. In the afternoon James Dobson helped cut hay with the machine. Heinr. helped him bind sheaves of wheat. I cultivated.

Wednesday the 26th
Stormy, but dry. James Dobson helped out for 1½ hours with the horses and the mowing machine. Heinrich helped him all day. I raked some of the hay cut the day before and stacked it. Brought one load in. From M.M.& M. Co. oatmeal 0.25 [missing] 0.25, molasses 0.10; total 0.60.

[27]   July & August 1899

Thursday the 27th
Nice weather. Brought in five loads of hay. Then stacked hay. For shingles 0.30.

Friday the 28th
Nice weather. Put the last of the hay into stacks and brought four loads in. All together that made 24 loads.

Saturday the 29th
Nice weather. From Johannes 30.00. Paid Dupee 24.50. H. Blumenthal 2.25. from M.M.& M. Co. for tobacco 0.10, sugar 0.30; total 0.40. Paid Nerriter 1.00, Weaver 0.50 borrowed on April 30. Total 1.50. Paid McGurk back a dollar that wasn't written down. For fertile eggs 0.25. Mini a book 0.13. Raked hay and brought in a small load.

Sunday the 30th
Very warm. Kept the Sabbath.

Monday the 31st
Very warm. Cultivated. Heinr. worked around the barn. In the afternoon took the horse to Dobsons. I cultivated potatoes in the afternoon.

Tuesday the 1st of August
Very warm. Heinr. worked on a bridge for James Dobson. I cultivated in the afternoon and worked the potatoes.

Wednesday the 2nd
Very warm. In the morning it was cloudy but it cleared off and it became a beautiful day. I worked with the youngsters on the potatoes. Heinr. for James Dobson. For oatmeal 0.25, rice 0.25, beans 0.25, tea 0.25, celery 0.05 soda 0.08, 10 yds. oilcloth @ 0.12½ = 1.25, waist = calico 0.24, spool thread 0.04; total 2.66. O.A. Marfileus ink 0.05, paper 0.10; total 0.15.

[28]   August 1899

Thursday the 3rd
Johannes 57.60, Independent 2.00. M.M.& M. Co. 34.77, J. Daugherty 0.50. P.M. Miller 0.10, N.B. Weaver 18.28, Nerriter 12.60, Gottenmyer 1.85. James Norn 1.02, John Dobson 1.00, Marfileus 0.56, Curney 5.00, Heinrich 0.25, School 0.75, Telfer 5.85, Geo. Wright 2.70.
As of 3 August 1899:
Outstanding receipts 9.30
Debts 138.53
Cash on hand 0.00
Beautiful day, very warm. Heinr. and Hinr. worked on the new barn to lay the floor. Laid the sills on posts buried in the earth. I worked the potatoes with the youngsters.

Friday the 4th
Very warm. In the course of the day Heinrich squared accounts with Earnest Knight and P. M. Miller; he also bought 50 cents worth of nails with his own money. Further he borrowed from Norn 1260 feet of lumber @ 7.00 per

1000 which makes $8.82. Heinrich worked in the P.M. on the barn; the youngsters and I cleaned potatoes and carrots.

Saturday the 5th
Very warm. From N.B. Weaver 10 lbs. nails @ 0.05, total 0.50. Heinrich & Hinr. worked on the barn. The youngsters and I picked potatoes and carrots. from M.M.& M. Co. sugar 0.30.

Sunday the 6th
Very warm. Kept the Sabbath.

Monday the 7th
Cool at night. Heinr. and Hinr. worked on the barn. The youngsters and I cleaned potatoes.

Tuesday the 8th
Cool at night. A.M. to school to bring a bill to Kroske 0.50. Bill Geo. Wright 2.40; pay Taalke 1.25,

[29]   **August 1899**

Heinr. 0.50; total 1.75. from N.B. Weaver 2 pair of hinges @ 0.20 = 0.40 and 2 hooks with steeples @ 0.05 = 0.10; total, 0.50. Heinrich & Hinr. worked on the barn. I cleaned potatoes with the youngsters.

Wednesday the 9th
Cleaned potatoes with the youngsters till 3:00 P.M. Then came a thunderstorm with rain and we stopped. Then worked in the barn. Heinr. Taalke & Hinr. picked blueberries. The weather was good. To Gottenmyer 1.00. I was to get from him 0.67.

Thursday the 10th
For iron from Dow 2.71; from Weaver for cheese 0.14, iron 5 lbs. @ 4¾ cts. = 0.25; total 0.39. Heinr. & Hinr. worked in the barn. The youngsters weeded potatoes. I went to town to get wood and to put a pane in the schoolhouse window. I will ask 1.00 for that. From M.M.& M. Co. for sugar 0.50.

Friday the 11th
Beautiful weather. Around noon a fierce thunderstorm. I cleaned potatoes all day. Heinrich worked on the new barn.

Saturday the 12th
From M.M.& M. Co. beans 0.25, oatmeal 0.25, baking powder 0.10, celery 0.05; total 0.65 from M.M.& M. Co. for lard 3.50, fatback 0.15; total 3.65 + 0.65 = 4.30. Heinrich worked a full day for James Dobson.

[30]   **August, 1899**

Sunday the 13th
Beautiful weather. Kept the Sabbath.

Monday the 14th
Beautiful weather. Very cool at night. From Dow 24 sections of 3/8" lath by
4'. Each section @ 0.02 = 0.24. From M.M.& M. Co. soap 0.25 = 0.50;
Heinr. cut oats; I bound sheaves and set them into shocks.

Tuesday the 15th
Nice. Cut and bound oats and put them in shocks. Paid Dow 1.00.

Wednesday the 16th
Taalkes birthday. From M.M.& M. Co. for chocolate 0.10. Cut and bound
oats, shelled peas and weeded potatoes.

Thursday the 17th
Beautiful weather. Hot. Cut and bound oats, shelled peas and cleaned potatoes. After school Kroske's work 0.2.5

Friday the 18th
Very hot. Shelled peas, cleaned potatoes and cut and bound oats.

Saturday the 19th
Shelled peas. Helped Beasons thresh. Cut and bound oats and brought three
loads of oats in. From M.M.& M. Co. sugar 0.30, bacon 1.25; total 1.55.
From N.B. Weaver a whetstone 0.05.

Sunday the 20th
Nice. Hot.

Monday the 21st
Very hot. A thunderstorm with rain around noon. Paid Peppel 1.00. Cut and
bound oats; Shelled peas.

Tuesday the 22nd
Nice, hot. Bound oats, shelled peas. Warm. Finished around noon. During
the storm the old sow gave birth to nine shoats. From M.M.& Co. cheese-
cloth 0.05, golddust 0.25; total 0.30. To Taalke 0.25.

Wednesday the 23rd
Nice, hot. Heinr. helped John Dobson thresh for half a day. Brought in the
oats and the peas at night.

[31]   **August & September 1899**

From M.M.& M. Co. 0.18 for Mini's skirt.

Thursday the 24th
Heinrich and I went to Dankert's to help with threshing. From M.M.& M. Co. sugar 0.30, cocoanut 0.10, mustard 0.10, molasses 0.05, lemon extract 0.10, raisins 0.25, apples 0.25, jelly 0.10, butter 0.15, spices 0.10; total for groceries 1.50, 1½ yd. netting 0.38, 1½ yd. lace 0.12, thread 0.05, pepper and steak 0.10; total 0.65.

Friday the 25th
Beautiful. From M.M.& M. Co. tobacco 0.10, tea 0.25, vinegar 0.05; total 0.40. From Gottenmyer beefsteak 1.00. Threshed 85 bu. of oats and 22 bu. of peas. I must pay the threshers the amount of 4.00.

Saturday the 26th
Beautiful, hot. Threshed for I. Johnson then took the straw into the barn. From M.M.& M. Co. a box of salt 0.85, tobacco 0.10; total 0.95. From N.B. Weaver cradle fingers 0.25. Credited 8.54 for milk from July.

Sunday the 27th
Beautiful. Kept the Sabbath.

Monday the 28th; Tuesday the 29th; Wednesday the 30th
Worked in the fields and in the barn. Took the census 4.00.

Thursday the 31st
Hot, dry. From M.M.& M. Co. children's clothes for 5.28, for pickles 0.25; total 5.53. Went to Patteron to see about the rent.

Friday the 1st of September
Hot and dry; Saturday the 2nd, was the same. from M.M.& M. Co. for cups 0.25, tobacco 0.10; total 0.35.

Sunday the 3rd
A.M. hot; P.M. cool.

Monday the 4th
Cool. From M.M.& M. Co. shoes for Heinrich 1.75. Cash for Heinrich (travel money) 10.00; total 11.75. Debt to Schauers for work 1.75.

[32]   **September 1899**

Tuesday the 5th & Wednesday the 6th
Worked the farm.

Thursday the 7th
Pulled stumps and piled them. In the evening of the 6th I burned my foot and was unable to work on the 7th. On the evening of the 7th Heinrich left us to try his luck at earning money up north. From M.M.& M. Co. clothes for Heinrich 5.00. Taalke's dress 0.54; total 5.54. I quit work at 4:00 P.M. because I was unable to go on with the burned foot.

Friday the 8th
In bed. The foot is no better.

Saturday the 9th
In bed. The foot no better. From M.M.& M. Co. tea 0.25, sugar 0.25, 50 lbs. flour. Salve from Dr. Grigg 0.25.

Sunday the 10th
In bed. The foot no better. Kept the Sabbath.

Monday the 11th
In bed. The foot no better. Hinrich had to keep the place running.

Tuesday the 12th
Still in bed. Called the Dr. at 2:00. From Marfileus carbolic acid 0.10. From M.M.& M. Co. bandages 0.10, cotton 0.06; total 0.16.

Wednesday the 13th
Still no better. The Dr. here for the second time. He brought Bittersalz. He found the wound better.

Thursday the 14th
Still in bed. Trying a salve from the doctor.

Friday the 15th and Saturday the 16th.
From M.M.& M. Co. shoes, etc. from Grigg powder 5.53.

Monday the 18th, Tuesday the 19th, Wednesday the 20th, Thursday the 21st
From Oscar Marfileus vaseline 0.20. From M.M.& M. Co. kerosene 0.50; Emma's shoes and stockings, Griggs's powder 1.38. For a stick of lab. vaseline 0.20.

[33]   **September & October 1899**

Friday the 22nd
Grigg's powder. Fair.

Saturday the 23rd
Sugar from M.M.& M. Co. 0.25, tea 0.25.

Sunday the 24th
Very rainy. Powder.

Monday the 25th
25 lbs. Eureka flour, baking powder 0.10 (flour to be paid with wheat).
Nerriter flour.

Tuesday the 26th
Grigg powder. 0.47.

Wednesday the 27th
Beeswax for salve, O.A. Marfileus 0.05.

Thursday the 28th
Emma's birthday.

Friday the 29th
Husked corn. Shelled some.

Saturday the 30th
For hat Mrs. Hartman 1.35. For shoes and stockings for Minnie, M.M.& M.
Co. 1.45.

Sunday the 1st of October
Prof. M. came to visit.

Monday the 2nd
Minnie for shoes 0.15. Nerriter for flour.

Tuesday the 3rd, Wednesday the 4th, Thursday the 5th

Friday the 6th
Gold Dust M.M.& M. Co. 0.25

Saturday the 7th
For Mrs. Holm 0.25

Sunday the 8th
Thanks be to God! I am finally able to sit up. Yesterday I was able already to
husk corn. Thanks be to God, for He is with us and His goodness lasts forever.

Monday the 9th
Beautiful weather. Husked corn and hauled the beans into the granary. Borrowed 25 lbs. of flour from Nerriter. Sold 6 pigs to Nehls for 4.50. Of that
paid Shauers 1.75.

Tuesday the 10th & Wednesday the 11th
Husked corn. Was not able with the children to husk much more than the pigs could eat.

Thursday the 12th
From M.M.& M. Co. 50 lbs. lard 3.75.

Friday the 13th
Husked corn. Beautiful weather.

Saturday the 14th
From M.M.& M. Co. 50 lbs. flour 1.00, sugar 0.25, tea 0.25, crackers 0.18; total 1.73.

[34]   October 1899

Sunday the 15th
Kept the Sabbath following Sunday School.

Monday the 16th
Husked corn. Heavy rains the following night.

Tuesday the 17th
Hauled two loads of wood for Karl from town. Paid Dow 2.00; this leaves an outstanding debt of 0.48. From N.B. Weaver 10 door hooks for the barn @ 0.05 each = 0.50. From M.M.& M. Co. baking powder 0.10, tobacco 0.10; total 0.20. From Marfileus for school: crayons 0.25 and a composition book 0.10, lead pencils 0.10; total 0.45.

Wednesday the 18th
Hauled three loads of wood for Karl from town. I should note that we got a calf (heifer) from Stölt a few days after I had burned my foot. We were to pay 7.00 but Stölt owed us 3.00 which left us with a debt of 4.00. After I had paid Peppel we still had a credit of 5.26 with M.M.& M. Co. resulting from September's milk. For stamps 0.10 and for Sunday School on the 15th 0.05.

Thursday the 19th
Hauled two loads of wood from town for Karl. Rain toward evening.

Friday the 20th
The Conference was here the whole day. Good weather.

Saturday the 21st
Conference. From the school 7.25. For postal cards 0.10 and sugar 0.25. Fixed the big barn door. Paid Dow 0.50 which leaves us free of debt there.

[35]   October 1899

Since I hadn't done anything with the school or Geo. Wright since the third of August, we only got 5.85 from Telfer.

Sunday the 22nd
The Conference visited. During the night and in the morning heavy rain and thunderstorms.

Monday the 23rd
Thunderstorm in the morning. Taalke for roosters 2.25. Spread manure. Hinrich and Fr. pulled carrots.

Tuesday the 24th
Hauled manure and pulled carrots. Of the latter we had about 5 saltbarrels full. It must have been about 10 bushel. On the 26th it rained all day as well as during the entire previous night. It was wet and muddy all around the new barn. Used the shovelplow to make drainage ditches and you could see that it did some good when we had finished.

Friday the 27th
Worked in the barn all morning. Delivered a load of hay (1000 lbs.) to Mrs. Gammon. Karl helped to load and weigh it. From Taalke for the hat Mrs. Hartman bought on September 30.

Saturday the 28th
Cloudy. For hay 5.85, insurance 2.27, paid Weaver account 4.50, Garries 1.69, flour 0.95. For the weighbill from weighing the hay 0.25—the wagon weighed 1360 lbs. ½ bushel peas 0.25.

Sunday the 29th
Nice. Kept the Sabbath. In the evening to Sunday School with Nehls to Barns church.

[36]   October & November 1899

Monday the 30th
Beautiful weather. Karl helped harrow the potato field and to plow. For hay 6.90.

Tuesday the 31st
Nice weather. Karl helped us plow. Paid for the threshing machine (see August 25) and instead of 4.00 the man only wanted 3.50.

Wednesday the 1st of November
Johannes 57.60; Independent 2.00. M.M.& M. Co. 71.10; J. Daugharty
0.50, N.B. Weaver 15.58; Nerriter 15.00 Gottenmyer 4.35; James Norn
18.84, John Dobson 1.00; Marfileus 2.00; Curney 5.00; Dr. Grigg 5.00;
Telfer 5.85 (Outstanding).
As of 1 November 1899:
Outstanding receipts 5.85
Debts 191.97
Cash on hand 8.51

We owe Stölt 4.00 (see October 18). Very raw and cold. Karl plowed his land
with our horses. From Monday the 18th of October it should be noted that
we borrowed from M.M.& M. Co. for sugar 0.25, pins 0.05; total 0.30
which should be added to the debt we owe from November 1. Then from
N.B. Weaver 5 lbs. of nails (bought on November 1) @ 0.04; total 0.20. For
overall material 0.80, light bulb 0.20 and hairpins 0.05. Willie's pants 0.25,
thread 0.20, matches 0.10 and plaster of paris 0.05; total 1.75. Burned heaps
on the fields all day.

Thursday the 2nd
Very raw and cold. Karl plowed his land with our horses again. I worked
around the barn, fixing things etc. From M.M.& M. Co. for cotton 0.07.

Friday the 3rd
Cold and raw. Slaughtered a pig. Karl plowed for us. From M.M.& M. Co.

[37] **November 1899**

for allspice 0.10.

Saturday the 4th
Heinrich's birthday. Beautiful weather. Karl plowed for us. I drained and
salted the pig we slaughtered yesterday.

Sunday the 5th
Beautiful weather. Kept the Sabbath. Brbr 2.00. In the evening a meeting in
the school with Mr. Matthews.

Monday the 6th
Beautiful weather. Karl came to help pull carrots and began to plow the land.

Tuesday the 7th
Nice. For a comb 0.10, for wool yarn 0.75. Traded wheat for the 50 lbs. of
flour that Nerriter had gotten during the time I suffered with the burned foot;
straightened that situation out. From M.M.& M. Co. for tea 0.25, pickles

0.25, soap 0.25; total 0.75. Karl stayed to help till noon. Sent for wooden shoes 1.95. For Milne's Arithmetic 0.65 (Mini).

Wednesday the 8th
Nice. Plowed. Drained and planted three prune trees (1.50).

Thursday the 9th
Nice. Karl plowed again with our horses on his own land. For almonds 0.05 from M.M.& M. Co. Cleared fields and burned them off. Got things for the school 0.25.

Friday the 10th
Nice. Karl used the horses on his own land. Cleared fields and burned them off. Slaughtered a pig. Nehls came to help.

[38]   November 1899

Saturday the 11th
Nice day, but a strong wind from the north. Karl used the horses on his own land. Cleared fields and burned them off as on the previous days. Salted the pig.

Sunday the 12th
Beautiful. Kept the Sabbath.

Monday the 13th
Nice day. Helped Karl in his barn for a quarter of the day otherwise I plowed. From M.M.& M. Co. for a lamp chimney 0.10, for a pancake turner 0.05.

Tuesday the 14th
Cloudy. Wet weather till 10 o'clock. Worked till then in the barn. Cleared fields and plowed. For a few days Heinrich has complained of headaches; he felt better today.

Wednesday the 15th
Cloudy. Plowed and drained fields.

Thursday the 16th
Nice weather. Plowed and drained fields. From M.M.& M. Co. for yeast cakes 0.04.

Friday the 17th
Nice weather. Plowed. At noon I had to quit because of a pain in my hip. In the afternoon Dupke from Kawhawlin came for a visit and stayed overnight. From M.M.& M. Co. for a bedsheet 1.00, for baking powder 0.10; total

1.10. Paid Dr. Grigg 0.50 for a checkup for Taalke. From Marfileus for machine 0.60 and for liniment 0.25; total 0.85.

Saturday the 18th
Cool and cloudy. Was only able to plow a few furrows before I had to quit because of the pain. Friedrich's birthday was yesterday. He and Heinrich celebrated it today.

Sunday the 19th
Beautiful day. Kept the Sabbath.

Monday the 20th; Tuesday the 21st; Wednesday the 22nd
Pretty nice weather. Pulled stumps and piled them up.

[39]   **November & December 1899**

Thursday the 23rd
Good weather. Plowed in the morning. Slaughtered a pig in the afternoon. Nehls and Karl came to help.

Friday the 24th
Daugharty came about hiring a teacher (school business 0.25). Several days ago spent 0.40 for freight on the wooden shoes.

Saturday the 25th
Good weather. Plowed and cleared the fields.

Sunday the 26th
Good weather. Kept the Sabbath.

Monday the 27th
Very thick fog during the night. Plowed. Fanny, the horse, was worked out in a manner of speaking. Since the 13th she fell down in front of the plow several times. I think that Karl is responsible for this. He brought the horses back on the 10th as wet from sweat as though they had been pulled out of the water. For spices 0.20 and for lamp chimneys 0.20; total 0.40.

Tuesday the 28th
Nice. Plowed. Fanny no better.

Wednesday the 29th
Nice. Gave the horses a rest. Spent the day in bed because of pain in my back and hip.

Thursday the 30th
Thanksgiving. Gave a speach in German in the school to a group of about 14 persons. Received from Kraus as honorarium 0.50.

December 1899. Regarding outstanding receipts, debts and cash on hand see the next page (40).

Friday the 1st
From M.M.& M. Co. tea 0.10 (see the following page). Plowed and drained.

Saturday the 2nd
Snow during the morning and afternoon. Then it melted. Plowed and drained.

[40]   December 1899

Johannes 51.60, Independent 2.00, M.M.& M. Co. 73.61, J. Daugharty 0.50, N.B. Weaver 15.78, Nerriter 15.00, Gottenmyer 4.35, J. Norn 18.84, John Dobson 1.00, Marfileus 4.00, Curney 5.00, Dr. Grigg 6.00, Stölt 4.00, Telfer 5.85, School 0.50, Prunetrees 1.50, Peppel 1.50
As of 1 December 1899:
Outstanding 6.35
Debts 204.68
Cash on hand 0.96

Friday the 1st
Add to Friday the 1st, 0.10.

Sunday the 3rd
Rather cold. Kept the Sabbath.

Monday the 4th
Very cold. Things in the barn froze. Jerry Waites ordered a load of hay to be delivered the following day. $10.00 per ton.

Tuesday the 5th
Very cold. Brought Mrs. J. Waites a load of hay which Proulx helped to load and which Stillinger weighed at 1930 lbs. This made 9.65. The woman had paid 2.00 in advance when she placed the order yesterday; this left the rest 7.65. For kerosene 0.50, and soda 0.07, baking powder, 010 [0.10?], yeast cakes 004 [0.04?]; total 0 21 [0.21?]. Mini borrowed 0.04 from M.M.& M. Co. for a yeast cake. For the weighbill (Stillinger) 0.25. For steeples and washers 0.05.

Wednesday the 6th
Very cold. Paid Peppel 1.50. For yarn 0.10, linen 0.15, tablets 0.10; total 0.35. A hard freeze but I let the animals out anyway and watered them in the barn.

[41]   **December 1899**

Wednesday the 6th
To the doctor again. In October Marfileus for medicine 0.25.

Thursday the 7th
Mini to the Doctor, 0.75 with medicine. Ten lbs. of nails from N.B. Weaver 0.40. The morning was dry. Burned and cleared fields. In the afternoon it snowed somewhat; continued to clear the fields.

Friday the 8th
Beautiful. The calves didn't come home in the evening. During the day began to put new sheeting on the pig pen.

Saturday the 9th
Good weather. Found the calves at Fecto's house. Worked on the pig pen.

Sunday the 10th
Good weather but damp. Kept the Sabbath. Brbr.

Monday the 11th
Rained the entire day. Received a U.S postal money order from Heinrich for 70.00. Drained. N.B. Weaver 2 lbs. nails @ 0.04 = 0.08.

Tuesday the 12th
Rain, snow, hail: raw weather. From M.M.& M. Co. 2 spools of thread @ 0.04; total 0.08. Drained.

Wednesday the 13th
Very cold. Worked on the pig pen and in the cow barn.

Thursday the 14th
Very cold. Made the cow barn as tight as I could. Found out that the taxes will be 62.29.

Friday the 15th
Very cold. Things in the barn didn't freeze though.

Saturday the 16th
Very cold. Found out that the taxes would be not 62.29 but 62.91 with the fees. (The drain taxes were 50.00.) I paid the drain taxes with drain orders and made 7.50 in the process. I immediately paid Gottmeyer 4.35, M.M.& M. Co. 5.00, Taalke 2.00. For Gold Dust 0.20, lamp 0.20, slates 0.60, stone blacking 0.05; total 1.05. Prune tree 1.50.

[42]   December 1899

Sunday the 17th
Nice weather. Kept the Sabbath. Brbr.

Monday the 18th
Windy and cold. Worked on the cellar.

Tuesday the 19th
Windy and cold. Worked on the cellar.

Wednesday the 20th
The day was nice but the previous night very cold. Pants for Heinrich 0.20, pants for Friedrich 0.20, Hinrich's stockings 0.25, tea 0.25, sugar 0.50; total 1.50. Borrowed from Taalke 0.80. Cleared and sawed.

Thursday the 21st
Nice weather. Sawed and cleared.

Friday the 22nd
Beautiful day. Worked a quarter of a day for Thoms; hauled logs and wood home with the horses. In the afternoon the cow Flora gave birth to a heifer calf. Cleared and sawed.

Saturday the 23rd
Nice weather. From M.M.& M. Co. rice 0.25, tobacco 0.15; total 0.40. Also onions 0.05; everything together 0.45. From Waites 1.00. Paid Taalke 0.80.

Sunday the 24th
Gave a sermon in the school on Phil. 4:4 (in German).

Monday the 25th
Beautiful day. Very cold. Celebrated Christmas.

Tuesday the 26th
Nice day. Very cold. Put manure on the fruit trees and brought in a load of firewood.

Wednesday the 27th, Thursday the 28th
Very cold and raw. Put manure in the chicken house and cut firewood.

Friday the 29th
Very cold and raw. Cut firewood. From M.M.& M. Co. 9 yds. flannel @ 0.05 = 0.45, stockings 0.25, braid 0.15, bleached cotton 0.12, thread 0.04; total 1.00. From Waites 2.00. For machine oil 0.10. Very raw and cold.

Saturday the 30th
For groceries 1.00. Very cold.

Sunday the 31st
Kept the Sabbath. Very cold.

[43]   **January 1900**

Monday the 1st

Johannes 51.60, Independent 2.00, M.M.&M. Co. 51.25, I. Daugharty 0.50, N.B. Weaver 16.18, Nerriter 12.60, J. Norn 18.84, John Dobson 1.00, Marfileus 6.00, Curney 5.00, Dr. Grigg 8.00, Stölt 4.00;—Telfer 5.85, School 0.50.

As of January 1 1900:

Outstanding receipts 6.35

Debts 176.97

Cash on hand 0.69

This is the financial situation on new year's day 1900. With this we enter the new year. To be sure there were many difficulties, but we were spared any really severe punishment from on high and even though my burned foot hurt quite a bit, it was after all a punishment that I deserved—a proof that we are God's children: Whom God loveth he chasteneth. We were richly blessed in spiritual things. I myself together with the children have learned much through the hand of the Almighty and even though Hinrich and Friedrich missed a lot of school, I am sure that they have made good progress in reading and writing. The harvest was meager but the Lord sent us help from another quarter: on March 18 Heinrich gave me 40.00 and on the 11th I received 70.00 from him and so I saw the helping hand of the Lord at work and therefore we will not trust in the strength of our own arms

[44]   **January 1900**

but rather trust in the Lord, who has ever been our help. He has never erred in the conduct of his affairs and his work and will come to a good end. For the work on the farm we have a 10 year old mare "Fanny" a 19 month old colt "Lizzie," and Heinrich's gelding "Prince"; three cows, "Nellie," "Blossom" and "Flora," all five years old, Taalke's cow, "Taalke Hiley," three years old; three young pigs born in August '99; 10 chickens and 2 roosters; in addition two yearling heifers, three calves born in 1899 and one calf born in December 1899. In the old barn there remains about a ton of old hay that is still good; in the new barn about 8 tons of hay for fodder and about 3 tons of straw. That leaves about 3 tons of hay available for sale. (The corn was used up by December 14, 1899.) We have about 15 bu. of potatoes, 6 bu. of peas, 50 bu. of oats, 3 bu. of wheat. Equipment includes a wagon, a plow, a harrow, a cultivator, a shovelplow as well as the necessary garden tools. We praise Thy name faithful Lord for all Thou hast done for us in the past and place our trust in Thee for the future.

[45]   **January 1900**

Tuesday the 2nd
Raw weather. Everybody kinda sick. Colds. My face swelled. Mini off and
on in bed.

Wednesday the 3rd
Mild weather. Mini better. My face even more swollen. Threshed the buckwheat and cleaned it. About a peck. I forgot to note on the monthly balance
that Waites owes me 4.65 for hay.

Thursday, the 4th
Milder. Wrote to the boys in Chatham as well as to Mr. Kausen. Cut wood
and cleared.

Friday the 5th
Good weather. Sold three tons of hay to M.M.&M. Co. @ 9.50 per ton for
Saturday.

Saturday the 6th
Loaded two tons and delivered them. Mr. Barthard helped me to load. Had
it weighed by Stillinger. The wagon weighed 1380 lbs. From N.B. Weaver
shoetacks 0.05. Licorice syrup from O.A. Marfileus 0.25.

Sunday the 7th
Kept the Sabbath. Brbr.

Monday the 8th
Beautiful weather. Delivered another load of hay which made together with
the two loads from the 6th 6020 lbs. That yielded 28.00 of which I took 1.00
to pay for the weighbills. Used the 27.00 to pay off debts. For miscellaneous
etc. 0.25. With that I had on hand 0.32.

Tuesday the 9th
Picked up Taalke's order from Sears and Roebuck. For paper, envelopes and
stamps 0.30. Assumed Heinrich's debts with M.M.&M. Co. in the amount
of 8.61.

Wednesday the 10th
Picked up things for the school: a record book, 6 slates, penholders 0.50.
M.M.&M. Co. for GoldDust 0.25. Hauled two loads of manure.

[46]   **January 1900**

Thursday the 11th
Owe James Dobson for staples for the big barn door 0.80.

Friday the 12th
Beautiful weather. Hauled manure.

Saturday the 13th
Beautiful weather. From M.M.&M. Co. tobacco 0.05, sugar 0.10, matches 0.10; total 0.25.

Sunday the 14th
Good weather. Kept the Sabbath. Nehls came for a visit.

Monday the 15th
Snowed the entire day. Threshed beans and repaired the gates. From M.M.&M. Co. waist lining 0.20. From Gottenmyer lard 0.50.

Tuesday the 16th
Snowed during the day. From N.B. Weaver a lantern 0.60. From M.M.&M. Co. bleached cotton 2 yds. @ 0.06 = 0.12.

Wednesday the 17th
Thaw, hail and rain. Cleaned some beans.

Thursday the 18th
Thaw. From M.M.&M. Co. petroleum 0.60. Visited for a while with Wendt.

Friday the 19th
Thaw. Sawed wood.

Saturday the 20th
Thaw. Sawed wood.

Sunday the 21st
Beautiful weather. Brbr. Kept the Sabbath.

Monday the 22nd
Beautiful weather. Sawed wood.

Tuesday the 23rd
Beautiful weather. Sawed wood. Had a letter from Johannes. He is giving me 21.60 which will reduce the debt owed him.

Wednesday the 24th
Very cold. Thawed during the afternoon and rained in the evening.

Thursday the 25th
Very cold. From M.M.&M. Co. soap 0.25. Attended a meeting at the cheese factory.

Friday the 26th
Very cold during the night and during the day everything froze in the horse barn. Ella's birthday. Cleaned beans. Very fierce storm.

Saturday the 27th
From M.M.&M. Co. cornmeal 1.00.

Sunday the 28th
Very cold. Kept the Sabbath. In the audience for Barnett.

Monday the 29th
Very cold. Went to the school because of Johnson's Fritz and because of the children about recess, 0.50.

Tuesday the 30th
Very cold and wet. Traded the remaining wheat for flour, about 250 lbs. From I. Lieberan for 5 bu. peas @

[47] **January & February 1900**

0.80 = 4.00; total 4.80 with the staples from Jan 11. The debt to Telfer less the 5.85 leaves 1.05 outstanding. From M.M.&M. Co. beans 1.91, tobacco 0.10; total 2.01. Received 10.00 in cash and 6.59 on credit for milk: total 16.59. Paid Taalke 8 for a dress.

Wednesday the 31st
Very, very cold. A hard freeze in the barn. In the morning the water in the kitchen had ice an inch thick. During the day hauled a load of wood; for us hauled a load of manure.

Thursday the 1st
Independent 2.00, M.M.&M. Co. 30.35, I Daugharty 0.50, N.B. Weaver 16.78, Nerriter 12.60, Norn 18.84, J. Dobson 1.00, Marfileus 2.53, Curney 5.00, Dr. Grigg 8.00, Stölt 4.00—Telfer 1.15, School 1.50, Gottenmyer 0.50; + Waites 4.65
As of 1 February 1900:
Outstanding receipts 7.30
Debts 192.12
Cash on hand 2.00

Thursday the 1st
For 0.05 shoetacks from N.B. Weaver should be added to the debt from January 6th. Johannes wrote me that Heinrich intended to give him back the 30.00 so I didn't include the 51.00 debt to him. From M.M.&M. Co. tea 0.15, sugar 0.15, baking powder 0.10; total 0.30.

Friday the 2nd
Very, very cold. Hauled a load of wood in from the field during the morning. In the afternoon with Nehls and Daugharty 0.50. In the evening we couldn't water the horses because of lack of water.

Saturday the 3rd
Very cold. Hauled firewood home.

Sunday the 4th
Somewhat milder. Kept the Sabbath.

Monday the 5th
Cold. From Gottenmyer lard 0.75. It should be noted that we had emptied the loft over the stalls by February 1 but that the loft (11 foot) in front of the stalls was filled up

[48]   **February 1900**

even with the loft above the stalls. In the old barn we still had about a ton of hay. This makes with the hay in the new barn about 7 tons available to feed the 3 horses "Fanny," "Prince" and "Lizzie" as well as the 4 cows "Nellie," "Blossom," "Flora" and "Taalke Hiley," the two heifers "Cherry" and "Quincey" and the three calves.

Tuesday the 6th
Very nice. Sawed some wood. Mini came home in the evening. In Standish 18 cases of scarlet fever had broken out and the school closed as a result.

Wednesday the 7th
Thaw. From M.M.&M. Co. soda 0.07, yeast cake 0.04; total 0.11. From O.A. Marfileus camphor 0.05, comb 0.15; total 0.20. For the school pen holders 0.05. Taalke's invoice number is 1327 i.e. Taalke's dress from Sears Roebuck & Co.

Thursday the 8th
It rained the entire night. All the snow had disappeared by morning. Lots of water standing in the fields. Drained them as well as I could given the frost in the ground.

Friday the 9th
Very cold. From M.M.&M. Co. coffee 0.12, sugar 0.25, tobacco 0.10; total 0.47. Sawed firewood.

Saturday the 10th
Nice. Collected the stumps scattered around the barn and piled them up.

Sunday the 11th
Very nice. Brbr: 0.47. Voted in Sunday School on the organ.

Monday the 12th
Very nice. With Nehls to Daugharty regarding hiring Hamilton as teacher 0.50. Also wrote the minutes of the meeting regarding the organ. Prince's foot was very bad.

[49]   February 1900

In the evening Nehls (now after I had seen Keifer who didn't want to come) and had a look at Prince's foot and behold there was a nail in it about an inch long. On the previous day Karl had already treated it with Corosine liniment. In the afternoon I washed the swollen part with hot water for 2 hours and in the evening the foot was already a lot better.

Tuesday the 13th
Very raw weather. During the night it had snowed. When I came into the barn Prince was standing on the sore foot and resting the other one. During the day sorted beans for seed. During the afternoon Proulx was here to visit Prince.

Wednesday the 14th
Very nice day but very cold. Nehls and Dankert came to help with washing Prince's foot. It seems to me that the foot is getting better.

Thursday the 15th
Very raw and cold. During the morning washed Prince's foot with Proulx. In the afternoon used Fanny to haul logs home for firewood.

Friday the 16th
It froze terribly during the night. In the morning water that had been fresh at 9:00 in the evening and which had stood on the stove in the washroom all night was frozen solid. In the afternoon Duncan and Nehls came to have a look at Prince's foot and believed it to be all right. From M.M.&M. Co. yeast cakes 0.08, baking powder 0.10, twine 0 08 [0.08?]; total 0.26.

Saturday the 17th
Beautiful day but very cold. Prince's foot better. Sawed firewood and hauled it home.

Sunday the 18th
Beautiful but cold. Kept the Sabbath. Flora was with Daugharty's bull 0.50. She should come fresh on November 29, 1900.

[50]   **February 1900**

Monday the 19th, Tuesday the 20th, Wednesday the 21st
Snowy. On Wednesday windy and snow flurries. Sawed firewood at home as much as possible. Prince's foot healing nicely. But we discovered a scratch or cut on Lizzie's hind leg. It was full of pus and quite swollen on Wednesday already. Washed the wound faithfully with hot water and applied Corosine liniment.

Thursday the 22nd
Washington's Birthday. Lizzie's leg no better. Washed it again with hot water and applied Corosine liniment. From M.M.&M. Co. Gold Dust 0.25, sugar 0.16, coffee 0.12; total 0.53. For butter 0.24. Remaining debts 0.29. Raw and cold all day.

Friday the 23rd
It seemed to me that Lizzie's leg was improving but it was still very swollen and pus ran freely. A thick lump had collected over the wound. Applied more Corosine liniment. Less cold. Looked for more logs to use for firewood and found several.

Saturday the 24th
Very cold. Snow flurries. Hauled some logs home and a load of pine lumber as well. Sawed wood for the large heating stove. Lizzie's leg was as before. Prince was completely healed. From Marfileus Corosine liniment 0.25, camphor syrup 0.05; total .30. From M.M.&M. Co. a broom for 0.30. Very raw weather.

Sunday the 25th
Fearfully cold. Kept the Sabbath. Three people at Sunday School: the elder Sonnschmitt, young Naiser and young Walton.

Monday the 26th
Somewhat milder.

[51]   **February and March 1900**

From M.M.&M. Co. for waist lining 0.30, thread 0.04; total 0.34. From Gottenmyer for lard 1.10. Ordered a book for the school 0.10 (Classification book) and wrote 2 contracts 0.50; total 0.60.

Tuesday the 27th
Very cold. Worked at home.

Wednesday the 28th
Somewhat milder. It snowed. Wrote to Monroe. From M.M.&M. Co. fine cornmeal 100 lbs. @ 1 ¼ cents = 1.25, 4 bu. and 5 lbs. peas @ 0.60 = 2.45, tobacco 0.10; total 3.80

Thursday the 1st
Independent 2.00, M.M.&M. Co. 36.32, I. Daugharty 1.00, N.B. Weaver 16.38, Nerriter 12.60, Norn 18.84, John Dobson 1.00, Marfileus 3.05, Gottenmyer 2.35—Telfer 1.15, School 3.15, Waites 4.65
As of 1 March 1900:
Outstanding receipts 8.95
Debts 108.99
Cash on hand 0.99

Thursday the 1st
Mild. Worked at home.

Friday the 2nd
Nice weather. Sawed some wood, so [incomplete sentence].

Saturday the 3rd
Nice weather. Sawed some wood. From M.M.&M. Co. coffee 0.12, sugar 0.10, coffee extract 0.05; total 0.27.

Sunday the 4th
Raw. Snow flurries. Kept the Sabbath. Very hard frost.

Monday the 5th
Milder. It should be noted that Ella owes me 100.00 as a result of a bet she lost to me several days ago. Sorted beans for seed.

Tuesday the 6th
Very raw and cold. Snow flurries. Stayed at home.

Wednesday the 7th
Raw and cold. Sorted beans for seed.

Thursday the 8th
Mini's birthday. She wasn't at home, however, and so I couldn't congratulate her. Sorted beans for seed and worked in the barn. In the evening sold the two young bulls to John Dobson for 18.00. 2.00 on hand.

[52]   March 1900

Friday the 9th
Beautiful day. Delivered the bull calves to John Dobson. Received 1.80 from Telfer. Heinrich took Fanny and the sled to Standish to pick up hay for Karl and hauled two bales. Received 15.00 from John Dobson as final payment for the bulls and subtracted the dollar owed him. From M.M.&M. Co. petroleum 0.60.

Saturday the 10th
Beautiful weather. Paid Nerriter 3.00, Marfileus 2.98. For a kettle 1.00, for shirting 0.30, buttons 0.06, for a shirt 0.50; total 0.86. Paid Taalke 2.00. For chocolate 0.10, Mini's Birthday. Thread 0.10, sugar 0.20, coffee 0.12, tobacco 0.10, hairpins 0.05; total 0.67. Writing material 0.10. For repairing a bucket 0.10.

Sunday the 11th
Raw with snow flurries. Brbr. 2.00.

Monday the 12th
Very windy and raw. Blossom came fresh. I was there to help. Both cow and calf were very weak. M. [sentence incomplete]

Tuesday the 13th
Thaw. Beautiful day. From M.M.&M. Co. things for the record (a tradebook which the Co. gave me) 0.71. From P.M. Miller for 6 milk cans 0.50, 6 plates 0.24; total 0.74. For 50 lbs. of flour 0.96. Received 1.00 from Barker for wheat lent him. Karl had a son.

Wednesday the 14th
Clear but very cold. Cleared and sawed.

Thursday the 15th
Raw, snow flurries. Worked at home.

Friday the 16th and Saturday the 17th
The same. From M.M.&M. Co. (Tradebook) 0.50. Looked for Timrick's advice/wheel [could be either] as on Tuesday the 13th.

Sunday the 18th
Clear but very cold.

Monday the 19th
Hauled three bales of hay from Standish for Karl. The cow Taalke very sick. From M.M.&M. Co. a corset jacket 1.00.

[53]   **March 1900**

Tuesday the 20th, Wednesday the 21st, Thursday the 22nd
Beautiful weather. During the day the snow melted where the sun hit it; during the night everything froze solid. Nehls came to look at the sick cow.

Friday the 23rd
Beautiful day. Taalke the cow gave birth to a bull calf; both cow and calf were very weak. Proulx was here to help with the birth. On the 20th Angus's house burned down. On the very same day our policy expired at noon. I renewed it on the following day: house and furniture, the barn, horses, cows, wagon, etc. granary, everything insured for 1400.00; the fees etc. come to 1.90. Forsyth lent it to me. Received back for Taalke 0.67. Mini for school stuff 0.20, tobacco 0.10.

Saturday the 24th
Beautiful weather. For butter 1.23. For Kaufmann 4.89. For groceries 1.63. For timothy 0.38; total. From N.B. Weaver for tacks 0.10.

Sunday the 25th
Nice day. Gave the cow Taalke about a pound of fatback. In the afternoon she made manure. A. Reigh preached in the P.M.

Monday the 26th
Nice. Filed the saw. Gave the cow linseed oil.

Tuesday the 27th
Nice. Sawed wood. From M.M.&M. Co. thread 0.04.

Wednesday the 28th
Nice. Sawed wood. The cow no better.

Thursday the 29th
Nice. Sawed wood. The cow no better.

Friday the 30th
Rain showers, snow and hail. Bought 8 bu. seed potatoes @ 0.60 = 4.80 from Nehls. The cow no better.

Saturday the 31st
Nice. Hauled firewood home. In the morning the cow Nellie gave birth to a dead calf, but the cow seemed well contented. From Nerriter bran 0.25. From Marfileus condition powder 0.25, turpentine 0.05; total 0.30.

[54]   **April 1900**

Sunday the 1st
Kept the Sabbath. Good weather.
Independent 2.00, M.M.&M. Co. 34.43, I. Daugharty 1.00, N.B. Weaver
16.93, Nerriter 9,85, Norn 18.84, Marfileus 0.30, Curney 5.00, Dr. Grigg
6.00, Stölt 4.00, Gottenmyer 2.35—school 3.15, Waites 4.65—Forsyth
(insurance) 1.90, P.M. Miller 0.74, Nehls 8 bu. Potatoes @ 0.50 = 4.00
As of 1 April 1900:
Outstanding receipts 7.80
Debts 107.34
Cash on hand 0.83

Monday the 2nd
Bought paper for school 0.25. From P.M. Miller 5 milkcans 0.50.

Tu. the 3rd, We. the 4th, Th. the 5th, Fr. the 6th, Sa. the 7th
Hauled manure every day. From M.M.&M. Co. for spices for the cow
Taalke 0.60. From Gottenmyer for fatback also for the cow 0.54. The cow
became terribly thin. I haven't seen the animal chewing a cud since the 12th
of March. Several times I beat her to get her up, gave her medicine etc. I gave
up hope and the intention to keep her alive till Rockwell Demond played the
doctor. He ordered one pound of fatback 3 times a day as well as black pepper, ginger and sage—one spoonful of each herb in a pint of water for two
or three days and then wait for an equally long period.

Sunday the 8th
Nice weather. Kept the Sabbath. Brbr.

[55]   **April 1900**

Monday the 9th, Tuesday 10th
Helped Timrick sell his house. Very raw and cold. Paid careful attention to
the cow and rubbed the horse's foot with Corosine liniment. From Marfileus
for camphor spirit 0.05. Gottenmyer for lard 4.00. For composition book
0.10. For diamond dye 0.10; total 0.20. Note that to the expenses on April
2 should be added from M.M.&M. Co. for cotton 0.45, for a spool 0.04;
total .049 [0.49?]

Wednesday the 11th, Thursday the 12th
Hauled manure. On the 12th, Maundy Thursday, the cow Taalke died.

Friday the 13th
Good Friday. Got a load of manure from town. Karl hauled it. The road was
in terrible condition.

Saturday the 14th
Good weather. Hauled two loads of manure from town. From M.M.&M. Co. cornflour 1.40, sugar 0.25; total 1.65. Grace Wübbena's tumor very large. Taalke up with her through the night.

Sunday the 15th
Nice weather. Celebrated Easter. Brbr.

Monday the 16th
Overcast and rainy. Hauled a load of manure from town and sent Timricks 5.00.

Tuesday the 17th
Rain during the night. The road was very soft. Hauled two loads of manure from town. Rain again toward evening.

Wednesday the 18th
Overcast. Drained fields the entire day. It was very wet and a lot of water standing in some places.

Thursday the 19th
Hauled two loads of manure from town.

Friday the 20th, Saturday the 21st, Sunday the 22nd
Attended a conference in Saginaw, fare 1.30, glasses 0.75, other expenses 0.20, collection 1.00. Borrowed 1.00 from Taalke, paid Nehls 2.00, Street-car 0.05. Other expenses, I can't remember what for, 0.50.

Monday the 23rd, Tuesday the 24th, Wednesday the 25th, Thursday the 26th
Hauled firewood and piled stumps. Paid 0.15 to have the ax filed, couvertee 0.05; total 0.20.

[56]   **April and May 1900**

Thursday the 26th
From Marfileus licorice syrup 0.25.

Friday the 27th, Saturday the 28th
Hauled manure from town. Scissors from N.B. Weaver 0.35.

Sunday, the 29th
Beautiful day. Karl's son buried. Brbr.

Monday the 30th
Nice weather. Hauled two loads of manure from town. From M.M.&M. Co. tobacco 0.10.

Tuesday the 1st of May
Independent 2.00, M.M.&M. Co. 39.49, I. Daugharty 1.00, N.B. Weaver 17.28, Nerriter 9.85, Norn 18.84, O.N. 1.00, Marfileus 0.60, Curney 5.00, Dr. Grigg 6.00, Stölt 4.00, Gottenmyer 6.35, Forsyth insurance 1.90, P.M. Miller 1.24, Nehls 2.00—school 3.45, Waites 4.65
As of 1 May 1900:
Outstanding receipts 8.10
Debts 116.55
Cash on hand 0.00

Tuesday the 1st
Nice weather. Hauled a load of manure from Standish.

Wednesday the 2nd
Good weather. In the morning Johannes and Heinrich came home. Received from Heinrich 39.00. From this paid out to Curney 5.00. From M.M.&M. Co. for 50 lbs. flour 1.00. Plowed in the forenoon. Paid Taalke 1.00, for an umbrella 0.50; total 1.50.

Thursday the 3rd
Plowed. Paid N.B. Weaver 5.00, Forsyth Insurance 1.90, for curtains etc. 6.16. From M.M.&M. Co. tea 0.25, for grapevines 2.00. After I noticed that the debts from May 1st didn't include the 1.00 from Taalke I realized that I had made a mistake on the second when I subtracted the dollar paid to her and correct the record here.

Friday the 4th
Johannes cultivated and Heinrich plowed. Cleaned the chicken house. From M.M.&M. Co. rice 0.25. Prince developed sore shoulders.

Saturday the 5th
Johannes cultivated and Heinrich plowed. Cleaned the backhouse. Paid Nerreter 4.50, Norn 4.00, Gottenmyer 3.00; total 11.50.

[57]   **May 1900**

Paid Hartmann 0.50. Tobacco 0.10. M. Miller 1.24. Received a card from Sears & Roebuck re. Invoice Nr. 330246. To Schauers for blacksmith work 0.25, bolts 0.08.

Sunday the 6th
Nice. Brbr. 0.50

Monday the 7th
Clear but cold. Johannes cultivated and Heinrich plowed and harrowed. I picked up trash and cleared fields. During the night and off and on all day rain. In the dry spells planted oats with peas.

Tuesday the 8th
Weather changeable. From M.M.&M. Co. for 2¼ bu. peas @ 0.85 = 1.91 and for repairing a pail 0.05. Heavy rain in the evening.

Wednesday the 9th, Thursday the 10th
Sowed oats and peas and harrowed them under. In the evening of the 10th Johannes and Heinrich made me a present of a new singletree harness.

Friday the 11th
Harrowed oats and peas under and plowed some and leveled off the planted fields.

Saturday the 12th
Six chairs from N.B. Weaver for 3.75; paid 2.50 which leaves a debt of 1.25. From M.M.&M. Co. for flour 4.50, Gold Dust 0.25, tea 0.25, yeast 0.04, matches 0.10, rice 0.24, oatmeal 0.25, sugar 0.25, tobacco 0.10; total 5.99. Gave Mini 0.05.

Sunday the 13th
Beautiful day. Sunday School 0.05.

Monday the 14th
Beautiful day. Cleared and drained fields. Nellie bred to Jim Dobson's bull 0.50; she should come fresh on Feb. 14th 1901.

Tuesday the 15th
Nice day. Cool and cold toward evening. Received another card from Sears & Roebuck with a note regarding the statement invoice # 357248. Cleared and drained fields.

Wednesday the 16th
Overcast, rainy. Cleared fields and drained.

Thursday the 17th
Overcast, rainy. Cleared fields and drained.

Friday the 18th
The same. Cleared fields. 2 clevises @ 12½ from N.B. Weaver.

[58]   May 1900

Saturday the 19th
Beautiful weather. Cleared fields.

Sunday the 20th
Nice. Rested. Brbr.

Monday the 21st
For seeds 0.30. Cleared fields.

Tuesday the 22nd
Cleared. Groceries from M.M.&M. Co. 0.95. From M.M.&M. Co. for carrot seed 0.12.

Wednesday the 23rd
Cleared fields. Blossom bred to Dobson's bull 0.50.

Thursday the 24th
Cleared fields. Nice weather.

Friday the 25th
Cleared fields. Nice weather.

Saturday the 26th
Cleared fields. Nice weather. From M.M.&M. Co. for groceries 3.09.

Sunday the 27th
Beautiful day.

Monday the 28th
Nice day. Planted beans and potatoes and harrowed.

Tuesday the 29th
Beautiful. Toward evening a thunderstorm brewing. Planted beans, harrowed and marked the fields to plant corn. From N.B. Weaver for a windowpane 0.50.

Wednesday the 30th, Thursday the 31st
Beautiful weather. Planted corn and potatoes. Corn about one bushel.

June 1900
Friday the 1st
Independent (Ireland) 2.00, M.M.&M. Co. 52.95, I. Daugharty 1.00, N.B. Weaver 13.78, Nerriter 5.30, Norn 11.08, O. Nachricht 1.00, Marfileus 0.60, Dr. Grigg 6.00, Stölt 4.00, Gottenmyer 3.00, Nehls 2.00—school 3.40, Waites 4.65.

As of 1 June 1900:
Outstanding receipts 8.10
Debts 102.71
Cash on hand 0.00

Friday the 1st
Planted potatoes all together 10½ bushel. The mare Fanny gave birth to a beautiful mare colt as she had two years ago with "Topsy."

Saturday the 2nd
Very cool, cold. Picked up a sewing machine from Pomeroy 48.00

Sunday the 3rd
Beautiful day. Cool. Brbr. Nerriter 0.10.

[59] **June 1900**

Monday the 4th
From N.B. Weaver two hooks @ 0.40; total 0.80. From M.M.&M. Co. groceries 1,84.

Tuesday the 5th
From M.M.&M. Co. for millet molds 0.55, 4 bu. corn @ 0.56 = 2.24, yeast 0.04, 2 yds. cotton 0.18, cash 3.00; total 6.01.

Wednesday the 6th, Thursday the 7th
Johannes and Heinrich had to go over to Karl's and work for him, plowed, harrowed, etc. Johannes went to Felix Proulx on the 7th.

Friday the 8th
Heinrich's birthday. Threatening storm as yesterday and the day before. Heinrich worked for Karl plowing, harrowing, etc. Johannes and I worked on the land clearing fields and logging.

Saturday the 9th
Logged and cleared. From M.M.&M. Co. for groceries 1.50.

Sunday the 10th
Threatening storm.

Monday the 11th
Beautiful day. Cleared fields. In the afternoon plowed. Fanny inoculated by Keifer 5.00.

Tuesday the 12th
Cold at night. Plowed. Johannes and Heinrich put up a fence for Karl. From M.M.&M. Co. for yarn 0.08.

Wednesday the 13th
Nice day though the night was cold. Plowed. From Cassidy an Hill patented share for the plow 0.40. From N.B. Weaver 2 screws 0.05. Watched through the night at Spooners. Blossom bred; should come fresh on March 13th.

Thursday the 14th
Nice weather. Heinrich and I plowed, Heinrich in the morning and I in the afternoon. Jake intends to leave and went to Munising in the evening. On the 13th meat from Gottenmyer 0.30.

Friday the 15th
Plowed. Beautiful weather.

Saturday the 16th
Plowed. In the morning the heifer Cherry bore a heifer calf. For groceries from M.M.&M. Co. 0.80.

Sunday the 17th
Clear but cool. Brbr.

Monday the 18th
Clear but cool. Heinrich plowed and I visited G. Lucks. Heinrich worked for Mrs. Angus.

[60] June 1900

Tuesday the 19th
Clear and cool. Heinrich plowed and I visited G. Lucks. Heinrich worked for Mrs. Angus. For Heinrich's hat from M.M.&M. Co. 0.20.

Wednesday the 20th
Nice day. Harrowed. Bushel corn sowed as well as ½ bushel millet, one peck buckwheat and about a quart of beans. From M.M.&M. Co. groceries 0.54. Heinrich worked for Mrs. Angus.

Thursday the 21st
Nice day. Threatened storm in the afternoon, we had two strong rain showers. Heinrich worked for Mrs. Angus. From N.B. Weaver nails for 0.40.

Friday the 22nd
Hot. In the morning a rain shower. About 9:00 Heinrich began to harrow in the seeds and had finished the job by noon. With that we had the newly cleared field planted. I found out that the same field is about 5 acres. Cultivated in the evening and picked up trash.

Saturday the 23rd
Hot. Cultivated and raked.

Sunday the 24th
Very hot. Kept the Sabbath.

Monday the 25th
Very hot. Oatmeal 0.25, rice 0.25, 50 lb. lard 4.25, 2 bu. potatoes 1.00, sugar 0.50, soap 0.25, cornmeal 0.38, Gold Medal flour 5.00, tea dust 0.25, yeast 0.04, 2 spoons 0.08; from M.M.&M. Co. total 12.25. From N.B. Weaver a milkpail 0.50, rope 0.40, and 8" file 0.12; total 1.02. Began to dig a well in the barnyard. Credit for Milk in May 1900: 1091 lbs. = 4.91.

Tuesday the 26th
Very hot. In the morning Heinrich and I dug the well. In the afternoon I went to the school 0.50. Heinrich made a drinking trough and a fence around the well. Received from the school 3.95. Heinrich was over to Angus' and quit working because the wages were too low. Stölt's heifer suffered a bad fall.

[61] **June and July 1900**

Wednesday the 27th
A storm during the night. Finished digging the well. Prince hurt himself badly when he tried to jump over a wire fence. Applied Corosine liniment to the wound.

Thursday the 28th
Thunderstorm during the night with very heavy rain. In the forenoon went to pick up a pump. Paid John Stölt 4.00. Then worked on the road with the horses, Heinrich and Stallinger. From N.B. Weaver a pitchfork for 0.45, two rakes 0.30, one pair of hinges 0.10, 9 lbs. of chain 1.08, a pump head 1.75, a 14 foot long pipe 1.40, 4 buckets 0.40, 1 qt. machine oil 0.09; total 5.57. The pump with chain, head, pipe and baskets cost 4.63; but now it won't be necessary to pull up water on a hook for 8 years.

Friday the 29th
Very windy but at least not cold. Heinrich got the pump working. He then made hay and raked. I cultivated the entire day.

Saturday the 30th
Very windy; cold. Heinrich, Hinrich, Friedrich and Emma weeded the carrots. From M.M.&M. Co. onions for 0.10, soap 0.10; total 0.20. From Marfileus sulfur 0.05. I cultivated. Sent Stölt 4.00.

Sunday the 1st of July
Beautiful, warm day. Brbr.

Monday the 2nd
Fine weather, warm. Very windy. Cultivated and raked. From Thurs. all Curk 2.00.
Independent 2.00, M.M.&M. Co. 77.64, I. Daugharty 1.00, N.B. Weaver 21.62, Cassidy 0.40, James Dobson 1.00, O.N. 2.00, Nerriter 5.30, Norn 11.08, Marfileus 0.65, Dr. Grigg 6.00, Gottenmyer 3.30, Nehls 2.00 Curney 5.00, Dr. Me. Curk 2.00, Pomeroy—Waites 4.65.
As of 1 July 1900:
Outstanding receipts 4.65
Debts 189.59
Cash on hand 0.00
Fanny refused to be bred—this already on June 11th.

[62]   July 1900

Tuesday the 3rd
Stormy, humid. Hoed corn. Fanny again refused to be bred.

Wednesday the 4th
Stormy. Celebrated the magnificent 4th. The white heifer was with a bull. She should accordingly come fresh on April 14, 1901.

Thursday the 5th
Very hot. From Waites 3.00, from the school 1.00; total 4.00. Paid Marfileus 1.35, M.M.&M. Co. 2.00, Cassidy 0.40; total 3.75. Groceries from M.M.&M. Co. for 0.90.

Friday the 6th
From M.M.&M. Co. baking powder 0.10, sugar 0.25, Paris Green 0.90; total 1.25. From Marfileus a comb 0.15, tablet 0.05, Paris Green 1.00; total 1.20. Spent the entire day attending to the potatoes. The children hoed corn. Heinrich raked hay and stacked some of it. In the evening brought in about ¼ load to the barn. In the evening a powerful electric storm with heavy rain.

Saturday the 7th
From M.M.&M. Co. a barrel of salt. Thunderstorms all day and rain. Heinrich cut hay during the afternoon. Raked and hoed.

Sunday the 8th
Cloudy and cold. In the evening lit a fire in the stove. Sunday School 0.05

Monday the 9th
Bright and clear. In the afternoon hauled three loads of the hay that was raked and stacked on Friday home. In the evening attended the annual synod, 0.50.

Tuesday the 10th
Overcast. Raked and stacked some hay anyway. A rain shower about 11:00 made us give it up. So far this year we have had bad luck with the hay harvest. In the afternoon Heinrich cut some hay and toward evening raked some of it together.

Wednesday the 11th
Very raw and stormy. A heavy thunderstorm with hail during the night. During the day we dried as much of the hay as we could.

[63]   July 1900

Thursday the 12th
Strong wind out of the northwest. Raked and stacked hay and hauled the cured hay to the barn, 5 loads. That makes 8 loads all together so far this summer that we have been able to get into the barn.

Friday the 13th
Stormy, hot, lightning. Cut hay, raked and stacked it. Brought a load home in the evening. On the 11th from M.M.&M. Co. 5 lbs. beans 0.30, sugar 0.25, yeast cakes 0.08, onions 0.05, rice 0.25; total 0.93. Further to B. for calico 0.36, thread 0.04; total 0.40.

Saturday the 14th
A powerful storm. Hot. Brought in 6 loads of hay; this makes a total of 15 loads so far this summer. From M.M.&M. Co. sugar 0.25, rice 0.25; total 0.50. From N.B. Weaver for 4" spikes 0.16.

Sunday the 15th
Very hot, oppressively humid.

Monday the 16th
Very hot, stormy. Heinrich cut the last of the hay. Heinrich and I worked in the barn. During the following night, or actually during the evening, there was a terrible storm, a cyclone with thunder and lightning and heavy rain and hail. For a while the beans and cabbage planted in front of the kitchen were under water.

Tuesday the 17th
Windy. Drained fields the entire day. In the low spots the back fields had
water standing more than knee deep. From M.M.&M. Co. ½ dozen eggs
0.06, a pound of butter 0.15; total 0.21. Over the weekend Heinrich had
made a rig for unloading hay by putting a pole on the west end and another
on the east end. I helped him a little.

[64] July 1900

Wednesday the 18th
Very nice weather. Heinrich went to work in the stave factory. I worked in
the barn during the morning. In the afternoon raked hay and stacked it.
From M.M.&M. Co. 2 shirts @ 0.50; total 1.00.

Thursday the 19th
Very beautiful weather. Brought in 6 loads of hay; that makes all together 21
loads that we were able to get in good condition in spite of the unfavorable
conditions under which we had to work. We also salted the hay at the rate
of about 15 lb. per ton as a rough calculation. From M.M.&M. Co. tobacco
0.40, sugar 0.50, eggs 0.18, baking powder 0.10, soap 0.25; total 1.43.

Friday the 20th
Stormy. From M.M.&M. Co. butter 0.23, cornmeal 0.29, salt 1.10, vinegar
0.10; total 1.72. Drained fields the whole day. Credit for milk for June 6.81.

Saturday the 21st
Drained fields the whole day. The water was knee deep in some places.

Sunday the 22nd
Hot. Brbr.

Monday the 23rd
Weeded the pig yard which was full of chamomile and goldenrod. Toward
evening there was a thunderstorm with heavy rain.

Tuesday the 24th
Overcast. Drained fields. From M.M.&M. Co. sugar 0.50, tea 0.25, butter
0.15, eggs 0.12, rice 0.25; total 1.27. From Marfileus a comb for 0.15.
Weeded.

Wednesday the 25th
Clear. Drained fields and weeded. Received from Heinrich 4.00. Paid
McGurk 2.00.

Thursday the 26th
Clear. Weeded. From Gottenmyer meat 0.36. From M.M.&M. Co. celery and onions 0.10.

[65] **July and August 1900**

Friday the 27th
Nice weather. Raked and stacked the wheat that Heinrich had cut for hay the night before. Heinrich mowed the remainder in the evening.

Saturday the 28th
Nice. Raked and stacked the mown hay. Brought two loads in. From M.M.&M. Co. sugar 0.50, butter 0.30; total 0.80.

Sunday the 29th
Beautiful day. Kept the Sabbath. A small thunderstorm in the afternoon. Paid Nehls 2.00.

Monday the 30th, Tuesday the 31st
Weeded the carrots. Beautiful weather.

AUGUST
Wednesday the 1st
Independent 1.00, M.M.&M. Co. 82.34, I. Daugharty 1.00, N.B. Weaver 21.78, James Dobson 1.00, O.N. 2.00, Nerriter 5.30, Norn 11.08, Marfileus 1.35, Dr. Grigg 6.00, Gottenmyer 3.60, Curney 5.00, Pomeroy 48.00— Waites 1.65, school district 0.50.
As of 1 August 1900:
Outstanding receipts 2.15
Debts 189.45
Cash on hand 0.00

Wednesday the 1st
Beautiful day. Weeded and cultivated. From M.M.&M. Co. sugar 0.50, butter 0.15, yeast cakes 0.08, potatoes ½ bu. 0.28; total 1.01.

Thursday the 2nd
Beautiful weather. Picked huckleberries.

Friday the 3rd
Nice day. Around noon Heinrich came home from the factory. From four o'clock he mowed some oats with the machine. Weeded, hoed cabbage etc. From M.M.&M. Co. butter 0.15, celery 0.05, pins 0.05; total 0.25. From Gottenmyer bologna 0.10.

Saturday the 4th
From M.M.&M. Co. oatmeal 0.25, rice 0.25, vinegar 0.10, soda 0.10, eggs 0.06; total 0.76. Raked the oats cut the previous day into piles and bound some of them to sheaves.

Sunday the 5th
Very hot. Brbr. From Marfileus 0.10.

[66]   August 1900

Monday the 6th
Very hot. From M.M.&M. Co. sugar 1.00, flour 0.65, butter 0.30, tea 0.25, powder 0.15; total 2.35. Picked up some wood to make a book case for the school. Pulled peas.

Tuesday the 7th
Very hot. Pulled peas and brought in oats.

Wednesday the 8th
Very hot. Pulled peas. Heinrich and Taalke alone and Hinrich went to Bentley.

Thursday the 9th
Very hot. Pulled peas and brought in oats.

Friday the 10th
Was over to Daugharty's then to Nehls about the bookcase West had made for the school, copied the Pumche {?}, it took the entire forenoon, 0.75. Pulled peas in the afternoon.

Saturday the 11th
Very hot. Brought in oats and peas. From M.M.&M. Co. butter 0.30, soap 0.25, eggs 0.12, yeast 0.08, tobacco 0.35; total 1.10. Received from E. Waites 1.55, of that gave Taalke 0.80. Pulled peas.

Sunday the 12th
Rainy.

Monday the 13th
Clear and then overcast. Heinrich returned from the mill. Mowed the remaining oats and then helped me pull peas. Fanny allowed herself to be bred as M.

Tuesday the 14th
Nice weather in the forenoon, pulled peas. Afternoon a violent thunderstorm. In the evening Heinrich helped pull peas, during the day he worked in

the factory. From M.M.&M. Co. butter 0.30, vinegar 0.10, cornmeal 0.25; total 0.65.

Wednesday the 15th
Nice. Pulled peas. In the afternoon rainy.

Thursday the 16th
Hot. Pulled peas; Heinrich helped me. Taalke's birthday; she is 19 years old and received presents from her younger siblings. She celebrated during the afternoon. Visited Gammons.

[67]   **August 1900**

Friday the 17th
Hot in the morning and threatening storm in the afternoon. Brought in oats and helped Dankerts and Sillos with the threshing.

Saturday the 18th
From M.M.&M. Co. flour, 1.25, lard 4.38, yeast 0.08, sugar 1.00, butter 0.30, rice 0.25, bran 0.35; total 7.61. From N.B. Weaver rope 0.20. For milk 7.10, cash 1.00. From Norn for lumber 1.00.

Sunday the 19th
Very hot and threatening storm. Brbr. Kept the Sabbath. During the night a long thunderstorm with rain.

Monday the 20th
Very hot. In the morning went to a school board meeting about hiring a teacher and setting up a contract, 050. The forenoon was very hot. Raked peas in preparation for bringing them in. Around noon there was a violent thunderstorm. Dankert got a sunburn.

Tuesday the 21st
Overcast. Hamilton 1.00. From N.B. Weaver spikes 0.40, nails 0.40; total 0.80. Tea dust 0.35, lamp oil 0.60; total 0.95. Raked peas and began to build an addition to the barn for extra stall space. Hired Miss Henderson as the teacher two weeks ago already and gave her a contract, 0.75.

Wednesday the 22nd
Nice. Brought in two loads of peas and worked on the new stalls. Hauled a load of manure from Waites.

Thursday the 23rd
Good weather, a shower of rain around noon. Had just gotten a load of peas in beforehand. Heinrich and Hinrich worked on the stall. Received from Heinrich 7.00, paid 2.00 to M.M.&M. Co. Mutual Home Insurance 5.60.

Friday the 24th
Good weather. Heavy fog during the forenoon. Brought in the rest of the peas in the afternoon and got everything ready for threshing. Began to cut corn on the 22nd.

[68]   August 1900

Paid Home Mutual Insurance (5.60). Gottenmyer for meat 1.00. Groceries from M.M.&M. Co. for 1.58. From Harry Blumenthal 2 blankets Tuesday the 1.00 = 2.00.

Saturday the 25th
Threshed grain: peas 61 bu., oats 80 bu. wheat 3.bu. Lefree's bill for the threshing 4.29.

Sunday the 26th
Hot all day, toward evening a violent thunderstorm and rain. Kept the Sabbath.

Monday the 27th
Heinrich worked on the stalls. The children and I worked on the straw stack and got most of it in the barn. Very hot.

Tuesday the 28th
Heinrich helped John Dobson with the threshing during the forenoon. From M.M.&M. Co. axle grease 0.10, matches 0.10, 50 lb. Gold Medal flour 1.25, soap 0.25; total 1.70. From N.B. Weaver 5 lb. spikes Tuesday the 0.04 = 0.20 and 10 lbs. 10d nails 0.40; total 0.60. From J. Norn 8 rafters 2" × 6" × 14' 0.80. Very hot. From M.M.&M. Co. 2 spools 0.08, 5 yd. denim 0.63, duck 0.60, trimming braid 0.05, sugar 0.25, tea 0.25; total 2.21. In the afternoon brought in some more straw.

Wednesday the 29th
Nice day. Pulled straw up into the mow with the horse. Till evening we were almost finished. Heinrich worked on the stall.

Thursday the 30th
Nice day. In the morning hauled a load of manure from Waites. Then pulled beans with the children. With all the rain you could hardly find the beanstalks for all the weeds. Heinrich worked on the stall. In the afternoon he and Hinrich hauled hay for Karl.

Friday the 31st
Nice day, hot. Cut corn and pulled beans.

[69]   **September 1900**

Saturday the 1st
Hot. Took the census, 4.00. The children cut corn. Heinrich and Hinrich worked on the stall. From M.M.&M. Co. sugar 0.25, butter 0.17; total 0.42.

Sunday the 2nd
Sunday. Kept the Sabbath. Brbr.

Monday the 3rd
From N.B. Weaver 10 lbs. of 10d nails 0.40. Picked up crocks for the school, 1.00.

Tuesday the 4th through Saturday the 8th
Cut the corn we had sown with Emma and Friedrich. Heinrich mowed four loads of clover, dried it and hauled it in. Made a hayrack, a good job. On the 8th from M.M.&M. Co. sugar 0.50, baking powder 0.10, onions 0.10, vinegar 0.10, flour 1.25, tobacco 0.35; total 2.40. From Nerriter for shingles, 3500 @ 1.00 per 1000 = 3.50. From N.B. Weaver for 14 lb. of roofing nails @ 0.05 = 0.70. Received from Heinrich 1.00, paid Nerriter 1.00. From O.A. Marfileus Algebra for 1.00.

Sunday the 9th
Kept the Sabbath.

Monday the 10th
Heinrich mowed the millet and buckwheat and then shingled the stall with Hinrich's help. Emma and Friedrich helped me cut corn. Delivered the shelves for the school in the evening. Have to take the census, received 4.00.

Tuesday the 11th
Very hot. Emma helped me cut corn all day. Heinrich and Hinrich worked shingling the new addition. Heinrich also pulled peas for Thoms for about a quarter of a day. Friedrich helped cut corn. The afternoon brought rain showers. From M.M.&M. Co. tea.

Wednesday the 12th
Nice, warm day. Received from the school 8.60.

[70]   **September 1900**

Thursday the 13th
Soldier's Reunion. The children attended; I cut corn and shocked it up: 44 shocks. On Monday the 10th Heinrich had sold the white heifer for 24.00 and had received 2.00 in advance which we paid to reduce our debt with

Gottenmyer. Taalke's shoes 1.75, other expenses resulting from the reunion 0.40; total 2.35.

Friday the 14th
Nice weather. Received 22.00 for the heifer. For shoes 2.00, other expenses 0.20, sugar 0.25, leaves 19.55. Came back from delivering the heifer. Cut corn and shocked it up; raked the millet and put it in stacks and also stacked up some of the buckwheat.

Saturday the 15th
Nice weather. Brought the millet in and cut and shocked corn. Clothes for the children 6.49, for harness hooks 0.20; total 6.79.

Sunday the 16th
Cold. Brbr.

Monday the 17th
Cold. In the morning the heifer Rosa lay dead in the barnyard. Nehls and I skinned her and sold the hide for 2.10. It weighed 35 lbs and sold for 0.16 per lb. For sugar 0.25, from M.M.&M. Co. cash 1.50. Cut corn the remainder of the day with Mini, Hinrich and Friedrich. Gathered it and set it up in 64 shocks.

Tuesday the 18th
Beautiful weather. Cut corn and set up 84 shocks. Hinrich helped till 4:00. Gave Heinrich 5.00. In the evening Heinrich left us and headed north. Paid Hamilton 1.00 for hauling milk in August.

Wednesday the 19th
The forenoon was dry but cloudy; in the afternoon rain. Set up 40 shocks. Trained the colt.

[71]   **September 1900**

Thursday the 20th
Bound up the corn we had cut. The children pulled beans.

Friday the 21st
Tied up corn in the morning but had to quit because of a headache. Attended Senne's funeral. Paid Pomeroy 16.00 against the amount owed on the sewing machine. Borrowed 1.00 from Forsyth and gave the dollar to Taalke to decorate mama's and Delie's graves.

Saturday the 22nd
Good weather. Husked 2 ¾ bu. corn (Mini and Emma). I tied up the cut corn and put it up in shocks, also set up the shocks that had fallen over.

Sunday the 23rd
Beautiful day. Kept the Sabbath.

Monday the 24th
Nice. Pulled the remaining beans, set up the fallen corn shocks and husked
1½ bu. corn.

Tuesday the 25th
Nice. Brought in the buckwheat. 7 shocks = 3 bu. husked corn.

Wednesday the 26th
Nice, hot. Had our buckwheat threshed at Thoms. Yielded 4 bu., paid 0.25.
Then husked 3 bu. and 2 peck of corn from 7 shocks. For hairpins 0.11.

Thursday the 27th
Nice. Cold during the night but no frost. Dug 11 bu. 2 peck of potatoes from
7 × 90 hills.

Friday the 28th
Nice. 2 bu. potatoes from 2 × 90 hills; that makes 13 bu. 2 pecks of red
potatoes all together. Husked 2 bu. of corn.

Saturday the 29th
Nice. Husked 5 bu. of corn. Hinrich and Emma plowed.

[Left space, but wrote nothing for the 30th; confusion in the following three
dates probably the result of his illness.]

Sunday the 1st
Very sick, stayed in bed.

Monday the 2nd
Some better, but still in bed.

Tuesday the 3rd
Some better, still in bed. The cow Cherry to Sonnschmitt's bull, 0.50.

[72]   **October 1900**

Independent 2.00, M.M.&M. Co.

[The writer left space for the usual list of debts and assets at the beginning of
the month, but never completed it.]

Wednesday the 3rd
Overcast. Threatening storm. Husked 4 bu. of corn from 16 shocks.

Thursday the 4th
Nice and warm. Husked 5 bu. from 28 shocks.

Friday the 5th
Nice and warm. In the afternoon a violent thunderstorm. Husked 8 bu. of corn from 20 shocks.

Saturday the 6th
Nice. Husked 6 bu. and 2 peck of corn from 22 shocks. In the afternoon a violent thunderstorm.

Sunday the 7th
Nice. Kept the Sabbath.

Monday the 8th
From M.M.&M. Co. lard for 4.50, flour 1.25, oil 0.60, sal soda 0.10, meal 0.25, onions 0.10, sugar 0.25, rice 0.25, yeast 0.08, tobacco 0.48, vinegar 0.05; total 8.11. Credit for milk (I think) 6.28. In addition I received 1.50 on September 17; that would make 7.78 all together. In the evening loaded a load of hay with Karl after I had made a rack on the wagon.

Tuesday the 9th
Sold a load of hay weighing 2180 to M.M.&M. Co. @ 7.50 per ton = 8.18; took 3.00 in cash and paid the weighbills 0.25 and paper 0.15. Received a letter from Heinrich.

Wednesday the 10th
Dug 15 bu. of potatoes from 540 hills (white ones) and brought in two bu. of corn. Answered Heinrich's letter.

Thursday the 11th
Dug 17½ bu. white potatoes from 810 hills. Went to prayer meeting in the evening.

[73]   **October 1900**

Friday the 12th
Dug 6½ bu. white potatoes from 180 hills. Went to bed in the afternoon because of a headache. Paid R. Forsyth back 1.00. In the forenoon went to conference.

Saturday the 13th
Dug 15 bu. from 360 hills and dumped them in the SW corner of the cellar. To conference in the forenoon.

Sunday the 14th
Conference and Brbr.

Monday the 15th
Dug 25 bu. of potatoes from 675 hills; dumped them in the SW corner of the cellar.

Tuesday the 16th
Dug 23 bu. of white potatoes from 540 hills; dumped them in the second southwest bin in the cellar.

Wednesday the 17th
Dug 19 bu. of white potatoes from 450 hills and dumped them also in the second southwest bin in the cellar.

Thursday the 18th
Dug 6 bu. of white potatoes from 115 hills and dumped them in the second bin from the south in the cellar. Paid Sonnschmidt 0.25 for the breeding of the cow on October 3rd. Dug 21 bu. of carrots with Taalke and Mrs. C.H. Wübbena. Husked 2 bu. of corn. We now have 140 bu. of potatoes in the cellar. Loaded a load of hay with Nehls.

Friday the 19th
Delivered a load of hay to Gottenmyer @ 8.00 per ton. The load weighed 1565 which made 6.26. From this paid off debt to Gottenmyer for 3.80, the weighbill 0.25, bologna 0.10, to Nerriter 2.00, from M.M.&M. Co. 1.00. Dug 6 bu. of carrots.

Saturday the 20th
Paid Hamilton 1.00 for hauling the milk in September. Dug 6 bu. of carrots and husked 9 bu. of corn from 18 shocks. From M.M.&M. Co. 50 lbs. Gold Medal flour 1.25, lamp chimney 0.05; total 1.30.

Sunday the 21st
Nice day. Kept the Sabbath.

Monday the 22nd
Nice day, cloudy and warm. Dug the rest of the carrots, 15 bu., which makes a total of 48 bu. Only 6 bu. of red beets and that was all the beets. Emma went to school.

[74]   October 1900

Tuesday the 23rd
Husked 20 corn shocks. Hinrich hauled 3 loads of manure. Overcast, miserable weather, showers off and on.

Wednesday the 24th
From M.M.&M. Co. shoes for Friedrich 1.50, soap 0.25; total 1.75. Husked 24 corn shocks. Hinrich hauled two loads of manure.

Thursday the 25th
Husked 16 corn shocks. Friedrich got sick and so I had to husk alone. Emma has also been going to school since Monday. Hinrich hauled in the corn from the shocks that had fallen over and also hauled some firewood and 7½ bu. of corn. From N.B. Weaver a fireback 0.75.

Friday the 26th
Husked 19 corn shocks. In the forenoon a violent thunderstorm with rain showers. Hinrich plowed the harvested potato fields.

Saturday the 27th
Overcast. Helped Proulx slaughter a pig. Husked 8 corn shocks; with that we are done with husking, those were the last. Karl used our horses to haul firewood from town. From M.M.&M. Co. pork, 0.24, starch 0.10, sugar 0.10, matches 0.10, butter 0.05; total 0.54.

Sunday the 28th
Nice day. Brbr.

Monday the 29th
Rainy. Lengthened tongue on the wagon and worked around the barn. From M.M.&M. Co. 2 yds. cotton @ 0.07 = 0.14.

Tuesday the 30th
Rainy. Build a small calf stall. It was filthy weather. Yesterday I sent the tugs [=traces] and harness straps which had been unsatisfactory back to Sears and Roebuck in Chicago under invoice # 330246 (see November 14th).

Wednesday the 31st
Rainy. Did a little logging during the dry spells.

[75] November 1900

Independent 2.00, M.M.&M. Co. 106,75, John Daugharty 1.00, N.B. Weaver 25,63, James Dobson 1.00, O.N. 2.00, Nerriter 5.80, James Norn 12.88, Marfileus 4.35, Dr. Grigg 6.00, Gottenmyer [no sum], Curney 5.00, Pomeroy 32.00, Harry Blumenthal 2.00, Sonomit 0.25, Home Mutual Ins. 2.80. Total owed: 206.66

Thursday the 1st
Raw and rainy. Nehls came to visit during the afternoon.

Friday the 2nd
Dry. Hauled home the rest of the corn. Some of it lay in water. It amounted to 12 bu. With that we had a total of 80 bu. of corn in the crib. Spend the rest of the day logging the rest of the old horse fence. From M.M.&M. Co. 5.00; the threshing machine cost 4.29 which I paid as instructed to John Rancourt. Attended a Republican rally in the opera house.

Saturday the 3rd
Dry weather. Started to make a road along the north-south fence. From M.M.&M. Co. rice 0.25, tea 0.10; total 0.35. Tobacco 0.10. On the 2nd went to see Daugharty about kindling wood. Lent Hall 0.50.

Sunday the 4th
Good weather.

Monday the 5th
Violent storm with hail during the morning. Many of the corn shocks were literally blown apart. In the afternoon hauled beans into the barn and piled them on ladders which we had laid on saw horses. The beans were soaked through as a result of the heavy rains we had on the 29th, 30th and 31st of October. On the following days

[76]   November 1900

we attempted to dry them out again. With that we had them all in the barn in as good a shape as possible.

Tuesday the 6th
Election day. Went to Standish in the morning. Then loaded a load of hay with Karl, set up the fallen corn shocks and sawed firewood.

Wednesday the 7th
Delivered the hay loaded yesterday to M.M.&M. Co. for 7.50 per ton. The load weighed 2188 lbs. which made it 8.20. Paid the weighbill of 0.25 out of that and then bought groceries: flour (Gold Medal) 1.25, soda 0.10, oil 0.60, sugar 0.10, onions 0.05; total 2.10. Then sold a load of hay to Owen for 9.00 per ton. Loaded it in the afternoon with the help of Mr. Heinrich Nehls. In the evening strong wind and snow.

Thursday the 8th
The snow had melted by morning but the ground was covered with a blanket of frost. I delivered the load of hay; it weighed 2100 lbs. which made 9.45. I paid the weighbill of 0.25 and then paid 2.80 to Mutual Home Insurance (I had already paid 5.60 on August 23rd), 5.00 to N.B. Weaver, for

camphor gum 0.20, for beverages 0.20, to Marfileus for a fine comb 0.10, to M.M.&M. Co. for print 0.06.

Friday the 9th
Nice day but cold. In the forenoon Hinrich wanted to haul wood with the horses for Mrs. Spooner. Prince, however, didn't want to cross a steam pipe by the factory and so came home. From M.M.&M. Co. 4 skeins of yarn 0.75. In the afternoon I plowed and the boys cut wood.

Saturday the 10th
Plowed and hauled two loads of manure. Meat 0.50.

[77]   November 1900

Sunday the 11th
Nice. Brbr.

Monday the 12th
Very raw. Had sharp pains on the left side of my chest. Scraped sand into the new stall. Toward evening I had to quit working because of the pain. Mini came home from her visit to Garners in Chapel Grove.

Tuesday the 13th
Snow flurries. Cold and raw. Hinrich brought Mini to school and brought Karl Richert's things from K. Wübbena home. In the afternoon scraped several more scrapers full of sand into the new stall. From Marfileus iodine 0.05 and castor oil 0.05; total 0.10.

Wednesday the 14th
Very cold. Was hardly able to scatter the sand I had hauled in the previous day. Managed to do it nevertheless with a grubhoe and a sledge. Started to build a new pig pen in the new stall. Received for Hinrich 0.75 from Charles Richert for the work he did for him yesterday. Had a note from Sears & Roebuck that the harness I had sent for repair would be returned on the 12th of November, the invoice # was R. Dept. Inv. # R 57773. Received a letter from Johannes. From M.M.&M. Co. 22 yds. print 1.23, spool 0.04, cotton 0.18, braid 0.15; total 1.59.

Thursday the 15th
Very cold. Worked on the pig pen. Hinrich picked up the repaired straps and put the harness back together. The Sears & Roebuck Company had replaced everything with new material; that is the 4 tugs, the 4 hamestraps and one bellyband.

[78]   **November 1900**

Friday the 16th
Somewhat milder. Yesterday brought Johannes' horse to Karl so that he could board it. For that reason I filled the floor above the new stall where the horse was with cornstalks on account of the cold. Toward evening it turned raw again and looked as though it would snow.

Saturday the 17th
Friedrich's birthday. Congratulated him. Overcast and snowy. Worked on the new stall and prepared for Sunday. From M.M.&M. Co. oatmeal 0.25, rice 0.25, onions 0.10, baking powder 0.10, yeast 0.08, soap 0.25, cornmeal 0.35; total 1.41. Shirting for Hinrich and Friedrich 0.75. P.M. Miller for plates 0.24. Learned that the Home Mutual Insurance Company has failed; now we are without insurance.

Sunday the 18th
Rain during the night and it continued all day. Had Sunday School with Nehls and his son Heinrich.

Monday the 19th
Rain during the night which continued all day. Fixed the old windows etc. Worked on the stall etc.

Tuesday the 20th
Overcast and damp during the night; during the day still overcast but dry. Drained fields as much as I could.

Wednesday the 21st
Overcast and stormy. It rained till about 8:00 in the morning. Went to see Daugharty about hiring a teacher, 0.50. Took in 0.50 on Thursday the 15th as well as 0.50 on Thursday as rent for the school; total 1.00

Thursday the 22nd
Overcast and stormy. Drained fields during the forenoon. In the afternoon Nehls came for a visit and stayed till 4:00. Afterward I drained fields again. Hinrich and Friedrich tried selling bluing and sold 6 boxes. From M.M.&M. Co. shoelaces 0.03.

[79]   **November 1900**

Friday the 23rd
The fierce storms and heavy rains of the last days blew down much of the corn and left much of it in the water. Tried to bring the corn in and stand it up against the fences. The ground was too soft for the horses and wagon and

so stood some of it against the tallest stumps. Traded the wheat for about 80 lb. of flour and left the buckwheat in the mill—the entire wheat and buckwheat harvest. From M.M.&M. Co. Gold Medal flour 1.25, lard 4.50; total 4.75. From Heinrich a day's wages as a credit at the mill 1.25. From N.B. Weaver 3 windowpanes @ 0.10 = 0.30.

Saturday the 24th
In the previous night heavy frost. Hauled two loads of manure. Let the horses out in the afternoon. Fixed the windows in the chicken house and removed the fences by the old camp. Raw and cold. For several nights I left the cow Flora in the boxstall with the expectation that she would have her calf. Mini, Emma, Hinrich and Friedrich were selling bluing door-to-door.

Sunday the 25th
Good weather. Taalke went to visit Sadie Henderson. Heavy frost during the night. Flora had a bull calf.

Monday the 26th
Good weather. Heavy frost during the night. Hauled two loads of manure. Saw the boar with the black sow; I expect accordingly that she will farrow on March 25th 1901. Reinsured the buildings for 3 years on November 29th, 21.00 with the North British and Mercantile Co.

Tuesday the 27th
Frost during the night. Hauled two loads of manure. H. and Fr. sawed wood. Many Gebothen [?] from the Ancient Order of Eleanors [?]. Owe Hamilton for hauling milk 1.50.

Wednesday the 28th
Frost at night. Picked up the buckwheat flour from the mill and a load of wood for the big

[80]   **November & December 1900**

stove.

Wednesday the 28th
From M.M.&M. Co. rice, 0.25, sugar 0.10, onions 0.10, tea 0.10, apples 0.10; total 0.65. From N.B. Weaver for shoetacks 0.10. From Gottenmyer beef shank for 0.20. Had previous meat purchases twice for 0.25 each time makes 0.50 additional.

Thursday the 29th
Celebrated Thanksgiving Day in the afternoon and attended a meeting in Standish. Kay arrived during the sermon. Afterwards went to see Dr. Grigg about the pains in my chest 0.50.

Friday the 30th
Overcast. Filed and sawed.

Saturday the 1st
Overcast. Sawed wood. Have sawed more or less a week long and have yet to find a single shinglebolt—the wood was very rotted. Fritz has sore legs and wasn't able to walk very well. Till now there has hardly been a chance to plow; the land was too soft and wet.

Sunday the 2nd
Good weather, overcast. Brbr.
Independent 2.00, M.M.&M. Co. 95.53, John Daugharty 1.00, N.B. Weaver 21.03. James Dobson 1.00, O.N. 2.00, Nerriter 3.80. James Norn 12.88, Marfileus 4.35, Dr. Grigg 6.50, Curney 5.00, Pomeroy 32.00, H. Blumenthal 2.00, North British & Mercantile Co. 21.00.

Monday the 3rd
Good weather. Plowed; it was pretty wet. The boys Hinrich and Friedrich sawed wood.

Tuesday the 4th
Same as on the 3rd.

Wednesday the 5th
Same as on the 4th

Thursday the 6th
Same as on the 5th. Went to welcome Geo Spencer. In the meantime Hinrich and Friedrich pulled two mighty stumps with the horses.

[81]   **December 1900**

Friday the 7th
Light frost. Plowed during the forenoon. Dug ditch in the afternoon with the scraper. Paid N.B. Weaver 0.45 for two ax handles. Heavy frost as evening came on and during the night.

Saturday the 8th
Heavy frost. Hauled two loads of manure from town. The children and also Taalke went to the school to practice for the Christmas program. Mini and Friedrich kept house. Mini was over at Karl's on Thursday and Friday. His wife was sick. Hinrich and Friedrich did the evening chores.

Sunday the 9th
Very cold. Brbr.

Monday the 10th
Very cold. Hauled 2 loads of cornstalks home and a load of manure from town.

Tuesday the 11th
Very cold. Hauled two loads of wood home as well as one load of manure from town which I used to bank up around the cellar. I had used the load from the previous day for the same purpose.

Wednesday the 12th
Very cold. Now somewhat milder. Hauled one load of manure from town and one load of wood. The wagon reach broke about 100 feet from the house just as I was about to haul another load. From M.M.&M. Co. sal soda for 0.10.

Thursday the 13th
Horribly cold. Spent the morning making a new reach for the wagon and hauled a load of manure from town during the afternoon. From M.M.&M. Co. cornmeal 0.33, matches 0.05; total .038 [0.38?]. Hinrich and Friedrich did the chores.

Friday the 14th
Same as the previous day. Hauled a load of wood home and one load of manure from town. It was very cold and froze in the horse stall and in the calf stall. Closed the blinds over the windows at night and tried to protect the things in the cellar against the cold as best I could.

Saturday the 15th
Terribly cold, milder in the afternoon. Hauled one load of manure from town as well as one load of wood. Paid James Dobson

[82]   **December 1900**

Paid James Dobson 1.00 with two bu. peas. From M.M.&M. Co. 4 yds. of print 0.25, spool 0.04, braid 0.05; total 0.30. From Marfileus rosin 0.10. Hauled one load of manure from town and one load of wood.

Sunday the 16th
Milder. Went to visit Nehls.

Monday the 17th
Milder. Hauled a load of manure from town. From M.M.&M. Co. soap 0.25, sugar 0.05, rice 0.25; total 0.55. From N.B. Weaver for a monkey wrench 0.85. From Gottenmyer meat 0.35. Received 55.00 from Heinrich.

Gave Taalke for her use 1.00, to Hinrich and Friedrich 1.00, to the other children together 1.00 as a Christmas present; total 3.00.

Tuesday the 18th
Foggy and damp. Hauled a load of manure from town. Paid Iexen [?] 13.00, paid M.M.&M. Co. 20.00. Put half a load of manure from the barn around the trees. Paid H. Blumenthal 4.00 for Heinrich and 2.00 against the debt; total 6.00.

Wednesday the 19th
Slight thaw. Hauled two loads of manure. Paid the Independent 2.00. Paid Marfileus 4.35; total paid out 6.34. In the evening attended a meeting conducted by Mr. Johnson. To Hinrich and Mini 0.25. Thanks be to our faithful Heavenly Father that it has been possible after all to pay off some of our debts. O.N. 2.00. Postage 0.20.

Thursday the 20th
In the forenoon hauled a load of manure. Nice weather. From M.M.&M. Co. for onions 0.05, candies 0.05; total 0.10. In the afternoon loaded a load of hay with Hinrich and Friedrich. From Dankert about 1½ bu. of corn for the 3 sows that have been with the boar since yesterday. Proulx also had two there since Tuesday and had brought 3 buckets full of corn to that point. Wrote to Heinrich and Johannes in the evening.

[83]   **December 1900**

Friday the 21st
Delivered a load of hay to M.M.&M. Co. It weighed 2635 lbs which came to 10.45 at 8.00 per ton. Paid 5.45 to M.M.&M. Co. and 5.00 to N.B. Weaver. Beautiful weather.

Saturday the 22nd
In the forenoon castrated the boar; Nehls, Burkhart and Dankert came to help. Then hauled a load of corn straw home. From M.M.&M. Co. a broom for 0.35, Gold Medal flour 1.25, lamp oil 0.03; total 1.63. Good weather.

Sunday the 23rd
Very soft and damp. Brbr. Hard freeze during the night.

Monday the 24th
Prepared for the Christmas festival around the Christmas tree in the evening. To M.M.&M. Co. for sugar 0.25, chocolate 0.14, prunes 0.24; total 0.63. Hauled a load of manure from Clarembean (town). Very raw weather and cold. To Gottenmyer for meat 0.40. In the evening took all the children at home to the Christmas tree in the school.

Tuesday the 25th
Celebrated Christmas.

Wednesday the 26th
Good weather. To M.M.&M. Co. for onions 0.10, yeast 0.08; total 0.18.
Threshed some beans.

Thursday the 27th
Good weather. Threshed beans. Paid N.B. Weaver 0.10 to repair the oil can.
To M.M.&M. Co. for petroleum 0.12.

Friday the 28th
Very cold. Threshed some beans and sawed some wood. Nehls come to visit
for a while.

Saturday the 29th
Cold. Filed the saw in the forenoon. To M.M.&M. Co. for syrup 0.30, pork
0.38, rice 0.25, thread 0.04, Lubrikens licorice syrup 0.25.

Sunday the 30th
Cold. Brbr. The cows stayed out the following night.

Monday the 31st
Cold and snow. Bought 2 cows from Schneider for 12.00 and wrote to Heinrich and Johannes about it. Karl sent us about two cords of shingle bolts.

[84]

[The page is lined out but left entirely blank.]

[85]   **January 1901**

Tuesday the 1st
M.M.& M. Co. 74.98, John Daugharty 1.00, N.B. Weaver 17.33, L. Nerriter
3.80, James Norn 12.88, Marfileus 0.35, Dr. Grigg 6.50, Curney 5.00,
Pomeroy 32.00, P.M. Miller 0.24, Schneider 72.00
As of 1 January 1901:
Outstanding receipts 0.00
Debts 226.08
Cash on hand 0.00

Praise to the Lord, the Almighty, the King of creation!
O my soul praise Him for He is thy health and salvation!
All ye who hear, now to His temple draw near!
        Join me in glad adoration!

These are our debts on New Year's 1901. The Lord who has been our help
till now will surely help us further so that we may pay them off. For working the farm we have "Fanny," 11 years old; Heinrich's horse born on the 7th
of June, 1897; "Nellie," "Blossom" and "Flora," the three cows, each 6 years
old; "Cherry," 2 years old, 4 calves, 3 pigs born in August '99, one of them
a boar castrated on December 22, 1900 and two of them sows, both for sure
carrying young; 12 chickens and 3 roosters; a good 7 tons of hay, about 3
tons of straw, about 6 loads of cornstalks, i.e. husked and standing corn
together; 100 bu. of potatoes; 75 bu. of peas; 60 bu. of oats. On farm equipment we have a plow, a harrow, a cultivator, a shovel plow, a mowing
machine as well as the necessary garden tools.

    We will praise Him for all that is past,
        And trust Him for all that's to come.

[86]   **January 1901**

Tuesday the 1st
See the previous page. Threshed beans. Hinrich and Friedrich celebrated by
going ice skating.

Wednesday the 2nd
Very cold. Threshed some beans. [Sold] the cows Nellie and Flora together
with Flora's calf born on November 25, 1900 for 63.00. Wrote to Johannes
and Heinrich about it and mailed the letter. Hinrich and Friedrich sawed
wood. Put a new handle on the ax.

Thursday the 3rd
Very cold but clear and bright. Brought in two loads of wood. The chores took a lot of time. Ordered lubricants from Albert Embury for 1.10. From M.M.& M. Co. sal soda for 0.05, seleratus 0.07, lamp chimney 0.05, onions 0.10; total 0.57. Last evening Johannes' horse over at Karl's was sick, today it seemed better.

Friday the 4th
Very cold but a little milder. Delivered to Nerriter 1¼ cord of shingle bolts and got a credit of 1.88. From N.B. Weaver a skillet for 0.25.

Saturday the 5th
Very nice weather all day. Robert Garner came to visit. Garner with his wife and daughter. From M.M.& M. Co. tea for 0.25, spices 0.10; total 0.35.

Sunday the 6th
Snowy. Kept the Sabbath.

Monday the 7th
It snowed fairly heavily during the night. From M.M.& M. Co. lamp oil for 0.60, lantern chimney 0.10; total 0.70. Paid N.B. Weaver 0.20 to repair an oil can.

Tuesday the 8th
Thaw and rain. Delivered the 2 cows Nellie and Flora together with the calf and received 63.00. Marfileus licorice 0.10. Then had Mini seen by Dr. Grigg 0.25. Then signed a note for 21.00 for insurance from the North British & Mercantile Co. (Forsyth).

[87]   **January 1901**

Wednesday the 9th
Good weather, cold. Went with Schneider to Sterling to buy a cow; didn't find any. From M.M.& M. Co. soap for 0.25.

Thursday the 10th
Big snow storm during the night with a heavy fall of snow. Went with Nehls and Daugharty to Standish to have the children vaccinated, 1.00. Then had Wilhelm's shoes repaired and helped around the house.

Friday the 11th
Snow flurries during the morning. Repaired shoes. Got the sled ready in the afternoon. Attended a meeting in the school regarding vaccination in the evening, 1.00.

Saturday the 12th
Very raw weather during the forenoon. Hauled in a sled load of firewood. In the afternoon hauled a load of shingle bolts to Nerriter which canceled our debt with him and paid a difference of 0.65. Praise be to God! To M.M.& M. Co. for rubbers and socks 2.50, onions 0.10, rice 0.25, baking powder 0.10, yeast cakes 0.04, Gold Medal flour 1.25; total 4.25. In addition paid 1.00 for the freight on a poplin [?].

Sunday the 13th
Beautiful weather. Brbr.

Monday the 14th
Snow and thaw. Went to school in the morning to repair a chair and write a letter to Cashnell, 1.00. Then went to Lewa to try to buy a cow. Didn't buy it. Hauled manure in the afternoon. In the evening went to visit Demond.

Tuesday the 15th
Thaw. Bought a cow in the forenoon. The cow was 8 years old. In the afternoon hauled manure.

Wednesday the 16th
Very raw. Off and on snow flurries. Did no work because I had a headache and wasn't feeling well. Mini was also in bed the whole day.

[88]   **January 1901**

Thursday the 17th
Stayed home because of the headache and not feeling well. Very raw weather. In the evening Mini was bad. Pills from Dr. Grigg. To M.M.& M. Co. for 2lb. lard 0.18, shoelaces 0.04; total 0.22.

Friday the 18th
Stayed home because of the headache and not feeling well. Good weather. Mini and Wilhelm, Hinrich and Emma all sick. I sawed some wood for the stove.

Saturday the 19th
Bright and clear but very cold. Went to the cheese factory meeting. Hauled a log home to be cut up for firewood. Went to Turphus about buying a cow but did no business. To M.M.& M. Co. for onions 0.10, lard 4.38, sal soda 0.05; total 4.53. To Gottenmyer for meat 0.20. The children all still sick.

Sunday the 20th
Thaw. Talked with Alf. Hall. Mini and Wilhelm better.

Monday the 21st
In the morning Taalke got up feeling well. After an hour, however, she felt sick again and had to lie back down. Ella, too, got sick. Hinrich felt somewhat better and Friedrich went alone to school.

Tuesday the 22nd
Very nice weather. At Proulx's everyone was sick. This morning Friedrich was also sick. Emma and Ella were as good as recovered. Taalke was still sick. Hinrich went alone to school. On the 21st to M.M.& M. Co. for 25 lbs. of cornmeal 0.38.

Wednesday the 23rd
Overcast. The children were feeling better; all returned to school. Mini stayed home on account of Taalke. I was in bed yesterday and today with a headache. To M.M.& M. Co. for Hinrich's shoes 1.25, three pair of stockings for 0.25; total 1.50. Toward evening Taalke felt better. Toward evening it snowed.

Thursday the 24th
Sick. A terrible headache and pain in my limbs.

[89]   **January 1901**

Friday the 25th
Sick. Pain in my limbs and a headache.

Saturday the 26th
Better. To M.M.& M. Co. for onions 0.10, 2 chamberpots @ 0.25 = 0.50, sugar 0.10, tea 0.10, Ella's shoes 1.75, Emma's rubbers 0.50, 1½ yd. calico 0.09, 2 spools of thread 0.08; total 3.27. We were all still a little bit sick.

Sunday the 27th
Raw and cold. Brbr. In Standish a lot of people were sick, also in Setkemant [?]. Only 4 children in Sunday School. Mrs. Benson's birthday. Astrid Benson was sick. Toward evening Taalke felt worse. To R.M.Forsyth for saltpeter 0.20. To O.A. Marfileus for a comb 0.10, licorice 0.25; total 0.35 (bought the day before).

Monday the 28th
Raw, cold. Sawed some firewood.

Tuesday the 29th
Very nice day. Sick. Mini at home yesterday and today. The teacher also sick. Taalke better again.

Wednesday the 30th
Cold. Sick. Mini went back to school. In the afternoon Mrs. Clarke (Bertha Kaschub [?]) came to visit. For that reason Mini stayed at home the following day (Thursday the 31st).

Thursday the 31st
In the evening Taalke got sicker. Taalke had a terribly sore throat. I sawed some wood. Mini and Mrs. Clarke went to visit C. Richert. In the evening it got very cold.

[90]   February 1901

M.M.& M. Co. 91.69, John Daugharty 1.00, N.B. Weaver 17.78, James Norn 12.88, Marfileus 0.80, Dr. Grigg 6.75, Curney 5.00, Pomeroy 32.00, P.M. Miller 0.24, R.M. Forsyth 0.20, British & Mercantile Co. Insurance 21.00, O.N. 1.00, Gottenmyer 0.20, Al Embury 1.10.
As of 1 February 1901:
Outstanding receipts 3.00
Debts 191.64
Cash on hand 32.00

Friday the 1st
To M.M.& M. Co. for lamp chimney 0.05. Received from Heinrich 40.00. Sawed firewood. Mrs. Clarke ended her visit.

Saturday the 2nd
To M.M.& M. Co. for soap 0.25, rice 0.25, soda 0.10, tea 0.15, Gold Medal flour 1.25; total 1.00. Paid 21.00 to Forsyth for the British and Mercantile Insurance Co. Paid Taalke 0.25 for groceries she had bought with her money. To Gottenmyer for meat 0.10.

Sunday the 3rd
Good weather but cold. Kept the Sabbath.

Monday the 4th
Very raw and cold. Went to Maple Green to see about buying a cow and bought one for 25.00. Paid 10.00 down; the people are to deliver the cow tomorrow in Standish.

Tuesday the 5th
Beautiful weather the entire day. Was in Standish to pick up the cow but the people never brought her.

Wednesday the 6th
Very nice weather. Hinrich and I went to get the cow. To avoid further unpleasantness I simply paid the remaining 15.00 of the 25.00. Paid P.M. Miller 0.39. Tobacco 0.25.

Thursday the 7th
Very nice weather. Sawed firewood.

Friday the 8th
Very nice weather. Sawed firewood.

Saturday the 9th
Very raw. Snow flurries during the forenoon. Hauled a load of manure from town and from Waites. To M.M.& M. Co. for a barrel of salt 2.25, sugar 0.15, rice 0.25, yeast 0.12; total 2.77.

[91]   **February 1901**

Sunday the 10th
Very cold and snowy. Brbr.

Monday the 11th
Paid Pomeroy 16.36. Licorice syrup for 0.25. On the 8th from M.M.& M. Co. onions 0.05. Very raw weather. Hauled a load of manure from Standish.

Tuesday the 12th
Raw. To M.M.& M. Co. for merchandise, i.e. 1½ yd. cooet [?] cloth 0.21, thread 0.04; total 0.25. Two clevises @ 0.15 = 0.30.

Wednesday the 13th
For [sewing] machine needles 0.17. To Elwell for meat 0.10. Very cold. Hauled one load of manure from town.

Thursday the 14th
Again very cold. To M.M.& M. Co. for 2 shirts 0.15. Taalke to visit McCaddy's. Brought in a small load of cornstalks and sawed some firewood.

Friday the 15th
Very cold. Hauled two loads of cornstalks home.

Saturday the 16th
Horribly cold. I had covered the potatoes well the night before. Brought in the last load of cornstalks. Hinrich was sick and was to the Dr. He needs glasses. To M.M.& M. Co. for baking powder 0.10, sugar 0.25, tea 0.25, one spool of thread 0.04; total 0.64. To Gottenmyer for meat 0.10.

Sunday the 17th
Snow flurries. Brbr.

Monday the 18th
To repair Mini's shoes and for a composition book 0.35. Hauled manure and hunted for Karl's horse.

Tuesday the 19th
Very cold during the night. Went to the circuit court about the Home Mutual Insurance Co.

Wednesday the 20th
Very cold during the night. Hauled manure.

Thursday the 21st
Very cold during the night. Hauled manure. To M.M.& M. Co. for Taalke's corset 1.00, 2 yds. shirting 1.25, buttons 0.10, thread 0.08, onions 0.10; total 1.35.

[92]   **February 1901**

Friday the 22nd
Washington's Birthday. The children and the teacher went for a sleigh ride. It was very cold and stormy. Hauled manure.

Saturday the 23rd
To Elwell for meat 0.25. Very cold. Hauled manure. Hinrich hauled several logs home.

Sunday the 24th
Very cold and raw. To Vance after Sunday School.

Monday the 25th
Beautiful weather. To Daugharty's about firewood for the school, 0.50. To M.M.& M. Co. for Gold Medal flour 1.25, rice 0.25; total 1.50. To Elwell for meat 0.20. Sawed firewood.

Tuesday the 26th
Very cold and raw. Sawed firewood. To N.B. Weaver for a file 0.13. To M.M.& M. Co. for a lantern chimney 0.05, spices 0.05; total 0.10. Give the job of firewood for the school to Armstrong, 0.25.

Wednesday the 27th
Very cold and raw. Sawed firewood.

Thursday the 28th
Very cold and raw. Sawed firewood. Had a sore throat. Hinrich came home early from school with a headache.

[93]   **March 1901**

M.M.& M. Co. 100.73, John Daugharty 1.00, N.B. Weaver 17.91, James Norn 12.88, Marfileus 0.80, Dr. Grigg 6.75, Curney 5.00, Pomeroy 16.00, O.N. 1.00, Gottenmyer 0.40, Embury 1.10, Elwell 0.45—from the school 3.75.
As of 1 March 1901:
Outstanding receipts 3.75
Debts 164.02
Cash on hand 0.00

Friday the 1st
Since new year's we have had a lot of sickness and generally poor health. The work didn't go forward very well. To R.M. Forsyth for 3 doses of worming medicine for the horses 0.50. For ½lb. saltpeter, 1 lb. resin 0.25; total 0.75. Sawed firewood.

Saturday the 2nd
To M.M.& M. Co. for 2 shirts for Hinrich 0.50, for Mini's dress 0.36; total 0.86. To N.B. Weaver 0.85 for a dishpan. Sawed firewood.

Sunday the 3rd
Very cold at night. Brbr.

Monday the 4th
Went to Keefer's auction but didn't buy anything. To M.M.& M. Co. for starch 0.10, matches 0.10, kerosene 0.60, onions 0.10; total 0.90. Hinrich's glasses cost 2.50; paid 1.50 which leaves a debt of 1.00 to C.H. Schoerpff. Very, very cold.

Tuesday the 5th and Wednesday the 6th
Very, very cold. Covered the potatoes in the basement as warmly as possible.

Thursday the 7th
Received a letter from Johannes and answered it. Last night was horribly cold. To M.M.& M. Co. for sugar 0.25, chocolate 0.14.

Friday the 8th
Mini's birthday. She came home and celebrated with Fidelia Proulx, Astrid Benson and Ann Johnson in addition to her little brothers and sisters. To M.M.& M. Co. for butter 0.16.

[94]   **March 1901**

Saturday the 9th
In the morning it snowed. Hauled shingle bolts into town, 1.90. Paid Scho-erpff 1.00, R.M. Forsyth 0.75. To M.M.& M. Co. for sal soda 0.10. The boys sawed firewood. I spoke with the folks at M.M.& M. Co. and learned that our debt with them as of the 7th amounted to 63.45 for groceries and 13.25 for cash advances received during the previous year; total 76.70.

Sunday the 10th
Very raw and rainy. Nobody at Sunday School.

Monday the 11th
Very raw. Kept the children at home from school. It was too wet and slip-pery. To Marfileus for sulfur 0.05. Got the wagon ready to load hay and got a load ready to deliver to M.M.& M. Co. in the afternoon. Raw, snowy and wet the entire day.

Tuesday the 12th
Butchered a pig in the forenoon. Nehls and Waites came to help. Nice weather. In the afternoon hauled the hay for a fee of 7.20 to the stave factory from which I received 1.20 in cash and 6.00 in credit from M.M.& M. Co. For soap from M.M.& M. Co. 0.25.

Wednesday the 13th
Very raw weather. Salted down the pig that we butchered yesterday. It must have weighed about 275 lbs.

Thursday the 14th
Raw and windy. To M.M.& M. Co. for spices 0.10, pepper 0.05, thread 0.04, silicia 0.20; total 0.39. Powerful thaw during the afternoon. Hauled a load of manure and shelled some seed corn.

Friday the 15th
Raw and windy. Received seeds from Embury which had been ordered on January 3rd, 1.10. Did some plowing in the forenoon and shelled some corn; hauled a load of manure in the afternoon. Peter Proulx had come home the night before.

[95]   **March 1901**

Saturday the 16th
Good weather. Hauled a load of manure. To M.M.& M. Co. for Gold Medal flour 1.20, onions 0.12, thread 0.04; total 1.36. To P.M. Miller for a comb 0.05, cloth pins 0.05; total 0.10.

Sunday the 17th
Beautiful weather, warm. Brbr.

Monday the 18th
Beautiful weather. Split firewood.

Tuesday the 19th
Very raw and windy with much snow. Went to circuit court. Yesterday the one sow gave birth to 10 little pigs. Several days ago I had shut her in a pen in the new addition to the barn that Heinrich had built.

Wednesday the 20th
The weather was somewhat more pleasant. Plowed and shelled corn.

Thursday the 21st
Very raw and windy. Plowed and shelled corn.

Friday the 22nd
Good weather. Threshed beans. To M.M.& M. Co. for yarn 0.75, 50 yd cotton 3.75, 1½ yd. lace 0.15, 8 spools 0.32, 5 yd. denim 0.75, 14 yd. outing 1.12, 5 yd gingham 0.25, 6 yd. duck 0.52, one belt 0.19, 35 yd. ticking 3.50, 4 yd. cult [?] cloth 0.50; total 11.80. R. Forsyth for envelopes 0.10. In the afternoon the cow Blossom gave birth to a heifer calf. The sow ate one of her shoats on Wednesday and another one today. Went to see Daugharty about a school matter (it had to do with the town treasurer transferring too little money), 0.50.

Saturday the 23rd
Good weather. Threshed beans.

Sunday the 24th
During the night and all day today thaw and rain. You couldn't get to the school and so there was no Sunday School. Went to Benson's to visit.

Monday the 25th
Thunderstorms and rain during the night. Called off school for a week at least. To M.M.& M. Co. for

[96]   **March 1901**

cornmeal 0.25, onions 0.10; total 0.35. Rain and thunderstorms all day as a result of which the snow and ice quickly melted and cakes of ice were floating in the ditches. Since the ice cakes tended to pile up and form dams at the weak places water was soon out over the road and made holes in a number of spots. In the afternoon I worked on the ice and water in order to keep the water off the land as much as possible.

Tuesday the 26th
Dry weather. Threshed beans.

Wednesday the 27th
Dry weather. Threshed beans and cleaned them. Had about 2 bu.

Thursday the 28th
Good weather, things dried off well. Hauled three loads of manure.

Friday the 29th
Good weather. Hauled one load of manure from the barn and one from town (Oakley). Delivered ¼ cord of shingle bolts 1.05. Paid Elwell 0.45 and 0.10 for a harness hook for Prince (checkbook); total 0.55.

Saturday the 30th
Good weather. The roads dried out very nicely. Hauled a load of manure from the barn and one from town (Waites). To M.M.& M. Co. for rice 0.25, sugar 0.25, tea 0.25, Mini's shoes 1.75, Emma's shoes 1.25; total 3.75.

Sunday the 31st
Kept the Sabbath. To Barnes' Revival meeting from Mr. Clark. Saginaw.

[97]   **April 1901**

Monday the 1st
M.M.& M. Co. 94.86, John Daugharty 1.00, N.B. Weaver 18.76, James Norn 12.88, Marfileus 0.85, Dr. Grigg 6.75, Curney 5.00, Pomeroy 16.00, O.N. 1.00, Gottenmyer 0.40, P.M. Miller 0.10.
As of 1 April 1901:
Outstanding receipts 4.25
Debts 156.60
Cash on hand 0.00

Monday the 1st
Election day. Hauled 2 loads of manure from town.

Tuesday the 2nd
Good weather. Hauled a load of manure from town. To M.M.& M. Co. to exchange Emma's shoes 0.25. To Barnes' Revival meeting.

Wednesday the 3rd
Good weather. In the morning Johannes and Heinrich came home. Worked around the house all day. Received 5.00 from Heinrich and 5.00 from Johannes for a new seed drill.

Thursday the 4th
Good weather. Maundy Thursday. Hauled manure.

Friday the 5th
Good Friday.

Saturday the 6th
Raw and windy. For shingle bolts 1.10. Paid Norn 5.00 which left a debt there of 6.00 according to the bookkeeper. For a meat knife 0.45, for an ax sharpener 0.50; total 0.95. At home cleared fields and piled up wood.

Sunday the 7th
Kept the Sabbath. Brbr.

Monday the 8th
Good weather. Strong wind. Cleared fields at home.

Tuesday the 9th
Good weather. To M.M.& M. Co. for oatmeal 0.25, sugar 0.25, yeast cakes 0.04, lamp chimney 0.05; total 0.25. To W.N. Honey for a wash tub 0.15. Cleared fields. To C. Schoerpff for repairing Harry's glasses 0.25.

[Written upside down at the bottom of the page] The money owed to J. Norn was 6.08 on April 6.

[98]   April 1901

Wednesday the 10th
Papa's birthday. Cleared fields.

Thursday the 11th, Friday the 12th, Saturday the 13th
Cleared fields. To M.M.& M. Co. for washing soda 0.10, mincemeat 0.25; total 0.35.

Sunday the 14th
Beautiful weather. Kept the Sabbath.

Monday the 15th, Tuesday the 16th
Cleared in preparation for building a fence along the road. Burned the area off as well as we could. To M.M.& M. Co. for tea 0.25.

Wednesday the 17th
Rainy. Cleared land in the afternoon. The cow Flora had a heifer calf during the previous night. The cow was well contented.

Thursday the 18th, Friday the 19th, Saturday the 20th
Raw and cold. Cleared land for the fences along the road. Pulled and burned stumps and used sticks of dynamite to shoot those we could not pull. To Charles Francis for sugar 0.25, onions 0.10, washboard 0.30, soap 0.25; total 0.90.

Sunday the 21st
Rainy and raw. Brbr.

Monday the 22nd
Rainy during the day. Sold a sow to F. Elwell for 12.50. I'm to pick up the money next Friday. Worked on the fence during the afternoon.

Tuesday the 23rd
Rainy during the forenoon. Dug holes and set posts for the fence. Received 11.50 for hay; gave 2.50 of it to Heinrich and 0.50 to Taalke to pay off debts.

Wednesday the 24th
Overcast and rainy. Let J. Dobson have 1225 lbs. of hay for 4.90; he is to pay in 2 or 3 weeks. Set posts and tamped them in. Received for hay 0.20. For shoes 1.25, 2 overalls @ 0.45 = 0.90; total 2.15. Paid Schoerpff 0.25 on the debt, to Honey 0.15, see April 9.

[99]   April 1901

Thursday the 25th
Received for hay 14.00. Sold it at 10.00 per ton. To Charles Francis for rice 0.25, oatmeal 0.25; total 0.50. Worked on the new fence.

Friday the 26th
Received 8.00 for hay. Sold it at 10.00 per ton. Gave Taalke 1.00, this left 7.00. Paid N.B. Weaver 10.00. For a milkpail 0.25; total 10.25. The red heifer born December 22, 1899 was bred to J. Dobson's bull.

Saturday the 27th
Beautiful day. Received 7.00 from Elwell for the pig (see April 22). For a seed drill 6.50, for a set of glasses 0.25. Home Mutual Insurance assessment 5.00. Received the rest from Elwell 5.50. For fruit trees 2.25. For 12 lb. spikes 0.42. To Taalke for Hinrich's suit 5.00.

Sunday the 28th
Beautiful day. Brbr.

Monday the 29th
Nice day. Put palings on the fence posts. Dug around the grapevines and planted 5 trees: 1 Bartlett, apricot, 2 Duchess cherry, 2 Clapps St. pear.

Tuesday the 30th
Nice. Plowed. Received for 11 bu. potatoes 2.20. Both Edward Proulx and his sister Melwa Proulx got married.

[100]   May 1901

M.M.& M. Co. 95.46, Ch. Francis 1.40, I. Daugharty 1.00, N.B. Weaver 8.76, Marfileus 0.85, Dr. Grigg 6.75, Pomeroy 16.00, O.N. 1.00, Gottenmyer 0.40—John Dobson 4.90, school 4.25
As of 1 May 1901:
Outstanding receipts 9.15
Debts 131.62
Cash on hand 11.58

Wednesday the 1st
Nice weather. Plowed. Fixed fence. Received 5.10 for 8½ bu. peas. Paid debt to Taalke 0.25. For flour 2.50, rice 0.25; total 2.75. Paid Norn 6.08. Collection Congregational Church 0.25.

Thursday the 2nd
Nice weather. Harrowed and picked up trash [from the fields].

Friday the 3rd and Saturday the 4th
To Bay City for Christ. Conference. Paid for the fare 1.15 and for riding in the electric car 0.20; total 1.35. The collection 1.00; total 2.35. Additional expenses 0.35; total 2.70.

Sunday the 5th
Went to the conference.

Monday the 6th
Nice weather. Plowed, harrowed and picked up trash. Johannes and Heinrich had harrowed in the 4 bu. of peas sowed on Friday and Saturday. Received 3.00 for 6 bu. of peas. To Charles Francis for sugar 0.25, rice 0.25.

Tuesday the 7th
Nice. Sowed oats and covered them with the harrow, 5 bu. over a good 2½ acres. We planted clover and timothy together with the oats and covered all the seed with the harrow. Hinr. 1d. Bred Blossom.

Wednesday the 8th
Nice day. Drained fields. Plowed for Karl and for King each half a day.

Thursday the 9th
Nice day. Cleared fields and drained. For Shakespeare's works 0.65. For Pilgrim's Progress 1.05.

Friday the 10th
Nice but overcast. For [crossed out] sugar 0.20, rice 0.25, oatmeal 0.25; total
1.80.

[101] **May 1901**

Saturday the 11th
Nice day but cool. Drained fields. Fixed the calf pen. Heinrich took the team
and worked for Karl. For Chase's Recipe Book 1.00.

Sunday the 12th
Very raw and cold. Brbr. Blair from Jersey City was there.

Monday the 13th
Cold. Heinrich went north. Johannes took the team and worked for Karl. I
worked on the grapevines and the fruit trees.

Tuesday the 14th
Cold. Sold a bu. of potatoes to Karl Wübbena for 0.20. From James Norn
420 ft. of flooring @ 18.00 / thousand = 7.71 for 2" × 5" × 12'. For eveners 0.15; total 7.86. To N.B. Weaver for 11 lb. 8d nails 0.38. For 6 bolts to
make it level 0.18; total 0.56. To Charles Francis for a lamp chimney 0.05.

Wednesday the 15th
Gave the children 0.50 to go to the circus. Sold David Mills 5 bu. of potatoes @ 0.20 = 1.00. Sold 2 bu. peas @ 0.60 / bu. = 1.20. Cleared and leveled.

Thursday the 16th
Leveled. Hauled manure. Received 1.80 for 3 bu. peas.

Friday the 17th
For Vermifuge 0.25, comb 0.15, for a drill 0.20; total 0.60. Plowed and
spread manure, ditched and drained.

Saturday the 18th
For groceries 1.80. For cleaning Hinrich's watch 1.00; total 2.80. For
Marfileus for rat poison 0.15. Plowed and ditched. Raw and cold.

Sunday the 19th
Kept the Sabbath. Wet weather.

Monday the 20th
To N.B. Weaver for linseed oil and a bucket 0.92. For repairing Mini's shoes
0.50. Began to lay the floor. For 4 lb. nails 0.28!!!

[102] May 1901

Tuesday the 21st
For 3 lb. nails 0.14. Laid the floor. Plowed. Wet weather, overcast.

Wednesday the 22nd
Plowed. Finished the floor.

Thursday the 23rd
Plowed. Beautiful weather. In the evening a violent thunderstorm with rain. It rained all night as well as the

Friday the 24th
entire day. Wet and overcast. Drained.

Saturday the 25th
Good weather. Tried to plow but the ground was too soft and it wasn't possible. Drained and fixed mama's grave. To Charles Francis for 50 lb. Gold Medal flour 1.25, sugar 0.25, yeast 0.08, vinegar 0.05, oil 0.60; total 2.23.

Sunday the 26th
Nice weather. Brbr.

Monday the 27th
Drained and plowed.

Tuesday the 28th
Plowed and cleared. Paid C. Francis 2.50. Owe 3.20 for 4 bu. corn @ 0.80, tea 0.40; total 3.60. To N.B. Weaver for a fork handle 0.15.

Wednesday the 29th
Wet and overcast. Plowed and picked up trash. Received from Hinrich 4.85.

Thursday the 30th
Dry weather. Sowed 4 bu. on the newly cleared field and covered the seed with the harrow. Picked up roots and other trash.

Friday the 31st
Dry weather. Plowed and picked up trash; also drained and fixed fence.

Saturday the 1st
Got a horse rake (24.00) from Cassidy. Got 640 feet of fencing from J. Norn @ 9.00 per 1000 = 5.76. To N.B. Weaver for 15 lb. nails @ 3.00 per 100 = 0.35. Nailed the boards onto the fence posts we had set. Good weather, very cool. To Taalke for Heinrich's suit 1.00, for Hinrich's shoes 1.50; total 2.50. For groceries 0.68.

[103]   **June 1901**

Cassidy 24.00, James Norn 13.47, M.M.& M. Co. 95.46, Ch. Francis 7.78, John Daugharty 1.00, N.B. Weaver 10.92, Marfileus 1.00, Dr. Grigg 6.75, Pomeroy 16.00, O.N. 1.00, Gottenmyer 0.40, Lämmerhirte 0.80—John Dobson 4.90, David Mills 1.00, School 4.25.
As of 1 June 1901:
Outstanding receipts 10.15
Debts 178.58
Cash on hand 1.85

Saturday the 1st
Bred Fanny. Expect her to foal May 6th 1902. Stud fee 10.00.

Sunday the 2nd
Nice weather. Brbr.

Monday the 3rd
Beautiful day, warm. Plowed and picked up trash. Sold 18 bu. potatoes @ 0.25 = 4.50. For groceries 0.50, difference 4.00.

Tuesday the 4th
Beautiful day, warm. Plowed and picked up trash. Harrowed some. Was interrupted for about 1¼ hours by the missionary Geo. Davis.

Wednesday the 5th
Beautiful day. Harrowed and marked the field for planting corn. Prince the horse took off with the marker and broke it. In the evening the cow Frenchi gave birth to a heifer calf. To Ch. Francis for lemons 0.10.

Thursday the 6th
Beautiful weather. Planted corn and marked the field. Mrs. Barnett came for a visit yesterday.

Friday the 7th
Cold. Planted corn. Received 1.75 for 5 bu. of potatoes; for groceries 1.10, difference 0.65. To Joe Gorton 2 bu. of potatoes @ 0.30 = 0.60.

Saturday the 8th
Cool. Planted corn and beans. Hinrich's birthday.

[104]   **June 1901**

Sunday the 9th
Beautiful weather. Brbr.

Monday the 10th
Beautiful, warm. Planted corn. Johannes sowed carrots etc. Set out tomatoes.
For groceries 3.05, for seeds 0.30; total 3.35. For meat 0.35. To Elwell for
meat on Friday 0.30.

Tuesday the 11th
Nice, warm day. Planted corn. Broke one of the corn planters. Also planted
several rows of potatoes. Johannes set out cabbage plants.

Wednesday the 12th
Nice, warm day. Planted potatoes. Johann plowed for Karl Richert. Received
5.00 from John Dobson and 0.10 as interest.

Thursday the 13th
Nice, warm day. Planted potatoes, all together 12 bu. Johannes worked for
Karl Richert with the horses the plow and the harrow.

Friday the 14th
Nice, warm. Planted some corn and Kaffircorn Johannes and Friedrich hoed
and weeded and also drained some. For groceries 1.00. To repair a tug and
shoes 0.35. For a whippletree 0.05; total 1.40. Paid on the debt to M.M.&
M. Co. 2.00. To Taalke 1.00 for Hinrich's suit. 0.25 shoes.

Saturday the 15th
Nice, warm. drained. Paid Mrs. Hartmann 0.25 for Mini's hat and 0.50 on
our debt. Mini's dress braid 0.16.

Sunday the 16th
Nice, hot. Brbr.

Monday the 17th
Hot. The little horse Topsy hurt herself on the rump. It was a cut 12" long
perhaps from barbed wire—a horrible sight. I took the horse to the Dr. He
closed the cut with 12 stitches. It cost 2.00 which I borrowed from Dieter
McGurk. To Marfileus for liniment 0.25; total 2.25.

[105] **June 1901**

Tuesday the 18th
Nice weather. Paid C. Francis yesterday for cornmeal 0.25, tea 0.10; total
0.35. Johannes worked in the garden. Friedrich and I cultivated.

Wednesday the 19th
Johannes and I worked on the road with the horses. For onion sets 0.10,
vinegar 0.10, for Mellencamp 0.15. Owe Fred Keller for sugar 0.25, rice
0.25, baking powder 0.10, soda 0.07 oatmeal 0.25; total 0.92.

Thursday the 20th
Cultivated and weeded. Beautiful weather.

Friday the 21st
Cultivated and weeded. Beautiful weather.

Saturday the 22nd
Bred Fun to Sonomit's bull. Fanny bred a second time. To Honey for repairing a horse collar 0.10. To Ward for screws for the cultivator 0.05. Cultivated and set out celery.

Sunday the 23rd
Nice. Spent the whole day in bed, tired, tired. See Tu. the 25th about Katie.

Monday the 24th
Hot. Cultivated. Johannes replanted corn. For cotton 0.25, thread 0.04; total 0.29 to M.M.& M. Co. To Robt. Forsyth for iodine and a brush for Nehls wrist 0.08.

Tuesday the 25th
Hot in the forenoon, thunderstorms and rain in the afternoon. To Ch. Francis for sugar 0.25, onions 0.10; total 0.35. Cultivated in the forenoon. Johannes worked in the garden. Katie, the white heifer, was bred to Proulx's bull on the 23rd.

Wednesday the 26th
Very hot. Cultivated and sowed beets. Cleaned up the garden. Received 7.25 from Hinrich. Then gave Hinrich 0.25, Honey 0.10, Ward 0.05, Elwell 0.35, Keller 1.22; total 1.94.

[106] June 1901

Thursday the 27th
Very hot. Cultivated. Johannes hoed in the garden. For groceries 2.30, dry goods 1.28. To McGurk 2.00 (see June 17th). To Johannes 0.50. Stationery 0.20 (Forsyth).

Friday the 28th
Thunderstorms and rain showers. Went to school in the afternoon to count books and take inventory, 0.50. Cultivated in the afternoon and worked in the garden.

Saturday the 29th
Hot. Cultivated and worked in the garden.

Sunday the 30th
Hot. Brbr.

[Added at the bottom of the page]
See June 7: Received 0.60 from Gorton on the 29th.

[107]   July 1901

Cassidy 24.00, J. Norn 13.47, M.M.& M. Co. 93.75, Ch. Francis & Grow
7.98, J. Daugharty 1.00, N.B. Weaver 10.92, Marfileus 1.25, Dr. Grigg 6.75,
Pomeroy 16.00, P.N. 1.00, Gottenmyer 0.40, Lämmerhirte 0.80, Stud fee
1.00, Sonomit 0.50—David Mills 1.00, school 4.75
As of 1 July 1901:
Outstanding receipts 5.75
Debts 187.82
Cash on hand 0.60

Tuesday the 2nd
Mowed and raked some. Hot.

Wednesday the 3rd
Hot. The sky threatened storm. Mowed, raked and cultivated. To Keller for
vinegar 0.10, cornmeal 0.20, sugar 0.25, soap 0.25; total 0.80.

Thursday the 4th
The glorious 4th. Johannes, Mini, Hinrich and Emma went to Bay City.
Taalke, Friedrich, Ella and Wilhelm went to Standish.

Friday the 5th
Stormy. Raw, yesterday as well. It rained off and on. Cut hay anyway.

Saturday the 6th
Violent storm. Brought in two loads of hay. To Keller for sugar 1.00, soda
0.10, 100 lbs. Gold Medal flour 2.50, rice 0.25, oatmeal 0.25, onions 0.10,
tea 0.25, yeast cakes 0.08, starch 0.10, apples 0.10, raisins 0.10; total 4.03.
To Elwell for meal 0.15. From the school district 7.50.

Sunday the 7th
Very cool. Rested and kept the Sabbath.

Monday the 8th
Very cool. Brought in two loads of hay. Emma, Friedrich and Wilhelm were
riding on the second load and fell off; Wilhelm hurt his right wrist. Took him
to Dr. Toothacker who set the wrist.

[108] **July 1901**

Paid Keller 4.83 (see July 6th) + 0.88 (July 3rd); total 5.75. The annual school meeting took place in the evening.

Tuesday the 9th
In morning hauled a load of hay in. Wilhelm back to Dr. Toothacker. Ordered a rat trap from Sears & Roebuck Co. and sent 0.65 in advance payment; total with the postal order 0.73.

Wednesday the 10th
Good weather. A violent thunderstorm in the evening. Brought in 2 loads of hay. From N.B. Weaver 2 rakes @ 0.15 = 0.30. From Marfileus sulfur for 0.10. Honey mended a tug 0.10.

Thursday the 11th
Good weather. Hauled home 2 loads of hay. To Keller for a barrel of salt 1.25. To Marfileus for 1 lb. of Paris Green 0.25. To Elwell for meat 0.22. In the evening we discovered that the cow Cherry had given birth to a heifer calf.

Friday the 12th
Beautiful weather. Made hay and brought home 3 loads. That makes a total of 12 loads so far.

Saturday the 13th
Very beautiful weather. Hauled in 3 loads of hay for a total of 15 loads so far. From Elwell meat for 0.25. The spotted heifer Katie was bully; bred her to John Dobson's bull.

Sunday the 14th
Very hot. Kept the Sabbath. Brbr. Bred the cow French to J. Dobson's bull.

Monday the 15th
Very hot. Cut and cured hay. Hauled 1 load to the barn for a total of 16 loads thus far. Wrote a teacher's contract 0.50.

Tuesday the 16th
Very hot, in the evening a thunderstorm and rain. Brought in 4 loads of hay for a total of 20 loads so far. The last load was not very big, however. Was over to the school with Dankert and Daugharty; gave the teaching job to Hall etc. 0.75.

[109]   **July 1901**

Wednesday the 17th
Hinrich worked in the garden. I brought in the rest of the hay: 2 loads; that makes a total of 22 loads. Mini used the horse rake to gather up what was left in the fields. Mini and Emma both felt sick with headaches. Praise to the Lord O my soul! Thou hast been our ever present help thus far and I stand amazed by Thy goodness and patience! With Thee all is grace; works count for nothing.

Thursday the 18th
Worked in the garden, weeding etc. Mini was very sick all morning. In the afternoon both she and Emma felt better. To M.M.& M. Co. for Hinrich's shoes 1.50, hairpins 0.05; total 1.55. To Francis and Grow for oatmeal 0.25, rice 0.25, 2 chimneys (lamps) 0.10, onions 0.10; total 1.35.

Friday the 19th
Worked in the garden. In the afternoon I went to Wentzel Barn. [?]

Saturday the 20th
Weeded potatoes. Cleaned out the beets and carrots and thinned them. Mini has gone to work in the kitchen for William Honey until August 1st. To Francis & Grow for lemons 0.30, vinegar 0.10; total 0.40. On the 19th Hinrich and Friedrich got a pet rabbit as a present from Heinrich.

Sunday the 21st
Stormy the whole day. Kept the Sabbath. Taalke and Johannes and Karl and Family went to Büy. [?] Karl Richert, his wife and child as well.

Monday the 22nd
Very beautiful weather. Weeded corn and hilled up the potatoes. Worked in the garden.

Tuesday the 23rd
Very beautiful weather. A thunderstorm and rain toward evening. Pulled stumps and piled them up. Made ready to pick berries. Received from Johannes 0.50.

[110]   **July 1901**

Wednesday the 24th
Beautiful weather. A small thunderstorm with rain during the night. Johannes, Taalke, Hinrich, Friedrich and Emma went berry picking.

Thursday the 25th
Overcast and rainy, wet weather. The children returned in the evening with 2 bu. of berries. Received a letter from Heinrich which I immediately answered. Received from Hinrich 7.38.

Friday the 26th
To Mrs. Hartmann for Mini's hat 0.50. To Elwell toward the debt 0.15 and for meat 0.35, sugar 0.50; total 1.00. Rubber for the preserves 0.17, sugar 1.00, tea 0.25, spices 0.10. Dr. Toothacker 1.50. Flour 2.50; total 5.62. To Johannes 0.50. Hinrich worked on Friday at M.M.& M. Co. for Mini's shoes 1.50.

Saturday the 27th
Rainy. Cleaned the well and put in a new casing at the top. Last night was stormy with much, much rain.

Sunday the 28th
Rainy and stormy. Kept the Sabbath.

Monday the 29th
Much, much rain during the night, thunder and lightning as well. Picked up wood for the well from Norn: 250 feet @ 9.00 per 1000 makes 2.25.

Tuesday the 30th
Finished work on the well at home. Pulled peas. Hinrich worked ¾ d. Good weather.

Wednesday the 31st
Worked on the well in the barnyard. Hinr. ¾d.

[111]   **August 1901**

Cassidy 24.00, J. Norn 15.72, M.M.& M. Co. 96.75, Ch. Francis & Grow 9,73, J. Daugharty 1.00, N.B. Weaver 11.22, Marfileus 1.50, Dr. Grigg 6.75, Pomeroy 16.00, O.N. 1.00, Gottenmyer 0.40, Lämmerhirte 0.80, stud fee 10.00, Sonomit 0.50, Keller 1.25—David Mills 1.00, school 1.25
As of 1 August 1901:
Outstanding receipts 2.25
Debts 196.62
Cash on hand 0.00

Thursday the 1st
Beautiful weather. Finished cleaning the well, installed a new casing, filled in around it and covered it. Hinr. 1d.

Friday the 2nd
Overcast and rainy. Built a box for the milk cans. Johannes mowed. Finished work on the well. Hinr. ¾d.

Saturday the 3rd
Good weather. Dusted the potatoes with Paris Green. Johannes mowed oats with the machine. Hinr. d. To Ch. Francis for lamp oil 0.60, for vinegar 0.10 [crossed out]; total 0.70. To Keller for sugar 0.25, rice 0.25, soap 0.25, matches 0.05; total 0.80. To Marfileus for liniment (Wilhelm's hand) 0.35.

Sunday the 4th
Good weather. Kept the Sabbath. Brbr.

Monday the 5th
Good weather. Raked the oats and peas into piles. For middlings 0.01. Accepted an organ for Minnie and for Taalke. Hinr. 1d.

Tuesday the 6th
Beautiful weather. Hauled the oats home, 4 loads. To Schoerpff for a watch spring 1.00. To N.B. Weaver for dynamite 7.50, 100 ft. fuse 0.75, 100 caps 0.90; total 9.15. Hinr. ¾ d.

[112]   **August 1901**

Wednesday the 7th
In the morning hauled home the peas that had been cut, 1½ loads. In the afternoon cleaned the grapes and weeded the beans. Hinr. ¾ d.

Thursday the 8th
Johannes blew out stumps and I pulled peas. Hinr. 1 d.

Friday the 9th
Overcast and rainy. Pulled some peas and blew some stumps out. Hinr. ¾ d.

Saturday the 10th
Very cool. Used the rest of the 100 sticks of dynamite to blow up stumps. Pulled peas. Hinr. ¾ d. To Keller for rice 0.25, sugar 0.10; total 0.35. To N.B. Weaver for 14 feet of fuse 0.14.

Sunday the 11th
Beautiful weather. Kept the Sabbath.

Monday the 12th
Nice but cool. Pulled peas. Hinr. ¾ d. Bred Katie; she should come fresh on May 30th, 1902.

Tuesday the 13th
Nice but cool. Pulled peas. Hinr. ¾ d. and Johannes worked for John Dobson.

Wednesday the 14th
Nice but cool. Pulled peas. Hauled 1 load home.

Thursday the 15th
Nice but cool. To Ch. Francis & Grow for vinegar 0.15, soda 0.10; total 0.35. Hauled home the rest of the peas, 1½ loads; a total of 4 loads. Unloaded 1 load and let the same load stand to be threshed. Fed the peas out of the straw.

Friday the 16th
Taalke's birthday. Congratulated her. Good weather. Pulled stumps and piled them up. Hinr. ¾ d. Rubie, the young heifer, got herself bred on the road. In the evening attended a school board meeting to accept the grades, 0.75. To Ward for shovel part 0.25. To W. Daugharty to put a handle on the shovel 0.10.

[113]   August 1901

Saturday the 17th
Beautiful weather. Pulled 2½ stumps and partly piled them up. Hinr. ¾ d. The chains broke very often; had no cold shuts and there were none to be had in town either.

Sunday the 18th
Beautiful weather. Brbr.

Monday the 19th
Overcast and rainy. Went to Standish for cable from Norn's mill that burned down but didn't get any. To Earnest Knight for cold shuts 0.30. Saw Topsy the horse; she looked good, the wound had healed. Johannes went north again on the evening to earn money after he had spent his entire sojourn here at home helping his father.

Tuesday the 20th
Good weather. Cut the standing corn. Taalke and Hinrich to the Sunday School picnic in B. Ella, Emma and Willie helped cut corn. Friedrich cultivated where the peas had grown. Prince jumped over the fence onto Proulx's land even though we had fastened a chain to his foot.

Wednesday the 21st
Stormy. A violent thunderstorm with rain during the afternoon. In the morning cut some more corn. Hinr. 1d. Received from Hinrich 5.20.

Thursday the 22nd
Good weather. Cut corn. These remarks about the weather and the work
apply to Wednesday the 21st and the remarks about the weather and work
done yesterday apply to today. Friedrich drove the horse for Vance. Hinr. ½d.

[114]   August 1901

Friday the 23rd
Thunderstorm and rain till 9:00. It had been raining since 4:00 in the morning. When things had dried off a little we cut corn. Hinrich plowed from 2:00
to 4:30. Because of the rain he didn't go to work in the mill. For soap 0.25,
rice 0.25, yeast cakes 0.05; total 0.58.

Saturday the 24th
Good weather. Cut corn. To Ward 0.25. On Saturday a week ago I felt very
sick during the afternoon and today again. From Mini 2.00.

Sunday the 25th
Good weather. Kept the Sabbath.

Monday the 26th
In the afternoon good weather. For 50 lb. wheat flour 1.15, for 25 lb. cornmeal 0.60. For 4 lbs. washing soda 0.10; total 1.85. Paid on debt to Francis
and Grow 2.00. To the Lord in the form of a cripple 0.20. Brought a load of
peas to John Dobson for threshing. Around noon there was a thunderstorm
with heavy rain. Got the peas threshed at John Dobson's just before the storm
broke. Hauled the load of peas to Schulz. Hinr. ½d.

Tuesday the 27th
Threshed at Schulz's and Proulx's. Brought the load of peas home and 7 bu.
of peas which we had threshed at Schulz's. To Taalke 1.00 for Hinrich's suit.
For stuff 0.25; total 1.25.

Wednesday the 28th
Nice and dry. Cut corn. Hinr. 1d.

Thursday the 29th
Nice and dry. Hot. Cut corn in the midday. Threshed for Proulx at Richard's
during the afternoon. Hinr. 1d. A violent thunderstorm during the following
night

Friday the 30th
with heavy rains. Cool during the day and dry. Took the census. Hinr. 1d.

Saturday the 31st
Beautiful weather. Took over the job (of cleaning the school) from Hall 0.25.
Cut corn. For clothes 0.82.

[115]   **September 1901**

Cassidy 24.00, J. Norn 15.72, M.M.& M. Co. 96,75, Francis & Grow 7.73,
J. Daugharty 1.00, N.B. Weaver 20.53, Schoerpff 1.00, Marfileus 1.85, Dr.
Grigg 6.75, Pomeroy 16.00, O.N. 1.00, Gottenmyer 0.40, W. Daugharty
0.10, E. Knight 0.30, Lämmerhirte 0.80, stud fee 10.00, Sonomit 0.50, Keller
2.40—David Mills 4.00, school 2.25.
Dr. Toothacker 8.00 (v. July 8th, Wilhelm's wrist)
As of 1 September 1901:
Outstanding receipts 3.25
Debts 214.78
Cash on hand 0.00

Sunday the 1st
Good weather. Kept the Sabbath.

Monday the 2nd
Good weather. Emma, Ella and Wilhelm to school. Mini and I cut corn.

Tuesday the 3rd
Good weather. Bound corn and set it up.

Wednesday the 4th
Hot. Good weather. Bound corn and set it up. Pulled some of the ripe beans.
To Marfileus for Mini's Montworth Geometry 0.85. Hinr. 1d. Received 3.55
from Hinrich. For a dinner pail 0.35.

Thursday the 5th
Hot. Good weather. Bound corn and set it up. Pulled the ripe beans. To
Marfileus for 1 lb. sulfur 0.10. Karl used the horses. H. 1d.

Friday the 6th
Hot, good weather. Bound corn and set it up. Pulled ripe beans. To N.B.
Weaver for 15 springs 0.05. H. 1d.

Saturday the 7th
Hot. Good weather. Bound corn and set it up. Pulled ripe beans. Toward
evening a violent windstorm. H. 1d. For Friedrich handtools 0.30, overall
material 0.29, repairing a pail 0.10, 2 spools of thread 0.08; total 0.77.

Sunday the 8th
Beautiful day. Brbr.

[116]   **September 1901**

Monday the 9th
Overcast during the morning, in the afternoon wet. Brought the school report home; from the school 6.25. To Keller 3.90 for flour and groceries. (2.43 owed). Paid Francis & Grow 2.00 on the debt. Paid Montgomery Ward & Co. 0.54 for a rat trap, for a chest strengthener 0.25, a collar 0.15, freight 0.66; total 1.50. From Marfileus for a book 1.30. Paid E. Knight 0.30 and W. Daugharty 0.10; total 0.40. H. ½d.

Tuesday the 10th
Overcast. Pulled beans. H. 1d.

Wednesday the 11th
Overcast. Worked on the road, 3.00. H. ½d. To N.B. Weaver for a corn knife 0.35.

Thursday the 12th
Heavy rain during the night. Not able to work on the road. Worked on building more racks for the corn so that they are ready when we begin to cut. To N.B. Weaver 1.00. H. 1d.

Friday the 13th
Dry. Made racks (wigwams) to set up the corn, about 700 all together. Then cut some of the standing corn, bound it and set it up. E. Knight repaired the scraper that got broken on Wednesday. H. 1d.

Saturday the 14th
Dry. Bound corn and set it up. In several places where I had turned it in the morning or last evening it still wasn't dry by nightfall. H. 1d. Taalke and Mini were to Mt. Forest, Chris Richert also, to pay for Johannes' horse.

Sunday the 15th
Heavy rains during the night; it simply poured.

Monday the 16th
Dry. Bound the rest of the cut corn and stood it up.

Tuesday the 17th
Dry. Cut corn. To Honey for shoe repair 0.25. To Francis & Grow for a lantern

[117] **September 1901**

chimney 0.05. H. 1d.

Wednesday the 18th
Good weather. Worked on the road, 3.00. H. 1d. The children husked corn.
From Hinrich 4.75. To Taalke for Hinrich's suit 1.00, 3.75 remaining. For
corn husking [?] 0.25.

Thursday the 19th
Good weather. Worked on the road, 3.00. For groceries 1.90. To Sonomit
0.50. The children cut corn. It froze last night. From Chris Richert for
Johannes' horse 24.00.

Friday the 20th
Good weather. Worked on the road, 3.00. The children cut corn. During the
night and into the morning it rained. To Taalke 1.00 for Hinrich's suit.

Saturday the 21st
Good weather. Cut corn and set it up. For groceries 0.65. Hinrich's shoes
1.50. Taalke paid.

Sunday the 22nd
Good weather. Brbr.

Monday the 23rd
Good weather. Set up corn. The children helped. Mini and Wilhelm went to
school. H. 1d.

Tuesday the 24th
Good weather, cold. Set up corn, the children helped. H. 1d. To Francis
Grow for Gold Medal flour 2.40.

Wednesday the 25th
Good weather, cold. Set up corn, the children helped. H. ¾ d.

Thursday the 26th
Good weather. Very beautiful and warm. Husked corn, 28 shocks. H. ¾ d.
To M.M.& M. Co. for stockings 0.45.

Friday the 27th
Very nice weather. Husked corn, 18 shocks; a total of 46. Worked alone—
the children had gone to the fair.

Saturday the 28th
Very fine weather. Husked corn. 21 shocks; total of 67. Worked alone—the
children had gone to the fair.

[118]　September 1901

Sunday the 29th
Good weather. For about a week now I have had nearly unbearable pain in my right side. Today it felt somewhat better. The children, too, weren't feeling well. Only Mini was healthy. All complained about sore throats, headaches etc.

Monday the 30th
Good weather. Husked corn with the children. 32 shocks, a total of 99 shocks. Taalke was quite sick toward evening and had to lie down. H. 1d.

Tuesday the 1st of October
Hauled a load of firewood from the factory. It amounted to 45 foot ["cord" crossed out]. From Keller & Co. cornmeal for 0.25, soap 0.25; total 0.50. Received for road work 12.00

[119]　October 1901

Cassidy 24.00, J. Norn 15.72, M.M.& M. Co. 97.20 + firewood, Fr. & Grow 8.23, J. Daugharty 1.00, N.B. Weaver 19.93, Schoerpff 1.00, Marfileus 2.80, Dr. Grigg 6.75, Pomeroy 16.00 O.N. 1.00, Gottenmyer 0.40, W. Daugharty or E. Knight scraper, Lämmerhirte 0.80, stud fee 10.00—David Mills 1.00, Road order 12.00
Dr. Toothacker 8.00
As of 1 October 1901:
Outstanding receipts 13.00
Debts 212.83
Cash on hand 0.00

Tuesday the 1st
Stormy. Hauled a load of wood from M.M.& M. Co., 45 foot. To Keller for groceries 0.50. Received for road work 12.00. H. 0.40. Husked 6 shocks; a total of 105 shocks.

Wednesday the 2nd
Cold. Took Karl's cow to Sonomit's. The children helped to husk 20 shocks; a total of 125 shocks. H. 1d.

Thursday the 3rd
Cold and raw. Taalke and Mini better again. H. ½d. Hinrich came home because of a toothache. Emma was sick and stayed in bed after school. Fixed a bell rope 0.50. Then husked corn with Emma's help, 10 shocks; a total of 135 shocks. I myself was in such condition that I was almost unable to work.

Friday the 4th
Cold. Emma and Hinrich both sick. Hinrich was to the dentist. I husked 23 shocks with Ella's help; a total of 158 shocks.

Saturday the 5th
A violent storm, from time to time like a hurricane. H. ¾ d. With the help of Mini and Emma husked 26 shocks for a total of 184 so far. to Schoerpff 1.00 for Hinrich's watch. Emma is better again.

Sunday the 6th
Good weather. Brbr.

Monday the 7th
Good weather. Heavy frost during the last few nights. Pulled the rest of the beans and piled them up

[120]   **October 1901**

to dry. Carried then some of the straw from the peas into the cellar to bed the potatoes in. Hauled the corn husked so far home: 45 bu. Hinrich had his tooth worked on a second time. H. ¾ d.

Tuesday the 8th
Good weather. Dug potatoes. 660 hills produced 13 bu. which we hauled home. H. ¾ d.

Wednesday the 9th
Rain during the forenoon as during the preceding night. Went to the school with Dankert in the afternoon and took the clapper out of the bell, 0.50. In the afternoon helped Proulx thresh at Vance's. Dug potatoes. Hinrich at home. Had his tooth filled for 4.50. Hauled the potatoes in, 8½ bu. for a total of 21 bu. Dug 300 hills for a total of 960 hills so far.

Thursday the 10th
Good weather. Dug 545 hills of potatoes for a total of 1505 hills so far. Put 18 bu. into the cellar; that makes 39½ bu. all together. H. 1d. Received a letter from Heinrich and 30.00.

Friday the 11th
Good weather. Dug 610 hills of potatoes for a total of 2115 hills. Hauled 12½ bu into the cellar for a total of 52 bu. H. 6 hours.

Saturday the 12th
Overcast and rainy, wet weather. Dug 325 hills for a total of 2440 hills. Brought another 14½ bu. of potatoes into the cellar for a total of 66 bu. Of these 2½ bu. are red and 2½ bu. are for seed.

Sunday the 13th
Heavy rain last evening that continued through the night. In the morning the cabbage and celery planted in front of the kitchen was completely under water. Kept the Sabbath.

Monday the 14th
Overcast but good weather. Toward evening it rained. During the day dug about 500 hills of potatoes. Brought in 7½ bu. for eating and 5 bu. for seed and stored them in the cellar for a total of 79 bu. so far, or about 69 bu. of potatoes for food. H. 1d.

[121]   **October 1901**

Tuesday the 15th
Very raw and cold. Dug the last of the potatoes, 360 hills for a total of 3300 hills. Hauled in 4½ bu. of seed potatoes and 4 bu. to eat for a total of 12 bu. seed potatoes and 73 bu. to eat. H. 1d. Taalke and Mini each got a coat for 6.00; total 12.00. The money order from Heinrich (see October 10th) 30.00

Wednesday the 16th
Beautiful weather. Dug beets and cut off the tops. 20 bu. in all in the cellar. Then pulled up part of the celery and replanted it in the cellar. Gathered up another ½ bu. of potatoes after the field had been cultivated. H. 1d. Received from Hinrich 2.78.

Thursday the 17th
Very raw and cold. Planted the rest of the celery in the cellar. Violent snow and hail. Pulled 12 bu. of carrots and brought them into the cellar. H. 1d. From Hinrich 0.50. Emma sick. We got the celery out of the water; the cabbage was still standing in it.

Friday the 18th
Very cold. Conference. Paid the dentist 2.00. Pulled the carrots and brought them into the cellar. H. 1d. Sent a letter to Engelke Jungjohann.

Saturday the 19th
Good weather. Conference. For groceries 100 lb. Gold Medal flour 2.40, soda 0.10, cornmeal 0.25, postage stamps 0.40, envelopes 0.10; total 3.25. From Mini received 2.00 from her wages at Honey's. Sold 4 pigs for 28.00 of which I got 24.00. Paid debts to Gottenmyer 0.80, for lantern chimneys 0.30, sugar and tea 0.50; total 0.80. Paid Francis 2.00. Outstanding from Elwell for the pig, 4.00. H. 1d.

Sunday the 20th
Attended conference, 3.00. Beautiful weather.

Monday the 21st
Paid M.M.& M. Co. 10.00, paid Norn 5.00; total 15.00.

[122] October 1901

Hauled in 3½ load of stalks from the husked corn. Husked 10 shocks of corn.

Tuesday the 22nd
Beautiful weather. Hauled the beans into the granary and husked 12 shocks of corn for a total of 202 shocks. H. 1d. The Ostfriesen News 2.00. Sent a letter to Johannes and Heinrich as well a letter to Stölt and Central Publishing House. For stockings 0.27.

Wednesday the 23rd
Nice weather. In the afternoon a violent storm from the northwest. Hauled corn home: 6 bu. from the shocks husked during the past two days and 12 from the present day makes all together 214 shocks and 51 bu. of corn. [To] Lämmerhirte 0.80. H. 1d.

Thursday the 24th
Cold and stormy. Husked 17 shocks for a total of 213 shocks. Got 10 bu. of corn for a total of 61 bu. of corn. H. ¾ d.

Friday the 25th
Good weather. Ella and I husked 29 shocks for a total of 242 shocks and hauled 16 bu. into the corn crib for a total of 77 bu. Hinrich, Friedrich and Emma all sick.

Saturday the 26th
Good weather. Mini and I husked 28 shocks for a total of 270 shocks. They yielded 10 bu. corn for the corn crib and a total of 87 bu. Hinrich was better. H. 1d. Friedrich and Emma still sick. Taalke bought clothes for the children, 4.00. Received from Elwell 4.00, v. 19th of October.

Sunday the 27th
Good weather. Kept the Sabbath.

Monday the 28th
Good weather. Husked 8½ bu. corn from 29 shocks making all told 95½ bu. from 299 shocks. To N.B. Weaver for hairpins 0.05. To C. Francis 0.15 for groceries. H. 1d.

Tuesday the 29th
Good weather. Husked 10 bu. of corn from 35 shocks; total of 334 shocks and 105½ bu. corn. Emma somewhat better. Friedrich was able to work again on Monday; Hinrich helped, too.

[123]   **October 1901**

Wednesday the 30th
Good weather. Husked another 23 shocks for 6 bu.; total 357 shocks and
111½ bu. corn. Hinrich helped Karl with the horses. Karl had a load of wood
for us. Two loads @ 0.50 = 1.00. To Honey for repairing Mini's shoes 0.20.
Attended a meeting at Daugharty's on account of Mini's Crosley's Language
system. Hinrich looked for the cows.

Thursday the 31st
Violent storm. In the afternoon heavy rain showers. Husked 24 shocks for 8
bu.; total of 381 shocks and 119 bu. corn.

[124]   **November 1901**

Cassidy 24.00, J. Norn 10.72, M.M.& M. Co. 88.20, Francis & McRae
6.33, John Daugharty 1.00, N.B. Weaver 19.98, Schoerpff 2.00, Marfileus
2.80, Dr. Grigg 6.75, W. Daugharty or E. Knight scraper stud fee 10.00, den-
tist 2.50, Toothacker 8.00, Keller 0.50—David Mills 1.00, school 2.50—
Honey 0.20, Pomeroy 16.00
As of 1 November 1901:
Outstanding receipts 3.50
Debts 199.03
Cash on hand 29.33

Friday the 1st
Good weather. Emma still sick. Husked 13 bu. corn from 28 shocks; total of
409 shocks and 132 bu. corn. Received 5.00 from Hinrich. H. 1d.

Saturday the 2nd
A hard freeze during the night. Emma still sick. Husked 27 shocks for 6½ bu.
of corn; total 436 shocks and 138½ bu. H. 1d. For groceries 0.25.

Sunday the 3rd
Good weather. Brbr.

Monday the 4th
Very raw and cold. Husked 24 shocks for 11 bu. corn; total 460 shocks and
149½ bu. H. ¾ d.

Tuesday the 5th
Cold. Husked 18 shocks for 7 bu.; total of 478 shocks and 156½ bu. corn.
H. 1d. Hinrich's skates 0.35

Wednesday the 6th
Milder. Husked 28 shocks for 12½ bu. corn; total of 506 shocks and 169 bu. Gloves from M.M.& M. Co. for 0.50, 3 spools of thread 0.16. From Francis yeast cakes 0.08, baking powder 0.10. H. 1d.

Thursday the 7th
Very raw and cold. Paid M.M.& M. Co. 2.62. To Francis 0.18. Husked 24 shocks for 8½ bu.; total 530 shocks for 177½ bu. corn. Karl had the horses for a third day. One day Karl had just Prince. H. 1d.

[125]　**November 1901**

Friday the 8th
Beautiful weather. Husked 11½ bu. corn from 28 shocks; total of 558 shocks and 189 bu. corn. H. 1d.

Saturday the 9th
Raw and cold. Husked 37 shocks for 8 bu. corn; total of 595 shocks and 197 bu. H. 1d. For Emma's shoes 1.50, Ella's dress 0.75, Mini's book 0.50; total 2.75. Paid Cassidy 12.00; total 14.75. To Francis for flour 0.65.

Sunday the 10th
Good weather. Brbr. Brought Topsy home.

Monday the 11th
Overcast, rain toward evening. Husked 55 shocks for 21 bu. of corn; total 650 shocks and 218 bu. corn. Thoms came to help. H. ¾ d.

Tuesday the 12th
Rain, hail and snow during the night. In the forenoon rather dry. Husked the rest of the corn: 9 shocks and 3 bu.; total of 659 shocks and 221 bu. In the afternoon it turned raw, cloudy and rainy again. H. 1d. In the afternoon Topsy broke her halter. When I was repairing it and tying her fast again the horse leaped against my shoulder. At first I hardly noticed it but later I discovered that I was pretty badly hurt and that I was hardly able to lift a pail of corn up onto the wagon. H. 1d.

Wednesday the 13th
Pulled cabbage and brought it into the cellar. Then banked up the house and went to see Dankert about hiring a teacher, 0.25. From Francis washing soda 0.05. From Marfileus vermifuge 0.65.

Thursday the 14th
Violent storm and cold. Sick the entire day. The shoulder blade hurt a lot. Puttered around the house a bit. H. 1d. Taalke's stuff from M.M.& M. Co.

1 spool 0.04, 4 yrds. goods 2.00, 4 yds. celicia 0.60, 1 yd. camcars 0.23, 4 yds. braid 0.32; total 3.19.

[126]   November 1901

Friday the 15th
The weather settled down and became a bit warmer. Cold. Hauled 3 loads of manure. The shoulder hurt bad, bad. H. 1d.

Saturday the 16th
Good weather. The ground was frozen hard. Hauled 1 load of manure. Hinrich came home. Received from Hinrich 4.05. After school I fixed the stove pipes, 0.25. For wood 1.00. For overalls for Hinrich and Friedrich 1.00 each; total 2.00.

Sunday the 17th
Friedrich's birthday. Brbr.

Monday the 18th
Good weather. Hauled in 4 loads of cornstalks. Paid Pomeroy 16.00, 17.04 with the interest. For stockings from M.M.& M. Co. 0.30. H. ¾ d.

Tuesday the 19th
Good weather. Hauled in 3 loads of cornstalks. For Gold Medal flour 2.50, soda 0.08, thread 0.16, baking powder 0.10; total 2.84. H. 1d.

Wednesday the 20th
Good weather. Hauled 2 loads of cornstalk home. Karl came to help out till noon. Pulled a stump in the afternoon. That made all together 9 loads of cornstalks and with the 3½ loads from the 21st a total of 12½ loads. H. ¾ d.

Thursday the 21st
Good weather. Fixed the school bell. It took till 11:00, 0.75. Then pulled 2 stumps; a total of 3 stumps with the one yesterday. Had a lot of trouble with the chain breaking. H. 1d.

Friday the 22nd
Overcast and rainy. To Keller for a barrel of salt 1.00, for matches 0.05; total 1.05. Harry didn't go to work. To Marfileus for iodine for my shoulder 0.05. Used the shovelplow to open the ditches. H. 1d. To M.M.& M. Co. for Taalke's shirting 0.75. Received 30.00 from the boys.

[127] **November 1901**

Sunday the 24th
Good weather. Brbr.

Monday the 25th
Very raw and cold. Butchered a pig that weighed about 130 lbs. Then pulled two stumps. H. 1d.

Tuesday the 26th
Very cold and raw. Put the boar in with the sows.
[Prepared the following order for Sears & Roebuck and then crossed it out.]

1 cellbrated lever spring tooth harrow	14.64
1 ladies fascinator, black	.40
1 ladies fascinator, white	.50
1 wool toque, navy blue	.40
1 doz. invisible sew-on fasteners	.08
1 skirt supporter, drab	.10

Paid Honey 0.25. To N.B. Weaver for rope 0.22, cold shut 0.03; total 0.25. From Ward 6 cold shuts 0.24. From Keller tea 0.25. Cashed the money order the boys sent. Found out that I could get a better deal on a harrow from Cassidy. Decided therefore to cancel the items on the order to Sears & Roebuck. H. 1d. Hauled manure and put it around the fruit trees and the grapevines.

Wednesday the 27th
Very cold. Picked up the harrow from Cassidy, 16.00. Paid Ward 0.24. Sick. H. ¾ d.

Thursday the 28th
Thanksgiving Day. Very, very sick.

Friday the 29th
Somewhat better. Great pain in the chest. H. 1d. Taalke bought stuff for the children and a table cloth. Pain, Pain!!

Thursday the 30th
Unable to work, but some better. H. 1d. To Keller for sugar 0.25. Received from Hinrich 4.10.

[128] **December 1901**

Sunday the 1st
Good weather. Kept the Sabbath.

Monday the 2nd
Cassidy 12.72, J. Norn 10.72, M.M.& M. Co. 92.44, Francis & McRae
9.28, J. Daugharty 1.00, N.B. Weaver 20.23, Schoerpff 2.00, Marfileus 3.20,
Dr. Grigg 6.75, Daugharty & Knight scraper . . . , stud fee 10.00, dentist
2.50, Dr. Toothacker 8.00, Keller 1.55—David Mills 1.00, school 3.75.
As of 2 December 1901:
Outstanding receipts 4.75
Debts 180.49
Cash on hand 17.61

Monday the 2nd
Very raw and cold. Pain in my chest. Salted down the pig butchered on Monday. Hunted up a little firewood around the barn. Then pulled another
stump. Friedrich to school. H. 1d.

Tuesday the 3rd
Very raw and cold. Pain in the chest. Didn't do any work. Hinrich didn't go
to work today because of the cold. Taalke and Mini canvassed.

Wednesday the Thursday the 4th
Nice weather. H. ¾ d. Paid taxes of 16.87. Stuff for quilts 3.61. Borrowed
from Taalke 2.87. Threshed some beans and cut some firewood. Still owe
Taalke for Hinrich's shoes and groceries; total 5.87.

Thursday the 5th
Beautiful weather. H. 1d. Threshed some beans and cut some firewood. 2 bu.
of potatoes froze. The house was almost completely banked up. Banked up
the cellar some more with a load of manure. H. 1d.

Saturday the 7th
Wet and cold. Piled another load of manure around the cellar. From Ch.
Francis & McRae Corosine 0.60, sugar 0.25. H. ½d.

[129]   **December 1901**

Sunday the 8th
Snow, rain and hail. Kept the Sabbath.

Monday the 9th
Good weather. Put yet another load of manure around the cellar. H. ¾ d.

Tuesday the 10th
Good weather. Light snow. One more load of manure around the cellar. A
lamp wick from Francis & McRae 0.01. H. 1d.

Wednesday the 11th
Good weather. Sawed some firewood. H. 6 hours. To M.M.& M. Co. for Hinrich's shoes 1.50

Thursday the 12th
Snowy. Went to school to measure the kindling wood from Dankert and to visit the school, 0.25. Sawed some firewood. H. 1d.

Friday the 13th
Rain all day. Shelled some seed corn. Drained fields. Received from Mini 4.05. Shoes and stockings for Hinrich 1.75. Flour 1.20, tea 0.25, soap 0.25, baking powder 0.16, embroidery floss 0.20; total 2.06. For 1 bu. potatoes 0.55. H. 1d.

Saturday the 14th
Snow during the night. Sawed firewood. For tea 0.25, shoelaces 0.05; total 0.30. To resole a pair of shoes 0.50.

Sunday the 15th
Very cold. Brbr.

Monday the 16th
Very cold. H. ¾ d. Sawed some firewood.

Tuesday the 17th
Milder. H. 1d. Sawed some firewood. Bred Sonomit's sow to our boar, 0.50.

Wednesday the 18th
Clear but cold. Things froze in the cellar and in the barn as they had on the 3 or 4 preceding days as well. H. 1d. See the remarks about the debt owed to Taalke. The shoes bought on the 11th were returned. From M.M.& M. Co. buttons for Mini's dress 0.08. Bred another of Sonomit's sows to our boar. Through an oversight the debts from 7th of December were not added in 0.85.

[130]   **December 1901**

Thursday the 19th
Very cold. Sawed some firewood. H. 8 hours. From M.M.& M. Co. 2 pairs of pants for Friedrich and Wilhelm @ 0.50 = 1.00. Waist for Friedrich 0.09; total 1.09 To Keller for sugar 0.50, vanilla extract 0.10, lemons 0.10, butter 0.16, chocolate 0.20, currants 0.10, raisins 0.20, eggs 0.10; total 1.46.

Friday the 20th
Very cold. Sawed some firewood. H. 1d. Went to visit Mr. Rug (Mrs. Demon's brother). Fee for breeding and feeding Proulx's sow, 0.50.

Saturday the 21st
Cold. Sawed some firewood. H. 1d. For Taalke 0.20 to buy things for
Christmas.

Sunday the 22nd
Good weather. Brbr.

Monday the 23rd
Thaw. H. ¾ d. Repaired a halter. Received from Hinrich 4.50. In the evening
the Christmas tree at home. Lots of fun. Received a cap and a pair of stockings from Taalke. But thank God I'm healthy! The greatest of God's gifts here
on Earth! For tea from Francis 0.25.

Wednesday the 25th
Celebrated Christmas. Kay and Matthews preached.

Thursday the 26th
Good weather. Butchered a pig. Nehls and Carl came to help.

Friday the 27th
Good weather. From M.M.& M. Co. 6 yd. calico @ 0.05 = 0.30. For
Friedrich's shoes 1.00, stockings 0.50; total 1.80. To Blumenthal for 1 yd.
of stuff 1.25. To N.B. Weaver for a file 0.12. To Ch. Francis & McRae for
matches 0.05.

   [131]   **December 1901**

Saturday the 28th
Good weather. Hauled some logs home. From Keller 25 lb. cornmeal @ 0.02
= 0.50.

Sunday the 29th
Beautiful weather. Brbr.

Monday the 30th
Nice weather. Sawed firewood and piled it.

Tuesday the 31st
New Year's Eve. A fierce storm and very cold. Tried to cut wood but it didn't
go well. Sorted beans for seed. Fearfully cold and stormy. All's well that ends
well. Taalke went to spend New Year's Eve with Gammons.

[132] **January 1902**

Wednesday the 1st
Praise to the Lord, the Almighty, the King of creation!
O my soul praise Him for He is thy health and salvation!
All ye who hear, now to His temple draw near!
        Join me in glad adoration!

We have reason to sing praises and give thanks! We have not known want!
On the contrary, we have enjoyed plenty! We have suffered no misfortune.
In the barn we have three horses, "Fanny," "Prince" and "Topsy," 11, 5, and
2 years old, respectively; four cows, "Fun," "Blossom" "French" and
"Cherry," respectively 6, 7, 10, & 5 years old; (Prince and Fun belong to
Heinrich); three heifers "Flora," "Katie" and "Rubie," each 2 years old; 4
calves; 3 pigs, i.e. one boar and two sows; 30 chickens. There are about 9
tons of hay for sale and then about 11 tons of hay and cornstalks for fodder. We have 170 bu. corn, about 1 load of unthreshed beans, ½ bu. beans
for food, and 5 bu. peas for seed. We have one wagon, a new harrow, a
horse-drawn rake, a mowing machine, a cultivator, and a seed drill. The rake
and the mowing machine belong to Heinrich. Along the road we have built
about 40 rod of very neat fence during the past year. The remainder of the
farm equipment includes yet 2 plows and a shovel plow.

[133] **January 1902**

Wednesday the 1st
Financially, we are as follows:
We owe
Cassidy 12.72, J. Norn 10.72, M.M.&M. CO.. 95.41, Francis & McRae
10.44, J. Daugharty 1.00, N.B. Weaver 20.35, Schoerpff 2.00, Marfileus
3.20, Grigg 6.75, Daugharty & Knight scraper [no amount], stud fee 1.00,
dentist 2.50, Toothacker 8.00, Sam Blumenthal 0.25, Keller 3.51, Taalke
8.74.
We have receipts outstanding from
David Mills 1.00, school 4.00
Sonomit will breed two of our cows in exchange for his two sows bred to our
boar.
As of 1 January 1902:
Outstanding receipts 5.00
Debts 195.59
Cash on hand 0.00

Wednesday the 1st
Good weather. Celebrated New Year's Day.

Thursday the 2nd
Violent storm. Sawed firewood. Attended Hartmann's funeral.

Friday the 3rd
Violent storm, very cold. Sawed firewood. Paid Keller 2.40 for 100 lb. flour, washing soda 0.10; total 2.50.

Saturday the 4th
The storm abated. Sawed firewood. To M.M.&M. CO.. for Mini's stockings 0.15.

Sunday the 5th
Good weather. Brbr. Wilhelm's birthday.

Monday the 6th
Good weather. Severe pain in my chest; rubbed it with iodine but it didn't help. Mini returned to Barnes'; Hinrich went to school.

Tuesday the 7th
Nice weather. Better. Sawed firewood.

Wednesday the 8th
Very nice weather. Pains in my chest. Karl returned the boar.

Thursday the 9th
Very nice weather. Nehls came and got the boar.

[134]   **January 1902**

Thursday the 9th
Very nice weather. Raincoat for Hinrich 4.00. To M.M.&M. CO.. for Ella' overshoes 0.35. Sawed firewood.

Friday the 10th
Beautiful weather. Sawed firewood. The children were at home because the teacher is sick. A free day for Hinr. Fr. Wilh.

Saturday the 11th
Raw and stormy. Hauled in logs and sorted beans for seed. Mini came home for a visit; she has been back at Barnes' since Monday.

Sunday the 12th
Raw and cold. Brbr.

Monday the 13th
Good weather. Went to see Daugharty about something. Richards and the teacher, 0.50. Diarrhea. Chest pains.

Tuesday the 14th
Good weather. Sawed firewood. Severe chest pains. To M.M.&M. CO. for Hinrich's canvas 0.75, 4 spools of thread 0.26; total 0.91; paid 0.50, owe 0.41.

Wednesday the 15th
Raw and cold. Sawed firewood. Frequent pain in my chest.

Thursday the 16th
Beautiful weather. Sawed firewood.

Friday the 17th
Stormy. Lay down all day because of the pain in my chest. Emma was sick.

Saturday the 18th
Good weather. The boys Hinrich and Friedrich hauled some logs home. I stayed lying down.

Sunday the 19th
Beautiful weather. Brbr. To Forsyth for drugs 0.40.

Monday the 20th
Good weather. Went to bed and tried to sweat, but was not able to. Snow during the night.

Tuesday the 21st
Good weather. Had more pain than before. Was it in the back or in the chest?

Wednesday the 22nd
Good weather. During the previous night I had a fly blister on my chest. I broke the blister and it felt better.

[135] **January 1902**

To M.M.&M. CO.. for Mini's waist 1.26.

Thursday the 23rd
Good weather. To Keller for kerosene 0.50. Mama has been dead for 8 years, gone home.

Friday the 24th
Good weather. Put up cabbage.

Saturday the 25th
Good weather. To Francis & McRae for groceries, sugar 0.25, chocolate 0.16; total 0.41.

Sunday the 26th
Good weather. Ella's birthday; she is 9 years old. Kept the Sabbath. Brbr. Very cold during the night.

Monday the 27th
Very cold and a severe storm. Threshed some beans.

Tuesday the 28th
Somewhat milder. Nehls brought the boar back. Karl's horse is sick. The stray heifer gave birth to a bull calf.

Wednesday the 29th
Not too cold. Sawed firewood.

Thursday the 30th
Not too cold. Sawed firewood.

Friday the 31st
Beautiful weather. Went to the Farmer's Institute. Wilhelm had a bad cough. To Marfileus for licorice 0.25.

Saturday the 1st of February
To Honey for repairing shoes (Ella's) 0.50.

[136]   February 1902

Cassidy 12.72, J. Norn 10.72, M.M.&M. CO.. 97.48, Francis & McRae 10.85, J. Daugharty 1.00, N.B. Weaver 20.35, Schoerpff 2.00, Marfileus 3.45, Grigg 6.75, Daugharty & Knight scraper, stud fee 10.00, Heasley 2.50, Toothacker 8.00, Sam Blumenthal 0.25, Keller 6.51, Taalke 8.78, R. Forsyth 0.45, Honey 0.50,—David Mills 1.00, school 4.50
As of 1 February 1902:
Outstanding receipts 5.50
Debts 202.31
Cash on hand 0.00

Saturday the 1st
Beautiful weather. Went to the Farmer's Institute. Sharpened the saw.

Sunday the 2nd
Very cold weather. Brbr.

Monday the 3rd
Very cold. Went to the meeting at the cheese factory and was elected secretary.

Tuesday the 4th
Very cold; storm. Cleaned beans.

Wednesday the 5th
Very raw and cold. To Francis & McRae for Gold Medal flour 2.40, rye flour 0.50, yeast cakes 0.08, coffee extract 0.05, coffee 0.10, sugar 0.25; total 3.38. Since the 3rd I think I have seen some change in the cow Blossom's udder. She has been dry for two months and until now I had had my doubts that she would come fresh.

Thursday the 6th
Beautiful, clear day but cold. Shelled corn for seed and chicken feed. Sold a peck of beans to Alfred Hall for 0.40.

Friday the 7th
Beautiful weather. Very cold. Emma stayed home [crossed out]. I stayed home.

Saturday the 8th
Good weather but very cold. Sawed firewood.

[137]   **February 1902**

Sunday the 9th
Beautiful weather. Brbr. Taalke hasn't felt well for several days but nevertheless went this evening to the Gospel meeting in the Methodist church.

Monday the 10th
Good weather. Cold. Threshed beans. To Keller for 25 lbs. coarse cornmeal 0.38, lamp chimney 0.05; total 0.43. Mrs. John Daugharty was saved following the Gospel meeting in the Methodist church.

Tuesday the 11th
Beautiful day, mild. Sawed firewood. Taalke to Dr. Warren, 0.35.

Wednesday the 12th
Raw and cold. Cleaned beans. Went to Standish to take inventory in the cheese factory with Gammon and Dobson, 050 [0.50?]. To N.B. Weaver for a grindstone axle 0.50 and cooking pot 0.85; total 1.35.

Thursday the 13th
Very beautiful weather. Rev. Thomley came to visit, then Miss Barbara Kelsch, then Nehls. Pulled Vance's heifer out of the well.

Friday the 14th
Very beautiful weather. Sawed firewood.

Saturday the 15th
Very beautiful weather. Very cold at night. Hauled manure. Taalke to Dr. Warren. To N.R. Forsyth 2.00. To Ch. Francis & McRae for oatmeal 0.10, sugar 0.25; total 0.35.

Sunday the 16th
Nice day. Taalke was somewhat better and went to the Methodist service in the afternoon and to the Gospel meeting there in the evening. I stayed at home.

Monday the 17th
Good weather. To Keller for thread 0.04, hairpins 0.05, darn needle 0.01; total 0.10. To Francis & McRae for a wash kettle 0.30. Went to see the Judge of Probate Mr. Decum.

[138]   February 1902

Tuesday the 18th
Very raw. A severe storm, cold. Stayed in all day.

Wednesday the 19th
Nice day. To Francis & McRae for a broom 0.35, 3 bowls @ 0.08 = 0.24; total 59. Sawed firewood.

Thursday the 20th
Very nice day. Sawed firewood. In the evening Nehls came to visit and stayed till 11:30. Taalke went to the Methodist church this evening as she had yesterday evening.

Friday the 21st
Very nice day. Sawed firewood.

Saturday the 22nd
Very nice day. Hauled manure. To Schauer for a whippletree 0.30, for a whippletree hook 0.05; total 0.35. In the evening a party for Mini.

Sunday the 23rd
Very nice. Brbr. Marfileus 0.05

Monday the 24th
Very nice. Hauled manure. Taalke to the Methodist church. Washed also during the day. Felt a lot better.

Tuesday the 25th
Very nice. Taalke to the doctor. He pronounced her no better.

Tuesday [Wednesday?] the 26th
Very nice. Had the last missions meeting in the Methodist church. Taalke and Hinrich were to N.B. Weaver for shoe tacks, 0.10. Hauled manure.

Thursday the 27th
Nice. Hauled manure.

Friday the 28
Windy and wet. Drained. Heard from John Niemann that Johannes and Heinrich would soon be coming home.

> *The month is at an end,*
> *But God is ever true;*
> *Whichever way I wend,*
> *I find His love anew.*

[139]   March 1902

Cassidy 12.72, J. Norn 10.42, M.M.&M. Co. 97.48, Francis & McRae 15.92, J. Daugharty 1.00, N.B. Weaver 21.80, Schoerpff 2.00, Marfileus 3.50, Grigg 6.75, Daugharty & Knight scraper   ,stud fee 10.00, Heasley 2.50, Toothacker 8.00, Sam Blumenthal 0.25, Keller 7.54, Taalke 8.78. R. Forsyth 2.45, Honey 0.50, Dr. Warren 0.35, Schauer 8.35—David Mills 1.00, school 4.50, Alfred Hall 0.40, cheese factory 0.50
As of 1 March 1902:
Outstanding receipts 6.40
Debts 212.61
Cash on hand 0.00

Saturday the 1st
Raw, windy and overcast. To M.M.&M. Co. for clothing material for Taalke 2.00. To Dr. Warren. Medicine from Forsyth 0.45.

Sunday the 2nd
Raw, snowy. Kept the Sabbath.

Monday the 3rd
Schoerpff for repairing glasses 0.15. During the previous night there was a large fire in Standish.

Tuesday the 4th
Nice weather. Heinrich's cow Fun was not chewing a cud in the morning. I went and got Barker to have a look at her. To Forsyth for Epsom salt 0.20. To Keller for coffee 0.14, sugar 0.25,; total 0.39. In the afternoon the cow Blossom gave birth to a heifer calf.

Wednesday the 5th
Very windy. Doctored around with the sick cow; by noon she was better. Had given her about 1½ lbs. of fatback.

Thursday the 6th
Severe storm. Stayed inside because of chest pains. Received from Keller 0.57 for 3½ doz. eggs.

Friday the 7th
Nice weather. Hauled 2 loads of manure. Chest felt better.

[140]   March 1902

Saturday the 8th
Sloppy weather, snow and rain. Wilhelm's birthday. (Editor's note: this was actually Minnie's birthday, not Wilhelm's.)

Sunday the 9th
Snow during the night and all morning. Brbr. Kept the Sabbath.

Monday the 10th
Good weather. Wilhelm's overalls 0.50.

Tuesday the 11th
Wet and overcast. Stayed in bed.

Wednesday the 12th
Same as yesterday. Stayed in bed. In the evening Johannes and Heinrich came home. Snow and rain. Received from Heinrich 5.00. For seleratus 0.08, sugar 0.25; total 0.33.

Thursday the 13th
Nice weather. Stayed in bed. Johannes and Heinrich sawed fence posts.

Friday the 14th
Nice weather. Took the old cellar down and salvaged the logs.

Saturday the 15th
Nice weather. Removed part of the roof on the old barn. To Keller for 100 lbs. flour 2.40. To Honey for 2 bolts 0.05, for a riveting machine 0.50; total

0.55. Paid Schoerpff 1.15. Paid Schauer 0.35, for a snapper 0.02, 2 bolts 0.05; spent a total of 0.07.

Sunday the 16th
Very raw and cold. Brbr.

Monday the 17th
A very hard freeze during the night. Had paid Honey 0.90 toward what we owe him on Saturday the 15th (see March 1st, 0.50).

Tuesday the 18th
Heavy frost during the night. Sold Vance ½ ton of hay for 3.50 and got another 0.50 for delivering it to town; total 4.00. Paid 0.50 for kerosene. Paid Ch. Francis & McRae 2.00 toward what we owe. Paid Taalke 1.50 for shoes. Paid 0.25 to repair Hinrich's shoes. To Forsyth for linseed oil and borax 0.15.

Wednesday the 19th
Good weather. For Hinrich's pants 0.50. The boys sawed; I threshed beans.

[141]   **March 1902**

Thursday the 20th
Nice weather. Sawed firewood and threshed beans.

Friday the 21st
Good weather. Sawed firewood and worked on the carrots and beets by myself in the cellar. In the evening one of the sows threw 10 shoats. The old sow was born March 19th, 1901. Also castrated the boar the same day.

Saturday the 22nd
Good weather. Burned the trash heaps from the old barn we had taken the logs from. To Francis & McRae for 25 lbs. cornmeal 0.50, sugar 0.25, coffee 0.13; total 0.88. To Honey for repairing Mini's shoes 0.45.

Sunday the 23rd
Good weather. Kept the Sabbath. Kept an eye on the fires we set yesterday.

Monday the 24th. Tuesday the 25th, Wednesday the 26th
Good weather. Sawed fence posts, shingle bolts and firewood.

Thursday the 27th and Friday the 28th
Good weather. Maundy Thursday and Good Friday. Collected the fence posts and piled them up. To Forsyth for medicine 1.00.

Saturday the 29th
Good weather. Sold shingle bolts for 1.50, bought meal for 0.15. To Keller for cornmeal 0.43, sugar 0.25, rice 0.25, raisins 0.10; total 1.03. Appointed supervisor of the census.

Sunday the 30th
Celebrated Easter. Rained the whole day, snow toward evening.

Monday the 31st
Overcast and wet, dried off toward evening. Cleaned some more beans. High wind.

[142]   April 1902

Cassidy 12.72, Norn 10.72, M.M.&M. Co. 99.48, Francis & McRae 14.80, J. Daugharty 1.00, N.B. Weaver 21.80, Schoerpff 1.00, Marfileus 3.07, Grigg 6.75, Daugharty & Knight scraper , stud fee 10.00, Heasley 2.50, Toothacker 8.00, Keller 11.36, Taalke 8.78, R. Forsyth 4.25, Honey 1.00, Dr. Warren 3.00—Alfred Hall 0.40, David Mills 1.00, school 4.50, cheese factory 0.50.
As of 1 April 1902:
Outstanding receipts 6.40
Debts 220.23
Cash on hand 1.25

Tuesday the 1st
Very raw and cold and windy. Logged and pulled stumps. To Heinrich for dynamite sticks 1.00. To Keller for soap 0.25.

Wednesday the 2nd
Very raw and cold. Cleared land for building a fence along the road as far as Proulx's.

Thursday the 3rd
Mild. To Keller for vinegar 0.20, 25 lb. lard @ 0.12 = 3.00, 2 spools of thread 0.20; total 3.40. To N.B. Weaver for 2 clevises @ 0.10 = 0.20, 8 cold shuts 0.25; total 0.45. Received for ½ ton of hay to be delivered 3.50. Cleared and burned. For repairing a tug [space left, but no amount entered].

Friday the 4th
Nice weather. Cleared and burned. In the morning the cow Fun gave birth to a bull calf.

Saturday the 5th
Went for 2 rolls of barbed wire, 5 bu. oats, 20 lbs. nails and steeples which we paid for with the hay money from the 3rd and with shingle bolts. Kept

0.07 left over. Paid 1.50 to Marfileus. To Keller for sugar 0.25. We owe Weaver for the barbed wire 0.03½ per pound makes 7.18.

[143] **April 1902**

Sunday the 6th
Good weather, Brbr.

Monday the 7th
Raw and cold. Election day. To Keller for 1 lb. tea 0.25 and ½ lb. tea 0.18; total 0.43. To Heinrich for dinner for everyone 1.50. Worked on the new fence. Dug holes and set posts.

Tuesday the 8th
Dug holes, set posts and attached the first pales.

Wednesday the 9th
Set up pales and attached three lines of wire. That is one beautiful fence! Then laid out a pig lot, dug holes and set posts. To Keller for tapioca 0.16, sugar 0.25; total 0.41. Received for hay 5.00.

Thursday the 10th
Papa's birthday. Received congratulations from all the children. Was given a pair of shoes and a cup and saucer, the latter from Karl. To M.M.&M. Co. for cloth, shirt sleeves, 0.15.

Friday the 11th
To Ch. Francis & McRae for Gold Medal flour 2.50, soap 0.25; total 2.75. To N.B. Weaver for steeples 0.06, jackknife 0.40; total 0.46. Severe storm, cold. Got the fence and the pig lot finished.

Saturday the 12th
Received for hay 3.00. Hauled manure.

Sunday the 13th
Good weather. Conference in Saginaw. Brbr.

Monday the 14th
Good weather. Cleaned [= gemuct?] the granary.

Tuesday the 15th
Good weather. To Keller for washing soda 0.10. Pulled stumps and piled them up.

Wednesday the 16th
Storm. Piled and burned stumps.

[144]   **April 1902**

Thursday the 17th
Plowed and picked up trash.

Friday the 18th
Plowed and picked up trash. To Keller for sugar 0.25. Johannes' birthday.

Saturday the 19th
Received 5.30 for sale of a pig. Outstanding at Gottenmyer's 8.00. Spent 0.75 for cornflour. Paid Honey 0.95 on the debt we owe. For allspice 0.05. Delivered hay to Wm. Daugharty: 1410 lbs. @ 8.00 per ton makes 6.01 and the weighbill of 0.25.

Sunday the 20th
Good weather. Brbr.

Monday the 21st
Good weather. Hot in the afternoon and a thunderstorm toward evening. Sowed 5 bu. of oats, clover and timothy on Saturday and Monday and covered them with the harrow. Sold ½ ton of hay to Wilson @ 8.00 per ton, 4.00.

Tuesday the 22nd
Violent storm. Delivered 1¼ ton of hay to M.M.&M. Co. @ 8.00 per ton; applied the 10.04 to reduce our debt. Received 5.25 from Wm. Daugharty; paid 0.25 for the weighbill which leaves 5.00: received 5.25 instead of 6.04. Paid Mr. Culbert the stud fee of 10.00. Owe Francis & McRae 0.03 was short buying groceries. Ditched and pulled stumps.

Wednesday the 23rd
Violent storm. Pulled stumps.

Thursday the 24th
Good weather. Piled stumps. H. 1d.

Friday the 25th
Good weather. Piled stumps and burned them. H. 1d.

Saturday the 26th
A severe thunderstorm with rain during the night which began already the previous evening. Received 8.00 from Gottenmyer. Paid J. Norn 5.00. Paid N.B. Weaver 3.00. For 3 apple trees 0.90, for cold shuts 0.56, groceries 1.25; total 2.71. Paid 0.16 interest on the stud fee.

[145]   **April 1902**

Sunday the 27th
Nice day, dry. Brbr.

Monday the 28th
Received 0.90 for 223 lbs. of hay. Piled stumps. The tugs and belly band broke; 0.15 to repair them. H. 1d.

Tuesday the 29th
Nice weather. Piled stumps and plowed. Paid 0.15 for repairing pails. For Hinrich's shoes and overalls 1.50 and 0.50. For a fashion magazine 0.25; total 2.40. To N.B. Weaver for corn planter 0.75. H. 1d.

Wednesday the 30th
Upon cleaning, our own peas proved to be unsuitable for seed. Borrowed from Francis & McRae 3 lbs. peas Tuesday the 0.90 = 2.70, 4 qt. timothy seed 0.47 and 4 qt. Alsyke clover seed 1.20, 100 lbs. Gold Medal flour 2.40; total 6.77. Strong wind. Received 0.50 from Gorton for hay. H. 1d.

[146]   **May 1902**

Cassidy 12.72, Norn 5.72, M.M.&M. Co. 89.59, Francis & McRae 24.35, J. Daugharty 1.00, N.B. Weaver 27.64, Schoerpff 1.00, Marfileus 1.57, Grigg 6.75, Heasley 2.50, Toothacker 8.00, Keller 16.45, Taalke 8.78, R. Forsyth 4.25, Warren 5.00—Alfred Hall 040 [0.40?], D. Mills 1.00, school 4.50, cheese factory 0.50
As of 1 May 1902:
Outstanding receipts 6.40
Debts 215.32
Cash on hand 1.53

Thursday the 1st
Good weather. Sowed 2 bu. of peas and covered them with the harrow. Picked up trash and cleared some more field and piled stumps. Received 4.00 for two shoats. Received 0.75 from Hinrich. H. 1d. To Taalke for shoes and Mini's clothes 5.00.

Friday the 2nd
Thunderstorm with heavy rain. In the afternoon dry. Drained and picked up trash. Traded 8 doz. eggs for groceries.

Saturday the 3rd
Good weather. Gave Sonomit 1055 lbs. of hay for 4.00; received 3.00, outstanding from Sonomit 1.00. Sold Benson 649 lbs. of hay; @ 8.00 per ton this

makes 2.10 of which I received 2.00 leaving 0.60 outstanding. Received 2.10 from Karl for hay and 2 bu. of potatoes. Got from Mrs. Gregory in Jonesville a barrel with Sunday School supplies. H. 1d.

Sunday the 4th
A violent thunderstorm with heavy rains during the night. Brbr.

Monday the 5th
Good weather. Drained and plowed. Gave Mini 1.00 for school.

Tuesday the 6th
Rained all day. Gave Mini 2.00 to make a dress. Pulled 2 stumps.

[147]   May 1902

Wednesday the 7th
Gave Mini 4.00 for a dress; for groceries 0.98; total 5.38. To P.M. Miller 1.30 for wallpaper. Pulled 21 stumps; total of 23.

Thursday the 8th
Pulled 24 stumps; total of 47. Good weather. To P.M. Miller for wallpaper 1.30.

Friday the 9th
Pulled 17 stumps; total of 64. Piled and burned some of them. Good weather.

Saturday the 10th
Sowed 2 bu. of peas and covered them with the harrow. Sold H. Sonomit 1025 lbs. of hay; Tuesday the 8.00 per ton this makes 4.10.

Sunday the 11th
Good weather. Brbr. Owe Taalke 0.25 for the collection.

Monday the 12th
Good weather. Pulled 24 stumps. H. 1d. Sold Charles Richert 3 bu. potatoes @ 0.70 per bu. = 2.10. Fun bully.

Tuesday the 13th
Good weather. Piled 18 stumps. H. 1d.

Wednesday the 14th
Good weather. Piled 25 stumps. H. 1d. Received 2.10 from C. Richert.

Thursday the 15th
Good weather. Sold Weaver 351 lbs. of hay for 1.40. Sold Parker ½ corn for 0.30. To Taalke 0.25, to Mini 1.85; total 2.10. Blossom bred to Sonomit's

bull. Received 2.00 from Hinrich. H. 1d. To Keller for sugar 0.25, tea 0.25; total 0.50. To P.M. Miller for wallpaper 0.10. Plowed.

Friday the 16th
Beautiful weather. Traded boars with Gammon. The one we got was born on April 11th and was a Chester white. Gave Mini 2.00 for school. H. ¾ d.

Saturday the 17th
Beautiful weather. Hauled manure. H. 1d.

Sunday the 18th
Beautiful weather. Brbr. McLean was there.

Monday the 19th
Hot. Thunderstorm in the afternoon. To Albert Embury

[148]   May 1902

To Albert Embury for seeds 0.47. For 90 lbs. of pork 6.51. Gave Heinrich 2.00 for shoes. Took 2 sacks of corn to the mill to be ground. Paid for the seeds in the evening. H. 1d.

Tuesday the 20th
Dry. Drained and traded 10 bu. of unshelled corn for flour. Plowed some. Paid 0.25 for saw sharpening. Paid 3.50 for 3000 shingles, 0.20 for roofing nails; total 3.70. Cherry gave birth to a heifer calf. Paid 0.07 for two bolts (on the Syracuse flywheel). H. 1d.

Wednesday the 21st
Dry and hot. Plowed and worked on the pig pen.

Thursday the 22nd
Dry weather. Sold 1450 lbs. of hay to W. Daugharty @ 8.00 per ton for 5.80. H. 1d. Plowed and worked on the pig pen.

Friday the 23rd
A thunderstorm with rain in the morning. Plowed and worked on the pig pen. H. 1d.

Saturday the 24th
Dry weather. Plowed and worked on the pig pen. Borrowed Karl's horse to help out.

Sunday the 25th
Beautiful weather. Katie the cow had a bull calf. Fanny the horse a filly. Kept the Sabbath. The calf born on the 20th died.

Monday the 26th
Cold. Received 5.80 for the hay sold on the 22nd. Paid Mergel a weighbill of 0.50. Received 2.00 for corn. Paid for tea and sugar 0.25. Plowed. Borrowed Karl's horse to help out. Paid M.M.&M. Co. 0.75 through Hinrich's work on May 3rd for Hinrich's shirts and Friedrich's shirt and pants, Ella's dress and credit of 2.50, Mini's shoes 2.00. H. 1.d.

Tuesday the 27th
Cold. Heinrich bought 0.80 corn [?]. Plowed and worked on the pig pen. Borrowed Karl's horse to help out. H. 1d.

[149] May 1902

Wednesday the 28th
Cold. Gave Emma 0.15 for entertainment on Friday evening at the school. Paid Robert Caldwell 0.50 for helping out; total 0.65. Plowed and worked on the pig pen. Borrowed Karl's horse to help out. H. 1d.

Thursday the 29th
A nice warm day. Plowed. Heinrich helped Carl Richert log as he had for half a day yesterday. Paid R.M. Forsyth 0.40 for Mini's medicine. Received 2.00 from Hinrich. H. 1d. Had Karl's horse to help out.

Friday the 30th
Decoration Day. Finished with plowing and started to harrow. To Taalke for 2 waists 1.50, overalls 1.00, roofing nails 0.25; total 2.75. Received from Hinrich 2.75. The cow Fun bred to Sonomit's bull. Heinrich shingled the pig pen. H. 1d.

Saturday the 31st
Nice and warm. Harrowed. Heinrich shingled the pig pen. H. 1d. Took Karl's horse back in the morning. Received 0.10 for corn (Kelsch).

[150] June 1902

Sunday the 1st
Cassidy 12.72, Norn 5.72, M.M.&M. Co. 188.84, Francis & McRae 24.35, J. Daugharty 1.00, Weaver 27.64, Schoerpff 1.00, Marfileus 1.57, Dr. Grigg 6.75, Heasley 2.50, Toothacker 8.00 Keller 16.95, Taalke 8.78, R. Forsyth 4.65, Dr. Warren 6.00, P.M. Miller 1.40—Alf. Hall 0.40, D. Mills 1.00, school 5.00, cheese factory 0.50, Benson 2.00, Sonomit Sr. 0.50, H. Sonomit 4.10, Parker 0.30 Wilson 4.00.

As of 1 June 1902:
Outstanding receipts 17.80
Debts 217.87
Cash on hand 3.26

Monday the 2nd
Violent thunderstorms and rain yesterday. Drained the entire day, i.e. Friedrich, Wilhelm and I. Heinrich and Hinrich hunted for the horse Topsy who had run away on Sunday. They found it in Moore's Junction.

Tuesday the 3rd
Several thunderstorms during the night. Nicer during the day. Drained in the forenoon and in the afternoon sorted and cut seed potatoes. Heinrich whitewashed the pig pen. For a fireback 0.75. H. ¾ d.

Wednesday the 4th
French heifer calf [written above the entry]
Good weather, cool. Harrowed and worked on the pig pen. H. 1d. For stockings 0.25.

Thursday the 5th
Good weather. Cool. Harrowed and worked on the pig pen; also cut eyes out of the potatoes. H. 1d. Gave Mini 2.25. On the 4th the cow French had a heifer calf.

Friday the 6th
Good weather. Paid Francis & McRae with 15 bu. potatoes. Harrowed and marked the field for potatoes and planting potatoes. H. 1d.

[151] **June 1902**

Saturday the 7th
Good weather. Heinrich planted 8 bu. of corn. Friedrich and I marked the fields for corn planting. H. 1d. Rain in the evening.

Sunday the 8th
Good weather, cool. Garners came to visit us.

Monday the 9th
Overcast and cool. Not at all good growing conditions, the fields are still very wet. Finished marking the fields. Have so far planted 13 bu. potatoes and also some corn. H. 1d.

Tuesday the 10th
Cool. Mini and I planted corn. Heinrich planted cabbage and worked in the garden with Friedrich. The school in Standish was closed because of an out-

break of smallpox. The cow Cherry was bred to Sonomit's bull; Sonomit's and we are now even. H. ¾ d. Gave Mini 0.30, for sugar 0.20; total 0.50.

Wednesday the 11th
Nice and warm. Planted corn: Mini and I in the forenoon, Emma helped in the afternoon. Heinrich traded corn for 150 lbs. of Gold Medal flour as well as for 1500 shingles, nails and spikes for the corn crib and 2 milk pails. H. ½ d.

Thursday the 12th
Good weather. In the morning the heifer Rubie had a heifer calf. I was tired and went to bed. H. 1d. Toward evening there was a thunderstorm with rain. Heinrich took the corn crib down. For ½ bu. corn 0.30.

Friday the 13th
Good weather. Was so tired I stayed in bed till noon. Had pain in my back and in all my limbs. In the afternoon cleared out around the fruit trees and around some of the grapevines with the youngsters. Received 4.75 from Hinrich, paid Taalke 0,05 leaving 4.70. Heinrich worked on the corn crib. H. 1d.

[signed] Jan Wübbena

[152]   **June 1902**

Saturday the 14th
Received from Wilson 4.00. For overalls 0.75, Wilhelm's overalls 0.35; total 1.10. Paid N.B. Weaver 1.00, P.M. Miller 1.40. For sulfur 0.10, cream of tartar 0.25; total 0.35. For Taalke's hat 2.00. From Mini left over from butter 0.52. For a mirror 0.25, comb 0.15, hair pins 0.05; total 0.45. The cow Katie was bred by an unknown black bull. H. 1d.

Sunday the 15th
Hot. Kept the Sabbath. In the afternoon there was a thunderstorm with rain. Since smallpox has become an epidemic in the area, all public meetings have been canceled.

Monday the 16th
Beautiful, warm weather. Drained fields during the forenoon. In the afternoon hoed potatoes. Heinrich worked on the corn crib. H. ¾ d. Hinrich's shoes. M. 110.

Tuesday the 17th
Beautiful, warm weather. Mini and I cultivated. Heinrich worked on the corn crib. For roofing nails 0.07. H. 1d. M. 113.

Wednesday the 18th
Beautiful, warm weather. In the afternoon stormy with a few brief rain showers. For Heasley 2.00. To repair Hinrich's shoes 0.25. To Keller for sugar 0.25, baking powder 0.10; total 0.35. H. 1d. M. 109. Heinrich worked on the corn crib. Emma and I cultivated.

Thursday the 19th
Beautiful weather. M. 121. Cultivated. Heinrich set up wood. In the afternoon plowed for John Dobson. H. 1d.

Friday the 20th
Beautiful weather. M. 121. Cultivated. Heinrich worked for John Dobson. Toward evening rain. H. 1d.

[153]   **June 1902**

Saturday the 21st
M. 124. Good weather. To Ward for a shovel 0.75. Paid for a scale 0.50. To Schoerpff for a brooch (Goldie Garner) 0.50. H. 1d. Heinrich plowed for Dobson. I hoed around the fruit trees. To M.M.&M. Co. for shoes bought two weeks ago for Heinrich 1.50. Paid Keller 0.35 with eggs, v. June 18th.

Sunday the 22nd
Good weather, but cold. Fun bred to Sonomit's bull. Kept the Sabbath otherwise.

Monday the 23rd
M. 130. Worked on the road: Heinrich with the team, I with a spade. H. 1d.

Tuesday the 24th
M. 124. I worked ½ day on the road. Heinrich worked for the road commission. In the afternoon cleaned up in the orchard. H. 1d.

Wednesday the 25th
M. 120. Began replanting corn. But about 9:00 it began to rain so we had to stop. Heinrich had worked till then for the road commission. H. ½ d.

Thursday the 26th
Good weather. M. 128. Drained till noon then replanted corn with Mini and Emma. Heinrich was busy elsewhere, clearing etc. H. 2 hours.

Friday the 27th
M. 127. Yesterday Hinrich received 5.25 for his work. Of that I received 2.72 after he got 0.50 for a hat and we had bought various groceries. In addition I had in safe keeping 1.02 from Emma which she had earned working for

Karl and Proulx. Hinrich kept 0.75 for the 4th of July celebration. The 0.40 from Saturday the 21st had been spent elsewhere. H. 1d.

[154]   June 1902

Saturday the 28th
M. 118. Good weather. For hold back straps 0.50, a cold chisel 0.10; total 0.60. H. 1d. Paid Wards 0.75 for the shovel (v. June 21st). Mini, Ella and I replanted corn. Heinrich, Friedrich and Wilhelm cleaned up around the barn.

Sunday the 29th
Good weather. Brbr. Public meetings no longer prohibited.

Monday the 30th
M. 128. Rainy. Friedrich, Ella, Wilhelm and I replanted corn as well as we could. Heinrich cut clover in the forenoon and cultivated potatoes in the afternoon. H. 4 hours.
Milk delivered in June
$$1451 \text{ lbs.} = 6.53$$
$$198 \text{ lbs.} = 0.88 \text{ (May)}$$
$$7.41$$
$$1.50 \text{ (Delivery, Armstrong)}$$
leaves   5.91
Credited on July 15: 6.37

[155]   July 1902

Cassidy 12.72, Norn 5.72, M.M.&M. Co. 90.34, Francis & McRae 19.20, J. Daugharty 1.00, N.B. Weaver 26.64, Schoerpff 1.50, Marfileus 157 [1.57?], Dr. Grigg 6.75, Heasley 0.50, Toothacker 8.00, Keller 16.95, Taalke 8.78, R. Forsyth 4.65, Warren 6.00—Alb. Hall 040 [0.40?], D. Mills 1.00, school 5.00, cheese factory 0.50, Benson 2.00, H. Sonomit, Jr. 4.10, Parker 0.30.
As of 1 July 1902:
Outstanding receipts 13.30
Debts 210.32
Cash on hand 2.39

Tuesday the 1st
M. 121. Beautiful. Replanted corn. Heinrich raked the hay which he had cut the day before and then hoed. Friedrich helped him. Hinrich and Ella helped me. For groceries 0.25, for bolts for the mowing machine 0.75; total 1.00. H. 1d.

Wednesday the 2nd
M. 121. Emma, Mini and I replanted corn. Heinrich stacked the hay and hoed. It rained during the forenoon so that we had to quit. The afternoon was dry but there was a hard rain toward evening. H. ¾ d.

Thursday the 3rd
Rain in the morning. Replanted corn and was finished by 9:00 (with that had spent 7 days to replant 7 acres. Had 34,039 stalks standing 3 feet in either direction which makes a good seven acres.) Then it dried off. Posted the announcement of the annual school meeting at five locations, 0.50. Raked hay and stacked it. Hinrich didn't go to work on account of the weather.

[156]   **July 1902**

Friday the 4th
M. 129. Celebrated the glorious Fourth. Very hot in the forenoon, thunderstorms and rain in the afternoon.

Saturday the 5th
M. 128. Dry and hot. Dried the cut grass and hauled home the cured hay which amounted to about 6 loads. To Gottenmyer for meat 0.25. To Keller for raisins 0.10. Had Karl over to help in the afternoon and Hinrich the entire day.

Sunday the 6th
Thunderstorm and rain in the morning. Kept the Sabbath.

Monday the 7th
M. 117. Violent thunderstorms and rain during the night. To Keller for salt 2.00. To M.M.&M. Co. for 10 yds. of shirting 1.00. To N.B. Weaver for a hay scale 2.25. H. 2 hours.

Tuesday the 8th
Hot. M. 140. Warned people about milk on behalf of the cheese factory, 2.00. Heinrich mowed hay. Weighing milk with Dobson's and our scale gives a 1 lb. difference. In the evening a school board meeting, 1.50. H. ¾ d.

Wednesday the 9th
M. 109. Rain and thunderstorms during the night. Received 7.00 from the school. Paid N.B. Weaver 5.00. Paid Francis & McRae 2.00, Schoerpff 0.50, Gottenmyer 0.35. For tea 0.25, sugar 0.25; total 0.50. Heinrich mowed for Karl. I weeded and hoed with the youngsters. Overcast the whole day. H. 1 hour.

Thursday the 10th
M. 121. Hauled in 4 loads of hay. That made a total of 10 loads. Cultivated potatoes and corn. H. 1d. Karl helped us during the afternoon.

Friday the 11th
M. 122. On the third of July Katie was bred by Gammon's on the road and Rubie was bred to Dobson's bull on July 8th. Brought in the rest of the stacked hay and then cultivated with Prince and Fanny, Prince with our own and Fanny with Proulx's cultivator. H. 1d.

[157]   July 1902

Saturday the 12th
M. 110. Cultivated with Prince and Proulx's cultivator. Heinrich hauled hay for Karl with Fanny. H. 1d.

Sunday the 13th
Beautiful weather. Kept the Sabbath. Brbr.

Monday the 14th
M. 140. Beautiful weather. Heinrich cut hay till 10:00 at Karl's with Fanny. I cultivated with Prince. H. ½ d. In the evening at the school meeting was reelected as director for three more years (till 1905).

Tuesday the 15th
M. 126. Beautiful weather. To Gottenmyer for lard 6.05, meat 0.35; total 6.40. To Keller for sugar 0.25, oatmeal 0.25, soda 0.10, molasses 0.10; total 0.70. For a Pitman bolt 0.15. Credit for milk 6.37. Heinrich cut hay with Prince and Lizzie. In the afternoon I raked the hay cut yesterday with Fanny and then hauled one load to the barn; this makes a total of 11 loads.

Wednesday the 16th
M. 126. Beautiful weather. Brought in 4 loads of hay. Of these we put one more in the east mow and the other three in the west mow. All together we now have 15 loads in the barn: 12 in the east and 3 in the west mow. H. 1d. In the afternoon had Karl over to help. Bought Emma's dress on Friday the 11th from M.M.&M. Co. for 0.90

Thursday the 17th
M. 131 [143 crossed out]. Beautiful weather. To Keller for sugar 0.25, rice 0.25; total 0.50. To Aug. Schauer for fixing the cultivator 1.00. To 10 cold shuts 0.40. Cut and raked hay. H. 1d.

Friday the 18th
M. 124. Cool and overcast. Brought in 6 loads of hay which we put in the west mow.

[158] **July 1902**

With that we had 9 loads of excellent quality hay in the west and 12 loads in the east mow for 21 loads all together in the barn. Karl was over to help all day. H. 1d.

Saturday the 19th
M. 127. Rainy and overcast. Didn't work today on account of the weather. Hinrich also at home. As much as possible we had a day of rest. To Keller for tea 0.23, sugar 0.25; total 0.48.

Sunday the 20th
Overcast and rainy. Kept the Sabbath.

Monday the 21st
M. 128. Overcast and wet in the morning. About 9:00 it cleared up and became a beautiful day. In the forenoon Peter Proulx cut the rest of our hay, about 2 acres. Hinrich was at home the whole day. He helped to pick the great numbers of Colorado beetles. In the afternoon he took Fanny and raked over the hay fields we had harvested on Friday. I hilled up the potatoes with Prince with the shovel plow. Heinrich had gone elsewhere to work on the previous evening already, i.e. to the telephone company. The children were all busy picking Colorado beetles from the potatoes.

Tuesday the 22nd
M. 135. Beautiful weather in the forenoon. I cultivated with Prince; Taalke hauled in the hay we had cut the previous day. Mini was back at Barnes'. In the afternoon there was a violent thunderstorm with rain. The first drops fell just as we were about to haul the first load of hay and so we didn't get any of it in. H. ¾ d.

Wednesday the 23rd
M. 126. (Yesterday evening) went with Dankert to Gammon about school bondsmen, 0.40. Katie bred to Lava's bull, 0.50.

[159] **July 1902**

Nice weather. Dried the hay cut on Monday and brought in 3 small loads for a total of 24 loads: 12 loads in the west and an equal number in the east mow. Taalke bought Emma shoes for 1.25; the money had been saved for

Mini's graduation exercises. Emma and Wilhelm took care of the potatoes. H. 1d.

Thursday the 24th
M. 111. Good weather. Hauled another 2 small loads of hay and put them in the west mow for a total of 15 loads there and 12 in the east, 27 loads all together. In the meantime Friedrich raked over some of the hay fields. Emma and Wilhelm worked on the potatoes. Mini had hurt her thumb in the morning and was unable to work in the hay.

Friday the 25th
M. 121. Good weather. Raked the remaining hay in windrows. Around noon there was a thunderstorm with rain and so we were not able to bring in the hay. Cultivated. H. 1d.

Saturday the 26th
M. 121. Good weather. Cultivated during the forenoon, i.e. Mini and I. Emma and Willie took care of the potatoes. Then brought in the last of the hay, a small load which we put in the west mow. With that we had 28 loads in the barn: 16 in the west and 12 in the east mow. In the afternoon there was a violent thunderstorm with rain. To Keller for oatmeal 0.25, sugar 0.25, rice 0.25, soap 0.25, baking powder 0.10; total 1.10. To M.M.&M. Co. for my shoes 1.50, miscellaneous 0.15; total 1.65. H. 7 hours.

Sunday the 27th
Thunderstorm with heavy rains during the night which lasted into the morning. Kept the Sabbath.

[160]   July 1902

Monday the 28th
M. 105. Good weather. Cultivated. Hinrich at home. Picked Colorado beetles from the potatoes; many of the vines were completely eaten away. Friedrich got 0.30 from Dobson for ½ day of work.

Tuesday the 29th
M. 120. Good weather. Cultivated. H. 1d. Received 7.47 from Hinrich. Picked beetles from the potatoes.

Wednesday the 30th
M. 108. Good weather. Cultivated. Picked beetles from the potatoes. H. 1d. For Hinrich's shoes 1.50, Friedrich's pants 0.30, miscellaneous 0.18; total 1.98, groceries 0.30.

Thursday the 31st
M. 122. In the forenoon heavy rain. Trimmed the hay in the east mow back. Worked in the potatoes in the afternoon—very, very wet. H. ¾ d.

Milk delivered in July: 3028 lbs.

[161]   August 1902

Cassidy 12.72, Norn 5.72, M.M.&M. Co. 87.52, Francis & McRae 17.20, John Daugharty 1.00, N.B. Weaver 23.89, Lava 0.50, Schoerpff 1.00, Marfileus 1.57, Dr. Grigg 6.75, Heasley 0.50, Toothacker 8.00, Keller 21.83, Taalke 8.78, R. Forsyth 4.65, Warren 6.00, Gottenmyer 6.40, Schauer 1.00—Alf. Hall 0.40, D. Mills 1.00, school 0.40, cheese factory 2.50, Benson 2.00, H. Sonomit, Jr. 4.10, Parker 0.30.
As of 1 August 1902:
Outstanding receipts 10.70
Debts 215.03
Cash on hand 5.47

Friday the 1st
M. 113. To Dankert and Gammon about whitewashing the school and buying curtains. Gammon will take the first job, I the second, 0.50. The children picked berries. Friedrich and I worked in the potatoes. H. 1d.

Saturday the 2nd
M. 125. Worked in the potatoes and ditched. To Keller for rice 0.25, oatmeal 0.25, sugar 0.25 [crossed out], matches 0.05, yeast cakes 0.08; total 0.63. H. ¾ d.

Sunday the 3rd
Beautiful weather. Brbr.

Monday the 4th
M. 116. Worked in the potatoes and sprayed. Ditched. H. 1d. Johannes cut oats.

Tuesday the 5th
M. 120. In the forenoon severe thunderstorms and rain. In the afternoon bought curtains for the school 0.50. Johannes cut the rest of the oats. H. ¾ d. To Keller for washing soda 0.50.

Wednesday the 6th
M. 109. Raked oats and weeded. H. 1d.

Thursday the 7th
M. 129. For hiring a teacher and writing the contract, 0.50. H. 7 hours.
Rained all day.

Friday the 8th
M. 108. Good weather. Mounted the device for pulling hay up into the barn
up in the

[162]   August 1902

peak of the roof. Neighbor Schulz came to help. Then dried as much of the
oats that had been cut as possible. Weeded the grapevines and cleaned up
around the fruit trees. H. 1d.

Saturday the 9th
M. 118. 130 [crossed out]. To Keller yesterday for sugar 0.25. Good weather.
Dried oats and hauled them in. 3 small loads and a small load of stubble.
H. 1d. To N.B. Weaver for a whetstone 0.05. Short rain showers during the
night.

Sunday the 10th
Kept the Sabbath. Good weather. Short rain showers during the night.

Monday the 11th
M. 115. Cold. A rain shower during the forenoon. Weeded potatoes as well
as the grapevines and picked Colorado beetles. Drained with the scraper. H.
1d.

Tuesday the 12th
M. 121. Good weather. Pulled peas and weeded corn. H. 1d.

Wednesday the 13th
M. 116. Good weather. A few short rain showers. Weeded corn. H. 1d.

Thursday the 14th
M. 124. Good weather. Cleaned beans and peas. Received 2.00 from Ben-
son. Gave the children 1.00 for Taalke's birthday and Taalke 1.00; total 2.00.
Hinrich at home, the factory has shut down.

Friday the 15th
M. 123. Received 4.10 from H. Sonomit. For flour 2.40, for plow points
1.00. Received from Hinrich 0.50, from M.M.&M. Co. 13.63 for 3028 lbs.
of milk. Paid M.M.&M. Co. 10 against our debt. Paid R.M. Forsyth 3.00.
Gave Mini 1.10 for a dress. To Keller for coffee 0.25, oatmeal 0.25, sugar
0.50, rice 0.25, soap 0.25, chocolate 0.24; total 1.74. To Parker 0.30, to
Schauer 0.25 for a rake tooth.

Saturday the 16th
M. 122. Paid Armstrong 1.00. Raked the clover hay and stacked it up. Good weather.

[163]   **August 1902**

Sunday the 17th
Good weather. Brbr. Attended Mrs. Coor's funeral and went to Elwell's for supper.

Monday the 18th
M. 66. Good weather. Pulled peas. Checked the kindling wood after school, 0.25. Hinrich picked berries.

Tuesday the 19th
M. 129. Brought in 1 load of clover hay and 1 load of peas. Put the hay up in the shed (addition over the stalls) and the peas in the barn. Back pain. H. 1d.

Wednesday the 20th
M. 118. Good weather. Pulled some peas. Helped Proulx thresh in the afternoon. H. 1d. Back and chest pains.

Thursday the 21st
M. 127. Nice weather. Mini and Taalke went to Benson's trial. Pulled peas. H. 1d. To see Dankert about the census, 0.10.

Friday the 22nd
M. 121. Nice weather. Brought in 2 loads of clover hay. This makes a total of 21 loads including the load from Tuesday. Of these 15 loads are in the east mow and 16 loads in the west mow. Received 5.30 from Hinrich. To Gammon about taking the census, 0.10. H. 1d. For groceries 2.00.

Saturday the 24th
M. 120. Took the census. For Mini's hat 2.00. H. 1d.

Sunday the 24th
Nice weather. To Forsyth for iodine 0.05. Received 12.00 from Heinrich the previous evening. Kept the Sabbath.

Monday the 25th
M. 116. Deposited 22.00 in the bank for Heinrich. Pulled peas. Heinrich at home because of a headache. To Forsyth for Kiens Kidney tea, 0.25. Severe pains in the back and chest. For Mini's skirt 0.39, for soda 0.10.

[164]   **August 1902**

Tuesday the 26th
M. 113. Brought in a small load of peas. Cut some of the standing corn.
Went to school and cleaned it for Willie Sonomit, 0.25. H. 1d.

Wednesday the 27th
M. 105. Taalke and Mini picked berries. Cut corn. H. 1d. Nice weather.

Thursday the 28th
M. 110. Cut corn and hauled a small load of peas home. Went to town to
pick up two window panes for the school, 0.25. To Keller for tea 0.23, sugar
0.50, oatmeal 0.25; total 0.98. H. 1d. Pulled some peas.

Friday the 29th
M. 114. Installed the two window panes in the school and hung 8 curtains,
1.00. Pulled some peas. H. 1d. To Gottenmyer 0.25 yesterday for meat.

Saturday the 30th
M. 112. Hinrich on account of the Pioneer Picnic at home. Bound the corn
that was cut. I pulled peas. To Keller for matches 0.10.

Sunday the 31st
Good weather. A heavy rain shower in the afternoon. Brbr.
Milk delivered during August: 2711 lbs. $\times$ 0.45 = 12.1995

[165]   **September 1902**

Cassidy 12.72, Norn 5.72, M.M.&M. Co. 77.52, Francis & McRae 17.20,
J. Daugharty 1.00, N.B. Weaver 23.94, Lava 0.50, Schoerpff 1.00, Marfileus
1.57, Dr. Grigg 6.75, Dr. Heasley 0.50, Keller 23.89, Taalke 8.78, R. Forsyth
2.85,* Warren 6.00, Gottenmyer 6.65, Schauer 1.25,—D. Mills 1.00, cheese
factory 2.50.
As of 1 September 1902:
Outstanding receipts 3.50
Debts 197.84
Cash on hand 5.00

Monday the 1st
M. 24. Good weather. Wrote school report, 2.00. H. 1d. Settled with the
school, 9.00.

Tuesday the 2nd
M. 110. Owed Cassidy 0.50 for a rake tooth v. August 15th. Dr. Toothacker
forgave our debt. Paid Francis & McRae 4.00, Schauer 1.25, Heasley 0.50.
H. 1d.

Wednesday the 3rd
Didn't weigh the milk (115 guess). Thunderstorm threatened during the forenoon. Cleared around stumps in preparation for pulling them. H. 1d. From Gottenmyer meat for 0.30.

Thursday the 4th
M. 115. Hauled in a good load of peas. Stormy. H. 1d.

Friday the 5th
M. 124. For Ella's shoes 1.50, Willi's shoes 1.50, apples 0.35; total 3.35. For Keller for soap 0.25, rice 0.25; total 0.50. H. 1d.

Saturday the 6th
M. 113. Overcast and stormy during the forenoon. Hauled in the last load of peas; that made all together 5 loads. Also hauled a small load of stones which we gathered up by the stumps. Then got the chains and blocks ready to pull stumps.

*The bill on August 1st was 5.80 rather than 4.65 of which we paid 3.00 on August 10th.

[166]   **September 1902**

Sunday the 7th
Nice day. Brbr. Went to Norn's house.

Monday the 8th
Nice. M. 118. Severe storm. About 3 stumps; had a lot of trouble with chains breaking. To Ward for a box of cartridges 7.50, 100 ft. of fuse 0.65, 50 caps; total 8.65—to be paid soon! H. 8 hours.

Tuesday the 9th
M. 118. Rain during the night. Hinrich at home. Blew about 40 stumps with the cartridges we bought yesterday. Raw and cold.

Wednesday the 10th
Paid Proulx 0.50 for 1 bu. oats. M. 120. Frost during the night, pretty hard. Hinrich and Taalke to Sterling; picked up Miss Schmelzer. Mini and I pulled stumps. Hinrich at home.

Thursday the 11th
M. 110. Good weather. Pulled stumps; the chains broke and the harness broke: a lot of trouble. Hinrich at home. Lundy's son buried.

Friday the 12th
M. 118. Nice weather during the morning, rain in the afternoon. About 9 stumps; it went better than the day before. Hinrich at home.

Saturday the 13th
M. 123. Good weather. Pulled stumps. Hinrich at home.

Sunday the 14th
Heavy frost during the night. Brbr. Nice weather.

Monday the 15th
M. 112. Nice weather. Piled stumps. In the evening Karl came and got the mowing machine to cut clover in the morning. Hinrich at home. Went to the Gospel Chapel with Hinrich and Mini in the evening.

Tuesday the 16th
M. 104. Nice weather. Made racks to stand the corn against when we cut it. Karl was using Prince and the mowing machine. H. 1d.

[167]   **September 1902**

Wednesday the 17th
M. 124. Nice weather. Made racks to stand the corn. Piled some stumps. Went with James Dobson to Frank Larou about watering the milk, 1.00. $2.78 for 26½ lbs. of cheese @ 0.10½ = 2.78.* To Keller for 50 lbs. flour 1.20.

Thursday the 18th
M. 105. To the cheese factory about Larou's watering the milk, 0.50. For 10 lbs. of cheese 1.00. To Cassidy for rake section 0.75 (v. Sept. 2nd; instead of 0.50 it was 0.75). For groceries 0.25. Received 14.13 for milk. Armstrong 1.75 for hauling milk. To Ward 2.00 for silk. Mini's skirt 0.05. For hinges 0.25. This leaves 10.08. Then to M.M.&M. Co. 5.00. To M.M.&M. Co. for cheese 2.78. Wet and overcast the entire day.

Friday the 19th
M. 102. To the Conference. To Halcro for mending tugs 1.15. Heinrich came home. More careful checking has shown that instead of having had 14.13 credited for milk, the amount was 12.20, or 1.93 less. Accordingly our debt is that much greater. H. 3 hours.

Saturday the 20th
M. 104. To the Conference. Heinrich with Mini and Friedrich piled the stumps we had pulled out.

Sunday the 21st
Section Conference.

---

* The same item is recorded on the 18th as well but only counts once.

Monday the 22nd
M. 107. Good weather but threatening storm. Piled stumps. H. 1d. Toward evening lit 8 piles of stumps.

Tuesday the 23rd
M. 112. Rainy. Burned the piled stumps. H. 1d.

[168]   **September 1902**

Wednesday the 24th
M. 102. Stormy. Piled stumps and burned them; the fence around the calf yard also caught fire. H. 1d. Received 2.00 from Hinrich on the 22nd.

Thursday the 25th
M. 104. Humid and overcast. Piled stumps and burned them. H. 1d. To Keller yesterday for sugar 0.25, rice 0.25, oatmeal 0.25, soda 0.02, baking powder 0.10; total 0.92. For Hinrich's overalls 0.50. H. 1d.

Friday the 26th
M. 100. Good weather. Cut 95 shocks of corn, 8 × 8 stalks to the shock. County fair; Hinrich, Heinrich as well as Taalke and Mini went.

Saturday the 27th
M. 95. Good weather. With Mini and Hinrich cut 60 shocks of corn by noon. Emma and Ella went to the county fair. Shocks 8 × 8 stalks. Hinrich at home. To N.B. Weaver for glass 0.20. For Heinrich a pair of tugs worth 14.00. James Dobson to Vance's about falsifying the milk, 0.20.

Sunday the 28th
Kept the Sabbath and rested.

Monday the 29th
M. 91. Cut 78 shocks @ 8×8 stalks; that makes 207 shocks all together. H. 1d.

Tuesday the 30th
M. 95. Humid and overcast all day. Puttered around some. H. 1d. To Keller for flour 2.40, kerosene 0.60; total 3.00.

In September delivered 2559 lbs. of milk = 11.51.

[169]   **October 1902**

Wednesday the 1st
Cassidy 12.72, Norn 5.72, M.M.&M. Co. 75.30, Francis & McRae 13.20, J. Daugharty 1.00, N.B. Weaver 24.14, Lava 0.50, Schoerpff 1.00, Marfileus

1.75, Dr. Grigg 6.75, Keller 29.51, Taalke 8.78, R. Forsyth 2.85, Warren 6.00, Gottenmyer 6.95—D. Mills 1.00, cheese factory 4.20

As of 1 October, 1902:

Outstanding receipts 5.20

Debts 195.99

Cash on hand 6.40

Wednesday the 1st

M. 93. Cut 84 shocks of corn @ 8×8; that makes all together 291 shocks. H. 1d. Johannes came home. Received 2.50 from Hinrich.

Thursday the 2nd

M. 98. It froze last night. Cut and set up 84 shocks @ 8×8; that makes 348 shocks all together. H. 1d.

Friday the 3rd

M. 103. Good weather. Cut and set up 80 shocks; that makes 455 shocks all together. Husked 3 shocks and fed the pigs. Helped Schulz to thresh. H. 1d.

Saturday the 4th

M. 98. Paid Ward 5.00 yesterday. Paid 1.50 for lard. To Keller for sugar 0.25. Helped Schulz with the threshing in the morning then worked over at Johannes' place. H. 1d.

Sunday the 5th

Brbr.

Monday the 6th

To Keller for oatmeal 0.25, rice 0.25, yeast cakes 0.04, bran 0.01, matches 0.05; total 0.60. To Sam Blumenthal for Friedrich's shoes and stockings 1.55. M. 94. H. 1d.

[170]   October 1902

Tuesday the 7th

M. 88. To Keller for tea 0.25. For Friedrich's overall 0.50. Dug 2½ bu. of potatoes yesterday and 16½ today; a total of 40 bu. H. 1th

Wednesday the 8th

M. 86. Heavy frost during the night. Dug 11½ bu. of potatoes for a total of 51½ bu. H. 1d.

Thursday the 9th

M. 70? (took some out of the can after weighing the milk). To Keller for sugar 0.25, soda 0.10; total 0.35. To N.B. Weaver 0.60 for 6 windowpanes 6" × 9". Dug 12 bu. of potatoes for a total of 63½ bu. H. ¾ d.

Friday the 10th
M. (72?) Dug 15 bu. of potatoes for a total of 78½ bu. H. 1d.
Beautiful weather.

Saturday the 11th
M. 72. Very fine weather. Dug 12 bu. of potatoes, a total of 90½ bu. H. 1d.
To Keller for sugar 0.50, ginger 0.05, cinnamon 0.05, nutmeg 0.05; total
0.65.

Sunday the 12th
Overcast. Kept the Sabbath. I had terrible pains in the left side. I have had
them ever since September 17th.

Monday the 13th
M. 82. Heavy rain during the night. To Toothacker to examine me and for
pills 0.25. Overcast during the day. Dug 12 bu. which makes 102½. H. 2/3
d.

Tuesday the 14th
M. 72. Overcast. Dug 15 bu. potatoes for a total of 117 bu. [sic] H. 1d

Wednesday the 15th
M. 70. Nice weather. Received 11.50 for milk and 8.54 for Hinrich's work
to the 11th. Of the 8.54 I received 0.25 for the orphanage in St. Joseph,
Michigan; that left 8.29.

[171]   October 1902

Last month I was paid 1.00 too much for milk and therefore received only
10.51 instead of 11.51. That made a total of 18.80 with the money from
Hinrich. Of that paid 8.00 to M.M.&M. Co., to Ward 1.65, for freight for
the school clock 0.25, for meat 0.50, to the Dr. for helping with my side 0.30,
to Armstrong 1.50. Borrowed from R.M. Forsyth for liniment 0.44. Paid for
licorice 0.50, for glass 0.30. H. 9 hours. To Taalke to buy clothes 6.40. The
liniment from Forsyth is No. 7264 or 1264 from Dr. Toothacker; I note that
for the following reason: if the liniment is good and if rubbing it three times
a day into my side and into the foot I injured this morning helps them heal,
then I will be able to buy more of it without a doctor's prescription.

Thursday the 16th
M. 60. Good weather. Hinrich worked for Wards and not for the factory
0.65. Johannes plowed. The children carried into the cellar about 5 bu. of
carrots, 1 bu. turnips and 10 peck red beets.

Friday the 17th
M. 64. After school went to the Pioneer Picnic 0.50. A lot of pain in my side and in my foot. To N.B. Weaver for sheet iron for under the stove 0.60.

Saturday the 18th
M. 66. To Keller for rice 0.25, oatmeal 0.25, sugar 0.50, tea 0.23; total 1.23. H. 1d. Overcast. Johannes built a bed for Wilhelm; I lay around and looked after my side and my foot.

[172]   October 1902

Sunday the 19th
Nice weather. Kept the Sabbath. A lot of pain. Thomley baptized 12 people from Johnsfield Methodist.

Monday the 20th
M. 28. Began cleaning out the well by the house. Johannes bought ½ ton of bran and ¼ ton of middlings for calf feed during the winter; he will begin on January 1st, 1903. H. 1d.

Tuesday the 21st
M. 56. A very heavy freeze during the night. Cleaned the well by the house. H. 1d.

Wednesday the 22nd
M. 50. It rained toward morning. Overcast and wet all day. H. 1d.

Thursday the 23rd
M. about 50, didn't weigh it. Cleaned the well by the barn and made it deeper. The children husked corn. H. 1d. Heinrich gave me 11.00 on Monday the 20th, delivered through Mrs. Karl Wübbena.

Friday the 24th
M. about 50, didn't weigh it. To Dr. Toothacker 0.50. Forsyth for quinine 0.25, Lard 1.08, for an overall 0.25, sugar 0.50, lamp wicks 0.05, matches 0.05, soap 0.25; total 2.93. H. 1d.

Saturday the 25th
M. not weighed. Plowed and husked corn. Mini had been at Barnes' since yesterday night; she came home this evening.

Sunday the 26th
Rainy and overcast. Kept the Sabbath.

Monday the 27th
Overcast. Husked corn. Mini went back to Barnes'. Couldn't find the colt in the evening. H. 1d.

Tuesday the 28th
Johannes left yesterday for the north. For Friedrich's rabbit 0.20, for bolts in the ploy 0.07, for pictures and frame 3.10; total 3.37. For tea 0.25, laces 0.05, thread 0.05; total 0.35. H. 1d. Found the colt at Armstrong's.

[173] **October 1902**

Wednesday the 29th
M. 40. Plowed with three horses, Fanny, Prince and Topsy. Husked corn. H. 1d. A lot of pain in my foot and side.

Thursday the 30th
M. not weighed. Plowed with three horses. Husked corn. H. 1d. Very windy. A lot of pain in my foot and side.

Friday the 31st
M. not weighed. Plowed with three horses. Friedrich was driving all three days. Topsy was sweating a bit toward evening. Have so far plowed every day from 11:30 to 4:00 P.M. Husked corn. H. 1d. A lot of pain in my foot and in my side. Frenchi's heifer bred to Peter Proulx's bull. For fish 0.25.

Delivered 1461 lbs. of milk in October.

[174] **November 1902**

Saturday the 1st
Cassidy 12.72, Norn 5.72, M.M.&M. Co. 75.30, Francis & McRae 13.20, J. Daugharty 1.00, N.B. Weaver 25.34, Lava 0.50, Schoerpff 1.00, Marfileus 1.57, Dr. Grigg 6.75, Keller 32.84, Taalke 8.78, R. Forsyth, 3.29, Warren 6.00, Gottenmyer 6.95, Sam Blumenthal 1.55—D. Mills 1.00, cheese factory 4.20.
As of 1 November 1902:
Outstanding receipts 5.20
Debts 202.51
Cash on hand 4.10

Saturday the 1st
M. not weighed. Plowed with three horses, Mini helped. From M.M.&M. Co. 15.00. Paid Cassidy 12.72, for a lantern 1.00, clovells 0.10, snaphooks 0.04, oatmeal 0.25, sugar 0.25, baking powder 0.10; total 14.49. Received credit for Hinrich 8.10. H. 1d.

Sunday the 2nd
Nice day. Kept the Sabbath. Brbr.

Monday the 3rd
Nice day. Plowed with 3 horses, Mini helped out. Husked corn and brought in beans. Took a good load on the wagon box to Francis & McRae paid 3.00. H. 1d.

Tuesday the 3rd
Overcast during the forenoon. Plowed with 3 horses. Paid Lava 0.50. Collection last Sunday 1.00. Election Day. To Forsyth for liniment 0.40, for spices 0.11. H. 1d. Heinrich's birthday.

Wednesday the 5th
Wet and overcast during the forenoon; rain in the afternoon. Plowed during the morning. H. 1d. Threshed some beans. Friedrich spent the entire day looking for the heifers and found them. Put them in the stall for the night and plan to do this every evening from now on.

[175] **November 1902**

Thursday the 6th
Very wet ground; tried to plow but it didn't work. Rained during the night and stopped toward morning. Had letters from both Heinrich and Johannes. From the former received 12.00 to put in the bank and 1.00 for me. H. 1d.

Friday the 7th
Beautiful, dry weather. For groceries 1.00. The ground was very wet. Tried to plow but couldn't. Drained as much as possible. H. 1d. Put 12.00 in the bank for Heinrich.

Saturday the 8th
Very nice day. The ground very wet. Plowed some. H. 1d. For groceries 1.00. Wrote yesterday to Heinrich. To Crecine 0.03 for an envelope for Heinrich's letter.

Sunday the 9th
Very nice day. Brbr. From Nehls 0.25 for the collection.

Monday the 10th
Very nice, dry weather. Plowed and husked corn. Friedrich went to help Carl Wübbena. To Keller for Gold Medal flour 2.40, tea 0 25, matches 0 05, oatmeal 0.25; total 2.95. To Gottenmyer for lard 1.65. H. 1d.

Tuesday the 11th
Wet and overcast, rain toward evening. Hauled in a load of husked corn, perhaps 20 bu. Plowed some but it didn't go well. H. 1d.

Wednesday the 12th
Very wet. Plowed some. Rain toward evening. H. 1d. Taalke attended Cadi's funeral.

Thursday the 13th
Dry weather and windy. Plowed some. Was to Rug's funeral. Received 8.92 from Hinrich and paid out of it to M.M.&M. Co. 3.00, Keller 3.00, for cabbage 2.00, sugar 0.25, envelopes, paper & poststamps 0.50, miscellaneous 0.17; total 8.92. H. 1d.

[176] **November 1902**

Friday the 14th
Overcast. Plowed. Hinrich's shoes 1.50, canvas 1.25, pants 0.50, from M.M.&M. Co.; total 3.25. H. 1d. Mrs. Carl Wübbena helped husk corn for ½ day.

Saturday the 15th
Dry. The ground was very wet; rain the night before. Plowed. Credit for milk 6.71, received 4.00. Paid Armstrong 1.50, Marfileus 0.50, sugar 0.25, spices 0.25, overall 0.50, Friedrich's birthday 0.20; total 2.70 [sic]. Elsewhere 1.30. H. 1d. To M.M.&M. Co. for Friedrich's and Wilhelm's jackets @ 1.25 = 2.50; see December 4th where the 2.50 is recorded.

Sunday the 16th
Kept the Sabbath. Brbr. S.S.

Monday the 17th
Good weather. Husked the rest of the corn. Emma and Ella went to school. Friedrich's birthday, 11 years old. Plowed. H. 6 hours.

Tuesday the 18th
Good weather. Plowed. To Keller for lamp chimneys 0.05. To N.B. Weaver for 2 pails @ 0.10 = 0.20. H. 1d. Hauled the rest of the corn home, about 15 bu., a very poor crop.

Wednesday the 19th
Beautiful weather. Plowed. Hinrich at home. Got the barn ready to bring in the corn straw. Received 70.25 from Dankert for Johannes; gave him a receipt for it.

Thursday the 20th
Beautiful weather. Hinrich at home. Hauled in the corn straw and set ten heaps afire.

Friday the 21st
Nice weather. Hinrich at home. Plowed and burned. Put Johannes' money in the bank as well as 5.00 for Heinrich which he had sent the day before and 6.00 for Mrs. Carl Wübbena.

[177]   **November 1902**

Saturday the 22nd
Raw and cold. Hinrich and Friedrich hauled Karl's cornstalks in after school. Measured Sonomit's firewood 0.25. From the cheese factory 4.20. Last evening a cheese factory meeting at home because of Mrs. LaRou and Vance. For a padlock 0.50, groceries 2.00, cold shuts 0.12, Taalke's shoes 1.50; total 4.12. Pulled half a stump and burned.

Sunday the 23rd
Kept the Sabbath. Nice weather.

Monday the 24th
Raw and cold. Plowed and got ready to butcher pigs. H. 1d.

Tuesday the 25th
Raw and cold. Butchered three pigs; Nehls came to help. Did some plowing. H. 1d.

Wednesday the 26th
Raw and cold, snow in the evening. Salted the pigs butchered the day before. Did some plowing. The pigs weighed together 275 lbs. Got ready for Thanksgiving (tomorrow). It should be noted that 6.57 rather than 6.71 was credited for milk on the 15th (0.14 less). Credit for milk in November 1.37. Received 5.62 from Hinrich and paid out of that 2.00 to M.M.&M. Co. and 0.50 for gloves. H. 1d.

Thursday the 27th
Thanksgiving Day. Hinrich at home.

Friday the 28th
Raw and cold. A hard freeze during the night. Hauled a load of manure. H. 1d. For stockings and clothes 3.12. to Forsyth for cough medicine 0.15.

Saturday the 29th
Raw and stormy all day, snow. H. 1d.

Sunday the 30th
Nice weather. Brbr.

Delivered 261 lbs. of milk in November.

[178]   **December 1902**

Norn 5.72, M.M.&M. Co. 76.51, Francis & McRae 10.20, J. Daugharty
1.00, N.B. Weaver 25.54, Schoerpff 1.00, Marfileus 1.07, Dr. Grigg 6.75,
Keller 32.89. Taalke 8.78, R. Forsyth 3.84, Warren 6.00, Gottenmyer 8.60,
Sam Blumenthal 1.55—D. Mills 1.00, school 0.50
As of 1 December 1902:
Outstanding receipts 1.50
Debts 189.40
Cash on hand 0.00

Monday the 1st
Good weather. Hauled 2 loads of manure. H. 1d.

Tuesday the 2nd
Good weather. Hauled 1 load of manure. To Keller for scrubbing brush 0.05,
washing soda 0.10, matches 0.05, yeast cakes 0.08, broom 0.35, oatmeal
0.21, rice 0.25, lamp chimney 0.05, G.M. flour 2.30, sugar 0.25; total 3.69.
To Ward for 2 lantern chimneys 0.20, shoe tacks 0.10; total 0.40. H. 1d.

Wednesday the 3rd
Raw weather, snow storm. H. 1d.

Thursday the 4th
Very cold. Just did chores. H. 1d. To M.M.&M. Co. for Hinrich's shoes 0.75;
that they are so cheap results from the purchase of jackets on November
15th, total 2.50.

Friday the 5th
Mild. Brought 2 loads of manure to the cellar. H. 1d. To Will Herten about
business guide.

Saturday the 6th
Raw and cold. Hinrich at home; went to the dentist. Cut some wood.

Sunday the 7th
Very cold. Kept the Sabbath.

Monday the 8th
Very cold; snow during the night. Hinrich at home.

Tuesday the 9th
Very cold. Hinrich at home. Hurt a finger badly on Monday afternoon while cutting. Hauled a load of manure.

Wednesday the 10th
Very cold but mild. Hinrich at home. Moved hay out of the west mow into the east. Barker's son buried.

Thursday the 11th
Cold and overcast. Hinrich at home. Sawed some wood.

Friday the 12th
Received 7.50 for Hinrich, owed for milk 16.00, on the 6th 4.00 from Heinrich; total 24.50. Paid taxes of 15.02. Paid Keller 6.00, Ward 0.40, tea 0.23, baking powder 0.10, sugar 0.25; total 0.58; snap hooks 0.05; everything together 22.05.

Saturday the 13th
Raw and cold. Hinrich at home. Sawed and skidded at Johannes' place.

Sunday the 14th
Nice day, but cold. Brbr.

Monday the 15th
Good weather, rain in the evening. H. ½d.

Tuesday the 16th
Raw and windy. Hinrich and Charles Gale sawed on Johannes' farm.

Wednesday the 17th
Raw and windy, cold. Hinrich and Friedrich sawed on Johannes' land.

Thursday the 18th, Friday the 19th, Saturday the 20th
Didn't have much luck all this week. Cut all together about 1½ cord of wood. Broke the reach on the wagon and fixed it. To Keller for coffee 0.25, sugar 0.25; total 0.50. For Christmas things etc. 2.45. H. ½d in the factory this week.

[180]   **December 1902**

Sunday the 21st
Wet and rainy. Brbr.

Monday the 22nd
Raw and cold. Moved hay out of the west mow into the east mow in the barn. Then skidded several logs on Johannes' farm. To M.M.&M. Co. for

Friedrich's and Wilhelm's pants @0.50 = 1.00. Bought a muffler 0.35, ribbon 0.07, mittens 0.65; total 1.77.

Tuesday the 23rd
Cold. For milk 10.00. To Keller 1.00, S. Blumenthal 1.55, Taalke 1.00, G.M. flour 2.40; on hand 1.50; groceries 2.55; total 10.00. Butcher knife 0.75.

Wednesday the 24th
Cold and very raw. Moved hay from the west to the east. Taalke went to trim the Christmas tree. Had the Christmas tree in the evening. Received a book, "Daily Light & Strength" from his friends as well as a pair of stockings and a chest protector from his children. For groceries 0.75.

Thursday the 25th and Friday the 26th
Celebrated Christmas. Hinrich went to Mrs. Richards' trial on Friday.

Saturday the 27th
Very cold. Hauled a sledload of wood from Johannes' farm, but the snow wasn't deep enough. Hinrich is sick. To Keller for Gold Dust 0.25.

Sunday the 28th
Cold. Brbr.

Monday the 29th
Cold. To Keller for soap 0.25. Snow till noon. Taalke to Barnes'. Hauled logs from Johannes' farm.

Tuesday the 30th
Johannes paid his taxes.

Wednesday the 31st
New Year's Eve. Cut wood and hauled 1 load of manure. Butchered two pigs.
    My figures for milk delivered: 11,579 lbs. = 100.16
    M.M.&M. Co.'s figures: 11,769 lbs. = 101.80

[181]   **January 1903**

Now thank we all our God
  With hearts and hands and voices,
Who wondrous things has done
  In whom His world rejoices,
Who from our mother's arms
  Hath blessed us on our way
With countless gifts of love
  And still is ours today.

Oh, may this bounteous God
  Through all our life be near us
With ever joyful hearts
  And blessed peace to cheer us;
And keep us in His grace
  And guide us, when perplexed
And free us from all ills
  In this world and the next.

All praise and thanks to God
  The father now be given,
The Son and Him who reigns
  With them in highest heaven;—
The one eternal God,
  Whom heaven and earth adore;
For thus it was, is now,
  And shall be ever more.

Martin Rinkart, 1644

Who should not praise Thee, Thou faithful Father in Heaven! Thou who hast not spared Thine own Son but has given him unto death that we might have salvation. How canst Thou not give us all since Thou hast given us him!?

[182]   **January 1903**

Thursday the 1st

Now we have lived another year and are 365 days older. It is now nearly 58 years that our loving Father has borne me with patience and long-suffering. They have passed as in a dream and I have not in all this time accomplished anything of consequence for the glory of God and the betterment of my fellow man! May things go better in the coming year! If I should live out this year, I would want to be able to say at its end to my children and to all people the same thing: "Follow the example I have shown you in the year 1903!"

By Thy grace grant me this for the sake of Christ, dear Father. We have not known want, rather we have enjoyed plenty. In the barn we have 3 horses, "Fanny," "Prince" and "Topsy." Prince belongs to Heinrich as well as a filly born on May 25th, 1902. There are 7 cows: "Fun," "Rubie," "Blossom," "French," "Katie," "Cherry," and "Molly." "Fun" belongs to Heinrich, "Rubie" to Johannes. There are 4 heifers of which one belongs to Heinrich, 13 calves of which 6 belong to Johannes, 2 sows, a boar and 30 chickens.

In the barn we have 20 tons of hay; we have already fed the cornstalks. In the cellar we have about 80 bu. of potatoes, 25 heads of cabbage, 20 bu. of carrots and 5 bu. of turnips. The farm equipment includes a wagon, a harrow, a mowing machine, a horse-drawn rake, a cultivator, a shovel plow, and a seed drill. The rake and the mowing machine belong to Heinrich. We have made 40 rods of fence along the road and have built a fine pig pen. We have pulled and burned about 300 stumps. We have about 250 lbs. of pork.

[183] January 1903

Financially we stand as follows:
Debts: Norn 5.72, M.M.&M. Co. 81.53, Francis & McRae 10.20, N.B. Weaver 25.54, Marfileus 1.07, Schoerpff 1.00, Dr. Grigg 6.75, Keller 30.53, R. Forsyth 3.84, Taalke 8.78. Gottenmyer 8.60—D. Mills 1.00, school 0.50.
As of 1 January 1903:
Outstanding receipts 1.50
Debts 183.36
Cash on hand 0.00

Thursday the 1st
Celebrated New Year's. Wrote a letter to E. Jungjohann.

Friday the 2nd
Moved hay from the west to the east mow. Measured Sonomit's wood (school), 0.25. Hinrich went to Mrs. Richard's trial.

Saturday the 3rd
It snowed and then a thaw. Cut wood and hauled manure.

Sunday the 4th
Good weather. Kept the Sabbath.

Monday the 5th
Sent Johannes' order. Johannes' taxes were 10.81; I paid 8.56 in cash and the rest with a round receipt [?]. It cost 0.14 to send the order:

| 15J1541½ | 1 24 inch stand with fam lasts | 0.45 |
| 14J9465 | 1 post auger, 8" | 1.65 |

9J5426	3 bales galvanized cattle wire	10.50
35J6030	1 Acme carpenter chest of tools	14.95
15J1801	1 combination shoe, harness & tinner's outfit	1.98
9J4754	1 Tyler's Safety Weaver No. 1	0.16
9J4754	1 Tyler's Safety Weaver No. 4	0.23
9J5597	Galvanized staples sufficient, according to wire	
	(3 bales cattle wire)	
	altogether [sic]	30.06
	with the taxes	38.56

[184]   January 1903

Monday the 5th
Good weather. Hinrich sick. The children to school: Friedrich, Emma, Ella and Wilhelm. Wilhelm's birthday. Hauled manure.

Tuesday the 6th
Very nice weather. Sawed wood. To M.M.&M. Co. for Mini's shoes 2.00, to R.M. Forsyth for Dimond dyes 0.30, to Keller for matches 0.05.

Wednesday the 7th
Very raw, snow flurries. Sawed wood.

Thursday the 8th
The little colt has been lame on the right hind leg for about the past 4 weeks. From the time that we noticed it, had her looked at by Proulx and Gammon and rubbed the spot daily with Corosine liniment, a large lump had formed which was this morning about the size of four or five eggs.

Friday the 9th
Lanced the colt's abscess in Proulx's presence. The pus ran out like a small stream of milk through a strainer. Sawed some wood.

Saturday the 10th
Washed the colt's lump and dusted it with sulfur. Received a card from Sears and Roebuck: the invoice number of Johannes' order from the 5th of January is 544516. To Keller for washing soda 0.10.

[185]   January 1903

Sunday the 11th
Nice weather, very cold. Kept the Sabbath.

Monday the 12th
To M.M.&M. Co. about the cheese factory; for that and for the meeting next Thursday 3.00. Delivered 11,769 lbs. (eleven thousand, seven hundred sixty-nine pounds) of milk last year. Was paid 0.86½ for 100 lbs; that made 9.88. Paid Keller 5.00, for groceries 3.40, for 8 foot pump and 16 foot chain and a basket 2.38.

Tuesday the 13th
Salted down the pig butchered on the 31st of December last year. Very cold. Proulx came to visit and acted as a doctor to the colt. The hip was very badly swollen. Applied turpentine, vinegar and eggs.

Wednesday the 14th
Snow flurries during the afternoon. Hinrich resoled my shoes. I fixed a hay rack in the cow barn. Cut wood during the afternoon.

Thursday the 15th
Thaw. Cleaned out the calf pen. Moved hay from the west to the east mow. Attended a meeting at the cheese factory. Gave Taalke 2.00 for a skirt, Keller 0.35 for syrup, for a feeding pail 0.10; total 0.45. To Marfileus for liniment 0.25 (see January 19th). Gave Mini 0.25 for a composition book.

Friday the 16th
Thaw, nice weather. Sawed wood in the forenoon and built a hay rack in the cow barn during the afternoon. In the evening the children went on a sleigh ride to Jarvis Center.

Saturday the 17th
Very cold and raw. Moved hay from the west mow to the east mow. Hauled wood in the afternoon.

[186] January 1903

Cleaned the pig pen and fixed it up as best I could; it is very cold in there. In the evening I got a letter about Johannes' order sent on January 4th. The things left the store in Chicago on January 15th. To A.H. Welles for Emma's shoes 0.99 and for Ella's shoes 0.99; total 1.98.

Sunday the 18th
Very cold but clear. Brbr. Heinrich and Karl came home in the evening.

Monday the 19th
Very cold, clear. Johannes picked up his things at the depot and paid the freight of 1.66. That makes a total of 40.22 spent for the taxes and the order. Got 1.44 back so have spent 38.78 in all. With that 1.22 for trouble and

Christmas present. It should be noted that the liniment from Marfileus bought January 15th cost 0.30 instead of 0.25, i.e. 0.05 more. To Welles for two quilts @ 1.25 = 2.50, one blanket 1.50; total 4.00. To Keller for a lamp chimney 0.05. For the 1.22 received Mini's pills 0.30, two bu. oats 0.80, sugar 0.25, lamp chimney 0.05. Now have two lamp chimneys. Sawed some wood in the afternoon.

Tuesday the 20th
Very cold, milder in the afternoon. Sawed wood.

Wednesday the 21st
Very cold, milder in the afternoon. Sawed wood. To A. Welles for a veil for Mini's face 0.25, Friedrich's stockings 0.10; total 0.35. Heinrich helped Karl.

[187]   January 1903

Thursday the 22nd
Heinrich, Taalke, Mini and Hinrich to Barrager and Mrs. Richards' trial. Sharpened a saw and hauled manure. To Keller for kerosene 0.50.

Friday the 23rd
Heinrich and Hinrich went to Johannes' farm and got the wood ready. I sharpened a saw.

Saturday the 24th
Moved hay from the west mow into the east mow. Heinrich and Hinrich hauled wood home. To A.H. Welles for Taalke's dress 0.95, a spool of thread 0.04, Harry's overall 0.39; total 1.38. To Keller for coffee 0.12, washing soda 0.10; total 0.22.

Sunday the 25th
Beautiful weather. Brbr. Br. Marten was there.

Monday the 26th
Thaw. Heinrich left. Farmer's Institute.

Tuesday the 27th
Thaw. Farmer's Institute. To Ward for 2 lantern globes 0.20. To Dr. McGurk 0.50 for Farmer's Institute membership and for sending Mini's letter with picture to Germany.

Wednesday the 28th
Thaw. Lengthened the pump. Bolts from the sled from the shoe. Cut some firewood.

Thursday the 29th
Thaw. To Schauer for bolts for the sled 0.05. To Keller for matches 0.05, needles 0.05; total 0.10. Fixed the sled and the door chain in the barn. Fixed the one heifer's kramen [?]. The cows were outside in the afternoon. Sawed wood.

Friday the 30th
Thaw. Sawed wood. Went to visit Nelson Nicolson.

Saturday the 31st
Thaw. Moved hay from the west mow into the east mow. Went to cheese meeting 1.00. To Ward for a pocketknife 0.25. Went to visit Harten.

[188]   **February 1903**

Norn 5.72, M.M.&M. Co. 79.76, Welles 11.48, Francis & McRae 10.20, N.B. Weaver 25.54, Marfileus 1.37, Schoerpff 1.00, Dr. Grigg 6.75, Keller 27.00, R. Forsyth 4.14, Gottenmyer 8.60, Ward 0.45, Taalke 8.78—D. Mills 1.00, school 0.75, cheese factory 1.00

Sunday the 1st
As of 1 February 1903:
Outstanding receipts 2.75
Debts 190.79
Cash on hand 0.00

Monday the 2nd
Raw, wet, hail. To Welles for Emma's rubbers 0.50. Wrote letters and sent them to E. Brouwer, Clara City, Minnesota; Mrs. J. E. Swalne, Harper Illinois; Mrs. L. Bruns, Dumont, Cutler Co. Iowa. In the evening to Br. Marten's meeting. H. 1d.

Tuesday the 3rd
Good weather. Wilson came to visit in the forenoon; Nehls in the afternoon. Fixed the lock on the chest and repaired the hay racks. To Keller for syrup 0.30, sugar 0.25, tea 0.15; total 0.70. H. 1d.

Wednesday the 4th
Very raw. Werner [?] Dankert visited and brought 10.00 for Johannes. H. 1d. In the afternoon lowered the bridge between the west and east hay mows.

Thursday the 5th
Very nice weather. Went to visit James Harten. Sawed some wood.

Friday the 6th
Nice. Came into the barn to find Mollie calving. She gave birth to a bull calf.

Saturday the 7th
Clear and very cold. To Welles yesterday for 2 spools of thread 0.05. To Forsyth for a comb 0.05. H. 1d.

Sunday the 8th
Very raw, snow. To Marfileus for licorice 0.25.

[189]   **February 1903**

Monday the 9th
Beautiful weather. Went to visit Hartens. Sawed in the afternoon and fixed a collar. H. 1d.

Tuesday the 10th
Got the cart from Schauer on Saturday. It cost 0.30. To Keller for a lamp chimney 0.05. Went to bed. H. 1d.

Wednesday the 11th
Snow. Received a letter from Johannes and answered it. In the afternoon visited the school with Dankert, 0.25. To Keller for a lamp chimney 0.05, washing soda 0.01 [0.10?]; total 0.15.

Thursday the 12th
Nice, thaw. To Francis & McRae for soap 0.25, syrup 0.30, sugar 0.50, oatmeal 0.25, apples 0.25, matches 0.05, baking powder 0.10, lamp wick #20 0.01, raisins 0.25, ginger 0.05, cinnamon 0.05, prunes 0.25; total 2.31. H. 1d. Mrs. Karl Wübbena sent for Taalke because she had injured herself on the head with an ax. H. 1d.

Friday the 13th
Good weather. Studied Dr. Charles' Recipe Book regarding Mini's rash and eye disease. H. 1d.

Saturday the 14th
Cold. Moved hay from the west mow into the east mow. Sawed wood in the afternoon. H. 1d. To Welles for Mini's stockings 0.10.

Sunday the 15th
Thaw. Brbr. Visiting pastor from Pinconning.

Monday the 16th
Very cold, the coldest day so far this winter. Lice on French, Blossom, Cherry and Katie; [rubbed] them with petroleum. Went to see Gammon after school about weights, measures etc.

[190] **February 1903**

Tuesday the 17th
Very cold. To Welles for papa's overall 0.50, thread 0.10; total 0.60. To Keller for tea 0.25. Went to bed because of pain in my chest and side. H. 1d.

Wednesday the 18th
Very cold. Stayed inside because of the cold. Fixed the cart. H. 1d. From Hinrich 9.00 (pay up to the 14th).

Thursday the 19th
Cold. To Keller for sprays 0.30, kerosene 0.55, salt 0.20; total 1.05. For flour to Francis & McRae 2.30. Filled out half of the crop report for the U.S. government at S. Hayes'. To R.M. Forsyth yesterday for Mini's medicine 0.65. H. 1d.

Friday the 20th
Very cold. For Hinrich's jacket and pants 5.25, Taalke's skirt 3.50; total 8.75. Sorted beans for seed. H. 1d.

Saturday the 21st
Cold. Moved hay from the west mow into the east mow. That emptied the mow. To Welles for exchanging Hinrich's shirt 0.25 for Taalke's skirt 0.50; total 0.75. Cleaned the calf pen. H. 1d.

Sunday the 22nd
Washington's birthday. Put hot stones on the left side of my chest all day; the pain was less. In the evening Blossom gave birth to a heifer calf.

Monday the 23rd
Thaw. To Francis & McRae 60 lbs. of lard 7.50. To McGurk 1.00 for oats, a bushel cost 0.42, bought it at the elevator. H. 1d. Sorted beans for seed. Telfer came to visit.

Tuesday the 24th
Nice weather. Sorted beans for seed and shelled corn. To Welles for Hinrich's shoes 1.50, for material to make Emma's apron 0.05; total 1.55. H. 1d.

[191] **February 1903**

Wednesday the 25th
Good weather. Cleaned the pig pen and fixed the calf stall. To Keller for washing soda 0.15. H. 1d.

Thursday the 26th
Good weather. Mrs. Barness came to visit. To Keller for syrup 0.30, sugar 0.25, pepper 0.05; total 0.60. Shelled corn. H. 1d.

Friday the 27th
Thaw, snow and rain. Shelled corn. Nehls came to visit. H. 1d.

Saturday the 28th
Thaw till 4:00 P.M. then it turned freezing. Cleared off the threshing floor, took the bridge away and cleaned the calf pen. H. 1d.

The month is at an end,
But not the Love of God.

[192]   **March 1903**

Sunday the 1st
Violent storm. In bed with a headache. In several places the water was over the road so that it was hard to get to Standish.
Norn 5.72, M.M.&M. Co. 79.76, Welles 15.06, Francis & McRae 22.31, N.B. Weaver 25.54, Marfileus 1.62, Schauer 0.30, Schoerpff 1.00, Dr. Grigg 6.75, Keller 29.95, R. Forsyth 4.94, Gottenmyer 8.60, Ward 0.45, Taalke 8.78, McGurk 1.00—D. Mills 1.00, school 1.25, cheese factory 1.00.
As of 1 March 1903:
Outstanding receipts 3.25
Debts 211.78
Cash on hand 0.00

Monday the 2nd
Storm during the forenoon; more able to work during the afternoon. Sawed wood. Friedrich at home. H. 1d.

Tuesday the 3rd
Good weather. Sawed wood. H. 1d.

Wednesday the 4th
Good weather. Sawed wood. H. 1d.

Thursday the 5th
Snow during the night then thaw. Received 9.00 from Hinrich; paid McGurk 1.00 (borrowed on February 23rd) and 0.50 (borrowed on January 27th). Paid Keller 3.00 (Keller told me the balance was 24.31 and also gave me a credit book). For Mini's medicine 0.65. For middlings 0.38, tea 0.30, yeast cake 0.04, baking powder 0.10, sugar 0.50, molasses 0.10, syrup 0.35, broom 0.35; total 2.04. Friedrich 0.10, thread 0.20 to Taalke 1.51 for chil-

dren's clothing. The balance with Keller worked out 2.64 in our favor; so much less that we owe.

[193] **March 1903**

Thursday the 5th
Thaw, very unpleasant weather. H. 1d.

Friday the 6th
Very heavy frost during the night; thaw during the afternoon. Sawed wood. H. 1d.

Saturday the 7th
Severe storm with rain during the forenoon. In bed with a headache and with pains in the chest and shoulders. Rain all day. H. 7 hours.

Sunday the 8th
Good weather. Very high water. Brbr. Mini's birthday. She got a copper tea kettle from Mr. Henderson.

Monday the 9th
Nice day. Went to Witts to buy a cow. Sawed wood. H. 1d.

Tuesday the 10th
Overcast and wet. Cleaned the calf pen, drained the pig yard and also cleaned the pig pen. Paid Schauer 0.20 to fix two cow bells. H. 1d.

Wednesday the 11th
Good weather. To Witts to buy a cow. Sawed and split wood.

Thursday the 12th
Beautiful weather. Sawed and split wood. H. 1d.

Friday the 13th
Beautiful weather. Sawed and split wood. H. 1d. Johannes came home in the evening.

Saturday the 14th
Good weather but overcast. In bed. H. 1d.

Sunday the 15th
Good weather. Brbr. Johnson and Matthews were here in the forenoon.

Monday the 16th
Nice weather. Johannes and Friedrich put up wire on the fence between the boards on the east half around the road. H. 9 hours. During the following night Rothie gave birth to a heifer calf.

[194]   **March 1903**

Tuesday the 17th
Good weather. Sawed wood. H. 1d.

Wednesday the 18th
Thunderstorms, wet and rainy. Fixed shoes and sawed wood. H. 1d.

Thursday the 19th
Good weather. To Keller for syrup 0.25, sugar 0.50, oatmeal 0.25, rice 0.25, seleratus 0.07, yeast cake 0.04, Best on Record flour 2.00, tea 0.40; total 4.06. To Blumenthal for overalls 0.75. To Ward for 2 pails @ 0.35 = 0.70. The roads were in miserable condition for traveling. Paid the express company 0.25 for Johannes; borrowed it from Webber. H. 1d.

Friday the 20th
Stormy. Received 8.62 from Hinrich then paid Keller 4.06 and 2.00 toward the debt. Paid Wards 0.70 for the parts bought yesterday and 0.45 towards the debt. Paid 0.60 for middlings and 0.05 for matches. Paid Webber back the 0.25 borrowed yesterday and received the same from Johannes. H. 1d.

Saturday the 21st
Nice weather. Johannes and Friedrich dug a ditch through the barnyard. Cleaned the calf pen. Cherry gave birth to a bull calf. H. 1d. Sold the calf to Gammon, see April 14, '03.

Sunday the 22nd
Good weather. Brbr.

Monday the 23rd
Overcast and wet. Dug the ditch in the barnyard longer and deeper. H. 6 hours.

Tuesday the 24th
During the night and all day a hurricane-like storm. Johannes fixed his gate and brought the ax and the saw home. Johannes had left yesterday. In bed; Friedrich as well. Delivered to Gammon the calf born Saturday. H. 7 hours. Very raw, cold weather.

[195]   **March 1903**

Wednesday the 25th
Good weather. To Gottenmyer for bologna 0.10. Nominated following the caucus as a member of the board of review. Hinrich at home.

Thursday the 26th
Good weather. Hinrich and Friedrich sawed over at Johannes' place. I cleared.

Friday the 27th
Nice weather. Hinrich and Friedrich sawed over at Johannes' place. I cleared.

Saturday the 28th
Nice weather. Hinrich and Friedrich sawed over at Johannes' place. I cleared. Gammon helped castrate four animals while they stood. Afterward I did the same to our two yearling bulls which still hadn't been fixed. They were born respectively on the 4th of April and the 25th of March, 1902. Also bred the cow Mollie to Gammon's bull today.

Sunday the 29th
Nice weather. Brbr. Bred Blossom to Gammon's bull, 0.50.

Monday the 30th
Nice weather. Piled up the stumps burned last fall. Hinrich worked 9 hours for William Woods; paid.

Tuesday the 31st
Nice weather. Piled up stumps burned last fall. H. 8 hours.
The month is at an end,
But not the Love of God.
Thanks be to God for He is good,
And His goodness lasts for ever.

[196] April 1903

Norn, 5.72, M. Cooperage Co. 79.76, Welles 15.06, Francis & McRae 22.31, N.B. Weaver 25.54, Marfileus 1.62, Schauer 0.50, Schoerpff 1.00, Dr. Grigg 6.75, Keller 22.31, R. Forsyth 4.94, Gottenmyer 8.70, Taalke 8.78— D. Mills 1.00, school 1.25, cheese factory 1.00
As of 1 April 1903:
Outstanding receipts 3.25
Debts 202.99
Cash on hand 0.00

Wednesday the 1st
Nice weather. Hauled manure. H. 1d. During the following night violent thunderstorms and rain.

Thursday the 2nd
Received 5.20 from Hinrich. To Mini for travel money 2.50. For groceries: syrup 0.30, sugar 0.50, baking powder 0.10, soap 0.25, tea 0.30, flour 0.60, oatmeal 0.25, kerosene 0.55, lemon extract 0.20; total 3.05. Paid 2.50; balance of 0.55 owed to Keller. H. 6 hours.

Friday the 3rd
Very raw and cold. Hauled manure. H. 1d. Mini to the conference in Saginaw.

Saturday the 4th
Very cold. Hauled manure. H. 1d. It should be noted that we owe Gammon 0.50 since March 29th; the debt is not included in the April 1st list.

Sunday the 5th
Nice. Conference in Saginaw. No meeting in Standish. Lost my glasses. The old sow died.

Monday the 6th
Nice. Election day. For 20 bu. H [written above the line] Mich. Wonder oats 13.00, 1 bu. recleaned aloike clover 9.00, 1 bu recleaned timothy 2.50, 1 bu. throughbred [sic] white Dent corn 1.50; total 26.00. Borrowed 28.00 from Nehls against a mortgage on Blossom and Cherry at six

[197]   **April 1903**

percent per year over twelve months, i.e. till April 6th, 1904. This makes the debt to Nehls 28.00 principal plus 1.68 interest for a total of 29.68. At the same time sent away and ordered for Schulz 1 bu. recleaned timothy 2.50, 1 bu. crimson clover seed 4.00; total 6.50 or 32.50 all together. For postage 0.02, for postal order 0.15; total 0.17. Paid 0.50 to have the mortgage written by S. Hayes. Schulz owes 0.06 as his share of the cost of sending the money.

Tuesday the 7th
Severe storm. Hauled manure. H. 6 hours. In the evening the little sow gave birth to a litter of eight shoats of which four died during the night. At

Wednesday the 8th
four o'clock in the morning she wanted to eat one more and killed it with her teeth. Took the remaining three shoats into the kitchen and put them in a boiler. Got 0.60 back from Mini. Hauled manure. H. 1d.

Thursday the 9th
Violent storm. Maundy Thursday. Hauled manure. H. 1d. During the night the three shoats died which we had wanted to raise without their mother.

Friday the 10th
Good weather. Good Friday. Papa's birthday. Congratulated by all the children. Hauled manure. Got word from the Hammond Seed Co. of the order sent on the 6th. The order has the number 43339 in case we would want to write to Bay City regarding it. To Francis & McRae for flour 2.30, a lamp chimney 0.05, molasses 0.10; total 2.45. H. 1d. To Henderson for five bandages 1.00.

[198]   **April 1903**

Saturday the 11th
Rain all day. Hauled one load of manure. H. 6 hours.

Sunday the 12th
Easter. Brbr. Good weather.

Monday the 13th
Heavy rain all day. About noon the cow Bessie gave birth to a bull calf. Very raw and cold. H. 4 hours. To Francis & McRae for middlings 0.19.

Tuesday the 14th
Heavy rains and storm all day. Stayed in bed. Got a heifer calf from Gammon for the one from Cherry he got on March 31st. This one was born on Good Friday, April 10th. H. 5 hours. To Francis & McRae for syrup 0.30, sugar 0.50, yeast cakes 0.08, tea 0.30, oatmeal 0.25, starch 0.10; total 1.53. Heinrich came home in the evening.

Wednesday the 15th
Overcast. Drained. Heinrich paid the 5.72 debt to Norn. H. 1d.

Thursday the 16th
Windy in the morning. At 6:00 the cow Rubie gave birth to a bull calf. Received 6.59 from Hinrich. To Hinrich for the Social Gleaner 0.75. For Emma's shoes 1.50, Hinrich's cap 0.50, linseed meal 2.00, oats 1.14, sugar 0.25, 6 milk pails 0.50; total 6.59. H. 1d.

Friday the 17th
Nice weather. Drained. Johannes came home during the morning. H. 1d.

Saturday the 18th
Johannes' birthday. Wished him luck. Got the shipping bill for the order of the 6th. Pulled two stumps, piled them up and worked on some other stumps. H. 1d.

Sunday the 19th
Nice weather. Brbr.

[199]   April 1903

Monday the 20th
Nice weather. Hauled manure and sand to the barn yard. H. 6 hours. To Francis & McRae for 10 lbs. middlings 0.13.

Tuesday the 21st
Nice weather. Hauled manure and sand to the barn yard. H. 1d.

Wednesday the 22nd
Very cold. Picked up 8 bags of oats and 2 bags of seed from the depot. To Keller for oats 1.00, 100 lbs. of flour 2.30, 2 lemons 0.05; total 3.35. To Francis & McRae for 55 lbs. of corn flour 0.77. H. 1d. Plowed.

Thursday the 23rd
Cold. Planted 22 grapevines with D.C. Henderson's help (¼ day) and also laid out the orchard. Johannes plowed. H. 1d.

Friday the 24th
Raw, rainy in the afternoon. Set posts among the vines. Cut fence posts. H. 6 hours.

Saturday the 25th
Nice. Johannes plowed. Hauled fence posts for the orchard and set some of them. H. 6 hours.

Sunday the 26th
Nice weather. In bed. The calf that was born on April 13th died. In the evening Fun gave birth to a bull calf.

Monday the 27th
Nice weather. Johannes plowed. I pounded in fence posts and with Mr. Henderson's help planted 8 fruit trees, the rest of the vines and set posts by each of them. H. 1d.

Tuesday the 28th
Nice and warm. Johannes plowed. Planted four more fruit trees. Got the 12 trees from Henderson and owe him 2.40 for them. Cut fence posts to length and cleaned the rest of the beans; had about ½ bu. H. 1d.

[200]   April 1903

Wednesday the 29th
Strong wind from the west, warm. Harrowed and worked on the orchard fence. H. 1d.

Thursday the 30th
Raw and cold, overcast and rainy. Received 7.25 from Hinrich and for butter 0.83; total 8.08. For 4 bu. oats 2.00, syrup 0.30, oatmeal 0.25, sugar 0.50, soap 0.25, molasses 0.10, washing soda 0.10; total 3.75. Paid 2.00 toward the debt with Keller. Paid 0.25 for freight on the clover seed, see the order of April 6th. Paid 0.30 for a hoe, 0.15 for spikes; total 0.45. Paid 0.50 for Hinrich's overall, for a collar 0.25. Cash to Taalke 0.37, cash on hand 0.50; total 1.63. Katie gave birth to a heifer calf. H. 1d.

[201]   May 1903

Mich. Cooperage Co. 79.76, Welles 15.06, Francis & McRae 27.54, Henderson 2.40, N.B. Weaver 25.54, Marfileus 1.62, A. Schauer 0.50, Schoerpff 1.00, Dr. Grigg 6.75, Keller 24.21, R. Forsyth 4.94, Gammon 0.50, Gottenmyer 8.70, Taalke 8.78, Nehls 29.68—D. Mills 1.00, school 1.25, cheese factory 1.00.
As of 1 May 1903:
Outstanding receipts 3.25
Debts 236.82
Cash on hand 0.00

Friday the 1st
Good weather but very cold. A hard freeze during the night. Johannes finished fencing in the orchard. I borrowed 1.75 from Taalke for clothes. H. 1d.

Saturday the 2nd
Good weather. Johannes worked on his own place with Friedrich. Traded Fanny off for a watch. Johannes castrated three bulls. I harrowed. Topsy was pretty tired in the evening.

Sunday the 3rd
Castrated four of Johannes' bulls last evening. Rain during the night and today. Kept the Sabbath.

Monday the 4th
Good weather. The ground was pretty wet. I sowed the 20 bu. of oats, but it wasn't enough so borrowed another 6 bu. @ 0.55, total of 3.30, from Francis & McRae. From Cassidy a bolt and an iron plate 0.15. To N.B. Weaver for 4 bolts 01.0 [0.10?]. H. 1d.

Tuesday the 5th
Good weather. Sowed 4 bu. to the 20 already sowed. Covered as much as possible with the harrow, about 6 acres in both days. Topsy couldn't go on;

toward evening got Karl's horse to help out. Sowed all together 24 bu. of oats. H. 1d. Mixed 2 parts of timothy to 1 part clover.

[202]   May 1903

Wednesday the 6th
Good weather. Tried to harrow with Karl's horse, but it refused to go on after a short time. In the afternoon I gathered up trash wood from the fields with the wagon. Johannes worked on his own place. H. 1d.

Thursday the 7th
Very cold during the night. Rothie bred to Sonomit's bull 0.75. Harrowed. Johannes worked on his own place. H. 1d. Got Karl's horse to help out.

Friday the 8th
Cold during the night, a hard freeze. Harrowed. Johannes worked on his own place. H. 1d. Traded butter for groceries worth 1.14. Borrowed Karl's horse and returned it in the evening.

Saturday the 9th
Good weather. Finished harrowing in the oats which Johannes had oversown with grass and clover seed. Johannes also plowed the orchard and part of the vegetable garden. Dug ditch through the oats and leveled a bit. Friedrich hunted for 3 lost yearlings but couldn't find them. Emma was sick and Hinrich stayed home as well because of a boil on his neck. It seemed that Katie was bully.

Sunday the 10th
Good weather. Brbr. To Alfred Embury for carrot seed 0.35. Still haven't found the yearlings.

Monday the 11th
Beautiful warm weather. Found the yearlings. Harrowed and leveled off the furrows we had plowed. Planted some potatoes. H. 1d.

Tuesday the 12th
Received 9.00 from Hinrich and paid out 0.75 to Kroske, 0.25 to him himself, 1.75 to Taalke (see May 1st) and for shirts 0.25; total 3.00. Balance due Francis & McRae of 1.92: for 5 bu. oats 2.50, for 2 barrels of salt 2.00, for flour 2.30, tea 0.30, cornmeal 0.32, oats 0.25, vinegar 0.20, matches 0.05; total 7.92. Paid 6.00 of this to leave a balance due of 1.92. To

[203]   May 1903

Schauer for bolts for the harrow 0.05. Harrowed. Johannes planted some beans and potatoes and sowed some carrot seed. Fun bred to Gammon's bull 0.50. H. 1d.

Wednesday the 13th
Good weather. Harrowed, three fourths of the time with Karl's horse. Johannes cultivated. H. 1d. Sold butter for 0.85 and bought sugar 0.25, a thimble 0.05, a comb 0.15, Fred's hat 0.25, Ella's hat 0.30, Wilhelm's hat 0.25; total 1.14 [sic]. Paid the balance with the due bill from the 8th of May.

Thursday the 14th
Good weather but cool. Harrowed, leveled the plowed out furrows. H. 1d. Johannes worked for Karl during the afternoon.

Friday the 15th
Good weather. M. 100. Cool. Harrowed. Johannes worked on his own place. H. 1d.

Saturday the 16th
M. 100. Harrowed. Johannes cleared with Friedrich, Emma and Wilhelm. For clover seed 1.80. Paid Schauer's debt of 0.55 as well as washtax [?] 0.25, bell 0.10, total 0.90. Sold butter for 1.10 and bought syrup 0.30, sugar 0.50, needles 0.05, twine 0.16, stockings 0.15; total 1.16, with Schauer's things all together 2.06 leaving a remainder of 0.84 cash in hand. H. 1d. H. 6 days this week.

Sunday the 17th
Good weather. Brbr. Warm.

Monday the 18th
M. 123. Harrowed. Johannes and Friedrich worked at Johannes' place. H. 1d.

Tuesday the 19th
M. 123. Harrowed during the forenoon. Johannes worked on his own place. Around noon a severe thunderstorm with rain. Slept during the afternoon. H. 1d.

Wednesday the 20th
M. 126. Cleared, Johannes and I. H. 1d.

Thursday the 21st
M. 131. Ascension Day. Hot. Katie bred to Gammon's bull. 0.40. H. 1d. Harrowed. Johannes planted beans etc. for ½ day. To Nehls for Hinrich's shoes 1.50.

[204]   May 1903

Friday the 22nd
M. 122. Harrowed. The fence between us and Schulz' and also between us and Karl caught fire. Put it out as best we could. H. 1d.

Saturday the 23rd
M. 122. Very cold during the night and all day. Harrowed a while. Fixed the fence between us and Karl. Marked some for corn planting but was prevented from continuing by a thunderstorm and rain. Picked out seed potatoes. H. 1d.

Sunday the 24th
Beautiful weather but cool. Brbr.

Monday the 25th
M. 124. Nice weather. Rothie bred again to Gammon's bull 0.50. To Keller for sugar, 0.25, syrup 0.30, sal soda 0.10, snaps 0.25, tea 0.25, oatmeal 0.25, oil 0.55, seeds 0.05, molasses 0.10; total 2.10. From Welles for cheese cloth 0.24. Marked fields. Johannes worked on his own place. Bessie covered by an unknown bull. H. 1d.

Tuesday the 26th
M. 126. Threatening weather. Marked fields for corn and potatoes and planted some corn. Johannes and Ella planted some more beans. Got 12 bu. of potatoes ready for planting. H. ¾ d. Had a violent thunderstorm with rain during the afternoon.

Wednesday the 27th
M. 133. Threatening weather. Planted corn and potatoes. Johannes worked on his own place.. H. 1d.

Thursday the 28th
M. 133. Unpleasant weather. A violent storm during the night. Friedrich, Wilhelm and I planted corn; the girls had gone to the school to practice for tomorrow's entertainment. Johannes worked on his own place. H. 1d.

Friday the 29th
M. 123. Raw and unpleasant. Hinrich at home. Planted

[205]   May 1903

potatoes during the afternoon. Received 9.00 from Hinrich. Paid on debt to Welles 1.50, to Taalke 2.00, to Keller 2.10 (debt, see May 25) and bought oats 1.00, corn flour 0.25, cornmeal for family use 0.40, flour 2.30, a hoe

0.35, 5 lbs. of nails 0.15; total 10.05. Balance of 1.00 owed to Keller. To Daugharty and Beaton for a hoe 0.35. For packing up the books after school etc. with Dankert 1.00. Johannes went to Bay City to the R.R. show. H. at home.

Saturday the 30th
M. 131. Cold. Planted corn. Johannes worked on his own place. H. at home.

Sunday the 31st
Pentecost. Raw and cold.
Delivered 1717 lbs. of milk by my scale in the month of May; 1719 according to the factory. Received 9.45 on June 24th.

[206]   [This page is blank.]
[207]   [This page is blank.]

[208]   **June 1903**

Mich. Cooperage Co. 79.76, Welles 15.30, Francis & McRae 32.60, Henderson 2.40, N.B. Weaver 25.64, Marfileus 1.62, Schoerpff 1.00, Dr. Grigg 6.75, Keller 25.21, R. Forsyth 4.94, Gammon 2.00, Gottenmyer 8.70. Nehls 29,68, Daugharty & Beaton 0.35, Sonomit 0.75, Taalke 8.78—D. Mills 1.00, cheese factory 1.00, school 2.25.
As of 1 June 1903:
Outstanding receipts 4.25
Debts 245.48
Cash on hand 0.00

Monday the 1st
M. 139. Good weather. Planted corn. Johannes worked on his own place. To Welles for Hinrich 2 shirts @ 0.39; total 0.78. H. 1d.

Tuesday the 2nd
M. 131. Beautiful weather. Planted corn. Johannes worked on his own place. H. 1d. To Gottenmyer for meal 0.30, to Marfileus for 1 lb. of Paris green 0.30.

Wednesday the 3rd
M. 131. Hot. Finished with the corn planting. Johannes worked on his own place. To Marfileus for a second pound of Paris green 0.30. To Keller for oatmeal 0.25, sugar 0.25, cornmeal 0.25; total 0.75. H. 1d.

Thursday the 4th
M. 131. Warm. Hoed and planted beans. H. 1d. Johannes worked on his own place.

Friday the 5th
M. 142. Warm. Hoed and spaded getting ready to plant cabbage. Cleaned up the fruit trees. Johannes worked on his own place. H. 1d. French gave birth to a bull calf.

Saturday the 6th
M. 142. Warm. Hoed and set out 40 cabbage plants. Johannes worked on his own place. H. 1d.

Sunday the 7th
Trinity Sunday. Kept the Sabbath. Brbr.

[209]   **June 1903**

Monday the 8th
Hinrich's birthday. Hot. Hoed. M. 126. Johannes worked on his own place. H. 1d. Delivered 3 bu. of potatoes to Armstrong @ 0.35 = 1.05 to be applied toward hauling the milk (1.50 per month).

Tuesday the 9th
Hot. Cultivated. M. 139. Johannes worked on his own place. H. 1d. Yesterday a young sow pig from Demond and another one from John Dobson; both 4 weeks old and born on April 10th. To Francis & McRae for sugar 0.25. Fun was bully.

Wednesday the 10th
M. 133. In the morning overcast and cold, later sunny and warm. Received 7.12 from Hinrich. For groceries = lantern chimney 0.10, 93 lbs. feed 1.20, 3 lbs. fine corn meal 0.62, soap 0.25, sugar 0.50, beans 0.25, baking powder 0.15, tea 0.30, matches 0.05, yeast cakes 0.10, salt 0.05, rice 0.30, oatmeal 0.25; total 4.02. Beef shank 0.40; total 4.42. To Gottenmyer's debt from June 2nd 0.30; grand total 4.72, leaves 2.40. Rothie died. Katie bred to Gammon's bull. H. 1d. To Taalke 0.75 for Friedrich's shirts, leaves 1.65.

Thursday the 11th
M. 144. Cold. Skinned Rothie. Cultivated and hoed. Mini's shoes 0.25, Taalke's pickles 0.10, Hinrich's overall 0.50; total 1.10, leaves 1.30. H. 1d. Paid Gottenmyer with the hide 1.85.

Friday the 12th
M. 134. N.B. There was an oversight yesterday involving Gottenmyer: instead of 1.85 it should have been 1.70; this is 0.15 less, so the debt is that much greater. Johannes worked on his own place. Cultivated and hoed. H. 9 hours.

Saturday the 13th
M. 144. Hinrich's overall 0.50, leaves 0.60. To Keller for 2 bu. of oats 1.00. Cultivated till noon. Rain during the afternoon and also the following night. H. 1d. Johannes worked on his own place. Picked up the cellar and cleaned the barn. Friedrich and Emma hoed beans in the afternoon.

Sunday the 14th
Rain till noon. Kept the Sabbath.

Monday the 15th
M. 136. Worked on the road. The children replanted corn. Johannes worked on his own place. H. 1d.

Tuesday the 16th
M. 141. Cold and warm, threatening storm, calm and windy. Toward evening a cold wind and stormy. Cultivated. Johannes worked on his own place. Friedrich weeded carrots. Emma went to Brocons. H. 1d. For Friedrich's shirt 0.25, for meat 0.40, leaves 0.00.

Wednesday the 17th
M. 147. Changeable weather: warm and cold, calm and windy. Cultivated. Johannes worked on his own place. Friedrich weeded carrots. Emma sick. H. ¼d.

Thursday the 18th
M. 147. To Marfileus for licorice 0.25 on Saturday the 13th. Changeable, stormy. Felt like rain in the afternoon. Cultivated. Johannes worked on his own place. Emma better. She and Friedrich weeded carrots. H. 8 hours. Hinrich's work consisted of loading piles. His daily wage for this was higher. To Francis & McRae for a lamp chimney 0.05.

Friday the 19th
M.M.&M. Co. . 151. to Keller for 100 lbs. bread flour 2.35, 4 lbs. washing soda 0.10, beans 0.25, Lincoln rolled oats 0.25; total 2.95. Very foggy during the morning. Cultivated and weeded. Johannes worked on his own place. H. 1 hour. Good weather.

Saturday the 20th
M. 140. To N.B. Weaver for shoe tacks 0.05. In the morning overcast, felt like rain. Cultivated. Friedrich and Emma weeded. H. 0d. H. didn't work.

Sunday the 21st
M. 120. To Keller for tea 0.30, sugar 0.25; total 0.55. Kept the Sabbath. Brbr.

[211]   **June 1903**

Monday the 22nd
M. 154. Cultivated till 10:00 then had to quit because of rain. Went to Dankert and Gammon with bills from Forsyth and Weaver 0.50. Johannes worked on his own place. H. 1d. Got 102 cabbage plants from Gammon.

Tuesday the 23rd
M. 137. Rained the entire day. Drained some. H. ¼d. Johannes worked on his own place.

Wednesday the 24th
M. 147. Overcast and wet. For milk in May 1719 lbs. @ 0.55 = 9.45. From that paid M. & Coop. Co. 3.45. Received 6.00 for Hinrich 6.12 [sic]. From that paid Keller 3.50 toward the debt and spent 0.50 for Lincoln oatmeal, 0.50 for rice, 0.50 for sugar, 0.35 for tea, 0.10 for pepper and 0.50 for baking powder; total 2.45. Dry in the afternoon; set out 100 cabbage plants. H. 1d. For meat 0.40. Johannes worked on his own place.

Thursday the 25th
M. 138. Beautiful weather. Drilled corn. Cultivated during the afternoon. Friedrich and Emma weeded carrots. H. 1d. Johannes worked on his own place. Gave Taalke 1.00 yesterday for shoes.

Friday the 26th
M. 152. Beautiful weather. Cultivated. Johannes worked on his own place. For oats 1.00. H. 1d.

Saturday the 27th
M. 138. Beautiful weather. Cultivated. Went to graduating exercises yesterday evening. Borrowed a cultivator from Proulx and worked with two cultivators. H. 1d.

Sunday the 28th
Hot. Brbr. Fun bred to Gammon's bull.

Monday the 29th
M. 154. Hot. Cultivated. Johannes worked on his own place. H. 1d. Went to school board meeting in the evening, 0.50. Received 4.50 from the school district.

Tuesday the 30th
M. 120. Good weather. Cultivated. To Taalke 0.50, to Hinrich for shoes 1.75, meat 0.50; total 2.75.

Milk in June, 3634 lbs.; the Co. had 3587, a difference of 47 lbs., see July 18th. H. 1d.

[212]   July 1903

Mich. Cooperage Co. 76.31, Welles 16.08, Francis & McRae 32.90, Henderson 2.40, N.B. Weaver 25.69, Marfileus 2.47, Schoerpff 1.00, Dr. Grigg 6.75, Keller 26.96, R. Forsyth 5.45, Gammon 2.00, Gottenmyer 7.00, Nehls 29.68, Taalke 8.78—D. Mills 1.00, cheese factory 1.00
As of 1 July 1903:
Outstanding receipts 2.00
Debts 243.47
Cash on hand 0.00

Wednesday the 1st
M. 123. Cultivated and weeded. Johannes worked on his own place. Hot. Violent storm. H. 1d.

Thursday the 2nd
M. 123. Cultivated and weeded. Johannes worked on his own place. Hot. H. 1d.

Friday the 3rd
M. 123. To Francis & McRae for tea 0.35, beans 0.50, rice 0.50, soap 0.25, flour 2.50, sugar 0.50; total 4.60. To N.B. Weaver for smooth wire 0.70, staples 0.06, oil 0.15; total 0.91. Posted notices about the annual school meeting (already paid). Threatening weather. Cultivated during the afternoon. Johannes worked on his own place. Hinrich at home.

Saturday the 4th
M. 148. Hot. Celebrated the Declaration of Independence. Slept all day. To Daugharty & Beaton for an oilcan 0.15. To R. Forsyth for paper and envelopes 0.20. Hinrich at home.

Sunday the 5th
Hot. Brbr.

Monday the 6th
M. 48 [sic]. Hot. Johannes mowed. Hoed and weeded. H. 1d.

Tuesday the 7th
M. 134. Hot. Johannes mowed. Raked, stacked and hauled two loads of hay in. H. 1d.

[213]   July 1903

Wednesday the 8th
M. 134. Hot. Hauled in 3 loads of hay. H. 1d. Total of 5 loads of hay in the barn.

Thursday the 9th
M. 128. Hot. Received 7.86 from Hinrich and paid Francis & McRae 4.60 on the debt and for oats 0.79, cornmeal 0.34, starch 0.10; total 1.23. For thread 0.26. To Gottenmyer for 65 lbs. of lard 6.30. Paid Gottenmyer 1.00. For meat 0.35, snap hooks 0.10. H. 1d.

Friday the 10th
M. 128. Hot. Cultivated. Johannes worked on his own place. H. 1d. To R. M. Forsyth for a comb 0.15.

Saturday the 11th
M. 118. Hot. Cultivated. Johannes worked on his own place. To Keller for yeast cake 0.04. H. 1d. For oatmeal 0.25.

Sunday the 12th
Nice warm day. Brbr.

Monday the 13th
M. 120. Cool, overcast. Johannes cut hay in the forenoon. Made a trough in the afternoon. To a school meeting in the evening. I mowed around the stumps.

Tuesday the 14th
M. 134. Cool and overcast. Johannes cut grass and then made hay. Hauled 3 loads home which makes a total of 8 loads. To Keller yesterday for sal soda 0.10, sugar 0.50, beans 0.25, needles 0.05; total 0.90. H. 1d.

Wednesday the 15th
M. 130. Cool and clear. Johannes cut hay. Brought in 7 loads which makes 15 loads all together of very good hay. H. 1d. To Francis & McRae for 1 lb. tea 0.25.

Thursday the 16th
M. 144. Beautiful, warm day. Johannes cut hay then raked and hauled in 3 loads of hay for a total of 18 loads. Karl helped us in the afternoon. H. 1d.

Friday the 17th
M. 131. Johannes raked and cut the last of the hay. Karl helped us with his horse. Brought in 8 loads of hay for a total of 26 loads. H. 1d.

[214]   **July 1903**

Saturday the 18th
M. 139. School board meeting yesterday evening about painting the school
and hiring a teacher, 0.50. For 3587 lbs. of milk in June received 19.73 and
paid out on the debts to Mich. Coop. Co. 15.00. For Mini's things 0.10,
papa's picture 1.75, corn flour 0.25; total 2.10. Turnip seed 0.10. To Daugharty & Beaton for an oil can 0.15 from the 4th of July; To Armstrong for
hauling the milk 1.50. Raked and hauled in 4 loads of hay for a total of 30
loads. Carl helped out for ½ day. H. 1d.

Sunday the 19th
To Welles the previous evening for 2 spools of thread 0.08. Today to
Marfileus 0.25 against the debt. Gave Taalke 0.40 for the dentist. Brbr. Good
weather.

Monday the 20th
M. 147. Nice weather but seemed like it might storm. Johannes helped Karl
with the horses. Friedrich and Emma went looking for the colt, came home
about 2:30 P.M. and then weeded and hoed the carrots. H. ¼d. To N.B.
Weaver for 216 lbs. of barbed wire @ 3.25 per 100 lbs. = 7.02. To 6 lbs. staples @ 0.03 = 0.18; total of 7.20.

Tuesday the 21st
M. 123. Stormy, much rain. Spaded and sowed some turnips. H. 6 hours.

Wednesday the 22nd
M. 129. Received 10.02 from Hinrich and then bought flour 2.45, soap 0.25,
oatmeal 0.25, beans 0.25, broom 0.35, vinegar 0.25, starch 0.05, tea 0.25,
fine cornmeal 0.25, coarse cornmeal 0.40; total 4.75. Gave Keller 2.00
against the debt. Gave N.B. Weaver 2.00 against the debt. For meat 0.20,
shoelaces 0.10. Hinrich at home.

Thursday the 23rd
M. 106. Hot. Hilled up the potatoes with the shovel plow. H. 1d. Weeded
carrots.

[215]   **July 1903**

Friday the 24th
M. 137. Friedrich and I weeded carrots. Johannes went with the horses over
to Karl. H. 1d. in the foundry.

Saturday the 25th
M. 110. Friedrich and I weeded carrots. Emma sick. Johannes went with the horses to Karl. H. 1d. in the foundry.

Sunday the 26th
The entire day in bed, tired. Kept the Sabbath.

Monday the 27th
M. 121. Johannes deepened the well. Received 2.12 for Hinrich. H. ½ day in the foundry, ½ day in the stave factory. The 2.12 was his pay for the last 2½ days in the foundry. In the evening Hamilton and Gammon were here about painting the school, see Thurs. the 13th.

Tuesday the 28th
M. 115. Johannes deepened the well. H. 1d.

Wednesday the 29th
M. 119. Jersey bred to Gammon's bull 0.50. To Francis & McRae for sugar 0.25, rice 0.25, tea 0.30; total 0.80. Paris green 0.25, machine needles 0.05, meat 0.30. Weeded. Johannes worked on his own place. H. 1d.

Thursday the 30th
M. 113. To school about the painting with Dankert and Gammon and Hamilton and Heinrich Sonomit, 0.75. To Taalke for an umbrella 1.50, stationery 0.10, Paris green 0.25. H. 1d.

Friday the 31st
M. 121. Johannes, Mini, Emma, Wilhelm, Karl and his wife picked berries. I weeded corn. H. 1d. Castrated the boar in the evening.
According to our scale delivered 3356 lbs. of milk in the month of July. Should have received 18.46 on August 18th, but received 18.26.

[216]   August 1903

Mich. Cooperage Co. 61.31, Welles 16.16, Francis & McRae 33.95, N.B. Weaver 31.80, Marfileus 2.21, Schoerpff 1.00, Dr. Grigg 6.75, Keller 25.90, R. Forsyth 5.80, Gammon 2.50, Nehls 29.68. Taalke 8.78, Gottenmyer 12.30.—Henderson 3.50, D. Mills 1.00, cheese factory 1.00, school 1.25.
As of 1 August 1903:
Outstanding receipts 6.75
Debts 238.14
Cash on hand 0.00

Saturday the 1st
M. 106. Nice day. Picked up the paint for the school, 0.75. To Francis &
McRae balance due on groceries 1.13. To Albert Embury for a board 16" ×
8' 0.15. Harrowed the pig lot. Friedrich and Emma weeded corn. H. 1d.

Sunday the 2nd
Nice weather. Brbr.

Monday the 3rd
M. 130. Johannes cut oats with the machine for ½ day. In the afternoon he
worked at his own place. I cut around the stumps with the scythe. Friedrich
and Emma weeded corn. Toward evening a thunderstorm with rain. H. 1d.

Tuesday the 4th
M. 120. Heavy rain during the night. To Keller for middlings 0.03, for rape
seed 0.08, matches 0.05, sal soda 0.10; total 0.26. Painted mama's grave
marker white. Johannes sowed the pig lot with rape seed. Johannes bred his
cow (Rubie). Dry weather. Hoed in the afternoon. Friedrich and Emma went
to look for the horses and came home with them in the evening. H. 1d.

[217]   **August 1903**

Wednesday the 5th
M. 109. Heavy rain during the forenoon, in the afternoon dry. Johannes and
Friedrich worked with Prince over at the former's place. Emma and Wilhelm
and I weeded corn. H. 1d.

Thursday the 6th
M. 107. To R.M. Forsyth for 2 brushes to paint names 0.05. To Marfileus
for a brush for the same purpose 0.10. To Gottenmyer for meat 0.48, to
Keller for oatmeal 0.25, sugar 0.50, tea 0.35, rice 0.25, cornmeal 0.37; total
1.67. Brought in 4 small loads of oats for a total of 34 loads with the 30
loads of hay. H. 1d. Picked up paint for the school, 0.50.

Friday the 7th
M. 106. Brought in three middling loads of oats which makes 37 loads with
the 30 loads of hay and the three loads from yesterday. Cut about 2 acres of
oats and raked as much. H. 1d. In the afternoon as we were unloading, Wilhelm was playing with the hook, got his hand caught in the block and was
badly hurt. Dr. A. Warren bandaged him, 2.00.

Saturday the 8th
M. 113. Went to Bay City on July 31st to Wilton Bookstore about seats for
the school, 0.25. This morning to Dankert and Gammon about seats in Jarvis

Center, 0.25. Hauled 4 loads of oats home; this makes a total of 41 loads of good fodder with the other loads of hay and oats. Wilhelm felt good. About 4:00 there was a thunderstorm and rain; we had just gotten the 4 loads into the barn. To Welles for waist goods 0.19. H. 1d. French's calf had a heifer calf.

[218] August 1903

Sunday the 9th
Good weather. Brbr.

Monday the 10th
M. 133. Went to see Dankert and the school about painting, 0.25. Raked oats; Johannes put them in piles. Schmelzer and his son came to visit. H. 1d. To R. Forsyth for salve for Willie's hand 0.10.

Tuesday the 11th
M. 104. Overcast sky. Brought in 5 loads of oats which makes with the hay and oats already in the barn 46 loads of good fodder. H. 1d. To Francis & McRae for p. barley 0.20, prunes 0.20; total 0.40.

Wednesday the 12th
M. 96. Painted the letters on mama's grave marker. On the one side: Here lies Catherine Louise Caroline, nee Jungjohann, wife of J. Wübbena in Johnsfield. Born 31 March 1855, died 23 January 1894. On the other side: My soul does now in Christ rejoice, and sings his praise with cheerful voice. Brought in another small load of oats. To Francis & McRae for feed 0.35, sugar 0.50; total 0.85. H. 1d. Went in the afternoon with Dankert and Gammon and an agent for school furniture to the school to see about new seats etc., 0.25. Took the cart to W. Daugharty in the evening to order paint, 0.75.

Thursday the 13th
M. 98. Good weather. Deepened the well in the barnyard. H. 8 hours.

Friday the 14th
M. 101. Good weather. Deepened the well in the barnyard and lengthened the pump by six feet. The well is now about 16 feet deep and the pump is about 2 feet from the bottom. H. 1d.

[219] August 1903

Saturday the 15th
Received 4.67 from Hinrich and 18.26 for milk; total 22.93. Paid on debts out of it to Keller 5.00, to A.H. Welles 10.00, to Francis & McRae 5.00; total

20.00. For a washboard 0.35, looking glass 0.25, comb 0.10, oatmeal 0.25, thread 0.05; total 1.00. To N.B. Weaver for 100 feet of fuse 0.55, 1 box dynamite 8.65, 50 caps 0.45; total 9.65. For 4 buckets for the pump 0.40. To Taalke for Hinrich's entrance to Uncle Tom's Cabin Show 0.25. On the 13th to Gottenmyer for meat 0.35. H. 1d.

Sunday the 16th
Nice day. Brbr. Reconciled with Nehls.

Monday the 17th
Milk not weighed (about 100 lbs.). In the course of the day Johannes, Friedrich and I blasted about 30 stumps. The youngsters weeded corn. Taalke and Mini at home. H. 8 hours. To Keller for tea 0.35.

Tuesday the 18th
M. 100. Yesterday from Daugharty & Beaton 50 feet of fuse 0.45. Today 20 feet of fuse 0.20. To Keller for 1 lb. raising 0.10, coconut 0.05; total 0.15. To Francis & McRae for cheese 0.17, sugar 0.50; total 0.67. H. 1d.

Wednesday the 19th
M. 101. To Keller for flour 2.60, sugar 0.50, oatmeal 0.50, washing soda 0.10, soap 0.25, yeast cakes 0.08, rice 0.50; total 4.53. Received 10.20 from Hinrich. Used it to pay Keller for the groceries today and 0.47 against the debt. Paid Gottenmyer 1.00 on the debt and 0.35 for meat. For Papa's shoes 1.50, Mini's stockings 0.30; total 1.80. Paid Armstrong 1.50. Hinrich went to the Orangemen picnic. In the evening went to Standish to see Daugharty about paint and oil, 0.75.

[220] **August 1903**

Thursday the 20th
M. 82. To Dankert and Gammon about taking the school census, 0.25. Brought the oil home. Daugharty & Beaton in Standish had no paint yesterday. Today he went to Saginaw. Good weather. Timrock and his eldest daughter for a visit. Johannes departed. Friedrich and I used the horses to pull stumps. H. 1d.

Friday the 21st
M. 103. Violent storm out of the southwest. Pulled 6 stumps for a total of 9 with the ones pulled yesterday. H. 1d.

Saturday the 22nd
M. 90. Good weather. Pulled 5 stumps (had a lot of trouble); that makes 14 stumps all together. To Welles for 10 yd. cotton 0.70, 6 yd. cotton 0.54, 2½

yd. embroidery 0.13, 1 yd. ribbon 0.05, pins 0.05, needles 0.05, 3 spools of thread 0.12; total 1.64. H. 1d.

Sunday the 23rd
Kept the Sabbath.

Monday the 24th
M.M.&M. Co. . 57. Good weather. Pulled one single stump; that makes 15. To school with Dankert and Gammon to take over Hamilton's work, 0.50. H. 1d.

Tuesday the 25th
M. 87. Good weather. Pulled one stump, makes 16. Burned. H. 1d.

Wednesday the 26th
M. 80. Good weather. Pulled one stump, makes 17. Lili covered by Gammon's bull a second time; she was covered on the 25th of May as well. H. 1d.

Thursday the 27th
M. 84. Rainy. Toward evening worked trying to pull a stump. H. 1d.

Friday the 28th
M. 81. The heifer that came fresh on August 8th covered by Gammon's bull. H. 1d. Pulled the stump started yesterday.

Saturday the 29th
M. 68. Rainy. Took the census. To Schauer to fix the anchor chain 0.50. H. 1d.

Sunday the 30th
Rainy. In bed.

Monday the 31st
M. 101. Took the census. Loaned the school 0.25 to pay the freight for school things from Bay City. Piled stumps during the afternoon. H. 1d.

Delivered 2554 lbs. of milk during August according to our scale and expected to receive 14.05 on September 15th. The cheese factory had 2532 lbs. and I got 13.95.

In the last days of August, perhaps the 31st, to Francis & McRae for sugar 0.25, tea 0.35, cornmeal 0.42; total 1.02.

[222]   September 1903

Mich. Cooperage Co. 61.31, Welles 7.99, Francis & McRae 33.02, N.B. Weaver 41.45, Marfileus 2.31, Schoerpff 1.00, Dr. Grigg 6.75, Keller 22.85,

R. Forsyth 5.95, Gammon 2.50, Nehls 29.68, Taalke 8.78, Daugharty & Beaton 0.65, Dr. A. Warren 1.00, Schauer 0.80, Gottenmyer 12.13.—Henderson 3.50, D. Mills 1.00, cheese factory 1.00.

As of 1 September 1903:

Outstanding receipts 5.50

Debts 238.18

Cash on hand 0.00

Tuesday the 1st
M. 80. Pulled stumps all day. H. 1d.

Wednesday the 2nd
M. 88. Helped Schulz thresh. Pulled 2 stumps; that makes 20. H. 1d.

Thursday the 3rd
M. 84. Pulled 2 stumps; that makes 22. H. 1d. To N.B. Weaver for paint dryer 0.15.

Friday the 4th
M. 84. Pulled 2 stumps; that makes 24. From the school 13.50. H. 1d.

Saturday the 5th
M. 84. Hinrich home. From the school 13.50. As of today everything is even with the school. Had a meeting yesterday evening at Gammon's. Papa got a new suit for 11.00. From Hinrich 8.92. For stuff for Mini's clothes 5.00. For groceries 4.25.

Sunday the 6th
Nice weather. Brbr.

Monday the 7th
M. 92. Rained all day. Presented the school report and had Dankert and Gammon sign it. H. 1d.

[223] **September 1903**

Tuesday the 8th
M. 88. Very hot. Built a bridge. To Tom Milne for lumber 2.48. Dug some potatoes. Piled the stumps we pulled.

Wednesday the 9th
M. 87. Yesterday got 10 cartridges, 12 feet of fuse and 5 caps from Daugharty & Beaton. For thread 0.05. To Welles for lining (Mini's dress) 0.75. H. 8 hours. To Francis & McRae for tea 0.35, shoe blacking 0.10; total 0.45. Rain, wet. Pulled 2 stumps; that makes 26 stumps.

Thursday the 10th
M. 63. Lots of rain during the night, a most violent thunderstorm. To Schauer for work done 0.80. Lots of rain. H. 6 hours. Conference prayer meeting. For Believer's Hymnbook 0.15.

Friday the 11th
M. 68. Good weather. To Welles for stuff for Mini's dress 1.16. Attended conference. H. 1d.

Saturday the 12th
M. 63. Conference. Beautiful weather. To Welles for stuff for Mini's dress 0.25. Went to conference. H. 1d.

Sunday the 13th
Conference. Mini baptized by Kay.

Monday the 14th
Rain, rain, heavy rain. M. 64. H. ½d. Piled three stumps in the afternoon. It was very wet and we had to quit on account of the rain.

Tuesday the 15th
M. 86. Overcast, rain in the morning. Received 13.93 for 2532 lbs. of milk in the month of August. From Hinrich to September 12th 8.32; that is 22.25 in all. Then paid Armstrong 1.50 and for sugar 0.50, oatmeal 0.25, lantern chimney 0.10, lamp chimney 0.05, tea 0.30, Papa's shoes 1.50, Hinrich's shirt 0.50, Wilhelm's overall 0.25, Mini's dress 6.25; leaves 11.05.

[224]   September 1903

To N.B. Weaver for Hinrich's dinner pail 0.40. Hinrich ½d. Pulled and piled 2 stumps for a total of 28 stumps so far this fall.

Wednesday the 16th
M. 73. Overcast with showers. Pulled 3 stumps which makes a total of 31. H. 1d. Taalke to the Dr. with a badly swollen eye, 0.75.

Thursday the 17th
M. 75 (estimated). Overcast in the morning; it only dried off later on. Pulled one stump for a total of 32. H. 7 hours.

Friday the 18th
M. 70. Good weather, cool. Pulled 3 stumps, that makes 35. H. 1d.

Saturday the 19th
M. 84. Nice weather, cool. Pulled 4 stumps, that makes 39. H. 1d.

Sunday the 20th
Nice. Brbr. Mini was taken into the Community of the Confessors.

Monday the 21st
M. 100. Nice, warm day. Cut corn, 24 shocks 10 × 10 and 8 shocks 8 × 8, Friedrich, Emma, Ella and I. Hinrich plowed in the morning. In the afternoon Karl took Prince to haul sand. Hinrich at home. 11 f. For second reader to the school in Standish, 0.75.

Tuesday the 22nd
M. 76. Nice weather. Plowed in the morning and burned in the afternoon. Karl had Prince in the afternoon. H. 1d. Paid freight for center leg of recitation seat, 0.75.

Wednesday the 23rd
M. 82. Nice. Afternoon very cold. Plowed in the forenoon and burned in the afternoon. Karl had Prince during the afternoon. H. 1d. 10 f.

Thursday the 24th
M. 86. Heavy frost during the night. Plowed during the forenoon and cleared during the afternoon. Karl took Prince for the afternoon. H. 1d. 10 f.

Friday the 25th
M. 87. Nice. County Fair. Hinrich at home. Plowed in the forenoon; Hinrich plowed. In the afternoon the children went to the fair. Pulled ripe beans. For freight + C.O.D. 0.75; took care of getting it to the school, 0.25.

[225]   **September 1903**

Saturday the 26th
M. 82. Nice day. County fair. Hinrich at home. Plowed in the morning, to the fair in the afternoon. Pulled ripe beans. H. 1d.

Sunday the 27th
Nice day. Brbr.

Monday the 28th
M. 81. Very heavy frost during the night. Nice day. Dug potatoes. Plowed in the afternoon. Received from Hinrich 6.80 for his work to September 26th. To Keller for flour 2.50, tea 0.35, soap 0.25, oatmeal 0.25, sugar 0.50, yeast cakes 0.08; total 3.90. To Page 0.20, Halcro for repairing a sailing glove 0.10; total 0.30. Hinrich spent 1.35 at the fair; the other children 0.25 together. Took it from the 10.30 (see previous page). Used the rest of the 10.30 for Mini's dress stuff = 8.70. H. 1d.

Tuesday the 29th

M. 91. Very heavy frost during the night. Dug potatoes. More than half were spoiled, rotten. By evening had about 52 bu. in the cellar. H. 1d. For Wilhelm's shoes 1.50, Hinrich's underpants 0.50; total 2.00.

Wednesday the 30th

M. 88. To Welles yesterday for Hinrich's stockings 0.15. Dug potatoes and put 11 bu. in the cellar for a total of 63 bu. Way more than half of the potatoes are rotten; it is hard to sort them. H. 1d. Delivered 2094 lbs. of milk in September by my scale and expect to receive 10.52 on October 15th. Received 11.60 on October 15th for 2110 lbs. of milk.

[226]   October 1903

Mich. Cooperage Co.61.31, Welles 10.35, Francis & McRae 33.47, N.B. Weaver 42.00, Marfileus 2.31, Schoerpff 1.00, Dr. Grigg 6.75, Keller 22.86, R. Forsyth 5.95, Gammon 2.50, Nehls 29.68, Taalke 8.78, Daugharty & Beaton 1.90, Dr. A. Warren 1.00, Schauer 0.80. Gottenmyer 12.13, Tom Milne 2.48—school 1.75, Henderson 3.50, D. Mills 1.00, cheese factory 1.00.

As of 1 October 1903:

Outstanding receipts 7.25

Debts 245.27

Cash on hand 0.00

Thursday the 1st

M. 79. Rain all day which began already during the night. Pulled some beans. H. 7 hours.

Friday the 2nd

M. 76. Good weather. Cut 50 shocks of corn 8 × 8 for a total of 82 shocks. H. 1d.

Saturday the 3rd

M. 73. To Francis & McRae yesterday for ground mustard 0.05, ginger 0.05, cloves 0.05, cinnamon 0.05, green peppers 0.05, mixed spices 0.10; total 0.95. Hauled a load of wood from Johannes' place. Cut and set up 80 shocks of corn for a total of 132 shocks. H. 1d.

Sunday the 4th

Nice day. Brbr. Mini. I went to bed.

Monday the 5th

M. 65. On the 1st bought a spade handle from Daugharty & Beaton for 0.25. Cut 52 shocks of corn for a total of 184 shocks. Friedrich plowed. H. 1d.

[227]   October 1903

Tuesday the 6th
M. 67. From Marfileus on the 1st of October Mini's language text 1.15. To
Keller today for onions 0.10. Helped John Dobson thresh in the morning;
in the afternoon cut 28 shocks of corn and set them up. This makes 212
shocks so far. H. 1d.

Wednesday the 7th
M. 72. Helped John Dobson thresh till 10:00 in the morning. There was a
violent storm and immediately afterward it began to rain and rained all day.
H. 7 hours.

Thursday the 8th
M. 72. Yesterday to Daugharty & Knight for work 0.15. To Francis &
McRae 0.50, tea 0.30, matches 0.05, vinegar 0.15, 5 gal. oil 0.60; total 1.60.
Cut 49 shocks today and set them up for a total of 261 shocks. In the after-
noon went to help Rob Feeto. Emma was sick as was Taalke. With that it
was Ella, Wilhelm, I and Feeto doing the cutting. H. 1d.

Friday the 9th
M. 70. Flora covered by Gammon's bull for the third time. Cut corn, bound
it and set it up: 6 hills to a sheaf, 36 sheaves to a shock. Set up 5 shocks. Went
to help Rob Feeto in the afternoon. H. 1d. To Francis & McRae for lantern
globe 0.10.

Saturday the 10th
M.70. Bound corn. Went to help Schulz in the afternoon. The ground was
very wet and soft, lots of water. H. 1d.

Sunday the 11th
Nice weather. Brbr.

Monday the 12th
Nice weather. M. 67. Karl's calves got out 3 times, took half a day to round
them up. Cut corn and set it up, 11 shocks 8 × 8 for a total of 272 shocks.
Set six of the other shocks back up. H. 1d.

[228]   October 1903

Tuesday the 13th
M.M.&M. Co. . 70. Good weather. Cut and set up 38 shocks 8 × 8 for a
total of 310 shocks. H. 1d. To R.M. Forsyth for Mini's phisiology [sic] 1.30.

Wednesday the 14th
M. 58. Cut and set up 41 shocks 8 × 8 for a total of 351 shocks. This corn is not ripe. The corn we cut on the 9th and on the following days is very green. H. 1d.

Thursday the 15th
M. 71. Overcast. Cut and set up 24 shocks 8 × 8 before noon for a total of 375 shocks; not ripe. Between showers we set up another 9 shocks during the afternoon. Makes 384. It rained off and on all afternoon. The corn is being completely ruined. The stalks just go kaputt as the weight of the water breaks them down. To Francis & McRae for sugar 0.25, tea 0.30, r. oats 0.25; total 0.80. To Gottenmyer for lard 0.10. H. 8 hours.

Friday the 16th
M. 66. Overcast and wet. Cut and set up 36 shocks 8 × 8 for a total of 420 shocks. That is all the corn. H. 8 hours.

Saturday the 17th
M. 66 (estimated). Rainy and cold. For 2110 lbs. of milk in September 11.60, for Hinrich's work till October 10th 9.24; total 21.02. To Francis & McRae 5.00, to T. Milne 2.48, to R.M. Forsyth for phisiology 1.30 (see October 13th), for 2 barrels of salt 2.00, ginger 1.00, 1 lb. tea 0.30, r. oats 0.50, 10 lbs. rice 0.50, w. soda 0.10, soap 0.25, vinegar 0.15, 100 lbs. flour 2.50, wicks 0.02; total 7.32. Gloves 0.20, apples 0.30, Emma's shoes 1.50, fine comb 0.20, coarse comb 0.15, overshoes 0.50, shoelaces 0.10; total 2.85.

[229]   **October 1903**

Saturday the 17th
To N.B. Weaver for nails 0.30, staples 0.15; total 0.45. To Gottenmyer for 7 lbs. of lard 0.84, meat 0.45; total 1.29. Fixed fence. Karl brought Prince and the harrow back. H. 8 hours.

Sunday the 18th
Good weather. Mini Brbr.

Monday the 19th
M. 76. Fine weather. In the forenoon brought about 40 bu. of carrots into the cellar. Taalke had pulled them and gotten them ready over the last few days. In the afternoon hauled to the barn several corn shocks that were wanting to fall over. Then did some plowing and husked corn. H. 1d. To Marfileus for Mini's physology [sic] 1.00 and 1 algebra 0.15; total 1.15.

Tuesday the 20th
M. 66. Fine weather. Husked some corn, about 8 bu, and put it in the crib. Also dug some potatoes although it was almost too wet to dig. H. 1d. Sold the three last yearlings for 50.00. Collected 5.00. To be delivered next Tuesday.

Wednesday the 21st
M. 62. Fine weather. Dug potatoes; most of them are soft and rotten. H. 1d.

Thursday the 22nd
M. 61. Beautiful weather, very cold in the afternoon. Eight more bushel of potatoes in the cellar; digging them was almost no work at all in the wet ground. H. 7 hours. We now have 70 bu. of potatoes in the cellar.

Friday the 23rd
M. 61. Dug and hauled 7 more bu. of potatoes to the cellar. H. 1d.

[230]   **October 1903**

Saturday the 24th
M.56. Good weather. Hauled the last firewood from John's farm. Husked 8 corn shocks which gave about 7 bu. and which we put in the crib; makes 15 bu. all together.

Sunday the 25th
Very nice weather. Brbr.

Monday the 26th
M. 76. Very raw and cold. Emma and I and Ella and Wilhelm husked 9 bu. of corn from 18 shocks for a total of 24 bu. in the crib. H. 1d.

Tuesday the 27th
M. 62. Very cold. There was a hard freeze during the night. Received 46.00 for 3 yearlings which makes 51.00 with the 5.00 received on the 20th. Of this gave Taalke 5.00 for clothes for the children etc., 5.00 to Marfileus, 5.00 to Forsyth, 0.80 to Schauer. Spent 0.18 for snaps and rings. To Dr. A. Warren for glasses 1.25. To Dr. Warren for dressing Wilhelm's hand on August 7th 1.00. Hauled in cornstalks. H. 1d.

Wednesday the 28th
M. 54. Had Lava dehorn 10 cows; @ 0.12½ each this makes 1.25. Mini stayed at home to husk corn (13 shocks). Friedrich and I hauled cornstalks in to make room to plow. H. 1d.

Thursday the 29th
M. 52 (estimated). Put 20 bu. corn (15 shocks) into the crib for a total of 44 bu. Paid Nehls 29.68. So far have husked 52 shocks. H. 1d.

Friday the 30th
M. 52. Husked 15 shocks for a total of 67. Wilhelm and I cut some wood at Johannes' place. H. 1d.

[231]   October 1903

Saturday the 31st
M. 51. From Hinrich to the 24th of October 8.50. For tea 0.30, clothespins 0.10, yeast cakes 0.08, sugar 0.50, washing soda 0.10, latchet 0.10, rope 0.25; total 1.43. From Henderson for pig 2.00. Husked 10 shocks which makes a total of 77 shocks and 13 more bu. of corn in the crib. H. 1d. Mrs. Wyatt came to visit. Took the glasses back to Dr. A. Warren (see October 27th) which reduced the debt by 1.25.

Delivered 1771 lbs. of milk by my scale in October and expect to get 9.74 on the 7th of November (see Nov. 19th). Received 9.55 for 1738 lbs. from the factory.

When filling out one of the crop reports for Washington I gave the following information:

corn	8 acres	140 bu. shelled corn (guess)
wheat	none	
oats	11 acres	160 bu. (guess)
flaxseed	none	
hay	12 acres	15 tons
potatoes	¾ acres	45 bu (more produced, but too many rotten)

[232]   November 1903

Michigan Cooperage Co. 61.31, Welles 10.35, Francis & McRae 31.32, N.B. Weaver 42.45, Schoerpff 1.00, Dr. Grigg 6.75, Keller 22.96, R. Forsyth 0.95, Gammon 2.50, Taalke 8.78, Daugharty & Beaton 2.15, Gottenmyer 13.52— school 1.75, D. Mills 1.00, cheese factory 1.00, Marfileus 0.61
As of 1 November 1903:
Outstanding receipts 4.36
Debts 204.04
Cash on hand 0.00

Sunday the 1st
Nice. Bbr.

Monday the 2nd
M. 70. Nice day. Husked 9 bu. of corn from 18 shocks for a total of 96 shocks and 13 bu. on Saturday and 9 today makes 66 bu. all together. H. 1d.

Tuesday the 3rd
M. 46. Beautiful weather. Heinrich's birthday. (*Ed. note:* Jan had an error of one day as to Heinrich's birthday.) Husked and put in the crib 10 bu. of corn and 18 shocks for a total of 132 shocks and 85 bu. corn. Since Monday I drained by opening the ditch with the scraper that leads from the east-west central collector to the pig lot. I spread the soil on the low spots where the potatoes were under water and rotted. The ground is still very soft and wet. H. 1d.

Wednesday the 4th
M. 47. Very raw and cold. Husked and put in the crib 6 bu. of corn from 10 shocks for a total of 91 bu. and 142 shocks. I drained with the horses. H. 1d. Spread some of the soil in the barnyard.

[233]   November 1903

Friday the 6th
M. 45. Very cold. There was a good freeze during the night, but by afternoon was able to drain. Husked 9 bu. of corn from 9 shocks and put them in the crib for a total of 100 bu. from 151 shocks. H. 1d. To Emma and Ella each 0.50 = 1.00 for a garden, for groceries 4.00, collection 7.00; total 12.00. H. 1d.

Saturday the 7th
M. 45. Another good freeze during the night. Drained in the afternoon. Husked 2 bu. of corn from 5 shocks and put them in the crib for a total of 105 bu. and 156 shocks. H. 1d.

Sunday the 8th
Beautiful weather. Bbr.

Monday the 9th
M. 60. Beautiful weather; in the afternoon at about 4:00 the sky clouded over and it began to storm. I drained with the horses. Taalke and Ella were both not feeling well. Mini, too, came home not feeling well. Emma, Friedrich and Wilhelm husked 8 bu. of corn from 18 shocks for a total of 113 bu. of corn in the crib from 174 shocks. H. 1d.

Tuesday the 10th
M. 44. Very raw and cold. A powerful storm blew all night. In the course of the day it cleared off and became nice. Husked and put in the crib 8 bu. of corn from 12 shocks; that makes 186 shocks and 121 bu. Taalke has been sickly for several days. Emma helped her out around the house. Friedrich plowed. H. 1d.

Wednesday the 11th
M.M.&M. Co. . 44. Very raw and cold. From Hinrich for work to the 7th of November 9.52. To Francis & McRae for flour 2.50, rice, 0.25, soap 0.25, matches 0.05, soda 0.08, chimney 0.10, sugar 0.50, oatmeal 0.50 tea 0.25; total 5.48. Friedrich's shoes 1.50, Taalke's shoes 1.75; total 3.25, spikes 0.10; all together 3.35.

[234]   November 1903

chamber 0.50, postage 0.04. To Joh. and Heinr. and to the U.S. Agriculture Department together 0.54. H. 1d.

Thursday the 12th
M. 36. Very raw and cold, snow and rain; a powerful storm during the night. Sorted corn for seed. Taalke went to James Dobson's place, also on the 11th. H. 1d. (P.S. The entry for this day applies to the 11th and the entry for the 11th applies to this day.) H. 1d.

Friday the 13th
M. 35. Very raw and cold. Friedrich plowed the pig lot. Husked from 9 shocks 4 bu. of corn for a total of 195 shocks and 125 bu. of corn in the crib. Went to Dankert and Gammon about hiring a teacher and taking care of the bill with Wilton, 0.50. H. 1d. Many shocks were blown over in the last storm; we set them up again in the course of the day.

Saturday the 14th
M. 34. Very raw and cold. Plowed in the afternoon, Fr. and I husked some corn—3 bu. from 5 shocks for a total of 128 bu. from 200 shocks. H. 1d. From the school 0.75 for freight for the center leg of the recitation seat. To Taalke for Emma's clothes [no sum given].

Sunday the 15th
Unpleasant and cold. Bbr.

Monday the 16th
Overcast and wet. To Armstrong 1.50 (see November 19th) for order to McGurk. Fr. plowed a little. It was no weather to work outside. H. 9 hours.

Tuesday the 17th
Very raw and cold. In the afternoon came a hard freeze. Fr. plowed. Husked from 6 shocks 3 bu. of corn for a total of 206 shocks and 131 bu. of corn in the crib. H. 1d.

[235]   **November 1903**

Wednesday the 18th
Very cold. It froze in the horse barn and in the pig pen. Hauled 10 shocks of corn onto the threshing floor and husked the same. It was, however, too cold. H. 1d. Put the windows in the cellar.

Thursday the 19th
Received 9.55 for milk in October. Of this gave Keller 1.90 for groceries, Taalke 5.00 for clothes for the youngsters. Sold the cow Bessie to Gottenmyer for 0.05 per pound. Butchered a pig in the afternoon; Dankert came to help, 0.50 for this and also for his help in selling the cow. Karl also helped butcher the pig. H. 1d.

Friday the 20th
Good weather but cold. Delivered the cow to Gottenmyer. For a cattle leader 0.15. To Armstrong 1.50. to Daugharty & Beaton for snaps 0.05, for husk pins 0.10. H. 1d.

Saturday the 21th
Good weather but cold. Husked 6 shocks of corn on the threshing floor for a total of 222 shocks with the 10 shocks for the 18th. Left the husked corn on the threshing floor. H. 1d.

Sunday the 22nd
Cold. Bbr. Kept the Sabbath.

Monday the 23rd
It snowed during the night. Husked 4 shocks on the threshing floor for a total of 226 shocks. Hauled in another 5 shocks. H. 1d.

Tuesday the 24th
Very cold. Received 19.30 for the cow. To Lava 1.25 (see Oct. 28th). Paid debt of 13.52 to Gottenmyer (according to his records we owed 15.33); this leaves 3.97. Received 9.52 from Hinrich for his work to November 21st; expect about 3.47 for milk to the 15th of November for a total of 12.99. Of this gave Taalke 9.00 for a coat, stockings 1.00, groceries from Francis & McRae 3.85; total 13.85.

[236]   November 1903

Paid Lava 1.25 (see October 28th). For cleaning a watch 0.75. Hauled 5 shocks onto the threshing floor; makes 231 shocks. H. 9 hours.

Wednesday the 25th
Very cold. Hauled 17 shocks onto the threshing floor for a total of 248 shocks. Cut some wood and hauled it home. H. 9 hours (see December 1st). (To Norn for wood 0.84.)

Thursday the 26th
Celebrated Thanksgiving.

Friday the 27th
Hauled in 4 loads of cornstalks. (18 shocks on the threshing floor makes 266 shocks.) Very nice weather.

Saturday the 28th
Snow all day. Sawed a bit more wood. H. 1d.

Sunday the 29th
Snowy and cold. Kept the Sabbath. James Harten buried. Was at the funeral. Barness preached on Ps. 23:4.

Monday the 30th
Nice weather. Cut wood. Emma and Ella to school. Wilhelm has complained for a week about severe pain in his limbs.

In November delivered 554 lbs. of milk according to my scale. Received 3.42 on November 24th. Over the summer delivered 14,560 lbs. and received 80.08.

[237]   December 1903

Michigan Cooperage Co. 61,31, Welles 10.35, Francis & McRae 31.32, N.B. Weaver 42.45, Schoerpff 1.00, Dr. Grigg 6.75, Keller 22.96, R. Forsyth 0.95, Gammon 2.50, Taalke 8.78, Daugharty & Beaton 2.30, Daugharty & Knight (see Oct. 8th and Dec. 15th), James Norn (see Nov. 25th and Dec. 15th)—school 1.75, D. Mills 1.00, cheese factory 1.00, Marfileus 0.61.
As of 1 December 1903:
Outstanding receipts 4.36
Debts 190.67
Cash on hand 0.00

Tuesday the 1st
Good weather. Sawed stumps. To Taalke to pay the Dr. for Wilhelm 0.50. To Francis & McRae for a lamp chimney 0.05. To Forsyth for the school for slates and pencils 1.00? H. 1d.

Wednesday the 2nd
Good weather, foggy. Sawed stumps. H. 1d.

Thursday the 3rd
Overcast and cold. Hauled several logs to the house and cleaned some beans. H. 1d.

Friday the 4th
Snowy. Threshed beans, hauled a few more logs home and also 9 shocks of corn to the threshing floor to husk; that made 275 shocks all together. H. 1d.

Saturday the 5th
Good weather. Cut wood. Emma, Ella and Wilhelm husked the corn we brought in yesterday. H. 1d.

Sunday the 6th
Beautiful weather. Bbr.

[238]   **December 1903**

Monday the 7th
Good weather. Cut wood. W.N. Honey died. H. 1d.

Tuesday the 8th
Good weather. Cleaned the outhouses at the school yesterday evening, 0.50. Cut some wood. H. 1d.

Wednesday the 9th
Overcast and snowy. Received 8.24 from Hinrich for his work to the 5th of December. For flour 2.50, tea 0.25, yeast cakes 0.08, matches 0.05, soap, 0.25, sugar 0.50, file 0.10, papa's rubbers snag proof 1.50; total 5.33. To Server for pulling two of Topsy's teeth and two of Fanny's 1.00, for distemper medicine 1.00; total 2.00. H. ½d. W.N. Honey buried. Taalke attended the funeral. To Mr. Woods from Hinrich for the cripple 0.25.

Thursday the 10th
Very nice weather. Brought the rest of the corn in to be husked; it made a total of 287 shocks as well as 3 loads of bound but unripe corn whose ears we will feed to the cow French to fatten her up. H. 1d.

Friday the 11th
Good weather. Sharpened the saw and did some sawing. H. 1d.

Saturday the 12th
Very raw and snowy. It was hardly possible to work outside. H. 1d. From
Francis & McRae a broom (school) 0.35. To Harry Blumenthal for felt boots
0.75, shoes for Friedrich 1.50; total 2.25. H. 1d.

Sunday the 13th
Very stormy and very cold, snow flurries. Sick all day.

Monday the 14th
The weather better but still very cold. To Welles for Hinrich's gloves 0.10,
and garters 0.75; total 0.85. To Norn from November 25th, 0.84. To Daugharty & Knight from October 8th, 0.15. H. 2 hours. Just did the chores.

[239]   **December 1903**

Tuesday the 15th
The weather better but still very cold. Just did the chores. H. 6 hours.

Wednesday the 16th
Milder. Cut some wood. H. 1d.

Thursday the 17th
Good weather, cold. Cut wood. H. ¾ d.

Friday the 18th
Nice weather, mild. Rev. Birdsall and a peddler came to visit. H. 1d.

Saturday the 19th
Wet and overcast, mild. Husked corn and sorted some out for seed. H. ¾ d.
[in the margin, an = to]

Sunday the 20th
Good weather. Bbr. To Francis & McRae (Sat. the 19th) for 5 gal. kerosene
0.60.

Monday the 21st
Good weather. Sawed up a stump and hauled it in. H. 1d.

Tuesday the 22nd
Good weather. Made a trough for the pigs. H. 1d.

Wednesday the 23rd
Good weather. Received 8.50 from Hinrich. Paid Francis & McRae for sugar
0.75, rice 0.25, raisins 0.25, oatmeal 0.25, chocolate 0.24, apples 0.50, tea

0.25, coffee 0.25, extract 0.05, lamp chimney 0.10, bran 0.50; total 3.39. Received 15.00 from the cheese factory for milk last summer. Paid taxes of 14.14. For 1 lb. of sulfur 0.10, rosin 0.10, stromonium 0.25; total 0.45. H. 1d.

Thursday the 24th
Good weather. Got ready for Christmas. Johannes and Heinrich came home last evening. H. 1d. Taalke bought blankets and things for Christmas, 5.50.

[240]   December 1903

Friday the 25th
Celebrated Christmas. Very cold.

Saturday the 26th
Very cold. Sharpened the saw. Uncovered hay for the horses. Hinrich at home. [in the margin, an = to]

Sunday the 27th
Very raw and cold, snow flurries. Kept the Sabbath. To Welles for Hinrich's rubbers 1.50.

Monday the 28th
Very cold. To Johannes for Hinrich's gloves 0.25. H. 2 hours.

Tuesday the 29th
Cold. Delivered 2 yearlings for Gottenmyer @ 0.05 per lb. dressed. To Welles for Friedrich and Willie each a pair of stockings @ 0.25 = 0.50, 2 spools of thread 0.08; total 0.58. To Marfileus for licorice 0.50. H. 1d.

Wednesday the 30th
Very raw and cold. Sawed some wood. H. 1d.

Thursday the 31st
Raw and cold. H. 1d. I fell off of a sledge load of cornstalks and hurt myself in the upper body. Not a very nice way to take leave of the year 1903. Nevertheless praise and thanks to God.

[245]   **January 1904**

Michigan Cooperage Co. 61,31, Welles 13.28, Server 2.00, Harry Blumen-
thal 2.25, Johannes 0.25, Francis & McRae 32.32, N.B. Weaver 42.45, R.
Forsyth 1.95, Norn, 0.84, Daugharty & Beaton 2.30, Gammon 2.50, Taalke
12.28, Keller 22.96, Schoerpff 1.00, Dr. Grigg 6.75, Daugharty & Knight
0.15, Marfileus 0.50.—School 2.60, D. Mills 1.00, cheese factory 1.00,
Marfileus 0.60.
As of 1 January 1904:
Outstanding receipts 5.21
Debts 205.09
Cash on hand 0.00

Friday the 1st
Celebrated New Year's. Very Cold.

Saturday the 2nd
Very cold and raw. Received 25.95 for the yearlings I delivered on December
29th. Of this paid Chamberlain & Henderson 22.00 for insurance till
November 23, 1906. For a pancake griddle 0.65. To Francis & McRae for
100 lbs. Henkel's bread flour 2.60. H. 1d.

Sunday the 3rd
Very, very cold. Lots of pain in my shoulder and in my side from the fall on
the 31st. Kept the Sabbath.

Monday the 4th
Very cold. For Hinrich's stockings 0.35, for the collection Sunday 0.25; total
0.60. H. 1d. Shelled corn.

Tuesday the 5th
Very cold. Shelled corn. H. 1d.

Wednesday the 6th
Nice weather. Received 5.37 from Hinrich for work to January 2nd. To
Keller for tea 0.30, sugar 0.50, yeast cakes 0.08, raisins 0.25, flour 1.30,
Atlas soap 0.25, oatmeal 0.25, rice 0.25, Union oats 0.25, onions 0.10,
matches 0.10; total 3.32. Taalke worked for Chamberlain.

[246]   **January 1904**

Wednesday the 6th
For shoelaces 0.15, stockings 0.30; total 0.45. To Server 1.00. To Johannes
0.25. For yarn 0.35. Cut wood, i.e. Fr. and Willie. H. 1d.

Thursday the 7th
Good weather. In the morning Mollie gave birth to a bull calf; in the evening Blossom also had one. Changed the pig pen and gave the animals fresh straw. H. 1d.

Friday the 8th
Beautiful weather. Cut firewood. To Francis & McRae for 2 lantern globes 0.20. H. 1d.

Saturday the 9th
Good weather. Cut firewood. To Welles for Hinrich's overcoat 6.00, thread 0.20; total 6.20. H. 1d.

Sunday the 10th
Good weather. Bbr.

Monday the 11th
Good weather. Cut firewood. Sorted potatoes: 5 buckets of bad ones for every bucket of good potatoes. H. 1d. Hinrich's pay was raised by 15%: instead of 0.85, from now on he will get 1.00 per day. Taalke worked as assistant clerk in the Register of Deeds Office (H. Chamberlain). She had helped out there one day last week.

Tuesday the 12th
Good weather. In the afternoon it snowed. Sorted potatoes and cut wood. I want to note that my fall on the 31st of December has made it so that I cannot do any work with my right arm. I sorted potatoes; Fr. & Wilh. cut wood.

[247] **January 1904**

Wednesday the 13th
Very raw and cold. It snowed the entire day. Sorted potatoes and cut wood. H. 1d. T. 1d.

Thursday the 14th
Good weather. In the forenoon Johannes and Heinrich hauled in 2 loads of cornstocks, 1 load of husked and 1 load of unhusked cornstalks. Friedrich and Wilhelm cut wood and sorted potatoes. H. 1d. T. 1d.

Friday the 15th
Good weather. Sorted the last of the potatoes. Friedrich and Wilhelm cut wood. Taalke at home. H. 1d. Received a letter from Cincinnati in answer to my inquiry about stove repairs.

Saturday the 16th
Very raw and snowy. Friedrich and Wilhelm cut wood. Taalke at home. H.
1d. Johannes hauled 2 loads of logs home; he had already brought 2 more
loads earlier.

Sunday the 17th
Nice weather. Kept the Sabbath.

Monday the 18th
To Francis & McRae on December 19th for oil 0.70 instead of 0.60; noticed
it on December 20th. T. 1d. H. 1d. To Francis & McRae for oil 0.70.

Tuesday the 19th
Good weather. Cut wood. H. 1d. T. 1d. Took the cow French to be
slaughtered.

Wednesday the 20th
Mild. Picked up the meat from the slaughtered cow, 382 lbs. Gottenmyer
kept some meat for which I can claim 21 lbs. of lard, see February 27th. For
Hinrich's work to the 16th of January 11.10, for the hide 2.55; total 13.65.
To Francis & McRae for washing soda 0.10, flour 2.60, tea 0.25, coffee 0.30,
yeast 0.10, roots 0.25, rice 0.50, gr. sugar 0.50, soda 0.08, 100 lbs. linseed
meal 2.00; total 6.68. Paid Gammon 0.50. Heinrich to the telephone line in
Gaylord. H. 1d.

[248]   January 1904

Thursday the 21st
Raw and cold. Sent to Wm. Resor & Co. in Cincinnati, Ohio for stove
repairs and wrote the order as follows:
Standish, Arenac Co., Mich. Jan. 21, 1904
Messrs. Wm. Resor & Co.
Cincinnati, Ohio
Enclosed with this find three dollars and ninety cents, for which please send
me

    one front grate   No. 9-21
    one bottom grate   No. 9-Monitor Stove
    one fire back
    ($3.90)

                        and oblige
                        Respectfully
                        [signed] Jan Wübbena

The order with a money order and postal stamp cost 3.97. Attended the Farmer's Institute. Very raw weather. For dinner 0.20. Mini's shoe repair 0.10. Taalke sick; to Dr. Toothacker 0.75 for examination and medicine.

Friday the 22nd
During the night lots of hail and heavy hoarfrost. For Hinrich's overall and jacket 1.00. To Welles for stiffening 0.08 Emma's coat. Went to bed. Taalke better. H. 1d.

Saturday the 23rd
Snow, otherwise good weather. Johannes hauled in 2 sledgeloads of logs for firewood. H. 1d.

The Wm. Resor & Co.
State Ave. North of Gent Street
Cincinnati, Ohio

[249]   **January 1904**

Sunday the 24th
Very raw and cold, snowy, windy. Kept the Sabbath. I went to bed.

Monday the 25th
Very cold, 23° below zero. Johannes and Friedrich hauled in 2 loads of logs. H. 6 hours. T. 1d.

Tuesday the 26th
Very cold. Johannes and Friedrich hauled 2 loads of logs home. H. 1d. T. 1d.

Wednesday the 27th
Milder. Paid 0.25 to join the Farmer's Institute Society on the 22nd. Johannes had his teeth repaired. In the afternoon he hauled in a load of cornstalks. H. 9 hours. T. 1d.

Thursday the 28th
Beautiful weather but very cold. To school to check the wood supply, Hall's firewood and because of Al Lawrence's son 0.50. Johannes and Friedrich cut wood. H. 1d.

Saturday the 30th
Beautiful weather but cold. Hauled in a load of cornstalks. Friedrich and Wilhelm cut wood. H. 9 hours.

Sunday the 31st
Very cold. Kept the Sabbath.

[250]   **February 1904**

Michigan Cooperage Co. 61.31, Welles 19.56, Server 1.00, Harry Blumen-thal, 2.25, Toothacker 0.75, Francis & McRae 33.32, N.B. Weaver 42.45, R. Forsyth 1.95, Norn 0.84, Daugharty & Beaton 2.30, Gammon 2.00, Taalke 12.28, Keller 22.96, Schoerpff 1.00, Dr. Grigg 6.75, Daugharty & Knight 0.15, Marfileus 0.50.—School 2.60, D. Mills 1.00, Cheese factory 1.00, Marfileus 0.61
As of 1 February 1904:
Outstanding receipts 5.21
Debts 211.37
Cash on hand 0.00

Monday the 1st
Very cold. All the children away; at home all by myself. Johannes left in the morning for Norn's camp, Taalke to Chamberlain, Mini and the youngsters to school, Hinrich to the stave factory. H. 1d.

Tuesday the 2nd
Since Friday the 29th of January we have been watering the cows in the river by Kings because our water is low. H. 1d.

Wednesday the 3rd
Very cold. Hauled 2 loads of cornstalks home as well as 2 loads yesterday. H. 1d. T. 1d.

Thursday the 4th
Very cold. Received the shipping bill for the stove repairs but the things themselves had not arrived at the depot. For that reason I wrote a postcard to the company in Cincinnati as follows:

[251]   **February 1904**

Standish, Arenac Co.
      Michigan, Feb. 4, 1904
Mrss. Wm. Resor & Co.
Cincinnati, Ohio
State Avenue, North of Gest St.
Dear Gentlemen:
I received your shippingbill [*sic*], dated the 26. of January, on the 30., but thus far the articles have not arrived at the Standish depot yet; after seeing the R.R. Agent here he advised me to write to you about the matter; please do something for me in the case and oblige
                              Respectfully
                              [signed] Jan Wübbena

Received 10.50 from Hinrich for his work to January 30th. From this paid 0.50 for licorice, for 2 cooking pots @ 0.50 = 1.00, an ax handle 0.20. to Keller & Armstrong for rolled oats, 09.20, chopping bowl 0.20, soda 0.07, yeast cakes 0.10, salt 0.05, lantern globe 0.10, one pail syrup 0.30, 1 lb. tea 0.25, 1 lb. coffee 0.15, sugar 0.50; total 4.77. To Mini for teacher's institute 0.10. H. 1d. Taalke at home.

Friday the 5th
Milder. To Harry Blumenthal 2.25. For Wilhelm's and Friedrich's overalls 1.00, Mini's rubbers 0.50, Hinrich's gloves 0.25, Hinrich's shirts 1.00, other 0.43; total 3.18. H. 1d. T. 1d. Hauled in a load of cornstalks.

[252] February 1904

Saturday the 6th
Overcast, thaw. Shoulder very sore, unable to work. H. 1d. Unloaded the cornstalks hauled yesterday. About 11:30 at night Cherry gave birth to a bull calf.

Sunday the 7th
Very cold. Kept the Sabbath.

Monday the 8th
Clear and very cold. Hauled a load of cornstalks home. H. 1d. T. 1d.

Tuesday the 9th
Clear and very cold. Hauled a load of cornstalks home. H. 1d. T. 1d.

Wednesday the 10th
Clear and very cold. To Standish with J. Dobson and Gammon to speed up the sale of the cows, 0.50. H. 1d. T. 1d.

Thursday the 11th
Clear and very cold. Hauled a load of cornstalks home. H. 1d. T. 1d.

Friday the 12th
Clear and very cold. Wrote
      To the
            C. H. & D. Ry Freight Depot Agent
            Guest Street Station
            Cincinnati, Ohio
      Dear Sir,
      I received a shippingbill (I think No. 1142 to your books) from the Wm. Resor & Co., Stove & Range Manufacturers, dated the 26. of February, on the 30., indicating one bundle of stove castings (repairs), but thus far the arti-

cles have not arrived at the Standish depot; please, do something for me in regard to hasten its coming and oblige

Respectfully your
[signed] Jan Wübbena

[253]   **February 1904**

Friday the 12th
Clear but very cold. Hauled in a load of cornstalks. H. 8 hours.

Saturday the 13th
Clear, very cold. H. 1d.

Sunday the 14th
Very cold and windy. Bbr. The roads are very hard to get through; the snow [sic] has driven the snow into drifts.

Monday the 15th
Very cold, colder than any day so far this winter, and windy. It seemed as though the air had turned to ice. The Republican County Club organized. H. 8 hours. T. 1d.

Tuesday the 16th
Very cold, just like yesterday. Fixed up the well. Very, very cold. H. 7 hours. T. 1d.

Wednesday the 17th
Very cold. Threshed some beans. H. 4 hrs., H. 1d [sic].

Thursday the 18th
Very cold, but some milder. Went with Dobson and Gammon to Welles about selling cows, 0.50. Received 10.50 from Hinrich for his work to Feb. 13th. Of that paid Francis & McRae for groceries: 5 gal. oil 0.65, tea 0.25, washing soda 0.10, Atlas soap 0.25, Roots 0.25, syrup 0.30, clothespins 0.10, onions 0.25, sugar 0.50, 100 lbs. flour 2.65, 10 milk pans 0.80, shoe tacks 0.10; total 7.30. Paid Server the doctor's fee owed him 1.00, paid Marfileus 0.50 on the debt. To LeRock for Friedrich's shoes 0.15. Taalke had already paid Toothacker 0.75; to Taalke for paying Toothacker 0.75 and for Ella's fascinator 0.25; total 1.00. H. 1d. T. 1d.

Friday the 19th
Cold, cold, but clear. Threshed some beans. H. 1d.

[254]   **February 1904**

Saturday the 20th
Clear and very cold. Received a postcard in the evening that my stove repair parts (see Jan. 15th, Jan. 21st, Feb. 4th and Feb. 12th) had arrived at the depot in Standish. Threshed some beans. Friedrich and Wilhelm cut some firewood. H. 1d.

Sunday the 21st
It snowed all day. Kept the Sabbath.

Monday the 22nd
Washington's Birthday. Very raw. H. ½d. T. 1d. Cleaned 2 bu. of beans.

Tuesday the 23rd
It snowed all night. Picked up the repair parts for the stove from Cincinnati, but they didn't fit. What is to be done? Bright and clear during the day, windy and not so cold. Cleaned out the pig pen. Paid the debt to Daugharty & Knight, 0.15. H. ½d. T. 1d.

Wednesday the 24th
Heavy frost and snow during the night. Threshed some beans. Cleaned 2 bu. of beans. Very strong wind and snow flurries. H. ½d. T. 1d.

Thursday the 25th
Heavy frost and snow during the night. Wrote the following postcard to Cincinnati:
>   Standish, Arenac Co. Mich. Feb. 25. '04
>   The Wm. Resor & Co.
>   State Ave, North of Gest Street,
>   Cincinnati, Ohio.
>   I received the repairs, of which you sent me the shippingbill on the 26. of January, and now they do not fit! I sent this order on the 21. of January:
>   one front grate   Ì
>   one bottom grate   û- for No. 9-21 Monitor stove.
>   one fire back   ì

[255]   **February 1904**

What am I to do now: Please, advise me about the matter and send me the right repairs;—I am very sorry. Shall I return the pieces?

The front grate, I want, opens like a door horizontally, I have no idea, how those repairs, you sent me, work.

Please, send me the right items as soon as possible, I am willing to pay freight; If I only could get the items soon, and oblige

Respectfully
[signed] Jan Wübbena

Further:

Dr. Chas. Hull

Maple Ridge

Arenac Co., Mich.

Standish, Feb. 25. '04

Dear Sir,

Some one informed me, that you want to trade of a farm horse for a good roadster; if this is the case, I believe, I can meet your demand; I have a four year old marecolt, to quick for its mate on the farm; this trait is a reason I want to part with it if I can do business to suit me.

If you think that this would meet your suggestions, come over and see

Respectfully,
[signed] Jan Wübbena

[256]   February 1904

Thursday the 25th

The weather was clear but very cold. Soled shoes and threshed beans. By times I was coughing so hard I could hardly get my breath.

Friday the 26th

Very cold. In answer to my order for stove repairs I received the following answer on January 27th. The order had been sent by postcard on January 21st:

The Wm. Resor & Co.

State Ave., North Gest St.

Cincinnati, O. 1/24

Gentlemen:

We are pleased to acknowledge receipt of your order of 1/24 for repairs which we enter for careful attention and prompt shipment.

Thanking you for the same and soliciting your further orders, we are,

Yours truly,
The Wm Resor & Co.
MEG

Friday the 26th

Very cold. Taalke at home. Washed. Made a calf trough. H. 7 hrs.

Saturday the 27th
Somewhat milder. To Standish for a window in the school, 0.80. Broken by Emma and Kitzmann's daughter, 0.50. Before that sold a pig to Gottenmyer for 0.06 per pound. To Marfileus for licorice 0.50, for postal cards 0.05. On the 25th received a reminder from Dr. Grigg about the 6.75. H. 1d. Answered Grigg's letter by postal card:

> Standish, Feb. 27. '04
> A. Grigg, M.D.
> N. Fayette Street 325
> Saginaw West Side
> D.G.: Have received your letter dated Feb. 24; will try to respond to the

request in course of next week. D.V.

> Respectfully
> [signed] Jan Wübbena

[257]   February 1904

Saturday the 27th
To Gottenmyer for 24 lbs. of lard @ 0.10 = 2.40. In addition the 21 lbs. of lard that he owes me for the beef (see Jan. 20).

Sunday the 28th
Nice day. Brbr.

Monday the 29th
Very, very raw. Handed over the three pigs sold to Gottenmyer on Saturday the 27th. Gusting snow showers all day; perhaps the most unpleasant day of the entire winter.

[258]   March 1904

Michigan Cooperage Co. 61.31, Nehls 19.56, Francis & McRae 33.32, N.B. Weaver 42.45, R. Forsyth 1.95, Norn 0.84, Daugharty & Beaton 2.00, Gammon 2.00, Taalke 12.28, Keller 22.96, Schoerpff 1.00, Dr. Grigg 6.75, Marfileus 0.50, Gottenmyer 2.40.—School 2.60, D. Mills 1.00, Cheese factory 1.00.
As of 1 March 1904:
Outstanding receipts 4.60
Debts 209.62
Cash on hand 0.00

Tuesday the 1st
    Dear Kitzmann!
    May God be with us!
    Our daughters broke a windowpane in the school. We are obliged to replace it. I have put one in; it cost 0.80 without figuring anything for my time. I would now like to inquire whether you would not like to bear half the cost and come to my aid with 0.40?
                              Yours in friendship,
                              [signed] Jan Wübbena

Tuesday the 1st
Put the boar and the sow together. Shoveled snow. In the barnyard it was higher than the fence in places. Had to dig the gate to the road out of the snow. H. 1d. T. 1d.

[259]   March 1904

Wednesday the 2nd
Thaw. Thunderstorm with rain in the evening. Stayed in bed because of tiredness and feeling sick. Heinrich came home in the evening. H. 1d. T. 1d.

Thursday the 3rd
Very heavy frost. Cold, very cold. Cleaned the rest of the beans, had all together 5 bu. Received an answer from Cincinnati, Ohio to my card of February 25th:
    Cincinnati, Feb. 29, '04
    Dear Sir: Wood repairs sent on Feb. 29, '04.
    Ship the casting back to Wm. Resor & Co.
    If you order casting again, order for wood.
    Coal linning [*sic*] are always sent, unless ordered for wood.
                              Yours truly
                              The Wm Resor & Co.
The above had been sent on a canceled postcard in an envelope with the shipping bill from Feb. 29th. T. 1d. H. didn't work.
    Johnsfield, March 4, '04
    A. Grigg M.D.
    N. Fayette Street 325
    Saginaw West Side
    Dear sir & friend:
    Enclosed with this find 6.75, which will respond to your request from the 25th of February.

Wishing you very much prosperity physically and spiritually I remain in friendship your

[signed] Jan Wübbena

[260]   **March 1904**

Friday the 4th
Very cold during the night. Received 16.38 for the pigs sold on February 29th, from Hinrich for his work to Feb. 29th 9.00; total 25.38. From this paid Gottenmyer 2.40 on the debt, to Dr. Grigg 6.75, to Taalke for things she bought 2.00, for sending the shipping bill to Cincinnati 0.02, postage 0.02 and postal note 0.10 for sending the money to Dr. Grigg; total 0.12. To Keller & Co. for rice 0.50, syrup 0.30, tea 0.30, onions 0.25, sugar 0.75, oats 0.25, flour 1.45; total 4.20; To Taalke to buy shoes for Wilhelm 2.00, overall 0.50; total 2.50. Paid on the debt to Daugharty & Beaton 2.30, to R.M. Forsyth 1.00. H. ¼d.

Saturday the 5th
Somewhat milder. Hinrich and Friedrich cut wood; Wilhelm and I did the chores.

Sunday the 6th
"Good" weather. Bbr. Big thaw.

Monday the 7th
Big thaw. Received 5.00 from the cheese factory. Of that 2.00 on the debt to Marfileus which made us even. There was a difference in the record between Marfileus and us of 1.50 to his advantage. Paid it. For chains on whipple-trees 1.00. Taalke found out that the 1.00 we gave R.M. Forsyth on the 4th paid everything we owed him. This lowers the debt by 0.95. H. 1d.

Tuesday the 8th
Wilhelmina's birthday. Heinrich and I cut wood. Thaw during the forenoon, heavy frost toward evening. H. 1d.

Wednesday the 9th
Good weather. Cleaned the pig pen in the forenoon. Heinrich built a new gate to the road. I went to bed in the afternoon.

[261]   **March 1904**

Wednesday the 9th
Went to bed in the afternoon. H. 1d. T. 1d.

Thursday the 10th
Very raw and cold. Heinrich hauled a load of cornstalks home. H. 1d. T. 1d.

Friday the 11th
Cold and raw. Stayed home and in bed. Heinrich brought in the rest of the cornstalks. H. 1d.

Saturday the 12th
Good weather. Sorted beans. H. 1d.

Sunday the 13th
Good weather. Kept the Sabbath.

Monday the 14th
Very raw. Johannes came home. H. ¾ d.

Tuesday the 15th
Better weather. Received 10.30 from Hinrich for his work to March 12. Of that paid Francis & McRae for matches 0.05, sugar 0.50, oatmeal Union 0.50, rice 0.50, syrup 0.30, tea 0.30, Atlas soap 0.25, washing soda 0.10, Henkel's bread flour 2.90; total 5.40. For an ax 1.15. Iron for Wilhelm's lock 0.10, Emma's stockings 0.25; total 1.50. Advertisement 0.15, freight for stove castings 0.40, coll. 1.03, swill barrel hoop 0.25, shoe blacking 0.10. To Taalke for clothes and shoes for the youngsters 1.38. H. 1d.

Wednesday the 16th
Very nice weather. Hinrich at home. Removed sheeting in the green room. Johannes and Heinrich worked over at Johannes' place. Hinrich at home.

Thursday the 17th
Nice weather in the forenoon, snow and snow flurries in the afternoon. Johannes and Heinrich worked over at Johannes' place. H. 1d.

Friday the 18th
Good weather. Things thawed out during the day, a hard freeze during the night. H. 1d.

Saturday the 19th
Thaw. Caucus. H. 1d. (14 + ¾)

Sunday the 20th
Nice weather. Brbr. Matthews was there.

Monday the 21st
Good weather. Johannes and Heinrich laid a floor in the green room. H. 1d.

[262]   **March 1904**

Tuesday the 22nd
Johannes and Heinrich went with Charles Johnson to Norn's sawmill. H. ¾
d. I went to bed.

Wednesday the 23rd
Beautiful weather; the snow melted nicely. H. 1d. Started to put up lath in
the green room.

Thursday the 24th
Good weather, the snow continued to melt. Put up lath in the green room.
H. 1d.

Friday the 25th
In the night powerful lightning and rain; in many places the water was over
the road. In the course of the day it dried up pretty well. In bed. Put up a little lath in the green room during the afternoon. Iester Dystant came to visit.
to N.B. Weaver for tacks 0.10. To Baumgarth for Mini's shoes 2.25. To Keller
for tea 0.30. H. 1d.

Saturday the 26th
Very cold. Gammon, Denco [?] and Proulx came to see me about the democratic caucus in the afternoon at the school. H. 1d. Put up some lath in the
green room. In the afternoon the cow Katie gave birth to a heifer calf.

Sunday the 27th
Very cold. Brbr. Taalke has been visiting at Barnes' since yesterday afternoon.
Wrote to Cincinnati:

> Standish, Arenac Co., Mich., March 28. 1904
> The Wm Resor & Co.
> State Ave., North of Gest street,
> Cincinnati, Ohio
> Dear Gentlemen:
> I received the repairs, of which you sent me the shippingbill on the 29.
of February, and now

[263]   **March 1904**

again they do not fit! Is it not too bad?! Having been informed by Mr. Baikie
from Omer, a hardwareman, I will renew the order again: the items have to
be for the

No. 9-21
ROYAL
MONITOR

one front grate
one bottom grate
one fire back
for wood.

With this order I send back the other bundle castings with a shipping-bill to it; and please, send me the right items as soon as possible, I am willing to pay freight and oblige

Respectfully,
[signed] Jan Wübbena
Standish, Arenac Co., Mich.

Could you let me have a catalogue?

Monday the 28th
Received 10.35 from Hinrich for his work to the 26th. From that paid Keller & Co. for 2 packages of Highland Rolled Oats @ 0.25 = 0.50, yeast foam 0.08, washing soda 0.10, kerosene oil 0.60, sugar 0.75, syrup 0.30, tea 0.30, salt 0.10, coffee 0.12, lamp chimney No. 1 0.05, Henkel's bread flour 100 lbs. 2.80; total 6.70. To Baumgarth for Mini's shoes 2.00, Emma's rubbers 0.60, my caucus of the 19th 0.20, postage 0.06. H. 1d. Put up lath in the green room.

[264]   March 1904

Tuesday the 29th
Put up lath in the green room. Nice weather. Katie covered by Gammon's bull, 0.50. H. 1d. Paid Gammon 0.50.

Wednesday the 30th
Very wet and overcast. The water was over the road in many places. Put up lath in the green room. H. 1d.

Thursday the 31st
Overcast and wet. Went to Standish about the sale of cheese, 0.50. That is already paid. H. 3½ hrs.

Maundy Thursday.
As the twig is bent,
so grows the tree.

To Daugharty and Beaton for 2 lbs. of lath nails @ 0.04 as well as for 2 lbs. yesterday; that makes 4 lbs. @ 0.04; total 0.16.

[265]   April 1904

Michigan Cooperage 61.31, Welles 19.56, Francis & McRae 33.32, N.B.
Weaver 42.50, Norn 0.84, Gammon 2.00, Taalke 12.28, Keller 23.26,
Daugharty & Beaton 0.16—School 2.60, D. Mills 1.00.
As of 1 April 1904:
Outstanding receipts 3.60
Debts 195.23
Cash on hand 0.00

Friday the 1st
Good Friday. Put up lath in the green room. Mini was to the children's festi-
val (our congregation's Sunday School). H. 1d. Received an answer from
Cincinnati to my letter of March 18th, first by postcard:

> The Wm. Resor & Co.
> State Ave., North of Gest St.
> Cincinnati, O. 3/9/04
> Gentlemen:
> We are pleased to acknowledge receipt of your order of 3/28/04
>   Repairs
> which we enter for careful attention and prompt shipment at once.
>   Thanking you for the same and soliciting your further orders, we are
>   Yours truly
>   The Wm Resor & Co.

[266]   April 1904 [J.W. had written 1903]

Friday the 1st
and then by letter:

> Cincinnati, March 30, 1904
> Mr. Jan Wubbena,
> Standish, Mich.
> Dear Sir:
> We are indeed sorry to learn that the castings shipped you on the 29th
of February is not what you want and wish to inform you that we will forward the castings, as per your letter of today, at once, with freight prepaid
and trust that it will reach you in good condition and be just what you
want.
>   We take pleasure in mailing you under separate cover our catalogue of
stoves and ranges and if there is anything that you think you can use we will
be glad to quote you a price.

With kind regards, we beg to remain,

> Yours respectfully
> The Wm. Resor & Co.
> [signed] E.N. Hake

E.H.-L.

Saturday the 2nd
Good weather but cold. Put up lath in the green room. H. 1d.

Sunday the 3rd
Easter. Kept the Sabbath. Brbr.

Monday the 4th
Election Day. H. 8 hrs.

[267]   April 1904

Tuesday the 5th
Good weather. Hauled 2 loads of manure. The ground is very soft. H. 1d.

Wednesday the 6th
Overcast and wet. Went to bed in the forenoon, put up lath in the green room in the afternoon. H. 1d.

Thursday the 7th
Nice weather. Worked in the green room in the morning; attended to cheese business in the afternoon. H. 1d.

Friday the 8th
Dry in the forenoon. Hauled manure. Bred the cow Mollie to Gammon's bull, 0.50. H. 6 hrs. In the afternoon a powerful thunderstorm and rain.

Saturday the 9th
Wet and overcast. Tried to haul manure but broke the reach on the wagon. Castrated three bulls; kept the one born to Mollie on Jan. 7th to use for breeding. Had a cheese meeting in Standish in the afternoon; Garner from Airline Road elected to my position. H. 1d.

Sunday the 10th
Good weather. Brbr. Toward evening snow and rain; it continued into the night. In the night the cow Fun gave birth to a bull calf.

Monday the 11th
On the 9th to Francis & McRae for rice 0.25, raisins 0.24, crackers 0.25; total 0.74. Received 10.50 from Hinrich today for work to April 9th. From that for Friedrich's shoes 2.00, overall 0.50, gloves for Hinrich 0.25; total

2.75. To Francis & McRae for rice 0.25, oatmeal 0.50, nutmeg 0.05, coll. 1.05, sugar 0.75, tea 0.30, washing soda 0.10, matches 0.05, paper & envelopes 0.20, snaps 0.05; total 3.80 [added on the side] Daugharty & Beaton shoetree 0.16; total 3.96.

[268]   April 1904

Monday the 11th
Cold and unpleasant all day. H. 1d.

Tuesday the 12th
Snow during the night. Very unpleasant. A lot of pain in my back and chest. Made a wagon reach. H. 1d.

Wednesday the 13th
Very cold. It froze pretty good, but it thawed where the sun was shining. Hauled manure. H. 1d.

Thursday the 14th
Mini paid Francis & McRae on the 12th, day before yesterday, 0.74 and to Gottenmyer 0.35 for meat. Hinrich's overall 0.50. Picked up the stove repairs at the depot; 0.50 freight. Sold hay for 1.75 to Karl Wübbena and delivered it. Hauled manure. H. 1d.

Friday the 15th
   Standish, Arenac Co., Mich., April 14.04.
   The Wm. Resor & Co.
   Cincinnati, Ohio
   Dear Gentlemen:
   I received the castings today, of which you sent me the shippingbill dated March 30, '04. The bottom grate was broken, but I can use it just the same, so there is not much lost.
   The catalogue, which accompanied your letter form March 30 I received also, for which I thank you very much; and I believe, I will make use of it in course of time. You mention in your letter, you want to forward the castings with freight prepaid, but I had to pay 0.50 before I could get the castings. What am I to do?

[269]   April 1904

Besides the shippingbill and the letter you sent me a bill of 0.80—dear friends: if you kindly will look up your books, you will find, that I sent you with the order of January 21 three dollars and ninety cents;—according to the bill some change should be due me. If you kindly will figure our business over, and if I have a claim on a money return, then please, send me

front grate	ì
bottom grate	û- 9-21 Royal Monitor for wood
fireback	ì

as many as I can get.

Respectfully,
Jan Wübbena

Friday the 15th
Taalke and Mini to the Conference in Bay City. A terrible storm the entire day. H. 4 hrs.

Saturday the 16th
Good weather. Deep snow. Sold 1000 lbs. of hay to Carl for 6.00. Hinrich at home. 4d 4h

Sunday the 17th
Nice weather. Kept the Sabbath.

Monday the 18th
Paid Gammon 0.50 yesterday. Sold Armstrong 1085 lbs. of hay @ 15.00 per ton = 8.14. To Welles for a pair of shoes bought on the 15th 1.50. Sold Hamilton 230 lbs. of hay @ 15.00/ton = 2.30. H. 1d. A very hard freeze.

Tuesday the 19th
Very hard frost. Hauled manure. H. 1d. Paid Taalke 2.00 for needles and c. (Friedrich) 0.15. H. 1d.

[270]   **April 1904**

Wednesday the 20th
Sold 590 lbs. of hay @ 15.00 per ton = 4.43.

Thursday the 21st
Sold 208 lbs. of hay @ 15.00 per ton = 1.56 and received 1.00 in cash from Lava; he still owes 0.56. Received an answer from Wm Resor & Co. to my letter of April 14th with 0.40 in stamps—the freight for the repairs. Sold Ch. Hamilton ½ ton of hay @ 15.00 per ton = 7.50. Paid McRae 10.00 for 20 bu. of oats. To Pomeroy for wagon bolts (wrench bolt) in evener 0.40. For freight to cheese 0.25. H. 1d. Heinrich came home last evening, the 20th. H. 1d.

Friday the 22nd
Katie bred to Gammon's bull, 0.50. Sold Gammon 230 lbs. of hay @ 15.00 per ton = 1.73. Hauled manure. H. 1d. For Hinrich's suit 8.00. To surveyor 0.50. To Taalke 0.50. H. 1d.

Saturday the 23rd
Thunderstorm and rain during the night. Hauled manure. H. 1d.

Sunday the 24th
Good weather. Kept the Sabbath. Spent the whole day in bed. Rain in the morning; good weather in the afternoon.

Monday the 25th
Good weather. Received 9.90 from Hinrich for his work to April 23rd. Received 7.00 from Hamilton. For Ella's shoes 1.75, for Hinrich's shoes 1.50, for stationery 1.00, for 1 Bbl. lime 1.20, spoon 0.05, ladle 0.10, tab 0.75, 1 bu hair 0.30. To Keller toward the debt 4.00, for coffee 0.15, tea 0.30, onions 0.25, 2 boxes of oats 0.50, Atlas soap 0.25, sal soda 0.25, pepper 0.10, yeast 0.10, sugar 0.75, molasses 0.10, ginger 0.05, flour

[271]   April 1904

2.80, broom 0.35; total 20.55. For thread 0.10. H. 1d

Tuesday the 26th
Good weather. Pulled stumps and piled them. Plowed some of the orchard. H. 1d.

Wednesday the 27th
Good weather but still a very cold blustery winter wind. Hauled manure, plowed the rest of the orchard and harrowed it. Also drained some. H. 1d.

Thursday the 28th
Heinrich hauled 2 loads of sand for plastering and then plowed. I worked on the lath in the green room. H. 1d.

Friday the 29th
Received 0.56 from Lava (see April 21st). Heinrich plowed; I worked on the lath in the green room. H. 1d.

Friday the 30th
Good weather. Planted strawberries in the orchard. Heinrich plowed. H. 1d. For Hinrich's stockings 0.25. Johannes came to visit in the morning. 6 d.

[272]   **May 1904**

Michigan Cooperage 44.15, Welles 25.14, Francis & McRae 33.32, N.B.
Weaver 42.50, Gammon 2.50, Taalke 10.28, Keller 19.26, Pomeroy 0.40.—
School 2.60, D. Mills 1.00, Gammon 1.38.
As of 1 May 1904:
Outstanding receipts 4.98
Debts 177.55
Cash on hand 0.00

Sunday the 1st
Good weather. Bbr. Kay and Johnson were there. Johannes departed in the
evening again without saying good-bye to me.

Monday the 2nd
Good weather. Plowed the rest of the 10 acres along the road out toward
Proulx's and then harrowed. In the morning Heinrich departed. H. 1d.

Tuesday the 3rd
Nicer weather. Picked up 20 bu. of oats (see April 21st); borrowed 5.00 from
the bank to be paid back with 7% interest on August 3rd. Cultivator 4.75.
Then harrowed. H. 1d. From P. Proulx for 200 lbs. hay 1.50.

Wednesday the 4th
Very fine weather. Harrowed. The 10 acres northwest along the road are
ready to plant to oats. Went to see if Dankert would drill them in on the 6th;
he agreed. Sold Armstrong 256 lbs. of hay @ 15.00 per ton = 1.92; he will
pay in the near future. H. 1d.

Thursday the 5th
Ordered from Sears, Roebuck in Chicago:

1017810	1 pair Men's six wood Stirrups	0.10
191652	1 Grant foot pump for bicycle	0.25
2411310	1 log chain	1.60
15Y703	1 pair of two-buckle tan blucher	4.50
24Y3538	4 Malleable Self Fastening Inc.	
	Clevises @ 0.07	0.28
		6.73

See May 8th, invoice No. is 30049. See May 11th.

[273]   May 1904

Thursday the 5th
The stirrups are for Friedrich and the log chain is for the family as well as the clevises for a total of 1.88. Taalke lent the 0.13 I was short. In the forenoon went to bed; in the afternoon got ready to sow the next day and dug stumps out of the pig lot. To Francis & McRae for timothy seed 0.50. H. 1d.

Friday the 6th
Beautiful weather. To Gottenmyer for meat 0.30. To N.B. Weaver for oil 0.05. To Francis & McRae for sugar 0.25. Had Dankert over to drill in the oats. Found out through the drill that the piece was 8 ¾ acres without the pig lot, half barn, pig pen and corn crib. 22 stumps, four ditches and a north-south road should be added to the area because they also occupy space. We sowed 2¼ bu. per acre and so had about 1 peck left over, but we had 2 sacks full left over. In addition we sowed 32 lbs. of timothy and 23 lbs. of clover seed for a total of 55 lbs. = 5½ acres. We were finished about 6 o'clock in the evening. H. 1d.

Saturday the 7th
Beautiful weather, thunderstorm brewing. Harrowed some for planting corn then from 4 o'clock in the afternoon began rolling in the oats planted yesterday with Benson's roller. H. 1d. 6d

Sunday the 8th
Good weather. Bbr. Received an answer from Sears Roebuck to my order from the 5th: the invoice No. is 30049.

[274]   May 1904

Monday the 9th
Rolled in the piece of land planted to oats with Benson's roller. H. 1d.

Tuesday the 10th
Sent 65 lbs. of milk to the County Line cheese factory 4 miles west of Standish. I had to sign a contract to send all I could spare from today till November 1. (I am not required to deliver on Sunday and I likewise have the right to keep as much as I want for my own use.) Plowed some more and then harrowed twice. Then planted with oats, grass and clover seed and harrowed it in. Then harrowed some for corn planting. The piece for corn is about 6 acres and was plowed last fall. H. 1d. To Francis & McRae for tea 0.35. Received a postcard from Sears & Roebuck that the valued order of May 5th has been sent. The date—when—is not mentioned.

Wednesday the 11th
Milk 63 lbs. Received 12.00 from Hinrich. For groceries to Francis &
McRae 1 gal. vinegar 0.15, rice 0.25, tea 0.30, gr. sugar 0.50, lamp chimney 0.05, syrup 0.30, flour 2.80, washing soda 0.10, baking powder 0.10,
onions 6.25, bluing 0.10, linseed meal 2.00, oatmeal 0.25, coll. 1.20, Emma's
shoes 2.00, Emma's hat 1.00,

[275]   May 1904

Hinrich's overall 0.50; total 11.85. Sold hay for 10.30 cash. Have to ask
Dankert for 1.00 for hay. To Daugharty & Beaton for 1 bbl. lime 1.15. Harrowed for corn planting. H. 1d

Thursday the 12th
Milk 62. To Taalke 0.15 (see May 5th), to Hinrich 0.25 after the show, to
Friedrich 0.10 for stirrups. For Hinrich's gloves 0.25, mirror 0.10; total 0.35.
Paid Daugharty & Beaton 1.15 for 1 bbl lime (see Wednesday the 11th). A
thunderstorm with rain during the forenoon; harrowed during the afternoon.
H. 1d.

Friday the 13th
Milk 82. Taalke came home sick in the afternoon on Wednesday; she was
better by Thursday morning, however. Sold 343 lbs. of hay to Gammon @
15.00 per ton = 2.55. It rained in the afternoon. Fixed harness, etc. H. 1d.
From Hamilton 0.50. To Emma 0.50 for an examination. Paid the bank 5.00
on the note from May 3rd. Refund of 0.75 from Emma's shoes and hat as
well as Hinrich's overall (see May 11th).

Saturday the 14th
M. 62 lbs. For washbasin 0.20, lantern chimney 0.25, hoe 0.35, rake 0.45,
stationery 0.15; total 1.40. Debt to Norn 0.84, to Francis & McRae 1.00.
Duckering [?] feedbarn 0.10. Freight for Sears Roebuck order, see May 5th,
0.51. To Ryland [?] a stud fee of 10.00 for Topsy. H. 1d. Harrowed for planting corn. Milk for the week 334 lbs.

[276]   [Blank page]
[277]   [Blank page]

[278]   May 1904

Sunday the 15th
Cold, cold. Bbr. Fun bred to Gammon's bull, 0.50.

Monday the 16th
M. 94? 99. Cold. The heifer Jersey gave birth to a bull calf in the morning and the cow Rubie had a heifer calf in the afternoon. Harrowed in preparation for planting corn. H. 1d.

Tuesday the 17th
Cool. M. 80. Harrowed for corn planting. Blossom bred to Gammon's bull, 0.50. To Keller for sugar 0.25. H. 1d. For Mini's tablet 0.05.

Wednesday the 18th
M. 90. Sold 100 lbs. of Hay for 0.75. Received a statement from Dr. McGurk according to which our debt is less than I thought: instead of the 61.31 noted on May 1st, we owe 44.15, 17.16 less. Received a statement from Welles according to which we owe 5.58 more: instead of 19.56 we owe 25.14; see May 1st. Today it is raining and so I can revise my statement for May 1st. Harrowed some more for corn planting in the afternoon. H. 1d. To Gottenmyer for meat 0.30.

Thursday the 19th
M. 80. Rain, rain all day. For hinges 0.40, postage and for Emma's, actually Friedel's, ring 0.12; total 0.52. Put feed cups in front of the cows, then went to bed. Didn't weigh the milk. Learned from Wilson, who hauls our milk, that our milk was found to have a butterfat content of 3.08%. H. 1d.

[279]   May 1904

[No entries between May 19 and May 28.]

Saturday the 28th
M. 108. Beautiful weather. Hauled manure and planted corn. For hiring teacher Hamilton, 0.45. Received 2.38 from Taalke for Dankert's hay from the 11th and the 25th of May. H. 1d.
Milk this week: 566 lbs.

Sunday the 29th
Good weather. Brbr. Kept the Sabbath.

Monday the 30th
Cool, cloudy sky. M. 154. Planted corn and hauled manure. H. 1d.

Tuesday the 31st
M. 132. Planted the garden and harrowed. H. 1d. Planted corn.
According to our scale delivered 1715 lbs. of milk in the month of May; see June 14th, 1713 lbs. according to the factory.

We will praise thee for all that is past and trust thee for all that is to come.

[280]   **June 1904**

Michigan Cooperage Co. 44.15, Welles 25.14, Ryland 10.00, Francis & McRae 33.42, Weaver 42.55, Gammon 3.50, Taalke 10.28, Keller 19.76, Gottenmyer 0.40, Lerock 20 [*sic*].—School district No.2 3.35, Mills 1.00, Gammon 3.98, Armstrong 1.92 (see May 14th).
As of 1 May 1904:
Outstanding receipts 8.28
Debts 189.40
Cash on hand 2.43

Wednesday the 1st
M. 105. Planted corn and worked in the orchard. H. 1d.

Thursday the 2nd
M. 108. To Dankert yesterday 190 lbs. @ 15.00 per ton = 1.43. Picked up wood for the windows and doors in the green room. Borrowed 2.00 from Robert Page. To Gottenmyer for meat 0.35. H. 1d.

Friday the 3rd
M. 118. Planted beans and potatoes. H. 1d.

Saturday the 4th
M. 120 (guess). Planted potatoes and cleaned up around the grapevines. Hinrich to Bay City to see Barnum & Bailey's show 2.00. For Hinrich to June 3rd 10.00. Milk for the week 451.

Sunday the 5th
Brbr. Violent thunderstorm around noon.

Monday the 6th
Storm brewing. The milk was returned; was sour. Fun bred to Gammon's bull, see May 16th. H. 1d.

[281]   **June 1904**

Tuesday the 7th
M. 116 lbs. To Francis & McRae for flour 3.00, rolled oats 0.25, cr. of wheat 0.30, rice 0.25, gr. sugar 0.75, apples 0.25, washing soda 0.10, onions 0.10, tomatoes 0.25, pork 0.80, oil 0.65, baking powder 0.10, coffee 0.30, tea 0.25; total 8.50. For glasses 0.75, for repairing Mini's shoes 0.15. H. Peterson's wife Patty was buried. Potatoes ½ bu. 0.60. H. 1d. Paid Robert Page the 2.00 which I had borrowed from him on June 2nd. Daisy bred to Gammon's bull, 0.50.

Wednesday the 8th
M. 140 lbs. (guess). Hinrich's birthday was celebrated by all. The heifer Lili didn't come home last evening. Friedrich looked for her and found her over at Johannes' place. She had given birth to a beautiful heifer calf. H. 1d.

Thursday the 9th
M. 138 lbs. Cleared. Heinrich came by to visit for a few hours; Johannes came in the evening. H. 1d.

Friday the 10th
M. 121 lbs. Cleared; Johannes helped. H. 1d.

Saturday the 11th
M. 131. Cleared; Johannes helped and Karl helped ½ day. Pansy bred to Gammon's bull, 0.50. H. 1d.

Sunday the 12th
Brbr. Beautiful weather. Ps. 42: 1-2, Joh. 20: 20.

Monday the 13th
M. 124. Cleared; Johannes helped. H. 1d.

Tuesday the 14th
M. 127. Received 1.92 on Saturday the 11th from Armstrong. Owe H. Blumenthal 2.75 for Hinrich's birthday drink. Cleared, Johannes helped. H. 1d. For 1713 lbs. of milk in May 8.56; still expect to receive 4.97. Averaged 3.7% butterfat.

[282]   **June 1904**

Wednesday the 15th
M. 100. To H. Blumenthal 2.75. Cleared. For meal 0.25, rice 0.10, onions 0.05; total 0.40. H. 1d.

Thursday the 16th
M. 123. Cleared; Johannes helped as he did yesterday. H. 1d. Set fire to several heaps in late evening.

Friday the 17th
M. 130. In the morning 80 paces of fence between us and Karl had burned down. Cleared and plowed. To Wilson for hauling milk in May 1.50. For oatmeal 0.40, sugar 0.25, Friedrich's and Mini's hats 0.60; total 1.25. H. 1d.

Saturday the 18th
M. 120. For hiring a teacher and writing the contract 0.75. For Emma's and Ella's clothes 1.50, for Hinrich's shoes 1.50, shoe polish 0.10. Daisy covered by Gammon's bull. H. 1d. Milk for the week 724 lbs.

Sunday the 19th
Beautiful weather. Brbr. Heb. 10 16-25.

Monday the 20th
M. 130 lbs. Cleared and plowed as well as on Saturday the 18th. H. 1d.

Tuesday the 21st
M. 50. Harrowed and picked up roots etc. H. 1d. To Gottenmyer for meat 0.35.

Wednesday the 22nd
M. 130 lbs. Received from Hinrich for his work to June 18th 12.00. From that paid Cooperage for the 3.00 lent on May 26th. To Keller for matches 0.05, yeast 0.08, flour 2.80, oatmeal 0.25, r. wheat 0.25, rice 0.25, 2 lbs. coffee 0.30, tea 0.30, Atlas soap 0.25, sugar 0.50, pork 1.00, molasses 0.10, nutmeg 0.05, ½ bu. potatoes 0.63, onions 0.15; total

[283] June 1904

7.96. Paid 6.59 leaving 1.46 owed to Keller. For Hinrich 1.25, graduation 0.50. to Francis & McRae for 20 qt. millet seed 0.90. Received the balance for milk from 1903 = 13.41. Paid M.M.&M. Co. 13.40. Planted about 2 bu. of potatoes. H. 1d.

Thursday the 23rd
M. 120. Worked on the road Johannes worked over at his own place as he had yesterday. H. 1d.

Friday the 24th
M. 128. For a daybook 0.35, mouth harps 0.20; total 0.55. Worked on the road. Rubie covered by Sonomit's bull, 0.50. H. 1d.

Saturday the 25th
M. 110. Johannes sowed 20 a. (Ed note: means acres.) millet seed in the uncleared piece of land and harrowed it in. I went to bed. In the afternoon Johannes cultivated corn and potatoes. H. 1d. Milk for the week: 668 lbs.

Sunday the 26th
Beautiful weather. Brbr. Eph. 1: 3-8, Is. 43: 21-26.

Monday the 27th
M. 121. Cultivated corn with two horses; Johannes helped. Was to Mrs. Barnes' funeral. To Mich. Cooperage Co. for casing for the doors and windows in the green room 2.50. To Francis & McRae for washing soda 0.05, sugar 0.50; total 0.55. H. 1d.

Tuesday the 28th
M. 130. Cold during the night. Cultivated; Johannes helped. H. 1d.

Wednesday the 29th
M. 126. Hot. Replanted corn and hoed beans. Set out 30 cabbage plants. H. 1d. Fidelia Proulx had a birthday, 12 years old.

[284] June 1904

Thursday the 31st [*sic*]
M. 136. Set out 100 cabbage plants and then spaded some. Johannes hauled a load of wood for building a new house. Replanted corn. H. 1d.

According to our scale delivered 3003 lbs. of milk in June.

Delivered 1750 lbs. in May; received 8.56.

This book is full.
It was begun in God's name
and it ends in His name.
Praise be to Him and thanks!

[The remaining pages of Jan Wübbena's manuscript are as follows:

285 & 286, blank.

288: 1903.
For the eggs and butter delivered March 24th received comb 0.15, Taalke's stockings 0.20, Mini's rubbers 0.50, hairpins 0.55.
For the eggs sold on March 26th received syrup 0.19, lamp chimney 0.05.
For the butter sold March 28th received 1 bowl 0.15, sugar 0.25, collection 0.05, molasses 0.10, buttons 0.10, ginger 0.05, lemon 0.05, stockings 0.15, cash 0.02; total 0.92.
For the butter sold on April 4th received assorted groceries.
For the butter sold on April 18th received syrup 0.30, soda 0.10, thread 0.8, forgotten.
April 22nd oatmeal 0.25, rice 0.25, onions 0.07.
May 8th butter shoelaces 0.05, molasses 0.10, sugar 0.25, rice 0.25, ginger 0.05, due bill 0.44.

289:   1903

Feb. 23, Mon.	received for butter	0.40
Mar. 7, Sat.	received for butter	0.65
Mar. 14, Sat.	received for butter	0.60
Mar. 14, Sat.	received for 1 doz.	0.15
Mar. 24, Tue.	received for butter	0.67
Mar. 24, Tue.	received for eggs	0.28
Mar. 26, Thr.	received for eggs	0.24
Mar. 28, Sat.	received for butter	0.92
Apr. 4, Sat.	received for butter	1.00
Apr. 18, Sat.	received for butter	0.57
Apr. 22, Wed.	received for butter	0.57
May 8, Fri.	received for butter	1.14

287, 290–293:   Herdsman's records of the livestock in table form giving their names, dates of birth, breeding, names of sire animals, dates of freshening and notes on the sex of their offspring and on their life.

294–298:   are lined out (three blocks to the page) to record money owed various creditors. There are spaces for Barnes, the Independent (N. Ireland), M.M.&M. Co., J. Daugharty, N.B. Weaver, L. Nerriter, Gottenmyer, J. Norn, John Dobson, O.A. Marfileus, Curney, Dr. A. Grigg, Telfer, J. Stölt, and Peppel. These spaces have at most one entry from the year 1899; apparently Mr. Wübbena abandoned this system of recordkeeping almost immediately.]

GLOSSARY OF TERMS USED IN JAN WÜBBENA'S FARM DIARY

by Catherine Wubbena

Airline Road   The road from Standish to Omer, so called because the telegraph poles, with lines, ran alongside this road. At the present time this is US 23.

Aloike clover   Probably a misprint. Should be Alsike clover.

Angus   Owner of a large farm on the western outskirts of Standish; Standish Community Hospital now stands on this site.

Arenac County Normal   The system of county normal schools was an institution which existed in various rural counties in Michigan. In order to provide a supply of teachers for the numerous rural grade schools a county would create what was known as a County Normal School, though in fact it would more appropriately have been called a program.

In the early years of this institution a few of the seniors in the high school at the county seat who desired to become rural teachers would be given special training by a teacher who assumed responsibility for the program as an extra duty. Later on the institution restricted training to high school graduates who spent an additional year in the high school undergoing more extensive training by the teacher assigned to the program. In either case these students were afforded an opportunity to do practice teaching in the town's grade school, which in those days was usually part of the same school building as the high school.

Upon satisfactory completion of the course the graduate was certified as a teacher for the county's rural grade schools, subject to periodically taking summer courses offered by the state system of teachers' colleges in order to maintain certification.

The system served rural Michigan well. It provided teachers from the rural areas that were better able than outsiders to adapt to the demanding nature of teaching eight grades in one room under almost primitive conditions.

In or before 1903 Arenac County created the first County Normal in Michigan. All of the Wubbena girls attended except Talka.

Gradually the need for these county normals died out, due to three things: (1) the improvement in the rural roads until they became passable under all weather conditions; (2) the concomitant increase in the trend to bus students to a centrally located larger school; and (3) the increased availability of teachers with more training from the state system of teachers' colleges. Arenac County terminated its Normal in 1957, the last Michigan county to do so.

Armstrong   A farmer whose farm was adjacent to John's farm. Their children had fun with the Wubbenas.

Baikie   A Scottish family in the nearby town of Omer. Years later his grandson William married Myrtle Wubbena (daughter of Charles).

Barker   A farmer living a mile west of Standish on M-61.

Barnes   Not identified. Probably was a member of the Gospel Hall or perhaps the minister at the Congregational Church. He seemed to do some preaching.

Barness   Preached at the Harten Funeral Home. Was this Barnes?

Barness, Mrs.   Probably Mrs. Barnes

Barnett   Not identified.

Barnett, Mrs.   Not identified.

Barns Church   Not identified.

Barrager   Not identified.

Barthard   Not identified.

Baumgarth   A shoe repair shop in Standish.

Beason   A farmer in the vicinity.

Benson, Mrs. Astrid   Members of a Swedish family whose farm was on the southwest corner of Johnsfield and Melita Roads.

Bentley   A small village several miles west of Standish.

Birdsall, Rev.   Not identified.

Bittersalz   Probably similar to Epsom Salts.

Blain from Jersey City   Not identified.

Bluing   A laundry compound used in the rinse water for white clothes in order to make them whiter.

Blumenthal, H.   One of two Jewish families; owned a clothing store on Cedar Avenue for many years.

Box of cartridges, fuse, caps   Equipment for setting off blasts of dynamite. Stubborn pine stumps were blasted out; remaining smaller roots left in the ground were dug out by hand with cant hooks or by the horses pulling with chains. Frightened horses and children were kept at safe distances during the blasting. Infrequently the person doing the work, in a moment of careless-ness, would be injured, perhaps losing fingers, a hand, etc. The entire family was apprehensive until father returned safe and sound to the homestead after a day's working on the stumps. Pulled-out stumps would most commonly be placed in piles and burned at a convenient time when no strong wind was blowing.

Brbr   Broke bread. Remembering the Lord on the Sabbath included pass-ing a loaf of bread to members. Each "broke" a piece of bread. This was fol-lowed by passing a goblet of wine, each member taking a sip.

Brocoms   Not identified.

Brouwer, E.   Of Clara City, Minnesota. Not identified.

Bruns, Mrs. L.   Of Cutler County, Iowa. Not identified.

Burkhart   Did carpenter work; was the father-in-law of Dankert.

Buy   Possibly the Saginaw Bay where there were places satisfactory for swimming. At that time it was most likely the beach called Timber Island.

Caldwell, William   A Johnsfield farmer. Harry lived with them for several months after his mother Catharina died.

Calicia and Camcara   Not identified. Perhaps a kind of cloth used for their sewing.

Cashnell   Not identified.

Cassidy   A Standish family. Mr. Cassidy drove horses with a wagon and delivered freight from trains to stores and businesses.

Cassidy & Hill   Not identified.

Chamberlain and Henderson   H. Chamberlain bought and sold property, was County Registrar of Deeds for a period of time, and later became a banker. Benjamin J. Henderson apparently worked with Chamberlain selling insurance; he had an office in the courthouse and was an energetic, colorful lawyer known to become somewhat profane as he pressed witnesses to tell more. Not related to D.C. Henderson.

Dr. Charles' Recipe Book   Probably a misinterpretation—more likely to be *Dr. Chase's Recipe Book*.

Chase's Recipe Book   A familiar item in homes; in addition to recipes it included many first aid measures and home remedies for various ailments. It was published as *Dr. Chase's Home Adviser and Everyday Reference Book* in 1894; later editions were published in 1904 and 1908. The edition at hand in the John Wubbena household is *Dr. Chase's Combination Receipt Book* published in 1915. Today it is a collector's item.

Cheese Factory   There were several small cheese factories in the area; one was in the north end of town, immediately east of the railroad and adjacent to the millpond (which site at present is a building occupied by Spartan Tire Co.). The cheese factory alluded to (February 3, 1902) may be the one located on the corner of present M-61 and Eight Mile Road known as the County Line Cheese Factory. Later, on February 12, he went into Standish to "take inventory" so the factory is probably the one in town.

Chest strengthener   An appliance or article used by Jan in an effort to rid him of his chest pains and improve his health.

Christ Conference   This must pertain to the "Christian Conference" held annually at the Gospel Hall.

Clarebean   Not identified.

Clarke, Mrs. (Bertha Kaschub)   Not identified.

Clevis   A U-shaped piece of metal used to attach one piece of equipment to another; a bolt had to be passed through holes in the two ends of the U after it had connected the two pieces. There were various sizes of clevises.

Codi   An Indian family living near the Bay. Some members attended the Gospel Hall.

Cold shuts   This must be related to the chains and other equipment used for pulling out stump roots after they had been blasted with dynamite.

Community of the Confessors   In the week after Minnie's baptism, she was accepted into the circle of Believers at the Gospel Hall, a group which participated in remembering the Lord's death by "breaking bread" from the broken loaf. See #4 on map [page 19].

Congregational Church   Talka was friendly with the pastor and his family; father Jan, too, had a warm relationship with the family and members of the church, which was located on the southwest corner of Court Street and Cedar Avenue. See #1 on map [page 19].

Coor, Mrs.   This may be a misprint for the name Coon—an Indian family and faithful Gospel Hall members for two generations.

Corosine   Possibly a form of liniment (used on a colt's leg).

Cradle fingers   Prongs, or tines, made of wood and attached to a handle in a curved manner; used to gather grain and hay which was laid flat after cutting with scythe or mower.

Crecine   A family living in Standish.

Curk   Not identified, but probably was McGurk, which appears to read as Mr. Curk.

Curney   Not identified.

Dankert   A family living a mile west of the Wubbenas. Their three sons and the Wubbena boys enjoyed playing pranks on each other as they grew up.

Dankert, Werner   Possibly Herman Dankert, one of the Dankert men whose farm was about a mile west of Wubbena's.

Daugherty, J.   A member of an Irish family living in town; helped with developing the school system in Arenac County.

Decum, Mr.   Judge of Probate. This name is probably a misprint. Mr. John W. Dunn was a lawyer who lived and practiced in Standish until a ripe old age, and courthouse records indicate that he was the judge of probate from 1900 to 1920.

Delie   Not identified. This may be a misinterpretaion of the name Daley. Baby Ella was kept by the Daleys who lived in Sterling.

Demond, Rockwell   A local "horse doctor."

Denco   Not identified.

Deo Volente   God willing.

Dobson, James and John   Members of the family whose farm was east of Wubbena's on the corner of Deep River Road and Johnsfield Road.

Dow   Sold building materials near Norn's mill.

Duckering, Thomas   Was "just over four feet tall and straight as a stick" (per Allan McCready). His daughter Ina married Judge Dunn. He had a feed barn located a block from Main Street. Those who drove horses into town tied the horse, with buggy attached, to a post along the street, or, if desired, paid a fee to have the horse and rig left at the feed barn. If the stay was to be a matter of several hours or overnight, the animals were fed for an additional fee. There was usually more than one feed barn located in town.

Dumond, or Dumund   A local "horse doctor" who also did some farming about one mile west of Standish. He helped to get Talka and Henry started with going to school in Standish the first autumn after they arrived from Germany.

Duncan   A Scottish family living in town. Daughter Myrtle married Charles Wubbena.

Dupee (also Dupius, and Dupres)   A French family, several members of whom lived on the road on which Charles' farm was located.

Dupke   A friend of the family; possibly a member of the Gospel Hall located in Bay City.

DV   See Deo Volente.

Dystant, Iector   Not identified

Elwell   Had a small meat market in town.

Embury, Albert   He and his family were long-standing friends and members of the Gospel Hall.

Eureka Flour   A brand of flour at that time.

Farmer's Institute   This was an annual affair that was much looked forward to and appreciated by local farmers. One of the promoters was the railroad company, their interest being related to the amount of freight for which the farmers would utilize the railroad. Speakers came from agriculture-related businesses and the Michigan Agriculture College (the forerunner of Michigan State University), or were progressive local farmers. The Institute would be held in one of the large buildings in one of the towns of Arenac County. This gradually developed into the Cooperative Extension Program for farmers which exists today and emanates from Michigan State University.

Farmer's Institute Society   This was a society that held periodic meetings throughout the year on various topics of interest to farmers of the region. Its purpose was twofold: first, to assist farmers by giving them the latest information on various agricultural aspects that would be of value to them; and second, to serve as a supportive network for the farmers and, through its ladies auxiliary, their wives.

Fecto   Not identified (Is it Feeto?).

Forsyth   Several members of this family were business people in Standish. One was a pharmacist, one a real estate dealer and the owner of the local Protestant Cemetery, another an insurance agent.

Francis, Charles   Had a grocery store on Cedar Avenue for many years.

Friedel   This may be Fidelia Proulx, nickname Feedell. She was a close friend of the Wubbena girls; her parents' farm was next door. She spent much time in the Wubbena home.

Friedrich   The German word for Frederick.

Gale, Charles Not identified.

Gammon, Mrs. Had a large farm on the present M-61 where the new state maximum security prison is now located.

Garner, Robert Not identified.

Garners Not identified.

Garries Not identified.

Gebothen from the Ancient Order of Eleanors Not identified.

Gorton, Joe Not identified.

Gottenmyer Two brothers who had a meat market on Cedar Avenue.

Gregory, Mrs. In Jonesville. Not identified.

Grigg, Dr. A general practitioner in Standish.

Gross Charles Francis' partner in the grocery store (?).

Grow Not identified.

Halcro A family living on North Main Street. Mr. Halcro and his son Ed repaired harnesses. After there were no more harnesses being used, they did cobbler work for many years, repairing boots and shoes. Some of the Halcro family attended the Gospel Hall Sunday School.

Hall, Alf Alfred Hall, called Fred Hall, had a flour mill near the Mill Pond. Eventually he rigged up equipment which produced electricity for his mill, and, for a stated number of hours per day, supplied electric power to some businesses and residences.

Hamilton Both Frank and Clara, son and daughter of George Hamilton who was the owner of the farm adjacent to John's farm on the west. Frank and Clara were teachers in the Johnsfield School. The whole family were close friends of the John Wubbena Family.

Hartman, Mrs. A member of a family of farmers. She trimmed hats for ladies.

Hayes, Sam A lawyer in town; always called "S.E.". He and his daughter Amy lived on South Forest Street.

Heasley Not identified.

Heinrich The German word for Henry.

Henderson, Miss This was Sadie Henderson, a member of a family who were close friends with the Hamilton family. Both families had migrated from Canada and were active in the Standish community.

Herten, Will Not identified (may be the same as Harten).

Hinrich   The German word for Harry.

Holm, Mrs.   Not identified.

H. 1d, H ½d, H. 4 hrs, etc.   This apparently was Jan's system for keeping a record of Hinrich's (Harry's) work which seemed to be at the stave mill. (This may be the Michigan Cooperage Co.) Staves were used in making wooden barrels.

Honey, W. N.   Had a general store. His son, Doug Honey was the freight agent at the Michigan Central depot for many years.

Hull, Dr. Chas.   Dentist in district of Maple Ridge, several miles north of Standish.

Iexin   Not identified.

Independent   The name of the local newspaper.

Ireland   Part owner of the old *Independent Newspaper*.

Jake   Not identified.

Jarvis Center   A school district located about two miles north of Standish. Minnie and/or Ella taught at this school for a short time.

Johannes   The German word for the name of Jan's son, John.

Johnson, I.   A farmer in the Johnsfield District.

Jungjohann, Engelke   The brother of Catharina (Jan's brother-in-law) who lived in the village of Neermoor in Germany. For several years following his death, the Wubbenas carried on correspondence with his widow, Aunt Lukke, and in fact William, his daughter Dawn, and his son William visited her in Neermoor in 1956.

Kaffircorn, also Kafircorn   A kind of corn used more for fodder than for grain.

Karl   The German word for the name of Jan's son, Charles.

Kaufmann   Not identified.

Kausen, Mr.   Not identified.

Kawkawlin   Taken from the Indian language. A village and district located a few miles north of Bay City.

Kay, James Sr.   A preacher from Bay City who conducted Jan's funeral service in 1907. He drowned while swimming in the Cass River. His widow and children were frequent visitors at the Wubbena home.

Keefer   Not identified.

Keifer   Perhaps a "horse doctor," not a veterinarian.

Keller, Fred   Co-owner of a grocery store with Charles Francis.

Kelsch, Miss Barbara   Probably Koelsch, one of a German family whose descendants continue to farm in the Johnsfield area. The farm is still located about a mile southwest of the old Wubbena place.

Kiefer   Perhaps another "horse doctor."

Kiens Kidney tea   Possibly a "remedy" for his backache.

Kitzman   A German family living a mile west of the Johnsfield school.

Knight, Earnest   A blacksmith who did many repair jobs. His shop was on Forest Avenue, the second or third building south of Cedar Avenue.

Kramen   Not identified.

Kraus   A German family in the Johnsfield District.

Krause, Ernst   Had a farm on what is presently M-61 about four miles west of Standish. Baby Fred was kept by them for nearly a year. Mrs. Krause (Louise) wanted to adopt Fred; Jan said "No."

Kroske   A Johnsfield German family; Mr. Kroske did much of the carpenter work when the Johnsfield School was built.

Lammerhirte   Not identified.

Larou, Frank   Apparently a person handling the milk as it was transported to the cheese factory. "Watering the milk"—a practice which had to be guarded against; in later years when milk was routinely tested for butter fat upon delivery to its destination, this practice was readily detected.

Lava   Not identified.

Lawrence, Al   A farmer whose farm was three miles west of Standish.

Lefree   Owner of a threshing machine which went from farm to farm.

Le Roc   Perhaps the French family whose name was spelled LaRocque.

Lewa   Not identified.

Lieberan   Not identified.

Lucks, G.   Not identified.

Lundy   Not identified.

M, Professor   This is M. Claus (according to a tape Henry made) who gave singing lessons at the Johnsfield School; the young Wubbena children learned much from him.

Mama's grave   This would be Catharina's grave, and at this time was located in the village of Sterling. Later, when Jan died in 1907, a cemetery had been located in Standish. Catharina was reburied by John, Charles, and

Henry next to their father's grave in the Woodmere Cemetery in Standish. See #6 on map [page 20].

M & M Co.   A business, the Mitts and Merril Co., located, along with other factories and mills, near the Mill Pond on the northern edge of Standish. They made sleighs for lumbermen and sold some household items. Bill Donnelly, a local historian, recalls that his father worked for this company.

Marfileus, Oscar A.   Had a pharmacy store in Standish as a very young man. Also sold stationery supplies. This store was later sold to Tom Milne. A local historian, Milton Bergeron, recalls that thirty years after this time Oscar was still a pharmacist, having a store in Holly, Michigan.

Marten, Br.   Not identified. To be preceded by Br., meaning Brother, would indicate he is one of the brethren (i.e., a member of the Gospel Hall). A few days later it is recorded Jan went to "Marten's meeting," so he must have been a preacher.

Matthews, Mr.   One of the "Nornites," and a brother-in-law of Mr. Norn. Probably preached the Gospel at "a meeting in the school."

McCaddy   A Scottish family, close friends of the Wubbenas and members of the Gospel Hall.

McGurk   A doctor who served many folks as the family physician in Standish.

McLean   Probably a preacher at the Gospel Hall.

Mellencamp   Not identified.

Mergel   Not identified.

Miller, P. M.   Worked for J. Norn. His wife had a lively millinery business in a storefront home on Beaver Street.

Mills, David   Not identified.

Milne, Tom   Member of a Scottish family. Apparently dealt in lumber. In the 1920s a Tom Milne was a pharmacist in Standish.

Milne's Arithmetic   A textbook used for years in the country schools.

Mini   Jan's pet name for Minnie.

Minis Crosley's language system   Not identified. Probably related to school studies.

M M & M Co.   Apparently the same company as M & M Co.

M109   These figures, with M, represent the number of pounds of milk hauled to the cheese factory on that day. One of the Armstrong boys apparently hauled the milk from each farmer to the cheese factory; each farmer paid the hauler based on the number of pounds hauled.

Monroe   Not identified.

Montworth Geometry   A textbook used at that time.

Moore's Junction   A community about three miles west of Johnsfield. It was near the junction of Adams and Moore's Junction Roads. There was a two-room school, post office, store, and Grange Hall. It was at the junction of two railroad spurs; these rails were for trains carrying out logs cut from nearby woods. In 1889 Joe Price was the postmaster. The post office was discontinued in 1907.

Mt. Forest   A community located several miles southwest of Standish.

Nachricht   Not identified.

Naiser   Not identified.

Nehls   A family with several members active in local government as well as farming.

Nehls, Heinrich   Henry remained a bachelor all his life. He liked the Wubbena girls.

Nerriter   A miller in Sterling who also did business in Standish. A part of his old mill still stands in Sterling.

Nicholson, Nelson   A member of Gospel Hall. The Nicholson house was located in Welles Addition.

Niemann, John   Possibly a member of the Nieman family, who were farmers in Johnsfield.

Norn, James   An immigrant from Scotland; a sharp businessman who owned several saw mills and stave mills in Standish, Sterling, Deep River, Omer, and briefly near West Branch. Very actively involved in working with Christians and a religious group; was a member of Gospel Hall. Because of his representation of this group, its members were called "Nornites."

Orangemen   Not identified; perhaps a lodge, or a group of immigrants from Ireland.

Ostfriesen News   This could have been mailed from Germany but was more likely to have come from a town in Iowa. Distant relatives and/or friends infrequently communicated with John and Talka.

Page, Robert   A man who bought and sold property all over the county at a profit.

"pales"   This is probably "poles" since they were setting up fences.

Parker Not identified.

Peppel A farmer, who with his descendants farmed for many years in the Johnsfield district.

"phisiology" Probably a misspelling of physiology. The context tends to indicate that the reference was to a textbook. (See entries October 13, 17, and 19, 1903.) Both R. M. Forsyth and Marfileus (local druggists) sold textbooks when I was a girl, so I assume they did in 1903.

Pioneer Picnic A potluck dinner and celebration, an annual summer event; it is unknown under whose auspices it was held.

Pomeroy A family name in Standish. In later years son Henry had a Chevrolet car dealership.

Proulx A French family whose farm was immediately adjacent to the west end of the Wubbena farm.

Ps. 42:1–2, Joh. 20:20 Reference is to these Scripture verses in the Bible as follows:

Psalms 42:1–2: *"As a hart longs for flowing streams,*
So longs my soul for Thee, O God.
My soul thirst for God, for the living God.
When shall I come and behold the face of God?"

John 20:20 *"When He had said this, He showed them his*
hands and side. Then the disciples were glad
when they saw the Lord."

Punche, or pumche Not identified.

R.R. Show A circus in Bay City. John loved a circus! Perhaps Ringling Bros?

Rancourt, John Had a large farm on the northwest corner of the present Cedar and Court Streets. He had several horses and apparently did custom work threshing grain.

Rape seed Also called canola. Little attention was paid to it by U.S. farmers at that time. By 1985, because of the attention being given to cholesterol, it was being planted and harvested in the United States; the oil extracted from it is low in saturated fat. European farmers have raised it for many years, and used it for feed for cattle and hogs.

Recitation seat In the country school there were two such seats, each long enough for about six to eight pupils to be seated. The teacher called each class to the front to be seated there for the lesson. The class period was about ten minutes in length, and pupils then were sent back to their desks. Then the teacher called the next class to be seated on the recitation seats. This went on for the total school day, with fifteen minute recess in mid-morning and mid-afternoon, and a one-hour lunch period. The school bell was rung at the end of each "break period."

Reigh, A.   A preacher in the Gospel Hall; family members were close friends of Minnie.

Richard   Not identified.

Richert, Karl   A family living in the South Branch school district, just south of Johnsfield.

Rug   Not identified.

Ryland   Had a hotel on the corner of Main and Cedar Streets.

Schauer   One of the "Nornite" families. Mr Schauer did blacksmith work. Their daughter Frieda was a long-standing friend of the Wubbena girls; she was a highly praised teacher in Detroit schools, and was singled out for recognition by Henry Ford I.

Schoerff, C. H.   Had a jewelry store and acted as an optician.

Schmelzer, Miss   May have been the daughter of the minister of the Lutheran church in Sterling.

Schneider   Not identified.

Schulz   Not identified.

seleratus   Possibly salt peter.

Senne   A family whose farm was about a mile west of Wubbena's. Their children and the Wubbenas' did a lot of singing together.

Server   A Standish family. Apparently Mr. Server did some veterinary work, and would have been called a "horse doctor" in those days.

Setkemant   Not identified.

Shinglebolt   A short log of cedar (or sometimes pine) for making shingles. The log had to be sound wood throughout with straight grain and no knots, and of a sufficient diameter and length. Such logs were not easy to find in most areas so when farmers did find them in trees they were cutting, they set them aside to sell to the local shingle mill for a little extra income. (See entry December 1, 1900.)

Sillos   Not identified.

Social Gleaner   This might have been the publication put out by the Gleaner Society.

Sonnschmitt   Not identified.

Sonomit   Not identified. Possibly Sonsmit.

Sonsmit   Not identified.

Spancer, George   Not identified.

Spooner, Mrs.   Baby Fred stayed with her for a period of time after his mother, Catharina, died. Mrs. Spooner showed some interest in Jan, but he "side-stepped the bait" according to a tape made by Henry.

Stallinger   Not identified.

"steeples"   This is probably staples, used when attaching fencing to posts.

Stillinger   Apparently had "drive-on" scales for weighing wagons, etc.

Stolt   Not identified.

Stube Factory   Not identified.

Swaive, Mrs. J. E.   Of Harper, Illinois. Not identified.

Telfer   Not identified.

Thomley, Reverend   Not identified.

Thoms   A neighbor whose sons Bill and Erie remained close friends of Fred and Bill Wubbena.

Timrick   A family apparently very close to the Wubbena family. Elsie Timrick and her mother visited the Wubbenas often.

Timrock   Probably a misprint for Timrick.

T. 1 d   Record of Talka's work at the office of H. Chamberlain.

Toothacker, Dr.   A general practitioner located in Standish for a number of years.

To the Lord in the form of a cripple 0.20   I do not understand the meaning, or implications, of this.

Turfus   A Scottish farmer living north of Standish. He and his sons and daughter were members of the Gospel Hall.

Vance   Not identified.

Vermifuge   A preparation for deworming; different preparations for humans and animals.

Waites, Jerry   A friend of the family. The Wubbena boys told of playing practical jokes on him.

Walton   Not identified.

Wards   Did lumber cutting. Apparently also sold shovels.

Weaver, N. B.   Had a hardware store on Cedar Avenue.

Welles, A. H. Owned a clothing store. Mr. Welles was interested in various manufacturing ventures. His plants were leased to others who made wooden tubs and pails and wooden handles. One company made barrels. A small settlement of homes about one mile east of Standish was called (and still is known as) Welles Addition.

Wendt, Otto A photographer. His business was located on the second floor over Schoerff's jewelry store.

Wentzel Barn Not identified.

West Apparently did carpenter work—"made the bookcases for the school."

Wilhelm German for William.

Wilhelm's birthday Noted on March 8. This seems to be an error; Bill's birthday was on January 5. Note that he writes on Saturday, February 22, "in the evening a party for Mini." This was probably an early celebration of her birthday, which was on March 8.

Wills Not identified.

Wilson A farmer located east of John's farm. Family members still own the farm on Sagatoo Road.

Wilton Not identified.

Woods, Mr. Not identified.

Wright, George Not identified.

Wubbena, Mrs. C. H. Apparently was Myrtie, Charles' wife.

Wubbena, Grace Charles' and Myrtie's second daughter.

Wyatt, Mrs. Lived in Standish and was a member of the Gospel Hall. Her daughter Laura married John several years after this.

Part Three

THE
WUBBENA FAMILY
TREE

WUBBENA FAMILY TREE

GENEALOGY DATA

The following pages set forth genealogical data for the descendants and antecedents of Jan and Catharina Wubbena, updated to reflect all information available to the compilers through June 21, 1995.

The first 45 pages reflect information pertaining to Jan and Catharina's parents and descendants. Following those pages is a set of charts setting forth what is known concerning the antecedents of Jan and Catharina.

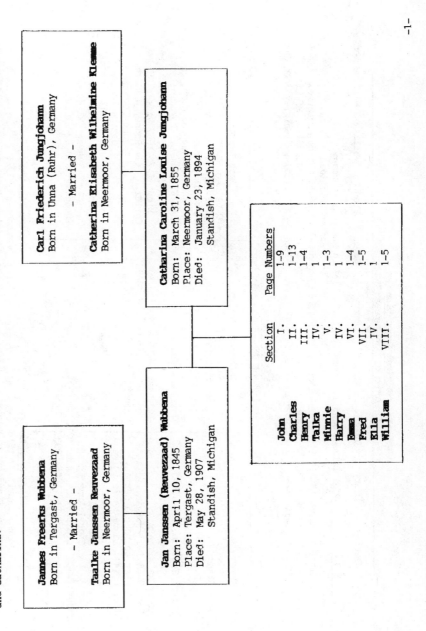

Carl Friederich Jungjohann
Born in Unna (Ruhr), Germany

   - Married -

Catharina Elisabeth Wilhelmine Klemme
Born in Neermoor, Germany

Catharina Caroline Louise Jungjohann
Born: March 31, 1855
Place: Neermoor, Germany
Died: January 23, 1894
        Standish, Michigan

James Freerks Wubbena
Born in Tergast, Germany

   - Married -

Taalke Janssen Reuvezaad
Born in Neermoor, Germany

Jan Janssen (Reuvezaad) Wubbena
Born: April 10, 1845
Place: Tergast, Germany
Died: May 28, 1907
        Standish, Michigan

	Section	Page Numbers
John	I.	1-9
Charles	II.	1-13
Henry	III.	1-4
Talka	IV.	1
Minnie	V.	1-3
Harry	IV.	1
Emma	VI.	1-4
Fred	VII.	1-5
Ella	IV.	1
William	VIII.	1-5

First Generation

(Children of Jan Janssen Wubbena)

John   Charles   Henry   Talka   Mimmie   Barry   Emma   Fred   Ela   **William Louis**

John Talkeus Wubbena   Born April 18, 1874 in Neermoor, Germany
Died July 6, 1954 in Standish, Michigan

Married: March 14, 1911 to Laura Mary Wyatt   [Born August 11, 1888 in Oneida, Ontario, CANADA
in Standish, Michigan   Died November 1, 1971 in Standish, Michigan]
Children (5): Wyatt Jan, Catherine Evelyn, Ruth Laura, Alice Jean Louise, and Shirley John Carl

Second Generation

(Children of John Talkeus Wubbena)

Wyatt Jan

Born: February 29, 1912
Place: Standish, Michigan
Died: April 10, 1981
         Dover, Delaware
Married: September 22, 1943
         Chicago, Illinois
         to Erika Wilharm
         Born 9-15-1921 Poznan, Poland
         [Later to become Germany]
Children (4): Laura Marie Luise
              Jan Helmut
              Kurt Wilharm
              Cheryl Anne Lurae
Address: 3001 Lititz Pike, Apt. #212
         Lancaster, PA 17606-5093
Phone: (717) 569-1650

Catherine Evelyn

Born: July 22, 1913
Place: Standish, Michigan
Married: No

Children: None

Address: 4406 S. Melita Road
         Standish, MI 48658
Phone: (517) 846-6620

Ruth Laura

Born: December 2, 1914
Place: Standish, Michigan
Married: August 3, 1938
         Standish, Michigan
         to William Clifford Tulloch
         Born 2-27-1910 Omer, Michigan
         Died 11-26-1987 Vassar, MI
Children (4): Rodney William
              John Truman
              Janine Louise
              Christine Mereda
Address: 6323 State Road
         Vassar, MI 48768
Phone: (517) 823-7089

Alice Jean Louise

Born: April 7, 1916
Place: Standish, Michigan
Married: December 12, 1945
         Le Havre, France
         to Irwin Kenneth Bittner
         Born 8-29-1919 Frostburg, MD
         Died 12-14-1970 Vassar, MI
Children (3): Theda Jean
              Ralph Kenneth
              Jacqueline Anne
Address: 6362 State Road
         Vassar, Michigan
Phone: (517) 823-2283

Shirley John Carl

Born: November 14, 1921
Place: Standish, Michigan
Died: May 9, 1972
         Standish, Michigan
Married: August 7, 1943
         Standish, Michigan
         to Jeannette Marie Noeske
         Born 2-26-1923 Standish, MI
         Died 7-2-1994 Saginaw, MI
Children: None
Address: 4700 Duprie Road
         Standish, Michigan 48658
Phone: (517) 846-9967

I. John – 2

-3-

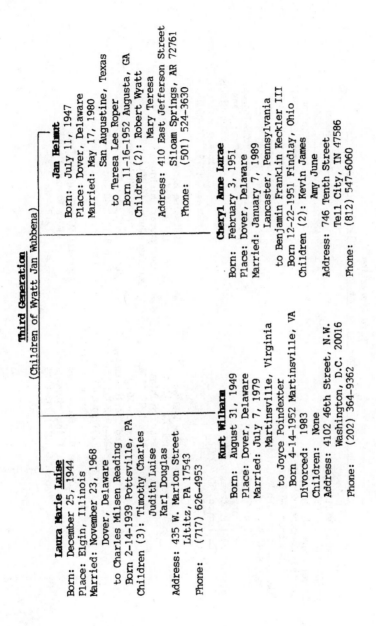

Third Generation
(Children of Wyatt Jan Wubbena)

Laura Marie Luise
Born: December 25, 1944
Place: Elgin, Illinois
Married: November 23, 1968
         Dover, Delaware
to Charles Milsen Reading
Born 2-14-1939 Pottsville, PA
Children (3): Timothy Charles
              Judith Luise
              Karl Douglas
Address: 435 W. Marion Street
         Lititz, PA 17543
Phone: (717) 626-4953

Jan Helmut
Born: July 11, 1947
Place: Dover, Delaware
Married: May 17, 1980
         San Augustine, Texas
to Teresa Lee Roper
Born 11-16-1952 Augusta, GA
Children (2): Robert Wyatt
              Mary Teresa
Address: 410 East Jefferson Street
         Siloam Springs, AR 72761
Phone: (501) 524-3630

Kurt Wilharm
Born: August 31, 1949
Place: Dover, Delaware
Married: July 7, 1979
         Martinsville, Virginia
to Joyce Poindexter
Born 4-14-1952 Martinsville, VA
Divorced: 1983
Children: None
Address: 4102 46th Street, N.W.
         Washington, D.C. 20016
Phone: (202) 364-9362

Cheryl Anne Lurae
Born: February 3, 1951
Place: Dover, Delaware
Married: January 7, 1989
         Lancaster, Pennsylvania
to Benjamin Franklin Keckler III
Born 12-22-1951 Findlay, Ohio
Children (2): Kevin James
              Amy June
Address: 746 Tenth Street
         Tell City, IN 47586
Phone: (812) 547-6060

Third Generation
(Children of Ruth Wubbena Tulloch)

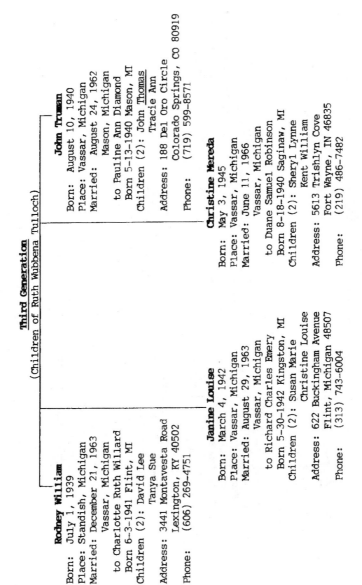

Rodney William

Born: July 1, 1939
Place: Standish, Michigan
Married: December 21, 1963
        Vassar, Michigan
   to Charlotte Ruth Willard
        Born 6-3-1941 Flint, MI
Children (2): David Lee
              Tanya Sue
Address: 3441 Montavesta Road
         Lexington, KY 40502
Phone: (606) 269-4751

John Truman

Born: August 10, 1940
Place: Vassar, Michigan
Married: August 24, 1962
        Mason, Michigan
   to Pauline Ann Diamond
        Born 5-13-1940 Mason, MI
Children (2): John Thomas
              Tracie Ann
Address: 188 Del Oro Circle
         Colorado Springs, CO 80919
Phone: (719) 599-8571

Janine Louise

Born: March 4, 1942
Place: Vassar, Michigan
Married: August 29, 1963
        Vassar, Michigan
   to Richard Charles Emery
        Born 5-30-1942 Kingston, MI
Children (2): Susan Marie
              Christine Louise
Address: 622 Buckingham Avenue
         Flint, Michigan 48507
Phone: (313) 743-6004

Christine Mereda

Born: May 3, 1945
Place: Vassar, Michigan
Married: June 11, 1966
        Vassar, Michigan
   to Duane Samuel Robinson
        Born 8-18-1940 Saginaw, MI
Children (2): Sheryl Lynne
              Kent William
Address: 5613 Trishlyn Cove
         Fort Wayne, IN 46835
Phone: (219) 486-7482

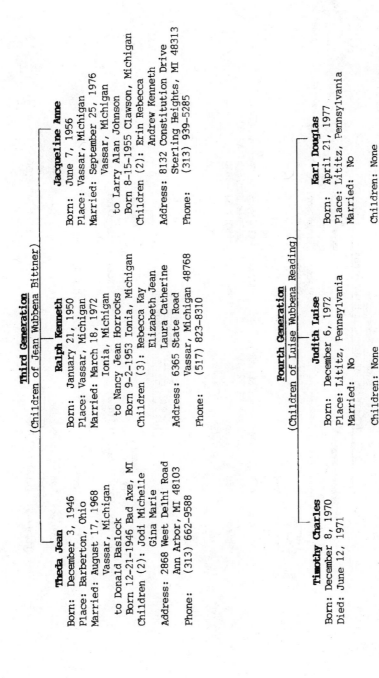

Third Generation
(Children of Jean Wubbena Bittner)

Theda Jean
Born: December 3, 1946
Place: Barberton, Ohio
Married: August 17, 1968
  Vassar, Michigan
  to Donald Baslock
  Born 12-21-1946 Bad Axe, MI
Children (2): Jodi Michelle
    Gina Marie
Address: 2868 West Delhi Road
  Ann Arbor, MI 48103
Phone: (313) 662-9588

Ralph Kenneth
Born: January 21, 1950
Place: Vassar, Michigan
Married: March 18, 1972
  Ionia, Michigan
  to Nancy Jean Horrocks
  Born 9-2-1953 Ionia, Michigan
Children (3): Rebecca Kay
    Elizabeth Jean
    Laura Catherine
Address: 6365 State Road
  Vassar, Michigan 48768
Phone: (517) 823-8310

Jacqueline Anne
Born: June 7, 1956
Place: Vassar, Michigan
Married: September 25, 1976
  Vassar, Michigan
  to Larry Alan Johnson
  Born 8-15-1955 Clawson, Michigan
Children (2): Erin Rebecca
    Andrew Kenneth
Address: 8132 Constitution Drive
  Sterling Heights, MI 48313
Phone: (313) 939-5285

Fourth Generation
(Children of Luise Wubbena Reading)

Judith Luise
Born: December 6, 1972
Place: Lititz, Pennsylvania
Married: No

Children: None

Address: 435 West Marion Street
  Lititz, PA 17543
  (717) 626-4953

Karl Douglas
Born: April 21, 1977
Place: Lititz, Pennsylvania
Married: No

Children: None

Address: 435 West Marion Street
  Lititz, PA 17543
Phone: (717) 626-4953

Timothy Charles
Born: December 8, 1970
Died: June 12, 1971

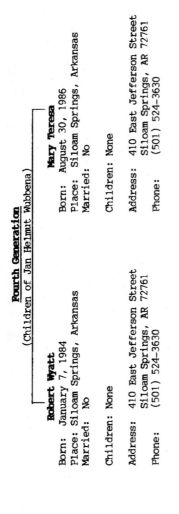

Fourth Generation
(Children of Jan Helmut Wubbena)

Robert Wyatt

Born: January 7, 1984
Place: Siloam Springs, Arkansas
Married: No

Children: None

Address: 410 East Jefferson Street
Siloam Springs, AR 72761
Phone: (501) 524-3630

Mary Teresa

Born: August 30, 1986
Place: Siloam Springs, Arkansas
Married: No

Children: None

Address: 410 East Jefferson Street
Siloam Springs, AR 72761
Phone: (501) 524-3630

Fourth Generation
(Children of Cheryl Wubbena Keckler)

Kevin James

Born: April 26, 1975
Place: Fort Wayne, Indiana
Married: No

Children: None

Address: 746 Tenth Street
Tell City, IN 47586
Phone: (812) 547-6060

Amy June

Born: July 15, 1977
Place: Lima, Ohio
Married: No

Children: None

Address: 746 Tenth Street
Tell City, IN 47586
Phone: (812) 547-6060

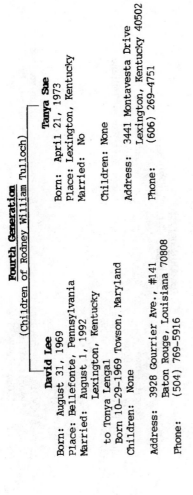

Fourth Generation
(Children of Rodney William Tulloch)

David Lee

Born: August 31, 1969
Place: Bellefonte, Pennsylvania
Married: August 1, 1992
    Lexington, Kentucky
  to Tonya Lengal
  Born 10-29-1969 Towson, Maryland
Children: None

Address: 3928 Gourrier Ave., #141
        Baton Rouge, Louisiana 70808
Phone: (504) 769-5916

Tanya Sue

Born: April 21, 1973
Place: Lexington, Kentucky
Married: No

Children: None

Address: 3441 Montavesta Drive
        Lexington, Kentucky 40502
Phone: (606) 269-4751

Fourth Generation
(Children of John Truman Tulloch)

John Thomas

Born: September 1, 1965
Place: Lansing, Michigan
Married: No

Children: None

Address: 49A Rosenveldt Street
        3025 RR Rotterdam
        The Netherlands
Phone:

Tracie Ann

Born: October 31, 1968
Place: Colorado Springs, Colorado
Married: July 29, 1990
    Colorado Springs, Colorado
  to John William Kruse
  Born 12-6-1967 Fort Collins, CO
Children (1): Paulina Joy

Address: 888 South Dexter, #707
        Denver, CO 80222
Phone: (303) 758-4194

Fourth Generation
(Children of Janine Tulloch Emery)

Susan Marie

Born: July 26, 1964
Place: Sault Ste. Marie, Michigan
Married: September 8, 1989
         Flint, Michigan
  to Michael Kevin Cox
  Born 9-2-1963 Flint, Michigan
Children: None

Address: 441 Burroughs Avenue
         Flint, Michigan 48507
Phone: (313) 742-8002

Christine Louise

Born: November 4, 1965
Place: Vassar, Michigan
Married: November 12, 1988
         Waltham, Massachusetts
  to Philip Charles Pedersen
  Born 12-10-1964 Brooklyn, New York
Children: None

Address: 25 Kettering Avenue
         Hampton, Virginia 23666
Phone: (804) 838-8199

Fourth Generation
(Children of Christine Tulloch Robinson)

Sheryl Lynne

Born: July 11, 1969
Place: Fort Wayne, Indiana
Married: August 14, 1993
         Fort Wayne, Indiana
  to Dan Heffern
  Born 1-27-68 Peoria, IL
Children: None

Address: 4010 N.Brandywine Dr, Apt.611
         Peoria, Illinois 61614
Phone: (309) 682-8435

Kent William

Born: March 17, 1973
Place: Fort Wayne, Indiana
Married: No

Children: None

Address: 5613 Trishlyn Cove
         Fort Wayne, IN 46835
Phone: (219) 486-7482

Fourth Generation
(Children of Theda Bittner Baslock)

Jodi Michelle

Born: August 3, 1969
Place: Ann Arbor, Michigan
Married: No

Children: None

Address: 2868 West Delhi Road
Ann Arbor, Michigan 48103
Phone: (313) 662-9588

Gina Marie

Born: December 10, 1970
Place: Ann Arbor, Michigan
Married: No

Children: None

Address: 2868 West Delhi Road
Ann Arbor, Michigan 48103
Phone: (313) 662-9588

Fourth Generation
(Children of Ralph Kenneth Bittner)

Rebecca Kay

Born: December 6, 1979
Place: Vassar, Michigan
Married: No

Children: None

Address: 2365 State Road
Vassar, MI 48768
Phone: (517) 823-8310

Elizabeth Jean

Born: February 18, 1982
Place: Vassar, Michigan
Married: No

Children: None

Address: 2365 State Road
Vassar, MI 48768
Phone: (517) 823-8310

Laura Catherine

Born: May 2, 1989
Place: Vassar, Michigan
Married: No

Children: None

Address: 2365 State Road
Vassar, MI 48768
Phone: (517) 823-8310

Fourth Generation
(Children of Jacqueline Bittner Johnson)

Erin Rebecca

Born: September 10, 1977
Place: Sterling Heights, Michigan
Married: No

Children: None

Address: 8132 Constitution Drive
Sterling Heights, MI 48313
Phone: (313) 939-5285

Andrew Kenneth

Born: September 26, 1985
Place: Sterling Heights, Michigan
Married: No

Children: None

Address: 8132 Constitution Drive
Sterling Heights, MI 48313
Phone: (313) 939-5285

Fifth Generation
(Child of Tracie Ann Tulloch Kruse)

Paulina Joy

Born: January 14, 1991
Place: Fort Collins, Colorado
Married: No

Children: None

Address: 888 South Dexter, #707
Denver, Colorado 80222
Phone: (303) 758-4194

II. Charles - 1

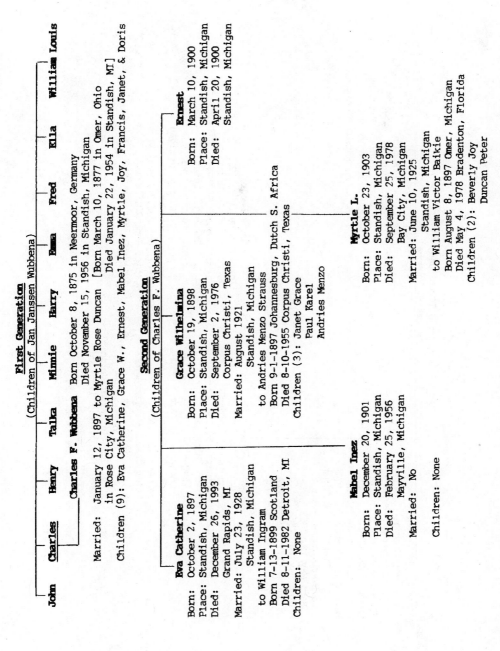

First Generation
(Children of Jan Janssen Wubbena)

| John | Charles | Henry | Talka | Minnie | Harry | Emma | Fred | Ella | William Louis |

Charles F. Wubbena Born October 8, 1875 in Neermoor, Germany
Died November 15, 1956 in Standish, Michigan

Married: January 12, 1897 to Myrtle Rose Duncan [Born March 10, 1877 in Omer, Ohio
in Rose City, Michigan   Died January 22, 1954 in Standish, MI]

Children (9): Eva Catherine, Grace W., Ernest, Mabel Inez, Myrtle, Joy, Francis, Janet, & Doris

Second Generation
(Children of Charles F. Wubbena)

Eva Catherine
Born: October 2, 1897
Place: Standish, Michigan
Died: December 26, 1993
        Grand Rapids, MI
Married: July 23, 1928
         Standish, Michigan
to William Ingram
Born 7-13-1899 Scotland
Died 8-11-1982 Detroit, MI
Children: None

Grace Wilhelmina
Born: October 19, 1898
Place: Standish, Michigan
Died: September 2, 1976
        Corpus Christi, Texas
Married: August 1921
         Standish, Michigan
to Andries Menzo Strauss
Born 9-1-1897 Johannesburg, Dutch S. Africa
Died 8-10-1955 Corpus Christi, Texas
Children (3): Janet Grace
              Paul Karel
              Andries Menzo

Ernest
Born: March 10, 1900
Place: Standish, Michigan
Died: April 20, 1900
        Standish, Michigan

Mabel Inez
Born: December 20, 1901
Place: Standish, Michigan
Died: February 25, 1956
        Mayville, Michigan
Married: No

Children: None

Myrtle L.
Born: October 23, 1903
Place: Standish, Michigan
Died: September 25, 1978
        Bay City, Michigan
Married: June 10, 1925
         Standish, Michigan
to William Victor Baikie
Born August 8, 1897 Omer, Michigan
Died May 4, 1978 Bradenton, Florida
Children (2): Beverly Joy
              Duncan Peter

Second Generation (Continued)
(Children of Charles F. Wubbena)

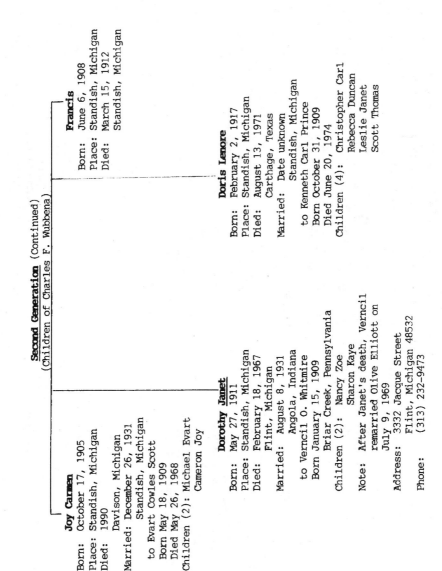

Joy Carmen
Born: October 17, 1905
Place: Standish, Michigan
Died: 1990 Davison, Michigan
Married: December 26, 1931 Standish, Michigan
to Evart Cowles Scott
Born May 18, 1909
Died May 26, 1968
Children (2): Michael Evart
Cameron Joy

Francis
Born: June 6, 1908
Place: Standish, Michigan
Died: March 15, 1912 Standish, Michigan

Dorothy Janet
Born: May 27, 1911
Place: Standish, Michigan
Died: February 18, 1967 Flint, Michigan
Married: August 8, 1931 Angola, Indiana
to Verncil O. Whitmire
Born January 15, 1909 Briar Creek, Pennsylvania
Children (2): Nancy Zoe
Sharon Kaye
Note: After Janet's death, Verncil remarried Olive Elliott on July 9, 1969
Address: 3332 Jacque Street Flint, Michigan 48532
Phone: (313) 232-9473

Doris Lenore
Born: February 2, 1917
Place: Standish, Michigan
Died: August 13, 1971 Carthage, Texas
Married: Date unknown Standish, Michigan
to Kenneth Carl Prince
Born October 31, 1909
Died June 20, 1974
Children (4): Christopher Carl
Rebecca Duncan
Leslie Janet
Scott Thomas

II. Charles - 3

Third Generation

(Children of Grace W. Wubbena Strauss)

Janet Grace

Born: May 31, 1926
Place: Standish, Michigan

Married: June 12, 1948
        Corpus Christi, Texas
to Richard Campbell Schneider
Born March 25, 1925 Enid, OK
Died March 29, 1991 Casper, WY
Children (3): Richard Harry
              Robert Andries
              Susan Grace
Address: 3500 Alpine Drive
         Casper, Wyoming 82601
Phone: (307) 234-4372 or
       (303) 249-0388 (in
       Montrose, CO)

Paul Karel

Born: June 27, 1930
Place: Standish, Michigan

Married: Date unknown
        Corpus Christi, Texas
to Patricia Ann Leighton
Born 8-30-33 Corpus Christi, TX
Divorced 7-5-? Austin, TX
Children (2): Christopher Paul
              Kimberly Alice
Married December 1992
        Manila, Philippines
to Catalina Cruz
Born on date unknown
Manila, Philippines
Children: None
Address: P.O. Box 1037
         Rota, M.P. 96951
Phone: 011 670 532 0772

Andries Menzo III

Born: February 14, 1932
Place: Standish, Michigan
Died: Sept.1989 San Antonio, TX
Married: Date unknown
        Corpus Christi, TX
to Janet Bowen
Born October 19, 1930
Divorced: 1970
Children (5): Michael Andries
              Andries Menzo IV
              David Marshall
              Leslie Janet
              Laura Diane
Married: 1979 Colorado Springs,CO
to Nancy ?
Born on date unknown
Children: None
Address: Unknown

Third Generation

(Children of Myrtle L. Wubbena Baikie)

Beverly Joy

Born: October 19, 1933
Place: Saginaw, Michigan
Married: June 10, 1955
        Ann Arbor, Michigan
to Roberto Rodriguez
Born 6-28-1930 Maracaibo, Venezuela, S.A.
Children (6): Roberto, Jr.
              William
              David
              Jose Luis
              Douglas
              Daniel
Address: 4307 10th Street Ct. E
         Ellenton, Florida 34222
Phone: (813) 722-2168

Duncan Peter

Born: March 6, 1936
Place: Saginaw, Michigan
Married: April 16, 1955
        Adrian, Michigan
to Jeannette Shannon
Born 1-23-1938 Omer, Michigan
Children (5): Nancy Dee
              Susan Marie
              Bruce Duncan
              Sally Lynn
              Michael Todd
Address: 1405 West White
         Bay City, Michigan 48700
Phone: (517) 686-3691

-13-

Third Generation
(Children of Joy C. Wubbena Scott)

Michael Evart

Born: March 23, 1937
Place: Flint, Michigan

Married: June 1, 1962
          Flint, Michigan
to Jacqueline Kirsh
Born 12-27-35 Flint, Michigan

Children (2): Michael Evart, Jr.
               Gregory John
Address: 2157 Holly Tree Drive
          Davison, Michigan 48423
Phone: (313) 653-5261

Cameron Joy

Born: December 10, 1936
Place: Unknown

Married: October 12, 1956
          Place unknown
to Richard Hinterman
Born on date unknown

Children (4): Debora Susan
               Rebecca Jane
               Julie Ann
               Victoria Lee
Address: Unknown

Third Generation
(Children of Dorothy Janet Wubbena Whitmire)

Nancy Zoe

Born: April 9, 1936
Place: Flint, Michigan

Married: June 20, 1959
          Flint, Michigan
to Carl Edward Brandt
Born March 6, 1934 Flint, MI
Children (4): David Carl
               Douglas John
               Rebecca Lynn
               Deborah Louise
Address: 1048 Stonegate Court
          Flint, Michigan 48532
Phone: (313) 732-5967

Sharon Kaye

Born: April 18, 1942
Place: Flint, Michigan

Married: April 30, 1963
          Flint, Michigan
to Larry McNenly
Born April 16, 1942
Children (4): Leslie Anne
               Jennifer Lynn
               Christopher Larry
               Nicholas Garrett
Address: 6317 Tanglewood Lane
          Grand Blanc, Michigan 48439
Phone: (313) 695-4274

Third Generation
(Children of Doris Lenore Wubbena Prince)

Christopher Carl
Born: April 14, 1945
Place: Flint, MI

Married: No

Children: None

Address: P.O. Box 149
Hempstead, TX 77445

Phone: (409) 372-3346

Rebecca Duncan
Born: February 12, 1948
Place: Shreveport, LA
Died: June 1992
Place unknown

Married: May 27, 1967
Place unknown
to Guy Bunyard
Born September 28, 1946
Children (1): Leslie Janet
Address: Route 1, Box 243 A
Carthage, TX 75633

Leslie Janet
Born: June 29, 1952
Place: Carthage, Texas

Married: August 21, 1971
Place unknown
to Norman Lee Copeland
Born on date unknown
Children (2): Bryan Lee
Holly Melissa
Address: 6824 N. Park Drive
Shreveport, LA 71107

Scott Thomas
Born: June 26, 1955
Place: Carthage, TX
Died: August 10, 1990
Lansing, MI

Fourth Generation
(Children of Janet Grace Strauss Schneider)

Richard Harry
Born: June 24, 1950
Place: Corpus Christi, TX
Married: November 23, 1974
Oklahoma City, OK
to Bonita Louise Reynolds
Born 12-16-49 Houston, Texas
Children (2): Benjamin Matthew
Nathan James
Address: 3113 N.W. 24th Street
Newcastle, OK 73065
Phone: (405) 392-4739

Robert Andries
Born: June 18, 1953
Place: Casper, Wyoming
Married: 1981
Napa, California
to Helen Kathleen Hulett
Born on date unknown
Children: None

Address: RR 4, Prairie Ridge
Ames, Iowa 50014

Phone: (515) 292-9296

Susan Grace
Born: February 1, 1957
Place: Casper, Wyoming
Married: June 16, 1979
Casper, Wyoming
to Kenneth Lee House
Born 9-27-56 Casper, Wyoming
Children: None

Address: 822 Spring Creek Rd.
Montrose, CO 81401

Phone: (303) 249-4490

Fourth Generation
(Children of Paul Karel Strauss)

Christopher Paul
Born: July 28, 1954
Place: Corpus Christi, Texas
Married: 1975
  Houston, Texas
  to Ellen Krahl
  Born on date unknown
Children (2): Catherine Grace
              Christopher James
Address: SFC Christopher P. Strauss
         HHC CMTC, Box 737, Unit 28208
         APO AE 09173
         [Sulzbach-Rosenberg, Germany]

Kimberly Alice
Born: September 22, 1962
Place: Corpus Christi, Texas
Married: No

Children: None

Address: 725 7th Avenue
         Salt Lake City, Utah 84103
Phone: (801) 363-2246

Fourth Generation
(Children of Andries Menzo Strauss III)

Michael Andries
Born: September 16, 1954
Place: Corpus Christi, Texas
Married: March 9, 1974
  Corpus Christi, TX
  to Linda Michelle Kilz
  Born on date unknown
Divorced on date unknown
Child: Son (Name unknown)
Address: 507 Middale
         Duncanville, TX 75116
Phone: (214) 780-7655 or
       Office (214) 220-1852

Andries "Buddy" Menzo IV
Born: September 25, 1955
Place: Corpus Christi, Texas
Married: Date unknown
  Place unknown
  to Peggy ?
  Born on date unknown
Children: None
Address: P.O. Box 71153
         Corpus Christi, TX 78415
Phone: (512) 882-5515

David Marshall
Born: February 26, 1957
Place: Corpus Christi, Texas
Married: Date unknown
  Place unknown
  to Name unknown
Divorced on date unknown
Children: None
Address: 3701 N. Creek Circle
         Corpus Christi, TX 78410
Phone: (512) 242-2973

Leslie Janet
Born: December 31, 1958
Place: Corpus Christi, Texas
Married: Date unknown
  Corpus Christi, Texas
  to Steve Swift
  Born on date unknown
Children (2): Son (Name unknown)
              Daughter (Deceased 1992)
Address: 1245 Logan Avenue
         Corpus Christi, Texas 78404
Phone: (512) 881-9276

Laura Diane
Born: October 20, 1961
Place: Corpus Christi, Texas
Married: Date unknown
  Place unknown
  to Name unknown
  Born on date unknown
Child (1): Name unknown
Address: Fort Bragg, North Carolina
Phone: Unknown

Fourth Generation
(Children of Beverly Joy Baikie Rodriquez)

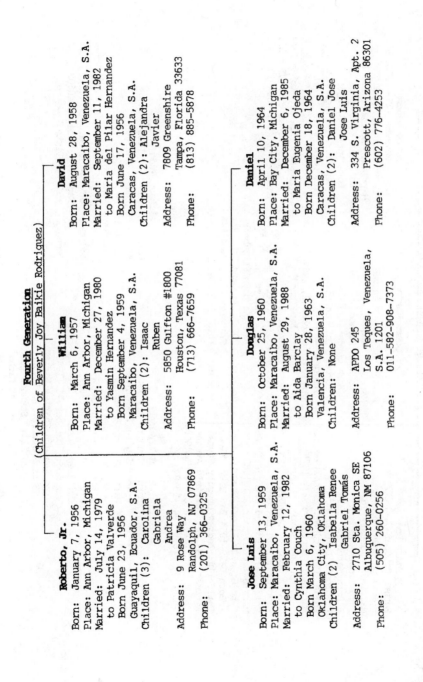

Roberto, Jr.
Born: January 7, 1956
Place: Ann Arbor, Michigan
Married: July 14, 1979
  to Patricia Valverde
  Born June 23, 1956
  Guayaquil, Ecuador, S.A.
Children (3): Carolina
  Gabriela
  Andrea
Address: 9 Rose Way
  Randolph, NJ 07869
Phone: (201) 366-0325

William
Born: March 6, 1957
Place: Ann Arbor, Michigan
Married: December 27, 1980
  to Yasmin Hernandez
  Born September 4, 1959
  Maracaibo, Venezuela, S.A.
Children (2): Isaac
  Ruben
Address: 5850 Gulfton #1800
  Houston, Texas 77081
Phone: (713) 666-7659

David
Born: August 28, 1958
Place: Maracaibo, Venezuela, S.A.
Married: September 11, 1982
  to Maria del Pilar Hernandez
  Born June 17, 1956
  Caracas, Venezuela, S.A.
Children (2): Alejandra
  Javier
Address: 7809 Greenshire
  Tampa, Florida 33633
Phone: (813) 885-5878

Jose Luis
Born: September 13, 1959
Place: Maracaibo, Venezuela, S.A.
Married: February 12, 1982
  to Cynthia Couch
  Born March 6, 1960
  Oklahoma City, Oklahoma
Children (2) Isabella Renee
  Gabriel Tomás
Address: 2710 Sta. Monica SE
  Albuquerque, NM 87106
Phone: (505) 260-0256

Douglas
Born: October 25, 1960
Place: Maracaibo, Venezuela, S.A.
Married: August 29, 1988
  to Aida Barclay
  Born January 28, 1963
  Valencia, Venezuela, S.A.
Children: None
Address: APDO 245
  Los Teques, Venezuela,
  S.A. 1201
Phone: 011-582-908-7373

Daniel
Born: April 10, 1964
Place: Bay City, Michigan
Married: December 6, 1985
  to Maria Eugenia Ojeda
  Born December 18, 1964
  Caracas, Venezuela, S.A.
Children (2): Daniel Jose
  Jose Luis
Address: 334 S. Virginia, Apt. 2
  Prescott, Arizona 86301
Phone: (602) 776-4253

Fourth Generation
(Children of Duncan Peter Baikie)

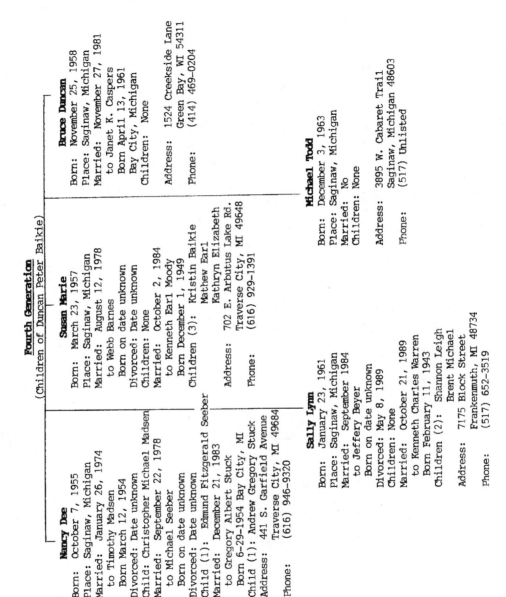

Nancy Dee
Born: October 7, 1955
Place: Saginaw, Michigan
Married: January 26, 1974
   to Timothy Madsen
   Born March 12, 1954
Divorced: Date unknown
Child: Christopher Michael Madsen
Married: September 22, 1978
   to Michael Seeber
   Born on date unknown
Divorced: Date unknown
Child (1): Edmund Fitzgerald Seeber
Married: December 21, 1983
   to Gregory Albert Stuck
   Born 6-29-1954 Bay City, MI
Child (1): Andrew Gregory Stuck
Address: 441 S. Garfield Avenue
   Traverse City, MI 49684
Phone: (616) 946-9320

Susan Marie
Born: March 23, 1957
Place: Saginaw, Michigan
Married: August 12, 1978
   to Webb Barnes
   Born on date unknown
Divorced: Date unknown
Children: None
Married: October 2, 1984
   to Kenneth Earl Moody
   Born December 1, 1949
Children (3): Kristin Baikie
   Mathew Earl
   Kathryn Elizabeth
Address: 702 E. Arbutus Lake Rd.
   Traverse City, MI 49648
Phone: (616) 929-1391

Bruce Duncan
Born: November 25, 1958
Place: Saginaw, Michigan
Married: November 27, 1981
   to Janet K. Caspers
   Born April 13, 1961
   Bay City, Michigan
Children: None
Address: 1524 Creekside Lane
   Green Bay, WI 54311
Phone: (414) 469-0204

Sally Lynn
Born: January 23, 1961
Place: Saginaw, Michigan
Married: September 1984
   to Jeffery Beyer
   Born on date unknown
Divorced: May 8, 1989
Children: None
Married: October 21, 1989
   to Kenneth Charles Warren
   Born February 11, 1943
Children (2): Shannon Leigh
   Brent Michael
Address: 7175 Block Street
   Frankenmuth, MI 48734
Phone: (517) 652-3519

Michael Todd
Born: December 3, 1963
Place: Saginaw, Michigan
Married: No
Children: None
Address: 3895 W. Cabaret Trail
   Saginaw, Michigan 48603
Phone: (517) Unlisted

Fourth Generation
(Children of Michael Evart Scott)

Michael Evart, Jr.

Born: May 24, 1963
Place: Lapeer, Michigan
Married: May 5, 1990
   Davison, Michigan
  to Tammy Beers
  Born 9-20-62 Flint, Michigan
Child (1): Michael Evart III
Address: 2057 Amy Street
    Burton, Michigan 48519
Phone: (313) 742-0074

Gregory John

Born: June 26, 1966
Place: Lapeer, Michigan

Fourth Generation
(Children of Cameron Joy Scott Hinterman)

Debora Susan

Born: September 23, 1957
Place: Unknown

Rebecca Jane

Born: June 17, 1960
Place: Unknown

Julie Ann

Born: January 20, 1962
Place: Unknown

Victoria Lee

Born: May 23. 1969
Place: Unknown

Fourth Generation
(Children of Nancy Zoe Whitmire Brandt)

David Carl

Born: November 14, 1961
Place: Flint, Michigan
Married: May 23, 1987
   Flint, Michigan
  to Susan Marie Flynn
  Born 2-21-65 Flint, Michigan
Children: None
Address: 8494 Bush Hill Court
    Grand Blanc, MI 48439
Phone: (313) 694-2298

Rebecca Lynn

Born: December 6, 1965
Place: Flint, Michigan
Married: February 10, 1990
   Fenton, Michigan
  to Anthony Edward Cubr
  Born 2-18-66 Detroit, MI
Children: None
Address: 5474 Floria
    Swartz Creek, MI 48473
Phone: (313) 655-6938

Douglas John

Born: January 17, 1964
Place: Flint, Michigan
Married: December 19, 1987
   Flushing, Michigan
  to Suzanne Marie Hackett
  Born 7-13-64 Flint, Michigan
Children: None
Address: 505 Pixley Lane
    Noblesville, IN 46060
Phone: (317) 877-2310

Deborah Louise

Born: November 16, 1968
Place: Flint, Michigan
Married: July 21, 1990
   Flint, Michigan
  to Michael John Staisil
  Born 12-13-67 Garden City, MI
Children: None
Address: 18 Banks, Apt. 404
    Cambridge, MA 02138
Phone: (617) 492-4379

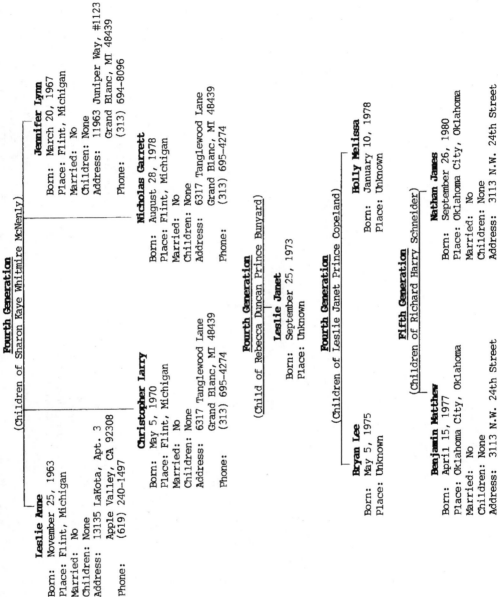

Fourth Generation
(Children of Sharon Kaye Whitmire McNenly)

Leslie Anne
Born: November 25, 1963
Place: Flint, Michigan
Married: No
Children: None
Address: 13135 LaKota, Apt. 3
         Apple Valley, CA 92308
Phone: (619) 240-1497

Jennifer Lynn
Born: March 20, 1967
Place: Flint, Michigan
Married: No
Children: None
Address: 11963 Juniper Way, #1123
         Grand Blanc, MI 48439
Phone: (313) 694-8096

Christopher Larry
Born: May 5, 1970
Place: Flint, Michigan
Married: No
Children: None
Address: 6317 Tanglewood Lane
         Grand Blanc, MI 48439
Phone: (313) 695-4274

Nicholas Garrett
Born: August 28, 1978
Place: Flint, Michigan
Married: No
Children: None
Address: 6317 Tanglewood Lane
         Grand Blanc, MI 48439
Phone: (313) 695-4274

Fourth Generation
(Child of Rebecca Duncan Prince Bunyard)

Leslie Janet
Born: September 25, 1973
Place: Unknown

Fourth Generation
(Children of Leslie Janet Prince Copeland)

Bryan Lee
Born: May 5, 1975
Place: Unknown

Holly Melissa
Born: January 10, 1978
Place: Unknown

Fifth Generation
(Children of Richard Harry Schneider)

Benjamin Matthew
Born: April 15, 1977
Place: Oklahoma City, Oklahoma
Married: No
Children: None
Address: 3113 N.W. 24th Street
         Newcastle, OK 73065
Phone: (405) 392-4739

Nathan James
Born: September 26, 1980
Place: Oklahoma City, Oklahoma
Married: No
Children: None
Address: 3113 N.W. 24th Street
         Newcastle, OK 73065
Phone: (405) 392-4739

Fifth Generation
(Children of Christopher Paul Strauss)

Catherine Grace

Born: January 15, 1980
Place: Austin, Texas
Married: No
Children: None
Address: c/o SFC Christopher P. Strauss
HHC CMTC, Box 737, Unit 28208
APO AE 09173
Phone: Unknown

Christopher James

Born: November 3, 1983
Place: Houston, Texas
Married: No
Children: None
Address: c/o SFC Christopher P. Strauss
HHC CMTC, Box 737, Unit 28208
APO AE 09173
Phone: Unknown

Fifth Generation
(Children of Roberto Rodriquez, Jr.)

Carolina

Born: January 10, 1983
Place: Pto. Fijo, Venezuela, S.A.
Married: No
Children: None
Address: 9 Rose Way
Randolph, NJ 07869
Phone: (201) 366-0325

Gabriela

Born: March 29, 1985
Place: Pto. Fijo, Venezuela, S.A.
Married: No
Children: None
Address: 9 Rose Way
Randolph, NJ 07869
Phone: (201) 366-0325

Andrea

Born: May 5, 1986
Place: Pto. Fijo, Venezuela, S.A.
Married: No
Children: None
Address: 9 Rose Way
Randolph, NJ 07869
Phone: (201) 366-0325

Fifth Generation
(Children of William Rodriquez)

Isaac

Born: July 8, 1985
Place: Houston, Texas
Married: No
Children: None
Address: 5850 Gulfton #1800
Houston, Texas 77081
Phone: (713) 666-7659

Ruben

Born: June 17, 1987
Place: Houston, Texas
Married: No
Children: None
Address: 5850 Gulfton #1800
Houston, Texas 77081
Phone: (713) 666-7659

Fifth Generation
(Children of David Rodriquez)

Alejandra

Born: July 15, 1984
Place: Caracas, Venezuela, S.A.
Married: No
Children: None
Address: 7809 Greenshire
Tampa, Florida 33633
Phone: (813) 885-5878

Javier

Born: July 21, 1985
Place: Caracas, Venezuela, S.A.
Married: No
Children: None
Address: 7809 Greenshire
Tampa, Florida 33633
Phone: (813) 885-5878

Fifth Generation
(Children of Jose Luis Rodriquez)

Isabella Renee
Born: October 30, 1989
Place: Albuquerque, New Mexico
Married: No
Children: None
Address: 2710 Sta. Monica SE
           Albuquerque, NM 87106
Phone: (505) 260-0256

Gabriel Tomás
Born: August 13, 1992
Place: Albuquerque, New Mexico
Married: No
Children: None
Address: 2710 Sta. Monica SE
           Albuquerque, NM 87106
Phone: (505) 260-0256

Fifth Generation
(Children of Daniel Rodriquez)

Daniel Jose
Born: March 23, 1986
Place: Los Teques, Venezuela, S.A.
Married: No
Children: None
Address: 334 S. Virginia, Apt. 2
           Prescott, Arizona 86301
Phone: (602) 776-4253

Jose Luis
Born: July 25, 1989
Place: Los Teques, Venezuela, S.A.
Married: No
Children: None
Address: 334 S. Virginia, Apt. 2
           Prescott, Arizona 86301
Phone: (602) 776-4253

Fifth Generation
(Children of Nancy Dee Baikie Madsen Seeber Stuck)

Christopher Michael Madsen
Born: August 3, 1974
Place: Bay City, Michigan
Married: No
Children: None
Address: 441 S. Garfield Ave.
           Traverse City, MI 49684
Phone: (616) 946-9320

Edmund Fitzgerald Seeber
Born: September 1, 1979
Place: Trenton, New Jersey
Married: No
Children: None
Address: 441 S. Garfield Ave.
           Traverse City, MI 49684
Phone: (616) 946-9320

Andrew Gregory Stuck
Born: July 17, 1984
Place: Saginaw, Michigan
Married: No
Children: None
Address: 441 S. Garfield Ave.
           Traverse City, MI 49684
Phone: (616) 946-9320

Fifth Generation

(Children of Susan Marie Baikie Barnes Moody)

Kristin Baikie Moody
Born: September 6, 1985
Place: Pontiac, Michigan
Married: No
Children: None
Address: 702 E. Arbutus Lake Rd.
           Traverse City, MI 49648
Phone: (616) 929-1391

Mathew Earl Moody
Born: July 28, 1988
Place: Pontiac, Michigan
Married: No
Children: None
Address: 702 E. Arbutus Lake Rd.
           Traverse City, MI 49648
Phone: (616) 929-1391

Kathryn Elizabeth Moody
Born: March 30, 1990
Place: Pontiac, Michigan
Married: No
Children: None
Address: 702 E. Arbutus Lake Rd.
           Traverse City, MI 49648
Phone: (616) 929-1391

Fifth Generation

(Children of Sally Lynn Baikie Beyer Warren)

Shannon Leigh Warren
Born: May 24, 1992
Place: Saginaw, Michigan
Married: No
Children: None
Address: 7175 Block Street
           Frankenmuth, MI 48734
Phone: (517) 652-3519

Brent Michael Warren
Born: May 24, 1992
Place: Saginaw, Michigan
Married: No
Children: None
Address: 7175 Block Street
           Frankenmuth, MI 48734
Phone: (517) 652-3519

Fifth Generation

(Child of Michael Evart Scott, Jr.)

Michael Evart III
Born: May 16, 1991
Place: Flint, Michigan
Married: No
Children: None
Address: 2057 Amy Street
           Burton, Michigan 48519
Phone: (313) 742-0074

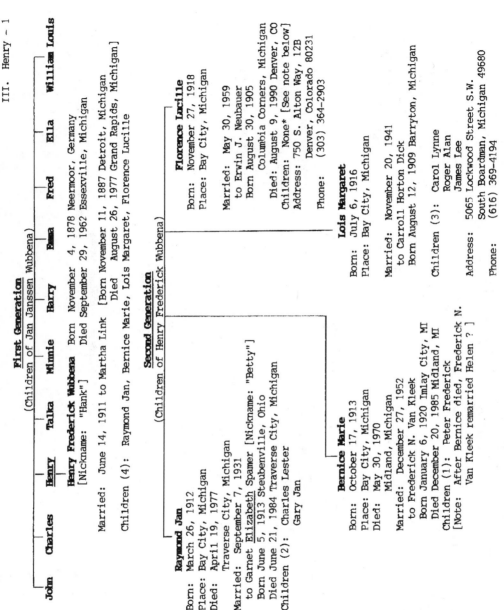

First Generation

(Children of Jan Janssen Wubbena)

John   Charles   **Henry**   Talka   Mimmie   **Harry**   Emma   **Fred**   Ella   **William Louis**

Henry Frederick Wubbena   Born November 4, 1878 Neermoor, Germany
[Nickname: "Hank"]   Died September 29, 1962 Essexville, Michigan

Married: June 14, 1911 to Martha Link   [Born November 11, 1887 Detroit, Michigan
                                            Died   August 26, 1977 Grand Rapids, Michigan]

Children (4):   Raymond Jan, Bernice Marie, Lois Margaret, Florence Lucille

Second Generation

(Children of Henry Frederick Wubbena)

Raymond Jan

Born: March 26, 1912
Place: Bay City, Michigan
Died: April 19, 1977
         Traverse City, Michigan

Married: September 7, 1931
            to Garnet Elizabeth Spamer [Nickname: "Betty"]
            Born June 5, 1913 Steubenville, Ohio
            Died June 21, 1984 Traverse City, Michigan

Children (2):   Charles Lester
                 Gary Jan

Bernice Marie

Born: October 17, 1913
Place: Bay City, Michigan
Died: May 30, 1970
         Midland, Michigan

Married: December 27, 1952
            to Frederick N. Van Kleek
            Born January 6, 1920 Imlay City, MI
            Died December 20, 1985 Midland, MI

Children (1):   Peter Frederick

[Note: After Bernice died, Frederick N.
          Van Kleek remarried Helen ?]

Florence Lucille

Born: November 27, 1918
Place: Bay City, Michigan

Married: May 30, 1959
            to Erwin J. Neubauer
            Born August 30, 1905
            Columbia Corners, Michigan
            Died: August 9, 1990 Denver, CO

Children: None* [See note below]

Address: 750 S. Alton Way, 12B
            Denver, Colorado 80231

Phone: (303) 364-2903

Lois Margaret

Born: July 6, 1916
Place: Bay City, Michigan

Married: November 20, 1941
            to Carroll Horton Dick
            Born August 12, 1909 Barryton, Michigan

Children (3):   Carol Lynne
                 Roger Alan
                 James Lee

Address: 5065 Lockwood Street S.W.
            South Boardman, Michigan 49680

Phone: (616) 369-4194

* [Erwin Neubauer had two children by his first wife Bernice Berge (Deceased).
They are Mary (Mrs. Fenton Judson Hood) and Thomas E. Neubauer.]

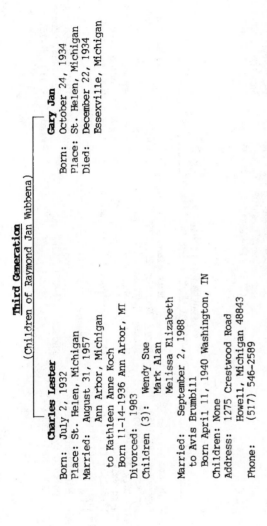

Third Generation

(Children of Raymond Jan Wubbena)

Charles Lester

Born: July 2, 1932
Place: St. Helen, Michigan
Married: August 31, 1957
          Ann Arbor, Michigan
  to Kathleen Anne Koch
    Born 11-14-1936 Ann Arbor, MI
Divorced: 1983
Children (3):   Wendy Sue
             Mark Alan
             Melissa Elizabeth

Married: September 2, 1988
  to Avis Brumbill
    Born April 11, 1940 Washington, TN
Children: None
Address: 1275 Crestwood Road
         Howell, Michigan 48843
Phone: (517) 546-2589

Gary Jan

Born: October 24, 1934
Place: St. Helen, Michigan
Died: December 22, 1934
      Essexville, Michigan

Third Generation

(Child of Bernice Marie Wubbena Van Kleek)

Peter Frederick

Born: August 20, 1956
Place: Midland, Michigan
Married: October 24, 1987
  to Nancy Lee Tonk
    Born June 6, 1955
      Midland, Michigan
Children: None
Address: 4840 Raymond Road
         Midland, Michigan 48640
    Phone: (517) 496-2970

Third Generation

(Children of Lois Margaret Wubbena Dick)

Carol Lynne

Born: October 26, 1942
Place: Ann Arbor, Michigan
Married: No

Children: None

Address: 32 Laurel Park
         Northampton, MA 01060
Phone: (413) 586-8982

Roger Alan

Born: May 13, 1945
Place: Los Alamos, New Mexico
Married: August 5, 1972
         to Gail June Stenning
         Born June 27, 1949
         Ypsilanti, Michigan
Divorced: January 9, 1986
Children (2): Darren Alan
              Kindra Sheree

Address: 505 Bruce Street
         Ann Arbor, MI 48103
Phone: (313) 747-9194

James Lee

Born: March 29, 1948
Place: Ann Arbor, Michigan
Married: June 13, 1970
         to Barbara Lee Tower
         Born April 11, 1948
         Ann Arbor, Michigan
Children (2): Michelle Suzanne
              Alisha Erin

Address: 1410 Saunders Crescent
         Ann Arbor, MI 48103
Phone: (313) 665-2847

Fourth Generation

(Children of Charles Lester Wubbena)

Wendy Sue

Born: September 18, 1959
Place: Ann Arbor, Michigan
Married: July 23, 1990
         to Edward Velez
         Born 12-5-1951 Brooklyn, NY
Child (1): Michael Stephen

Address: 3107 Summit Avenue
         Union City, NJ 07087
Phone: (201) 865-5133

Mark Alan

Born: February 22, 1961
Place: Ypsilanti, Michigan
Married: No

Children: None

Address: 3507 172 Street, S.W.
         Lynnwood, WA 98037
Phone: (206) 743-2145

Melissa Elizabeth

Born: September 16, 1968
Place: Howell, Michigan
Married: November 30, 1991
         to Kevin Lorren B. Davis
         Born 1-29-63 San Jose, CA
Children: None

Address: 1335 S.W. 66th Ave, #315
         Portland, Oregon 97225
Phone: (503) 292-1511

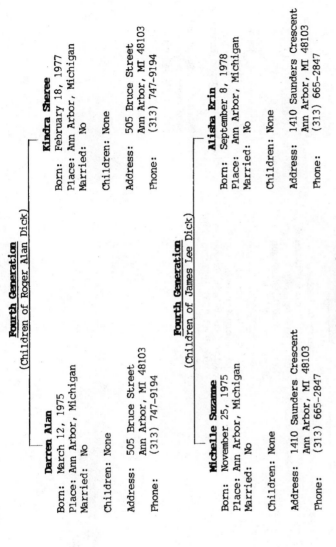

Fourth Generation
(Children of Roger Alan Dick)

Darren Alan

Born: March 12, 1975
Place: Ann Arbor, Michigan
Married: No

Children: None

Address: 505 Bruce Street
Ann Arbor, MI 48103
Phone: (313) 747-9194

Kindra Sheree

Born: February 18, 1977
Place: Ann Arbor, Michigan
Married: No

Children: None

Address: 505 Bruce Street
Ann Arbor, MI 48103
Phone: (313) 747-9194

Fourth Generation
(Children of James Lee Dick)

Michelle Suzanne

Born: November 25, 1975
Place: Ann Arbor, Michigan
Married: No

Children: None

Address: 1410 Saunders Crescent
Ann Arbor, MI 48103
Phone: (313) 665-2847

Alisha Erin

Born: September 8, 1978
Place: Ann Arbor, Michigan
Married: No

Children: None

Address: 1410 Saunders Crescent
Ann Arbor, MI 48103
Phone: (313) 665-2847

Fifth Generation
(Child of Wendy Sue Wubbena Velez)

Michael Stephen Velez

Born: November 22, 1991
Place: North Bergen, New Jersey
Married: No

Children: None

Address: 3107 Summit Avenue
Union City, NJ 07087
Phone: (201) 865-5133

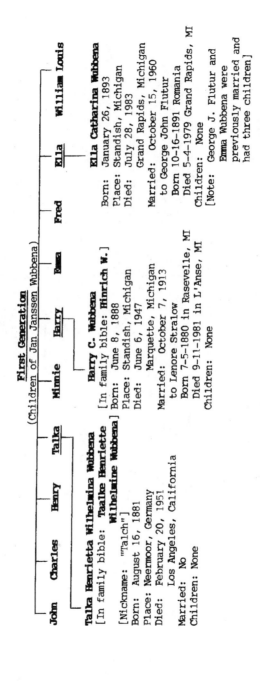

First Generation
(Children of Jan Janssen Wubbena)

John   Charles   Henry   Talka   Minnie   Harry   Emma   Fred   Ella   William Louis

Talka Henrietta Wilhelmina Wubbena
[In family bible: **Taalke Henriette Wilhelmine Wubbena**]

[Nickname: "Talch"]
Born: August 16, 1881
Place: Neermoor, Germany
Died: February 20, 1951
      Los Angeles, California
Married: No
Children: None

Harry C. Wubbena
[In family bible: **Hinrich W.**]
Born: June 8, 1888
Place: Standish, Michigan
Died: June 6, 1947
      Marquette, Michigan
Married: October 7, 1913
      to Lenore Stralow
      Born 7-5-1880 in Rasevelle, MI
      Died 9-11-1981 in L'Anse, MI
Children: None

Ella Catharina Wubbena
Born: January 26, 1893
Place: Standish, Michigan
Died: July 28, 1983
      Grand Rapids, Michigan
Married: October 15, 1960
      to George John Flutur
      Born 10-16-1891 Romania
      Died 5-4-1979 Grand Rapids, MI
Children: None
[Note: George J. Flutur and
      Emma Wubbena were
      previously married and
      had three children]

v. Minnie – 1

First Generation
(Children of Jan Janssen Wubbena)

John   Charles   Henry   Talka   **Minnie**   Harry   Emma   Fred   Ella   **William Louis**

Catherine Elizabeth Wilhelmina Wubbena   Born March 8, 1887 Standish, Michigan
[Nickname: "Minnie"]   Died April 1, 1974 Elgin, Illinois

Married: July 8, 1913 to Louis William Gabler   [Born   April 30, 1884 New York, New York
         Standish, Michigan   Died October 16, 1966 Elgin, Illinois]
Children (4): Marie Ella Muriel, Margaret Henrietta, Louis William, Jr., John George

Second Generation
(Children of Catherine Elizabeth Wilhelmina Wubbena Gabler)

Marie Ella Muriel
Born: June 2, 1915
Place: Elgin, Illinois

Married: June 18, 1949
         Elgin, Illinois
to William Ervin Ford
 Born 12-22-1900 Elgin, IL
 Died 2-10-1970 Elgin, IL
Children: None
Address: 37 N Jane Drive, Apt.4
 Elgin Illinois 60123
Phone: (708) 742-8185

Margaret Henrietta
Born: March 2, 1919
Place: Elgin, Illinois

Married: December 28, 1971
         Tracy City, Tennessee
to Everett Pickett
 Born 5-18-1910 Gruetli, TN
 Died 8-19-1992 Nashville, TN
Children: None
[Note: Everett had 6 children*
from his previous marriage to
to Lucille Pickett (Deceased)]
Address: Box 143-D, Route 1
 Tracy City, TN 37387
Phone: (615) 592-6541

Louis William, Jr.
Born: May 12, 1927
Place: Elgin, Illinois
Died: December 1, 1992
Married: August 28, 1948
         Hamburg, New York
to Frances R. Redding
 Born 6-21-1929 Hamilton,Ont.CAN
Divorced: 1980
[Note: Frances now lives at
612 Woodlake Road, Virginia
Beach, VA 23452, (804) 486-8231]
Children (4): Marilyn Joy
              Suzanne Carol
              Randall William
              Ronald Louis
Married: June 23, 1984
 Norfolk, VA
to Lillian Jackson
 Born 9-16-1925 Norfolk, VA
Children: None
[Note: Lillian has daughter,
Brenda Lambert, from a previous
marriage and a granddaughter,
Whitney Fowlkes.]
Address: 1024 Josephine Crescent
 Virginia Beach, VA 23464
Phone: (804) 424-7379

John George
Born: August 1, 1933
Place: Elgin, Illinois
Died: December 21, 1933

*Children of Everett Pickett:
Harold   )
Charles Edward) Twins (Chatanooga, TN)
JoAnn (Mrs. Dan Sargent)(Tracy City, TN)
Juanita (Mrs. Evan Davis)(Chicago, IL)
Pat (Mrs. John Hutchieson)(Dearborn, MD)
Elizabeth (Mrs. Pavlik)(Colonial, NJ)

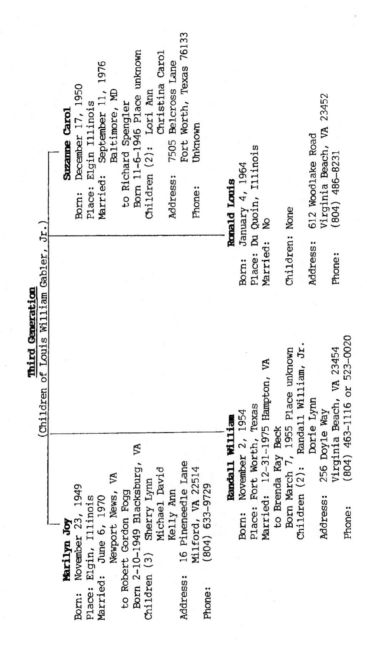

Third Generation
(Children of Louis William Gabler, Jr.)

Marilyn Joy

Born: November 23, 1949
Place: Elgin, Illinois
Married: June 6, 1970
  to Robert Gordon Fogg
  Born 2-10-1949 Blacksburg, VA
Children (3) Sherry Lynn
  Michael David
  Kelly Ann
Address: 16 Pineneedle Lane
  Milford, VA 22514
Phone: (804) 633-9729

Randall William

Born: November 2, 1954
Place: Fort Worth, Texas
Married: 12-31-1975 Hampton, VA
  to Brenda Kay Beck
  Born March 7, 1955 Place unknown
Children (2): Randall William, Jr.
  Dorie Lynn
Address: 256 Doyle Way
  Virginia Beach, VA 23454
Phone: (804) 463-1116 or 523-0020

Suzanne Carol

Born: December 17, 1950
Place: Elgin Illinois
Married: September 11, 1976
  Baltimore, MD
  to Richard Spengler
  Born 11-6-1946 Place unknown
Children (2): Lori Ann
  Christina Carol
Address: 7505 Belcross Lane
  Fort Worth, Texas 76133
Phone: Unknown

Ronald Louis

Born: January 4, 1964
Place: Du Quoin, Illinois
Married: No

Children: None

Address: 612 Woodlake Road
  Virginia Beach, VA 23452
Phone: (804) 486-8231

Fourth Generation
(Children of Marilyn Joy Gabler Fogg)

Sherry Lynn

Born: April 2, 1971
Place: Radford, Virginia
Married: No

Children: None

Address: 16 Pineneedle Lane
Milford, VA 22514
Phone: (804) 633-9729

Michael David

Born: March 11, 1976
Place: Waynesboro, Virginia
Married: No

Children: None

Address: 16 Pineneedle Lane
Milford, VA 22514
Phone: (804) 633-9729

Kelly Ann

Born: August 12, 1977
Place: Richmond, Virginia
Married: No

Children: None

Address: 16 Pineneedle Lane
Milford, VA 22514
Phone: (804) 633-9729

Fourth Generation
(Children of Suzanne Carol Gabler Spengler)

Lori Ann

Born: September 27, 1977
Place: Baltimore, Maryland
Married: No

Children: None

Address: 7505 Belcross Lane
Fort Worth, Texas 76133
Phone: (817) 292-1912

Christina Carol

Born: May 2, 1979
Place: Baltimore, Maryland
Married: No

Children: None

Address: 7505 Belcross Lane
Fort Worth, Texas 76133
Phone: (817) 292-1912

Fourth Generation
(Children of Randall William Gabler)

Randall William, Jr..

Born: May 12, 1979
Place: Virginia Beach, Virginia
Married: No

Children: None

Address: 256 Doyle Way
Virginia Beach, VA 23454
Phone: (804) 463-1116 or 523-0020

Dorie Lynn

Born: June 11, 1982
Place: Virginia Beach, Virginia
Married: No

Children: None

Address: 256 Doyle Way
Virginia Beach, VA 23454
Phone: (804) 463-1116 or 523-0020

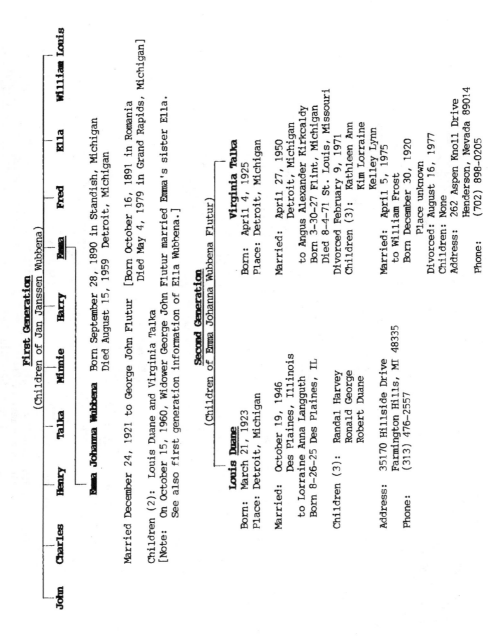

First Generation
(Children of Jan Janssen Wubbena)

John   Charles   Henry   Talka   Mimie   Harry   **Emma**   Fred   Ella   William Louis

Emma Johanna Wubbena   Born September 28, 1890 in Standish, Michigan
                            Died August 15, 1959 Detroit, Michigan

Married December 24, 1921 to George John Flutur   [Born October 16, 1891 in Romania
                                                    Died May 4, 1979 in Grand Rapids, Michigan]

Children (2): Louis Duane and Virginia Talka
[Note: On October 15, 1960, Widower George John Flutur married Emma's sister Ella.
        See also first generation information of Ella Wubbena.]

Second Generation
(Children of Emma Johanna Wubbena Flutur)

Louis Duane

Born: March 21, 1923
Place: Detroit, Michigan

Married: October 19, 1946
          Des Plaines, Illinois
to Lorraine Anna Langguth
Born 8-26-25 Des Plaines, IL

Children (3): Randal Harvey
               Ronald George
               Robert Duane

Address: 35170 Hillside Drive
          Farmington Hills, MI 48335

Phone: (313) 476-2557

Virginia Talka

Born: April 4, 1925
Place: Detroit, Michigan

Married: April 27, 1950
          Detroit, Michigan
to Angus Alexander Kirkcaldy
Born 3-30-27 Flint, Michigan
Died 8-4-71 St. Louis, Missouri
Divorced February 9, 1971
Children (3): Kathleen Ann
               Kim Lorraine
               Kelley Lynn

Married: April 5, 1975
to William Frost
Born December 30, 1920
          Place unknown
Divorced: August 16, 1977
Children: None
Address: 262 Aspen Knoll Drive
          Henderson, Nevada 89014

Phone: (702) 898-0205

VI. Emma - 2

Third Generation
(Children of Louis Duane Flutur)

Randal Harvey

Born: May 20, 1948
Place: Detroit, Michigan
Married: October 7, 1972
    New Era, Michigan
  to Anne Marcia Gowell
    Born 9-7-49 New Era, MI
Children (6): Heather Anne
    Autumn Lynn
    Randal Harvey
    Misty Starr
    Crystal Dawn
    Matthew Duane

Address: 3950 N. Anderson Road
    Ludington, MI 49431
Phone: (616) 843-8119

Ronald George

Born: November 23, 1950
Place: Detroit, Michigan
Married: August 8, 1975
    Farmington Hills, MI
  to Sue Jeanette Shobe
    Born 1-15-55 Detroit, MI
Divorced: January 1980
Children: None
Married: December 28, 1983
    Novi, Michigan
  to Amy Jolgren
    Born 5-10-62 Detroit, MI
Children (3): Christy Carol
    Mandy Lorraine
    Charles Duane

Address: 1166 S. Kellogg Rd.
    Brighton, MI 48116
Phone: (313) 227-2187

Robert Duane

Born: June 10, 1952
Place: Detroit, Michigan
Married: August 18, 1973
    Farmington Hills, MI
  to Marti Jane Daumler
    Born 5-3-54 Kokomo, IN
Children (2): Sara Marie
    Timothy John

Address: 30023 North Stockton
    Farmington Hills, MI 48336
Phone: (313) 477-9818

Third Generation
(Children of Virginia Talka Flutur Kirkcaldy)

Kathleen Ann

Born: October 30, 1951
Place: Detroit, Michigan
Married: October 8, 1971
    Place unknown
  to Roy Waller
    Born 4-7-49 Detroit, MI
Children: None
Address: 5430 South Dorchester
    Chicago, IL 60615
Phone: (312) 955-9085

Kim Lorraine

Born: November 8, 1954
Place: Detroit, Michigan
Married: April 26, 1975
    Southfield, MI
  to Dr. Alan Myers
    Born 1-25-55 Place unknown
Divorced: 1991
Children: None
Address: 1942 Magnolia Drive
    Henderson, NV 89104
Phone: Unknown

Kelley Lynn

Born: January 30, 1962
Place: Detroit, Michigan
Married: December 13, 1987
    Hendersen, Nevada
  to Tony Ray Hulsey
    Born 1-19-55 Place unknown
Children (1) Ryan Ray
Address: 1907 Spode
    Henderson, NV 89014
Phone: (702) 434-8820

Fourth Generation
(Children of Randal Harvey Flutur)

Heather Anne
Born: August 30, 1976
Place: Ludington, Michigan
Married: No

Children: None

Address: 3950 N. Anderson Rd.
Ludington, MI 49431

Phone: (616) 843-8119

Autumn Lynn
Born: September 22, 1977
Place: Ludington, Michigan
Married: No

Children: None

Address: 3950 N. Anderson Rd.
Ludington, MI 49431

Phone: (616) 843-8119

Randal Harvey
Born: April 30, 1980
Place: Ludington, Michigan
Died: May 5, 1980

Misty Starr
Still Born: July 31, 1981

Crystal Dawn
Born: May 13, 1983
Place: Ludington, Michigan
Married: No

Children: None

Address: 3950 N. Anderson Rd.
Ludington, MI 49431

Phone: (616) 843-8119

Matthew Duane
Born: July 2, 1986
Place: Ludington, Michigan
Married: No

Children: None

Address: 3950 N. Anderson Rd.
Ludington, MI 49431

Phone: (616) 843-8119

Fourth Generation
(Children of Ronald George Flutur)

Christy Carol
Born: August 8, 1986
Place: Southfield, Michigan
Married: No

Children: None

Address: 1166 Kellogg Road
Brighton, MI 48116

Phone: (313) 227-2187

Mandy Lorraine
Born: February 13, 1988
Place: Southfield, Michigan
Married: No

Children: None

Address: 1166 Kellogg Road
Brighton, MI 48116

Phone: (313) 227-2187

Charles Duane
Born: July 12, 1989
Place: Southfield, Michigan
Married: No

Children: None

Address: 1166 Kellogg Road
Brighton, MI 48116

Phone: (313) 227-2187

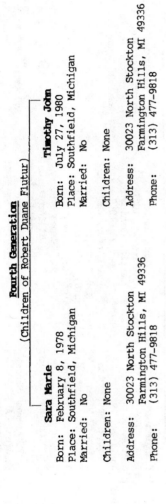

Fourth Generation
(Children of Robert Duane Flutur)

Sara Marie

Born: February 8, 1978
Place: Southfield, Michigan
Married: No

Children: None

Address: 30023 North Stockton
         Farmington Hills, MI 49336
Phone: (313) 477-9818

Timothy John

Born: July 27, 1980
Place: Southfield, Michigan
Married: No

Children: None

Address: 30023 North Stockton
         Farmington Hills, MI 49336
Phone: (313) 477-9818

Fourth Generation
(Child of Kelley Lynn Kirkcaldy Hulsey)

Ryan Ray

Born: October 19, 1991
Place: Las Vegas, Nevada
Married: No

Children: None

Address: 1907 Spode
         Green Valley, NV 89014
Phone: (702) 434-8820

First Generation
(Children of Jan Janssen Wubbena)

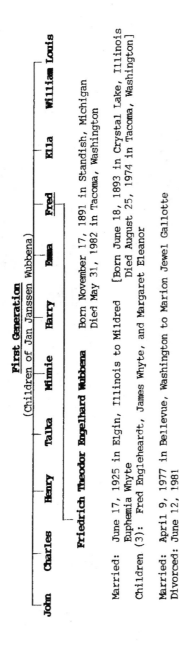

John   Charles   Henry   Talka   Mimie   Harry   Emma   **Fred**   Ela   **William Louis**

Friedrich Theodor Engelhard Wubbena   Born November 17, 1891 in Standish, Michigan   [Born June 18, 1893 in Crystal Lake, Illinois
Died August 25, 1974 in Tacoma, Washington]
Died May 31, 1982 in Tacoma, Washington

Married: June 17, 1925 in Elgin, Illinois to Mildred Euphemia Whyte
Children (3): Fred Engleheardt, James Whyte, and Margaret Eleanor

Married: April 9, 1977 in Bellevue, Washington to Marion Jewel Gallotte
Divorced: June 12, 1981
Children: None

Second Generation
(Children of Fred E. Wubbena)

Fred Engleheardt
Born: April 4, 1926
Place: Marquette, Michigan
Married: April 24, 1948
         Seattle, Washington
to Muriel Bernice U'Ren
Born 4-25-30 Seattle, WA
Children (3): Dawn Christine
              Diana Kay
              Douglas Fredrick
Address: 10376 Fremont Street
         Yucaipa, CA 92399
Phone: (714) 797-6768

James Whyte
Born: November 14, 1927
Place: Seattle, Washington
Married: July 23, 1949
         Bellevue, Washington
to Ruth Lorraine Lorentz
Born 6-7-27 Butte, Montana
Children (4): Linda Jean
              James Gregory
              William Hobson
              Christine Joann
Address: 4212 Oak Grove
         Carrollton, TX 75007
Phone: (214) 394-5793

Margaret Eleanor
Born: September 30, 1934
Place: Seattle, Washington
Married: June 10, 1955
         Seattle, WA
to Richard Carl Spangler
Born 4-7-31 Seattle, WA
Children (3): Michael Timothy
              David Richard
              Carol Jean
Address: 1837 Skyline Drive
         Tacoma, WA 98406
Phone: (206) 752-2230

VII. Fred - 2

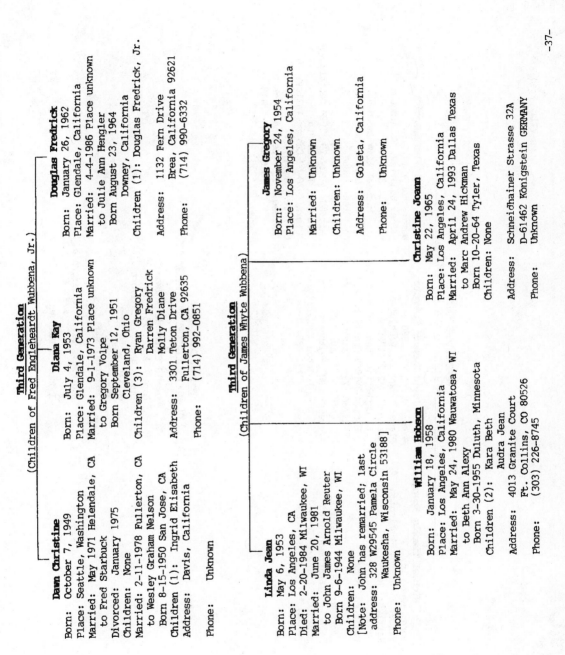

Third Generation

(Children of Fred Engleheardt Wubbena, Jr.)

Dawn Christine

Born: October 7, 1949
Place: Seattle, Washington
Married: May 1971 Helendale, CA
to Fred Starbuck
Divorced: January 1975
Children: None
Married: 2-11-1978 Fullerton, CA
to Wesley Graham Nelson
Born 8-15-1950 San Jose, CA
Children (1): Ingrid Elisabeth
Address: Davis, California

Phone: Unknown

Diana Kay

Born: July 4, 1953
Place: Glendale, California
Married: 9-1-1973 Place unknown
to Gregory Volpe
Born September 12, 1951
Cleveland, Ohio
Children (3): Ryan Gregory
Darren Fredrick
Molly Diane
Address: 3301 Teton Drive
Fullerton, CA 92635
Phone: (714) 992-0851

Douglas Fredrick

Born: January 26, 1962
Place: Glendale, California
Married: 4-4-1986 Place unknown
to Julie Ann Hengler
Born August 23, 1964
Downey, California
Children (1): Douglas Fredrick, Jr.

Address: 1132 Fern Drive
Brea, California 92621
Phone: (714) 990-6332

Third Generation

(Children of James Whyte Wubbena)

James Gregory

Born: November 24, 1954
Place: Los Angeles, California
Married: Unknown

Children: Unknown

Address: Goleta, California

Phone: Unknown

Christine Joann

Born: May 22, 1965
Place: Los Angeles, California
Married: April 24, 1993 Dallas Texas
to Marc Andrew Hickman
Born 10-20-64 Tyler, Texas
Children: None

Address: Schneidhainer Strasse 32A
D-61462 Königstein GERMANY
Phone: Unknown

Linda Jean

Born: May 6, 1953
Place: Los Angeles, CA
Died: 2-20-1984 Milwaukee, WI
Married: June 20, 1981
to John James Arnold Reuter
Born 9-6-1944 Milwaukee, WI
Children: None
[Note: John has remarried; last
address: 328 W29545 Pamela Circle
Waukesha, Wisconsin 53188]

Phone: Unknown

William Hobson

Born: January 18, 1958
Place: Los Angeles, California
Married: May 24, 1980 Wauwatosa, WI
to Beth Ann Alexy
Born 3-30-1955 Duluth, Minnesota
Children (2): Kara Beth
Audra Jean
Address: 4013 Granite Court
Ft. Collins, CO 80526
Phone: (303) 226-8745

Third Generation
(Children of Margaret Eleanor Wubbena Spangler)

Michael Timothy Spangler
Born: June 16, 1957
Place: Kirkland, Washington
Married: No

Children: None

Address: 8439 E. Imperial Hwy.
Apartment #203
Downey, CA 90242
Phone: (213) 862-5812

David Richard Spangler
Born: April 12, 1960
Place: Longview, Washington
Married: 12-21-1985
to Catherine Chandler Burdette
Born 4-8-1960 Charleston, WV
Children (2): Kristin Elizabeth
Lauren Elise

Address: 907 Heathgate
Houston, Texas 77062
Phone: (713) 486-7010

Carol Jean Spangler
Born: April 16, 1961
Place: Longview, Washington
Married: 8-6-1983
to Michael Alan Snowden
Born 11-5-1952 Tacoma, WA
Children: None
Divorced: 1988
Married: May 29, 1994 Seattle, WA
to Paul Tami Sakata
Born 4-20-62 Castro Valley, CA
Children: None
Address: 1512 Second North
Seattle, WA 98119
Phone: (206) 283-3619

Fourth Generation
(Child of Dawn Christine Wubbena Nelson)

Ingrid Elizabeth Nelson
Born: April 25, 1979
Place: Orange, California
Married: No

Children: None

Address: Davis, California

Phone: Unknown

VII. Fred – 4

Fourth Generation
(Children of Diana Kay Wubbena Volpe)

Ryan Gregory Volpe

Born: May 11, 1979
Place: Fullerton, California
Married: No

Children: None

Address: 3301 Teton Drive
Fullerton, CA 92635
Phone: (714) 992-0851

Darren Fredrick Volpe

Born: December 12, 1983
Place: Fullerton, California
Married: No

Children: None

Address: 3301 Teton Drive
Fullerton, CA 92635
Phone: (714) 992-0851

Molly Diane Volpe

Born: February 18, 1990
Place: Fullerton, California
Married: No

Children: None

Address: 3301 Teton Drive
Fullerton, CA 92635
Phone: (714) 992-0851

Fourth Generation
(Child of Douglas Fredrick Wubbena)

Douglas Fredrick Wubbena, Jr.

Born: 1 October 1992
Place: Whittier, California
Married: No

Children: None

Address: 1132 Fern Drive
Brea, California 92621
Phone: (714) 990-6332

Fourth Generation
(Children of William Hobson Wubbena)

Kara Beth Wubbena
Born: October 29, 1982
Place: Akron, Ohio
Married: No

Children: None

Address: 4013 Granite Court
          Ft. Collins, CO 80526
Phone: (303) 226-8745

Andra Jean Wubbena
Born: August 16, 1985
Place: Fort Collins, Colorado
Married: No

Children: None

Address: 4013 Granite Court
          Ft. Collins, CO 80526
Phone: (303) 226-8745

Fourth Generation
(Children of David Richard Spangler)

Kristin Elizabeth Spangler
Born: April 15, 1989
Place: Royal Oak, Michigan
Married: No

Children: None

Address: 907 Heathgate
          Houston, Texas 77062
Phone: (713) 486-7010

Lauren Elise Spangler
Born: June 25, 1992
Place: Webster, Texas
Married: No

Children: None

Address: 907 Heathgate
          Houston, Texas 77062
Phone: (713) 486-7010

VIII. William - 1

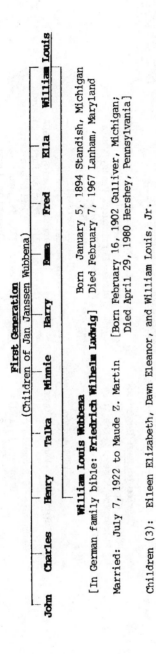

First Generation
(Children of Jan Janssen Wubbena)

John	Charles	Henry	Talka	Mimmie	Emma	Harry	Fred	Ella	William Louis

William Louis Wubbena
[In German family bible: **Friedrich Wilhelm Ludwig**]

Born January 5, 1894 Standish, Michigan
Died February 7, 1967 Lanham, Maryland

Married: July 7, 1922 to Maude Z. Martin   [Born February 16, 1902 Gulliver, Michigan;
Died April 29, 1980 Hershey, Pennsylvania]

Children (3):   Eileen Elizabeth, Dawn Eleanor, and William Louis, Jr.

Second Generation
(Children of William Louis Wubbena)

Eileen Elizabeth
Born: September 4, 1924
Place: Marquette, Michigan
Married: September 9, 1947
         Ann Arbor, Michigan
         to Robert Keith Catt
         Born May 2, 1923
         Freeport, Michigan
Children (3):   Shari Eileen
                Richard Keith
                Marjorie Ann
Address: 200 East Felshaw Street
         Gaylord, MI 49735
Phone: (517) 732-5071

Dawn Eleanor
Born: April 5, 1926
Place: Marquette, Michigan
Married: April 4, 1948
         Ann Arbor, Michigan
         to Burton B. Hendricks
         Born February 10, 1923
         Traverse City, Michigan
Children (2):   Charles Michael
                Lea Monette
Address: 56 Brownstone Drive
         Hershey, PA 17033
Phone: (717) 534-2962

William Louis, Jr.
[Nickname: "Weemo"]
Born: March 7, 1930
Place: Marquette, Michigan
Married: June 2, 1953
         West Point, New York
         to Marie Joan Schroer
         Born March 11, 1931
         New York, New York
Children (2):   William Philip
                Jon Kevin
Address: 3607 Spruell Drive
         Silver Spring, MD
                          20902
Phone: (301) 949-9719

-41-

Third Generation

(Children of Eileen Elizabeth Wubbena Catt)

Shari Eileen Catt Waldo

Born: April 8, 1950
Place: La Crosse, Wisconsin
Married: June 26, 1971
  to Raymond F. Gilmore
  Born August 27, 1948
  Grayling, MI [Divorced 1974]
Children (1): Betsy Jean Gilmore
Married: March 1, 1975
  to Gary F. Waldo
  Born March 8, 1938
  Grand Rapids, Michigan
Children (1): David Robert Waldo
Address: 2485 Fischer Road
  Gaylord, MI 49735
Phone: (517) 732-1588

Richard Keith Catt

Born: February 20, 1952
Place: La Crosse, Wisconsin
Married: June 16, 1979
  to Sheila M. Christenson
  Born March 18, 1950
  Niles, Michigan
Children (2):
  Sarah Hahn Catt
  Rachel Elizabeth Catt
Address: 1542 Lendale
  Ludington, MI 49431
Phone: (616) 845-7528

Marjorie Ann Catt Shev

Born: October 10, 1955
Place: Chicago, Illinois
Married: July 24, 1976
  to Keith K. Shev
  Born December 4, 1954
  Detroit, Michigan
Children (4):
  Nathan Andrew Shev
  Janelle Renee Shev
  Karee Leigh Shev
  Lindsey Erin Shev
Address: 2490 Potter Road
  Traverse City, MI
  49684
Phone: (616) 947-0218

Third Generation

(Children of Dawn Eleanor Wubbena Hendricks)

Charles Michael Hendricks

Born: September 14, 1955
Place: The Hague, Netherlands
Married: No

Children (1): Vanessa Joyce

Address: 56 Brownstone Drive
  Hershey, PA 17033
Phone: (717) 534-2962

Lea Nanette Hendricks Carswell

Born: December 4, 1957
Place: Harrisburg, Pennsylvania
Married: September 5, 1981
  Hershey, Pennsylvania
  to Glen D. Carswell
  Born August 31, 1955
  Goderich, Ontario, CANADA
Children (2): Douglas Burton Carswell
  Emily Dawn Carswell
Address: 2735 Kingswood Lane
  Gloucester, Ontario
  K1T 2G3 CANADA
Phone: (613) 523-7780

VIII. William - 3

-43-

Third Generation

(Children of William Louis Wubbena, Jr.)

William Philip Wubbena

Born: August 30, 1959
Place: Rio de Janeiro, Brazil, S.A.
Married: January 26, 1991
     College Park, Maryland
to Ann Marion Garvey
Born June 2, 1964
     Washington, D.C.
Children: None

Address: 4621 Edgefield Road
     Bethesda, MD 20814
Phone: (301) 530-7992

Jon Kevin Wubbena

Born: October 15, 1961
Place: West Point, New York
Married: May 3, 1986
     Hummelstown, Pennsylvania
to Michaelann Louise Rosario
Born September 7, 1962
     Harrisburg, Pennsylvania
Children (2): Jon Kevin Wubbena, Jr.
            Caitlin Marie Wubbena

Address: 315 Greenland Drive
     Lancaster, PA 17602
Phone: (717) 394-1451

Fourth Generation

(Children of Shari Eileen Catt Waldo)

Betsy Jean Gilmore

Born: October 10, 1973
Place: Gaylord, Michigan
Married: No

Children: None

Address: 2485 Fischer Road
     Gaylord, MI 49735
Phone: (517) 732-1588

David Robert Waldo

Born: June 6, 1979
Place: Gaylord, Michigan
Married: No

Children: None

Address: 2485 Fischer Road
     Gaylord, MI 49735
Phone: (517) 732-1588

Fourth Generation
(Children of Richard Keith Catt)

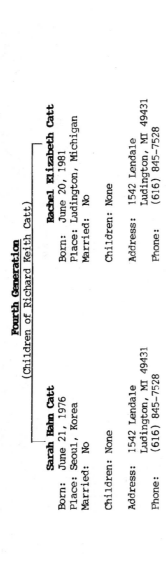

Sarah Hahn Catt

Born: June 21, 1976
Place: Seoul, Korea
Married: No

Children: None

Address: 1542 Lendale
Ludington, MI 49431
Phone: (616) 845-7528

Rachel Elizabeth Catt

Born: June 20, 1981
Place: Ludington, Michigan
Married: No

Children: None

Address: 1542 Lendale
Ludington, MI 49431
Phone: (616) 845-7528

Fourth Generation
(Children of Marjorie Ann Catt Shev)

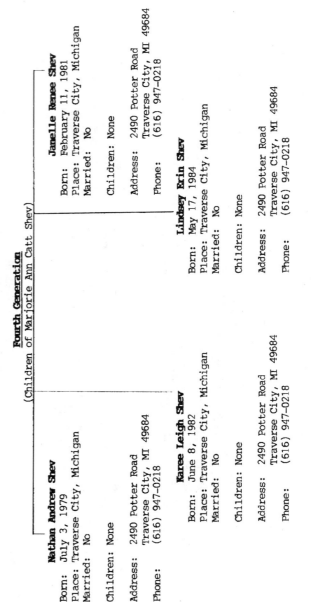

Nathan Andrew Shev

Born: July 3, 1979
Place: Traverse City, Michigan
Married: No

Children: None

Address: 2490 Potter Road
Traverse City, MI 49684
Phone: (616) 947-0218

Karee Leigh Shev

Born: June 8, 1982
Place: Traverse City, Michigan
Married: No

Children: None

Address: 2490 Potter Road
Traverse City, MI 49684
Phone: (616) 947-0218

Janelle Renee Shev

Born: February 11, 1981
Place: Traverse City, Michigan
Married: No

Children: None

Address: 2490 Potter Road
Traverse City, MI 49684
Phone: (616) 947-0218

Lindsey Erin Shev

Born: May 17, 1984
Place: Traverse City, Michigan
Married: No

Children: None

Address: 2490 Potter Road
Traverse City, MI 49684
Phone: (616) 947-0218

Fourth Generation
(Child of Charles Michael Hendricks)

Vanessa Joyce Hendricks

Born: March 3, 1992
Place: San Diego, California
Married: No

Children: None

Address: 56 Brownstone Drive
Hershey, PA 17033
Phone: (717) 534-2962

Fourth Generation
(Children of Lea Monette Hendricks Carswell)

Douglas Burton Carswell

Born: January 4, 1988
Place: Ottawa, Ontario, CANADA
Married: No

Children: None

Address: 2735 Kingswood Lane
Gloucester, Ontario
K1T 2G3 CANADA
Phone: (613) 523-7780

Emily Dawn Carswell

Born: September 20, 1990
Place: Ottawa, Ontario, CANADA
Married: No

Children: None

Address: 2735 Kingswood Lane
Gloucester, Ontario
K1T 2G3 CANADA
Phone: (613) 523-7780

Fourth Generation
(Children of Jon Kevin Wubbena)

Jon Kevin Wubbena, Jr.

Born: December 30, 1987
Place: Arlington, Virginia
Married: No

Children: None

Address: 315 Greenland Drive
Lancaster, PA 17602
Phone: (717) 394-1451

Caitlin Marie Wubbena

Born: August 5, 1990
Place: Alexandria, Virginia
Married: No

Children: None

Address: 315 Greenland Drive
Lancaster, PA 17602
Phone: (717) 394-1451

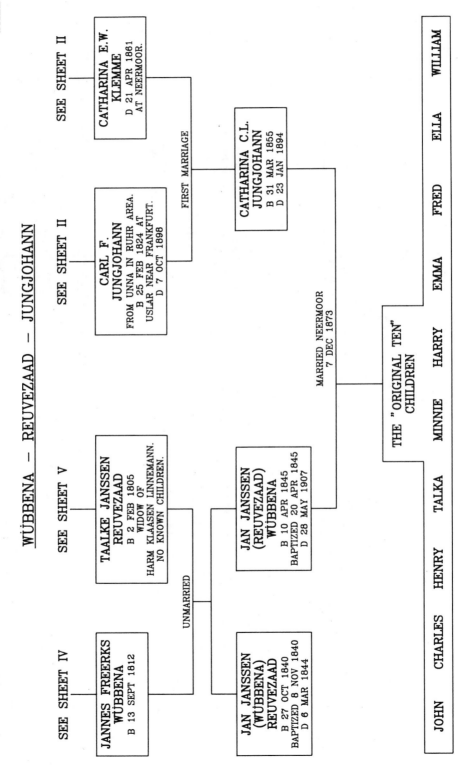

SHEET II

JUNGJOHANN – KLEMME

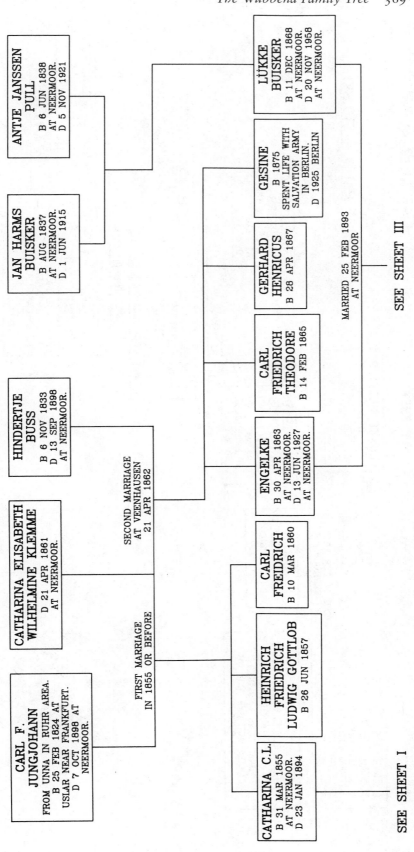

CARL F. JUNGJOHANN
FROM UNNA IN RUHR AREA.
B 25 FEB 1824 AT
USLAR NEAR FRANKFURT.
D 7 OCT 1898 AT
NEERMOOR.

CATHARINA ELISABETH WILHELMINE KLEMME
D 21 APR 1861
AT NEERMOOR.

HINDERTJE BUSS
B 6 NOV 1833
D 13 SEP 1898
AT NEERMOOR.

JAN HARMS BUISKER
B AUG 1837
AT NEERMOOR.
D 1 JUN 1915

ANTJE JANSSEN PULL
B 6 JUN 1838
AT NEERMOOR.
D 5 NOV 1921

FIRST MARRIAGE
IN 1855 OR BEFORE

SECOND MARRIAGE
AT VEENHAUSEN
21 APR 1862

CATHARINA C.L.
B 31 MAR 1855
AT NEERMOOR.
D 23 JAN 1894

HEINRICH FRIEDRICH LUDWIG GOTTLOB
B 26 JUN 1857

CARL FREIDRICH
B 10 MAR 1860

ENGELKE
B 30 APR 1863
AT NEERMOOR.
D 13 JUN 1927
AT NEERMOOR.

CARL FRIEDRICH THEODORE
B 14 FEB 1865

GERHARD HENRICUS
B 28 APR 1867

GESINE
B 1875
SPENT LIFE WITH
SALVATION ARMY
IN BERLIN.
D 1925 BERLIN

LÜKKE BUISKER
B 11 DEC 1868
AT NEERMOOR.
D 20 NOV 1958
AT NEERMOOR.

MARRIED 25 FEB 1893
AT NEERMOOR

SEE SHEET III

SEE SHEET I

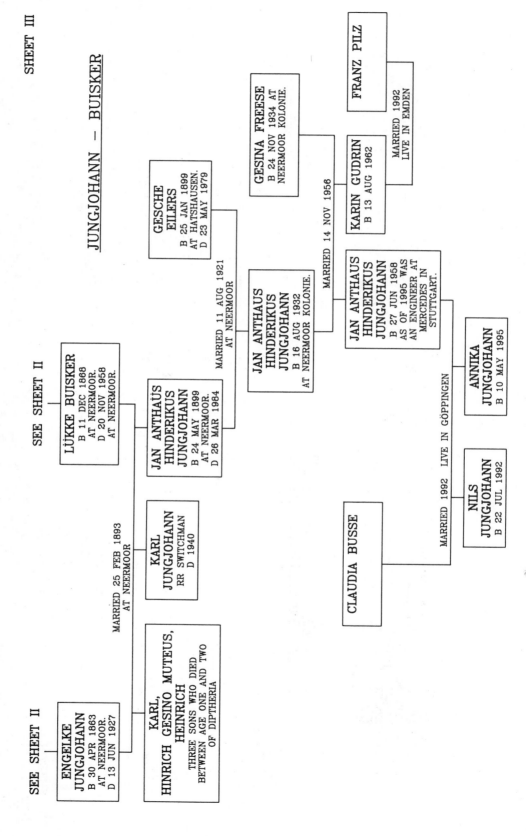

SHEET IV

WÙBBENA

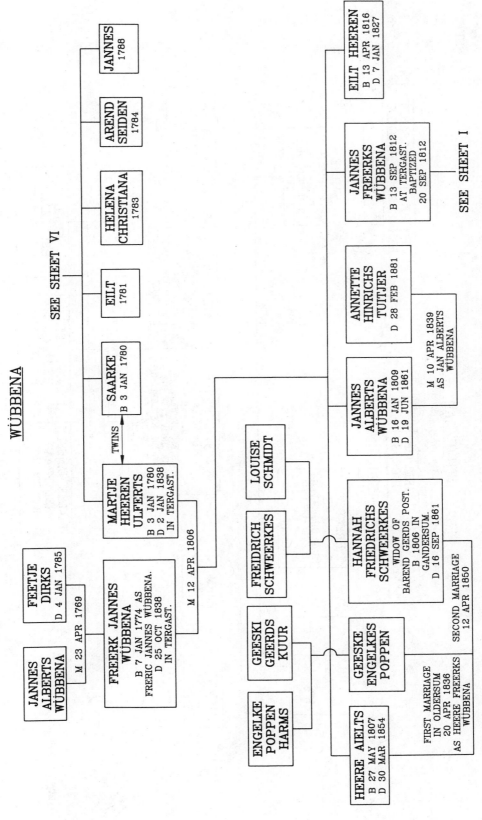

SEE SHEET VI

SEE SHEET I

JANNES
1788

AREND
SEIDEN
1784

HELENA
CHRISTIANA
1783

EILT
1781

SAARKE
B 3 JAN 1780

EILT HEEREN
B 13 APR 1816
D 7 JAN 1827

JANNES
FREERKS
WÙBBENA
B 13 SEP 1812
AT TERGAST.
BAPTIZED
20 SEP 1812

ANNETTE
HINRICHS
TUITJER
D 28 FEB 1881

JANNES
ALBERTS
WÙBBENA
B 16 JAN 1809
D 19 JUN 1861

M 10 APR 1839
AS JAN ALBERTS
WÙBBENA

TWINS

MARTJE
HEEREN
ULFERTS
B 3 JAN 1780
D 2 JAN 1838
IN TERGAST.

FEETJE
DIRKS
D 4 JAN 1785

FREERK JANNES
WÙBBENA
B 7 JAN 1774 AS
FRERIC JANNES WÙBBENA.
D 25 OCT 1838
IN TERGAST.

JANNES
ALBERTS
WÙBBENA

M 23 APR 1769

M 12 APR 1806

LOUISE
SCHMIDT

FREIDRICH
SCHWEERKES

HANNAH
FRIEDRICHS
SCHWEERKES
WIDOW OF
BAREND GERDS POST.
B 1806 IN
GANDERSUM.
D 16 SEP 1861

SECOND MARRIAGE
12 APR 1850

GEESKI
GEERDS
KUUR

ENGELKE
POPPEN
HARMS

GEESKE
ENGELKES
POPPEN

HEERE AIELTS
B 27 MAY 1807
D 30 MAR 1854

FIRST MARRIAGE
IN OLDERSUM
20 APR 1836
AS HEERE FREERKS
WÙBBENA

SHEET V

REUVEZAAD – WILKEN

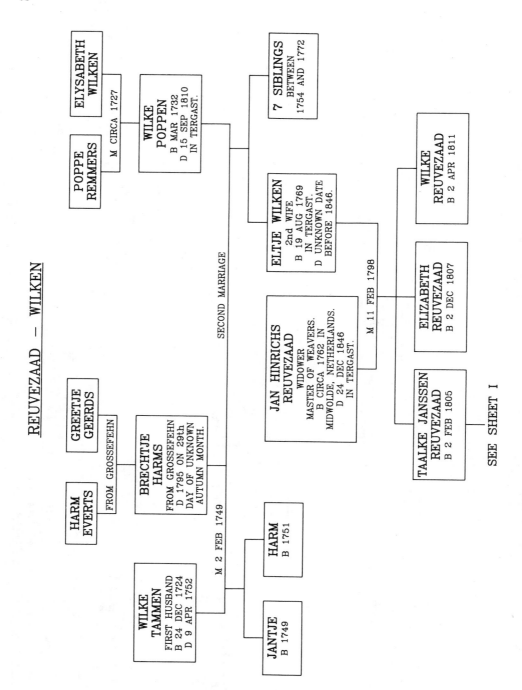

SHEET VI

ULFERTS

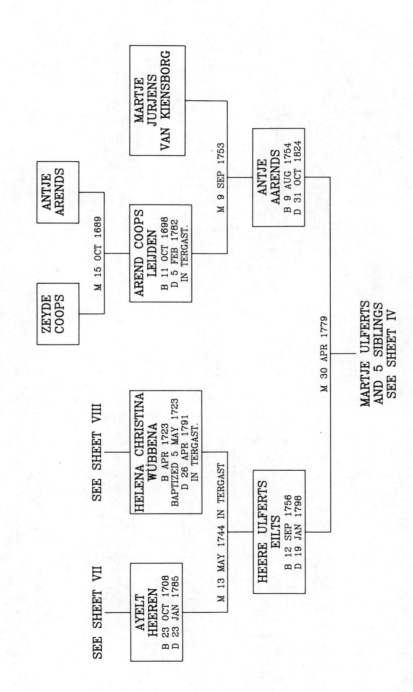

ZEYDE COOPS

ANTJE ARENDS

M 15 OCT 1689

AREND COOPS LEIJDEN
B 11 OCT 1698
D 5 FEB 1782
IN TERGAST.

MARTJE JURJENS VAN KIENSBORG

M 9 SEP 1753

ANTJE AARENDS
B 9 AUG 1754
D 31 OCT 1824

SEE SHEET VII

AYELT HEEREN
B 23 OCT 1708
D 23 JAN 1785

SEE SHEET VIII

HELENA CHRISTINA WUBBENA
B APR 1723
BAPTIZED 5 MAY 1723
D 26 APR 1791
IN TERGAST.

M 13 MAY 1744 IN TERGAST

HEERE ULFERTS EILTS
B 12 SEP 1756
D 19 JAN 1798

M 30 APR 1779

MARTJE ULFERTS
AND 5 SIBLINGS
SEE SHEET IV

SHEET VII

ULFERTS
(CONTINUED)

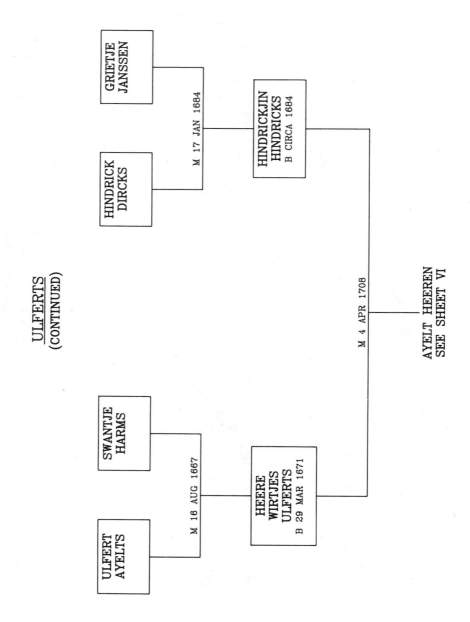

GRIETJE
JANSSEN

HINDRICK
DIRCKS

M 17 JAN 1684

HINDRICKJIN
HINDRICKS
B CIRCA 1684

SWANTJE
HARMS

ULFERT
AYELTS

M 16 AUG 1667

HEERE
WIRTJES
ULFERTS
B 29 MAR 1671

M 4 APR 1708

AYELT HEEREN
SEE SHEET VI

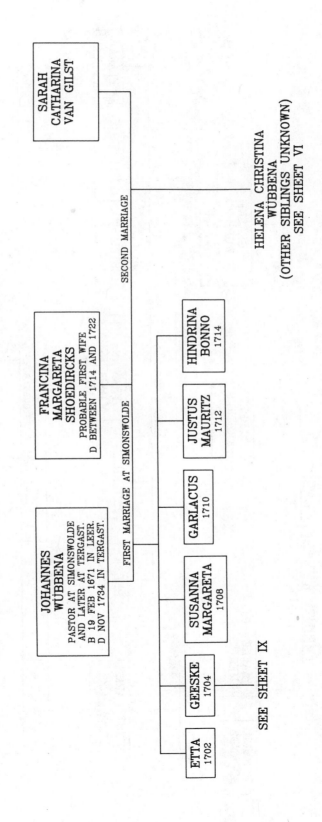

WÜBBENA – VAN GILST

JOHANNES
WÜBBENA
PASTOR AT SIMONSWOLDE
AND LATER AT TERGAST.
B 19 FEB 1671 IN LEER.
D NOV 1734 IN TERGAST.

FRANCINA
MARGARETA
SHOEDIRCKS
PROBABLE FIRST WIFE
D BETWEEN 1714 AND 1722

SARAH
CATHARINA
VAN GILST

FIRST MARRIAGE AT SIMONSWOLDE

SECOND MARRIAGE

ETTA
1702

GEESKE
1704

SUSANNA
MARGARETA
1708

GARLACUS
1710

JUSTUS
MAURITZ
1712

HINDRINA
BONNO
1714

HELENA CHRISTINA
WÜBBENA
(OTHER SIBLINGS UNKNOWN)
SEE SHEET VI

SEE SHEET IX

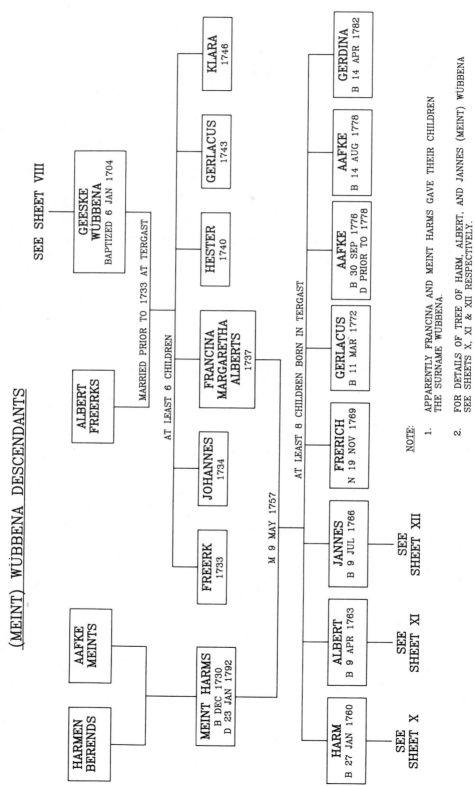

SHEET IX

(MEINT) WÜBBENA DESCENDANTS

SEE SHEET VIII

NOTE:

1.   APPARENTLY FRANCINA AND MEINT HARMS GAVE THEIR CHILDREN THE SURNAME WÜBBENA.

2.   FOR DETAILS OF TREE OF HARM, ALBERT, AND JANNES (MEINT) WÜBBENA SEE SHEETS X, XI & XII RESPECTIVELY.

SHEET X

HARM (MEINT) WÜBBENA
(CONTINUATION FROM SHEET IX)

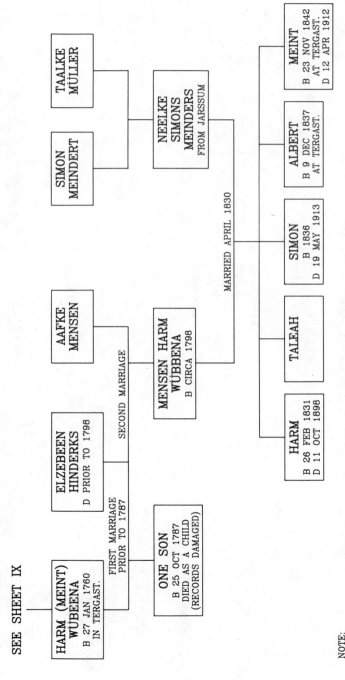

SEE SHEET IX

HARM (MEINT) WÜBEENA	
B 27 JAN 1760 IN TERGAST.	

FIRST MARRIAGE PRIOR TO 1787

SECOND MARRIAGE

ELZEBEEN HINDERKS
D PRIOR TO 1798

AAFKE MENSEN

SIMON MEINDERT

TAALKE MÜLLER

ONE SON
B 25 OCT 1787
DIED AS A CHILD
(RECORDS DAMAGED)

MENSEN HARM WÜBBENA
B CIRCA 1798

NEELKE SIMONS MEINDERS
FROM JARSSUM

MARRIED APRIL 1830

HARM
B 26 FEB 1831
D 11 OCT 1898

TALEAH

SIMON
B 1836
D 19 MAY 1913

ALBERT
B 9 DEC 1837
AT TERGAST.

MEINT
B 23 NOV 1842
AT TERGAST.
D 12 APR 1912

NOTE:

MENSEN HARM WÜBBENA WITH HIS WIFE AND 4 SONS EMIGRATED TO
THE MID-WEST. THEIR DESCENDANTS CONSTITUTE WHAT WE IDENTIFY
IN THIS BOOK AS TRIBE #2.

SHEET XI

ALBERT (MEINT) WÜBBENA
(CONTINUATION FROM SHEET IX)

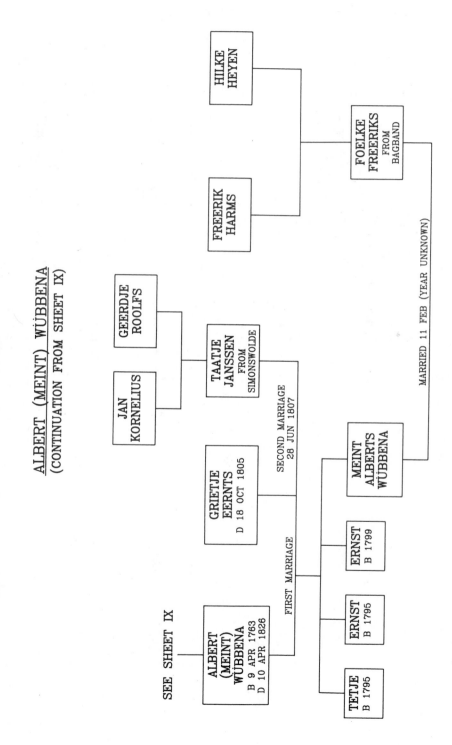

SHEET XII

JANNES (MEINT) WÜBBENA
(CONTINUATION FROM SHEET IX)

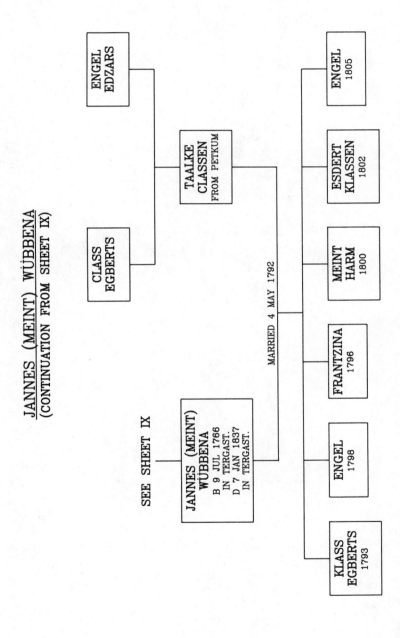

SEE SHEET IX

JANNES (MEINT)
WÜBBENA
B 9 JUL 1766
IN TERGAST.
D 7 JAN 1837
IN TERGAST.

CLASS
EGBERTS

ENGEL
EDZARS

TAALKE
CLASSEN
FROM PETKUM

MARRIED 4 MAY 1792

KLASS
EGBERTS
1793

ENGEL
1798

FRANTZINA
1796

MEINT
HARM
1800

ESDERT
KLASSEN
1802

ENGEL
1805

Part Four

A PHOTOGRAPHIC
HISTORY OF
THE WUBBENA FAMILY

From the Old World

The interior of the Tergast, Germany, Evangelical Reformed Church dated about 1921 is little changed from when Jan Wübbena was baptized here in 1845. Jan's great-great-great-grandfather, Johannes Wübbena, was pastor here from 1711 to 1734.

The exterior of the Tergast, Germany, Evangelical Reformed Church circa 1925

Train crossing guard's house in Neermoor circa 1900–1930. This is the house in which Karl Jungjohann lived and in which his eldest daughter, Catharina, was born. It is not known who the people standing in front of the house are.

The same house circa 1940–1950. It has since been torn down.

A typical farm scene in Tergast during World War I

A typical worker's house in the center of Tergast circa 1925

The old Tergast vicarage, where Pastor Johannes Wübbena lived while serving as a pastor in the early eighteenth century, and the new school to the right, circa 1950

A typical modern-day farmhouse in the Tergast area

Lükke and husband Engelke
Jungjohann, Catharina Wübbena's
brother. He was a tailor and they
lived in Neermoor.

A scene of the Neermoor skyline, probably in the early 1900s

A street scene in Neermoor around 1900

Scenes of modern-day Neermoor circa 1975

One of the most famous of the ancient "stone-built houses." See Appendix B for letters of Pastor Fassbender to Dawn Wubbena that tell of the significance of these houses.

Typical topography of this part of Ostfriesland. This particular scene shows where the Leda River enters into the Ems River. Note the dike. It is possible to judge its height from the sheep grazing in the foreground.

The house of Jan Jungjohann's parents after renovation. Neermoor-Kollonie (Rorichmoor)

Jan Jungjohann's parents on the day of their golden wedding anniversary, August 11, 1971

The family of Jan Jungjohann at the baptism of Jan's granddaughter Annika on September 3, 1995. *Left to right:* Gesine Jungjohann, Jan Jungjohann, Claudia Jungjohann, Karin Pilz holding Annika, Claudia's parents. *Front:* Jan Jungjohann, Jr. with son Nils

Jan and Catharina Wübbena and Their Children

Jan Janssen Wübbena
(April 10, 1845–
May 28, 1907)

Catharina Louise Wübbena
(March 31, 1855–
January 23, 1894)

Johnsfield School circa 1900. Jan Wübbena is the man with the beard standing in the aisle in the back. Frank Hamilton, the teacher, is the man in the white shirt and tie standing in the back.

Left: The Wubbena family burial plot, Woodmere Cemetery, Standish, Michigan. *Right:* Jan Wübbena's farmhouse on Johnsfield Road circa 1913. This is the new farmhouse that Jan and his sons constructed circa 1905.

Above: John T. Wubbena circa 1897 (April 18, 1874–July 6, 1954)

Left: John, the lumberjack (first row, fourth from left) circa 1898, Upper Peninsula of Michigan near Munising

Wedding picture of John and Laura Wubbena, March 14, 1911

Above left: Charles F. Wubbena (October 8, 1875– November 15, 1956)

Above right: Myrtle R. Wubbena, wife of Charles (March 10, 1877– January 22, 1954)

Right: Charles and Myrtle (Myrtie) with daughter Eva circa 1898

Henry F. Wubbena (November 4, 1878–September 29, 1962). *Right:* Martha, wife of Henry (November 11, 1887–August 26, 1977)

Henry working for Michigan Bell Telephone Co. circa 1936

Talka H. Wubbena circa 1946 (August 16, 1881–February 20, 1951). *Right:* Talka as a World War I army nurse in 1918. Picture taken while she was stationed at Letterman Hospital, San Francisco.

Talka as a student nurse in charge of a ward at University of Michigan Hospital in Ann Arbor circa 1914. Talka is the person sitting at the desk.

Minnie Wubbena (March 8,
1887–April 1, 1974). High
school graduation picture,
Standish, Michigan

Wedding picture of Minnie and husband
Louis Gabler, July 8, 1913

Harry C. Wubbena circa 1914
(June 8, 1888–June 6, 1947)

Harry and wife Lenore
circa 1914

Emma Wubbena circa 1917
(September 28, 1890–
August 15, 1959)

Emma and husband George Flutur,
Standish, Michigan, on 1922
post-wedding trip

Fred T. E. Wubbena as a
soldier in World War I
(November 17, 1891–
May 31, 1982)

Fred and Mildred Wubbena
with Fred Jr., 1926

Ella C. Wubbena (January 26, 1893–July 28, 1983). High school graduation picture circa 1911. *Right:* Ella as a health nurse at Moody Bible Institute, Chicago, Illinois, circa 1942

Ella with husband George Flutur, 1973

William L. Wubbena circa 1950
(January 5, 1894–
February 7, 1967)

Maude Z. Wubbena
(February 16, 1902–
April 29, 1980)

William L. Wubbena
at age of twelve,
1906

William as a soldier in
World War I

The Original Ten in 1921. *Left to right:* (Front row) Henry, John, Charles; (Back row) Minnie, Harry, Talka, Emma, Bill, Fred, Ella

The Original Ten in 1946. *Left to right:* Henry, Charles, Fred, Bill, Talka, Minnie, John, Ella, Emma, Harry

The four sisters circa 1915. *Left to right:* Minnie, Ella, Emma, Talka

The six brothers with their wives in 1946. *Left to right:* Laura and John, Myrtle and Charles, Henry and Martha, Harry and Lenore, Bill (Maude is absent), Mildred and Fred

Attendees at the 1946 reunion in Standish on the lawn at Charles' home. *Left to right:* (Standing) Len's mother, Lou Gabler, Minnie, John, Laura, Myrtle, Charles, Bill, Jean Bittner, Emma, Myrtle Baikie, Janet Strauss, Henry, Martha, Jim, Mildred, Fred Jr., Muriel, Fred. (Front row) Lenore, Talka, Harry, Beverly Baikie, Margaret Wubbena, Ella, Andries Strauss, Paul Strauss, Grace Strauss. *Note:* Dr. Andries Strauss took this picture.

The John Wubbena Family in 1948. *Left to right:* (Front row) John Tulloch, Rodney Tulloch, Christine Tulloch, Janine Tulloch, Luise Wubbena; (Middle row) Theda Bittner, Jean Wubbena Bittner, Ruth Wubbena Tulloch, Catherine Wubbena, Laura Wyatt Wubbena, Jeannette Noeske Wubbena, Erica Wilharm Wubbena, Jan Wubbena; (Back row) Kenneth Bittner, William Tulloch, John Wubbena, Shirley Wubbena, Wyatt Wubbena

The Nursing
Tradition of
the Wubbena Women

by Catherine Wubbena

Nursing has been a tradition among the women of the Jan Wübbena family. Talka prepared a composite photograph of the fifteen registered nurses that as of September 1950 were either daughters (3), daughters-in-law (2), or granddaughters (10) of Jan and Catharina [see facing page]. Succeeding years have produced several additional nurses who could be added to this group.

The ideal of the dignity and worth of life begets the idea that one must not live in vain. In no other work than in the health professions is one more aware of this. Nurses have the privilege of being a part of the very existence of their patients—their social and emotional well-being as well as their physical well-being.

Talka and those who followed after her appreciated their great privilege and responsibility, and were aware of the rewards, intangible as well as tangible, that come with this commitment. This is the true professional attitude.

We wonder which inherent traits transmitted down from Jan and Catharina were influential in steering members of subsequent generations into the nursing profession. There must be commonalities which were the forces in determining the "turns of the road" which led each one to choose this field as her life's work.

Facing Page: Registered nurses in the family as of circa 1945. Compiled by Talka Wubbena. Several nurses have graduated since this was compiled.

The 1993 Family Reunion

The pictures on the following pages were taken at the Wubbena Family Reunion held August 20–22, 1993, at the Quality Inn/Forward Conference Center at West Branch, Michigan.

The family of John and Laura Wubbena. *Left to Right:* (Back row) Larry Johnson, Jacquie Johnson, Catherine Wubbena, Ralph Bittner, Jean Bittner, Joe Fraam, Nancy Bittner, Donald Baslock, Richard Emery, Janine Emery, Carol Yops, Ruth Tulloch, Kent Robinson, Christine Robinson, Duane Robinson, Charlotte Tulloch, Rodney Tulloch, Ben Keckler; (Front row, kneeling or sitting) Elizabeth Bittner, Laura Bittner, Rebecca Bittner, Andrew Johnson, Erin Johnson, Theda Baslock, Jodi Baslock, Cheryl Keckler

The family of Charles and Myrtle Wubbena. *Left to right:* Janet Schneider, Roberto Rodriquez, Beverly Rodriquez, Jeannette Baikie, Duncan Baikie, Nancy Brandt, Carl Brandt

The family of Henry and Martha Wubbena. *Left to right:* Roger Dick, Mark Wubbena, Charles Wubbena, Avis Wubbena, Carol Dick, Lois Dick, Carroll Dick, Jim Dick

The family of Louis and
Minnie Wubbena Gabler:
Margaret Pickett (*left*)
and Muriel Ford

The family of George and Emma Wubbena Flutur. *Left to right:* (Back row) Robert
and Marti Flutur, Ronald and Amy Flutur, Randall and Ann Flutur, Virginia Frost,
Lorraine and Duane Flutur; (Front row) Sara and Tim Flutur; Mandy, Charlie, and
Christy Flutur; Heather, Matthew, Autumn, and Crystal Flutur

The family of Fred and
Mildred Wubbena:
Richard Spangler and
Margaret Spangler

The family of William and Maude Wubbena. *Left to right:* (Back row) Philip and
Ann Wubbena, Jon and Michaelann Wubbena with Caitlin, William Jr. and Marie
Wubbena, Dawn and Burton Hendricks, Eileen and Keith Catt, Shari and Gary
Waldo; (Front row) Jon Wubbena, Jr., Betsy Gilmore, David Waldo

Part Five

THE ORIGINAL TEN—
THE STORY OF
WHAT HAPPENED TO
JAN AND CATHARINA'S
CHILDREN

JOHN T. WUBBENA
(1874–1954)

"O Mein Papa—To Me He Was So Wonderful"
by His Daughter, Catherine Wubbena

In American history it is likely that the role of the traditional, generational farm family will be replaced by the modern computer-advised agri-businessman. It is happening now, in 1991; the eighty-acre farm which my father proudly cleared of pine stumps, and plowed and cultivated and reaped with his horses, is being overshadowed by farms of five hundred to one thousand acres as the average size. Even this size is not enough for some farms to fully utilize their powerful and expensive machinery; the farmer rents another five hundred acres to "make it pay."

If Dad could stand at his back door today and survey his fields, he would find it difficult to recognize his life's labor. The two barns still stand, the house is still here, the old brooder house is used for a woodshed. The corn cribs are gone; the hen house has been razed. The buggy shed with attached grainary became, with many storms and much sun, a beautiful gray with the patina of old boards; it gradually fell apart and the timbers and posts were put on the wood pile. Fences and gates have long been removed for the practical movement of tractors and machinery. It is now all one acreage with neither cows nor horses in sight. But the creek still runs through the same way it did despite the building of I-75, which destroyed and filled in the old beaver dam. And there are still eighteen acres of woodland in the southwest corner. Our garden plot is where he located it, but there is no fence around it because there are no hens to get in and scratch out the seeds and growing things. One post rail with support of two posts still stands under the maple tree where there used to be a small gate for getting in and out of the garden. The rail has a deep crack in it, a convenient indentation for filling with bird feed. How many more years will we have it, unrotted and whole?

John T. Wubbena bought his eighty acres from Mrs. Elizabeth Hensler who had come from Saginaw. Prior to her ownership, many, many surrounding acres had been lumbered over by a Mr. Yawkey whose headquarters were in Chicago. He left the territory with huge stumps squatting on the landscape. I recall those white pine stumps as being as large in circumference as those of redwoods we saw in California! As we helped Dad pick up wood and bring it to the house by the wagonload, we would find the remnants of the narrow gauge railroad that had been used to transport the logs to lumber camps in the Glover Switch and Moore's Junction areas, a few miles northwest of the Johnsfield area.

Mrs. Hensler and her son had lived in a small building amidst old trees and stumps. The same roof sheltered not only Mrs. Hensler but also the two oxen; a thick dividing wall separated her living quarters from the stable. A heavy wooden ox yoke hung in our barn for several years. For a while after he bought the farm Dad continued to live with his father and sisters on the Old Place as he worked on clearing his own land. No one lived on the road leading to his place. The road was just a pair of wagon tracks through the woods and stumps. The road was forced to end at his place because there was no bridge for crossing the creek that ran through his acreage. After two or three years he built a house, and later a barn. For years Mrs. Hensler's building was used as a grainary, and in her stable Dad placed a large tank which held the kerosene which was used in the lamps in the house and lanterns in the barns. An addition which Dad put on the grainary was used to shelter the two-seater buggy (called a Democrat) and a cupboard that held his hand tools.

The deed to Dad's farm is dated May 27, 1902. He paid $500.00 for his eighty acres. The deed is signed by H.A. Chamberlain and Lizzy Grier. Mr. Chamberlain was a landowner and banker. Miss Grier was Arenac County's registrar of deeds for many years. She was a dear gentlewoman who contributed much to the fabric and character of early twentieth-century Standish and Arenac County. A few years after my father started clearing his place and putting up buildings, others moved in and soon the road from our place to what became M-61 was filled with the farms of young families. Directly across the road from Dad's place was that of Jacob Yarger, who came up from Hastings, Michigan. He and Dad were to become close friends, helping each other with harvesting crops and watching the young children of both families grow. A noteworthy event was the barn-raising on the Yarger farm. The barn was the epitome of what a barn should be. The lumber and beams were selected personally by Mr. Yarger, some having been obtained by his driving his horses and wagon miles away in order to obtain exactly what he wanted. It was a sad day in 1986 when, with the snow very deep, the road barely passable, and the temperature hovering near zero, that landmark barn went up in smoke.

Another event that brought the two families especially close was the illness and subsequent death of Aletha Yarger, Jake's wife, in 1917. There were four little children needing care. Mom and Dad grieved as much as if it had been a sister who had died. After a few years Mr. Yarger married a widow, Mrs. Dora Dankert.

Bordering Dad's farm were neighbors who became friends and who exchanged work as well as ideas. To the north of Dad's land and on the west side of our road were the farms of William Armstrong, Charles Logan, Bill Logan, Phillip Koelsch, Sr., Gus Benson, and Will Lawrence. The Armstrongs moved from Oklahoma via a covered wagon, the reverse direction of what we studied in history books about the westward movement. On the South were the Adrians and John Kemp; on the west were Mike Nigl (few years later sold to Frank Haas) and Charlie Hamilton. Whenever a road was put through, each farmer had to cede (no recompense) some land, running the length of his property; this was thirty-two feet wide from the center of the road to his fence line. Eventually all these men worked together to build the road, using their horses and scrapers to dig the ditches along each side of the road. Each man was responsible for putting up fences along his own farm, digging post holes with manually operated diggers, and stretching the barbed wire. Not only were fences built along the roadways, but the farm was separated into fields, which meant more fence-building. Fence posts were cut from the cedar trees on the property. Gates were made from poles. As Dad built up his herd of cows from two to fourteen, these fences kept the crops safe from their grazing. Horses were also pastured nights; they were in the harness working hard all day. Each farmer kept his share of the line fences in repair. No livestock got into his neighbor's crops. Robert Frost's poem "Good Fences Make Good Neighbors" was a highly respected truth.

To pay for his farm my father worked in the lumber woods as a lumberjack. He was a bachelor until the age of thirty-seven. He helped his father on the Old Place at the same time he took care of his own farm. He spent winters in the lumberwoods and became a skilled woodsman capable of doing almost all the specialty work, including scouting ahead of the crew and "blazing" the trees that were to be felled. The axe used for blazing was smaller in size than the commonly used one. In later years he used to gaze at the Lumberman's Monument on the banks of the Au Sable; he understood what each workman's tools and responsibilities were. His facial expression would reflect the awe and love he had for that work. Some winters he was in the woods near Wolverine and Frederic in the Lower Peninsula, and some times in the Upper Peninsula near Munising and L'Anse. He seemed to prefer the Upper Peninsula.

When he felt he could be a full-time farmer, he gave up the work in the woods. His brother Charles at the age of twenty-two years had married Myrtle Duncan in 1897. Charles bought a farm which abutted the back of his father's farm and so he, too, helped with his father's farming. The poor tired team of horses had to take care of the Old Place, John's farm, and Charles' farm. No wonder Dad always spoke of them (the horses) with affection and took care to see that they got as much rest as he could provide. As each brother could afford it, he acquired horses and horse-drawn machinery of his own. The horses on Grandpa's farm were named Prince and Topsy. Dad's first horses were Gyp and Queen. As Dad's sisters grew up to be students at the high school in Standish, and later as teachers in the county, they had to travel with the horses hitched to the buggy. The sisters usually boarded at some home near their schools and came to their father's Old Place for weekends. This meant that one of the brothers drove them to and from their boarding places.

Dad was embarrassed by the name of Talkeus so, when it was not for legal papers, Dad would say "T" stood for Thomas when asked about it.

John Talkeus (my Dad) married my mother, Laura Mary Wyatt, on March 14, 1911. They were married by a Methodist minister in the parlor of the Wyatt's home on Court Street in Standish. The Arthur Wyatts had moved to Standish from Hagersville, Ontario, Canada. Arthur had been born in England and brought to Manitoba, Canada, by his father. His mother remained in England with his two sisters. He never saw his mother again. He later moved to Ontario, always working for farmers in the area. When in Standish he worked in the local lumber mill, and had a few dairy cows on the edge of town. He bottled and peddled milk to folks in Standish. Grandma Wyatt (née Catherine McConachie) was born near Hagersville, Ontario, of Scottish ancestry. At the time they moved to Standish they had two daughters; Laura was four and Evelyn was two. My dad was a young man of eighteen as he stood by the depot in Standish watching folks get off the train. He noticed a family of four, including a plump little girl who was wearing a bright red coat, get off the train. Nineteen years later, when Mom was twenty-three and Dad was thirty-seven, he married that girl.

Mom was fourteen years younger than Dad. Their actions and interests did not reflect this great difference in their ages. As a young woman Mom had worked for two or three years in the Belding Silk Mills in southwestern Michigan in the City of Belding. Two or three young girlfriends from Standish also worked there. The silk manufacturing company owned a large boarding house near the mill in which all the workers lived. There were rules for living and eating in the boarding house, so Mom had a taste of what college dorm living might be. At another time she went to Detroit where she lived with her Aunt Minn for four or five months. Minn trimmed some of the hats that her husband, Ralph Rothschild, manufactured. At that time Grosse Pointe was emerging as the locale for the residences of wealthy, elite Detroiters. Mom remembered learning to trim hats under Aunt Minn's direction. When clientele drove up in their carriages, each lady was placed in the fitting rooms in such a way as to prevent any other person from seeing the kind of hat and trimming that other ladies were getting. Aunt Minn and her husband went to Paris, via steamship, twice a year to buy silks, satins, laces, etc. for their business. This was very impressive to Mom as a young woman of about twenty-one or twenty-two years. By the age of twenty-three she was married. She continued to trim hats for family members and friends. She seemed to be able to select the right shape of hat for a particular head and shoulders, and the angle at which the hat should be worn. Of course, when the wearing of hats was no longer fashionable, her expertise was no longer in demand. But she still liked to wear a hat even if others did not, and she always looked "perky" in her selections.

As I look back I recognize her adventuresome spirit and show of independence as she left home to work in Belding and (later) in Detroit with her aunt. She liked to read, but it was usually something related to current events. Dad liked to read thought-provoking material; Mom preferred lighter stuff. Dad was sentimental and quick to express and show love and affection. Mom tried to submerge her real feelings under a veneer of physical activity. Her feelings were private and it was a rare moment when she permitted them to show.

Dad built a house on his property, with the help of a carpenter, in 1904 or 1905. The house was a one-and-one-half story structure with an ell jutting out. Downstairs there were three rooms and upstairs there were two rooms and an attic. Between 1905 and 1911, while Dad continued his work in the lumberwoods, young couples rented his house for short periods of time. During some of the periods when Dad lived in his house, his sister Emma lived with him for some months. After he married, his young teenaged brother Bill lived with him and Mom periodically. My parents always had a warm, loving spot in their hearts for Bill.

One piece of wood Dad used in his house was a plank obtained from a huge oak tree cut from the front yard; this was used for the sill of the front door. Later, when the house was remodelled in 1932, Dad insisted that the sill and the door be used for the back door. We still step over that sill a dozen times a day and open and close that door.

When we were young my father called the farm Clover Blossom Farm. After a few years, as he got more cows and separated the milk and sold cream (instead of whole milk), he called it Crescent Creamery Farm. "A crescent is something which is growing" was his explanation. I preferred the name Clover Blossom—the image of clover blossoms was more attractive.

Cream and milk were hauled in ten-gallon cans to the creamery or milk factory by the milk man who picked up the cans at the gate by the road. Night and morning, after the milking was done, Mom washed milk pails and strainers. There was no running water and no electricity. In summer the utensils were washed at the pumphouse located on the edge of the garden next to the barnyard. In winter this was done in the house. The cream separator also was washed and scalded. This was a more detailed job, since the separator was made up of intricate little parts.

A responsibility Dad took on was that of darning his own socks, gloves, and mittens. His mother had taught him to darn when they lived in Germany. He took satisfaction in putting the big needle and yarn above and then under the traverse thread/yarn. When he worked in the lumber woods he did all of his own darning and so he just continued doing it winter evenings after he was married. This relieved Mom of that tedious job, but she did lots of patching work. Dad praised her for her neat patching jobs and she was proud of his praise. Another thing Dad praised her for was the bread she made. It was always of a perfect texture. Because of all the work she had to do, she was usually doing everything in a hurry. This included her bread-making. I can still see her slapping that dough around and punching it. Through the years, as I tried to duplicate her efforts, I realized how essential was all that energy she used to punch her bread! When young, we didn't really appreciate that homemade bread. Years later, as we ate "store bread," minus the aromas, the texture, the taste, we remembered!

For a few years Mom churned some of the cream and delivered butter in little crocks to some of the families in town. Eggs were gathered in late afternoons. On Saturdays they were taken to town in crates where they were traded for groceries. This was "women's work." Dad would not have a car. This meant that Mom drove the horses and democrat to town to do the trading. She always spent an hour or so with her parents and two sisters who lived in town. On Sundays we always rode in the two-seater democrat to town to have dinner with Mom's parents. In the afternoon, at two-thirty, we went to Sunday School. Dad and Mom did not go to Sunday School. They were tired from their week's labors and rested and visited with Grandpa. As my brother Wyatt got old enough to help Mom with the horses, Dad stayed home. We walked the half-mile to the Gospel Hall, with Grandma and Aunt Evelyn helping us as we walked along to rehearse the Bible verses we were to recite to our Sunday School teacher. On a warm day in the summertime, Grandma would buy a quart of ice cream on our way home to her house. We sat on their big shady porch relishing root beer floats made with the root beer she made from a concentrate. Having no electricity or refrigeration on the farm, this was a real treat. We could never stay past four or four-thirty; the chores at home needed to be done. As soon as we were able to sit on a milk stool and hold the milk pail securely between our knees, Dad expected us to help with the milking. We climbed in the mow and threw down the hay using pitch forks. Then we put the hay in the mangers where the cows' heads were locked in their stanchions.

The greater part of most of the farms was still woods and brush. Farmers working at clearing their land would set a match to a brush pile. There were two summers in particular when forest fires threatened the community. The summer drought meant fire could spread rapidly. Neighbors helped each other beat out the flames, which would flare out of control with every breeze. Frightened horses were made to plow furrows to make a brake in an effort to prevent flames from getting near farm buildings and livestock. For days the air was blue and heavy with the odor of burning wood. Mom and Dad took turns sleeping at night so that one of them could stand watch and sound the alarm for help from, and to, neighbors. No buildings in the community were lost to forest fire.

Dad always worked right along with us. Mom helped with certain jobs, but she also had the cooking and housework to do. It was usually Dad and we four children who did field work. Wyatt, being the oldest, had to take the lead in learning "how to" and then he would teach me; I in turn transferred it on to Ruth and Jean. Shirley was not born until Wyatt was nine years old; we older four were each born only eighteen months apart so the time difference in age meant Shirley did not work closely with us. When Wyatt first plowed, I heard Dad tell Mom with quiet pride that Wy did a fine job of holding the plow in the furrow and made straight and neat headlands. We girls were never allowed to plow, but we did hold the cultivator that was pulled by one horse. The plow was pulled by at least two horses and often by three. The person holding the handles of the implement walked behind the horses, up and down the field, I cannot even guess how many times a day. This person was usually Dad. As time went on he was able to afford implements like plows and cultivators with seats for riding. As the years went on some of Dad's mares gave birth to colts. These were needed as the farm work increased, or as income was supplemented through the sale of a horse or two. Dad "broke in" some of the young colts to work. He was patient and gentle with them; his horses never reared up or ran away. Dad's creed was, "Be good to your land and your land will be good to you." He rarely used chemical fertilizer; cow and horse manure and the rotation of crops maintained optimum growth conditions.

Before we ate supper the horses had to be unharnessed, watered and fed; the cows had to be brought in from pasture and watered and fed. We children kept the water pumped in the tank in the barnyard. Dad often reiterated, "A good farmer does not eat until his animals are fed."

In wintertime the cows were milked before supper, and even though done before six o'clock, it was necessary to carry the kerosene lanterns from stable to stable. In summertime, when daylight prevailed until 9 or 10 P.M., milking was done after supper, after the full day's work in the fields. Tired as he was, Dad was always ready to sing some of the old songs, tell us about his boyhood in the "old country," and listen to us tell him and Mom about our school lessons and fun of the day. Mom was usually busy with food and cleaning, so was a silent bystander, but Dad was an active participant as we told him about homonyms, synonyms, and antonyms. He drilled us on the multiplication tables and the capitals of the forty-eight states. There were many discussions about the meanings of words. He insisted that we memorize Lincoln's Gettysburg Address and the twenty-third Psalm. We couldn't just recite them, we had to put expression, inflection and emphasis in the places where he thought appropriate. In the old house he sat in his rickety rocker in the dining room, and with his pipe in his mouth, read us such stories as *Black Beauty* and *Beautiful Joe*. I strained to swallow back the tears, and his hand would pat my cheek.

In preparing for the annual Christmas program at the Johnsfield School, we rehearsed in front of him at home. We were not to use the expressionless droning chant of words typical of school children shy about reciting their parts. And there was always the possibility of the dreadful disgrace of having stagefright at the last minute, with our minds going blank; so we had to know our poems and parts in the plays so well that we couldn't possibly "freeze." Ruth always made a big hit at these programs. She was a cute little girl with beautiful curls and she spoke with a slight lisp.

In the new house (the remodeled version done in 1932 by Mr. Charles Kitchen of Detroit) he again sat in a rocker, a new one given him by his sisters for his birthday. It, too, was stationed by the dining room window, but the dining room was now in a different place. The rest of the family would spend the evening in the living room but Dad held out for his quiet area. When he got disgusted with Mom over some disagreement he would say, "I'm going to my housetop," and would settle in his chair. The housetop was in reference to Proverbs, Chapter 25, verse 24: "It is better to dwell in the corner of the housetop than with a contentious woman and in a wide house."

It was on Dad's lap in this spot that Shirley heard all the old stories, told

Dad about *his* school day, and delighted both Dad and Mom with his singing of songs that were different from the ones the rest of us had learned several years before. Dad taught all of the grandchildren the Bible stories and about the "Old Country." He played the mouth organ and, as he could afford it, bought and played a small accordion purchased through the Montgomery Ward catalog. He had learned to play the accordion when working in the lumberwoods. As he sat in his chair, the dining table was close to the left arm of his chair. On the table were always his Bible and the dictionary. Several times in an evening his chair would creak and we knew that he was reaching for one book or the other.

Mom, too, must have had her hands full. But she taught us to play Flinch and Authors. Her sisters, Evelyn and Alice Wyatt, were generous at times of birthdays and Christmas, so we had such games on hand. Dad and Mom had no money to spare for buying games. These aunts also supplied us with story books. I remember Mom reading aloud a chapter a night from *Little Lord Fauntleroy, The Secret Garden, Little Women*, and *Rebecca of Sunnybrook Farm*. These activities could be done only during the winter months around the lamplit table; summer, spring, and fall were busy with field work and chores. Most of the time, during those seasons, we sat on the front porch where we sang as we listened to Dad's and Shirley's music. Neighbors, young and old, would come to visit while we young ones played our own version of baseball and field hockey (called "shinny") and a game called Duck on the Rock. Or, Dad and Mom would visit neighbors, taking us children, usually walking on the unlit and sparsely traveled dirt roads.

When snow was on the ground it was common to have one country school visit another on a Friday afternoon. The student body was transported by horse-drawn sleigh. Because he enjoyed it so much, Dad was the most frequent driver. He loved watching the spelling matches between the competing schools; there were also adding matches and geography matches. The teacher of each school would take turns administering the questions and would referee results. Dad knew all the teachers within several miles of our school (Johnsfield) and they knew him!

Dad loved to read. He rarely missed Malcolm Bingay's daily column in the *Detroit Free Press* or Clarence Buddington Kelland's stories in the old *Saturday Evening Post*. James Oliver Curwood and Gene Stratton Porter were favorite authors, probably because their settings were in woodlands. He would tell us the Old Testament stories in *every detail*, with graphic descriptions as well as the moral applications. Those I remember are: Lot's wife turning to salt; Noah and the Ark; Jonah and the big fish; Cain and Abel; Daniel in the fiery furnace; and Samson's loss of hair after Delilah's tempting, followed by the regaining of his strength with hair regrowth and the subsequent crashing down of the temple. He told us about the scandalous lives of Jesse James and his brother (and sang the song that tells the story, too); the assassinations of Presidents Lincoln and McKinley; Eva and Topsy in *Uncle Tom's Cabin*; as well as about Simon Legree and Eliza's crossing the ice of the Delaware River in her bare feet. Oh, he knew them all! When he worked in the lumberwoods he and the lumberjacks passed books around to each other. Mom raised an eyebrow when he started telling some of these stories; if he persisted, she would really scowl at him so we knew something was wrong. The dusty books were in a box at the back of their closet. Two I remember seeing were *The English Orphans* and *Dora Deane*, both written by Mary J. Holmes.

At times, with an expression of wistful regret he would say, "I should have spent my money for an education, not this farm." When we were old enough to appreciate the scope of his knowledge and wisdom, we would quickly rush forward with the remark, "But, Dad, you are educated!"

He would not join a church, a lodge, a club or an organization. Neighbors belonged to the Grange, the Masons, and/or one of the churches. In later years he did join the Farm Bureau. He seemed to feel he should not commit himself to any one creed or set of rules. He was fiercely loyal to his community, state, and country. He never failed to vote in any election; he served on the township election board many, many times, always walking the two miles back and forth to the township hall. He was called to jury duty two or three times and took that as a very grave responsibility. He would not think of evading his share of the local road and bridge work, or of letting the condition of fences and general appearances decline in quality.

When working in the lumberwoods one of the workers apparently needed some ready cash and so raffled off an expensive, high-quality gun. Dad won it. He had no use for guns and never would have one around. He gave this one to his brother Fred, who was in his late teens. Dad did not appreciate the high value of the gun, but Fred apparently did; he spoke glowingly about that gift for many years to come.

Dad made a raft from posts and boards and taught us how to use poles as punts. We had lots of good times punting around on the dam and down the creek when there was water enough to float us. He made whistles from willow twigs; they had a lovely, soft, sweet tone. He taught us to recognize birds' eggs, to differentiate between the eggs of sparrows, larks, robins, wrens, etc. He taught us the differences in pine trees' needles. He kept his eye out for tree trunks and limbs that would be good for future wagon tongues and eveners, a wagon box and/or rack, and for the ever-needed fence posts and gates. These would be oak, white ash, pine, and cedar. He never bought handles and knobs; he whittled them out from wood. Many of them are still in evidence in various places in the barns and woodshed.

For some reason Dad felt a special kindness for Mrs. Matilda Wilson. She was a widow who spoke with a thick Swedish accent. She lived on the farm she and her husband, Swan, had made tillable. After his death she continued living there with her children. She wore long skirts and flat shoes and a cotton hand-made bonnet. She always preferred to walk rather than drive a horse; she walked very rapidly, so her skirts flapped as she padded along. She was less than five feet tall, was very wrinkled, and had crinkly-smiling eyes. She often needed help with heavy work, repairing her horses' harnesses, and understanding some legal matters pertaining to taxes, etc. Dad always tried to help her. Her farm and woods were about one mile away, on the present Sagatoo Road.

Most jobs on the farm Dad could do by himself, but he wanted company more than he wanted our help. And we always had interesting conversations as we worked. For instance, we children were assigned to turn the handle of the cream separator, the churn, the washing machine, the clothes-wringer, the pump, and the big grindstone.

Dad helped his friend and neighbor, Charlie Hamilton, fill his ice house every winter. Ice was cut on Saginaw Bay, brought in by horses and sleighs in big chunks, and packed in sawdust in Hamilton's ice-house. In summer, when we had company and needed ice to make our food cool, we got a chunk of ice from Hamilton's. Once in a great while we made ice cream when someone supplied the ice-cream freezer. Other than that, my parents saw no need for an ice-house of their own.

Neither Mom nor Dad would tolerate violence or roughness towards humans or animals. Dad was noted for his success in "breaking in" colts and in handling his calves. If he ever swore, it was not around us children or Mom, though I cannot believe he worked all those years in the lumberwoods without having picked up some rough language. His gentleness and sense of propriety even extended to his opinion of public drinking fountains. Whenever he saw a woman bent over drinking at a fountain with water gushing up to her face he would say, "Women shouldn't drink there; it's not ladylike." We had one cheap saddle which Dad had acquired somewhere in his past. We kids always rode bareback on our workhorses' broad backs, and when we got the cows from pasture we usually walked since it was too much bother to ride. However, when the city cousins came to visit, they always took turns riding with the saddle.

The telephone came into the country areas about 1916. Mom really appreciated having it but Dad scoffed at it, calling it the "visiting box." For years our number was 15F21. The 15 meant we were on line 15; 21 meant that when two long and one short rings came in, we were to answer. About six other families' rings came in on the same line, each household having its own ring. If someone's ring were heard coming in at night, there was concern that there was grief or trouble in that family. Perhaps neighbors "listened in" to be helpful or for other reasons. The radio and television came to our home later than into other homes in our community. Dad never liked them, but eventually we got both. Dad did not spend much time in front of them except for a President's speech or a boxing match. He loved to watch boxing matches (he had watched the men box evenings in the lumber camps) and he knew all about Jess Willard, Jack Dempsey, Gene Tunney, Max Baer, and Joe Louis. He liked to hear Kate Smith sing on the radio.

Mom followed the Detroit Tigers baseball team, first on radio, then on TV. Wyatt, too, liked the Tigers, and at least once every summer while he was still home, he and Mom would go to Detroit to watch a game. Another annual event Mom never missed was the Kentucky Derby. She studied the sports writers' items in the newspaper and when the big Saturday arrived she had her list of horses' names with their jockeys written out with her choice of winner. What amazed us was she was often right! She loved to watch the harness races at our County Fair. Shirley usually arranged for her to have a choice seat in the grandstand; she not only enjoyed the racing, but also the kinship she felt with old friends who, year after year, were there, too. She did this right up until a year before she died; she was eighty-three when she died.

There was a period of about fifteen years when every summer a boy cousin would spend the summer months from mid-June to the end of August on our farm. Their parents wanted to get their boys out of the cities and "learn to work" under Dad's tutelage. Usually there was only one boy at a time with Dad and Shirley; once in a while it would happen that two would be here at the same time. These boys, in sequence of years as they passed by, were Duane Flutur, son of Dad's sister Emma Wubbena Flutur; George Postif, son of Mom's sister, Evelyn Wyatt Postif; Charles Head, son of Mom's Aunt Edith McConachie Head; and Billy Wubbena, son of Dad's brother Bill. These boys always worked long days in the fields and then returned in late summer to their respective cities (Detroit, Saginaw, and Washington, D.C.) tanned and calloused. Then they returned at least once more, sometimes even two or three additional summers for more of the same. By this time Charlie Hamilton had given Dad and Shirley his Model A Ford at a bargain price. The boys had great fun driving on the country roads, the highlight being to go out to White's Beach on Saginaw Bay (six miles straight east of our place) for a cooling evening swim. At that time there was still no electricity or running water in the house. "Many hands make light work," but still Mom had the cooking to do (wood-burning cook stove) and clothes to wash. Wyatt, at that time, was working as a linotype operator and/or pressman for the weekly newspaper in town, *The Arenac County Independent*. He was a big help to Mom, always seeming to sense just what would help her the most. Shirley's nature and personality were such that an easy camaraderie was established and all the boys worked well together and with Dad. It was the rule that everyone should eat at the same time; all feet under the table together. And the verse from the Bible, "Those who do not work, cannot eat," was a frequently stated remark and carried much weight with the city lads. An incident Shirley liked to relate was about when he and Billy (we always called him Billy, not Weemo) were cleaning stables and hauling manure to the field. Billy stood on the tractor as Shirley drove, watching the manure fly out the back end of the spreader. Several hens were following them, pecking away at the ground. Shirl said, "There are your eggs for breakfast in the morning." Billy would not eat another egg that summer!

Another visitor was Grandpa Wyatt's sister Harriet, who came from England when she was a young woman. She had been trained to be a milliner and found a job in Detroit working for Mr. Ralph Rothschild, one of the members of that famous banking family. He was a widower with two sons and owned a hat manufacturing business in downtown Detroit. After a few years she married him and later, as his widow, was considered by us to be well-off. She was always called Aunt Minn (rather than Harriet) and carried herself with a stately dignity. She clung to her British accent and English mannerisms, as well as to her dark auburn hair until the day she died. She wanted my brother Wyatt to have a sheep, so she, Wyatt, Dad, and Grandpa Wyatt made a big project of driving to a sheep farm near West Branch where they purchased a ewe which Wy named Rachel. Rachel was in Wy's care for several years and bore a lamb every year. Dad would help Wy take his pen of sheep to the county fair every September, and was as proud as Wy at the prizes the sheep won. Several years later, after Mom's parents had died, Aunt Minn spent a winter at our place. Being a widow at the time, and lonely, she was happy to be with Mom and Dad on our farm. Dad enjoyed her company, eccentric as she was. She always carried on a lively conversation with Dad, too, as they bantered back and forth. She scolded Dad for smoking his pipe, but her criticism went unheeded. Smoking a cigar was for Sunday.

Another winter Mom's Aunt Mida spent several months with Mom and Dad; only Wyatt and Shirley still lived at home at the time. Her husband, Tom Wyatt, brother to Grandpa, had died a few years earlier. Her sons had their own families and farms so she sold her farm. All of them lived on Wyatt Road in Arenac Township. She suffered severe arthritis and was relieved to have the attention and care given by Mom and Dad. She lacked the verve of

Aunt Minn Rothschild, but was a gentle and interesting conversationalist; Dad and Mom were happy to have her company.

Every few years there was a Wubbena family reunion. I think these were instigated by Dad's four sisters, who did much of the detail planning. Everything always worked out fine. Folks stayed at our place on the farm or with Uncle Charles and Aunt Myrtie in town. The overflow would sleep in the fresh hay in our barn. Some meals were eaten at our place and some at the Charles Wubbena home. Many of the old friends were invited to be present for the meals and fun during the three to five days the reunions lasted.

The one exception to the reunion's being held in Standish was the one held in 1933. This was held in Elgin, Illinois, with the Gablers as hosts. Part of the entertainment was to attend the World's Fair held that year in Chicago. It was decided that Dad and his three daughters would attend; Mom and her two sons stayed home to do the milking and take care of the farm work Dad was unable to do before he left. I drove our 1930 Plymouth sedan, which Wyatt and I had bought in 1931. I was twenty years old, and had driven to Detroit a couple of times as well as to Bay City fairly often. Uncle Charles rode with us, but Aunt Myrtle remained at home. We had a wonderful time with no incidents to detract from the joy and fun. The reunion in 1936, held in Standish with all details handled by Wyatt, was special in that it celebrated fifty years since Jan Wubbena and family had landed in the U.S.A. (See end of this section for the article on that reunion that was published in *The Arenac County Independent* in July, 1936.)

When I was graduated from the University of Michigan School of Nursing in June, 1937, all the family attended the ceremony. That is, all except Dad attended — he insisted that he be the one to stay at home to do the chores, "because I won't look so good all sun-burned, etc. among those university folks." No coaxing on my part changed his mind. When Jean was graduated in 1940 from the Henry Ford Hospital School of Nursing he felt he could go. Shirley was old enough to be trusted with the chores for one day. After the ceremony in the auditorium of the School of Nursing, as Dad was moving down the center aisle, Henry Ford I rested his hand on Dad's shoulder and told him how glad he was to see him there. That not only made Dad's day and was worth the trip, it was an incident he loved to tell for years to come!

When we reached high school age, we children lived in town with Grandpa and Grandma Wyatt. One by one, as we left home, the next younger assumed the jobs of those who had left. In this way it seemed that Mom and Dad were gradually weaned from our daily help. Spring, summer, and fall we would come home to help with field work some evenings and on weekends. Mom and Dad never hinted that we should stay home from school; they always managed somehow without us. As Shirley grew older more of the farm work fell on his shoulders. A tractor seemed to be the practical way to use his time and talents. The horses were getting older and slower. We all grieved, especially Dad, when it was decided that the horses had to go; working with them was too hard on Dad's health. Gyp and Florrie were sold to Joe Martin; Fred and Chief lived on our farm until they died. Dad would never drive a tractor or a car. He watched Shirley accomplish three or four times as much work as he had with his horses, and acknowledged and appreciated that the right decision had been made. There were times when a tractor was too big to get into a tight corner, or the soil was too wet and soft for the big wheels of a tractor; he couldn't resist saying, "Get a horse!" with a teasing look in his eye. One summer day in 1948 he went to his Brother Charles' farm to help him with a job there. Dad was holding the reins of Uncle Charles' horses as they were pulling some piece of equipment. Charles' horses were light-weight and rather flighty compared to the way Dad's staid Belgian breed work horses had been. They became startled at something and began to jump around. Dad felt he couldn't be disgraced by letting the horses get away, so he hung on to the reins and was dragged several rods before he finally let them go. The resulting injuries were fractured ribs, punctured lungs and many scrapes, bruises and lacerations; after two or three days there was the added complication of paralytic ileus. He was cared for in the little Standish Hospital where Dr. Malcomb Dolbee ministered expert medical attention. I left my job in Detroit and took care of him on the night shift. Jean and her husband, Ken Bittner, and their baby, Theda, were living with Mom and Dad that summer while looking for a place to settle down after both of them had retired from their stint in the army in World War II. It was fortunate that Jean was thus available and so could "special" Dad on the daytime shift. Dad was frail and weak for several months. We were grateful that he survived. Up until that time he had always criticized people for "running to the doctor," and accused doctors of "keeping people coming to them." After his accident he had nothing but praise for what doctors and nurses did and had gained insight into what goes on in hospitals. He lived six more years after this accident. He was never again as strong and zestful as he had been before that accident.

One of the most remarkable changes in farming was brought about by the presence of electricity. Rural Electrification laws, on the federal level, finally helped Consumers Power Co. financially to install the posts and wires down what Consumers was to call South Melita Road. In 1938, Mom and Dad had the thrill of turning on a switch and seeing the lights come on. Until the day he died Dad approached a light switch with a bit of pomp in evidence; then with the light on, he walked back to his chair with an expression of, "What a joy to have this kingly touch!" The lights in the barn and in the yard, the motor which pumped the water into the tank for cattle and horses, the motorized elevator for transferring bales of straw and hay from the wagon to the hay mow, and the warmer in the brooder house for the little chicks which he bought every spring were all blessings for Mom and Dad. Before electricity, after a cold winter night when the pump would be frozen, Dad would carry out the teakettle and pour the boiling water down into the pump; now he and Shirley rigged up a heat lamp which clamped onto the pump and was turned on before going to bed when the weather forecast warranted it. The whole family, and especially Mom, appreciated the refrigerator, washing machine with electric motor (rather than one to turn by hand, or with gasoline motor), toaster, iron, and reading lamps by our beds. All these conveniences, taken for granted by most folks, were wonderful, glorious enhancements to our daily living. These appliances and equipment were not acquired all at once; only as they could be paid for were they added to the homestead.

Ruth was the first to get married. In 1938 she married Bill Tulloch, who taught in the Standish High School at that time. There was no big wedding; she and Bill went to the minister's house. Wyatt was called by the Selective Service process into the army. After the Pearl Harbor attack, we did not know for many months where he had been sent; our mail to him and from him was addressed APO. Those were agonizing months for all of us, and especially for Mom and Dad at the time of D-Day and the Normandy invasion. Soon after we were relieved to learn that he had been stationed in Iceland. Throughout this time he had become acquainted with a girl in Elgin, Illinois, named Erika Wilharm. While he was still in the army, but had returned to the U.S.A., he and Erika were quietly married in 1943 in Chicago in front of a minister. During this same summer Shirley married Jeannette Noeske, a local girl whose parents were farmers a little north of Standish. At that time she was a teacher in the country schools. They, too, were married with only the minister and two attendants present. Jean had joined the Army Nurse Corps, and while stationed in France in 1945 married Kenneth Bittner, a young man from Meyersdale, Pennsylvania. The staff of their hospital unit had a joyful distraction from their duties as they planned and executed the celebration of their wedding there in LeHavre. When Duane Flutur was married in 1946 to Lorraine Langguth, the wedding took place in Des Plaines, near Chicago. Dad, Mom, and I attended. Duane was like a son and brother to us. A year or two later when George Postif was married in Detroit, again Mom, Dad, and I attended. George, too, was like a son after having spent several summers on the farm. Because of the circumstances of all these weddings, Dad would say, "Not a one of my own children did I see as they got married, but I went all the way to Chicago and Detroit to see Duane and George tie the knot!"

Some more traveling that Dad liked to reminisce about was when in February 1949 he and Mom came to Detroit to see me graduate from Wayne State University. From there we took the train to Dover, Delaware where Wyatt and Erika were living with their two children. It meant a lot to Dad to see Wy's home, the newspaper plant where he worked after getting out of the army, and the farming in Delaware and neighboring states. From Dover we went to Washington, D.C., where Uncle Bill and Aunt Maude escorted us around to see the sights. What impressed Dad the most were the Supreme Court Building and the Lincoln Memorial. Mom was most thrilled by attending a concert by the Marine Corps Band for which Aunt Maude had extended herself to make possible. Uncle Bill put Dad and me on the train for our return to Michigan. Mom remained with Wyatt in Dover for several weeks. Erika was not well; she and Wyatt had two small children and so Mom was a big help to them at that time. Dad was exhausted but as he and I rode along on our return trip he relived all the highlights of his visit. Prior to this time he had felt he could not leave the farm for any period of time. Shirley, now grown and married, was pleased to do what he could to see Dad have such an eventful vacation.

About this time Shirley started taking flying lessons. From early childhood, he had held a strong fascination for airplanes and flying. After a few years he became a member of the Flying Farmers Organization and a part-owner of a plane. Dad regretted Shirley's lack of whole-hearted interest in farming, but just as he had refrained from discouraging any of us from the pursuits we followed, so he put no stumbling blocks in Shirley's path when he took off to answer the urge to take to the skies. Having less than 20/20 vision he was turned down when he tried to enlist in the Air Force. However, this did not deter his flying private planes. Dad would not go up with him, or in any plane, but the rest of the family had frequent short flights with him. Shirley was especially pleased when Mom would go up with him.

Shirley and Jeannette lived with Mom and Dad when first married. After a few years they had a mobile home placed in the yard. They bought the farm Uncle Charles had on the corner of Dupree and Proulx Roads. While still belonging to Charles, the house on the farm had had renters in it, and was vandalized and burned. After Dad died, Shirley and Jeannette had a new house built on their own property. Throughout those years, before Shirley died in 1972, he farmed both his farm and Dad's farm.

It was a great blow to the entire Wubbena family when Uncle Harry died in June 1947. He had worked almost all his adult life as a freight agent and telegraph operator on the Duluth South Shore and Atlantic Railroad. He and his wife Lenore, née Stralow, had lived in the vicinity of Trout Creek and Bruce's Crossing in the Upper Peninsula. They had no children. Harry was fifty-nine years of age, and his was the first death in the family since their father, Jan, died. I was working in Detroit and did not own a car. Aunt Emma made plans for me to drive Duane's car, and she and I stopped in Standish to pick up Mom and Dad, and we continued on to Bruce's Crossing to attend the funeral. Despite the sadness of the occasion, Dad was glad for the opportunity to see the territory where he had worked in the lumberwoods. He was not prepared for the changes in the cities and towns, especially near Munising. He had often told us about one of the hospitable lumberjacks who would take some of the men to his home in Munising to have a meal of fish, fresh from Lake Superior. Fish was Dad's favorite food. The host's wife, whose name was Tootsie, was a beautiful blonde (Dad's words) who always made the men feel most welcome. On our return trip, after the funeral, we took the time to drive around Munising until Dad got his bearings, and so we were able to locate Tootsie, now a widow, living where she and her husband had always lived. We remained in the car as Dad walked to her as she stood on the lawn. After talking a few minutes Dad came back to the car wearing an expression of disbelief and almost shock. "She sure has changed! No teeth! Her hair isn't blonde, and she's quite fat!" were his words. He apparently felt she didn't see the aging effects of time in him. After that we never again heard Dad rave about the beauteous Tootsie.

Aunt Talka had had a severe illness shortly after World War I. She was not expected to live. Minnie and Ella, who were close to her, would phone every few days to report on her condition. I was about five or six years old. Wyatt and I were frightened when, on two occasions, Dad had nightmares about Aunt Talka, and walked in his sleep, calling out to her and talking about her. She survived, living for over thirty years after this illness. The last several years of her life she was confined to a wheelchair.

Dad and Uncle Charles liked to get together and reminisce. Uncle Charles was a great storyteller. He would make the telling of a single anecdote last an hour or so, always bringing into his story many funny observations and details that other folks would miss. Dad did not have this knack, but he appreciated Uncle Charles' version of an episode.

Dad would not do field work on Sundays. He had an innate respect for God's laws. He saw neighbors haul in hay, harvest beans, beets, and corn on Sundays but he was satisfied to do only the chores necessary for the care of horses, cattle, and chickens. When someone said to him that he lost money by letting rain fall on hay and grain which could have been harvested on Sunday when weather was threatening, his reply was, "God doesn't look at the harvest time in Fall as His pay day." God honored him for this stand because it seemed that his income, although at poverty level by some standards, was enough for our needs. We kids did not know we were poor. To Dad the rightness of what one did was more important than the money it produced. He did not waver from this belief.

For many years he wrote the "Johnsfield News," a weekly column for *The Arenac County Independent*. He always headed his column with a joke. Members of the community made frequent comments of appreciation to him. There were no errors in grammar or spelling; vocabulary was very fitting, with choice of words just right for his description of the local event or activity.

To have as many of his family as possible home for a holiday was his chief joy. He especially loved having the grandchildren. He could act like a kid with them, seeming to reach their level of understanding regarding everything in which they were interested. Good times also were spent with the families of Alec and Flora Milne of Sterling, and Bert and Emma Sivier of Standish. The children of these families were in school together with us for years, and the bonds formed were closer than with many relatives.

In June, 1954 Dad was taken to the Standish Hospital with what proved to be a massive myocardial infarct. He lived for about 10 days and died on July 6. He was conscious and alert. Again Jean and I "specialed" him. He wanted some of Mom's good oatmeal and she was pleased to take it to him, but was disappointed when he said it wasn't the same as it used to be. A day or two before he died, with oxygen catheter and I.V. tubing connections, he thumped with his brown work-worn hand on his bedding and sang *I'm a Child of a King*, which begins with, "My Father is rich in houses and lands, He holdeth the wealth of the world in His hands! Of rubies and diamonds, of silver and gold, His coffers are full, He has riches untold."

The last verse is, "A tent or a cottage, why should I care? They're building a palace for me over there! Though exiled from home, yet still I may sing; all glory to God, I'm the child of a King." We had not sung this hymn very often, so I was surprised to hear him sing it now. He must have felt the words were especially meaningful as applied to his life.

He had learned the first Psalm as a boy in Germany; he often recited the English version as a grown man. I write the first part of the Psalm here because, for me he was like a tree planted by the rivers of water which brought forth fruit in his season. Here are the first three verses of Psalm I:

Blessed is the man that walketh not in the counsel of the
    ungodly, nor standeth in the way of sinners, nor
    sitteth in the seat of the scornful.

But his delight is in the law of the Lord; and in His law
    he doth meditate day and night.
And he shall be like a tree planted by the rivers of water,
    that bringeth forth fruit in its season; his leaf
    also shall not wither; and whatsoever he doeth shall
    prosper.

Article printed in the Arenac Independent *of Standish in July 1936 regarding the reunion celebrating the fiftieth anniversary of the immigration of Jan and Catharina*

Wubbena Family Hold Reunion

Sunday, to celebrate the 50th anniversary of their arrival at Standish after a trip across the Atlantic from Germany, eight members of a family of ten, and their families, gathered at the John Wubbena home in Johnsfield, where they all joined in reminiscing and revelry. Two members, Fred, of Washington, and William, of Colorado, and their families were unable to attend. Four of the members, John, Charles, Henry, and Talka, were born in Germany and made the trip with their parents to this country.

Mr. and Mrs. John Nelson of Bentley were guests of the family for the day. Mr. Nelson came across from Germany on the same ship with the Wubbenas, and has also made his home in this vicinity since. Mr. Nelson enjoyed some of the stories told and also told several. He told how the little Wubbena children, upon their arrival in New York, drew much attention to their noisy wooden shoes as they clattered up the 40 steps to the hotel common to immigrating people. Mr. Nelson is now 82 years of age.

During the pot-luck dinner at noon relatives enjoyed reading a letter from Fred Wubbena of Seattle, Washington, who was unable to attend. This letter was sent air mail.

Those present for the event were Miss Talka Wubbena and Mr. and Mrs. Louis Gabler and son, Elgin, Ill; Miss Ella Wubbena, Chicago; Miss Catherine Wubbena, Ann Arbor; Meredith Taylor, Ohio; Mr. and Mrs. George Flutur, children, Duane and Virginia, Mrs. William Ingram, Detroit; Mr and Mrs. H. Wubbena, Bruce Crossing; Mr. and Mrs. Henry Wubbena and family and Mr. and Mrs. Raymond Wubbena and son, Essexville; Mr. and Mrs. William Baikie and Miss Mabel Wubbena, Omer; Mr. and Mrs. Verncil Whitmire, Flint; Mr. and Mrs. Evart Scott, Flushing; Mr. and Mrs. Charles Wubbena, Mrs. A. M. Strauss and sons and Miss Elsie Reetz, Standish.

Old neighbors and friends who called during the day were Mrs. Richard Haas, Mr. and Mrs. Mike Eichinger, Mr. and Mrs. Fred Wenkel,

Mrs. Louise Krause, Mr. and Mrs. Robert Peppel, Mr. and Mrs. Carl Spamer of St. Helen and Mr. and Mrs. Bert Sivier.

One of the poems recited by John T. Wubbena to children

I.   *Once there was a bad boy*
     Playing on the floor
     First he slapped his sister
     Then he slammed the door.
     And that night at supper
     While the others ate
     Then this little bad boy
     All alone did wait.

II. *Once there was a good boy*
     And he tried to do
     Everything for Mama
     That she asked him to
     Never was he punished
     Never left was he
     Always was this good boy
     Happy as could be.

III. *Oh it is the right way to be good and kind*
     And it is the best way Mama's word to mind
     And the Lord will help us if we really try
     And He watches o'er us from His home on high.

Memories of My Father
by His Daughter, Jean Wubbena Bittner

How did we get here? Mom never had babies—we always knew her as being pleasingly plump; Dad, hard-working around the farm, always found the babies! Winter months were spent hauling animal refuse from the accumulated pile from cleaning stalls, out to the fields to fertilize next spring's crops. In February 1912, on the twenty-ninth day (it was leap year), while busy at the job, Dad found a squirming infant in the pile and took it to Mom for a wash-up. It proved to be a boy. They were delighted and gave him Mom's maiden name, Wyatt, and Grandpa Wubbena's first name, Jan.

Summers were hot and busy, the hottest and busiest part was spent harvesting hay for the winter feed—mowing, raking, and making haycocks to be loaded on the wagon and then hauled to the barn. Hoisting a haycock to the wagon one sweltering day in July, Dad found a whimpering little baby girl. No swaddling clothes were needed in the heat so he hustled her in to Mom. The little toddling boy hugged her and pointed at Grandma Wyatt who was present for the day. Pleased at his suggestion, they named her Catherine after both grandmas—Catherine Wubbena and Catherine Wyatt.

December month was spent hauling and chopping wood for both the cook stove and pot-bellied heating stove. Dad always claimed he got two "sweats" out of the wood—one from cutting, and again while reading his paper. (His chair was always parked by the stove and near a window for light.) While sweating over the chopping block he heard a baby cry and sure enough, under the pile already cut was a poor little girl baby, blue with cold. He put her under his jacket out of the wind and rushed her in to the warm arms of Mom. So Ruth joined the other two children.

In those days paved roads were unheard of, and with April showers the roads were full of ruts with gushing water as the wagon wheels rolled along. Looking down in one of these puddles Dad saw a little arm and leg—he jumped off the wagon and pulled her out. She gave him the sweetest smile; immediately he dubbed her "Babe" and that is what the family called her. Only Mom stuck to the name Jean.

In the fall the corn was cut and put in rows of shocks to be hauled into the barn where husking took place later in the winter with shelter from wind and snow. In November, busy hauling in shocks, there was a little fella under one shock screaming his lungs out, thrashing hands and legs to keep warm. There had been a young man riding his bike through the county selling encyclopedias to earn money to go to college. He headquartered at our house while covering that territory. His name was Shirley Hameron, a very likeable chap who helped Mom with the dishes. So the new baby was named Shirley after this man.

Dad's stories of where he'd found each baby always added merriment as all five kids would hang around his chair to hear over and over again how they got into the family.

Dad was a good storyteller and had a good imagination. While corn, beans, and potatoes were being hoed he would take the middle row with girls flanked on both sides of him. When the girls began to lag, he'd start a story and we'd hoe like a house afire to keep up so we wouldn't miss any of it.

But we did our utmost *not* to do a sloppy job; we knew that meant a bite of an ear lobe if any weeds were left standing. I believe, however, that many missed standing weeds were purposely unnoticed; I reckon dusty, sweaty ears weren't very tasty.

We heard a good many of the Bible stories that way, too. Wyatt was usually cultivating with one of the horses in the same field with Dad and the girls. Shirley was just a baby, in the house with Mom during these times.

Dad and Mom seemed to know how much our self-invented games helped in our growth. Summer mornings before heading for the field work we "watched cows" so they could graze along the road side thus saving pasture. It took about two hours for the dew to dry off and that was about the time for the cows to have had their fill. At this point they would be put into our own woods for the remainder of the day. While watching cows we made up games. A favorite game was "shinny," a sort of field hockey we played in the yard. With the dew dried, crops could be hoed or harvested as the need required, so it was back to field work for the remainder of the day.

Uncle Charles' daughters and their city boyfriends seemed to especially enjoy these games and often came out to the farm to visit. Winter nights, in bright moonlight and crisp air, we delighted in using the wide sleigh bed on which we played King of the Mountain. Neighboring young folks usually came to play with us, their fathers not being as generous about letting them use equipment for such things at their own homes.

When the huckleberries were ripe in July and August Dad would take a day off, hitch up the team on the wagon, and load in a bag of hay for the horses. Mom fixed a basket with homemade bread and summer sausage—a delicacy we'd just learned about though it may have been invented long before. We thought we were in paradise when we could smack over it. When the berry patch was reached, we'd take off in different directions under our straw hats, swinging our syrup pails which each would try to fill with berries ahead of the other siblings. After despairing at the time it took to fill them, we'd wander toward the horses and wagon only to find that Dad had already beat us there and would be sitting with his back against a tree munching the bread and summer sausage. We weren't long in joining him. Only Mom would be left picking as she dreamed of the huckleberry pies her "pick" would make on the cold winter days.

Everything was canned in those days as we had no freezers or other way of preserving the food. Fruit, vegetables, and meat (beef and pork) were all "put up" for the winter.

We always looked forward to the Fourth of July. We'd hurry with hauling in a couple loads of hay with a promise from Dad and Mom that we could go to White's Beach on Saginaw Bay, a distance of five or six miles away. Again, the wagon was used for the "cost" of a bag of hay for the horses. The kids wore their bib overalls to be used as bathing suits. Neighbor Charlie Hamilton had a cottage there at the beach which he generously opened to us all to change clothes and to eat the potluck dinner that we, relatives and neighbors, had brought. Oh, that molasses cake that Mrs. Hamilton could make. I can still taste it! What a glorious day! Sleepy kids all the way home after that play time in the water—almost too weary to go to the woods and bring the cattle home for milking.

The Great Depression hit in the late '20s and early '30s just when we were all to graduate from high school. What money there was went back on the farm for seed, fertilizer, etc., so there was no ready cash for the three dresses needed for graduation—one for baccalaureate on Sunday night; one for the "Class Night" when the valedictorian gave his/her speech and the Class Will and the Giftatory were read (the latter two being humorous); and one dress for the real graduation night for the send-off and receiving of diplomas. "Hitherto the Lord hath provided" and did again; He saw to it that as the time came for each girl to graduate, a cow had a calf. Dad gave each girl a calf, then, with which to buy her graduation dresses. As the Depression years moved along, it turned out that Catherine's calf brought $24.00 in 1930; Ruth's income from her calf in 1932 was half that, and in 1933 Jean's calf brought in half of Ruth's amount. But prices were down accordingly, and each was able to buy her three dresses and participate in graduation activities with pride and a smile.

My Grandfather Wubbena
by Theda Bittner Baslock

John Wubbena was my grandfather. My earliest memory of him, and also the first thing that comes to my mind now, is the comfort of his lap as he sat in his rocker by the window in the dining room. The delicious aroma of his pipe as he held me close and told wonderful stories. Stories that were like old friends when I heard them again in Sunday School lessons from the Bible. Eventually it dawned on me why these stories were as familiar as family.

Another memory that is pure Grandpa is the skin-the-cat game that he played with all of us at one time or another. The child bends over forward and reaches between his legs where Grandpa grasps the eager hands and flips the child over in a sort of somersault. It delighted him as well as us.

One thing that he did just for me happened when Grandpa had to move a calf. I tagged along as he put a rope and a halter on that calf. Oh, did I want to walk that calf. But I was only five or so and Grandpa knew full well that I couldn't hold on to that calf. I pleaded and promised not to let go. Bless his heart, he let me try. Of course I got dragged and the calf got loose. Dear Grandpa picked me up, dusted me off, gave me a hug, and never said, "I told you so." I always deeply appreciated that he let me try.

It was Grandpa who introduced me to the roughness of a calf's tongue as it sucks your hand—all the way to your elbow it seemed—without ever biting. And Grandpa who showed me how good a slice of bread and butter is with sugar all over the top of it. These are my most cherished memories of Grandpa. What a dear man!

Memories of Grandpa
by Ralph Bittner

In 1954, I was preoccupied more with running through sprinklers and watching DC-3's dart in and out of clouds than I was with pondering Grandpa's words of wisdom. Most four-year-old minds work that way, I think, but had I known that that was to be our last year of earthly coexistence, I'm not sure but I would have approached the situation much differently.

And so my memories of Grandpa aren't very vivid—more like a smattering of vignettes. I remember being bounced on his knee in the dining room at Standish while he sang a tune in German. The aroma of his pipe was strong enough to make my nostrils twitch. I remember watching him swing an ax to clear brush from the swale here at our home in Vassar. And I vaguely remember his funeral—lots of gray-haired people in black or gray suits and dresses, arriving in cars covered with the gray dust of Arenac County.

Thanks in part to some letters from Grandpa to Aunt Ruth Tulloch, I feel I know him a little better today than when I was sitting on his knee. The nuances surface in his writing. (He seemed fond of slinging around twenty-dollar words; e.g., one letter was signed "Your Proletariat Pa".) I'm sure he was great fun. Not that we have control over such things, but I'm sorry that either he died too soon or I was born too late.

A Grandson's Memories of John T. Wubbena
by Rod Tulloch

We always looked forward to visiting the Wubbenas, at least once we got by the whiskers. When we arrived, he had always saved a good batch of whiskers to rub against our soft cheeks. He used to squirt milk at us from the cow and tell us we were supposed to catch it in our mouths. He used to tell us lots of interesting stories. We were not sure we could believe everything he told us. He enjoyed pulling our legs and we were very gullible. I also remember him as never going to the bathroom. Everyone else had to make their trip out back, but he never seemed to go. He tried to teach us German—

counting and simple stuff—with not much success. He used to smoke his pipe quite a bit. I don't remember if he let us try it, or if we wanted to.

I remember his funeral as quite an occasion. A great number of people came. Afterward everyone gathered at the old homestead and had a good time celebrating Grandpa's going to heaven, which was the way he would have wanted it, I think.

I Remember Grandpa
by John Tulloch

Grandpa was a warm, loving man who had a great sense of humor. My brothers and sisters and I would fight for his attention, which if won could be rewarded with a "whisker burn"; he would rub his chin stubble on some part of your face or neck that could leave you with something to remember him by for as long as a week! He would always have stories to tell and questions to ask that could make you feel you were one of the most special little people around.

He had a black Collie dog that he had trained to catch sticks that you threw up into the air. We had never seen such things and I wondered at the time if he had some magic way he could talk to animals to get them to do what he wanted.

I would love to go around the barns and garages and see the amazing door latches and little labor-saving devices and curiosities he fashioned out of wood. He built us a weather vane with a four-bladed propeller and a tail. He made the propeller by taking two ¾" × ¾" cross-section pieces of pine and carving off the diagonal sections away from the center of the pieces to form air foils and then carefully notching them in the center to join them together. He drilled a hole in the center of this assembly to form the pivot point of the propeller. He mounted this to a stick with a tail on it that could pivot on a pole. This absolutely fascinated me. I built several like it as a young child, with varying degrees of imperfection, but the lessons were invaluable.

Grandpa was a connoisseur of words. He read the dictionary from cover to cover several times. He loved the subtle nuances in the meanings of words. He also liked to poke fun at the English language. He had a litany of inconsistencies he would recite. "If mice is the plural of mouse, why isn't hice the plural of house?" he would ask. And he had dozens more such questions.

Grandpa had memorized hours of poems, humorous poems mostly, but some serious and heavy ones. I have listened to him recite some of these poems. They could take a large part of an hour. Even as a child normally bored with that sort of thing I was entertained.

He was born in Germany and I would ask him to tell stories of that place. He was quite vague about this. He would tell me some stories and some poems in German, but very little. He spoke English with no accent whatsoever. This seemed strange in later years when I was going to high school with third-generation German-Americans who spoke English with thick German accents. Many of them spoke German exclusively at home, and their grandparents often were not able to speak English. Grandpa's father told him when they moved to America that they were Americans now and they would cease to speak German and assume the American way of life.

I remember Grandpa. He is one of the best people I have ever known.

Memories of My Wubbena Grandparents
by Tina (Christine) Tulloch Robinson

Some of my earliest family memories go back to visits to Grandpa and Grandma's farm on Sunday afternoons. The hour-long drive to Standish from Vassar was filled with anticipation at seeing my cousins and playing in the hayloft and barn. There was always a good chance that there would be a new batch of cuddly kittens to hold. The smell of good food would be there to greet us along with various aunts bustling around the kitchen with Grandma. But, always, there was Grandpa, either finishing his chores or waiting for our arrival with obvious delight. He made no secret about it: he loved his grandchildren and loved having them around him. He took turns hoisting us younger ones up on his lap, while he grilled the older ones about their schoolwork and other activities. (Later, I loved having him ask me those demanding questions. He was quick to praise high report card grades and achievements.)

Going with Grandpa to do his chores was always exciting and just a touch worrisome at times. To him the daily routine was so familiar that he couldn't seem to help teasing us once in a while. I remember being held up to a cow's nose while she sniffed and nuzzled me, but Grandpa put me down when I showed great distress. We enjoyed following him when he milked the cows (sometimes squirting a shot into the waiting mouth of a clever cat). He told us about the different types of hay, which types of grass and grain made better feed, etc. We often stopped to examine a plant or flower that caught his interest and, again, he would draw from his vast store of knowledge to add to ours. He didn't simply stop to smell the roses—he studied them. Time was precious and a person should spend it bettering himself one way or another, Grandpa felt.

Grandpa's affection for us had a rough kind of teasing quality that made me a bit cautious. Often he would rub his bristly whiskers against our cheeks until we hollered, or he would squeeze us just to the edge of comfort. And he simply loved to coax us into smoking his pipe. I hovered between feeling it an honor and a torment, because I invariably got sick after each attempt. But I can still feel the bliss of sitting on his knee, knowing that I was loved and treasured by an important man—a man *I* loved and treasured.

Christmases were especially wonderful, warm family times. Following a hearty, jovial meal, the piano became the center of a carol sing-a-long, with plenty of enthusiasm and encouragement for showcasing special talents. If any grandchild had learned a new tune to play on the piano, or other instrument, this was the time to perform. Solos, tricks, dances, riddles and jokes were rewarded with approval. This was also a good time for the family stories to be repeated and appreciated, such as the different locations around the farm where Grandpa had found each of his five children. They weren't born, he just stumbled upon them and took them home to Grandma.

Even though my nickname, Tina, given to me by a nurse in the hospital when I was born, was used by all other friends, family and acquaintances, neither Grandpa nor Grandma could bring themselves to use such a frivolous misuse of the perfectly good name of Christine. To Grandpa, I was his "Little Christina." All correspondence was addressed to "Christine," and I felt lucky to have two names that I liked.

Each and every birthday, we could count on receiving a shiny, brand-new silver dollar in the mail from Grandpa and Grandma. A letter was sometimes included written in Grandpa's neat, carefully crafted handwriting. He always commented on my return thank you notes, letting me know that he read them with interest. Once, I made such a point of thanking them, and enumerating all the things I could use the money on, that he sent a second dollar!

I was ten years old when Grandpa died. Looking back, I can see the impact on our lives of those early experiences and ideals that Grandpa left us. He believed in the value of hard work, both physical and mental. He believed in the importance of fun. And he believed that family came first. I'm a fortunate person to be a member of that family.

My Grandfather, John T. Wubbena
by Jan Helmut Wubbena, son of Wyatt Jan Wubbena

John T. Wubbena was the eldest of a family of ten children, six of whom were boys. He raised a family of five, two of whom were boys. The elder of them, Wyatt, was my father. Wyatt had four children, two boys and two girls, and I am the elder of his sons.

I have no recollections of my paternal grandfather, because our only meeting was during the first year of my life. But that does not mean that I have no impressions of him based on what I have been told!

I was named after my *great*-grandfather, Jan Janssen Wübbena, who brought his wife and family of four, including John T., then twelve years of age, to the New World in 1886. When John T. gave his elder son, my father, the name Wyatt Jan he gave him the Dutch form of John; the name that was given to *his* father. (The German form of John is Johannes.)

John T. keenly desired to have the Wubbena surname continue on in his grandchildren. When my father was about to become a father for the first time, John T. already had three grandchildren, but all were of the Tulloch name. "Jan" for Wyatt's first son was evidently a foregone conclusion for everyone in Michigan, and they referred to the unborn baby as "Jan." Well, "Jan" turned out to be Luise! When the second baby in my family was underway, it was kept a secret, lest it be another "disappointment." By then John T. had six grandchildren, only one of the Wubbena surname, it being my older sister. Two months prior to my birth Grandma and Aunt Kate visited my family in Dover, Delaware, where we lived, and of course they could not have failed to observe that another was underway. Upon their return to Standish they managed to keep it a secret until the baby came.

I arrived at 1:18 A.M. on July 11, 1947, and my dad called his folks around breakfast time that morning. Grandpa was out tending the cows, so Grandma got the news and informed him of the arrival of the "heir to the name" when he came in to eat. I'm told he was speechless with elation. The very same day he penned a letter to my folks; I have that letter in a scrapbook, and it's a treasured memento.

Even though evidently he disliked travel, he had to see the heir for himself and thus made his only visit to Dover the following February. A favorite family story is an incident that concerned his short layover in Wilmington en route to Dover. He must have been fiercely self-sufficient, because my folks had offered to pick him up in Wilmington, but he insisted on getting to Dover on his own. He got off the train and proceeded to the taxi stand and asked to be taken to the bus station. The driver probably looked him over and said, "Sure!" Proud of his accomplishment in having made the connection in Wilmington, he bragged about it when he got to Dover. My father said, "But, Dad, you didn't have to take a taxi to the bus station—it's right down the street from the train station." "Oh no," he said. "The taxi driver took me for a nice long ride!"

CHARLES (CARL) FRIEDRICH WUBBENA (1875–1956)

by His Niece, Catherine Wubbena

Charles, born October 8, 1875, was the second child of Jan and Catharina Wubbena. His place of birth was Neermoor, Germany. He was one and one-half years younger than his older brother, John. He and John were close companions all of their lives. The third child of the family, Henry, was three years younger than Charles. These three brothers spent a happy childhood together in Neermoor with their mother while their father was away from home for months at a time as a seafarer in the German Merchant Marine.

At a very young age Charles and his brothers skated on the dikes in the community. They told us about eating eels which their mother fried. They attended school, where they had two school masters. The older one was kind, but the younger one was very strict and stern and they were afraid of him.

By 1886 Jan and Catharina felt the war machine was breathing closer and closer to young German boys, and so the little family of three sons and one daughter (Talka) moved to the United States. They lived on the little farm one and one-half miles southwest of Standish, Michigan, on what was later to be called Johnsfield Road.

Like John and Henry, Charles also had only four months of formal schooling in this country. When he left Germany he was in the sixth grade; he was placed in the third grade in the Standish school. After four months in school their father felt it was necessary for the boys to get jobs wherever they could. Charles helped with cutting wood and hauling it to customers in town. At the same time he worked with his father helping with the farming, milking their two cows, and taking care of younger brothers and sisters.

Through arrangement with their father, a Mr. Samuel Hoobler had the three brothers work on his farm for several months. Their wages were the education Mr. and Mrs. Hoobler provided during evenings around their dining room table. This was a valuable time for the boys. The instruction was not only in English and good grammar, but concurrently as they were being exposed to this they experienced using equipment and machinery common at that time in the community. In addition, "rubbing elbows" with the Hooblers and their children, and the consequent acquisition of manners, attitudes, and even clothing styles, proved invaluable. John and Henry did better with reading and writing; Charles was noted (all of his life) for his ability in math.

Charles was the first of the Wubbena children to get married. At age twenty-two he married Myrtle Duncan, who was twenty years old. Her parents and brothers and sisters lived in Standish. The wedding took place in Rose City on January 12, 1897. Charles worked part-time helping to put up telephone poles and lines in and around Rose City and West Branch. After living a few months in Rose City, which is about twenty miles north of Standish, and a few months in Clare, he and Myrtie (the name she was always called) bought an eighty-acre farm which abutted the south side of his father's farm. Charles and John and their father all joined forces as they farmed all three farms with the same team of horses and the same implements. As roads were built and other farmers moved in, Charles' farm was divided by Dupree Road; half the farm was on the north side of this road and the other half was directly across on the south side. Eventually Charles built a house and two barns on the north side of Dupree Road, which ends at his farm. The road which starts at the Wubbena farm and runs south, perpendicular to Dupree, is the Proulx Road. Charles' farm was one mile from John's farm "as the crow flies"; traveling by road made it almost two miles away.

Charles and Myrtie were the parents of nine children. Because they lived in the Johnsfield School District, the children attended that school until, in 1919, they moved to the town of Standish. Two of the children were boys: Ernest, born in March, 1900, died when two months old, cause unknown. Francis, born June 6, 1908, died at the age of four years on March 15, 1912. The whole family was sick with strep throat and/or pneumonia at the time of Francis' death. Both boys were buried in the Woodmere Cemetery in Standish. The little boys' deaths were a terrible grief to their parents. The older three daughters helped with the farming. Eve, Grace, and Myrtle worked side-by-side with their father. Mabel was frail and could not do the heavy work. The girls were relieved when the family moved from the farm into Standish.

Charles continued to farm for many years, driving back and forth from town to his farm. The property in Standish included a barn, so there was a place there for his horses. This home was on East Cedar Street on the southeast corner of the intersection with Lapeer Street. It was almost directly across from the school, which was for both high school and elementary students. This made it easy for the daughters to attend school.

Myrtie enjoyed living in town and became active in the Ladies Aid and other activities of the Methodist Church. She loved to read, as did Charles; as the girls grew, they found great enjoyment in reading. An enviable part of their living room was a huge bookcase filled with books. Uncle Charles liked to tell me about the books as he was reading them. Two of his favorites, to which he often referred, were *The Three Musketeers* and *Les Miserables*.

Rather than be redundant in telling his story, it might be well to include here an article taken from the weekly newspaper, *The Arenac County Independent*, dated August 16, 1940, printed when Charles retired as mail carrier.

Charles Wubbena Retires as Mail Carrier on No. 3

Charles Wubbena is out of a job—but he isn't worrying a great deal, except that he will miss his daily calls upon approximately 250 people along the route of Standish Rural Free Delivery No. 3.

Everybody knows that Charlie has been a carrier on No. 3 for a long time, but many will not realize that he is now a retired man, cannot carry mail for Uncle Sam any longer and is now on a pension to live as he pleases—not forced to sort out mail every morning. Charlie has been getting down to the local post office early every morning for the past 22½ years. He got so much into the habit of doing that stunt that he still wakes up early—then 'comes to,' snuggles back into the covers and takes an extra snooze.

Charlie says he is going to miss that daily trip through the country, a trip of 28 miles at first and finally strung out to the extent that he was making 34 miles when the day of retirement came last Thursday. For 15 years he drove the route with a horse (sometimes two horses when the roads were heavy with mud) and finally, when the roads were so improved that he could conveniently handle a car, he invested in a Model T Ford and for the past 15 years he has been driving a car—but, of course, not the original Model T.

Mr. Wubbena has been in the service since May 1, 1918. That was when Glenn Beardsley was called into the service in the World War. When Glenn returned, Charlie was transferred to Turner for three years. Glenn was taken ill and passed away and Wubbena was called back to fill the vacancy and has carried mail on Route 3 ever since. Ed Kiley has acted as his relief, but Ed was never called upon to relieve the regular carrier because Charlie was never ill while on the job for 22½ years. The only time he required relief was when he took his vacation. This is a record of which he is justly proud. It is interesting to note that Charlie was the third man in line between Beardsley, himself and Clyde Thompson for the job of carrying mail back in 1922. Thompson was in line for the position, but he, too, was called into the service and never returned, having passed away while across the water in active service.

Charlie's "big thrill" while hauling mail was back in the early part of his service, when, following extra-heavy spring rains, the water had crossed the highway near "The Cut" in Arenac Township. He was driving along carefully when his horses suddenly reared up and refused to go on. But suddenly they gave a leap and jumped over a wide expanse of water. He could not determine just why the horses went through those actions until he arrived at that same spot after the waters had subsided and saw a hole over four feet in depth. "If those horses had not had the instinct to go over that hole, I might never have had the privilege of being retired at this time," he said.

Today's retired carrier came to this country with his parents, Mr. and Mrs. Jan Wubbena, when he was 11 years of age. His parents came to escape just what America is about to enter, martial training. They did not want their family of boys to experience that period of training in Germany—they wanted to go to "free America." He was born in the northwest corner of Germany in Hanover Province, October 8, 1875.

His parents settled in Johnsfield, though Charlie himself later lived at Rose City and Clare, spending a year in each community. His father and himself both worked in the woods, the work being very hard for his father, as he had not experienced that type of labor while in Germany. He had always been a seafaring man and was not required to do much manual labor. Charlie finally settled in Johnsfield and operated a farm there from 1899 until 1919 when he moved to Standish.

While on the farm, he recalled with a great deal of pleasure, the time he sold 26 tons of baled hay for $26.00 per ton. Other crops were sold somewhat in the same high proportion. "Folks back in those days, or prior to the period of those high prices didn't have the Welfare to help them out—they just had to dig in and do the best they could with the little they had to do with, but we survived and perhaps we were better off, than the people today who get a boost from the government. And another thing, this pension given to the rural carriers isn't a gift by any means. Off every pay check we received each month, there was a three and one-half percent deduction and placed to our credit—to accumulate over the years and added to our pension fund we are to be paid after we are retired. So you see, we really pay for our own pension. And that's all right with me."

It was while in Rose City in 1897 that he married Miss Myrtle Duncan on January 12. Both Mr. and Mrs. Wubbena worked hard to make their farming operation successful. Charlie was employed part time on the telephone lines while engaged in farming. It is interesting to note that Mr. and Mrs. Wubbena are the parents of seven children, all daughters: Mrs. William Ingram, Detroit; Mrs. A. M. Strauss, Standish; Miss Mabel Wubbena, teaching school at Omer; Mrs. William V. Baikie, Omer; Mrs. Everett Scott, Flushing; Mrs. Verncil Whitmire, Flint; Miss Doris Wubbena, registered nurse at University of Michigan Hospital at Ann Arbor. Charlie also has five brothers and four sisters living in various parts of the country: John, Johnsfield; Henry, Essexville; Harry, Bruce Crossing; Fred, Seattle; William, Washington, DC; Miss Talka Wubbena, Elgin, Ill.; Mrs. George Flutur, Detroit; Mrs. Louis Gabler, Elgin, Ill.; Miss Ella Wubbena, Moody Bible Institute, Chicago, Ill.

Charlie has enjoyed his service as a rural mail carrier out of Standish, but a bit of pathos came over him when he recalled that many of his patrons had answered the call and passed on during his time. He named off several family names that are only memories among the people of today but whose families at one time were the people around whom the main activities of their various communities took place and they were also the families to lay the foundation for a growing and enticing section of the community area adjacent to Standish.

Don't be surprised to see Charlie going the rounds of his old route some day—just to keep acquainted with the folks. He still loves his old job and the yearn to carry mail will probably be with him always.

Good luck to you, Charlie, and may you enjoy your retirement.

Until other arrangements are completed, Ed. Kiley will carry mail No. 3.

As the above article suggested, Charles did make the rounds after his retirement, to visit the friends he made along his route. The roads he traveled in making the thirty-four miles of his rounds included these: Pine River, Hickory Island, Hale, Stover, State (also called Arenac Road), and Saganing. David Restainer, who lives on Arenac Road, recalls that at one time the bridge was out on Stover Road, so about fifteen mail boxes were clumped together on Hansel Road where folks had to go to pick up their mail. Dave also remembers that the distance Charlie traveled was so great that, when the weather was really bad and roads were difficult to travel, Charlie would change his team of horses about half-way through his trip.

His horses had to be well-trained and obedient. They pulled the buggy up to the mailboxes and stopped every time at just the right spot so that Charles could reach through the window and place mail in the box. The buggy's canopy was mostly homemade by Charles. I think it was made of wood and was painted black. It was rather high, and made one think of the buggies driven by the Mennonites. But Charles needed apertures that were placed for the convenience of his work. His rig was recognized with affection as he made his rounds.

Charles liked horses and enjoyed studying the features he deemed important. He would squint his eyes as he palpated a horse's joints and muscles, studied the condition of the teeth, stood back and looked closely at the horse's gait and movements. A neighbor in town was Tenhaus Rancourt, who lived with his family of three daughters and one son on the southwest corner of East Cedar and Cass, two blocks from Charles' home. Like Charles, he had a barn at the back of his property. The two of them would discuss horses by the hour. In addition to his house, barn, and small acreage in town, Tenhaus had a large farm located at the northwest corner of West Cedar and Court Street. There was a huge barn on this farm where Tenhaus kept several horses. It was there that Charles and Tenhaus would do their "bargaining" as they sometimes made horse trades and sales to each other. Tenhaus' son Edgar would race his father's horses at some of the county fairs. The farm was turned over to Edgar in 1938 (information derived from the Arenac County Register of Deeds). Some years later the farm was owned by George Cuttle, then by his son Lyle Cuttle.

As a matter of interest, Edgar Rancourt and Olga Panasiuk were librarians for the Standish library housed in the "Pump House" on North Main Street. This was in the late 1930s and early 1940s as the country was recovering from the Great Depression. In August 1992 the new Standish Library, called the Mary Johnston Library, was opened. The library is located on a corner of what was the Rancourt farm.

John Raynak and his family lived at the south end of Lapeer Street; Charles and Myrtie's house was the first house on Lapeer, at the intersection with East Cedar. Mr. Raynak was fittingly called "Big John." He was the blacksmith for the community. The quality of his work was much praised and admired. If "Big John" couldn't fix it, nobody could! His blacksmith shop was located immediately west of the railroad tracks on Beaver Street. There were several trees on his property which shaded his outdoor forge in summertime. When we read Henry W. Longfellow's poem "The Village Blacksmith" in school it was always Big John and his shop that formed the picture of Longfellow's smithy. Charles and John had much smithy work done by Mr. Raynak. Charles and Myrtie liked the Raynak family. There were several children who grew up with the Wubbena children. Both families grew vegetables, which they exchanged back and forth. When there were hard times and sickness in the families there was much empathetic support given each other.

Throughout these years, as Charles carried the mail and also farmed, the daughters were busy with gaining an education and working here and there. By 1993 all the daughters had died.

So what was once a flourishing, active family, which filled the little town of Standish with their songs, their smiling faces at their various workplaces, and their earnest aspirations to "do better," is now gone. Not one member of their next generation lives near Arenac County.

After his retirement Charles kept busy planting a few crops on his farm, using horses for the work, but traveling by car back and forth to his home in town. It should be noted that of the six Wubbena boys, only Charles and Fred drove cars. John, Henry, Harry, and Bill evaded that responsibility, always leaving the driving to other members of their families. They just didn't like "motors," and their functioning parts were to always remain a mystery to them.

Charles fitted up a shed on his farm with a little stove, an old rocker, and boxes of books. The house had been ruined by renters so his shed had to serve as his "roof-top" to which he would withdraw when his houseful of women in town became a little too active for him.

An attractive feature of their farm was the grove of about fifty beautiful maple trees. The grove was located a few rods north of the barns. When two or three of the families got together this was a lovely place to eat picnic meals. The trees began to die after Shirley and Jeannette bought the farm. Shirley's black angus cattle were allowed to graze around the trees. The trees' final destruction came from the purgation of wells drilled in a futile search for oil. Still remaining are the several old maples bordering the lawn.

For years John and Charles had done work on the family plot in Woodmere Cemetery, which is located on US 23 a mile northeast of Standish. In earlier years they had placed the gravestones, making a big job of pouring cement and fixing the curb sides. As Talka died, then Myrtie, then Charles' daughter Mabel, they selected and placed the stones for each one. In these later years they continued to spend time snipping grass and keeping the plots neat.

Charles made fun of any pretense or sham and made a long, amusing story of a fancy dinner he had attended in town. Apparently he felt the "dog" had been laid on a bit thick. One got the point from hearing him tell, "we even had olives, and we had napkins," in a slow, drawling emphasis that only he could express. He belonged to the Masons and attended most of their meetings. He was not always whole-hearted in supporting their opinions. He was careful about telling Brother John any secrets but he told enough to convey the fact that he was looking askance at the hypocrisy of some brother

Masons. More than once, he said, "I hate anything and anybody that teaches hate."

Uncle Charles' measured speech whenever he praised or criticized reminds me of this passage from the *Book of Sirach* (The New American Bible Translation):

> As the test of what the potter molds is in the furnace,
>   So in his conversation is the test of a man.
> The fruit of a tree shows the care it has had;
>   So too does a man's speech disclose the bent of his mind.
> Praise no man before he speaks,
>   For it is then that men are tested.   Sirach 27:4–7

Charles served on the County Welfare Board for several years and this work involved much of his time and interest. The Welfare Board was the forerunner of what became known as the Social Service Department, which is under state jurisdiction rather than under the county as was formerly the case. Charles could relate many comical and interesting anecdotes about his experience on the Board. It could readily be seen that he was a level-headed and conservative member of the Board. His insight into human nature's frothy foibles and deceiving behavior, as well as his discernment of the sincere striving and industrious attempts at self-sufficiency, were often praised by other members of the Board.

Charles' wife, Myrtie, died January 22, 1954, in Standish after several years of failing health. With all of his daughters except Mabel married and gone from home, Myrtie and Charles were very close companions during these latter years, with Charles caring for her every wish and need.

After her death he felt lost without Myrtie and would drive out to John's place for a few hours or a meal. The two of them would sit and visit for hours, usually outdoors under a tree. For years they had done this, but now with Myrtie gone, he came more often. Looking out the kitchen window we could see them, each smoking his pipe, with legs crossed in an identical manner, chortling over some joke or escapade in the community of their younger days. On cool days they sat in the living room. Their conversation was interesting and uplifting; especially Charles, more than John, remembered details and the amusing aspects of incidents. They exposed the positive side of almost everything.

John died in July of 1954. After that loss Charles was really lonesome and the aging process became very apparent. He spent some time with daughter Myrtle (Mrs. Bill Baikie), who lived in Omer, a distance of about six miles. His daughter Grace (Mrs. Andries Strauss), who lived in Corpus Christi, Texas, came up to Michigan for periods of time to provide some companionship. Charles continued to visit my mother, who was also widowed but had Shirley as a daily (and even more frequent) visitor. One time as he sat visiting with Mom he made the comment, "You know, Laura, a person can become very selfish living alone." This revealed a lot about Uncle Charles' nature. He was a selfless person, and in his quiet way did many generous and helpful things for others. It bothered him that age was slowing him down and he felt that he was not useful to others any more. An earlier example of his willingness to be helpful whenever possible was his service to the folks on his mail route. Some of the people were elderly and/or disabled and without transportation. When requested, Charles obligingly delivered packages down the road to some friend for them, and even shopped in town for a package of tobacco or loaf of bread, delivering it the next day when making the rounds with the mail. At the time it happened Charles did not find it amusing, but as time passed he enjoyed telling about the time the federal postal inspector visited the post office. The inspector decided he would make the rounds with Charlie, and sat beside him in the Model T as it traveled the dusty roads. As they drew near to Mrs. _____'s home, there she stood by the side of her mailbox. "Good morning, Mr. Wubbena. Please take this package to _____." Charlie squirmed as he said, "But I can't do that. I'm not allowed to." Her quick rejoinder was, "But you did on Monday." Poor Charlie just muttered, "But I can't now." They drove on. The inspector never said a word.

A widow, Mrs. Lucia, and her three sons needed a place to live. The old house on the Old Place was vacant, and had been allowed to fall into disrepair. Charles spent energy and money to fix the house to a level of comfortable occupancy and then moved them in. He helped the boys find odd jobs but also encouraged them, at the same time, to keep on attending school. The family had some hard years, but Charles stuck by them. In later years their gratitude was often expressed. Few people knew that he was often there in the background giving help to folks who needed it.

Even before old age reached him, he walked with a trudging gait rather than a smart step. His face was triangular in shape, and the pointed chin seemed to get more pointed as he grew older. His pale blue eyes were small and deep-set; he resembled the picture we have of his father. It seems to me that he and Fred looked more like their father than did any of the other brothers and sisters. When he grinned his wide grin, and with his fun-filled pointed little eyes, his face was almost elfin-like.

His home in Standish was sold, and he spent his last year or two in Omer living with Myrtle and Bill Baikie. They lived a very active life in their community and their contacts with people were of great interest to Charles. He became very hard of hearing, but never sat off in a corner. He was usually a participant in whatever was going on. As time moved on he suffered with cancer and some heart problems. He resisted hospital care and wanted to die quietly with his family. And so Myrtle, with the help of some of her sisters, took care of him at her home until he died on November 15, 1956. He had lived a full and enjoyable sixteen years after he retired from his mail-delivery work. He would have been pleased to know that the farm he loved became the property of another Wubbena, Shirley, the youngest child of his brother, John.

Memories of My Grandfather, Charles Wubbena
by Beverly Baikie Rodriguez

Charles Wubbena married Myrtle Duncan, who was "Pennsylvania Dutch." They had seven girls and two boys (both boys died when they were little).

He used to tell that he was trapped into marriage. He was so good-looking that he always had to carry a stick "to keep the girls away." One day Nanny, as we called her, made an elderberry pie and in his excitement he put down his stick and started in on the pie—and she nabbed him. Her answer to this was always, "Now, Charlie, you know that's not true!" She didn't have much sense of humor.

He did like tall stories. Sometimes he told of when he was little in Germany. (He was ten when he "came over.") His grandma didn't have any teeth so his parents made the kids take turns chewing her food for her. Then she could swallow it.

Supposedly the night they left Germany the kids tied the hens' feet together, passing the string under the roost, so when they woke in the morning and tried to hop off they would all hang by the feet.

When he was young he worked in a sawmill and there partially lost his hearing. After that he had the farm. Sometimes we could ride the horses while he plowed, but by that time they lived in Standish. He had a pair of matching black horses of which he was proud. There was also a mule named Maude.

He would drive out to the farm when he was older by the back roads as he felt he could be "a danger on the highway." My mother worked in the fields when she was a girl and had a sun stroke; later she was always bothered by the heat.

He also was a mail carrier, but had retired by the time I can remember.

For a while in Standish they took in boarders. A young man lived over the garage and they had someone upstairs.

When I was born he told my parents they didn't need to worry that I would go to Hollywood. So I went to nursing school—almost by tradition. I am glad I did.

When we were little we would go visit every Saturday (after piano lessons). We'd get on his knee and beg for stories. He'd take what seemed like a long time before he'd begin. Most were short like "The Man Who Couldn't Shiver," which was about a man who had everything, but was unhappy because he just couldn't shiver: His wife tried everything she could think of and one day found the fish vendor going by and bought the lot—fish, ice, the works, and dumped it on his tummy while he was napping, and did he shiver!

The stories were never the same and were always "embroidered." I don't know if any were originals but when I was little I thought they all were. I was disappointed to find the Prodigal Son came from the Bible.

He would sing "Down went McGinty to the bottom of the sea, and he must be very wet, as they haven't found him yet, dressed in his best suit of clothes." It had several verses.

He also told of a man who went fishing with his wife. When they got to the boat they found the rope was cut. He said it was cut with a knife. She, being a contrary woman, said, "cut with scissors." They argued as they got in and pushed out on the lake. Finally, exasperated, he told her not to say scissors again or he'd throw her in the water. She couldn't swim, but she said, "Any fool could see it was cut with scissors." So over he threw her and she went down, but as she did so she stuck her hand out and made a scissors motion with her fingers.

Another of Granddaddy's stories was about a man with one arm missing—people always bothered him by asking how he lost it. Finally one day he said, "If I tell you how I lost it, will you quit asking questions?" They promised, and he said, "It was chewed off!"

If we cried he'd say, "Quick, Myrtle, get a cup and we can save these tears for soup."

He also told us to save donut holes for him. If you bite into a donut without thinking, the hole is gone, so you carefully have to pluck it out first and thread it on a string. He always had string in his pocket and would take it out and show how many he had collected.

He also did tricks with the string. He'd cut a piece in two and then put it in his mouth and "chew the ends back together." And pull it out and have one piece.

He'd also have us watch very patiently while he'd blow smoke from his pipe out of his ears. He'd puff some rings first and then let some out of his ears—but only once.

He could do number tricks, too, like what day your birthday will fall on in three years.

One time he came to our house with Uncle Bill. Uncle Bill could throw his voice from the bathtub. And he also taught me a hat trick.

The movies Granddaddy liked best were Tarzan movies.

Nanny had diabetes and got senile quite young. Then she would call me Doris and kept asking who that man was that took care of her. She didn't know him, but he was kind to her. She caught her apron on fire one day making oatmeal and Granddaddy rolled her in a rug to put out the flames. Finally she had to go to a nursing home.

Before that happened we had a family reunion. Lots of people came from all over. Lots of cousins we hadn't met before. I remember Aunt Len got the kids out of the kitchen by telling us the watermelons were out in the garage and if just one disappeared she wouldn't tell. After dinner my brother and I teased Wendy—Eva's dog—by having her chase balls that we pretended to throw. She'd really run until she got tired.

My dad and maybe Vernce jacked up Lew Gabler's car (i.e., put it on blocks) and put a potato in the exhaust. When Lew got in to leave and put it in reverse nothing happened. So the people said, "Ask Bill (Baikie), he's a mechanic." Dad looked under the hood and made some diagnosis and said try again—gun it. The potato shot out and everyone laughed. Lew got out and found it jacked up.

That was the last reunion I remember.

Granddaddy went to Texas to see Grace with us once after Nanny died. We were there for Janet's wedding.

Later he got cancer of the intestine. By that time I was in college, so he came to stay his last days at our house. He didn't want a colostomy or to go to the hospital for a chance of maybe having five more years. He'd had a good life, he said.

He always spent a lot of time reading. On TV he liked boxing! But Elvis Presley's movements would send him to the bedroom. Also when he had a lot of pain he'd just stay in his room.

I went to his funeral. He's buried in Standish next to Nanny.

HENRY WUBBENA
(1878–1962)

My Grand Ole Dad
Memories of My Father, Henry Wubbena

by Lois Wubbena Dick

Henry was the third child of Jan and Catharina Wubbena and was born in Neermoor, Germany, on November 4, 1878. He was seven years old when he came to America in July of 1886. He carried the nicknames of "Hank" and "Webb."

In spite of the limited amount of food when he was a child, he grew into a tall, thin man: he was over six feet tall and weighed approximately 170 pounds. Basically he had good health and still had some of his own teeth when he died at the age of eighty-three.

His life during his childhood was simple and centered on the family. The poverty and hardships the family endured, and surviving the loss of their mother after her death at the age of thirty-nine, made a strong bond in the family. Their father appreciated music and the children entertained themselves by singing—all had good singing voices and sang in harmony. The sense of humor that each of the original ten children possessed must have helped them through the difficult times. I do not recall Dad ever being bitter about hardships the family went through. He had high esteem and much love for each brother and sister, and had only good things to say about each of them. Each child had his own Bible. Every evening the family sat around the table and read the Bible by candlelight or kerosene lamps.

Henry began working in a lumber camp at the age of fifteen. When he was sixteen years old he lost a ring finger in an accident at the camp. In 1902 at the age of twenty-four he began working for the Northeastern Telephone Co. in Pinconning, Michigan (now the Michigan Bell Telephone Co.); he was transferred from West Branch to Bay City in February, 1909.

Martha Link, who lived on a farm near West Branch, visited a friend who was a cook at a lumber camp. Martha's friend introduced her to John Wubbena, who was working at the camp. Sometime later John invited Martha to his home in Standish where she met John's sisters and his brother Henry. Henry was working near West Branch at the time and he and Martha began their courtship. After Henry was transferred to Bay City in 1909 Martha found employment in Bay City.

Martha Link and Henry Wubbena were married June 14, 1911 at the home of Mary and Frank Link, Martha's parents, who lived on a farm near West Branch. They were married by a young Lutheran minister. When the minister counselled them before the wedding he told them that this was his first marriage to perform. Henry replied that this was their first, also.

Henry came to West Branch for the wedding by train from Bay City. He was met at Lorenger, a train station about three miles from the Link home. Martha and her brother, Frank, met him with a horse and buggy.

Martha's sisters cut pine boughs and used them to form an arch under which the bride and groom stood. Martha's brother Frank and Henry's sister Minnie were their attendants. About forty guests witnessed the ceremony and were served a delicious dinner.

Martha had arisen at four A.M. that day to help with food preparation and to bake the wedding cake. Martha and her sisters had picked wild strawberries to serve over homemade ice cream. The ice cream was in a cylinder-shaped container (used in homemade ice cream freezers). Martha's mother plunged the container in the warm water in the reservoir of the kitchen stove, and the round disk of delicious ice cream came out in one piece. It was then sliced and served with the sweetened wild strawberries. A white linen tablecloth and napkins that Martha had hemmed was used and hemlock greenery decorated the table.

The newlyweds took the train that same evening to Bay City where they had rented a house on Second Street. They had little furniture, so they turned a washtub upside down and covered it with a linen tablecloth where they spread the lunch Martha's mother had sent with them. Martha had a hope chest of cedar filled with linens, many of which she had embroidered. Some of the wedding gifts they received were a library table, a mantle clock, a rocker with brown leather upholstery, and another oak rocker with no upholstery. The house had gas lights. They had a garden there and Martha canned vegetables they raised. Milk was delivered to the house by a milkman with a milk wagon pulled by horses.

Henry would often be out of town for two or three days at a time putting up telephone poles and stringing telephone lines to expand telephone service to other areas of Michigan. Occasionally he would be gone two or three weeks at a time repairing damage from a storm. His work was out-of-doors and they had no insulated clothing at that time. During the winter months, it was not unusual for him to wear two sets of long underwear, two pair of woolen trousers, and two pair of woolen stockings to face the winter elements. Martha would buy the woolen clothing in the summer months when it was on sale and made sure there was an ample supply to carry through the winter months. Henry walked across the Straits of Mackinac from St. Ignace to Mackinaw City—a distance of five miles—for what reason I do not know. However, this was unique because the Straits do not always freeze over.

Martha would pack nourishing food as there were no restaurants out in the country where Henry worked. The dinner bucket was made of aluminum. It was round and had three compartments stacked on top of each other. These were held in place by wire clamps. Martha would put hot coffee or soup in the bottom compartment, the "main course" in the middle compartment, and the fruit and dessert in the top one. The heat from the hot foods would help keep the other foods from freezing. In spite of all efforts, many lunches were eaten while frozen. Foods that were packed were pieces of meat, hard-boiled eggs, chicken, cheese, homemade bread and butter sandwiches (Henry preferred this to having the meat in a sandwich), cake, cookies, home-canned fruit, or fresh fruit in season. Apples were available during most of the winter months.

Their four children were born in Bay City. They saved their money and in 1919 they purchased a house located on a three-fourths acre lot at the corner of Scheurman Street and Borton Avenue in Essexville, which is a village adjacent to Bay City. The address was 901 Scheurman St.

I am Lois Wubbena Dick, the third child born to Martha and Henry. I remember nothing about Bay City. My first memory is that of a wagon pulled by a horse stopped in a street. The wagon was piled high with furniture with a chair precariously perched on top. The wagon contained the belongings of Martha and Henry being moved from Bay City to their Essexville home. Very vivid is a man with a black-brimmed felt hat perched in the front of the wagon with the reins in his hands. I looked up at this figure, too young to realize that he was my father and would have great influence on my life. I looked up to him then at the age of almost three years, and as I grew older looked up to him and respected him as a man and as my father throughout his life. He was a Grand Ole Dad.

Mom and Dad were happy with this property they bought in Essexville.

It had mature fruit trees: apple, cherry, crabapples, Bartlett pears, green gage and purple plums, a strawberry patch and a large garden area. There was a barn so they were able to have their own cow and chickens.

The house was wood frame. The first floor had a parlor (which they used as a bedroom), kitchen and pantry, dining room, and living room with a pot-bellied stove that burned hard coal for fuel. There were two bedrooms and a sewing room upstairs. The stovepipe from the potbellied stove in the living room went up through one of the bedrooms and that was the only source of heat for the upstairs. There was a porch on the north and south sides of the house and a stoop that faced west toward Scheurman Street that opened into the parlor. The pantry had a dirt floor. Vegetables and apples were stored there during the winter months. Shelves above held the many jars of food that they raised and Martha canned. This room was cooler, so leftover foods were kept there also. There was no such thing as a refrigerator in those days.

There was a cistern (a reservoir that collected rain water from the eave troughs) under the kitchen floor. There was a door in the floor of the kitchen that could be raised to the cistern below. Water from the cistern could be pumped to the kitchen sink to be used for the laundry, hand washing, bathing, etc. There was a pump in the yard that supplied well water for drinking and cooking. This water was pumped and carried in by pail.

We were warned of the danger of falling into the cistern and were told never to open that door! Sometimes during the winter months the water around the pipe in the cistern would freeze. Dad would put on rubber hip boots, raise that door, and climb carefully down into the cistern. Mother would hand him buckets of boiling water to pour around the pipe to thaw it. Even though I was very young I sensed the danger as he precariously positioned himself in that hole! I was so relieved when that door was closed!

Monday was wash day. Mother would "sliver up" a bar of P&G soap Sunday night. A boiler was filled with water and on Monday the water was heated on the wood stove in the kitchen. The soap and the cotton clothing were added and boiled. Mother had a long wooden pole that she used to shift the clothes and to lift them out to be rinsed. Woolen clothes were carefully washed in lukewarm water by hand. Dad would put up the clothesline before he went to work as he could stretch the line tighter than Mom. The clothesline would sag from the weight of the wet clothes and then be propped up by a clothespole. Clothes were hung outdoors during the summer months and during the winter months if it was not too cold. When it was cold Mom wore clean white gloves to protect her fingers while handling the cold, wet clothes. I recall her bringing in some yet partially frozen snow-white clothes and "draping" them around the coal-burning stove to finish drying. Oh, what a fresh smell they had! On severe cold days, lines were strung inside the house.

The clothes were wrung through a hand-turned wringer and still had a lot of moisture in them. The moisture would collect on the cold window panes (no storm windows or thermopanes then) and Jack Frost painted fancy designs.

Mom and Dad worked hard and worked as a team, and made many sacrifices for their family. Dad turned his paycheck over to Mom. She was the manager and a good one. She was able to put a part of the paycheck in the bank and when American Telephone and Telegraph Co. offered their employees the opportunity to participate in a stock plan, they had a certain amount of money withheld from Dad's pay to buy AT&T stock. Dad milked the cow before he went to work. Of course, when he was out of town, Mom took on that job. The larger garden was plowed, but the two of them spaded the area under fruit trees where the plow could not make long furrows. We children helped as we were able. A string between two stakes marked each row. Then, with a hoe he would make a series of holes along the line of the string, and we would put the number of seeds in the hole that he instructed. Then he would cover the seeds with dirt and firm the soil with the back of the hoe. Both Mom and Dad weeded the garden as needed. Many times people out for a walk stopped and admired the clean, producing plot. At harvest time Mom and Dad got up earlier than usual to pick the peas, beans, corn—whatever was "just right" for canning. The kids, when we got up, helped shuck, clip, husk, or whatever was necessary to prepare the vegetables. They were then blanched in boiling water for a certain length of time, and then plunged into cold water before we put them into sterilized glass jars and sealed them for processing. The corn was removed from the cob with a sharp knife after blanching, and the kernels were put into the jars. I often wondered how many ears of corn it took to fill one jar of kernels! The sealed glass jars of vegetables were put in a copper boiler that held sixteen quart jars. They were processed under boiling water the length of time (hours) required for preservation. Often times it would be midnight when the processing was completed. Dad helped Mom remove the hot jars from the boiling water and Mom would tighten the cover, check each jar for leakage, and run a knife at the edge of the zinc cover to make sure of a good seal. It was rare that a jar spoiled. Tomatoes, chili sauce, catsup, peaches, pears, cherries, strawberries, and relishes were canned by the "open kettle" method. Then there were the jams, jellies, marmalades, and fruit "butters." Peaches were the only thing they did not raise themselves. Up to four hundred quarts were canned a summer.

We kids would load fresh vegetables in our wagon and go from door to door selling them. Mother would tell us what to charge and then say, "Heap the basket." We also sold eggs and quart pails of milk to the nearby neighbors.

In 1925 they had a larger house built on the far end of the lot facing Borton Avenue (906 Borton Avenue). It was a two-story house with a dormer at the front and back, and a porch across the front. The outside was stucco on the first level with stained shingles on the second level. It had large rooms with oak floors, woodwork and built-in cabinets of oak. When planning the house the floor plan had an option of a fireplace in the living room for an additional $125.00. I remember Mom and Dad considering this and we kids encouraging them to have a fireplace. However, Mom and Dad, being conservative, felt they should not borrow any more money. They had saved their money and had to borrow only $1,500. On the first floor there was a large kitchen with eating "space," a dining room, a bedroom, bathroom, and a living room stretched across the front of the house. At the end of the living room was an open stairway leading to the upstairs where there were three large bedrooms and a large room with partial bath and built-in linen closet. A coke furnace was in the basement. There was a large fruit cellar in the basement, laundry tubs, and a toilet. Yes—there was inside plumbing! The barn was torn down and a garage was built for the old house and for the new house.

The old house was sold, but the people did not make any payments and moved out in six months. The Depression had hit and property was not moving. Two or three other tenants rented the house but often were not able to pay their rent. It was finally sold to Archie and Catherine Des Jardenes.

Dad had saved his money and bought a forty-acre farm with a house on the property in Johnsfield. After he was transferred to Bay City working for the telephone company, he felt he had a more secure job and opportunity than farming. Before he sold the farm he rented it; although the tenants were unable to make payments, he let them stay on. Dad eventually was able to sell the farm.

In August 1911, the first year they were married, and every summer thereafter Dad suffered from a skin eruption or eczema affecting his arms, areas behind his knees, and his face—especially his forehead. Mother tried every remedy the doctors prescribed or anyone suggested. He was miserable with the burning and itching and isolated himself; he stayed in bed when it was severe. He got the most relief from bathing with a solution of cornstarch and soda, and boric acid compresses. Mother changed the compresses and kept them moist. To prevent scratching he would pat his bandaged face to help relieve the itching. One summer Dad took the bus to Ann Arbor and went to the University of Michigan Hospital. In about ten days he returned home and his skin was completely clear. We were all *so* happy. The next morning his skin had broken out again. He took the earliest bus back to Ann Arbor and the doctors said they could do nothing more for him.

There were no paid sick days and no hospital insurance at that time, and Dad felt he could not lose his pay. He always took his two-week vacation the last two weeks of August, when his skin problem was at its worst.

For two summers a group of men at the telephone company rented a cottage on Saginaw Bay, and the men scheduled their vacations so it could be spent at the cottage. Dad would walk home from the cottage, pick the ripe vegetables, and bring them back to the cottage—a trip of about five miles each way! There were no conveniences at the cottage. Friends and relatives came out to visit us while at the cottage—I doubt if this was much of a vacation for either Mom or Dad. But we did learn to swim in the (then) clean water of Saginaw Bay.

Dad never drove a car and did not want to. When Raymond was old enough to get a driver's license, Dad and Mom bought their first car—a blue, second-hand, four-door Dodge sedan. We were able to go to Standish to visit the Charles and John Wubbena families, and to West Branch to visit our grandparents and Mother's family there.

In 1928 our family and some of our Standish relatives—a caravan of four cars—went to the Upper Penninsula to visit relatives there. Cars at that time had running boards where supplies could be carried. There was a "gate" attached to the running board and to the fenders to keep the load in place and secure. The doors on that side of the car could not then be opened, and passengers had to get in and out of the car on the opposite side. The supplies included a tent, bedding for our family of six people, cooking utensils, pails, dishes, flatware, food, towels, and clothes. There were no plastic or polyesters back then.

We crossed the Straits of Mackinac by ferry boat and camped at St. Ignace our first night out. During the night there was a severe thunderstorm with heavy rain. Bedding and clothes got wet and had to be hung on a clothesline between trees the next day to dry before we continued on our trip.

The terrain in the U.P. was more hilly than we were used to, and the clay roads a concern, for fear they might be slippery if wet.

Our first stop was in Marquette to visit Uncle Bill, Aunt Maude, and family. They warmly greeted this mob of people and had arranged with neighbors and friends for some of us to stay overnight. Marquette was also hilly. We made certain that the brakes were set correctly on the hill and the wheels turned toward the curb.

From Marquette we went on to Trout Creek to visit Uncle Harry and Aunt Lenore. Again, neighbors and friends housed some of the relatives. I do recall my sisters, Bernice and Florence, and I were assigned to a folding bed in Uncle Harry's office. During the night the bed tipped and dumped the three of us against a roll-top desk. There was little room to manipulate, but we managed to upright the bed without disturbing the other residents. I have no idea how this mob of people of all ages were fed at either home or how they managed this group. It certainly was quite an undertaking for all concerned!

One of the highlights of the trip, I remember, was seeing the Pictured Rocks (they are an attraction for tourists yet today). Large blueberries or huckleberries were growing wild. Everyone picked them and filled every available container.

Mother, though not educated, had a lot of common sense, good judgment, and insight. She was ambitious, and an excellent organizer and manager. She was good, kind, and generous. I remember her feeding "hobos" who came to the door. She never let them in the house, but would prepare a plate of food and have them eat outdoors.

Mother was an excellent cook and baker and served well-balanced meals. Her house was immaculate. She always told us to clean thoroughly and in the corners. She also said to buy good things and they would always look nice and last. Good clothes would not be a fad, would fit better, and would not fade or shrink when washed. We were also told repeatedly to take care of what you have or you will never have anything.

For a short time we had a roomer who was a consultant at the cement plant in Essexville. Mother would often have him join us for dinner or would send a "treat" up to him in his room. She would have a visiting preacher for dinner, and when there was a church conference she would have some of the out-of-town people stay overnight at our house. She would cook and bake for days to help with food supply at the conference. She made many of our clothes, hemmed sheets, made pillowcases, and did much mending.

Mother had been a Lutheran. It was through Dad's sisters that Mother was converted, and became a member of the Gospel Hall. Mother went to Sunday morning meetings and often to prayer meetings on Wednesday evening. When there was a series of nightly special meetings with a visiting preacher, Dad and we children would attend. The kids went to Sunday School every Sunday afternoon. New Year's Day the Gospel Hall had a special program for children called "Sunday School Treat." Each child was assigned a group of Bible verses by his Sunday School teacher to be recited by memory at the event. We rehearsed our part until we met Mom's and Dad's approval. Children received a small paper sack of candy and peanuts—the Sunday School Treat!

It was Mother who wanted us to take music lessons. Raymond took violin lessons for six years. He did well while taking lessons but after a few years the best he could do was saw off "Turkey in the Straw." Mother saved pennies and bought a Grinnell piano for $550. She wanted her three girls to take piano lessons and so we did—each for at least three years. We practiced for a half-hour each morning before going to school and another half-hour after school. We played at recitals and school functions and our parents were always there (I hope with pride). We took the bus to Bay City for our lessons—five cents fare each way. Each of us had an item to purchase (a pound of butter, lard, peanut butter, etc.) to make use of the bus fare. Lessons were one dollar each.

When relatives needed medical care in Bay City, the mother of the patient (and sometimes the recuperating patient) stayed with us. Aunt Mertie stayed with us when Grace had a mastoid operation, and Aunt Laura stayed when Shirley had his appendix removed.

Dad enjoyed radio programs, especially Amos and Andy, Al Jolson and Jack Benny, and was interested in boxing.

He played the jewsharp and the mouth organ. He sang to us by the hour—songs apparently the Original Ten sang at home—and hymns. He knew every word of them all by memory. Many times we fell asleep on his lap (if we were lucky) or sitting at his feet.

There was a request in the Michigan Farmer magazine for the words to "The Irish Jubilee." Dad meticulously wrote out the words to this lengthy song and sent them in. Some time later he received a book, *Call of the Wild*, for his efforts.

He was very patriotic and civic minded. He served as councilman in the Village of Essexville for many years and took that commitment very seriously. He also served on the school board for years.

Dad loved to read. We had a 10- or 12-volume set of the World Book Encyclopedia. He referred to this source of knowledge many times, and read through the complete set at least twice. He had an excellent memory and pointed out landmarks whenever we traveled.

Dad's pay was cut down to one-third of the normal amount during the Depression. The telephone company employees worked two days one week, three days the next and then had the third week off. With this plan no one was laid off. We were fortunate as we had *some* money coming in. Mom and Dad managed with the garden and the food that was stored. They helped many families who were less fortunate. I remember Mother feeding some of the children in the neighborhood, bathing them, and washing their hair. She would let them wear some of our clothes until their clothes that she had washed dried. She said that you might be poor, but you can be clean.

Mother always wanted her children to go to college, "Because I never had the chance." Raymond wanted no part of college because he had met his one and only love. After high school Bernice attended the Bay City Junior College for two years. I had graduated from high school in 1933 at the age of sixteen (I was seventeen in July). I wanted to go to the University of Michigan School of Nursing, but at that time students had to be eighteen years old to be admitted. Bernice and two of her friends wanted to complete their degrees. There were no jobs available and money was scarce. It was Mother who figured a way to make her goal possible. Raymond and Betty moved into our house and kept house for Dad and Florence, who was in high school at the time. Mother rented part of a house on South Division Street near Packard Street in Ann Arbor. The house had been converted into a two-family house. It had a large living room, dining room, small kitchen, and pantry on the first floor. There was a large "dormitory-style" room upstairs with closets and bathroom. Mother encouraged me to go to the LS&A College in hopes that I would take the five-year nursing course in which I would get my BS degree in nursing. I did take courses in the LS&A College for one year, but all I wanted was to be a nurse. In 1934 I entered the School of Nursing and had to stay at the nurse's dormitory, Couzen's Hall. Bernice's two friends paid room and board, and a law student from Bay City had his lunch and dinner with us. Mother did this for two years. Bernice received her BA degree, majoring in English and Latin. Bernice took summer courses after that and received her master's degree.

Mother enjoyed Ann Arbor and took advantage of free music recitals, programs, and lectures that were offered. She showed much interest in the courses "her students" were taking.

The Statue of Liberty was unveiled in October 1886, so the Wubbena family did not see it when they arrived from Germany in July of 1886. Dad always wanted to see it. In 1938 Dad, Mom, and their three girls went out East with Bernice doing the driving. We stayed in tourist homes, private homes that rented rooms to travelers. They had neon signs or signs in the yard to advertise. In New York City we took the boat to the Statue of Liberty. We all climbed the many stairs on the inside—it was quite a thrill for all of us and an emotional experience for Dad. We took in West Point Academy, Washington, D.C., Gettysburg, Mount Vernon, and Niagara Falls. On our return Dad wanted us to have the experience of taking the boat from Cleveland to Detroit, an overnight trip. We put the car on the boat in the evening and had no cabins even though they might have been available. What a long night it was—sitting on wooden slatted chairs in the cold, damp night air—even though it was summer! As we neared Detroit, Dad started rounding up his flock. He spotted Mother with her big brimmed hat and made a rush to get her coralled, but ran into a mirrored wall which had her reflection.

When there was no one at home to drive the car, Mother took driving lessons and did very well. This enabled her and Father to visit friends, and to go to Standish to visit Charles and Mertie, and John and Laura. However, those years were short. Mother had an inherited eye disease: Fuch's Corneal Endothelial Dystrophy in both eyes. Corneal transplant is the only treatment for that disease and at that time corneal transplants were not too successful and the surgery was not recommended until she could no longer see to get around. The surgery was never performed.

Mom and Dad enjoyed their family. They often told some of the "cute" things we said or did as children. The two of them hid the Christmas tree, and after we children went to bed on Christmas Eve they brought it in and trimmed it, so it was a complete surprise to us when we got up Christmas morning. We had candle holders that clamped onto the branches of the tree. The candles were lit only on Christmas Night and watched closely because of the danger of fire. Santa left only a pair of mittens, stocking cap, candy mints, and perhaps one toy. Mother spent days baking and making candies. Our Christmas dinner was always special with the best linen tablecloth, napkins, and china. We had all the trimmings even though we were alone.

The big house had served Mom and Dad well, but finally the four children left home. They sold the big house in 1947 and moved into a smaller house that Raymond had built at 1113 Borton Avenue, Essexville. It was a two-bedroom cozy home, and they were very comfortable there. For many years they had a garden at this location also, until Raymond sold the vacant lot.

They also enjoyed their grandchildren. They often took the bus to Ann Arbor to visit us, and many times took one of our children back with them for a visit. These visits were treasured experiences for our children. Dad would play "Skin the Cat," "Chee Chee," and "The Victim Game." He always had stories, puzzles, and games to entertain them. He took them to the fire station and for walks. When they went to the dairy to buy milk, he would buy them an ice cream cone—a real treat.

After Dad retired, the county hired him to accompany patients being transferred from Bay County to the Traverse City State Hospital by car. At times he read water meters for the Village of Essexville. He also helped his grandson, Charles, fold and deliver newspapers.

In 1949, while at a family Christmas dinner at our home on Hutchins Street in Ann Arbor, Dad had his first slight stroke (now called TIA). He had several more as the years passed and then developed congestive heart failure. In spite of Mother's poor vision, she managed to care for him at home except when he was hospitalized for short periods. She kept his medications in certain locations, and the location determined the time the medication was to be administered as she could not read the labels. She marked on paper when she gave him medication. Dad passed away in his sleep on September 30, 1962, in his home at 1113 Borton Avenue, Essexville, Michigan.

I do not remember my mother or my father ever saying, "I love you." However, things they did or said gave us the feeling of security and being loved. This was evidenced on my wedding day when Dad said to my husband, "Be good to her or we'll take her back!" We had dental care, medical care when needed, and we were encouraged to further our education and to always do our best. I hope they realized how much they were loved and appreciated by their children.

I'm proud of my heritage and grateful to be a twig on two sturdy family trees. Henry was a good man, honest, and a good citizen, husband, and father. He was well-liked and respected by the men he worked with and by all who knew him. I loved him and was proud of him—he was my Grand Ole Dad.

Mother adjusted to her life without "Daddy" at 1113 Borton Avenue. Daughter Bernice who lived in Midland phoned her every day. Bernice and her husband Fred did her shopping and other chores on weekends. Their son Peter was her pride and joy. Neighborhood children were frequent visitors and Mother shared with them her homemade cookies and other treats.

As her vision worsened and her hearing became impaired, we were concerned about her safety and persuaded her to sell her house, which she did in May 1965.

She spent winters in Denver with Florence, and summers in Ann Arbor with me. She did what she could to help in a busy household as long as she was able. She was so appreciative of everything and anything that was done for her. Many times she said how good her sons-in-law Erwin Neubauer and Carroll Dick were to her.

A hearing aid did little to alleviate her increased deafness and cataract surgery did not improve her vision inasmuch as she still had the Fuch's Corneal Endothelial Dystrophy and she was declared legally blind. As time went on she spent most of her daytime hours sitting in her room. Often when I came home from work I could hear her praying.

She began to dread air travel even though we arranged assistance for her. Then she did not want to go to Denver because she wanted to die in Michigan.

In the early 1970s homes in our quiet neighborhood in Ann Arbor were being burglarized. Houses all around us were broken into—some more than once. I was working and Dick was gone days at a time building the house in South Boardman. There was evidence that there was an attempt to pry open our back door. When the well-patrolled house of Judge Elden next door was a target, we became alarmed. Our fear was that someone would break into our house, and that they would harm Mother. After discussing the situation with her, and other family members, it was agreed that she would go to Rest

Haven Homes in Grand Rapids, Michigan, a retirement facility with a medical wing for those needing nursing care, which she did in the summer of 1973.

Rest Haven is affiliated with the Gospel Hall and Mother was content with the fellowship and the tender loving care she received there. In the fall of 1974 Mother fell and broke her hip. From that time on she became more bedridden and her world became very small. Whenever we visited she was mentally alert and content and showed interest in people she knew.

When Aunt Ella and Uncle George moved to Rest Haven, Ella visited with Mother and checked on her. We moved to South Boardman in 1976. When we visited Mother, Dick would take Aunt Ella out for lunch and I spent the time with Mother.

A few times we brought Aunt Ella back to South Boardman to spend a couple of days with us. These were treasured times. She would play the organ and sing and tat—her fingers would fly as the thread went in and out of that shuttle! And we would visit! She would tell us about her visits at Margaret and Everett Pickett's in Tennessee and how much she enjoyed the fresh fruits and vegetables from their garden. What a sense of humor she possessed. She was a delightful houseguest. She returned to Grand Rapids by bus.

After Mother began having medical problems, it was comforting to know a loved one was there to check on her. I frequently called Aunt Ella for an update on Mother, and she would call me if there was a change in Mother's condition.

Complications of age gradually took their toll. Mother crossed the "swelling tide" at Rest Haven on August 26, 1977, at the age of eighty-nine and was laid to rest next to her dear "Daddy" in Elm Lawn Cemetery, Bay City, Michigan.

PS: Little things I remember about my Dad:

Eileen—a funny name: "I lean against a post."

When we children cried, he'd say, "Get the bucket and collect the tears for goldfish."

If we spilled something or bumped into something, "Knock the horns off the animal."

If something did not go right, "It went haywire."

He told us that if we went to jail all we'd get to eat was bread and water. (That was enough to keep us out!)

Do a good job and you'll get ahead.

When asked about the warm weather on his wedding day, June 14, 1911, he said, "Yes, it was thawing."

He gave much importance to reputation.

A policeman was our friend.

On December 29 Dad excitedly told us that he had heard that a man was coming to Bay City that day with as many eyes as there were days in the year. Then, after a slight pause and softly, he added "Yet."

On December 30 he would tell us that a man was coming that day who had as many noses as there were days of the year, then add, "Yet."

Dad called Mother "Mom."

Mother called Dad "Daddy."

Additional Memories of My Parents
by Florence Wubbena Neubauer, Daughter of Henry Wubbena

My parents, Henry and Martha Link Wubbena, were married at my mother's home in West Branch, Michigan, on June 14, 1911. Minnie Wubbena and Frank Link were attendants. During the evening there was a shivaree. This custom consisted of a noisy reception by uninvited guests for the newly married couple on their wedding night, using kettles, horns, etc. as noisemakers. In order to get rid of them the groom was expected to pay the demonstrators with food, drinks, and money so that the newlyweds could have some privacy. Dad received the reputation of being the most generous groom in town.

They went to Loranger's (a train stop) by horse and buggy to catch the midnight train to Bay City, where Dad worked. On arrival they went to the home they had rented on Second Street.

All of their furniture had not arrived and they had no dining table. They upset the wash tub, spread it with a tablecloth Mom had made, and had a lunch Mom's mother sent with them. Included was a jar of pickled herring that Dad loved.

All four of their children were born at the house on Second Street. As time went on, Mom and Dad realized they had outgrown the house and they looked for another place to live. In the spring of 1919 they found and purchased an older home on three-fourths of an acre in Essexville, a village adjacent to Bay City. They moved in June of 1919. Both Mom and Dad worked long, hard hours to make the place liveable. Canning and preserving vegetables and fruits kept them busy in the summer. They had their own chickens.

In the fall they purchased a Holstein cow. We had our own milk, cream, butter, and cottage cheese. We sold milk to a neighbor and also to Dad's boss, who came to our home from Bay City to get it. He also purchased a loaf of Mom's home-baked bread twice a week when she baked it.

Our family doctor was the same Doctor Warren that took care of Dad when he had his finger amputated. Dr. Warren had moved his practice from Standish to Bay City. We had the usual childhood diseases and some that were more severe. Throughout our illnesses we were never neglected. Mom gave us good nursing care. She took our temperatures routinely and gave our medications on time with plenty of fluids. She bathed and sponged and kept us as comfortable as possible. She kept good records. Sometimes when she called the doctor he would say, "Well, you know what to do." During periods of long illnesses Dad sat with us in the evenings so Mom could get some much-needed rest.

Sundays were church days. They got up at the usual time, took care of the cow and milk, froze six quarts of ice cream. Mom put the roast in the oven and prepared vegetables for the noon meal before she caught the nine o'clock streetcar for the ten o'clock morning meeting of the Gospel Hall in Bay City. Dad always put the vegetables in the oven according to Mom's instructions so that dinner could be almost ready when Mom returned at twelve. We always had dinner in the dining room on Sunday. We children caught the two o'clock streetcar for Sunday School at three. Very often friends dropped in on Sunday afternoon and had Sunday night supper with us at five. We caught the 6:30 streetcar for the night meeting at 7:30. When we got home, we finished the ice cream that was left as there was no way to keep it frozen for a longer period.

On Monday Dad always helped Mom fill the copper boiler to get hot water to wash. During the early years she washed on a washboard and there was a hand roller to squeeze water out of the wet clothes. Clothes were always rinsed twice. When Dad was home on vacation one year, he observed Mom washing clothes on a washboard. He thought about this and then quoted a passage from the Bible to support his decision. He told Mom to go and buy an electric washer. She chose an Apex and what a labor-saving device it was! During the winter the clothes were hung around the house to dry.

The whole year was planned and well organized. They always took advantage of the January white sales and Mom hemmed sheets, pillow cases, dish towels and hand towels. Mom made her own house dresses, aprons, and sewed for us three girls.

Spring house cleaning followed with wall washing, airing of mattresses and cleaning of coil bed springs, carpet beating, washing windows and curtains, and polishing furniture. On her hands and knees, using a scrub brush, Mom cleaned the carpets by washing them on the floor with ammonia water and rinsing them in clear water. Any necessary redecorating was done at this time.

Then came the garden with canning and preserving of fruits and vegetables for the winter. Eggs were very expensive during the winter months when the chickens did not lay. So, in the summer months when eggs were plentiful, Mom put many dozen in water glass to preserve them for winter baking. We had fresh eggs for eating only during the summer months.

We were all assigned chores and in the evening when the daily work was completed, we children gathered on the corner with the neighbor children to play summer games. These included "Hide and Seek," "Pussy Wants a Corner," "Pom-Pom Pull Away," and "Lay-Low." Sometimes we played baseball in a vacant lot nearby. When there were not enough players, we played scrub, a version of baseball with few players. When we were older, we picked cherries, raspberries, and strawberries at truck gardeners nearby for our own spending money.

In the fall Mom and Dad purchased a quarter of beef and a pig. Mom canned meat, made sausage and head cheese, and on a Saturday she and Dad fried out the lard. Mom's brother, Garrett, always smoked the hams for us in his smokehouse. Mom and Dad also made sauerkraut on a Saturday. Mom cut the cabbage while Dad stomped it in the crocks with a large wooden mallet.

Then came preparations for the Christmas holidays. Baking consisted of fruitcake, lebkuchen, springerle, pfeffernusse, and frosted sugar cookies. Candy consisted of divinity, seafoam, fudge, and homemade hand-dipped chocolates.

The Christmas tree was always a big part of our Christmas and we always had the prettiest one in the neighborhood! Mom and Dad took such pride in trimming it. Some of our ornaments were hand-painted. During the holiday season they sang "O Tannenbaum, O Tannenbaum" and "Silent Night" in German with the other carols. They had Madam Schumann-Heink's Victrola record of "Silent Night" sung in German. They always felt that no one could sing it as she did.

Friends from the Gospel Hall dropped in frequently and we would have a good hymn sing. I remember when friends from the G.H. had a sleigh ride and ended up at our house for a hymn sing and refreshments. Our parting hymn was always "God Be with You Till We Meet Again."

As we children were growing we again outgrew our house. In 1925 Mom and Dad had a custom-designed house built on our land where the crabapple tree had stood. The folks had the barn at the old house torn down and a garage built for each of the houses. Our new home's many conveniences made us feel as if we were living in luxury! We were proud of it and were taught to take care of it.

The following year the Consumers Power Utility Company installed a gas line in front of our home. Mom and Dad purchased a gas stove with a rubbage burner on the side for the kitchen. They moved the wood stove to the basement, where it was often used for baking and canning. In later years they heated the home with gas.

Dad was known for his good sense of humor and Mom always went along with it. She said she married him for his winning ways. One time we were cleaning dresser drawers and found a box of treasures Mom had stored there. Among these were hat pins, decorative combs for hair, a pair of glasses, and two postcards Dad had sent to her. One read I.W.W.K.H.N. Being curious we asked her what that meant. She laughed and told us the story.

Before they were married or had any strings attached, the telephone company sent Dad up north to install telephone lines. While he was gone, Mom dated one of her other boyfriends and Dad heard about it. He wanted to let her know that he knew it and he figured out a way. He sent the card with only the letters on it. After considerable thought and study it dawned on her. The song "I Wonder Who's Kissing Her Now" was popular. He had simply taken the first letter of each word and sent it to her. They laughed about that many times over.

Dad often presented us with thought-provoking puzzles and had a clever answer to help us remember it. One time he asked if a person got more tired by standing or walking. After we expressed our opinions, he told us that a person got more tired standing. When he walked he always had one leg in the air resting.

Both he and Mom tried to humor us out of our tantrums but were not always successful.

Dad often sang old songs to us as he rocked in his brown leather upholstered oak rocker. Neighbor kids were there often and enjoyed the entertainment. We all learned the songs and as we grew older we sang along with him.

Dad never wanted to drive a car and they did not purchase one until Raymond was old enough to get a driver's license. Their first car was a 1927 four-door, blue Dodge sedan. Life again became much easier as we had our own transportation. Periodically we were able to take weekend and day trips to visit Mother's family in West Branch and Dad's brothers and their families in Standish. We always looked forward to these trips because we played with our cousins and became aware of and enjoyed the humor the Standish cousins had inherited from their parents.

The Great Depression came in 1929. Dad called Mom to tell her that the stock market had crashed and the banks in Bay City were closing their doors. After talking things over, Mom walked to the Essexville bank and drew out their small amount of savings. The following day that bank closed also.

Men were out of work and there were no jobs available. Soup lines were long. People were losing their homes and real estate was dirt cheap. Mom and Dad had always purchased their flour, sugar, and navy beans in large quantities, and I remember Mom taking staples to people who had little.

Ray also worked at odd jobs only. He and Betty moved in with us. We shared what we had.

The old house was sold, but the buyers were unable to make the payments. The folks allowed them to live there if they could make the interest payments only.

In 1935 Bernice had received her BA degree in education, specializing in teaching Latin and English; Ray was working full time at the Chevrolet plant in Bay City; and Dad's employment was better. Raymond and Betty had a home built on Scheurmann Street, a short distance from where we lived. Later Ray went into the contracting business and built houses. Mom always said how important it was for the contractor to make suggestions in order to make the houses more convenient. This Ray did and people were very happy with his work. When he could purchase only green lumber, he went out of the contracting business. He then got a job in Plant Protection at the Chevrolet plant in Bay City. Things were improving.

By 1938 all of the children had left home but me, and Mom learned how to drive in order to assure continued mobility. Finally, when I left, there was no need for the big house. They sold it and purchased a smaller one that Raymond and Betty had built for themselves when he was in the contracting business. It was a white, well-insulated, Cape Cod–style house with green shutters. It stood on a corner lot. It was shaded with lovely, large maple trees. It was a two-bedroom, one-bathroom home, and had a living room, dining room, kitchen, and full basement. It had birch floors and woodwork throughout with gas heat. They were very comfortable.

Some years later, when Dad had sufficiently recovered from a hospital illness, the doctor asked Dad if he wanted to go home. Excitedly, Dad asked, "Can I? Oh, yeh, Mom and I have it so nice!" It was a sharp contrast from his first home in the United States.

Dad and Mom celebrated their fiftieth wedding anniversary in June of 1961 by holding open house during afternoon and evening hours from Monday through Friday one week in their home. During this time, friends stopped in. They received gifts, flowers, and cards. Some cards were from friends from early married life. They relived the great times they had had together. On Sunday the children hosted a dinner party at the Republic Hotel in Bay City for the family and relatives who lived in the area. Some had attended their wedding. Everyone seemed to enjoy the memories of their wedding day.

In later life Mom and Dad reflected on the past and mentioned the many changes that had taken place during their lives together. They had four children of whom they were mighty proud. Raymond ended up as a finish carpenter for the University of Michigan. Bernice had a master's degree and taught Latin and English for many years. Later she worked for Dow Chemical as a secretary. After Lois reared her three children she worked at the University of Michigan Health Service and retired from that health care facility as Director of Nursing Services. Florence got a diploma in nursing from the University of Michigan and a BS degree at the University of Colorado. She completed the course work for a master's degree in nursing administration. She retired from the position of a contractor specialist for the federal government's Medicare program. All of the children were loving, devoted, and caring. All were happily married.

Our parents' lives were complete, full, and happy. Their life's work together had ended and they were ready to receive their reward.

Henry Wubbena's Forty-one Years with the Telephone Companies
by Lois Wubbena Dick

Installing telephones and placing new lines in the early 1900s was a lot different than today.

Henry began working for the Northeastern Telephone Company as a lineman at Pinconning, Michigan on July 5, 1902. The company was building a long distance line from Bay City north to Alpena at the time. His first job was digging holes and setting up poles.

The line crew of twenty to thirty men traveled with horses and wagons and lived in tents along the route. The moveable camp was composed of a kitchen and mess hall, a man's camp, and an animal and equipment camp — all under canvas. Henry always said that the food furnished the men was very good. For a ten hour day he was paid one dollar including food and lodging. Before the lines were strung, trees along the right-of-way had to be cut to protect the wires.

This toll line extended out of Bay City to Standish and from there to Pine River, then north along the Detroit and Mackinac railway to Alpena. By the time the crew broke camp for the winter on January 26, 1903 at Alpena, two feet of snow stood around the tents.

During the winter of 1902–1903 Henry assisted in building exchanges at Pinconning and Standish. In the spring of 1903 he went out with the toll crew which built the line north of Standish to Gaylord and on to Elmira where it connected with the Bell System. By the time the circuit was strung between Gaylord and Elmira, the crew had to dig through four feet of snow on the level before they reached the ground and could start digging the holes for the telephone poles. He helped install the toll line from Gaylord to Cheboygan, finished in 1904; from Alpena north to Millersburg in the same year; and from West Branch to Rose City in 1905. Still more difficult conditions were encountered in Alpena and Presque Isle counties. Rock formations were found there, and it was necessary to blast holes for the telephone poles instead of digging them.

At each new town Henry helped build exchanges, backed up the switchboard, ran lines to phones in the towns, and installed the phones. In 1924 it was estimated that Henry had set about 17,000 poles for new lines and about 3,000 in repair work, and that he put up about 1,000 miles of copper wire in circuits.

Exchanges in those days were often established in the same building with some other business that would likely be open for long hours and perhaps on Sundays. Drug stores were favored locations: in Gaylord, Fox's drug store; in Rose City, Karcher's drug store; in Standish, Forsyth and Downer's drug store. At West Branch the exchange was in Grant French's insurance office. The manager of the business where the exchange was located furnished the telephone operator, and many pioneer switchboard operators in northeastern Michigan sold bottles of liniment between calls from the telephone subscribers. The manager received a percentage of the telephone business for looking after the exchange.

When a call came in to the exchange, a light on the switchboard turned on. The operator then plugged in at the light and that made the connection. The operator had earphones and a mouthpiece into which she spoke. The operator would answer and then direct the call. Very few people had a phone in their own home. If the party did not have a phone, someone would have to notify that person, and he would come to the exchange (or to a phone) to receive the message and return the call. Local boys were often paid to notify people that they had received a call.

People who had phones were on a "party line"—more than one person on one line. The incoming call was identified by the number of rings, and the number of rings were assigned to a certain party. It was not unusual to have the operator and the other people on the same line listen to the conversation. In many cases news and gossip spread very fast.

In some rural areas where there were no businesses nearby, the exchange was in a private home. I was told that around 1910 or 1912 in the area in which I now live (Boardman Township in Kalkaska County) there were three exchanges in one home: the local Farmer's Co-op Company; The Swaverly, a private company; and what is now known as the Michigan Bell Telephone Company. The latter handled the long distance calls.

On January 1, 1909, the Northeastern Co. was purchased by the Michigan State Telephone Company, now the Michigan Bell Telephone Company. Henry was transferred from West Branch to Bay City shortly thereafter and started work there February 15, 1909. The offices and the exchange were located in a building at Fourth and Washington Avenues. (That area is now a parking lot. The Michigan Bell building is now located on Center Avenue and occupies the whole block between Madison and Monroe Avenues.)

Henry often recalled the devastating sleet storm on Washington's Birthday, 1922, that paralyzed the service in the Bay City area. Henry was in charge of the repair crews that worked day and night for nearly three weeks to restore service in that section of the state. It was nearly six months before all the damage caused by the storm was remedied.

When the lines north of Bay City were out of commission one day in late March, 1924, Henry went out early the following morning to determine what equipment and how many men would be needed to restore service. The company estimated that service could be restored by evening, but because of Henry's unusual familiarity with the circuits, he and his associates were able to have the first circuit opened by ten o'clock that morning.

Henry retired from Michigan Bell Telephone Company at the age of sixty-five. He had been employed as a senior stockman the last two years. He was proud of the fact that in all of his years of service, he had never had a serious accident. He was also proud to be a member of the Telephone Pioneers of America.

Memories of My Grandfather, Henry Wubbena
by Carol Dick, Daughter of Lois Dick

The most outstanding things about Henry were:

a. His restraint. I never heard him say anything bad about anyone.

b. His 'Mark Twain' sense of wry humor and imagination. For example, he called his razor-strap "The Persuader," in the event that a child might need some "encouragement" to behave! And, God is smart, putting ears in a convenient place to hang your glasses on. Or, an easy way to count cows: count the legs and divide by four.

His imagination was reflected by the stories he told: a story about the little man who grew from Henry's sawed-off finger (the result of a lumber camp accident); and his poem about the chicken (vs.) the incubator (where he could *imagine* how both felt!) [see the poem page 489].

c. He had a few riddles and jokes to entertain us. In short, Henry was charming and wonderful!

Some of the stories I've heard *about* him are:

1. Martha said of him, "He had winning ways."

2. He sobbed at Lois' wedding (a surprise to me, since he was so reserved).

3. When his son, Raymond, was offered a promotion, Henry's advice was to choose happiness; not what the "world" would have him do, but his *own* intrinsic satisfaction.

4. His son, Raymond, fell off the roof of the house one Christmas Eve. My guess is that Henry's vivid imagination could fuel any child's imagination to the extent that he could try to sight "The Magic Elf" himself!

5. He got a JOLT while working on the telephone wires, and lived to tell about it!

6. He had dental work done without pain medications (to save money?).

He was tough, but also a kind and gentle man. I adored him!!

Stories Told Me by My Grandfather, Henry F. Wubbena
by Charles L. Wubbena, Son of Raymond Wubbena

He, Henry, retired from the Michigan Bell Telephone Co. He had helped set most of the telephone poles north of Bay City in the early days of telephone. The men would live in tents and boarding houses while working on those lines and were gone from home for weeks at a time.

He related to me how he was called out with another lineman on a holiday because of some "trouble." They knew just about "where" the trouble was, but were not sure of exactly which pole, so they flipped a coin. Grandpa "lost" so the other man had to go up the pole. It proved to be his last pole climb; he was electrocuted on the pole. Grandpa would always point that pole out to me whenever we went over the Third Street Bridge in Bay City. He would always wipe a tear away when we passed or when he spoke of his "experience."

When he was a little boy on the farm his parents had always cut his hair. They only went to town on special occasions, so he didn't know all the proper methods of etiquette. But his parents had always told him to knock on a stranger's door, and that's what he did when he first went to the barber shop in town!

He was going to town one time and he asked his mother if there was anything she wanted. She thought, "He can take these two letters to the post office," and so she gave him the money for the stamps. When he came back he put the nickel back on the table for her. She asked, "Didn't you mail the letters?" He said, "Yes." "Well, didn't you buy stamps?" she said. His reply: "No, I put the letters in the slot when they weren't looking!"

He, Henry, retired from the Michigan Bell Telephone Co. in the 1940s, and for two years helped me deliver papers in Essexville, Michigan. He was always willing to help me and take me fishing when I was growing up. I remember going ice fishing and he told me to be careful of the ice spud when putting a hole in the ice; of course I knew I could do it, no problem. But— you guessed it—the spud went through the ice down into the water of Saginaw Bay. The first thing I did was look down at him. He acted like he wasn't watching, but he was. He wanted to know why I looked at him. Well, my Dad (Ray Wubbena) drove about twenty to twenty-five miles back home for the rake and we fished out that spud. I have that spud today and every time I see it the memories return.

I remember sawing up logs or old utility poles for kindling wood for their furnace. They had always burned coal so they burned a lot of logs also. I am determined that he always gave me the "hard end of the saw," because I would always tire before him, even if we switched ends! He was always a hard worker. He could cut all day long, with or without my "help."

Grandpa never owned a gun so we never went hunting together. I do remember going to his house, or him coming to ours, to listen to "Amos-n-Andy." (This was way before TV.) In all the times we spent together, and all the things we did together, I never heard him say a bad word about anyone or, for that matter, about anything. He certainly was a great friend and grandfather.

Memories of My Grandparents, Henry and Martha Wubbena by Peter Frederick VanKleek, Son of Bernice Wubbena VanKleek

Being so young when Grandpa died,* I have more memories of Grandma. Some things I remember are the weekends spent in Essexville. Grandpa and

---

*Ed. Note: Peter was six years old when Henry Wubbena died.

Grandma would take me down Burns Street to the park at the river. The main stop on these outings would be the swings. To my pleas of higher, higher, Grandpa would dutifully push. At that time there was still a beach there, and by the time we started home I usually had my pockets stuffed with pretty rocks and shells. It was on one of those outings that I received my first recollection of ice cream cones. To Grandma's cries of "Not so fast!" I polished off most of Grandpa's treat.

On these stays, Grandma would often make a treat that I wish I could taste again. Though I can't remember what it was, she always served it in small white bowls with wheat stem decorations on the side. I could always count on being reminded not to take such big bites. Grandma would ask Grandpa to go get a shovel to help me eat.

To a child the garage, with all of Grandpa's tools and telephone equipment, was a wonderland. I imagine he was glad when I went home and he had a chance to straighten up the mess I left.

Saturday nights were always spent in the living room. The two shows that I remember watching on TV were *Lawrence Welk* and *Mitch Miller*. Grandma and Grandpa would sing along with Mitch and I was coaxed to join in and follow the bouncing ball. Grandma had a vibrating footstool that I would drag out of the hall closet and sit on during these evenings. I often wish I had that old stool now. That hall closet also held another treasure that I would drag out and leave around the house: the small bars of soap that Grandma kept for company. I used to love to smell the different brands.

Every few months I'll drive to Essexville and visit the riverside park I mentioned earlier. On these trips I always drive by the house on the corner of Burns and Borton and slow down. I can still picture the inside in great detail. I sure do miss Grandma and Grandpa and thank the Lord for the privilege of having a wonderful family and childhood.

Songs Henry Wubbena Used to Sing

Set forth below are songs that our father, Henry Wubbena, used to sing. Of course, we all knew them and sang them, too. (LWD & FWN)

The Irish Jubilee
A short time ago, boys, an Irishman named Doherty
Was elected to the Senate by a very large majority.
He felt so elated that he went to Dennis Cassidy
Who owned there a barroom with a very large capacity.
He said to Cassidy, "Go over to the brewer

For a thousand kegs of lager beer and give it to the poor.
Go over to the butcher shop and order up a ton of meat.
Be sure you see the boys and girls have all they want to drink
and eat.
Send out invitations in twenty different languages
And don't forget to tell them to bring their own sandwiches.
They've made me their senator and so to show my gratitude
They'll have the finest supper ever given in this latitude.
Whatever the expenses are, remember I'll put up the tin
And anyone who doesn't come, be sure you do not let him in."

Cassidy at once sent out the invitations.
Everyone that came was a credit to his nation.
Some came on bicycles because they had no fare to pay
And those that did not come at all made up their minds to stay
away.
Two by three they marched into the dining hall
Young men, old men, girls that were no men at all.
Blind men, deaf men, men who had their teeth in pawn,
Single men and double men, men who had their glasses on.
Before many minutes, nearly every chair was taken
Till the front rooms and mushrooms were packed to suffocation.
When everyone was seated, they started to lay out the feast,
Then Cassidy said, "Rise up and give us each a cake of yeast."
He then said, as manager, that he would try to fill the chair.
We all sat around and we looked at the bill of fare.

Pigs heads, gold fish, mocking birds and ostriches
Ice cream, cold cream, Vaseline and sandwiches.
There were blue fish, green fish, fish hooks and partridges
Fish balls, snow balls, cannon balls and cartridges.
Then we ate oatmeal till we could hardly stir about.
Ketchup, hurry up, sweet kraut and sauerkraut.
Dressed beef, naked beef, beef with all its dresses on
Soda crackers, fire crackers, Limburger cheese with tresses on.
Beef steaks and mistakes were down upon the bill of fare.
Roast ribs, spare ribs, ribs that we couldn't spare.
Reindeer, snow deer, dear me and antelope.
The women ate the muskmelon. The men say they can't elope.
Red herring, smoked herring, herring from old Erin's isle.
Bologna and fruit cake, sausages a half a mile.
Hot corn, cold corn, corn salve and honeycomb.

Reed birds, read books, sea bass and sea foam.
Fried liver, baked liver, Carter's little liver pills.
Everyone was wondering who was going to pay the bills.

For dessert we had toothpicks, ice picks and skipping rope.
We washed them all down with a big piece of shaving soap.
We ate everything that was down on the bill of fare,
Then looked on the back of it to see if any more was there.
The band played horn pipes, clay pipes, and Irish reels,
And we danced to the music of the wind that shook the barley
fields.

The piper played old tunes, spittoons so very fine
Then in came Piper Heidrick and handed him a glass of wine.
They welted the floor till they could be heard for miles around.
When Gallagher was in the air, his feet were never on the
ground.
As fine a lot of dancers you never cast your eyes upon,
And those that could not dance at all were dancing with their
slippers on.
Some danced jig steps, door steps, and highland flings.
Murphy took his knife out and tried to cut a pigeon wing.
When the dance was over, Cassidy then told us to join hands
together

And sing this good old chorus:
Should old acquaintance be forgot
Wherever we may be
Think of the good old times we had
At the Irish Jubilee.

Florella

Down in the valley where the violets fade and bloom
There lies our own Florella in her cold and silent tomb.
She died not broken-hearted nor of sickness' lingering spell,
But in an instant parted from the home she loved so well.

The moon was shining brightly; the stars were shining too,
When up to her bedroom window her jealous lover drew.
"Come, love, and let us wander down by the meadows gay,
And undisturbed we'll ponder and name our wedding day."

Deep, deep into the forest he led his love so dear.
"It's all for you, dear Edward, that I should linger here.

The way seems dark and dreary, and I'm afraid to stay.
Of wandering I've grown weary. I would retrace my way."

"Retrace your way, no never. No more these woods you'll roam.
You must bid farewell for ever to parents, friends and home.
For in these woods I have you and from me you cannot fly.
No human hand can save you. Florella, you must die."

Then kneeling down before him, she pleaded for her life,
When into her lily-white bosom, he plunged his deadly knife.
"What have I done, dear Edward, that you should take my life?
I've always been kind and loving, and would have been your wife."

"Farewell, dear loving parents, your face I'll see no more.
Each night you'll wait my coming at our little cottage door.
Dear Edward, I forgive you," was her last and parting breath.
Her pulse had stopped its beating. Her eyes were closed in death.

The birds sang in the morning and mournful was the sound,
When they found our own Florella lying upon the ground.
She died not broken-hearted nor of sickness' lingering spell,
But in an instant parted from the home she loved so well.

Methusilah

Methusilah ate what was put on his plate
And never as people do now
Did he note the amount of the calorie count,
He ate because it was chow.
He cheerfully chewed each morsel of food
Unmindful of doubts or of fears
That his health might be hurt
With some fancy dessert
And he lived over 900 years!

When Pa Is Sick

When Pa is sick, He's scared to death,
An Ma an' us just hold our breath.
He crawls in bed, an' puffs an' grunts,
An' does all kinds of crazy stunts.
He wants "Doc Brown" an' mighty quick
For when Pa is ill, he's awful sick.
He gasps and groans, an' sort of sighs,
He talks so queer, an' rolls his eyes.

Ma jumps an' runs, an' all of us,
An' all the house is in a fuss.
An' peace an' joy is mighty scarce—
When Pa is sick, it's something fierce.

When Ma Is Sick

When Ma is sick, she pegs away.
She's quiet, though, not much to say.
She goes right on a doin' things,
An' sometimes laughs, or even sings.
She says she don't feel so well,
But then it's just a kind of spell,
She'll be all right tomorrow sure,
A good old sleep will be the cure.
An' Pa he sniffs an' makes no kick,
For women folk is always sick.
An' Ma, she smiles, lets on she's glad,
For when Ma is sick, it ain' so bad.

Leghorn Hens
by Henry Wubbena

Two leghorn hens one nice spring day
Conversed about the modern way.
One said now in this day and age
Production seems to be the rage.
We lay our eggs the same old way
Into the nests of straw and hay.
Our master gathers them in store
Just as he did in days of yore.
I think it's time to set and hatch,
It takes three weeks to bring a batch.
An incubator stood nearby
And heard this hen both talk and sigh.
He then spoke up and said aloud:
"You chickens need not feel so proud,
I'll do your hatching for you now.
We do not need you hens no how.
I'll show you how to do these tricks
I'll hatch about a thousand chicks
While you are setting to bring about

> Just ten or twelve or there about."
> The hens when all this they heard
> Said, "We will take him at his word.
> We need not lay or set these days,
> Our master had the modern ways.
> Vacations now are all the go
> We will take ours now also."
> For two weeks not an egg was laid.
> The master wondered what had made
> His fowls quit laying when they should,
> He always had been feeding good.
> When he inquired the hens replied,
> "That the incubator there inside
> Had told them that they were no use
> And scoffed at them with much abuse,
> That they decided to retire
> And let the master just admire
> That new fandangled modern hen."
> They hoped he'd change his mind by then.
> The master said, "Get busy you!
> I've got the hatcher that is true.
> But keep on laying right along
> The incubator there was wrong.
> Without the eggs he cannot hatch
> So hurry up and lay a batch."

The following letter was found among the papers Henry had put away. It is handwritten on paper with a letterhead, which reads: Headquarters, Army Air Forces Pilot School, Office of the Post Signal Officer, Hendricks Field, Sebring, Florida. It is not dated, but since the writer refers to Henry's retirement being the following day, the letter must have been written on November 20, 1943. The noteworthy feature of this man's thoughts is the high regard in which Henry was held by his fellow workers at the Bell Telephone Company. The letter reads:

Dear Henry,

On this eve of retirement, I wish to congratulate you on ending your long and faithful career with the Bell Telephone Company. I am sure you are deserving of your anticipated long desired vacation.

Your friends are many and spread throughout the land and I know their memory of your faithfulness will live for many years, and the management will more than ever realize your true worth.

I recall the calendar you kept and upon which you used to record the weeks remaining before retirement. The speed in which these weeks have passed makes one realize more than ever that time truly has wings.

Do you recall the many times I drove to Bay City for a visit with you and Grant and others. After these visits I could go back to my job with a much brighter outlook on different phases of my own life, because that sweet disposition of yours neutralized to a great extent that sour and rugged one which I possess.

As a matter of fact Henry, I also have gotten a great deal of pleasure in the many letters from Dave Larson and others in Saginaw. Dave keeps me posted on Central Division activities and I have appreciated this just as all men appreciate home news when far from home and during times like this.

I would like no one thing better than to be present at your party, but though I cannot be there in body I will be thinking of you.

Best of luck and enduring happiness I am your friend—

(signed) Dewey Solomon

Not only was Henry faithful in his work for the phone company, he was faithful in caring for the business affairs of his family's old farm. Among his papers are also pages of the meticulously kept records of the finances concerned with rental fees, the annual paying of taxes, and his prorating of these money amounts among the four older children (i.e., John, Charles, Henry, and Talka). One wonders how it was decided that Henry would be the one to take care of this aspect of handling the old place. It must be that Henry's inborn ability to handle such matters had been recognized by his siblings.

TAALKE HENRIETTA WILHELMINE WUBBENA

(1881–1951)

by Her Niece, Catherine Wubbena

Taalke was born on August 16, 1881 in Neermoor, Germany, the fourth child of Jan and Catharina. She was named for her father's mother whose name had been Taalke Janssen, née Reuvezaad. She was nearly five years old when her parents brought her and her three older brothers to Standish, Michigan, in July 1886. Because of her young age, she had not attended school while living in Germany.

The Johnsfield School came into existence in 1894. Up until that time the children living in the vicinity of the Wubbena family went to school in town (Standish). Access to school records of 1894 and earlier is not available. By word of mouth we learned that John, Charles, and Henry attended school in Standish for four to six months. We do not know for what period Taalke attended. Her name is never listed in the record book of the Johnsfield School; the first Wubbenas to be listed are Minnie and Harry in September 1894. In later years listed are Emma, Freddie and Willie. So we assume Taalke attended neither the Johnsfield School nor Standish High School. Her mother died January 23, 1894. Taalke was twelve-and-a-half years old. There were six children younger than she, so she (and her father) felt it necessary for her to forego any further formal schooling. She did the best she could with cooking and keeping house for the family. Kind neighbors and friends were generous with help. Her mother had taught her some of the needlecrafts and so she was fairly skilled in knitting and some sewing.

Her cooking skills were lacking. The family referred to her bread as "a big mistake," but Talka pluckily kept baking it and would even take a loaf to a needy family or a grieving neighbor. In one of her letters to my dad, dated April 12, 1926, she refers to all the corn meal mush they ate as they ran around barefoot in those early years.

The name Taalke was shortened by the family by omitting one of the "a's." The final "e" was not silent in German, but was pronounced as an "a" and so her name came to be spelled Talka in English. For some unexplained reason members of her family often called her Talch, and we of the next generation called her Aunt Talch.

When living in Germany, home life was sheltered, comfortable, and surrounded with the culture of generations of tradition and the security of an established reputation of a family name. Talka was frail and her mother worried about her health, so she was indulged with tidbits and goodies. Uncles and aunts living nearby yielded to strong-minded Talka's whims and wishes, so she was accustomed to having her own way by the time they sailed for America. The changes in living conditions and the parents' attention to the pressing demands of getting acclimated to country life in the United States meant Talka's expectations received some severe jolts.

By summer of the next year after arrival in Standish her mother had a new baby girl (Minnie). Talka was maturing rapidly by the time another baby (Harry) arrived in June 1888. It would seem she could not have enjoyed the luxury of a period of teen-age thrills and "foolishness." By January of 1894, after her mother died, she was a mother-figure; she became her father's right-hand helper as he struggled with being a productive citizen, father, and supportive aide to his children's teachers. Talka studied at home while her younger brothers and sisters did their homework, so her basic elementary education was the equivalent of that of an eighth grade graduate.

The older brothers were working away from home much of the time. Jan was home evenings but away at work throughout the daytime. Talka had to maintain order in behavior as well as with the housekeeping. Despite being six years younger, Minnie was Talka's closest ally and tried to support her in all her efforts. The brothers were fun-loving and liked to play tricks on the girls. Talka, being "in charge" and easily upset by their pranks, was their favorite target. When Talka was about fifteen years old, John and Henry were working in town. One time when walking home after their day's work one said to the other, "What can we do to tease Talch and the girls?" A member of a neighbor family had been ill for several days, and the Wubbenas had been quite concerned. So, with straight faces, John and Henry said to Talka, "Poor Mr. _____ (Moessner, I think) died today. It's too bad. He was a good man. He'll be really missed by us all."

Talka immediately turned to Minnie, "Oh, my, the poor folks. We'll go right down." So, changing to what they thought would be proper, they put on their black dresses and hats, Talka wrapped up a loaf of her bread, and away they went on foot. When they knocked on the neighbor's door, who should open the door but the man who was supposed to have died. Poor Talka and Minnie! They did their best to maintain their composure, but couldn't completely hide their discomfiture. They had to tell why they had come. The neighbor and his family, knowing the Wubbena boys, understood how the girls felt and tried to soothe their embarrassment. But when the girls got back home their brothers were subjected to a tongue lashing, and not only on that day but for weeks afterward. Despite the teasing and pranks, there was never harshness or any sign of disloyalty when help for one another was needed. The bond of love and concern is expressed in every letter written throughout all the years of their lives.

Talka's father, Jan, came to feel that he needed to examine himself and declare a new commitment to Jesus Christ. He became interested in the preaching of the Gospel Hall Brethren. He became a born-again Christian* and entered into a whole-hearted fellowship with the Gospel Hall members. His daughters accompanied him to the services, became close friends with other young folks in the assembly, and even entertained preachers and their families in their home. Minnie, Emma, and Ella followed in their father's footsteps, and also became born-again; and for the remainder of their lives they were closely allied with the Gospel Halls in whatever cities they lived. Talka, however, like her brothers, maintained an independent position, feeling her Christianity could be expressed more adequately through close ties with folks who had a wide range of church memberships.

As the children grew and became somewhat self-sufficient, Talka decided to try working in town for a few hours a week. The Congregational Church was located on the southwest corner of the intersection of Court Street and West Cedar Avenue. Talka did some housework for the minister and his family, never missing an opportunity to learn and gain experience concerning how other folks lived and what their religious beliefs were. She was noted for

---

Ed. Note: The phrase "born-again" has become much used in recent years. The term has become trite, and tossed about a bit flippantly. In earlier years the full meaning applied to one who has, in a spiritual way, gone from "rags to riches." The nothingness of one's self is overwhelmed with the sense of the worth He places on each person—"I am something. He died for me. I am His child." The words of I John, chapter 3, verse 2 are full of meaning: "Beloved, *now* we are the sons of God." There is the assurance of being a new creature, i.e. "born again." The prayer expressed in the hymn, "Teach me, Lord, on earth to show, by my love how much I owe" comes from a full heart, and the gratitude from being born again.

her indomitable spirit; she never felt inferior nor did she lose pride in maintaining a dignified self-image. Throughout the years, more than once, I heard her refer to keeping "a stiff upper lip." For some period of time she worked in the office of the County Registrar of Deeds. I never heard how this came about or for what period of time she worked. The person holding the office of Registrar of Deeds was Harvey Chamberlain. He was a demanding taskmaster and later became a hard-headed businessman in the city of Standish. But Talka learned a lot, and spoke highly of Mr. Chamberlain. She also earned a salary which enabled her to help her sisters until they were qualified to be school teachers.

By 1910, three years after her father's death, she came to realize she needed the equivalent of a high school diploma to be admitted to a school of nursing. I do not know who or what influenced her to want to become a nurse. By the very nature of her makeup one can appreciate how self-demanding she would be; she would not accept a second-rate school program, nor would she acknowledge that she might lack the native ability to acquire the credentials that a top-notch program would expect from anyone aspiring to become a graduate. So, at the age of twenty-nine and with a stiff upper lip, she took courses at what was then called Ferris Institute in Big Rapids, Michigan. This school is now called Ferris State University. Then, at age thirty, she met the prerequisites and was admitted to the University of Michigan Nursing Program. At that time admission requirements were: students must be between twenty and thirty years of age, of sound health, with the physical and mental capacity for the duty of nurses (the interpretation of this last criterion is left to one's imagination). Favorable references from upstanding citizens of one's home environment carried great weight with the admissions committee. Talka had proved her worth and so references were readily forthcoming. I quote from the Bulletin published in May 1991 for the celebration of the centennial year of the School of Nursing: "Members of the first graduating classes emerged as leaders, charting the course toward our present systems for professional nursing education. They were pursuing training for nursing practice at a time when this was not commonplace and opportunities were limited. Formal instruction was scanty. Work with patients extended over long-hour days and seven day weeks. Whatever didactic teaching was provided occurred during the evening. From written accounts of students of that day, it is apparent that those women realized that in order to achieve their ambition to be 'trained nurses' they had to develop their own strategies for overcoming fear, for dealing with the adverse circumstances that characterized student life and for challenging the many limits that were imposed upon women and nurses."

And meet those challenges she did! In 1914 Aunt Talch was presented with her diploma and a few weeks later she had her certificate from the State Board of Nursing proving she had passed the exams and could now sign her name with R.N. attached. She was thirty-three years old. She had made many new friends with whom she would be closely associated for years to come.

For several months she did private duty nursing in the community surrounding Ann Arbor. In those days "private duty" was done in patients' homes where the nurse could not evade interaction with her patients' families. Doctors recommended specific nurses for their patients' needs. Talka had emerged from training with a commendable reputation and so did not want for practice of her profession. She had many humorous and interesting tales to tell of her experiences as a private duty nurse. Despite the fact that she enjoyed this area of nursing, she felt the call to join the Army Nurse Corps, and on January 16, 1918, she entered the service where she remained until May 1920. Her first assignment was to Letterman General Hospital in San Francisco. She later served in Vancouver, Washington. She became disabled while in the Army, having contracted tuberculosis of the bone. After being a patient in several hospitals she was released to her sister Minnie's home in Elgin, Illinois, where she made her home for the remainder of her life. She was confined to a wheelchair these later years.

Included here are two clippings which tell of her death on February 20, 1951, taken from the *Detroit News* and the *Arenac County Independent*.

Detroit News, February 25, 1951

NURSE HEROINE OF 1919 DIES
Devotion to Duty in Epidemic Recalled

Standish, Mich, Feb. 24—Arenac County's heroic nurse of World War I was buried here today. She died Tuesday in Los Angeles.

Funeral services for Miss Taalke H. Wubbena, 69, whose devotion to duty as an Army nurse robbed her of her own health, were held in the Howard funeral chapel.

Miss Wubbena was cited for her work during the influenza epidemic of 1919. The disease killed hundreds of soldiers at the California camp at which she was based.

Weakened by the long hours of work she later contracted tuberculosis of a bone and spent many years in a wheelchair.

Surviving are three sisters, Mrs. Minnie Gabler, of Elgin, Ill., Mrs. Emma Flutur, of Detroit, and Miss Ella Wubbena, of Standish, and five brothers, John and Charles, of Standish; Henry, of Bay City; Fred, of Seattle, Wash., and William, of Washington, D.C.

Arenac County Independent, February 28, 1951

OUTSTANDING WAR NURSE IS DEAD
Miss Taalke Wubbena Dies of Heart Ailment

Miss Taalke Henrietta Wubbena, outstanding Arenac County war nurse of World War I, died last Tuesday night in Los Angeles, Calif., where she had been spending the winter, following a heart attack. She was 69 years of age. The remains were flown from Los Angeles to Detroit and from there to the Howard Funeral Home here where funeral services were held Saturday afternoon. Burial was in the Woodmere Cemetery. William Ferguson of Detroit, a friend of the family, conducted the services.

She was born August 16, 1881, in Province Hanover, Germany, and came with her parents and three of her brothers to Standish when she was four years of age. When she was twelve years old the family was left motherless and Taalke became an able assistant to her father in rearing the youngest children. Her father died 13 years later.

After the children were old enough to be left she attended the University of Michigan at Ann Arbor where she was graduated as a nurse in 1914. She entered the United States Army from Elgin in 1918 and remained in service until May 20, 1920, after serving as a nurse in the Letterman General Hospital in San Francisco, Calif. She became disabled while in the Army and was hospitalized at the Letterman General Hospital and the Hines Hospital in Chicago, Ill. She was finally transferred to the home of her sister, Mrs. Minnie Gabler, in Elgin, Ill., where she continued to make her home.

In her wheel chair, she was cheered by her many friends but she, too, contributed much to her friends by her wise counsel and understanding sympathy. She was a life member of the Richard F. Jacobs Chapter, No. 54, Disabled Veterans of Elgin, and of the Jane A. Delano Post, American Legion, of Chicago.

Left to mourn their loss are three sisters, Mrs. Minnie Gabler and Miss Ella Wubbena of Elgin, Ill., and Mrs. Emma Flutur of Detroit; and five brothers, John and Charles of Standish, Henry of Essexville, Fred of Seattle, Wash., and William of Washington, D.C.; a number of nieces and nephews and a host of friends. Preceding her in death, besides her parents, was her brother, Harry, of Bruce's Crossing, in 1947.

The death of Miss Taalke Wubbena, sister of Charles and John Wubbena, revealed an interesting human interest happening. The event took place during World War I. Roscoe O. Bonisteel, present regent of the University of Michigan and up for re-election at the approaching April 2 election, was stationed at Vancouver, Wash., in the service of the United

States Army. He was stricken with a severe case of the flu, which spread over the entire country at that time, and when complications set in chances for his recovery were so slight that doctors, in consultation, agreed that his family should be notified. His nurse was standing by and from the conversation of the doctor and patient, learned that Bonisteel was a resident of Ann Arbor. She revealed to him that she was a graduate of the University Nursing School and through their mutual interest, she told him "not to worry, she would stand by and 'pull him through.'" "She did just that," Bonisteel revealed in a visit at the *Independent* office last Saturday, "and that is the reason I am in Standish today — to pay tribute to a nurse who gave her best to save my life." It was soon after World War I that Miss Wubbena was stricken with a malady that caused her to spend the rest of the days of her life in a wheel chair.

While living in Elgin throughout these later years, she taught English to German-speaking folks who came to the house. Some teaching was as a private tutor, and some was to several at a time as a class. Being skilled as a knitter, she taught knitting to young folks who were interested. Having a wide range of interests, she was exceptionally alert to all that was going on in the world; her pupils were exposed to conversations and discussions which proved helpful to them in more than the formal subject matter which had been the objective for their coming to her. One such person was Toni Ochs, a young woman who had come from Germany. She had no relatives or friends; someone directed her to Aunt Talch who discerned that this young lady had superior intellect as well as winning ways. With Talka's encouragement, teaching, and (?) financial help, Toni went to the University of Michigan where, after a few years she earned her Ph.D. degree. In the meantime she worked for doctors who wanted valuable medical literature translated from German. She spent many hours in the carrells of the main library of the University. Lois and I were student nurses at the time and felt privileged to become friends of Toni, subsequent to Aunt Talch's arranging our getting together. After a few years of this kind of work, Toni married Dr. Davis, one of the doctors she had worked for, and lived in Dexter, Michigan, which is close to Ann Arbor and the life she loved among the medical/university intelligentsia. She also taught English at the Pioneer High School in Ann Arbor.

Toni is an example of just one of the young folks whom Aunt Talch guided and even prodded along the way to levels they might never have aspired to reach. Throughout my years of working and teaching in Detroit and Flint, and through contacts with older nurses in the Professional Organizations and U of M School of Nursing Alumnae activities, it has been a thrill and a joy to have many women come to me to see if my name

"Wubbena" has any relation to Talka. Their faces always beamed with their memories of her abilities as a nurse, her love of fun, and even in some instances, their mutual help in getting out of the trouble into which some of their pranks had led them. She was older than her classmates and thus was helpful in times of crisis.

She loved to keep in contact with her old classmates. Here is her contribution to the newsletter printed for her class reunion held in October 1950, which was one year before she died. The Miss K referred to is Miss Kusterer who was a secretary at University Hospital for many years, and in later years "took care" of the Alumnae affairs.

October 15, 1950

Dear Miss K____

It was truly heart-warming to receive your little note and I got a real thrill when the Directory reached me with so many familiar names of those who meant so much to me during our training days. How I yearned to be at the Reunion, but circumstances over which I had no control, prevented my being present. I could picture Mary Ware Currah, Lottie Ludington, Augusta Nieusma Spencer, Lela Reagan and other classmates having a real Gab-fest and much merriment over events which occurred during our school days.

The outstanding report of the hospital which I received was about the beautiful new Maternity Building. Beautiful from the standpoint of design and interior decorating, and the efficient labor-saving equipment. So very complete in every detail. The girls also wrote of the warm, friendly feeling which prevailed — no one standing back waiting to be introduced, etc. How I would have enjoyed being with them, but even as is, I have been enjoying the reports sent me and have a mental picture of all the happy fellowship and kindred feeling that exists, especially among our nurses.

With 7 of the 15 nurses of the Wubbena family as alumnae, the U. of M. School of Nursing is especially dear to me and I am always interested in hearing of its progress.

With hearty greetings to you,   Cordially yours.
Talka H. Wubbena,
"Class of 1914"

Talka tried to attend class reunions, but it was a physical hardship for her. While Lois and I were students she came to Ann Arbor and we tried to help her get to the various functions of the Alumnae programs. She enjoyed the contacts and attention given her, and especially that given her from Roscoe Bonisteel, a lawyer in Ann Arbor and a regent of the University. I think that was perhaps the last time she attended, preferring to write notes for the newsletters.

There were several summers when she spent a few weeks at Cedar Lake, Indiana, at a church-affiliated camp. In a letter to my dad while she was there, she referred to herself as "a sort of camp nurse." In addition to health matters I'm sure she was mentor in other areas also.

She maintained connections with the old friends of Standish, not only through letters but also through subscribing to the *Arenac County Independent* throughout all of her later years. Whenever she was in Standish she was busy on the phone, and many old friends would come to the house to visit in person.

Aunt Talka never lost her sense of being "big sister." Her words and attitude always reflected the everlasting and ever-present responsibility she had felt since she was twelve years old: my brothers and sisters are mine to help and encourage, and I'm here, ready and willing, if needed.

It could never be said that she was *bland*. Anything that was worth her attention received the full measure of all that she could muster from her store of learning and experience. She and her brother Charles were alike in that both had the keen ability to discern temperament and aptitudes of those with whom they came in contact. This ability served them in good stead as they dealt with others throughout their lifetimes.

In physical appearance it was Charles, Talka, and Fred who had the triangular face with a pointed chin which their father shows in the pictures we have. All had blue eyes and fair skin, and a lazy curl in their hair. Grandpa was short in stature and very round-shouldered even before he reached old age. His children were all of an average height with Henry, Bill, and Fred being near or over the six-foot mark. Before being confined to the wheelchair, Talka was slender and maintained a dignified bearing. She had the Wubbena gift of being able to enter into a situation with sensitivity to the full range of the pain or joy felt by those with her. She could get "to the point," sometimes with a little sharpness in her tone or words, but always with an empathy that kept others from being hurt. And above all, she could laugh. "Keep a stiff upper lip and have fun while doing it"—that was Aunt Talch!

| |

Letter to Henry and Martha from Talka shortly after they were married.

Nurses Home, Ann Arbor

June 19, 1911

Mr. and Mrs. Henry Wubbena

My dearest brother and sister,

As you must now be in your new home, and a letter addressed there will reach you, I'll write you a letter tonight. Suppose you are sitting on the porch tonight making plans for the future. Wish it were so I could walk in on you. I think I feel more than a sister's interest in you, and it doesn't seem long ago that you and I were playfellows, and I fell into the dobbin, and now you are a dignified married man. I rejoice in your new happiness and hope that it may never be dimmed by sorrow, and my dear new sister I am glad to welcome you in the family circle, and that he made so good choice of one to stand by his side thru all his future. Though the way may sometimes be rough, I hope that you may have a long and prosperous life together. How I wish I could have been with you on your happy day, but I had to be content by only thinking about the event and work away with my thoughts over there. I however had a nice box from home containing some of the "good things" which you people had. Received your nice letter Martha and also the invitation, but you understand my dear how it was. I expect to go home the latter part of August for two weeks and will surely plan on spending a couple days there, and you may both spend a Sunday at home anyway while I am there.

Just had a postal from Minnie since the wedding, saying she would write me a long letter telling me everything the next day and how beautiful the wedding was, so expect a long letter from her tomorrow. Hank said he had a lot of the furniture bought and was staying at the house. I would like to have been a mouse in the corner and heard you two do all your planning. Never mind, I'll be there too some day. Have you had your picture taken, if so you must surely remember poor me down here. I was so glad that circumstances were that the other girls could go, and now I wish you would both go and see them as often as possible, and if Hank can't always get away have the better half go and stay a few days once in a while, as that will please them so much, and Martha dear, as you are so much nearer to them now than I am, you can kind of give them a little sisterly advise now and then, and Hank of course does likewise. It seems so strange that so much is taking place while I am so far away. I get quite lonesome when I get to thinking, but I like it here very, very much, and am gaining wisdom right along.

Now I must be closing, as the lights must be out at 10:45 P.M. Hope you'll both write me a long letter, and may you both have a long happy prosperous life, is the wish of

Your old maiden sissy

Talka

PS: As to the wedding gift I will bring that when I come on my vacation, See?

| |

The last letter by Talka for the Original Ten's Round Robin, written a couple of weeks before she died.

Los Angeles 13, California
(1951)

My dear ones all

The only thing that is wrong with this place is that there are so many miles between me and all you dear ones. Fred is nearest and he is far away at that. I think of you all in the cold while here people are going about without any wraps on. Last week it was really hot, even for this climate, but now it is just comfortable. I'm writing this in front of a wide open window, in the bright sunshine. The only ones on the sick list in the R.R. letter are Bill and Mirtie and in Bill's letter to me today he writes that with a complete rest the M.D. thinks he will be O.K. by March lst, then Mirtie has been ailing but diabetes can be controlled by diet and medication so all is well as far as the physical conditions are concerned. This is truly an interesting place. People are here from all over the world of every tribe and nation, all ages and all sizes. There are two retired farmers here, brothers from Iowa, and it is so interesting to see what an enjoyable time they are having. They remind me of John and Cha's.; German, too, and I have a good time talking German to them. I am very nicely situated in a private room and in the heart of the city. Today a lady took me to several of the big stores and note this, Bill dear, she took me to Clifton's for dinner. I had on only a cloth cape for a wrap and it was very warm and nice. Then I have much company. Several nurses here who served with me in World War I and other friends, too. So many people wonder that I'm here all by myself but I get along very well. Several Elgin people in the city, too, who come to see me. They bring me oranges and grapefruit which grow in their gardens. Last Monday a former Elgin boy, a friend of Louis, Jr., and his wife came and took me for a long ride and this is truly interesting territory, the ocean on one side of the highway and mountains on the other. One marvels at the wonders of God's handiwork. However, I think these dear natives who know nothing of throwing snowballs, making snow men and sliding on the ice have missed something, too. Then, too, they tell me in the midsummer it gets very hot here so that's not so nice either. My, but was I thrilled to see the account of Catherine being sent to Minneapolis for that special course. The Elgin folks are hoping she may stop there en route. I also read about her in the news bulletin of the U. of M. which I will attach hereto. That dear girl is so worthy of all the good things that may come to her. As you say, John, we can truly be grateful for all of Jan's offspring. Last Saturday Fred, Jr. and family visited me here. Such a fine young couple they are. So full of business as well as humorous.

We miss the nice big clasps that Harry used to put on the letters. By By, my dear ones. How I love you all nobody knows. May God bless and keep you everyone.

Talch.

MINNIE WUBBENA GABLER (1887–1974)

Memories of My Mother

by Louis Gabler

Minnie from Standish, Michigan, and Louis from Elgin, Illinois (and New York City), seem like an unlikely match. They met because of their mutual interest in things of God, His word, the Bible, and His Son, Jesus Christ. Both these young people loved the Lord Jesus Christ as Lord, controller of their lives, and Savior from the penalty of sin. Both tried in their own way to live lives pleasing to God because of this relationship.

Mr. Hoehler was an itinerant preacher or pioneer missionary in one of the Dakotas. He and his wife Dora were participants in a Bible Conference at Bay City, which Minnie attended. They became good friends. (In later years Mrs. Hoehler came to live in the Gabler home as "Aunt Dora.")

Minnie heard the hymn, "God Will Take Care of You," and it became one of her favorites. She asked the Hoehlers if they had a copy of the words. Their negative reply and attempt to sing it from recall encouraged them to tell her of one Louis Gabler of Elgin, Illinois who, in the business of distributing Gospel literature, might possibly have music, too.

She wrote. He replied with not just the words and/or the music, but with a whole hymnal. Along with the book, he enclosed a note saying he'd checked off several other hymns which he enjoyed also.

The note and the neatly penned checks throughout the hymnal convinced her that she really should investigate this gentleman further. She wrote again, thanking him. And he responded again—and again.

The correspondence continued for several months and then she invited him to attend another conference at Bay City. (Was this a covert invitation to get family approval?) When he arrived, he readily located her sitting with two other ladies, her sisters, in the auditorium.

It was about three years later they were wed.

At the ripe old age of sixteen, Louis had left his parents in New York City to live with his Aunt Marie (Schmidt) in Elgin. There he built several houses, one of which was to become home for his bride and himself.

Mom (Minnie) was a patient, quiet, humble person. Yet she had a beautiful sense of timing and humor. An excellent cook, she could make a meal for one or a thousand—reminding me of the feeding of the five thousand—such was her talent in the kitchen. A capable seamstress, she could make a pair of socks live for decades. While one could outgrow an article of clothing, seldom was one able to wear it out. Clothing repairs were done with finesse and never looked patchy.

The trait of generosity for those in need was another foremost attribute. The house was always open for kin, troubled persons, someone in need, and even itinerant preachers who frequented our little community.

She was the one who gave much of her life to care for Talka during her invalid years. The two of them spent hours in the kitchen—not just cooking, but reminiscing and solving the problems of the world, neighborhood, community and family.

The days of the Depression must have been difficult, but we children would never have known. People without work were pitied, and helped as much as possible. Transient men often stopped by the house for a handout.

We raised chickens, so there were always eggs in the house and chicken dinners of different types were not uncommon fare. As the indigent or homeless would stop by, Mom would usually prepare an egg sandwich while the person would pull weeds from the garden, cut grass, or do some task around the house in "payment"—a lesson in generosity, assistance, and earning one's way through life.

The house was always immaculate, and yet it seemed always in need of cleaning or dusting, according to Mom. Laundry was done once weekly. Dad had a clothesline pattern from the house to several trees in the yard, getting the ultimate length in a minimum of space. On both the coldest and hottest days the clothes were hung to dry—most times outdoors, but occasionally in the basement. In the winter it was not unusual to see the frozen clothes stiffly waving in the freezing breeze. Yes, in time they did dry as the sun helped evaporate the crystals of ice.

Our laundry was in one corner of our basement. There was a gas hot plate for heat to boil dirty clothes to get them still cleaner! A big copper tub with a copper lid was always stored right there on, or next to, the hot plate.

Next were the dual laundry tubs complete with hot and cold running water along with proper drainage. The adjoining wall had the cumbersome water softener unit.

In front of the laundry tubs stood the Horton washer, plugged into the single hanging electrical socket which also held the one light bulb with the metal pull-down chain switch. The detergents of the day were Gold Dust Powder and Fels Naphtha soap bars, which were shaved or cut into cubes and put into a device much like a metal tea strainer and then swished around in the boiling hot water.

Sad to say, we were not always aware of the dangers of these new devices. Often, when the basement floor or the laundry area was drenched with water during wash day, someone would feel the unpleasant jolting tingle of electricity upon touching the washer or switching the light. Fortunately, there never were any serious injuries from this.

An instance of unexpected pain came as Mom tried to extricate some clothing from the wringer. It grabbed her arm before she was able to hit either the switch or the release lever. That laundry seemed to be the center of excitement on many occasions.

An exceptionally dirty load of clothes called for drastic measures. Using the copper tub to heat water on the hot plate, the greasy clothes were put in the boiling froth along with good doses of Gold Dust or the Fels Naphtha shavings.

One such occasion almost resulted in tragedy. Mom concluded that the addition of even MORE Naphtha should enhance the cleaning process. As long as the tub was covered, it ought to be safe — or so she reasoned.

The liquid Naphtha was added and hastily covered. All went well until the lid was lifted. A violent explosion sprayed our Mom on the face and both arms with boiling, soapy water as well as the now-flaming Naphtha! The burns were vivid in a hurry, but by God's grace, though painful, they healed quickly. Fortunately, there was no other damage. No one remembers if the clothes were any cleaner!

Lou, Sr., had built a chute from an upstairs (i.e., second floor) closet, through the kitchen and into the laundry area of the basement. This saved Minnie many a step. Instead of carrying the heavy loads of laundry through the house and into the basement, they were just dropped down the chute and sorted at a table down there in the basement.

He had drilled ventilation holes in the 'reservoir' at the bottom of the chute. A hinged door was designed to drop the clothes onto the table or into a basket for sorting. On occasion some of the clothes, or strings, would protrude through these vents. For some reason these threads appeared as unkempt as a dried, weedy field. And what does one do with a field to clean it up? One burns it, of course! One match in the hands of a naive child with a creative bent could be either innovative or disastrous. The latter proved to be the case as the child began to burn off the threads protruding from the vent holes.

It took only a few seconds for the entire stack of clothes to burst into flames and stream up the chute, which now was a chimney of flame.

A pale, frightened boy ran up the stairs interrupting a group of visiting ladies. Without saying a word, Mom ran into the basement and bravely used a garden hose (already attached in one of the laundry tubs) to extinguish the fire. She really should have gotten a medal for that one. Once again she did suffer some burns on her hands and arms. And not one person, apparently, thought to call the fire department!

When Minnie finished high school, she became a local school teacher. She loved the children she taught and was conscientious in her work. Later she went to Ferris Institute in Big Rapids, Michigan, to get her teaching certificate. She did well and inspired her own children some years later to continue their education, which each of us did.

Mom had many tricks to entertain us. One, inherited by a granddaughter, Marilyn Gabler Fogg, was to twist the corners of her mouth into opposing directions and switching them, thus giving the illusion of a horizontal figure eight, flipping and reversing itself over and over. Tis much more comical seen than described, and takes a real talent and gift.

Minnie was the quiet one—the timid one of the girls. It seemed that she was always the last to speak, and never ever wanted to be in the foreground. Like her older brother, John, it was always difficult to get a good picture of Min. If she would consent to pose, it was just that—a fixed, mysterious smile not unlike the Mona Lisa—feet together, a rigid stance. One dasn't laugh— or get tickled in front of the camera! It was all serious business! However, like John, she was caught unaware on occasion.

She, like the rest of the family, was musically inclined. Although I never heard or saw her play an instrument, she was always ready with a vocal rendition of a hymn or an old folk tune. Her repertoire seemed as endless as her stories. At work in a hot kitchen she'd be humming. In the basement doing the laundry, she'd sing above the din of the machinery. Outdoors while hanging the clothes to dry or weeding flower beds she'd be heard singing or even sometimes whistling a happy tune. Often the tunes were befitting the mood and just as often they were inspirational or humorous to lighten or change the mood of the moment. It's not surprising that her children picked up these musical settings and memorized many a hymn or song. Even some of the classics were ingrained in this way.

Radio was in its infancy and, as such, was suspect in the Christian and religious community. It took a while for it to become legitimate in our house-hold. Unless I'm mistaken, it was Talka who first 'fell from Grace' and bought a gothic-shaped Philco. Our Dad didn't vocally protest, that we know of, but it seemed to be a while before he caught the vision of the teaching and evangelization possibilities. And then came the radio programs—Amos and Andy, Fibber McGee and Molly, and Edgar Bergen and Charlie McCarthy. A radio then became a fixture in his bedroom as well as his "office."

Mom should have been named "Patience"! I can't recall ever hearing her complain. She may have cautiously questioned some actions or statements, but never complained. Even when she was wronged, she never acknowledged she had been!

The sense of humor was always there (typically Wubbena!), even in the toughest of times. As kids, we were never told much of our parent's younger years and how *they* were parented. But, oh, how we picked up on the sto-ries they'd tell on each other.

Talka would mention the name Hank Nehls in a way that we knew that in their younger years such an individual must have had an interest in our Mom—and pursued this interest with more than just thoughts. The same with Dad—the name Clara Krause struck a few raw nerves when mentioned in his presence. Christmas, birthdays, Valentine's Day, Mother's Day, and others always brought cards and gifts to both Talka and Minnie with "From Henry (or Hank) with Deepest Love" written in a childish scrawl. The response was most gratifying when Mom would respond that she must remember to write him a thank-you note! Naturally, that brought embar-rassed protests from the true giver!

Much of Mom's teaching came from personal experiences. One such les-son to her children was on the wise use of finances. She told of the carnival which came to Standish when she was a child. The family sacrificed to let the kids see the bright lights and the fun times. As I recall her account, each was given a whole quarter—25 cents. That was probably equivalent to a ten dol-lar bill in today's recreation dollars.

Min spotted a vendor who sold hairbrushes—for 25 cents! She bought one and thus had no more to spend the entire day. All the rest feasted on hot dogs and other wholesome entertainment while poor Minnie languished with her hair brush. No amount of begging for even a loan of a penny or two pro-duced any sympathy or extra monies.

There probably were many morals to that story, such as: the hairbrush lasted longer than any of the entertainment. But on the other hand, the mem-ories of the good times probably outlasted the hairbrush. I guess the greater lesson was that one should learn how to set priorities, and then live with the satisfaction that you lived up to them. In other words, make your choice and then be content that you did the best you knew with what you had at the time!

The wealth of the family could never have been measured in dollars and cents. Poverty was an unknown word except when used for those much less fortunate. I guess none of us who were raised during the Depression years (the late 1920s and 1930s) knew that we were poor or had any idea that we would be considered impoverished when measured by the standards of the 1990s. Under the tutelage of our Mom, Minnie, we learned to appreciate the smallest of favors. We enjoyed the simplest of meals—but were they really all that simple? We were always well-fed, weren't we? Yes, our clothing had been frugally repaired rather than purchased new. But we were always well and warmly clothed.

Does anyone today remember a darning egg? No, it's not an egg which a hen failed to hatch. It was used to set a 'platform' on which to darn (i.e., mend) holes in socks.

Letters from Minnie

Elgin, Ill. (Sun P.M.) Apr 14, 1940

Dear Brother John and Family,

About a year ago we were at your house to help celebrate the big birthday and what a happy day we had! We talked of it all the other day, and my, another year has already rolled around and its time again to wish our good big brother John a happy birthday and many more.

We've just returned from taking Margaret back to Evanston. She had to be back on duty at 1:30 so she packed our lunch before meeting and then we ate it in the car. On our way home we stopped and called on a friend who lives on a fifteen acre farm near Chicago. He wants to get on a bigger place because he says he cannot rotate the crops for lack of room as he should to save his land and one cannot buy manure, so the land needs rest. One year they made $20,000 from onions only from that 15 acres but since then garden products have been very much cheaper and besides that the ground not producing so well.

All is fine here. We are looking forward now to TH's return which, God willing, will be in early May. As the time draws near I think I am more lonesome for her than I've been when I knew she wasn't coming.

The boys have been raking the lawn and trying to help clean up but its really been too cold to do much gardening. Our greatest job in a way is to find things to keep them busy but now Lee has a paper route (Chicago Tribune) for an hour or so in the morning before school and Clarence has one after school. They surely have done well to accomplish that, especially Clarence who doesn't read much. He is such a dandy willing little helper but is too nervous to settle down. He may outgrow that tho. D.V., Lee will graduate on May 10. He had to go back to the orphanage for a sort of examination about a month ago—kind of a questionnaire telling what kind of work he's interested in especially, etc. If he finds a job in Elgin he'll stay here but if he doesn't, they'll find him something. He's been talking much of joining the Navy. We haven't discouraged it at all—not knowing what the State would do about it but in our own hearts we would sort of dread to have him go in that company even tho the discipline would be O.K. The poor children! When one thinks how much they're discussed, etc. (I mean all those orphanage children) and subject to people's whims, etc. one feels so tender to them. And yet the State has done so much for them financially, which is almost detrimental to their character building, in a way. We'd surely miss them in many ways if they were to go. There has been no welfare worker here to see them since before Christmas.*

How are you all? Em mentions the youngsters often. She's surely fond of them, and often mentions how true blue they are.

Do you think you'll ever come this way? We'd be <u>so</u> glad to have you. As you know one can easily make the drive in a day. We have not heard from Hank's (outside of the RR) directly for a long long time. I hope Bea is O.K. and that Martha is well and strong again by this time.

How is Aunt Mida? After the weather gets warmer and she can get right out in the sun 'twill make her feel some better, I hope. That arthritis is so extremely painful.

Next Sunday is Ella's Sunday home. D.V. She comes home every other Sunday and Muriel comes two out of three. M. comes home on Saturday night and then she and Ella go home together. They're only about 4 or 5 miles apart.

Elle has a number of snapshots of little Rodney. My, he must be sweet. I know you enjoy him immensely. Am so glad they're not too far away but that you can see him occasionally. Those little fellows surely are precious. Well, I guess they're precious all along the way. We surely enjoy Louis. He's been doing very, very well in school. Now he's in the 8th grade since Feb. and for some reason or other it has been just very hard for him. I guess his teacher is sort of hard to understand too (Muriel and Marg. both had her too). He brings home so much work to do. Now it seems as if the light is beginning

---

Ed. Note: The boys referred to here are Lee and Clarence Green, who were Minnie and Lou's foster sons and lived with them for several years.

to dawn on him (Ha). He had the flu and was out for nearly three weeks. Of course that didn't help either. He's just about made it up now and is able to carry on without but very little help, whereas at first I helped him every day.

Have you set any hens yet? Lou says he thinks he'll set two and then buy extra chicks too. We can get from 12 to 17 eggs from our flock. They're all White Rocks. We can easily sell all the eggs we don't use.

I had the nicest letter from Mildred not so long ago (I never hear from her). She wrote how they'd had a baby calf on Valentine's Day and when the boys and Fred came home they (She and Marg) had told the menfolk they had a Valentine for them. Little Marg. must be very sweet.—There are so many miles between us all. It seems such a little while since all of ours were so little, not?

Now I must wish you a very happy birthday, <u>dear</u> John, and hope you have many more and that each succeeding year will bring increased happiness. I surely enjoyed your good birthday letter. I just look forward to getting them and you and Charles <u>never</u> disappoint me. Thank you so much.

Much love to you all and write when you can. Kind regards to Aunt Mida.

From Minn's

| |

Postmarked Chicago – July 22, 1941 – Tues A.M.
Dear Folks: your good cd. and letter came this a.m. Thanks so much. I am so thrilled at your going to see Wy. Give him my love. It will do you all so much good to <u>see</u> him. One can accomplish so much more in an hr's visit than in many letters. Dear good boy. I also had the cutest booklet cd. from Jean and a lovely cd. from Evelyn too. Everybody's so good to me.

I came two wks ago today but had a severe sore throat and cold so had to stay a wk. before the oper. which was last Tues. Oh, how we all praise the Lord that there's no malignancy. I feel very comf. only weak. Lou and Louis were here Sunday. He is getting on O.K. and says Louis is a real helper. Talch is at Cedar Lake. We took her the day before I came never thinking of anything like this. Elle and Mu and Marg come every day. Lee visited with his folks in Cedar Rapids, Ia, over the 4th holidays (2 wks). Then he came home and said he was going to get work there. One can't blame him for wanting to be with his own. He had such a good job ($7 a day, many times) tho in the factory. In a way 'twill be much easier when I get home then, but we'll miss him. He bo't himself a 2d hand car and will get to see us tho'.

We had such a good time at Bill's and am sure you will, D. V. 'Twill do you good to talk things over with him. We wish you a safe journey and that the weather may not be too hot. We read Wy's letters in Arenac.*

Much much love, dear folks and come to see us when you can and thanks again.

Lots of love to dear Wy.

Minn

I think I'm going home Sat. D.V. Muriel will go with me.

Our Elgin Home

by Muriel Gabler Ford, Daughter of Minnie Wubbena Gabler

Minnie and Louis had four children. Marie Ella Muriel Gabler was born in 1915. Talka, who was a registered nurse, was there to assist in the delivery and postnatal care. Margaret Henrietta was born in 1919, Louis, Jr. in 1927, and John George in 1933. John George died at the age of 5½ months.

Louis was a very good provider and was very industrious—raising chickens, and having a very large garden as a "hobby," in addition to his work in the watch factory. His employment at the watch factory lasted just short of fifty years, until the watch business was curtailed and there were large layoffs. His chicken business not only supplied meat for his family, but excess eggs for sale. Uncle Harry would send crates of blueberries from northern Michigan during the season, and Louis would sell them. He loved to shop for groceries, taking the children along to show them how to find bargains and pick out the best produce. The children also were taught how to feed the chickens, gather the eggs, and do gardening.

From early infancy we were taught the Word of God and the way of salvation. We were taken to Sunday School and church services regularly. As we participated in the Sunday School programs, etc. we were routinely "drilled" in our pieces and Bible verses during family devotions at supper time. There also were the weekly Bible verses to learn for Sunday School. With her teacher's background, Mom was a good mentor. We were taught reading the Scriptures even to the genealogies in the Old Testament (good discipline). The Bible verses learned in this way were recalled many times and were a real help along life's way. As a result of this training, we children not only learned of our need of salvation (because Scripture says "All have sinned and come

---

*Ed. Note: The *Arenac Independent*, the Standish newspaper.

short of the Glory of God," Romans 3:23) but accepted the Lord as our Savior in our teens—the best decision anyone can make—and a treasure for life and eternity.

Our parents were a very hospitable couple. Our home was always open to company. We often had "hymn sings" with our guests. Usually as they left, we would all join together to sing a parting hymn, generally, "How Good Is the God We Adore" or "Praise the Savior, Ye Who Know Him" or "Once More Before We Part."

When Aunt Talka became an invalid, Louis erected a ramp to enable her to get from the house to the car. He never complained as he helped her and loaded the car with her extensive luggage and paraphernalia (wheelchair, bench, lunch baskets, water jug, etc.).

Aunt Talka was a very generous person. At Christmas time she made gifts for her friends. She knit a great many goodies, could crochet, and even had a sewing machine she used to make some of her clothes and gifts for others. Lou devised a hand control for her to use instead of a foot or knee control. She sometimes went along in the car with Lou to deliver her Christmas presents, dressed as a Santa. She helped in the home where she could. Many times when company came for a meal, she would do the sitting-down jobs in the kitchen, such as preparing the vegetables.

She inaugurated a "Shut-Ins" picnic for the community. An area was reserved in one of the local parks, and the shut-ins were invited to come on a special day to get better acquainted. It was potluck, helped by donations from merchants. Libby Goll, who had a nursing home, also provided some of the food and transportation. This event was an annual affair for several years. Shut-ins from surrounding towns also joined the group.

In the year 1933, the Chicago World's Fair and the Wubbena family reunion in Elgin took place. A tornado hit Elgin just the day before the guests arrived. The reunion went on without any delay. Minnie was pregnant with her fourth child during the planning, etc. Activities were sightseeing, visits to the Fair, and reminiscing.

Talka and Elle [Ella] were very helpful during the Depression years. Work was scarce in the watch factory, and there were layoffs. Lou worked only two days a month as a fireman—so different from his regular precision work on the intricate watches. He did any kind of extra jobs he could find as a handyman. Talka and Elle would help buying coal, etc., but on a loan basis. Talka's friend, Libby Goll, was generous in sending baskets of food—especially for the holiday meals. Louis' baker friend would give him a basket of left-over baked goods on Saturday afternoons. We would share them with needy neighbors. Uncle John would send us a frozen goose at Christmas time—something we children always looked forward to. We always enjoyed the delicious goose dinner. Even had goose grease applied to our chests when we had chest colds during the winter months!

About 1937 a young woman named Alice Bosch came to Elgin from Romania. She was introduced to our family through a mutual friend, who thought our family would be able to give her "family" support, most especially because Uncle George Flutur was also from Romania. Minnie helped her learn English as she would come and visit with Aunt Talka.

Several other young women also came for lessons in English—one worked at the nursing home that Libby Goll had only a few blocks from our home. And then Sophie Brenner, who had emigrated from Germany, used to come and bake goodies for us, besides having her English lessons. These young women kept in touch for many years. Sophie moved to New York and married. She would send Talka fabrics for her handwork, etc. Alice, the young woman from Romania, married and still lives in Elgin, and still recalls the happy times she had in our home. She just celebrated her eightieth birthday.

During World War II housing was a problem, and many single family homes were converted to multiple-unit dwellings. The Gabler house was no exception. An apartment was made on our second floor—still leaving bedrooms for our family; and then part of the basement was also converted into an apartment. These were rented to young couples or single young folks who were employed in the factories on "war projects" and as a result more lasting friendships were made. When Margaret moved back to Elgin to work as a school nurse, she moved into one of the apartments, which proved beneficial when Mom and Dad needed help because of Dad's failing health and Mom's visual problem.

In later years Aunt Dora Hoehler, the elderly widow of Charles Hoehler, was homeless and came to live with us to spend her last few months in our home. As mentioned earlier, Charles was instrumental in Minnie's and Lou's meeting each other. This hospitality was just an example of the kindness our parents showed through the years.

At another time they "housed" an elderly couple from an old folks home when it had a fire. Old Stimpson Payne was very hard of hearing, and recollections of his hearing problems are still vivid in our memories—with the "horn-like" hearing aid he used.

Talka's death in 1951 was a traumatic experience for all of us. Arrangements were made for the funeral in Standish with burial in the family plot. The Gablers journeyed from Elgin to Standish by train, and were given the responsibility of identifying her remains at the funeral home in Standish. This procedure was done in the rear of a furniture store adjacent to the funeral home. Quite an experience! Elle was still living with the Gablers at that time and was very helpful.

Elle retired from her nursing career to marry George Flutur (Aunt Emma's widower). She had been "school nurse" at Moody Bible Institute in Chicago for many years. Then she had moved to Elgin to become an industrial nurse at the Illinois Tool Works (Shakeproof). After Aunt Emma passed away, Aunt Elle corresponded with Uncle George, and later married him in Detroit. They made their home there until George's health deteriorated, at which point they gave up their home to move to a retirement community (Resthaven Homes) in Grand Rapids, Michigan. They lived there until the Lord took them Home.

Louis had several strokes before he passed away. He was in a nursing home for about a year and a half—much to Minnie's grief. She and Margaret were no longer able to give him the necessary care. It was a hard decision to make, and it was more difficult yet to see him so helpless in the home. At this point he also had a personality change, which made it even more difficult.

Minnie and Margaret sold the homestead and moved to a home Margaret purchased. Minnie lived for several years longer, but lost her central vision. This proved to be very frustrating to her. She often said that she loved to read, but never had time until she "retired," and then her vision failed her. She was a very patient person, and had the grace that very few persons have these days. She developed gallbladder trouble a few weeks before the Lord took her home. As she was passing into His presence, she whispered, "The Lord Jesus is My Savior." What a precious memory that is for us!

Muriel and Margaret both became nurses. Through the encouragement of Talka both took the five year nursing program which led to a Bachelor of Science degree. Both became instructors in nursing schools. Muriel married William Ford, and in 1949 became a homemaker until just before Bill's death in 1970 when she again donned her uniform to be an office nurse in the family physician's office. Margaret continued her career as nursing administrator in the Elgin Public Schools and then helped to establish the associate nursing degree program in Elgin Community College—a post she held until she met and married Everett Pickett from Tennessee in 1974. After their marriage they made their home in Tennessee on a "mountain top." Everett, too, went home to be with the Lord in August 1992.

Louis, Jr. was married to Francis Redding and had four children—Marilyn (Bob) Fogg (mother of three children), Sue (Richard) Spengler (mother of two girls), Randy (Kay) (father of two children), and Ronnie, single, who lives with his mother. Lou had several interesting careers. He was minister of music in several churches. Most recently until his retirement in

1992 he was involved with the media for the U.S. Navy in Norfolk, Virginia. He and Lil whom he married in 1983 made their home in Virginia Beach, Virginia. In December 1992 Lou was also taken home to be with the Lord as a result of a massive heart attack while shopping.

Truly the Gablers had their lives enriched by the presence and influence of the different Wubbenas. In this way God has blessed us all with the heritage left by Jan and Catharina Wubbena. We should thank Him for it.

Here are the words of the hymns mentioned earlier:

God Will Take Care of You

Be not dismayed whate'er betide
God will take care of you;
Beneath His wings of love abide,
God will take care of you.

Chorus:
God will take care of you,
Thro' every day, O'er all the way;
He will take care of you,
God will take care of you.

Thro' days of toil when heart doth fail,
God will take care of you;
When dangers fierce your path assail,
God will take care of you.

All you may need He will provide,
God will take care of you;
Nothing you ask will be denied,
God will take care of you.

No matter what may be the test,
God will take care of you;
Lean weary one, upon His breast,
God will take care of you.
Civilla D. Martin

Praise the Savior

Praise the Savior, ye who know Him!
Who can tell how much we owe Him?
Gladly let us render to Him
All we are and have.

Jesus is the name that charms us;
He for conflict fits and arms us;
Nothing moves and nothing harms us
While we trust in Him.

Trust in Him, ye saints, forever;
He is faithful, changing never;
Neither force nor guile can sever
Those He loves from Him.

Keep us, Lord, O keep us cleaving
To Thyself and still believing,
Till the hour of our receiving
Promised joys with Thee.

Then we shall be where we would be,
Then we shall be where we should be;
Things that are not now, nor could be
Soon shall be our own.

Thomas Kelly

How Good Is the God We Adore

How good is the God we adore,
Our faithful, unchangeable Friend;
Whose love is as great as His pow'r
And knows neither measure nor end.

'Tis Jesus the First and the Last,
Whose Spirit shall guide us safe home.
We'll praise Him for all that is past,
And trust Him for all that's to come.

Joseph Hart

A 1967 Writing by Minnie

It is a good policy to review one's conversion occasionally, and I thank Mrs. Govan for asking me to write mine out. Our whole family of ten children were taught from infancy that we were sinners and that the Lake of Fire would be our final destiny if we did not accept the Lord Jesus Christ as our Savior. We attended Sunday School and Gospel meetings conducted by the Brethren who had the Gospel Hall as their meeting place in Standish, Michigan. In October 1901 two evangelists, Mr. Thomas Touzeau and Mr. Thomas Dobbin were holding Gospel meetings. We had had a series of gospel meetings often, but these meetings seemed to be effective in reaching the younger generation, as several of the children of these Christians were saved at that time. There were Alice Wyatt Barr, Evelyn Wyatt Postif, Margaret Turfus DeWitt, her brother Harvey, Earl Black and Mrs. Agnes DeFord: among them was my sister Emma, who has gone to be with the Lord. I was very much troubled, but I don't remember a time that I didn't think seriously about getting right with God, but now I became intensely interested and disturbed because I wasn't saved. It seemed I had a stubborn and rebellious heart. I would lie awake night after night thinking of verses and hymns we had learned. On October 22 on a Sunday morning I confessed to myself and God that I was a sinner and that the Lord Jesus died for me. It brought relief, but I didn't feel satisfied, as it seemed all the others had special verses to rely on, but then by myself — I didn't know where to look, but in Romans 5:8 I did find that "God commendeth his love toward us, in that while we were yet sinners, Christ died for us." It was that which gave me definite assurance. "I yielded myself to his tender embrace" and from that day I thank our heavenly Father for his great love. Now at the age of three-quarters of a century I can testify to the goodness and care of our heavenly Father. Mrs. Govan also asked for my favorite hymn. There are many choice hymns that I love, but a special one is #336 in Redemption Songs:

> Vs 1 Loved with everlasting love,
>   Led by grace that love to know,
>   Spirit, breathing from above,
>   Thou hast taught me it is so!
>   Oh, this full and perfect peace!
>   Oh, this transport all divine!
>   In a love that cannot cease
>   I am His, and He is mine.   *(Repeat)*

> Vs 2 Heaven above is softer blue,
>   Earth around is sweeter green!
>   Something lives in every hue,
>   Christless eyes have never seen.
>   Birds with gladder songs o'erflow,
>   Flowers with deeper beauties shine,
>   Since I know as now I know
>   I am His, and He is mine!   *(Repeat)*

> Vs 3 Things that once were wild alarms
>   Cannot now disturb my rest,
>   Closed in everlasting arms,

Pillowed on the loving breast,
Oh, to lie forever here,
Doubt and care and self resign,
While he whispers in my ear
I am His, and He is mine!   *(Repeat)*

Vs 4 His forever, only His;
Who the Lord and me shall part?
Oh, with what a rest of bliss
Christ can fill the loving heart!
Heaven and earth may fade and flee,
First-born light in gloom decline,
But while God and I shall be
I am His and He is mine.   *(Repeat)*
Signed Minnie Wubbena

Memories Regarding Jan Wübbena's Daughters
by Muriel Gabler Ford and Margaret Gabler Pickett

The Standish family was very poor. As the boys grew older and little Minnie was not yet in school, one of them asked her why she didn't put on a dress over the little black petticoat that she was wearing day after day. She told her own children many years later, that the comment was one she never forgot, because she had no dress!

Grandma died as a result of a complication of childbirth when the tenth child, William, was born. This left Aunt Talka as the oldest Wubbena woman, age twelve years five months, to try to manage the younger children and the household. What a responsibility for such a young girl with six younger children to be cared for!

Aunt Ella, Uncle Bill, and Uncle Fred were fostered out to neighbors who would have adopted them, but Grandpa would not allow that to happen. Aunt Ella often told us how many homes she had been in during that year or two that they were fostered out. I don't remember how many there were, but I do recall the older ones telling us that she was pretty with blonde, curly hair.

Aunt Ella always said she thought that her Daddy loved her "special," and as a child she was always at his side. She would follow him around the farm and during his rest periods he would hold her and visit with her.

Grandpa must have done that with all of his girls, because Emma told how she helped him in the fields and how Aunt Talka was often upset because Aunt Emma would never help her in the house, because she would be out in the fields with her dad.

Aunt Talka had to be taken out of school at the age of twelve or thirteen to help at home. She always wanted to have an education. It became one of her priorities in life. She felt that a good education was one of the ways to "get ahead in life," so it became her major goal.

Grandpa nourished these desires of the girls. He became a civic leader, partly to help his family succeed. He and the neighbors started the first school in the area. After all, he had ten children, all of whom needed an education and he made sure that they got as much as he could provide for them. He served for several years as the director of the school board of that local school.

Grandpa believed that "Travel broadens the mind" and he instilled this proverb into his children. The Wubbena women believed this intensely. As a child, I remember, that for our vacation my dad, a common workman, would take us on a trip somewhere—maybe to Detroit or Standish or Niagara Falls, or maybe farther away, depending on the finances available. Aunt Ella provided the gas, Aunt Talka provided the car, and Dad was the chauffeur, but we all benefited. Those trips are memorable to this day.

Grandpa was also very conscientious to see that his children heard and learned the Word of God. Minnie was saved at the age of fourteen. Minnie trusted the Lord as her personal Savior and followed Him conscientiously throughout her life. She was called "The Little Angel" by her brothers and she lived a life pleasing to the Lord. She prayed fervently for the salvation of her siblings to the day of her death and almost every time she visited any of them, she took the opportunity to ask them if they were saved.

All of the Wubbena women earned their own way to further their education and they inspired us Gabler children to do the same. Aunt Talka finished high school and became a bookkeeper at the county courthouse. There she earned the money to go to Ann Arbor, Michigan to become a nurse.

Aunt Ella, the youngest daughter, went to work as a bookkeeper. When she moved to Elgin, she attended a technical school for bookkeeping. Upon graduation from that, she continued to work as a bookkeeper in Elgin, and she, too, was influenced by Aunt Talka and Aunt Emma to go into nursing. So she was accepted into the Sherman Hospital School of Nursing for training. Upon graduation, the director of the school asked Aunt Ella to become her assistant. She worked as Assistant Director of Nursing for a time and then resigned to take a position as Director of School Health at Moody Bible Institute where she stayed for about twenty-five years.

Aunt Ella and Aunt Talka enthusiastically supported the college education of the Gabler children and they helped us find what they thought were the best schools available at the time.

Although each of us helped to pay for our education, and also the Army helped Louis pay his way, Aunt Ella and Aunt Talka provided substantial funds for us to have "the best" that was available. Any further education beyond the bachelor's degree was completely our own responsibility.

They were a great help to our family during the Great Depression years and provided things that we would have suffered for. Our Dad was a common laborer and those were hard years for him, but he was a hard worker, always found jobs when he was laid off, grew huge gardens, and provided well for his family in hard times. We children were never aware of the struggle that our family had during those Depression years. Our parents were people of great faith in God. We thank the Lord for giving us Christian parents who were faithful to Him and taught us early in life to love the Lord as our personal Savior and to allow Him to be our guide throughout our lives. Each of us accepted the Lord as Savior in our early teens and none of us has ever regretted that we learned the way of salvation at an early age and accepted it when we did. We praise the Lord for our heritage.

In later years, the four Wubbena women always sang to us some of the songs that they had learned in their childhood. They encouraged the Gabler children to become interested in art and music and to learn to sing and play musical instruments. Their influence in our home along these lines brought a love to each of us for the fine arts.

We have happy memories of these Wubbena women. We are proud to have had the experience of having them live with us in our home. We appreciate their influence upon each of us.

Memories of Another Generation of the Wubbena Clan by Louis Gabler, Son of Minnie Wubbena Gabler

A TRAIN RIDE

To a child, train travel in those days was as exciting as trans-world air travel is today. But it was not nearly as comfortable. The trip to Bruce Crossing or Trout Lake, Michigan, from Chicago was, at the same time, dirty and uncomfortable but pleasurable, thrilling and boring, exciting and monotonous, tedious and interesting, noisy and hypnotizing, stirring yet tranquilizing.

I don't ever recall making the trip overnight. And yet, there was always the picnic basket filled with sandwiches, meticulously wrapped in waxed paper, pickles in the jar with rubber seal to prevent leakage, fresh fruits and washed veggies for snacks (potato chips, fritos, etc. were still unknown), perhaps dry popcorn, and treat of all treats . . . homemade cookies!

Then there was the carefully wrapped and bundled thermos bottle of hot coffee for the adults and the green insulated gallon jug filled with *real* lemonade . . . and if we were lucky, there might even be a chunk of ice in the jug (cubes were an even rarer commodity). The bigmouth aluminum cups were enclosed in the lid and used for both coffee and other drinks; paper cups were unknown until we discovered the folded paper cups outside the restroom door on the train.

Occasionally, there was a diner car on the train. For us, that was just a "walk-through" experience. Prices were prohibitive in those Depression and post-Depression days. Even the vendors walking through the cars selling sandwiches, candy and drinks seemed to be way overpriced. At the numerous stops, boys would walk through the cars shouting the headlines and the names of the newspapers they were trying to sell.

For entertainment, there was always the fast-moving scenery at the windows: watching the billows of smoke clouding the scenery as the coal-fired (not diesel oil) steam locomotive (the engine) puffed its way up grades . . . and then seeing that same smoke filtering through the cracks of the window frames in the winter or boldly flowing into the open windows in the summer (no air conditioning then!) . . . and on into the clothes and the lunches. And then there was the hypnotic clickety-clack of the wheels rhythmically popping over the joints in the rails. The mournful moan of the train whistle and the crescendo and decrescendo of the clanging crossing bells made the musical background for conversation or mesmerized rest.

For a child the train restrooms held much more intrigue than the facility at home. Flushing the toilet was especially entertaining. Where else could you look down through the toilet and watch the rails and ties whiz past? But then the thought crossed one's mind: Why would anyone want to walk the rails if they knew how the toilet on the train flushed?

Watching and listening to the drone of the conductor as he collected the tickets from the passengers, I was always curious how he always knew who got on the train at which station and their destination! At the same time I was annoyed by the persons who bought their tickets from him. Why didn't they get to the station early enough to buy their tickets there? The conductor had enough to do without taking his time to remedy their inconsideration.

How about the change of conductors during the trip? How did the new man know the destination of each of the passengers? What happened to the money collected by the previous conductor? These all-wise individuals seemed to know everything. They announced the exact time of arrival at the next station along with the name of the station, then reminded passengers of their luggage. Which, by the way, was almost always totally carry-on, stored in open overhead racks as well as on and under seats. It was not uncommon to see a conductor awaken a sleeping passenger as the train approached his destination.

Parents and other kin used many different ruses to maintain a decent amount of justice and discipline with traveling children. In our family, police were always portrayed as helpful and friendly, except that for creators of disturbances, they were administrators of swift and thorough justice.

Then there were others who administered justice and discipline. Aunt Ella, though single, had an uncanny imagination and was creative with children. She went to great lengths to describe a man-like creature called a "boo." These creatures, who never bathed or shaved, wore big, wide suspenders to keep their heavy canvas, filthy work pants (fore-runners of Levis?) and faded flannel shirts covered by heavy jackets of varying descriptions depending upon the mood of the hour. Some might be wearing jackets of animal fur they had skinned themselves. If one had the courage to really stare and look at their head, they were seen to wear strange caps or hats unlike any seen around the city. At the feet were huge, hob-nailed, cleated shoes or boots. They were known to often carry hatchets, axes, and even huge knives. It only stands to reason that their main dietary fare was unruly children!

Of course, approaching logging country we were certain to see many people who fit these descriptions. At my tender age, I had no idea of any kind of description of a lumberjack!

Sure enough, before we even left suburban Chicago, my imaginative aunt was nudging me and pointing toward the door of our railroad car. In walked the biggest man I have ever seen. He fit her description of a "boo" perfectly! Seizing a prime opportunity, my aunt whispered carefully, in German so no one else would be able to understand, "Oh, my! Here's a boo now! What if he sits with us?"

I could feel my heart . . . almost hear it! My eyes were stretching out of their sockets as they grew wider and wider and my mouth dropped further and further open.

Wouldn't you know, he sat down directly across the aisle from us in the seat where he could easily keep his eyes on me. Breathing was no longer part of me! Staring at him in my near catatonic state must have given the poor man a fright, too, for he soon changed seats to where he couldn't see this frightened little appetizer. I was convinced that he was elsewhere watching from another location, but I dared not turn around to verify.

In reminiscing, I can still almost feel the additional shaking of the seat as my aunt tried her best to stifle her laughter, as I became the more alarmed thinking that the boo would get her for laughing at *him*!

Boy, did I ever behave on that trip!

DETROIT

One of the main reasons (or excuses) for at least an annual trek from Elgin to Detroit was the Bible conference. Meetings morning, afternoon, and evening kept the schedule quite full for several days.

The Fluturs (that was Emma and George with Duane and Virginia) lived within an easy walk of the Masonic Hall where the conferences were held. How exciting to take that walk with Duane and "Gin." There was usually a Cord* parked on the street along the way. It was always due close scrutiny as well as much comment, conjecture, and dreaming.

Then there were the lawn bowlers and other athletic activities just across the street from the Masonic Hall. In spite of all the attractions along the way, we who walked would usually beat the adults who *drove*!

Arriving at the Masonic Hall, our (the kids') first goal was to scope out the "book store." My, what goodies they had there. (I believe it was operated by the Pell Brothers of Grand Rapids?) Toys, pencils, pens, buttons, flags, all kinds of colorful, creative things for Sunday School teachers and Bible teachers to use to boost attendance or give as awards for different occasions. Bumper stickers were still unknown in those days or else they would have been prominent.

Adults thrived on the superb Bible teaching available at all of the meetings. We kids used to head for the balcony whenever released from the invisible chains of our parents. If I do say so, the balcony was an ideal spot; misbehavior was seldom a problem. Although I do recall one hot day. There were those of us who found our place at the windows of the balcony. We could easily survey the activities outdoors, enjoy what little breeze came our way before any of the rest of the congregation had the benefit, and at the same time give cursory attention to the Bible teaching and occasional music.

Apparently one preacher or teacher of the hour was very conscious of all the activity in the balcony. He chose the passage from Paul's writings where someone fell to his death from the window during his (Paul's) sermon. I fully believe that got our immediate attention.

One of the hardest tasks of any child is to listen. (Some adults have the same problem, too.) Our parents would go on and on about the wonderful teaching and glorious singing. I really can't recall the sermons or lessons too well, nor can I truthfully say that they meant that much at that time, but the fact that Mom and Dad had us there did make a *lasting* impression. It really did pay in years to come. Memories of that unaccompanied, undirected,

---

*Ed. Note: An expensive car of that era.

congregation's singing remain as nothing short of glorious, harmonious sound.

A fond memory of the conference (and I hope this doesn't smack of sacrilege) was the odors of the meal being prepared while we were supposed to be concentrating on the lesson. What the mind failed to absorb, the digestive system turned to wild growls of imagination and anticipation.

The kind ladies from the various assemblies (churches) took their time to work in a hot, steamy basement kitchen and dining hall. The food smelled delicious all the way upstairs into the auditorium and tasted just as good when we finally got to the dining room. Of course, the windows downstairs were open as were the windows in the auditorium. It had to be a challenge to keep both the kitchen noises minimal as well to deter the smells of the baking hams, turkeys, and/or roasts. They were good cooks! And good waitresses. Although it was probably a strain to hear, the speakers were "piped" into the dining hall/kitchen area for all who wanted to hear.

One of these fine "waitresses" made a particularly big impression on me. Because of the crowd at one particular meal, we youngsters had the privilege of sitting as a group away from our parents. This sweet lady was taking orders for beverages . . . milk, Koolaid (Ugh! Or even "Yuck" in those days), tea or coffee, and, of course, water (no ice). For some reason, I created quite a stir among the waitresses as well as the family members sitting at the next table when I asked for tea. (Hot. Iced tea was quite a luxury in the North in those days.) Evidently it was quite a shock as I'd never before had anything stronger than milk and I sure didn't care for the thoughts of coffee. My thought processes were really developing for I reasoned that I could easily get seconds of tea but not of milk. And so it was!

Traveling the roads was not near the comfort as we know it today. In the earlier cars (1925 Dodge and previous) there were *no* heaters and certainly no thought of air conditioning. This meant that the winter trips called for heated and wrapped bricks on the floor of the car. The horse blanket (made with horse hide with the fur left on!) draped over the knees, feet, and bricks. The poor driver just froze! No defrosters! Much wiping with the hand-operated wiper blades, and towels in the hands of the co-pilot, was the order of the day in the cold November weather.

And, of course, the packed picnic lunch with the thermos bottle of hot coffee for the ladies and the green insulated gallon jug for those who didn't drink coffee was readily available. No fast food back then . . . and it was also the Depression era.

Preparations for the trip included being certain that the men had fresh haircuts, not just for looks, but so George wouldn't have to cut hair!!! Don't ask why. George was a barber and had a nice shop in the basement on Marquette Street. Personally, I looked forward to his cuts whenever the great occasion availed itself. He used the best powders and bay rum!

George made some delicious pickles. I *never* have found any others that compare in any way! They were not a traditional dill; the flavor was indescribable. And then, Em always managed to make the very best peanut butter cookies. What a thrill it would be to find a package of them included in our picnic lunch for the trip home. And then, more specially, sometimes she'd put in an extra package of these culinary delights just for me! Em, like Minnie, was an excellent cook!

The dining room was in the center of the house at Marquette Street. Off that were the bathroom, two bedrooms, living room, and kitchen. To get to the "attic" bedroom, we'd go thru Gin's animal-bedecked bedroom. The attic was the best room in the whole house. It was Duane's room, and, of course, it was secluded enough to please any boy! From that vantage point we could survey the entire neighborhood, and if no adults were watching we could climb out on the front porch roof!

One time Emma had some beautiful fruit on the dining room table. It was at absolutely the peak of maturity. The apple was especially appealing (no pun intended). The temptation was too great for me. I had to have at least a bite. Then I could turn that bite side down so it wouldn't be seen. That bite proved to me that all things are not as they appear . . . the fruit was *wax*! The bite was never repaired, to my knowledge! We'll not discuss any disciplinary actions taken by either parents or kin.

Gin's room, although a part of the thoroughfare to the upstairs, seemed to be a rather set-apart or even "holy" spot. It was no place for any play time except for the girls. At the same time, it held an attraction for me because of all the animal figurines she had on her table and bookshelves. Each had its name and Gin was very knowledgeable of the breeds represented. Her favorite was the cocker spaniel. Her live one (Cocker) was quite a singer. Whenever someone sat at the piano to play (it was a player piano, too) that dog would sit on the bench and howl to the delight of the majority of those present.

Then there was the popular, attractive alley behind the garage. What a wonderful spot . . . secluded and yet so available for the neighborhood games relegated to the rather busy streets back home.

Cars in the big city were always garaged. Not only were there cars in these "domesticated out-buildings," but all the garden tools and supplies: the reel-type, hand-pushed lawn mower, a rake, a shovel, a hoe . . . no electric- or gasoline-powered equipment back then! Still the yard was always well manicured and kept. It must have taken at least a half hour to mow the lawn, but it was always so neat!

The day came when Duane was old enough to have his own car. Earnings from delivering the *Detroit Free Press* and other odd jobs provided him with enough cash for a beautiful Model A Ford coupe with a rumble seat and all! In the rear window he put part of the wrapper from an "Oh Henry" candybar. The "Oh" was deftly and meticulously cut off. This gave the classy old machine a bit more distinctive individuality. The car was aptly named "Henry."

There was much celebration in the camp when Duane was tapped for a job at the Star Cutter Co. before he even left high school! An accomplished draftsman already, he 'jes growed' from there. (I think that among my memorabilia there is a Star Cutter Co. pencil that was "loot" Duane gave me as a gift.) Shortly thereafter (as maturity came) Gin got a job with the phone company. That, too, was excitement and good righteous brag material. (Never did get a spare phone from her, though!) Both these folks are still known to be a great credit to the Wubbena name even though they never carried it per se.

Always there were lengthy discussions concerning travel time and fastest routes between Elgin and Detroit. Both Duane and George were known as fast, though safe, drivers. And so it seemed that no matter what route we would take, we could never make the trip in as short a time as the Fluturs.

We who are a bit less daring used to be quite concerned when we heard of them cruising down the gravel country lanes near Standish traveling seventy and eighty miles per hour. Now that's fast even by today's standards. Sometimes we even rode with them. When confronted with the perspiration on our pale faces, they'd tell of others they'd known who would pass the power poles in a blur.

We were always excited when the Fluturs and the Gablers got together. The melding of the Wubbena heritage surpassed the "outsiders'" names and backgrounds to become a firm foundation for generations to come.

TALKA

Apparently it became the honor and responsibility of both John and Talka, the oldest son and daughter of the clan, to raise the family in their early years. Somehow the mothering instincts seemed to hover over Talka for years. It just seemed that all the rest looked to her and John in many ways, and the concern for the welfare of each was always apparent in their conversation as well as their action.

Talka became an invalid either during World War I or shortly thereafter. She had been an army nurse and had become afflicted with bone tuberculosis. Her right leg had to be immobilized which necessitated her use of a wheelchair in order to get around at home and in public.

About 1925 Talka first made her home with Minnie and her husband Louis. During the time she was with them she was occasionally hospitalized at Sherman Hospital in Elgin and Hines Veterans Hospital (Speedway) in Hines, Illinois, and she periodically "rested" at a nursing home, Resthaven in Elgin.

Louis was quite inventive. Realizing that Talka would want to get around, he designed and built: (1) a trunk for the rear of the 1925 Dodge (the original predecessor of the trunk in use today?) along with (2) an adjustable rack for Talka's wheelchairs (for she eventually had several for different occasions). This combination extended the car by probably three to five feet, and so he equipped it with the necessary safety reflectors and lights way ahead of the time they became required by law. That rack was so adaptable that it was used not only on the 1925 Dodge, but also on the 1935 and 1941 models. I don't recall its use on the Frazer or any of the later models.

When the front porch was enlarged and screened, he designed an elevator operated by a series of pulleys and a heavily waxed sliding rail or track so Talka could be lowered and raised almost into the car! Without this, Talka would slide onto a wide, beautifully finished board (assured to be splinter-free) with extended handles and then be carried from either her bed or her wheelchair to the car or other destination by two strong people. (Talka had become quite "large" in her later years.)

It may have appeared to some that the care of Talka was more of a burden than the fact. Sure, there were inconveniences, but she undoubtedly carried at least, if not more than, her fair share of the load.

Talka was a master seamstress and knitter. She could carry on a normal conversation with anyone, and still knit a sweater, a pair of mittens, or other fancier works and never miss a stitch or comment! Her hands and fingers flew. Those mittens were held in place on the sweaters or jackets with a knit cord traveling from the mitten on one side, through the sleeve, across the inside of the back of the garment, down through the other sleeve, and to the other mitten. An ingenious Wubbena way to prevent the loss of valuable TLC-made mittens.

As warm as these mittens were, they were absolutely no good for making and/or throwing snow balls. They got wet and then so cold they'd freeze. Of course, they weren't made for that kind of treatment. But they *were* warm when used as intended.

Not only the family was blessed with the fruits of her labors! Mr. Geirtz, who was the mailman on their route for as long as anyone could remember, always, but *always*, had a fresh pair of Talka's mittens to wear, especially at Christmas time. He also wore Talka-crafted sweaters along with his duly authorized uniform. She had a computerized memory bank in her head to file sizes for everyone . . . except growing children.

Many needy children, too, were given those famed mittens and sweaters. Even if they only looked needy, Talka was the loving donor. Her mothering instincts went far beyond her family.

She was a frequent visitor to Bible Conferences like Winona Lake and Cedar Lake, Indiana, where she'd spend weeks at a time. Conferences at Moody Bible Institute and Moody Memorial Church in Chicago were special to her, too. All of these institutions really catered to her needs as a handicapped person.

Resthaven was a beautiful nursing home operated by a friend of Talka's, Miss Libbie Goll. Whenever Talka felt she was in the way at Minnie's (i.e., spring cleaning, painting, etc.) she'd retreat to Resthaven. (She was *very* conscious of any stress factors that appeared.)

Resthaven was a beautiful place, and the care she needed was there. Someone of the family would visit her at least once daily and bring her mail and family chatter. It didn't take her long to get homesick.

Her bedroom at home looked across a vacant lot toward one of the (then) main highways and she could pretty well survey the neighborhood activities from there or any other place in the house. The awnings over her two windows shaded her, but never hid her from the view of passers-by. She could be seen from the street, sitting there doing—you guessed it—her knitting.

Her friendship with Miss Libbie (as she was called around the house) benefited the whole family, who got the same royal treatment Talka did! On such special occasions as Thanksgiving, Christmas, New Year's, Easter and others, there would be a knock at the door on the evening before. A gentleman would deliver the total dinner, including fresh baked bread, fresh veggies, and then the rest of the meal all ready to be cooked. The joke always seemed to be that the family didn't dare to prepare anything, just sit and wonder, for there was never any promise of anything coming from the hill. And pride and decorum dictated that we wouldn't ask!

Talka had friends world-wide. But close to home was one celebrity she met at Resthaven. Helen E. Duff was frequently seen walking down the street singing hymns and just enjoying life. She would come into the house and seat herself at the piano and play quite well. At first people thought she had caught the wrong elevator and hadn't quite gotten to the top. But in reality, the person we called Miss Duff was Dr. Duff! A well-published hymnwriter, her name was found as author and composer of many of the hymns in most of the hymnals found in our home. On learning of her accomplishments, the attitude of the household turned quite quickly to one of respect and admiration.

But that's the way it was with many of Talka's friends.

JOHNSFIELD

To describe Standish, the word "quaint" should cover it. The tiny "business district" included the newspaper office where the *Arenac County Independent* was published. Wyatt, John's eldest son, seemed to be the number one man there. Down the street was Buddy Strauss' office; he was another in-law all the way from South Africa and a capable dentist. The homes always seemed well-kept and the pride of ownership showed in more than just the buildings. Most seemed to have good-sized vegetable or floral gardens as well as individualized landscaping reflecting the personalities of the owners as well as their independence.

Trees in the yards and porches on the houses seemed to say "We're glad you came our way. Just come and sit a spell." Yes, the neighbors were just that . . . neighbors. Everyone knew what was going on all around town.

John and family lived out in the country on the old homestead in a locality called Johnsfield. His place was called the Crescent Creamery Farm. (Does anyone know where the name originated?) The only way to find the place was to ask directions. Leaving metropolitan Standish, it seemed one would course and weave through nicely fenced pasture, grazing, and grain fields to get to Johnsfield. Pulling into the yard, on the right was a barn or shed surrounded by farm wagons of various sizes, hay rakes, sickle bar mowers, and various other types of horse-drawn farming equipment.

In the shed was Wyatt's and/or Kate's Ford. Passing through the gate from the road, the drive broadened between the house and that shed toward the barn. That way it accommodated both incoming and departing traffic of cars and farm equipment and the horses could turn around in the yard to park the equipment. No, there was no paving either on the road or the driveway, so there was plenty of dust on the dry days, and an abundance of mud in the rainy season.

There sat the big white house on the left of the driveway. We could usually plan on seeing our beloved Uncle John with pipe in mouth, paper or book in hand, rocking on the porch. That is, unless there was field or barn work to be done. He was always a welcome sight, and a Wubbena welcome was always the best!

Aunt Laura was never too busy to come out to the porch to greet the guests as they arrived. She'd make her way either through the living room or out the back door, wiping her hands on her apron as she approached, and then each one was greeted with open arms, a kiss and a hug . . . sometimes even a tear or two.

Somehow we'd all make our way, generally through the living room, into the huge kitchen. The monstrous, black, wood-burning cookstove dominated the wall to the right where we entered and cautiously avoided tripping over the pail of water. Not only could that pail serve as an early American fire extinguisher, but it was used to fill a reservoir for hot water on the range . . . for baths, shaving, cooking, or whatever use one had for it!

On the outside wall, set between the windows, was a big white porcelain sink set into a wooden "counter." No spigots were in sight. One quickly learned that this was the farm! The only running water came out of the pump at the right of the sink. Ice cold for drinking and just as cold for anything else! (There was still another pump outdoors, too.) Were there some storage cabinets over the sink?

It seems there was a small table with chairs in the kitchen; no refrigerator, nor do I recall an icebox. There were other quaint ways of keeping things necessarily cool.

Just off this good-sized kitchen was the enormous dining room. It seemed the table was at least a small city block long. And then when the aunts, uncles, brothers, sisters, cousins, and in-laws got around it for a meal . . . now that was a crowd! However, there was always plenty of room for all in the generous Wubbena spirit, and all the girls pitched in for the preparation.

Today, the other room from the kitchen would be called the mud room. Here were hung the coats, jackets, heavy outer wear, and the boots, which were cleaned *before* one entered even the mud room, were stacked neatly under the hangers. Some pantry shelves were there, but the most intriguing thing was the cream separator. I was only fortunate enough to see it operate on a few occasions. What a miraculous invention! As the raw milk was poured into the oval-shaped bowl on top, someone would turn the crank at just the right speed and out of two separate spigots would come the two milk products: cream from one and milk from the other. There was a real trick to turning the crank. Too fast and the cream was of the wrong consistency, even partially whipped; too slowly and rich milk came from both spigots! The cream spigot always flowed so much more slowly than the other, and that was mystifying to a young mind.

Actually, this room must have been a rear porch which was now closed in. Just beyond the outside door was a small stoop and a short flight of stairs. Several feet from these stairs was a small wooden structure which seemed to attract an undue number of flies. Commonly called a privy, it explained the absence of a necessary room found in modern homes.

Tissue as we know it today was indeed a luxury. The cleansing commodity was more than likely either the old newspapers (But *never* the *Independent*!) or well-crinkled pages from a usually obsolete Sears Roebuck or
Montgomery Ward mail order catalogue. Even when well-crinkled, one soon
realized that none of these were the most comfortable to use.

Directly behind this was the barn which housed the horses, pigs, and
cows, mingled with chickens, cats, and other critters. The pigs' and cows'
homes faced the house, while the horses made their abode at the end of the
barn. Right outside the pigpen there was a hand-operated corn sheller. (For
the enlightenment of the city folks this took the kernels off the cobs.) Right
along the fence at the pigpen was the feeding trough. Every city child should
have the opportunity to see these animals "make pigs of themselves." A real
life education. Just walking past them with an empty bucket created pig
havoc!

Going into the barn during milking time was a real eye-opener. The
unwary could easily be surprised by a shot of milk in the face aptly aimed by
Uncle John, Wyatt, or Shirley. The cats in the area were always ready for a
treat of fresh, warm milk, too . . . right from the cow.

The horses were huge workers! They were gentle enough to ride for the
city guests, and still strong, big, and usually willing enough to pull the heav-
iest of equipment. I don't ever recall seeing a tractor or mechanical device
on the farm, except that during threshing time there was a motor-driven community thresher that traveled from farm to farm. John used its services for
threshing.

There was a fence traveling from the road to beyond the barn, separating
a hayfield from the yard. Harvest was a dusty job, and a back-breaker when
haying time came around. The horses pulled the rake, which made windrows
of the ripened hay. Praying for several days of dry weather, the hay lay there
until Uncle John determined it was dry enough to stack in the barn. The
back-breaking part came when the hay was loaded onto the wagons for
transport to the barn. Three-tined forks were used to pick up the hay and
swing it onto the wagon in one rhythmic, sweeping motion. The horses
seemed to sense just when to move and how far as the windrows of hay were
devoured by the wagon and those who were pitching the hay. No hay balers
were available then.

During the hay season I always envied Duane Flutur. He always got to go
to the farm to help! Me? I suffered from hay fever and felt I was considered
a liability for that kind of work . . . and I was.

In the evening after the chores were done and supper dishes were stashed
and tables set for the next meal, everyone would gather in the living room.
Story-swapping time for all. Another one of the beauties of being a Wubbena:

the kids were an integral part and not just an acknowledged entity. There on the inside wall separating the living room from the kitchen was the pump organ. In amongst the stories, someone would suggest a song and those who remembered would join in the singing. Then Shirley ("Toe") and Duane (called "Toot" for some reason) would break out their guitars and sing or lead the bunch in singing. Good music, good humor, great fellowship and camaraderie.

Then off to bed (?) at least to try to sleep; adults in the house and all the kids in the barn! This was all a great time of family togetherness, no griping, and positive fun challenges for all! This is how we were raised as Wubbena kin. What a heritage is ours!

CALIFORNIA

German was always the language of comfort in our house. The grand occasions when the Wubbena girls would get together was like Octoberfest. To be unilingual was a tragedy in that group! How the Deutsch would flow!

It stands to reason, then, that this would overflow into family conversations, too. All of the family understood and spoke quite fluent German in those days. How we'd laugh when the "girls"—Min, El, Em, and Talch— would, without warning, switch from English to German whenever they wanted to communicate something confidential or secret. The switch, at times, would be so fast, and yet so apparent, that it would capture the attention of all present and what a laugh! Everyone understood the tale perfectly!

The tale was told of Talka's childhood in Standish. Apparently she had a suitor (in whom, she claimed, she had no interest). He appeared to be the type who didn't have his roof completely shingled. His joy and delight was to skip and hop through metropolitan Standish singing to the top of his lungs as he followed Talka, "I asked Mr. Ribbenaw (Wubbena) if I could have Pelky (Talka) Ribbenaw . . . climbing down the golden stairs."

Talka was a generous person to our family. She would voluntarily and confidentially finance many of our travels. Wherever and whenever we'd tour, even for short trips, Dad would be asked to stop the car and, with the rest of us, to check the roadside for flowers to pick. Splendid idea, even in the deserts of Arizona and some of the other states we were privileged to visit.

You see, this was a code. Rest stops for the rest of us were quite simple. But Talka, being handicapped, had us beat! She always carried a bedpan! The last question as we left home usually was, "Talch, hast du deine bedpan?" (Translation: "Talka, do you have your bedpan?") The only way to empty it was out the rear door or window of the car on her side. Imagine the appearance of that side of the car on a long trip!

On one trip to California we took Talka to the Willard Hotel in Los Angeles, a part of BIOLA (the acronym for Bible Institute of Los Angeles) University at that time. We left Elgin in a heavy snow storm. Dad had purchased some miraculous windshield wiper blades especially for this trip. As the snow would hit them, it would melt and leave a residue on the windshield which kept it from freezing. We thought surely the snow would let up before we got to Springfield, Illinois . . . then St. Louis . . . then anytime before dark.

Our destination was Rolla, Missouri, and a tourist cabin village there. (Motels were still in the future.) There was no indication of the storm abating. Road signs (the few that there were in those days) couldn't be seen and darkness slammed down on us making it even more hazardous.

It was hard to distinguish the road, but we were fortunate that there was a car ahead blazing the trail for us. As we began the treacherous trek down a hill, we saw another car making its way down the opposite side of the wide valley. It appeared this car was traveling much too fast for the road conditions.

As we watched it approach, the car swerved past and missed the car immediately in front of us, and then struck our left front turning us toward the right side of the road, and then nudged the left rear so we headed into a rather steep embankment. We began climbing the embankment uncontrollably and then eased over, coming to a stop completely upside down!

Two panicky voices were heard. Mine was telling dad to shut off the ignition (which his pained, bruised knee had already done) and Talka's kept saying "Em can't breathe." As miracle after miracle unfolded from the accident, we learned that Talka had landed sitting on Emma's face. No wonder she couldn't breathe.

We always carried a good supply of food stuffs, for meals were picnics most of the trip. Our overnights were in cottages which hopefully had cooking facilities (all for $3 or less a night!). There were two dozen eggs in the trunk of the car . . . not one was even cracked! All the adults wore eyeglasses, yet none were even maladjusted! Talka's wheelchairs were secure and unharmed on the rack at the rear of the car!

Sure, all of us had bruises and sore muscles, but there were absolutely no debilitating injuries. Passers-by quickly gathered around and offered assistance. Some went on by and contacted a wrecker to fetch us out of that white wilderness. It surely took hours before they arrived, and by that time the car had been righted.

Sleep came hard that night. By morning the decision was made to continue on the way. Battery acid had dripped onto some of the upholstery and some of our clothing, ventilating both! There was a distinctive dent in the roof over the left rear window (which was broken out). Other than these things, the car ran well for the balance of the trip. We did feel that we looked like the folks in *The Grapes of Wrath* as they traveled west. That was the old '35 Dodge which took us on that eventful trip.

Dad always had the knack of foresight and planning ahead. On this same trip, we were aware of the dangers of drinking just any water and so Dad packed a bottle of his own vintage wine hidden in the depths of the trunk of the car. (The 1935 Dodge had dual trunks: one accessed from behind the back seat, and the other from outside in the rear.)

As we approached the boundary of California and Arizona we were stopped. These were inspection stations not unlike the ones found between the United States and Canada or the United States and Mexico. We were required to empty the trunks and open all the luggage! What a surprise when the back of the seat was folded forward. Embarrassment prevailed when the bottle of wine showed its face. The vestiges of Prohibition were still alive and well.

Poor Dad. His weak response and only defense was a faltering, "That's for medicinal purposes only." It truly was, but could we really believe the officers accepted that? Then, on the way back home, we took another route. Not because of the wine, although it was still intact, but for the scenery.

For souvenirs we'd purchased several bushels of oranges and even had the opportunity to pick some of our own.

When we approached the Arizona border again, we stopped as directed. The officers wanted to confiscate all of our oranges! After much ado, we were persuaded and allowed to peel every one of those oranges and then proceed! It seems there was something on the skins of the California orange which the Arizona Department of Agriculture didn't want to threaten their crops.

We enjoyed them all the way home anyway!!!

AN ELGIN REUNION

When Dad built our house, he was very creative. It was built with the future in mind, and yet never did it have a semi-completed look. The basement was a complete unit. In years to come, it became a small apartment. It was in fact a gathering place for the kids of the community, or the kids of visitors when the adults wanted to be alone in the living room upstairs. In the summer it was always cool and seldom damp, while in the cold northern Illinois winter, it provided a dry, warm, open play area heated by the huge warm air or hot water furnaces (whichever was appropriate for the season).

There was a gas "hot plate" available for cooking, but used primarily for heating laundry water, and a "fruit cellar" which was equivalent to the storage cellars folks used to dig in the ground to keep potatoes, apples, and such.

Dad always bought canned goods by the case, potatoes, flour, and sugar by the hundred pounds, and fruit by the bushel. All kept very well in this separated, tightly closed corner of the basement.

In those days, people who worked together seemed to socialize more than today. It was traditional that Dad had his co-workers and their spouses over for a potato pancake supper. Tables were rough boards set on top of sawhorses, and benches weren't much more than boards on short legs. The tables were covered with cloth covers (paper covers weren't yet available). Tableware was borrowed from participants and neighbors.

The basement looked like an old country church supper set-up. Dad donned his apron and cooked potato pancakes until everyone was totally incapacitated by their own gluttony! The mingled odors of those suppers stayed in the house for weeks, and the success of the occasion was the topic of conversation for months to come.

In fact, the success was so great that the idea to have a family reunion joining both Mom's and Dad's families soon became reality!

The basement was the main dining hall for the meals. Adults ate first and then the children. No, we didn't miss a thing. While the adults ate, we were on our own, and we thoroughly covered the neighborhood with the games of tag, variations of hide and seek, and other active and wild games until called to the meal. There was always plenty of food and plenty of action.

Always the cousins from both sides of the family swapped stories about adventures both real and fictional . . . and no one was able to discern the difference. Some may have doubted the truth, but no one dared voice the doubt. The older cousins seemed to gravitate toward the adult groups, rallying in their dreams and sharing in their hopes. The younger ones seemed to be more intent on physical activities, especially running and causing the adults their share of anxiety and grief. There is no recollection of any major, significant problems with such a group, and to this day there is still a strong sense of camaraderie.

There were the picture sessions: first individual families; then Dad's clan; then Mom's clan; then the combination of both; then the cousins, etc., ad infinitum! When one considers the eleven from Dad's side and the ten from Mom's side and all of their offspring, that was quite a crowd. A compatible crowd, I might add. Can you imagine the time it took to feed, to photograph, and even to just corral this bunch for any reason at all?

No, not all were able to attend. There were those from Seattle, Los Angeles, Denver, Upper Michigan, and other points.

Although this event would be newsworthy today, I don't recall any media publicity on that day at all. All we have (and it's great) is the fun of reminiscing.

THREE INARO

Living on the edge of the city limits had its benefits in the early 1900s. The lack of meaningful building codes and restrictions could easily have caused plenty of neighborhood friction. But in those days, neighbors communicated and had respect for one another without the need for legal entanglements.

Long before the World War II Victory Gardens were conceived, Dad kept at least one garden with enough fruit and veggies for us to enjoy, for Mom to can and preserve, and for the neighbors to share in the benefits (as they, too, would share their bounties with us).

Along with the garden, Dad raised chickens—enough for us to eat and to keep us supplied with the freshest of eggs. There were enough eggs to keep me busy Saturdays, taking my little red wagon around the neighborhood selling eggs for fifteen cents a dozen. How it pained Dad to raise the price to a quarter because of inflation! The mature hens were sold live for a quarter each.

Saturday was a day, too, to prepare for those special Sunday dinners. This meant butchering a couple of hens for baking or frying. While Mom was in the kitchen baking bread (it was much more economical than spending ten cents a loaf at the store), pies, and/or cake, and preparing those garden vegetables, Dad and I would be in the basement cleaning the chickens.

Occasionally, treat of all treats, Mom made chicken and dumplings. These were fluffy clouds which would billow to form a luscious, edible cover over the stewed chicken. Then the whole stew was put in the oven for a few minutes until a brown-tinged crust was formed. That was eating!

One spring when the new chicks arrived I asked Dad about the possibility of raising a few ducks along with the chicks. After considerable discussion, he agreed. He gave me the privilege of going to the feed store to buy a couple. There in a pen were three squeaking, lonely hatchlings. How could anyone *dare* to separate them? When I got home with the trio, I was quite hesitant about putting them in with the chicks. But I did. First response: the chicks, apparently concerned that the ducks had more than their share of beak, tried to help the ducks by pecking at their broad beaks quite violently.

It wasn't long before the ducks began their retaliation by grabbing the chicks by their tiny, fuzzy tails, even to the point of de-skinning some of them! As they matured, a mute truce was apparently drawn and observed.

An old washtub set in the ground soon served as a "lake" for the ducks. Although they were allowed to roam while the chickens stayed in the pen, the three never left the yard or wandered off without me or Bingo, our dog. If ever I needed to leave the yard without the procession of three ducks, I'd put them in the pen with the chickens. Whenever I'd cut grass, they'd follow up and down the rows. When it came time to cut the neighbors' yards, they'd proceed in perfect alignment all the way there. Then as I'd collect the clippings (to use as a forage for the chickens), they'd enjoy romping in the moist, fragrant cuttings in the wheel barrow. Tiring of that, they'd once again line up behind me and the trusty muscle-powered lawnmower.

It never bothered me that they'd not been named. They always came and responded to our various imitation duck calls. Mom, in all her Wubbena wisdom, felt that as they were such close family pets, each should have his or her own identity.

It was our custom (and a good one, too) each evening following "supper" to have our daily Bible readings. We were reading Psalm 23, a particularly short passage, on this day. As we completed the sixth verse, Mom exclaimed, almost irreverently, "There's the name for your ducks!"

And so they were named Shirley, Goodness, and Mercy—simply because they followed me all the days of their lives!

PICKING BERRIES

The gravel roads cut through the forests were straight as the trees were tall. It was like going down a long, dark, green corridor. The sun could hit the road for only a few short hours daily. It seemed that no light at all could get to the ground through those thickly leafed trees . . . it looked like night in all that shade.

It was blueberry season, and we were visiting Uncle Harry and Aunt Len in northern Michigan. With the density of the woods, it was hard for us to comprehend that anything, even blueberries, could grow beneath them.

The appointed day came and we walked with buckets and boxes for probably a quarter-mile before allowing ourselves to be swallowed by the darkness of the woods.

All was so quiet in the forest. The only exceptions were the occasional, unusual bird call (were they real?) and the rattle and rustle of the leaves, pine needles, and cones as we or some unseen animal disturbed them. It truly instilled a quiet reverence in each of us. As we were awestruck by the cool and quiet, we whispered any conversation and questions, and almost walked on some of the most luscious blueberries in my memory. Before we were allowed to pick, Aunt Len cautioned us to continue our walk further and keep our eyes open. We hadn't asked permission to pick berries!

As we walked still deeper into the woods, Aunt Len pointed out some huts in the darkness . . . and then we could faintly discern some figures quietly standing and watching us. We were to stay still as she went and asked permission not only to pick berries, but to come onto their land.

It seems we were actually trespassing on an Indian reservation—we were about to pick their livelihood. Yes, they were good to us and even helped us to select and pick the berries—enough for us to carry several crates full back home on the train.

UNCLE HARRY

Harry was a railroad man. Sounds like a likely title for a country western song, doesn't it? He was a stationmaster for several of the smaller stations in Upper Michigan.

His wife, Lenore (Len) was a tall, slow talking, fast driving lady of the North Woods to me. As did Harry, she always had a kind word to say about everyone and everything. Both were always ready and eager to entertain. (This, too, seems to be a true Wubbena trait.)

One of their several stations was Trout Creek. The very name stirs the imagination of a fisherman! As I recall, their house was directly across the tracks from the station. There were two tracks and a siding there. At the time there wasn't much more than a general store and a station. I'm unaware of the local industry at the time.

On one of our several visits there, a train derailment caused quite a stir in the community. By the time we arrived, most of the tracks were cleared and repaired and all wreckage removed except for one passenger car which was still off the tracks. A beautiful specimen, I asked Uncle Harry what was to be done with it. He said that if I wanted it, I could have it. But I had to leave it there.

Of course, I hoped to move it to Elgin. How proud I was! All kinds of plans were made by me for the placement in the yard at home. How I bragged to the neighborhood kids about my fancy railroad car. They'd see when we got it in the back yard and we could all play in it!

But I never got it moved. So as far as I know that car is still there . . . and still is mine . . . Uncle Harry said so.

One day in Trout Creek while we sat at the little station bay window surveying the tracks for signs of incoming trains, Harry started to teach me the use of the telegraph key. He actually had someone on the line send simple alphabets, etc., and then I was expected to reply in kind. That was OK. But then the difficult part came! Harry expected me to write down the messages as they came: first the alphabet, then the sending station code, then the receiving station code. All this was not too hard. He handed me the pencil. The key began to chatter and I tried to write. Harry had given me a pencil with a rubber lead.

Then there was Bruce Crossing. Harry and Len lived in an apartment over the general store right next to the station. All I remember about that thriving metropolis is the crossroads in front of the store and the railroad on the other side. For being so far in the "boonies," it was quite a modern store. But that's all there was.

One of the beauty spots not far away was Agate Falls. Haven't seen it since, but it was a sight of apparent true untouched wilderness. Harry claimed it was one of the outstanding trout fishing holes.

Harry had a place of his own not too far from Bruce Crossing. It may have been in suburban Bruce Crossing. Numerous times we were invited to spend some time in his log cabin. If memory serves me right, there was a stream with a bounty of fish just outside the back door. A natural "freezer" made of logs kept venison, bear, fish, and wild fowl for summer consumption. The logs were of such insulating quality that no ice or freezing mechanism was needed (or am I dreaming).

Memories of Harry are very, very warm. Somehow the impression was that Harry and Len were a whole lot like brother and sister. And yet, it was apparent that they were indeed husband and wife. When Harry passed away, Len tried to contact and even visit all of Harry's kinfolk to ask if she could remarry should the opportunity arise! Did she?

THE WORLD'S FAIR REUNION

All indicators tell us that the year was 1933. The Chicago World's Fair was in its prime. How the planning began or went ahead is unknown to me, but it must have really steamrolled. How it came to center in Elgin, Illinois, at Minnie's home is still more hidden history. But that's where it was. Talka and Ella were living with Minnie and her husband Louis (William Gabler). Emma and her husband George (Flutur) were probably the first to arrive for the festivities.

It seemed to be a sweltering evening. Dinner was long gone, there was no TV to watch, and radio, although still a novelty, was not all that captivating. What then? Those were the days that people really got acquainted with one another.

How the word got around, I really don't know. Sitting around the dining room table, the discussion was centered on the terror of the tornado which devastated downtown Elgin in 1926. Many of the stores were wiped out and the whole area looked like a battleground. Dad Gabler made the remark that we could expect a tornado every seven years.

Sure enough, as we sat around the table, the lights went out, the candles were lit and then extinguished because of the fire hazard. The wind blew. The lightning flashed with the accompanying roar of thunder. Rain with heavy hail battered the house and yard. We debated moving to the basement, but transporting Talka and her wheelchair was somewhat of a problem. The children did go to the basement and had a time playing games, totally unaware of the possible dangers. Yes, in the dark.

How the word ever got around in those days, we'll never know. We learned of the devastation and at daybreak tried to tour the town. Property damage was overwhelming and yet I don't recall any loss of life. Even an orphanage on the west side of town was uniquely damaged. Each of the dormitories had the north wall nicely peeled away from the building. Shelves and trinkets were all intact and, of course, the rooms on that side of the house were wide open to public scrutiny.

As more of the Wubbena clan arrived, the city-wide, narrated tours increased. It must have been quite a sight with the Gablers' 1925 Dodge leading the Michigan folks in their Fords through the business district, industrial areas, and then the tornado-damaged residences and farms. The big storm provided much entertainment and conversation throughout the entire reunion.

It's difficult to recall the housing arrangements, but it seems that there were those who slept on the floor, others in the basement, and did others sleep in friends' or neighbors' homes? The basement was the general dining hall for the entire group. Short sawhorses supported planks and boards which served as tables. There was a gas hotplate in the basement along with more-than-adequate washing facilities. The women, both laws and in-laws, seemed to revel in the meal preparation as they recalled childhood and told current tales on spouses and offspring. A grand and glorious time.

Even with a crowd like this, which could be noisy and fun-loving, there was always the time of thanksgiving for the bounty our God had provided, and such gratitude for the privilege of being together one more time. Yes, there was always much praise, too, for the heritage and solid parental influence. There was the undergirding of the older ones who responded so well and freely when their parents were called to be with the Lord they loved. I never recall overhearing any negative reactions about being raised by older brothers and sisters or of the heavy responsibilities unloaded at such tender ages. No cry for, or about, the lack of government support or welfare. Mutual needs seemed to be met by mutual family assistance and encouragement. "You CAN do it!," was the battle cry.

The sequence of arrival for this reunion is of no consequence. Some seemed to stick in the memory while others aren't just dim, but not recalled at all. Were it not for some pictures, one could not really remember their presence. Is that cruel to say? Not really. Those were probably more significant with their quiet, humble ways of support.

I remember Bill arriving in his crisp military uniform, boots polished to a mirror finish as was his Sam Brown belt. (Oh, how I admired and coveted that!) Every crease was in its proper place, and not a spot or piece of lint to be found. Where he had been is clouded, too, but his arrival was as if a general had come to grace our presence. How proud everyone seemed to be. Was it possibly pride in the younger brother coming home to the family?

The Fluturs had already arrived. Did some of the Standish folks come with them? Was it Catherine or Wyatt who drove? Naturally all of them drove Fords. The conversation among the men was always about the best and fastest routes, gasoline consumption, speed and average speed. Duane and Shirley took the wheel, but with someone else in control. There were always those significant points of interest used as reference points for comparing routes and necessary stops. There was always the lunch packed, saving the sheer terror of spending on meals at a high-priced restaurant. There were the Coldwater and Lansing rest and gas stops. The Studebaker Proving Grounds near South Bend, the smoke around the south side of Chicago, and many others, depending on the route different ones preferred and used.

Whatever their point of origin, it was Lenore, Harry's wife, who drove. They, too, had their Ford . . . or did they come by train, since Harry was the railroader? Len had the reputation of being a fast driver. Then, too, in those days being a woman driver did her reputation behind the wheel absolutely no good. At one time she lost control of the car and had quite a serious accident, rolling the car over and all. I don't recall ever seeing Harry behind the wheel. Maybe he was a better copilot/navigator than pilot!

Fred, Henry, and Charles undoubtedly were there at this reunion, too. There are group pictures in existence that show them there. In my mind they were the quiet, contemplative ones. Although it seems that even in humor (and there was much of that) that generation of Wubbenas were noted for weighing carefully each word they spoke. And that's why people listened!

Can anyone tell . . . did not the Gabler clan join with the Wubbena reunion during that time? There are vague recollections of both families together and multitudes of cousins running about the neighborhood and generally getting in one another's hair. It seemed the age groups naturally gravitated together and there was a good melding of families.

Was it a whole week the Wubbenas were together, or did they come together for a period of time when all could be together as a total family and then leave whenever? It's hard to visualize a grand exodus. There were always plenty of hugs and kisses by both laws and in-laws. That was the origin of "kissin' cousins," for sure!

How did the animals fare in all this? There were always pets around.

How did they cope with the mob? How did the neighbors cope? Apparently the general behavior was more than acceptable. Secretly, I think that the neighbors enjoyed the extra burst in population, rather than just tolerated it.

The turnout was so very gratifying for all the family . . . or should I say families? But that's the Wubbena clan, isn't it! The family that sticks together . . . that's Wubbena! Charles, Henry, Fred, Harry, and Bill had all "been around" while John stayed on the farm and gave it his best. Going to Chicago must have been not only exciting and revealing, but also quite traumatic.

One of the favored spots, we'd call it a tourist trap today, was Maxwell Street. There was absolutely no room for any type of vehicle on the street during business hours. Police were obvious in every block. While there were shops with the traditional oak doors and glass store fronts, the bulk of business was transacted from carts and booths under umbrellas and awnings right on the street itself. Ladies were not encouraged to carry their purses, and the menfolk were told to keep their hands on their wallets.

The appetizing odors of Jewish and other foods being cooked with more than sufficient garlic and other pungent spices, mingled with the strong odor of unwashed bodies and cheap perfumes to either nauseate or whet one's appetite. But no one dared eat from the vendor's trays and wagons, not even the fresh fruits and vegetables.

Dad Gabler proudly showed off his bargain purchase of twelve pair of socks for a dollar! Sure enough, there were twenty-four socks, but not one matched another, and several had good-sized holes in them. So much for the bargain days!

On to the Fair.

The sky ride seemed to go on forever.

Every country had outdone itself in displays and promotions. As one would expect, the exhibits were manned by those who were fluent in their native tongue. That is exactly what intrigued the group at the Black Forest, the German exhibit. It seemed the older Wubbenas found camaraderie among the native Germans. I'm sure they compared history notes and hunted for kin even then.

Surveying all the wonders of the known world at that time, most were intrigued with sights and scenes from different nations.

Here it was that John made his famous statement. On looking back at the crowds on Maxwell Street, and then the vast sea of people at the fair, his wondering comment was, "Where do they all come from? What do they all do?"

THE STANDISH REUNION

Dad Gabler was the oldest in his family. Mom's brother, my Uncle John, was the eldest in his. It seemed the lot of the eldest in each family to host the family reunions.

Uncle John was a farmer, working the family farm now called the Crescent Creamery. There's no way I could ever recall the number of cattle he had nor how many acres of land which were on the farm. The community was called Johnsfield after my grandfather—the German immigrant merchant marine turned farmer.

It was always an exciting time to travel to Standish, for all of Mom's kin (except Uncle Bill and Aunt Maude, and Uncle Fred and Aunt Mildred) were within minutes or short hours distant. The primary thing was seeing Uncle John and Aunt Laura. The memorable greeting was the picturesque scene of him sitting on the farmhouse porch in his straightback rocker, pipe in mouth, always reading and Aunt Laura with her winning smile nearby popping snap beans or making something with those gnarled hands.

When we arrived, making our way through the array of farm wagons and equipment up the short dirt drive to the porch, the greetings were always the warmest. The fragrant smells coming from the old farm kitchen and the huge wood cookstove made the welcome seem even warmer.

Although the farmhouse was typically large (at least in my memory), sleeping facilities were always at a premium. The floor was the most desirable, it would seem—at least until someone suggested that the young folks (I was never certain that the term included me because I was a "child") sleep in the hay loft.

That was exciting! Being the youngest of all the cousins present had both its advantages and its disadvantages. It was a distinct advantage to have the adult community on your side for special treats and attention. The downside of the younger age came from the cousins who felt it their responsibility to make certain the younger charges were able to withstand the necessary taunts, jokes, general trickery, and juvenile sufferings.

Sleeping in the barn was a special thrill. Especially after numerous visits to the horse pens which were on the end of the barn; educational contacts with the cows and being the recipient of squirts of warm, fresh milk in the face when turned in the wrong direction; the lasting memory of the strong, pungent odors of the pig lot; and the dust of the dried hay wreaking havoc in the sinuses of those suffering from hay fever. The visions of all these, coupled with the sight of chickens and pigeons scampering through the hay lofts, overshadowed the excitement the older ones tried to foster.

Sure enough, night fell. Each of us was given our quota of soft, thin summer blankets—no pillows. Finding a crescent-shaped area of hay (not unlike a small Greek theater) we did our best to soften the hay—but it still poked and stuck!

What does a group of kids (excuse me, young folks) do after it gets dark in the barn when there are absolutely no lights? The barn doors were left open, and we could still see stars through the few cracks in the walls.

Stories!!! That's it! Tell ghost stories. You've never seen anything on TV today which would begin to compare with those stories. With a certainty, I'm convinced to this day that every one of them was meant to make a petrified person out of me! How thankful I was that it was dark and no one could see how pale I turned. Nor could they see me creating my own earthquake!

During lulls in the stories, it had to be mice taking their night-time vigils and tours seriously. They were heard as if they were elephants. Then the horrors were told of those imagined relatives who never returned from a night in the barn and it was presumed that the mice did away with them. They were never seen again nor given the courtesy of decent burial! There was never anything left to bury!

Morning finally came—and none too soon!

At breakfast I was honored to sit near the head of the table between Uncle John and Mom. At my tender age and naivete, dentures were a total unknown. Suddenly, Uncle John caught my eye and popped out his lower dentures with his tongue. Imagine the shock in this finite little mind.

With the speed of lightning and the force of a locomotive I punched Mom in the ribs. By the time she looked, the dentures were back in their appointed place and all appeared normal—until, well, this procedure kept going for quite a while. My curiosity was never satisfied during the term of that memorable reunion at Uncle John's farm.

THE EXCURSION

Somehow, as children of the Depression era, we really didn't realize either our misfortunes, or how fortunate we really were. Sure, we saw the poor fellows on the street corners in the big city, selling apples, pencils, or anything for which there might be a market of any size.

Still, in all this, it seemed our family was able to pool enough resources to buy new cars periodically and to travel on short trips in the early thirties.

One such excursion took us on a boat trip from Chicago to Milwaukee. Leaving the mile-long Navy Pier aboard the SS *Grand Rapids* was an adventure in itself. One of my aunts (Aunt T) who lived with us was confined to a wheelchair due to a military-related illness she incurred in the first World War. Travel with her was always innovative and interesting.

Dad was most creative in making arrangements and making certain of her comfort.

We had the run of the ship. Aunt Talka was content to sit at the stern of the ship. The breeze was not quite as brisk because the superstructure deflected much. There was always a group of people around her. The wheelchair was a unique sight, especially aboard ship. The rest of us would wander the ship and then check on her frequently.

Milwaukee from Lake Michigan was most interesting. Of course, one of the primary sightseeing stops was one of the breweries. Prohibition was over and the beer flowed freely. No members of the family were even interested in drinking any, but we did take the tour.

There were other sights and opportunities for spending hard-earned cash. This was evidenced by the heavily filled shopping bags being carried back aboard the SS *Grand Rapids*. Some were carried quite unsteadily by those who apparently stayed too long at the brewery.

Nonetheless, the friendliness displayed by all aboard was interesting to say the very least. The kids were comparing the souvenir toys they bought. Adults were comparing prices of wares they'd found useful. Most stayed close to their shopping bags and boxes.

After a tour of the ship on its return cruise, Aunt Ella came back to Aunt Talka to check on her comfort. It was cold by this time, but Aunt T was well covered and enjoying the trip. Since the evening chill was doing its thing, most of the passengers went indoors for the warmth and comfort of the ballroom and whatever other rooms were open to the general public.

Aunt E spotted a fairly loaded shopping bag left beside Aunt T's wheelchair. Aunt T was unaware of the bag and had no knowledge of any owner. She made a remark which led Aunt E to think it was trash and garbage. Back then, ecology was unknown as a word or conscious effort. No sooner had she thrown the bag overboard and watched it disappear in the wake of the big ship than a lady approached both of them asking (in very broken English) if they'd seen a bag. She began describing contents to which both our aunts could give no affirmation. The poor little lady went on her way asking others if they'd seen anything. When we were in the car, well on the way home, there was at first laughter. But then the seriousness of the whole incident hit home.

How often the family thought of how they might contact that little immigrant woman. All those who were involved have passed away. But they left us a lesson in respecting the property of others and in keeping our lakes and wetlands clean for all to enjoy.

SAGINAW BAY

Dad had six brothers and four sisters. Mom had six brothers and three sisters. Not all on either side were married but still, the proliferation of nieces, nephews, and cousins, along with the aunts and uncles was something with which to contend at any reunion, even when some were unable to attend.

Rather than gather at any home, one year someone in their wisdom decided to lease a cottage on Saginaw Bay. It had, allegedly, plenty of rooms for all of Mom's family who could attend. It had a beautiful screened porch surrounding three sides of the house facing the placid waters of the bay on Lake Huron. This was ideal for Aunt Talka who was confined for life in a wheelchair, and also perfect for the observation of the horde of cousins and their activities.

The rear "porch" served as an extension of the kitchen, and did we ever need it! The range in the kitchen was electric and the stove on the back porch was kerosene and temperamental. It usually taxed the patience of all of the uncles to get it operating for any one meal.

Sleeping quarters were where they could be found. The adults, of course, had their choice of bedrooms while the offspring found their pallet in the living room or on the porch. Some of the more venturesome slept out-of-doors, at least the first night. Bugs did their share of interrupting sleep as well as meals.

There was no grass, only abundant sand and dust.

The water was ideal for the gathering. White, soft, sandy beach; gentle, sloping water's edge; enough grasses in the water to keep a low surf and yet the grass was far enough away from the shoreline to give ample room to play in the shallow water.

A short distance from the house was a building with a long pier. The assumption was that the building was a weekend bait shop or a fishing cabin. If only we'd taken the signs seriously!

Prohibition had just ended. We noticed the cars arriving at dusk the second night. At dark, the lights on the signs began their brilliant flashes, and the band began to play. The party got to be more than just boisterous. There was little sleep to be had for either the revelers at the nightspot or our little gathering!

The next morning there was a boat tied up quite close to the "honky tonk." The men of our group made their way to the building presumably to register their complaints about the night's entertainment! It was of no avail.

It turned out that the vessel was the mail boat! When the pilot tried to back out from the pier, he was hopelessly stuck. It took all the men as well as the young cousins to push that little tug out into deeper, navigable water.

At the end of the pier, the water was still shallow enough for us children to keep pushing the tug. The poor fellow kept backing for the longest time before he dared try to turn around.

For days we cousins had a great time playing in the trough the boat had made.

Never were we able to keep the night sounds from the tavern away. But did we ever have a good time with the kinfolk during the day.

"One Man Crusade" Goes Round the World
by Louis W. Gabler, Jr.

I was interested in "A Literature Crusade As I Saw It" by John Montgomery in the June-July *LOI*. It called to mind a literature crusade carried on for over fifty years from a home in Elgin, Illinois. It began in a small upstairs bedroom, and finally expanded to the basement.

When I was a small child our family would take me with them on frequent trips to Chicago—"the city." This was quite an excursion until cars became better built and equipped. Among the hot bricks needed in winter, jugs of drinking water needed in summer, and repair kits all year round were always a box or suitcase loaded with gospel tracts. Hitchhiking was then in its prime, and when we passed the pilgrims of the road Dad would select a group of tracts and prayerfully drop them from the car window. And in "the city," wherever a group of people stood near the road out went the tracts. This would be considered litterbugging today, but the leaflets were usually snatched from the ground before they could blow away.

After Sunday dinner Dad would pack the Gospel Suitcase, and he and I would walk up the hill to the busy intersection of state highways 20 and 35. When the cars stopped for a signal we'd go down the lines and give several tracts to each driver. Very few ever refused. Eventually a police permit was needed and was readily received.

Then came the "Gospel Bombs," a selection of leaflets attractively rolled in bright cellophane wrappers. Now a number of young people from the Elgin assembly and from other churches were becoming interested. They would meet together to fold tracts and make "bombs," and to pray and share fellowship, then go out to several street corners. Occasionally some took to bicycles and toured the rural areas, dropping "bombs" by mailboxes and handing tracts to everyone they met.

Results? Only eternity will reveal these in total. Letters used to arrive from all around the world telling of wonderful salvation experiences following the reading of tracts. Other letters asked for tracts to use in winning others to the Savior. Once a hastily scribbled note from a wanderer in Washington confessed he'd been ready to take his own life when a gospel tract blew across his path, and the Holy Spirit showed him the way of salvation and joy. Similar stories are too numerous to tell.

Our distribution of tracts was strictly a work of faith. Not once were its financial needs made known to anyone: Dad taught us that the Lord saw the needs before we did and He would provide. And time after time he told how the Lord had provided for His work. Even when the ready cash was not in hand, if a new printing was needed to fill distribution needs Dad would order it. It often "happened" that on the day the delivery truck was to arrive the mail would bring the money to cover the cost of printing, delivery charges and enough postage to send several orders.

The monies received for this ministry were *never* touched for family or household needs. We were all informed that this was the Lord's money, to be used for His work alone. Even during the lean years of the Depression, when times of temptation must have been overwhelming, the Lord's money was left untouched.

This literature crusade extended around the world; how this happened no one can really say. As is always true with our God, when we are willing to let Him lead, even a small piece of paper can quietly begin a world-wide Pentecost.

Dad was incapacitated by physical infirmity, and it appears that his dream for the Central Gospel Tract Depot has seen its fruition. But his life for his Savior was a testimony to his family, as well as to others. His interest and love for the Saints was shown in his concern for and support of small, struggling assemblies. His love and concern for the unsaved was revealed in his ever ready testimony in print and speech. Though he became physically unable to do much, surely the Lord will continue to use his testimony for years to come.

HINRICH (HARRY)
C.W. WUBBENA
(1888–1947)

by His Niece, Catherine Wubbena

Harry was the first son of Jan and Catharina to be born in the United States, on June 8, 1888. Knowing that one of the requirements for being president of our country was to be native-born, Grandpa Jan looked proudly down on him and exclaimed, "Just think, he can be president of the United States!"

Of all the American-born children, Harry was the only one who was baptized in the German Reformed Church, the same denomination as their old congregation in Germany. This was very important to Grandma; one of her most strongly felt regrets was that the other children born in the United States were not baptized in that church.

In order to obtain Harry's baptism he had to be taken to Bay City, where the nearest German Reformed Church was located. When only a few weeks old, Grandma took him by train, no doubt spending money which was counted out and prayed over. She was impressed and pleased with the train conductor's solicitous treatment of her and baby Harry. This treatment would not have been forthcoming from a person of a similar position in Germany.

In the old German Family Bible the birth of each child is recorded including the *full* name of each. Harry is listed as "Hinrich C.W." There seems to be no explanation for what "C" and "W" stand for. In later years the initial "C" is used, but not "W." Observing that a name was used for more than one child, I wonder if, regardless of the fact that these two names are also used for some of the other sons, "C" is for Carl, and "W" is for Wilhelm.

Harry would have been five and one-half years old when his mother died.

Since we have not heard of his being cared for by some neighbor or friend, it would seem that Talka immediately served as surrogate mother. In the Johnsfield School record for January 18, 1894 to July 7, 1894, and with Gertie Daugharty as teacher, Harry is listed as being five years old and in the Chart Class. His grades were: Orthography 70, Reading 88, Writing 80, Mental Arithmetic 38. A few lines above in the same book we see Minnie's name, who at age six was in second grade and whose class marks were 98, 90, 90, 85, 95! By the term September 2, 1895 to May 8, 1896, and with Alma Bassett as teacher, Harry is in the second grade and his marks are: Orthography 75, Reading 90, Writing 87, Mental Arithmetic 90, Arithmetic 95. The teacher's written comment is "restless" whereas by Minnie's name the comment is "very studious." The following year the comment by Harry's name is "very studious." Records following this year are incomplete. It seems that, instead of going to high school, he took some classes at Ferris Institute in Big Rapids, Michigan. He worked for a brief time with his older brothers in the lumber woods and for some periods helped to put up telephone poles and lines.

He liked to have a good time, and was somewhat of a worry to his father. The letters written to him by his father indicate that there was some concern. (See two letters included in Part One.) Below is a "poem" found among my father's (John's) papers in Harry's handwriting and with indication that Harry is the author.

The Harry's in Johnsfield
About 1907

Two Harry's on a wintery night
With Maidens young and fair
Straight to a party held that night
These young folks did repair.

Now Hamilton's is a jolly place
There is fun and joy galore.
They helpt themselves to candy
Until they could eat no more.

But the Harry's soon came to grief
For Will and Art did say
"Come on, sweet maids, we will take you home
Because the Harry's are bound to stay."

The Harry's then did have the laugh
For the night was dreadful cold
And Will and Art did all the work
While they to each other told

Of all the pleasures they had that night
With these two maidens fair
And Will and Art did all the work
And they stood the frosty air.

Now boys, if you will take our advice
And heed a little care
Don't rush these girls so much,
And you are sure to find a snare.

The girls were the Senne girl (I've forgotten her first name), and the other an Armstrong girl. The Harry's were Harry French and myself. The teacher was Miss Hamilton. I must add, too, the best teacher I ever had. Will and Art were the Willett boys, brothers.   [end of Harry's comment]

Some explanation regarding names used in the poem:

1. The Hamiltons were good friends and neighbors; their farm abutted John's farm on the west; daughter Clara wrote a wonderful tribute to Grandpa Jan and used it for one of her English papers at the University of Michigan. She and her brother Frank became teachers in Arenac County, having taught some of the younger Wubbenas in the Johnsfield School. Charlie Hamilton helped his father on their farm and took care of his mother after his father died. He loved kids and was kind and generous to both John's and Charles' offspring.

2. The "Senne girl" was Stella Senne whose family lived about a mile west of the old Wubbena home; several children in that family kept in touch with the Wubbenas as they, one by one, all moved away.

3. The "Armstrong girl" was no doubt Elnora who recently celebrated her one-hundredth birthday in our vicinity. The Armstrong farm was next to John's farm, on the north.

4. Harry French belonged to a family living in the community of South Branch next to Johnsfield.

5. The Willett boys, Will and Art, were from a family living on what is now M-61, and their house still stands, being presently occupied by Sam Kovalcik.

It would seem that they all had good times together! At the time Harry wrote this "poem" he would have been eighteen or nineteen years old.

Harry learned to be a telegraph operator (at Ferris Institute, I think) as well as to become knowledgeable about the intricacies of movement of freight on railroads. He was involved with this kind of work throughout his adult life. He eventually worked for the Duluth, South Shore and Atlantic Railroad after being graduated from Ferris Institute in approximately 1907.

After getting fairly well established in his work in Trout Creek, he saw possibilities for a spot for his younger brother Fred, so Fred soon found a niche in the Upper Peninsula where his talents could be used. After Grandpa Jan's death, young Bill was in need of more support and guidance than his sisters could give him at home so he spent some time in the Upper Peninsula with Harry and Fred. After a period of time spent there, Harry wrote John, saying Bill needed his (John's) supervision so Bill left the U.P. to live with John for a period of several months. (See copy of letter appended to William's story by William, Jr.)

Harry married Lenore Stralow on October 7, 1913. She lived in Hancock, Michigan, at the time, and the wedding was apparently held in that city. She was a tall woman with dark eyes and a keen sense of humor (a characteristic which Uncle Harry would definitely consider to be essential). She was a nurse and continued to do visiting nurse and public health nursing throughout many years after their marriage. Harry died on June 6, 1947; Lennie lived to be 101 years of age, dying on September 11, 1981.

All brothers and sisters, with the exception of Fred, were able to attend Harry's funeral. The funeral service was held in Ewen, a town south of Bruce Crossing. It was a very sad gathering. At the comparatively young age of fifty-nine, he was the first of the Original Ten to die. His illness and cause of death were related to complications of liver disease.

Both Harry and Len were active in the Masonic Lodge as well as in the Brotherhood of Railway Workers. The positions they held required quite extensive traveling. I recall their visiting at our place in Standish several times. When I was about five years old they came for a short visit. With company present, Mom (Laura) was having some difficulty with getting the supper meal prepared. Aunt Len pitched right in; the dish she prepared which everyone ate with gusto was of salmon, hard-cooked eggs and small potatoes with a cream sauce over all. Cooking on the wood-burning stove didn't upset her one bit. She always maintained equanimity and a poised demeanor, along with her love of fun. Her dark eyes would dance with merriment. Harry was proud of her, and often sat quietly by while she was in the limelight. Len's mother lived with them for several years. Harry was very solicitous of her, (he called her Grandma), and seemed to love her a lot.

Copied below is a letter Harry wrote to my parents (John and Laura) after he and Len had attended the Wubbena reunion in 1946. Harry died one year after that. He appeared to be frail at the time of the reunion, but asked no special favors or treatment. Of course, Len was right with him, being attentive and caring. Harry had a soft, gentle voice and spoke slowly with a bit of a drawl. His sisters, in telling of early events, would mock his speech as they quoted him. He was of average height so when he and Len stood side-by-side she was just an inch or so taller. Noted in our pictures one sees that John, Harry, and Bill had hairlines in which the bossae of their foreheads are prominent. (My brother Shirley's hairline was similar.) The picture of Grandpa Jan shows a forehead with a more modified curvature of the same hairline.

In the fall of 1935 a car full of us young folks visited the Upper Peninsula. Wyatt, Jean, Shirley, and I stayed two nights with Harry and Len at Trout Creek. They appeared to be delighted that we visited them. They took us to the Porcupine Mountains and the Lake-of-the-Clouds as well as to waterfalls and other scenic spots. I remember having delicious meals, some eaten in the open as picnics and others in their upstairs apartment. I think Uncle Harry wished he had had children of his own. He treated us with the love and consideration with which he would probably have treated his own children.

Set forth below is a copy of his obituary as printed in a newspaper near their home, as well as a small item taken from their Lodge newspaper.

From the local newspaper, in June 1947:

LAST RITES FOR H WUBBENA

Bruce Crossing—Masonic funeral rites for the late Harry C. Wubbena were held in St Mark's Episcopal Church in Ewen at 2 P.M. Monday. The Rev Norman Thurston of Ontonagon officiated.

Pallbearers were Eino Stenfors and Thomas Nordine, Bruce Crossing; Hugh Sommers and Dr. John H. Wilson, Ewen; Heino Anderson and Joseph Elliott, Jr., Kenton. Interment was in Maple Grove Cemetery.

Mr Wubbena was born in Standish, Mich., June 8, 1888. He attended grade school there and was graduated from Ferris Institute in 1907. He was employed by the Duluth South Shore railroad for the past 37 years.

Coming to Bruce Crossing in 1915, he moved to Trout Creek two years later. He was employed in Seney for several years and in 1936 returned to Bruce Crossing.

In April Mr Wubbena became seriously ill and received medical treatment at the Duluth clinic. For the past seven weeks he was a patient in St. Mary's hospital in Marquette.

He passed away early Friday morning, June 6. The body was taken to the Ewen church Monday morning.

Mr. Wubbena was married to Miss Lenore Stralow of Hancock on October 11, 1913. In addition to his widow he is survived by five brothers: Fred, Seattle, Wash.; William, Washington, D.C.; Henry, Bay City; and

John and Charles Wubbena, Standish; and four sisters; Mrs. George Flutur, Detroit; Miss Talka H. Wubbena, Mrs. Louis Gabler, and Miss Ella Wubbena, Elgin, Ill.

Out of town relatives who attended the funeral were: Mr. and Mrs. William Wubbena and son, William Jr., Washington, D.C.; Mr and Mrs. Henry Wubbena and children, Raymond and Berniece, Bay City; Mr. and Mrs. John Wubbena and daughter, Katherine, and Mr. and Mrs. Charles Wubbena, Standish; Mr. and Mrs. George Flutur, Detroit; Mr. and Mrs. Louis Gabler and the Misses Talka and Ella Wubbena, Elgin, Ill.; Mr. and Mrs. Vernon Casperson, Eau Claire, Wis.

Friends who attended were: Mrs. Etna Gandsey, Viginia, Minn.; Mr. and Mrs. Lawrence Sain and daughter, Lauryle, and Mrs Edna Brower, Marquette; Mr. and Mrs. Cleo Hughes and Mr. and Mrs. Louis Hughes, Battle Creek; Charles Danialson, L'Anse; E. N. Olson, Marquette; Mr. and Mrs. A. C. Ware and Mr. and Mrs. David Sexton, Paulding. A large group of friends from Bruce Crossing attended the rites at Ewen.

Notice published in the newspaper of the Order of Railroad Telegraphers.

H. C WUBBENA, GENERAL CHAIRMAN OF DIVISION 74, DIES

It was with the deepest regret that we learned of the death of Brother Harry C. Wubbena, General Chairman of Division 74, who passed away at 4:00 P.M., June 6, at Marquette, Michigan.

Brother Wubbena had been a continuous member of the O.R.T. since September 10, 1909, and was General Chairman on the Duluth, South Shore and Atlantic Railway for more than twenty years. He was highly respected and well liked by all who knew him. Our sympathy is extended to his good wife, who is Grand Secretary-Treasurer of the Ladies Auxiliary, and to the other members of the family.

Letter written by Harry to his brother John subsequent to the 1946 reunion of the Original Ten in Standish.

Bruces Crossing, Mich.,
August 19th, 1946

Dear John, Laura and All:-

That was the best reunion ever, we were so glad to see you all and you all looked so nice and we want to thank you for the very nice time you showed us.

We arrived home about 6 P.M. Saturday night and Grandma made the trip fine, we would stop about every 50 miles and get out and walk, stayed at St. Ignace over night, then the nice part of it was not a car trouble all the way.

John am sending you the blanks we spoke of, if you need more you can get them from the Judge of Probate there, they don't cost any thing.

Grandma, Tookie, Len and I are going to the cabin for dinner, I go to work tomorrow morning.

We all join in for thanking you again for the very nice time you gave us.

Your loving brother,
Harry

Some Memories of Uncle Harry and Aunt Lenore
by Margaret Gabler Pickett, daughter of Minnie Wubbena Gabler

Lou just loved going to see Uncle Harry. Uncle Harry would take him (at about age three to five years) onto some of the trains which stopped at the station. They never had any children of their own, though they loved all children. They always entertained us highly.

Aunt Lenny wove rag rugs for people far and near. She had hundreds of pounds of rags in her upstairs alongside her loom.

She loved flowers. I remember going to their home in Trout Creek when her entire front yard was a flower garden.

Uncle Harry had a cabin in the woods farther north where he and his hunting buddies would enjoy a week or so of hunting every now and then.

They sent us blueberries and trout in Elgin almost every year for a long time. When we visited them we always had fresh berries—blueberries, raspberries or blackberries—with real cream.

One year after I was older and apparently away at school or something, Harry and Len took the folks and little Lou to Lake Superior for a picnic when they came up for a visit. Lou was only a toddler and they tied a diaper over his shoulders while he was on the beach. But the poor kid got such a sunburn that he cried all night and got blistered. Mom related many years after and often how Aunt Lennie bathed Lou with vinegar and cool water to relieve the soreness. The folks loved to go there and always received a royal welcome.

EMMA CATHARINA
JOHANNA WUBBENA
FLUTUR
(1890–1959)

by Catherine Wubbena, Niece of Emma Wubbena

Emma Catharina Johanna Wubbena was born on September 28, 1890, in the family home located on Johnsfield Road in Standish, Michigan. She was the seventh child born to Jan and Catharina Wubbena and was their third daughter. She died on August 15, 1959, in Detroit, Michigan. Her mother died in January 1894, which means that Emma was only four years old at the time of her mother's death. There were three siblings younger than she. She was a young woman of seventeen when her father died in 1907.

In the old Record Book of the Johnsfield School Emma is listed as being in the Chart Class (now called Kindergarten) at the age of four and her teacher was Lottie Gibbon. In the second grade, at the age of six, her teacher was Alma Bassett. The grades for her second grade class were recorded as: Orthography 90, Reading 90, Writing 85, Mental Arithmetic 75, Arithmetic 80. The comment made for general status was "very good." She was in the fourth grade in November, 1899, with Frank Hamilton as teacher. Records are incomplete for the years she progressed from the third grade through the eighth grade.

Throughout these years her oldest sister, Talka, was cook and house-keeper for the brothers and sisters. The older brothers and their father worked (i.e., had employment off the farm) to contribute to the family income. John built a house on his own farm in 1905; for several weeks, through two or three summers, Emma lived with John. Minnie, three years older than Emma, was teaching school in the county as soon as she was graduated from high school. Ella was staying with Talka and Minnie in the old home, along with the younger brothers.

When Emma was graduated from Standish High School in 1907 she was able to pass the test administered by the County School Commissioner and was thus granted a teacher's certificate which qualified her to teach in the country schools. Their father had died in May 1907. Emma was hired as teacher of the Worth School. At that time the school was located on Huron Road (now M-13) on the northeastern corner of Worth Road and Huron Road. She was the teacher in this school from September 1908 until June 1917. Because of this lengthy tenure most of her students had no other teacher throughout their elementary schooling. One of her pupils was Lillian Kohn, née Adrian, who remembers many incidents of those school days. Lillian was in Chart Class at the age of seven in 1910. She was graduated from eighth grade in 1917 at the age of fourteen. This was Emma's last year to teach; she left teaching to enter Nurse's Training at Harper Hospital in Detroit in 1918.

While teaching, Emma had board and room with Mr. and Mrs. Chamberlain (Ed and Nell). Their farm was adjacent to the schoolyard, with a large apple orchard east of the school building, extending up to the Chamberlain's house. This meant that Emma had only a short walk every morning and late afternoon. Since she, with the help of some pupils, took care of the furnace and sweeping and dusting, this was a convenient arrangement.

Lillian Kohn remembers that there were always from fifty to fifty-two pupils in the one-room school. Some family names, besides her own name, Adrian, were: Raymond, Gauthier, Sovey, Metevia, Rhinehart, Jasman, Near, Pintoski, Cross, Chovin, Cartier, Johnson, Bressette, Bublitz, Lalonde, Guerin, Applegate, Krupa, Soztak, vanRumden, Mary Mitchell (an Indian), and Nelson Webb. Nelson was noted for his neat appearance; he dared not play rough games, or even go outside into the schoolyard. Emma tried her best to show him it was fun to play, and that his mother and aunt wanted him to have a good time. But he rarely relaxed enough to appreciate this. There was no such thing as a school counselor in those days. This role was left to the teacher.

The bonds were close between pupils and teacher; parents, too, became "family" with their teacher. Spending supper and overnight with one of the families was common. Joys and sorrows, births and deaths were as much a part of school life as were studies from textbooks.

In those days trains ran on the Michigan Central Railroad. The tracks were a little east of Chamberlain's house. On Friday nights Emma took the train from Worth to Standish; on Sunday evenings she returned to Worth via the train. There was no depot at Worth; the train stopped upon being flagged. Mail was brought in twice a day; one train from the north, and one train from the south. A mail bag of outgoing mail was hung up; the passing train grabbed the bag and left the incoming mail in a bag also on the hook. In addition, several freight trains ran daily.

The post office was in one room of the home of the DeRosia family. At one time it was called the Saganing Post Office; this was later called the Worth Post Office. The Metevias had a general store on Worth Road west of the railroad, and Bressette's general store was east of the railroad. Worth Corner was busy for another reason; logs from several lumber camps located west of Worth were brought in through the week by horse and wagon (sleighs in the winter time) and stacked by the railroad. On Sunday several flat cars were stationed on the tracks. Men from the camps came in on Sundays and loaded the logs on the cars. These were then taken down to Bay City and Saginaw to the big lumber mills.

Emma had golden blonde hair and blue eyes. Her skin was pink, and she blushed easily. She was impulsive; she had a ready smile; she shed tears easily over someone else's hurt and sorrow. She was lithesome, and worked rapidly and with no waste of motion. She played the organ and piano "by ear." When teaching at the Worth school, she and her students put on programs of singing and recitations and plays. The community was their audience. She organized box socials. This meant that girls and young ladies, and married women, too, packed delectable cold lunches in boxes. The box was usually a shoe box, but also could have been any other container. The important thing was the container was beautifully decorated with crepe paper, artificial flowers, ribbons, etc. Some articulate man was asked (by the teacher) to be the auctioneer. By some sly maneuvering a boyfriend or husband was usually able to recognize his sweetheart's box. Lots of teasing, flirting, and joking took place. Proceeds were turned over to the teacher, who in turn bought some needed item(s) for the school, such as a dictionary or other library books, a flag, or a patriotic picture for the school wall.

A memorable event which I recall was when Aunt Em took Wyatt and me to Elgin, Illinois, to visit her sister Minnie Gabler and family. It was when she had a few days of vacation at Christmas time. That was in 1917 so I was four years old and Wy was five. Mom and Dad took us by horse and sleigh to Worth, and watched as Aunt Em took us aboard the train. I do not remember changing trains along the way, but it must have been necessary. At the Gablers' house I cried at bedtime, and the aunts comforted me. Wy was embarrassed and scolded me, saying "you *wanted* to come!"

On our way home the train was packed with soldiers in uniform. The world was preoccupied with World War I and soldiers were on the move. Aunt Em learned that the soldiers were suffering from measles. About a week later Wy and I had measles, and so did our local playmates, and soon the whole Johnsfield School was infected. I do not remember having heard how Aunt Emma and the Worth School students fared.

When Emma decided to change vocations from teaching to nursing, she felt like she was deserting her own family when leaving the friends she had made at Worth. Many tears were shed and promises made to "keep in contact." I do not recall hearing why she selected the Harper Hospital School of Nursing in Detroit. Perhaps it was because Harper's quality and leadership were recognized not only throughout Michigan but also throughout the eastern United States. Harper Hospital's history and fame for quality care dates back to the Civil War.

At this time Talka had been graduated from the University of Michigan School of Nursing and, after doing some private duty nursing, she had become an army nurse assigned to army hospitals, where she took care of World War I soldiers. This was a factor, too, in Emma's decision to become a nurse.

A few years after this, the Worth School was moved to Worth Road to a point about one-fourth mile west of M-13. It continued to be used until 1944 when the county schools were consolidated and students began to be bussed into Standish. The building stood idle until it became used by a Mr. Shoultes for a garage for car repair; he still uses it today for this purpose. The building retains the form of a country schoolhouse.

While studying nursing, Emma had many amusing incidents occur. She frankly told us about the bumbling and embarrassing predicaments in which she found herself. She was afraid of doctors, and in those days nurses were expected to be "handmaidens" to doctors. When assigned to the operating room she was told by the head nurse not to enter one specific room. When Emma asked why she was told, "Because God is in there." Her curiosity aroused, she felt she had to see who was God, so she made an excuse to peek in. There was the chief surgeon who glared at her and loudly exclaimed, "Get out of here!" After that she felt he glared at her every time he saw her in the hall.

Another time, when a patient went into shock while on the table, the surgeon called "Trendelenberg." Emma dashed out into the hall, telling one and all, "He wants Dr. Trendelenberg! He wants Dr. Trendelenberg!" She was subjected to scolding by head nurses and teasing by her classmates when she learned that Trendelenberg was a position of lowering the patient's head and raising the feet by cranking the operating table. Knowing how pink Emma's face could get, I imagine it was really pink as she felt the humiliation. Years afterward she was still resilient enough to tell us younger nurses about her trials and tribulations.

While living in the student nurses' dormitory at Harper, Emma went to the Gospel Hall in downtown Detroit. This was the same assembly of Christians with which her father, sisters, and she had been associated in Standish; many Standish folks had migrated to Detroit to work in the auto factories which had started to boom in those years. So she had acquaintances in Detroit, and soon had many new friends, too. Among these friends were several young men who had come from Romania to get away from war-torn Europe. George Flutur was one of these men. He was a handsome, dark-haired fellow, and soon he and Emma were a "couple." When she let her brothers and sisters know they were contemplating marriage, they all wanted to meet him and pass their approval. In the summer of 1921 the brothers and sisters held one of their reunions in Standish. Among other activities was a picnic-day on Saginaw Bay at the then-popular Timber Island; Emma brought George.

The brothers asked George if he was going to let Emma be the boss and handle the pocketbook. George said, "No." So the brothers ducked his head under the water. When he was let up for air, they asked him again. Again, he said, "No." The third time he was held under the water they rubbed gravel in his scalp. He still said no. So the brothers gave up, evidently feeling that Emma was getting a man of strong character! They were married in Detroit on December 31, 1921. The word "Flutur" means butterfly in Romanian. George was a barber, and Emma did private duty nursing up until she had two babies of her own.

Ford Motor Company was growing by leaps and bounds, and Henry Ford I had established the five-dollar-a-day wage for all workers, so George went to work at Ford's. He continued to be a barber for years to come and had a barber chair set up in the basement of their home where he took care of customers and friends.

Emma was generous with time and the giving of tender nursing care to neighbors, friends, and relatives. She lost her slender figure along the way but retained her buoyant spirit and that so-characteristic joyous glow of hers, despite the depressing and/or worrisome circumstances that come to everyone with everyday living.

Emma had not learned to cook as she grew up; as a young married woman she was not noted for being a good cook. As time went by she gleaned helpful hints and instructions from friends and relatives and, after a few years, her reputation as a cook was changed. Her three older brothers, John, Charles and Henry, gathered at the Flutur's house on Marquette Street one day in May, about 1940. She served them a sumptuous meal. The brothers were generous with their praise; with brotherly frankness they told her what a marked improvement had been made. One thing on Emma's menu was brussel sprouts. As the dish was being passed I heard Charles mur-

mur to Henry, "What is this?" In reply, Henry muttered, "I think, it's called brock-o-lie."

She tried to follow George's directions in preparing foods the Romanian way but, I think, never attained the flavors and tastes he had remembered. One project they carried out every year in late summer or fall was to go to the farmer's market in Detroit and buy hot, hot peppers. They worked together putting these in pickling solution in jars. George (but no one else) enjoyed them all winter.

The two Flutur children, Duane and Virginia, grew up in the neighborhood on Marquette Street, not far from Grand River Avenue. When he was about eight years of age Duane began to spend summers on John's farm in Johnsfield, near Standish. His parents wanted him to experience farm work, with Emma's oldest brother John serving as his teacher and supervisor. Thus he, Duane, was removed from the influence of city life in the summertime when children, with no school life or studies, might pick up bad habits. George and Emma yearned over their young son, especially the first summer when he was being calloused and tanned with field work which he did side by side with John's children. He and Shirley (John's youngest child) spent many hours working and having fun together. Duane returned to the farm for three or four summers. After that time period he had built up a paper route in Detroit and his parents felt he was ready to assume this regular job in the city throughout both the summer and winter.

Virginia, the Fluturs' daughter, loved animals. She spent a few days of every summer on the farm where she rode the horses and brought the cows up from pasture and fed the cats and dogs. When of high school age, she would bring a girlfriend with her to share her enjoyment.

Emma was hospitable to one and all. She was pleased when several nieces decided to study nursing. She had regarded nursing as a high calling for herself, and so felt these younger girls were wise to also enter the profession. She loved to hear them tell of their experiences in hospitals and nursing classes, and served many a hearty meal to them as they sat around the dining table with her and George.

Duane and Virginia each got married, and in time there were grandchildren. Now Emma felt her life was crowned with blessing. In 1954 her brother John's illness and death brought real grief. A couple of days before he died she spent some time with him in the Standish Hospital. Her lips were thin and tense with the strain and grief she felt. She and he had always had a special warmth for each other, dating back to their days of struggle as they supported and comforted each other, first when their mother died; then when their father died; then when she needed help getting back and forth to high school; and last as she needed a big brother's approval and advice as she functioned as a schoolmarm at an age younger than most young women were when they graduated from high school. She was a very generous and loving woman. She could flare up with a quick-tempered reaction, but this was always followed immediately with evidence of insight and understanding of the total situation. She was a vital part of the Original Ten.

The following letter from Emma to John and Laura was postmarked from Harper Hospital in Detroit. She was a student nurse with nine weeks yet to go. The event to which she refers is a gathering of family members in Standish, at Timber Island on Saginaw Bay, for the Fourth of July. The "secret" must be Mom's pregnancy; Shirley was born the following November. Her heart and thoughts are still with the "Worth People," the folks in the school district where she taught. "Rudy" is Rudy Bublitz; she and he enjoyed each other's company, and this could have developed into a marriage but she once confided to me that her man *had* to be a professed child of God, and Rudy was not. But her eyes "sparkled" when she spoke of him. I think she and George never did go to Romania (spelled Roumania before World War II). The "planning together by Laura and Mertie" was in reference to getting food, beds, etc. ready for the reunion.

It would seem that this was the occasion for the introduction of George to Em's brothers and sisters. This was the time when the brothers ducked George's head under water in an effort to force him to yield the pocketbook control to Emma after they were married. (See account of the incident in the above story.)

June 15, 1921
Tuesday Eve.

Dear loved ones,

Laura's nice letter came yesterday. I'm glad everyone is planning on coming and hope I'll be able to get away too. I intend doing social service work at that time and may get Sunday off too, if so I can go with Eve Sat. night, D.V. George thought of coming Monday and Tues. but perhaps you'd rather not have him Laura. You have a houseful and you'd not know him well enough in two days to learn his good qualities. You'll no doubt all wonder like Ella did. The first time she saw him, she said "Where did you get that coon?" Coon is right, but he's a good one. He got a Ford last week and sometimes speaks of driving up, but he won't be efficient enough in that line before then.

George just called up and said to give you his love. I saw Alice last night. She's happy as usual.

Yes, I'll keep your secret. I think it is best too that the rest don't know, as Minn will just worry etc. Yes, Eve was right. The doctor thought it best she shouldn't go but you know how she is. She came home on Saturday. I never hear from the boys. I do hope Martha will go after all. Am glad the garden is fine. We've had radishes, lettuce, onions etc.

Last night we celebrated Mr. and Mrs. Muir's 40th anniversary and also the founding of the meeting here at the hall. We had a lovely time. Meeting lasted until 10:30 p.m. and I tell you the babies were restless.

I am very glad for you and John. I know it is very hard for you Laura, but God will bring blessing to you. I only hope every one of the 5 will be saved. No one knows how the grace of God keeps one out of things, and this world is getting worse and worse. Wouldn't our good old father enjoy the children! I'll be so proud if I ever have any.

I am in the children's ward now and they're into everything. I don't wonder at mother's being tired out and nervous but I surely like them too.

Give any of the Worth people my love, Laura. How are all of Adrian's? I hear Rudy is married. Helen has a good man, but I'm thankful for my Roumanian instead.

George plans so much on going back to Roumania, as soon as possible. We will rent a furnished apartment until after we return, D.V. We may never go, but he surely talks enough and plans enough about it now. I tell you it makes my heart go "pit-a-pat" when I think of putting my foot on the plank in New York Harbor, but God will take care of us, as we are His. George took out his first papers today, so I won't have to change my citizenship, as I'd have had or will until he gets his second. That's why I'm so anxious to get home the 4th too as we may be gone next year.

I finish nine weeks from last night, D.V. I'll certainly have to get busy. I hope Mabel is o.k. again. It's nice you and Mertie can plan together. I so hope I can go. Give Charles my love. Tell Mertie I'll write her one of these days too.

With much love to you all.
(signed) Em

Memories of Emma
by Duane Flutur, Son of Emma, and His Wife Lorraine

Emma never worked at nursing in a hospital after she was married. However, I can remember her nursing everyone that got sick in the neighborhood for one thing or another, giving shots, etc. I remember her sitting up all night with some that were seriously ill. She'd always get home in the morning in time to get us off to school. Speaking of school I remember, too, that if we had problems with homework she would help us.

She was an immaculate housekeeper! Every Monday morning she would wash and I remember she used the sudsy water to wash the front porch. Another ritual for Mondays was washing the dog!

She was an excellent cook, too. Saturday morning ritual was a pancake and sausage breakfast. I remember getting a lot of pigs-in-the-blanket and stuffed peppers to stretch the meat during the Depression. She did a lot of entertaining, especially preachers who would come to town for a series of meetings. Dad Flutur always gave them haircuts as this was his trade and he had all the barber equipment in the basement. I remember, too, he would always take his barber bag along when we would go for family reunions or visits to Standish or Elgin.

It was Mom's delight when the four sisters would get together. She'd clean and bake and prepare for them for days before their arrival. They would always talk in German when they were together.

Mom often took trips with the Gablers when we were older and could fend for ourselves.

She taught Sunday School at Central Gospel Hall for years. Even today we meet some of her former students and they recollect what a special teacher she was.

She whistled and sang a lot as she was working. She was always happy and pleasing.

Birthdays and Christmas were special times and she always made a special meal and cake for our birthdays. Christmas dinner was fit for a king! The linen table cloth and good china and silver were used. Dessert was always Christmas bread pudding with rum butter sauce.

Reading the Bible and Bible study books was a big important time of our lives. Every night we'd read the Bible after supper at the supper table. I can remember her teaching us verses and choruses to sing, or say, at the Sunday School programs. If we did a good job there was a special reward. Going to Sunday School and church meetings was a number one priority. Our whole lives revolved around the Church Assembly and activities, family and neighbors.

I remember Dad and Mom took in a foster child, a little girl named Elaine, for several years. Don't know or remember any of the particulars of it.

We moved to Monte Vista Avenue in 1943. I can remember Mom was delighted to have a larger house.

Another thing we remember about her was her love of nice clothes and hats. Some of her hats were really beautiful.

She loved her grandchildren with a passion, but because of her not feeling well she never did much babysitting with them. We lived with one house between us for eleven years. The boys (Randy, Ron, and Rob) remember running in and out, sometimes for cookies and sometimes when they were in the doghouse with us. They remember her singing and playing piano with them and making up stories. She was not well at all for several years before she died. She was operated on (hysterectomy) in September 1958. It was malignant. She had radiation treatments and we took her every day for three weeks for the treatments. In June she started not feeling well and she died in August 1959.

Added Recollections of Emma (Mom)
by Lorraine Flutur

Duane and I were married October 19, 1946. I can remember the first time I came to Detroit and met Duane's parents. Emma really treated me like I was special and we got along great from day one. After our wedding she held a big open house reception for us at the Monte Vista address. All the folks and friends from Detroit that didn't come to the wedding in Illinois came to see us. She worked so hard in preparing the food, etc. for that. Over one hundred friends came to welcome us and congratulate us.

During the early years I spent a lot of time with her. We were very good friends. Being new to Detroit I had few friends and she filled the gap. We'd shop together often. When we lived one door from them I took her shopping every week and drove her wherever she needed to go. She was my best friend and loved me as a daughter. If I ever told her of something I needed or wanted she would tell Duane and I would have it. She was an excellent example to me of a loving wife and mother. It left a big void in my life when she died.

| |

Letter from John T. Wubbena (and family) to Emma Wubbena Flutur (and family):

Standish Mich.
July 29, 1931

Dear Folks:

Received your nice letter, Em; but it was to Laura and I also read it so you will pardon me if I write and tell you something about <u>my boys</u>. I enjoy both of them. They both are very busy boys I tell you. That little Duane gathers eggs and if there is any of them hens wants to hatch he shuts them in a coop by themselves he would make a very good poultry man as he is very enthusiastic about the chickens. Between him and Shirley they keep the water tank full of drinking water for the cows and horses, bring Jean and I a fresh drink when we work in the field and during haying they drove the team on the hayfork, one day we had to deliver one cow and two veal calves to Sterling and we put the two calves in the democrat and Jean drove the horses and the little boys came along and changed about walking with the cow. I led the cow all the way but the little boys changed off walking behind but we got them to their destination safely. Mr. and Mrs. McConachie and 2 children of Detroit, Mr. and Mrs. Wyatt of Standish and Mrs. Sheldrake of the Soo were here today and I let Duane and Shirley take the horses to show them how they could ride. Everybody had a good time. When Duane came here I had to help him on and off the horses but now he leads them in the ditch or close to a stump and he can get on and off just as good as Shirley and sometimes they hitch up the dog and play with him. We usually let the little boys sleep till 7:30 mornings.

We have the hay and oats all in, have the barn full, filled up over the pigs and chickens and over the calfpen and then built a stack of 5 loads of oats outdoors, the little boys did part of the raking. Wyatt Jr had his vacation during haying and he helped us out in good shape, as he is big and strong, but the oats Jeanie and I had to handle ourselves, Jean built the stack and she did well. It is very dry here just now, we need rain very bad, the corn leaves are curling up and the 'tatoes need rain bad too.

Otherwise all our crops are very nice. Mr. Wilson, that shaky old fellow, you know, died at 5 o'clock this afternoon, the funeral is to be Saturday, he had been very weak for a long time.

Talka's birthday is drawing nigh again, My, but how time goes, in 6 yrs I'll be as old as Pa was when he died, I hate to think of it, but am very thankful for my good health and my fine children.

Now Dears, don't worry about that little boy, every one here, also Yargers, like him very much and you can leave him till you get ready to get him, you say to ship him when we get a chance, but we want to see you'se too, but I know what it means to you, it takes time as well as money to travel but please come if you can, as to Shirley, thank you for the invitation, but I don't know how we'd get him back as Wyatt Jr and Catherine are both working and no one else here drives the car, but we'll see if it can be arranged.

Come when you can but don't hurry on account of Duane as every one here loves him.

Lovingly John, Laura and the kids.

Thoughts about My Grandmothers, Emma and Ella Flutur
by Robert Flutur, Son of Duane and Lorraine Flutur

I have been asked to remember some thoughts about my Grandmother Emma Flutur. I did not have the opportunity to really get to know her well as she died when I was seven years old. The thoughts that I do remember are ones of a lady that showed much love in her life. I can remember her babysitting my brothers and me; we played with the toys that she had under the dining room window. I can remember feeling very special and very loved when I was with her. I really did not understand all the pain she was going through as cancer took its toll on her body. I do remember feeling a void in my short life as I stood in front of the house realizing that my Grandma was never going to be in it again.

It was very difficult for Grandpa Flutur also. When I heard he was going to marry Grandma's sister, I did not know what to think. I was excited for Grandpa but I was also a little leery about having Grandma's sister as my grandmother. Aunt Ella and Grandpa were married in our living room and looking back, Grandma Ella must have been a little scared. It would be hard enough having three boys as your own children, but now she had three boys as her grandchildren.

Being single all her life and then getting married had to be a big adjustment for her. She had to learn how to cook. I can remember going to their house for dinner and having her prepare her favorite dinner, Swiss steak. We had that dinner many times for the first few years. She became very proficient cooking for us at family gatherings at her home.

I always enjoyed talking to her about all the countries she traveled to. One time in the seventh grade, I had to do a special report on the land of Egypt. I asked Grandma Ella if she would come to school to talk about her travels to Egypt. As she was talking and sharing her experiences, I felt very proud having her as my grandmother.

Grandma Ella and Grandpa moved to an apartment in Redford. I was dating Marti, my wife to be, at the time and we were invited to dinner. We had a very nice dinner, and afterwards she read the passage from Ecclesiastes chapter twelve. This chapter deals with remembering God when you are in your youth. It talks about the problems of getting old. As we sat around the table, she shared her experiences with old age and the effects on her work and life for Christ. It had a profound effect on me. Every time I read or share this passage, I think back to the special time shared around that small dinner table with two very special people.

Grandma Ella had to take on more and more responsibility as Grandpa lost control of his mind. I remember when she made the decision to move to

Rest Haven Nursing Home in Grand Rapids. It meant giving up much for herself but she was thinking of what was going to be best for Grandpa and herself. We would go and visit often and she was always upbeat and on the move as much as possible. It must have been very hard for her at times but we could laugh about certain situations that would happen between her and Grandpa. As Grandpa got worse he would even forget who Grandma Ella was. Once he woke up and asked her why they were sleeping together because they were not married. She had to get out the marriage license to show him that they were truly married. Even with these difficult times I never saw her faith in Christ waver or fail.

When Grandma Ella was nearing the end of her life, we had her over at our house. Our children Sara and Tim loved playing doctor and they asked Grandma Ella if she wanted to play with them. She was always good for an operation or two on the kids so she started playing with them. After a while, the children wanted to operate on her. As you know, during the operation, they usually put you to sleep. The children had her lay down and pretended to put her to sleep and then proceeded to operate on her. When it came time to wake her up after the operation, the children could not because she really had fallen asleep! We let her sleep and had a good laugh with her after she woke up.

As I look back on both my grandmothers, I see a common thread that ties them together. That is the love they had for the Lord. I have looked at many people in the twilight of life and many of them were miserable and defeated people. Even though Grandma Emma died at a young age, I feel she would have been very much like Grandma Ella was. Grandma Ella had a glow about her that only a strong faith in Jesus Christ can give. She had her trying times, and I am sure she was difficult to live with at times like all of us are, but I saw a strength and faith that never wavered. When she looked at you, you could sense and feel not only the love she had for you, but you could see the love of Christ in her eyes. As I read and think about Ecclesiastes 12, I know that Grandma Ella was a living example of this passage. She not only remembered her Creator in her youth, but all of her life.

FRIEDRICK (FRED) THEODOR ENGELHARD WUBBENA (1891–1982)

Notes on the Life of My Father, *Friedrick Theodor Engelhard Wubbena*
by His Daughter, Margaret W. Spangler

Copied from his birth certificate: Friedrick Theodor Engelhard Wubbena was born on November 17, 1891 in Standish, Michigan, to Catharina Louise Caroline Jungjohann Wübbena and Jan Janssen Wübbena. He was the eighth of ten children. The family was poor but happy and industrious.

Fred completed the eighth grade at the Johnsfield Public School. The graduation program, Class Day exercises dated May 29, 1909, shows Will Wubbena as the class vice-president and Fred as the treasurer. There were two others in the class: Addie Beausoliel and Abbie Bell. The teacher was Oakley Johnson.

Fred went to Ferris Institute in Big Rapids, Michigan, with one of his brothers, possibly Bill. They passed the telegraphy course very quickly as they had "played" using the Morse code as kids. Their minds were always working, it seems.

From there he worked as an agent and auditor for the DSS&A System Railroad and seemed to be very close to Harry. Harry worked for the railroad at this time, too. Fred had board and room (i.e., he lived in a rooming house where he ate his meals) in the towns wherever he was assigned. In one new town he saw two girls walking down the street and said, "Who is that fat slob?" The fellow to whom he addressed the question answered, "That is my sister." The moral doesn't have to be stated, does it? After that Fred was always careful to never say anything negative about anyone.

On September 7, 1918, Fred enlisted in the Army. His Honorable Discharge states that he was a railroad agent with knowledge of the railroad accounting and telegraphing when he joined, and a sergeant when he was discharged on May 20, 1919. During the war he left his storage trunks at Harry and Len's. He sang his way through World War I with the Victory Quartet. He had a lot of fun singing—entertaining wherever he went. He was a good dancer and loved to dance with the girls in every town.

After the stint in the Army Fred moved to Upper Michigan. He began working for the Weidman Lumber Company in Trout Creek as office manager and as the person in charge of all purchases, including mill and camp supplies.

Mildred Euphemia Whyte, born June 18, 1893 in Crystal Lake, Illinois, graduated with the Class of 1916 of the Training School for Nursing at Passavant Memorial Hospital in Chicago, Illinois. She had various nursing positions after this. Some included private duty where the nurse was on duty twenty-four hours a day, sleeping in the same room as the patient. Then on January 6, 1918, she joined the Army Nurse Corps and served until she was "relieved from active service in the military establishment" on March 13, 1919. In June 1922 Mildred "completed the work and passed the examinations" of the one-year course for public health nurses in the School of Applied Social Sciences at Western Reserve University in Cleveland, Ohio. After this she worked as a Public Health Nurse in Grundy County, Iowa, driving around the countryside in a little Ford visiting schools and tending to the ills of the people. She really enjoyed the personal gratification she received from helping people directly.

It was in the Army Nurse Corps that Mildred met Talka, Fred's sister, who had also joined the Army Nurse Corps. Talka and Mildred served together in Vancouver, Washington, I believe. While in the army Talka got very sick with tuberculosis and was sent to Elgin, Illinois, to be near her sister, Minnie. Mildred's folks also lived in Elgin. Two of Minnie's sisters (Ella and Talka) also lived in Elgin. The Wubbena sisters felt that Fred and Mildred would be a good match, but it took several years before their plans came to fruition: for Fred had to come to Elgin from Michigan to visit Talka at the same time that Mildred would come from Iowa to Elgin to visit her parents. Finally they met at Talka's bedside, and Fred asked to take Mildred home. On the way they stopped and had milkshakes. Fred had some buttermilk, too. Mildred thought his capacity was quite amazing! They corresponded for several months and Fred wrote Mildred that this was one Christmas she was not going to spend with her folks. So at Christmastime 1924 Mildred went up to Trout Creek, Michigan, where Fred was working in the office of Weidman Lumber Company. During that visit he proposed marriage.

Fred married Mildred Euphemia Whyte on June 17, 1925 in Elgin, Illinois. As one can see, they were both mature adults by that time. Fred said that he waited to get married because if he married the right person and life was grand, then that one was worth waiting for; and, on the other hand, if he married the wrong one, then he wouldn't have to live with her so long. Win either way!

Their oldest son, Fred, was born April 4, 1926, which was nine months and ten minutes after they were married, according to Father Fred.

Fred calculated that the trees and lumber stands in Upper Michigan were not going to last a long time, so he looked elsewhere. He read the newspapers and watched the weather reports. The mild temperatures made Seattle look good to him. In 1927, after working seven years for Weidman Lumber Company, the family of three moved to Seattle, driving over muddy roads. Fred worked selling insurance when they first were in Seattle. He said later that he had never worked so hard and made so little money on a job.

It was at this time that he began to study diligently to better himself. He took accounting from LaSalle Extension University and loved it. He said that an accountant can know more about a business than the owner. The accountant knows if there is a profit, or if money is being lost and where. Furthermore, an accountant can walk in anywhere and by having a look at the books know the status of the company.

James Whyte Wubbena (son #2) was born in Seattle on November 14, 1927 at home with the doctor in attendance. This was because Emma had had her children at home and had said that it worked out well. Being in a new, rather strange city might have further influenced this decision.

During the 1929 crash Fred and Mildred watched the stock market go down, down, down. Here they were in a strange city, far from everyone, with the economy bad! They had bought a two-bedroom home in Seattle near the University of Washington. When the economy became still worse (January 1934) they bought a little place in the country, about thirty miles from downtown Seattle. At least, they felt, on those five acres they could feed the kids! They rented out the house in town and Mildred's father came out to build a home for them by adding on to the little house on the property.

Daughter Margaret Eleanor Wubbena was born on September 30, 1934 in a Seattle hospital while the new house was being constructed.

Fred continued to study accounting through LaSalle. Early in 1934 he went with Colby Steel and Engineering Company, which manufactured industrial cranes. His eventual title was treasurer of this company. During World War II the shipping business began to expand worldwide. This company prospered, being one of the first to build shipboard cranes which made loading ships more efficient. Mark R. Colby, the owner, sold the company to the important persons in the company in 1949. The new partners all worked hard and then they sold this new company, Colby Steel and Manufacturing Company, to Lockheed Aircraft Corporation in 1960.

Being sixty-nine years old, this was a timely transition into retirement for Fred.

In 1967 they moved to Longview to be near daughter Margaret. When Fred was seventy-seven years old, the Spanglers built an addition onto their home. At that time he worked very hard helping to dig the crawl space under the new addition. He worked with great gusto, digging like a man much younger than he was.

After Fred's retirement he and Mildred traveled and kept good track of their family. Mildred passed away on August 25, 1974 with diabetes that had come on later in life. Fred passed away on May 31, 1982, past the age of ninety. His body had just worn out. He was hospitalized about three weeks before passing away and during that time he requested that "Oh, What a Beautiful Morning" be sung at his funeral. So it was!

I appreciated many things about my father. He was very optimistic; he never fussed when things went wrong, he would just dive in to fix them. Mildred, my mother, said that that was an important trait for her husband to have. He helped various family members as they were getting started. If there was ever a sincere need he would help.

As a father Fred was very strict and definite. His children all had to take sufficient piano lessons to be able to play hymns. At one time I was going to the Cornish School in Seattle, and getting excellent classical training, but my father took me out because the music was getting too far away from "Old Black Joe."

Fred told many stories that left great impressions. When he and his siblings were kids they were stealing apples (Dankart's, maybe) one night when the neighbor came out. The kids somehow got into the turnip patch and started throwing turnips at the neighbor. He had a flashlight, so he was a wonderful target.

Fred's folks fed so many itinerant preachers Fred used to say that he was fifteen years old before he knew that a chicken had anything more than a neck. One of the requirements for being a preacher was that one must enjoy eating chicken, Fred would say.

Their father would come to school and visit as a member of the school board. After questioning he would say, "Let us sink." Then he would want to hear all the kids sing, and if he didn't hear one of his own distinctly he would say, "Emmy, Villie, Freddie, vere are you? Vy don't you sink?"

When Fred was working in Upper Michigan in the 1920s in the office of the Weidman Lumber Company, he was highly influenced by Stanley Weidman, who was a millionaire. At one point Fred was asked by Stanley to give a man some money as a loan, and Fred looked with askance, almost begrudgingly, as he gave the man the money. Mr. Weidman took Fred aside and told him, "When you give someone something it is gone. Don't wonder any further what will happen." He told him he should have given the man the money with enthusiasm and good wishes.

One of Fred's questions was, "What are pants, singular or plural?" The correct answer is singular at the top and plural at the bottom.

At one of the reunions in Standish, the brothers, upon returning home one night after they had been out partying, walked near people who were lined up sleeping in the hay. Perhaps it was Hank who said, "Now folks, this is the mortuary. We have to identify the dead." They seemed to have fun over all subjects—nothing was out of scope.

Fred did a lot of entertaining—ventriloquism, sleight of hand, and tricks. He could get out of handcuffs. When he was in his twenties, several times while wearing only a bathing suit he had handcuffs put on him, then he dove into Lake Superior and came out carrying them. He loved to be the middle of the show, and people got a kick out of him.

One admirable ability he possessed was that he could bend over and readily pick up a four leaf clover. Anywhere he was, he could find one quickly and easily.

If Fred were here he would say that life had been good to him. We can truly say that Fred had been good to life, and that he had made a definite contribution!

Family Memories
by James W. Wubbena, Son of Fred Wubbena

I recall Dad saying that his brother, John, saw him working in a blacksmith shop when he was very young, swinging a hammer, and said to him that "swinging a pen is a lot easier than swinging a hammer." This prompted Dad to seek out the "ways of the pen!"

Practical jokes abounded in the family. Brother Harry was the station operator at Bruce's Crossing or some small town near there. Harry faked a telegram to one of the prominent men in town, stating that this man had won a new car. Harry told him that he should buy drinks for everyone, which the man did. A day or so later, Harry sent the man another faked telegram to disregard the first telegram. It said that the company had made an error and the car would not be awarded.

Dad was a strict disciplinarian with a conservative outlook. He had an abundance of enthusiasm for life in general, was full of good humor with a fun-loving attitude, and loved music and singing. He was strong for getting results and taking "action," because, as he said, "That's all people see!" He said many times, "It's *who* you know, not *what* you know!" I used to think he was wrong about that when I was young, but having seen it work, I realize he was right! The "who" gets you there, and the "what" keeps you there!

He had a few other favorite sayings:

Fine feathers make fine birds!
Talking without thinking is like shooting without aiming!

A short poem he often recited was:

As a rule a man's a fool
When it's hot he wants it cool
When it's cool he wants it hot
Always wanting what is not
As a rule a man's a fool.

Dad had this poem framed and hanging on his office wall:

Life's Mirror

There are loyal hearts, there are spirits brave,
There are souls that are pure and true,
Then give the world the best you have
And the best will come back to you.
Give love, and love to your heart will flow,
A strength in your utmost need.
Have faith, and a score of hearts will show
Their faith in your word and deed.
For life is a mirror of king and slave,
'Tis just what you are and do;
Then give to the world the best you have,
And the best will come back to you.

Madeline S. Bridges

Songs that Dad used to sing:

He's Never Done Anything Since

One day, my brother, he picked up a pin!
He's never done anything since!
He went up to a man and he stuck it in him!
He's never done anything since!

The man hollered "Murder," my brother was glad!
He kicked him a mile, and then he was sad.
For the man who he stuck with the pin was his Dad!
He's never done anything since!

Two Old Maids Lived Together

Two old maids lived together
And neither was to blame;
The reason was that one old maid
She couldn't change her name.

A burglar to their room went
To rob them he did try,
He had a cold which made him sneeze,
And one old maid did cry:

Wake up! There's a man in our room!
He came to see me I presume.
Don't give me the worst—for I saw him first
If you do my poor heart will burst.

Oh the burglar thought he'd met his doom!
For he couldn't get out of that room!
"Just give me one kiss, that will fill me with bliss!"
And the burglar fell dead in the room.

In a Hotel Lived a Boarder

In a hotel lived a boarder
Who bordered on his gall.
All other boarders paid their bills,
But he paid none at all.

The landlord to his room went
And found that he had fled;
A letter on the table lay,
And this is what it said:

"Kind Sir, I am leaving in haste!
For, in fact, I'm not stuck on your place!
If you do not get rash, I will send you the cash
The mortal price to pay for my hash!

I've a dozen or so of your spoons,
And I hope to get rid of them soon!

If you do not object, I will send you the check!
To collect from the man in the moon!"

The Laughing Song

As I went around the corner
I heard some people say:
Here comes that same old darky
And he's heading right this way

His feet are like a snow plow
His mouth is like a trap
I couldn't keep from laughing
To see the darky's gap!

And now I laugh! With a Ha Ha
And a Ha Ha Ha Ha Ha
And etc.

Letters from Fred to His Brother John and Family in Standish
Compiled by John's Daughter, Catherine Wubbena

Perhaps the best way to depict what Uncle Fred was like, in the eyes of us
Michiganians, is to use the letters he wrote to my father, John. I'm sure he
must have written more letters throughout the years, but these are the ones
my parents had stored away with letters from other relatives and friends. Perhaps his own children don't know he utilized the techniques and property
as described in these letters with the intention of developing in them the character and abilities he wanted to see. But, then again, they felt the guiding
hand and sensed the urgency he felt as he encouraged them in their daily living; what they probably are not aware of is his writing so much of what
revealed his longing and aims to his big brother and surrogate father, John.
His wife, Mildred, to whom he refers in every letter, was his true mate and
a supporter of all his endeavors. I'm sure, in her gentle and calm way, she
often played the moderator as he impulsively and enthusiastically aspired to
carry out his plans.

| |

Friedrich Theodor Engelhard (as spelled in the German Family Bible)
wrote to his brother John and Laura fairly often. A visit in person was infrequent, but his letters reveal that his thoughts and affection were concerned
with the folks "back home."

A letter written January 26, 1912, is tattered and faded, but most of it is readable. It is typewritten on Duluth, South Shore and Atlantic Railway Co. stationery and is written from "Station Agent's Office, Wetmore, Mich." This letter follows (some words are not readable):

January 26, 1912

Dear Brother John:

Well how is the old kid? am fine as can be, and am getting fat, I tell you that I have the . . . in the snow at all, and I tell you that is fine dope, we have plenty of snow here now, and last night it was 38 below zero, but that . . . do not go out, just go out to go to work and home again, and meet the . . . and get in some coal.

Yes that Joe Jasper is around, . . . but have not met him yet. Say I saw a fellow that knows you and Hank. His name is Charlie Gogran, he knows you well, he worked in camp with you and Hank, he said how you used to sing, he lives about two miles from here, he also has some fine sisters.

How is farming these days, now is the time I like to farm in the winter time, but best of all I like this.

Have not written anywhere for a long time so you can see I am getting along fine as can be, I have a good place to board and a good bed, get three meals a day what more does a fellow want?

Have a dandy girlie here, but not married yet, and do not expect to be for some time yet.

Say I traded that watch I got from you, I have a dandy now, it is a seventeen adjusted South Bend movement, I spoke to the fellow that sold the watch, the dealer I mean, it cost new, $53.00, I gave $11.00 to boot, and well pleased, with the deal I made, I refused $35.00 from the dealer, that sold the watch in the first place, so guess I am not stung any.

What is doing around home, John? anything? nothing around here, just a lot of work these days, lot of wire work, as the trains are mostly all late.

Tomorrow night I expect to go to a party, had a dandy envite, so guess I will except it, from a dandy kidd, so you can not blame me can you?

Next Sunday a bunch of Telegraphers expect to go to the Soo, and I am expected to go along, have my pass now, so it is a sure thing that I am going.

I know a dandy girl at the Soo so will probably see her too, but I am not going for that, guess the telegraphers are going to plan for a strike, am not sure yet, just the union men . . . you know I belong . . . well I do, and carry $500.00 insurance . . . the whole boodle when I die, worth more dead than alive, what. . . .

I do not know when I will be able to take a trip home, not for a while yet anyway.

Well John I do not know of anymore news to write you, only that I am well and get all I want to eat.

So I will ring off, hoping you will write a card at least and let me know if you get this o.k. will address it to Bill, then you will get sooner, as I do not know how the thing is at home, and you do not have a mail box at your home, have you?

Now be a good kid, and if you do not hear from me, just make up your mind I am well as telegraphing does not cost us anything, if something should go wrong.

I am as ever your loving brother.

Fred (signed)

A second letter accompanies the one above, also written January 26, 1912. It would seem that Fred is being properly businesslike in repaying John for a $15.00 loan:

January 26, 1912

Mr. J.T. Wubbena
Standish, Mich.
Dear Sir and Brother:

Attach . . . find $15.00 which is due you what I owe you, and. . . .

Thanking you for past favors . . . hope to have the opportunity to return them some day.

Please advise if you receive this at your earliest convenience.

Again thanking you,

I am your loving brother

F.E. Wubbena (signed)

op'r

| |

The next letter found among my parents' papers is dated May 31, 1925. It is typed on Weidman Lumber Co. stationery; the town is Trout Creek, Michigan. The short letter follows:

Mr. and Mrs. J.T Wubbena
Standish, Michigan
My dear folks:

How are you all, will take just a minute, June 17th, at 11 A.M. at 320 Center St., Elgin, Ill. Freddie takes unto himself a wife, Miss Mildred E. Whyte and would like to see you present. I know how it is, but it being the last man in the Wubbena family, who resisted the temptation of this matrimonial adventure the longest, would be much pleased if you could be present.

Yes, it lots of fun to plan, and arrange affairs on the eve of my bachelorhood years, as have only about two weeks more, to muss em up, then I muss her up. Oh, my, but this is exciting, you know I'm supposed to be part coo-coo, but I know what's going on all the time.

The weather has been very cold, just warmed up yesterday, and today its hotter than H---. I do hope its cool, on the day of my serious adventure.

Must run along, loads of love, and lovingly, Yours, Fred E.W. (signed)

| |

The following letter was written from R.F.D. No. 2, Box 29, Kirkland, Washington, and is dated July 13, 1936. This is the year of the celebration of the fiftieth anniversary of the Wubbenas' arrival in the United States. My brother Wyatt sent out printed invitations (he printed them at the place of his employment, *The Arenac County Independent*). He also arranged for the food to be brought in and he put up tables on John and Laura's lawn. Photographs show tables placed all across the front lawn. Some meals served during the three- or four-day affair were held at Charles and Myrtie's place in town. Folks slept wherever space could be found in John's home and barn floor and hay mow, at Charles' house, at Grace Strauss' house in Standish, and at Myrtle Baikie's house in Omer. I (Catherine) and Lois were student nurses at the University of Michigan at the time, but we were privileged to get away for the one day when the speeches were made. Fred's letter is in an envelope addressed to John with the instruction typed on the outside of the envelope: "to be opened at the table July 19th and read by Miss T.H. Wubbena, R.N., please." This is Fred's "speech":

> R. F. D. No.2, Box 291,
> Kirkland, Washington.
> July 13th, 1936

To the Wubbena Assembly:

It is with sincere regret that we write you this letter in lieu of being in your presence on this, the half century anniversary of the Wubbenas arriving at Standish.

When we consider what that great decision of our dear parents meant to them, the self sacrifices, the energy, the very courageous move. It certainly took courage and adventure to leave their loved ones, and their country so that we should not be soldiers in the German Army. We realize that—Had that decision not been made—there is no doubt in my mind, that some of us children would have paid the supreme sacrifice for the Fatherland during the world war.

Our father certainly was an outstanding man, and very sincere in his ideas,—every evening Bible study—There is not one of his children that was put to the test he was, left with ten children, and would not part with one of them—How thankful we can be that we were not adopted out. That richly deserved tribute given our father at his funeral when all stores closed, is an appreciation of what other people thought of him, and with these high ideals in mind, we are trying to live a life and raise our children that they will be a credit to dear Jan.

To you, who were born on German soil and who carried on when our parents passed on—we needed your advice thru our adolescent years, and you so wisely and kindly directed us, we are grateful for your efforts and unselfish service.

I shall never forget how one of the girls would get at the piano, and the wonderful sings we had together. What a home, and what a full life—laughter, work, scraps, weeping and song. John married Ella and me at one of Mins or Ems school programs. We toiled and struggled and weeped and worked.

How we would like to have you all come and pay us a visit. How wonderful if Jan and Mother could walk in on us, and just walk in on your program today. I believe they would not be disappointed. That is the responsibility we have, that is, to let Jan and Mother walk in on us, if it were possible, and inspect the job we have done, and find that their decision fifty years ago, really matured. That all the Wubbena Children are not now in the German Army, but are in Good Old United States of America.

In closing we invite you all to come out to the Pacific Northwest, either individually or collectively. We most certainly will try and make it as pleasant for you as we can. What a wonderful country this is.

Loads of love to you all, and while we are not in your presence, we are with you in spirit, and we will be thinking of you. While you are around the piano, please sing that grand hymn that Dad loved so well "How Firm A Foundation" and dedicate that to his memory.

> Lovingly yours
> Fred E.W. (signed)
> R. F. D. No.2, Box 291
> Kirkland, Washington.

| |

This next letter, written from the Kirkland address, is dated April 13, 1943. It is Fred's birthday message to my dad, John, who was sixty-nine that year.

It reveals the "props" of what Fred was using to help his children to become self-sufficient, honest, hard-working citizens. He also shows that he remembers that my dad liked to eat fish, and that he was very generous in sending the Pacific salmon. I remember that Dad was very pleased with the gift, but scolded Fred for spending so much money. Here is the letter:

Kirkland, Washington,
R. F. D. #2, Box 477,
April 13th, 1943

Dear brother John,

Next Sunday April 18th is the anniversary of your birth. How I wish we could spend it together, have a good visit, and a smoke together, and talk of our younger days, when we worked, toiled with the seat out of our pants, and money was real tough to get, and lots of substantial food, the kind that is good for one. Lots of vegetables, and lots of hard work.

We have five acres, and it sure is a God send to us, we still have our home in Town, but will never move back to it, I do not believe, as we like to sticks so very much. We have three head, one heifer a year old, and a yearling steer to be butchered this fall, have a nice little pig growing, will butcher him in a month or two, and have a dandy cow who supplies us with milk and butter, and lots of it.

Several months ago, the boys came in, and said "Dad we want to talk to you, this is serious business" they came in my study, and closed the door, when that door is closed, that means no one is to come in, as I have lots of people come in with their problems, I have a typewriter, adding machine, and a dandy business library there, and can look up any problem that involves business, so the door is closed. They said, "Dad we want to borrow $1,000.00, we will give you our note for it, and pay you interest" Boys what are you going to do with it, that is a lot of money? We want to buy a tractor, Disc, plow and harrow—and do custom work. I thought it over a few minutes, and they now own a tractor, disc, plow and harrow, Last Thursday, Friday was no school, and Thursday, Friday and Saturday they earned $80.00 with their equipment, it is one of the best investments I have ever made, it keeps the boys busy, and they plow or work every night after school, earn not less than $5.00, and sometimes $7, and $8. I do not butt in on their business at all, only advise them, as to good business methods. They are doing a dandy job in the neighborhood.

I'd give anything for a good visit with you and Laura, the Wyatts were very good to us when we were kids and needed kindness, and then you get Laura into the family, she is a dandy mother, and a good wife. I really wish you would come and pay us a visit, we have it real nice, I work very hard at the office, but it is good for me. I enjoy my work, and manage to keep eating.

Mildred is the same good girl I married some years ago, is a very capable mother, wise, kind and very considerate of others, a hard worker, as is the entire family, and yet have lots of fun.

Yesterday I had a fish Company send you a 15 pound frozen Salmon, Mildred bakes them, and stuffs them, and really are they good? I hope this reaches you in first class condition, and I know it will, as this man ships them all over the country. If it does not arrive in first class condition, please let me know, and we will send you another. I tried to get you a fresh salmon, but that was out, the best he could was send a frozen salmon. Please keep in touch with the Express office so as to get it as soon as it arrives.

We all wish you a very Happy birthday, and only wish we could be with you and enjoy a good visit. We are all well, and are not sorry we came out on the Pacific Coast, the climate is just wonderful, the girls are beautiful, and everything is just right to make life worth living.

Loads of love to you, and your very fine family.

> Lovingly
> Fred (signed)
> Fred and Family

| |

Another birthday letter is written April 15, 1947. By this time Dad was seventy-three years old. The letter follows:

> R. F. D. #2, Box 477,
> Kirkland, Washington.
> April 15, 1947

Mr John T. Wubbena
    R. F. D.
    Standish, Michigan

Dear John:

Friday the 18th, you first saw the light of day, and I know our Dad and Mother must have been very much pleased. Congratulations John, I only wish we could spend the day together, I would do my utmost to make it pleasant for you.

Why don't you, Charles and Hank drive out here, bring your wimmin along too, but you sure will see a lot of country, and you will also admit that we are in at least a part of the best of it. I just wish you could look us over, and give us a good inspection, and I think you and Charles could give me some good tips on what to do and what not to do.

Jim is going to the University, and Fred Jr. is in carpenter work, and studying architecture, likes it very much, but wishes he had studied more while in school, but that is water under the bridge, and its too late now.

Margaret is going to school, and likes it, and is getting to be quite a girl, full of fun, and a fair worker, but will sluff off if she can, well, that is common among children.

Today is Payday here, and tomorrow Payday at Prescott Iron Works, and the day after at the American Foundry Company, these paydays are busy days for me, but I rather enjoy it, as I see all of the employes, have a word with them, perhaps not much, but at least an exchange of words.

The weather has been just wonderful out here, plowing and lots of folks are putting in their gardens, the Boys have been very busy plowing, every minute they have they plow, we have some things in, but not enough, they get $3.00 per hour, and are busy as can be.

John is it possible to get a <u>plank</u> scraper like you have, if you can pick one up, really I wish you would, that is one of the slickest things yet, and we could use it on my place some, and also on Fred Jrs. place, if you can buy one, please do so, I'll be glad to send the money now, or as soon as I hear from you, please send it Auto freight, and delivery is made by Kirkland Auto Freight, be certain to specify that delivery is made by Kirkland Auto freight, as then they will deliver it right in our yard, those Kirkland Auto freight boys know us, and are friends of ours, Plank scrapers are not known in this country, corn knives are not either, Charles got some Corn knives for me several years ago, and they are really good.

Well, John, Many Happy Returns of the day, and I just wish we could have a good old visit, and discuss the past, as well as the future, How I wish you could pay us a visit, I know you would think we have a pretty good set up, also see me in my work shop, where I work, have nice offices, and am my own boss, and no one pays any attention to me, I have keys to every door Colby owns, as well as the Safes and strong boxes.

Loads of love, and write when you can.

Lovingly yours
Fred and Family

P. S. If you find a Plank Scraper, ship it to

  F. E. Wubbena,

  R. F. D. #2, Box 477,

  Kirkland, Washington.

  Auto Freight – Kirkland Auto Freight Delivery.

| |

The next letter is dated August 6, 1947, in an envelope with the Colby Steel and Engineering Co., 525 Central Building, Seattle 4, Wash. It is addressed to Dad at the Standish Hospital. This is a day or two following the accident Dad had with Uncle Charles' horses. At this time Fred did not understand how serious were the injuries Dad had sustained.

> 538 Central Building,
> Seattle 4, Washington.
> August 6th 1947
> Wednesday

Dear brother John:

Well, I just got back from lunch and the bank, also called at a Tailors, he called me and said he had some new cloths in, and wanted me to look at it, I want two new suits, but the stuff or material is too light, and no deal, he will call me later.

How are you today? When you get well enough to travel, just let me know, we will have you come out by train or buss, but I believe train is better, you and Laura are going to take a vacation, if you come by train you can get a lower berth, and sleep and keep on riding right along, eat sleep, and just look out of the window, if on the other hand, you want Catherine to drive you out, we will arrange that too, it would sure be nice if Catherine could drive you out, if you have a good car, but brother it wants to be a good car, it is a long ways, and coming thru the mountains you must have good brakes. We will see.

The weather is just grand here, very dry, and hot, but cool mornings, fact Mildred lit a fire in the Trash burner to warm up the kitchen this morning, and it really felt good.

We have a nice baby calf at home, both mother and calf doing fine, she is going to be a very gentle cow, easy milker, and will have lots of sense.

Well, John old dear, I must get to work, just wanted to get a line off to you, and let you know I am thinking about you, and would very much like to sit along side of you and talk to you, but as distance will not permit, we do the next best thing.

Wasn't it luckey for you, that you had Catherine? also Jean, they sure are dear kids.

> Loads of love to all of you.
> Fred.

| |

This next letter, dated the following day, August 7, 1947, shows that he is thinking of brother John.

538 Central Building,
Seattle 4, Washington.
August 7th, Thursday 1947

Dear John:

No news from you since last Monday. I wonder how you are getting along. Everything is being done for you that it is possible to do for you, you have two of the best nurses East of the Mississippi River, I have the best one West of the Mississippi, so you see we have them in our family havn't we?

Last spring Mildred purchased 200 baby chicks, they delivered two hundred five, two quit, so we have two hundred three left, and I guess about half of them are roosters, last Saturday we killed eight, and sold them as friers, tomorrow morning Friday I deliver twelve to a Hospital, Mildred sold them yesterday, so I'll be in the chicken butchering business tonight, we have started to dump the roosters, receive 48 cents a pound for them, and they weigh about three pounds, that is she receives 48 cents a pound from the hospital, but when we sell only one or two to a person its 55 cents a pound, we just take the feathers off, no drawing done at our place.

We are all very busy around our place, Fred Jr. in the carpenter business, and Jim is with a contractor, and doing very well, both come home every night, so that makes it nice.

One of the Boys in the office just came in and announced that he is a proud papa, and handed me a nice cigar, do you care to smoke it? I do not care so much for cigars, but I do suck a seven horse power pipe.

Well, John I must close and get to work, I expect Miss Gibb in a few minutes with a report to go over. Loads of Love.
                    Fred.
2 sticks of gum for the Nurses. F. E. W.

| |

On August 21, 1947, he is writing to Dad, again showing his thoughts are concerned with John's convalescence.

538 Central Building,
Seattle 4, Washington.
August 21st 1947

Dear brother John:

Well, I am just going to take a few minutes and pen you a few lines, not that there is anything new, but just to have a little visit with you.

Mildred, Mrs. Wilson (Mildreds Cousin) from near Chicago, her daughter, our daughter Margaret, Miss Ruth Lorentz, and Muriel U'Ren who was with us last summer just left the office a short time ago, I wanted them to go to lunch with me at the Artic Club, but they had to do their gadding, and refused, Muriel is the girl who was weighed when weighing sheep, if you remember, she really is a nice girl, she and Fred Jr. chum it, and are pretty thick, and then Ruth is the girl whose gate Jim swings on, she is also a very fine girl. Nothing but the best.

John how are you coming? Do you feel your oats yet, or are you still doing as the Nurses say you must? Isn't it tough to have to do as these Nurses say, do they demand anything of you that you can't do? Well, if they are reasonable its not so bad, but if they should ask the impossible, and beyond all reason, then of course it is time for you to call on me, and see if I can't help you, and fix things so it is agreeable to you. I'm a good fixer John, you know me? I'm especially good with Nurses, I married one, and I have studied her reactions to certain things, of course all Nurses do not respond to the same technique, and all must be handled differently, that is with a process involving special skill and knowledge, and I feel I have just that. So call on me if you are in any difficulty. So much for the Nurses, and am glad that is settled.

I just got a call on the telephone, and we are to have a meeting, so will ring off, I suppose I'll just sit there and smoke, and say about ten words during the entire session. Loads of love, and Love and kisses to the Nurses.
Lovingly Fred.

| |

The next letter is dated March 3, 1954. This would be four months before Dad died, and is the last letter written by Fred which I can find. When Dad was growing weaker, just two or three days before he died on July 6, 1954, he said with real feeling, "I wish I could see Fred." Thinking there was something weighing heavily on his mind I said, "Why? What do you have to tell him?" His reply was, "Oh, I'd just like to have a good talk with him." When I talked to Fred on the phone I told him of Dad's wish. But I guess Fred could not get away at the time. The March letter is as follows:

3155 Elliott Avenue,
Seattle 1, Washington.
March 3d 1954

Dear John and Family:
Your letter is received, and we regret very much that you have decided not to pay us a visit, it really would be wonderful if you came out here and

inspected our operation, and give us some practical tips how and where we are doing things right or wrong. I know you would enjoy the trip, as well as this country, and anyhow you have never been in our home, and it really would please us very much to have you.

You and Charles talk about it some more, just because your deaf, that is one of the weakest excuses one really could think of, we also have some deaf folks out here, and they manage alright, at least I see some with a cable wrapped around their neck and anchored in their ear, and they are still breathing.

I know you would have a wonderful time on the train, that is the group, of course if you were traveling alone, it would be different. I think Hank could manage you alright, get a big bag of OLD CROP, and several pipes, and a box of matches, and you're all set until you arrive out here, then we'll take care of you.

Heard over the radio that you have had a bad snow storm there, we havn't had any snow for some time, weather is just like spring, trees are budding out some, have a man trimming our fruit trees today.

Feel sorry for old Charles, I'll bet he gets very lonesome, nice if you two could visit a great deal, keep his mind off his troubles, for that reason, or that reason among others I wanted you to come out here, you could look after Charles, and he could look after you, and Hank could kinda be manager of the two of you. Think it over some more.

Love to all of you.

Fred.

| |

Two letters to me that tell us a little bit more of what Fred was like:

538 Central Building,
Seattle 4, Washington.
Friday August 15th, 1947

Catherine:

A letter yesterday, so we will have to send the Nurses some gum, but no letter no gum, that is how we work here.

Glad to learn John is holding his own, and I think perhaps a little better, it may be a long drawn out affair, but he will make it I believe. I do not think he will ever be strong and do heavy work again, but then, he has done his share anyway, don't you think? Glad you are pouring the Malted Milks into him.

I have to laugh how John keeps his mind on his business, you know just a year ago now, we were altogether, and enjoying each other, before I left on my vacation, I got a lady in my place here, and told the Officers of the various Companys I represent, to "Pay attention to that Lady, and if they did not, it would cost them money, and to do as she said." This lady is a very capable woman, married, she is a Certified Public Accountant, and honest, smokes a great deal, but she does know her business law, and figures. Catherine, do you know when I returned, everything was up to the minute, a few things that I had started, and were hanging fire, she just left them, and I finished them up when I returned, Why you know, I was never missed, and am not as important around here as I thought I was, so John can take the trip out here, and Shirley will never miss him, Oh, he might for a day or two, but I doubt that now, as John hasn't done anything around there for two or three weeks now, and the trip out here will be a month or two, and Shirley can worry along a little longer without him, and John will be appreciated that much more when he returns, and while he is out here he will be regaining his strength.

I do appreciate very much how well Shirley is handling matters, as his good wife Jean, isn't that her name, she sure is a hustler, and they are a very good team. You know Catherine — John and Laura sure have done a wonderful job on raising a family, all work and are hustlers, and not a blank in the lot, all full of fun and laughing, no grunters, and all can work, and all have a good balanced brain too, and think. I just hope our family turns out as well.

Both boys worked the last two days, Fred Jr. as Carpenter, he gets $1.85 an hour, and Jim gets $1.25 an hour, but the last two days a neighbor, about a mile from our place called up and said he had a lot of hay out and would the boys come up and help haul it in after supper, well the boys got home from work at 5. p. m. eat, jump in the Jeep and haul hay until 9.00 p. m. The fellow paid them each $6.00, he wanted to pay them more, but the boys said that was enough, it is not the money, but consideration for the neighbor that I like, and that they are capable of doing the job, and that the neighbor likes them, they sure can work.

Last Saturday we killed 30 young roosters, friers, all five of us were at it, we get from 52 cents to 55 cents a pound for them, now tomorrow Saturday again we kill 24 I believe it is, Mother takes the orders, and then on Saturday we do commit murder, I sure do hate that job, but it has to be done, that is Mother's and Margaret's project.

Sold a cow, and got rid of a calf, so have only one cow now, and she is a young heifer, and kinda dumb, fusses when you milk her, as all these young ladies do, but we will educate her, and she will turn out all right, she is gentle as a kitten, very lonesome since the older cow left.

Well Cathie and Jean, I must get to work, thanks again for the letter, and Hope John snaps out of it, and I think he is making it. More Power to you John.

Love and kisses to you all.

Fred.

| |

538 Central Building,
Seattle 4, Washington.
August 19, 1947

Dear Katherine:

Your very nice letter arrived last night, and sure glad John is out of the woods, or at least we may expect so, if you are letting him sit up a little, that is very encouraging. Glad he is that far, glad Wyatt was there to pay you a visit, and the four Wubbena girls also, I'll just bet they talked and talked while they were there, you know all the Wubbenas are claterers, I get to talking, and Mildred says "Bubble, Bubble, Bubble." She (Mildred) sure is a dandy.

We have some of Mildreds relatives here from the east, and last night she had ten at the table, and she manages that just as easily as three, is a very good manager, and always good natured.

You know Catherine — Had I known that Wyatt was going to locate in Delaware, I would have liked to have him come out here and look us over, I feel very confident he would have located out here, but I hesitate to steal John's kids, this climate is just ideal, and the people are moving in this State, property is going up, building and building, and more building, and the City as well is growing, growing, I certainly am glad we moved out here when we did.

Well, I received a letter, so I'll just have to send the Nurses some gum, letter, Gum, no letter, no gum, that is how I work.

How is your mother? What appears to be wrong with her? I know she was an old horse on a long race when we were there, poor kid, she has worked very hard, and we are all getting older, time just creeps up on us, and we get worn out like an old cultivator, or an old Ford, sometimes there is a groan or a grunt in us, and sometimes we do not respond.

Well, Cath Old Top, thanks for the letter.

Love and kisses to you all.

Fred.

ELLA CATHARINA ELISABETH WUBBENA
(1893–1983)

by Her Niece, Catherine Wubbena

Ella, the ninth child of Jan and Catharina Wubbena was born in Standish on January 26, 1893. She was three days less than one year old when her mother died. Her father took baby Ella to a Mr. and Mrs. Daley who lived in Sterling, Michigan, a distance of six miles from Standish. Newborn baby William was placed in someone else's home, and two-year-old Fred was placed in still another home. Children Minnie, Harry, and Emma stayed at home to be cared for by their father, older brothers and Talka. Neighbors also helped with the children's care. Their father made weekly visits to the three families where the younger children were being kept. I do not know how old Ella was when her father brought her back to the motherless family circle. She was with the Daleys long enough to have bonds of love established because in a year or two they had a baby daughter whom they named Ella. Ella Daley and Ella Wubbena maintained a relationship for the remainder of their lives.

In the record book of the Johnsfield School, Ella's name first appears November 1899 at age six: she was in the second grade. Her grades were listed as: Reading 97, Writing 100, Arithmetic 98, Geography 93, Language 100, Physiology 92, Spelling 98. The teacher was Frank Hamilton. Ella attended Standish High School after completing the eight grades at the Johnsfield School. She also did her share of the work at home. My father (John) told us that she was a very thorough and reliable worker, albeit a slow one. She was shy and quiet, preferring to stay in the background when her brothers and sisters were playing tricks on each other; someone else would make the first move in helping her find a job rather than for her to take the initiative in doing so.

When she was graduated from Standish High School in 1911, as part of the program for the graduation exercises she and Alice Wyatt sang a duet. Alice was my mother's younger sister and had a rich soprano voice. Ella sang a lovely soft alto. The song they sang was "Whip-poor-will"; there were parts where the bird's song would be an echo, and was a wonderful showcase for Ella's alto voice to come into play. The two young ladies received much acclaim for their contribution to the graduation program.

Ella passed the teacher's exam and thus was qualified to teach in county schools upon completion of high school. She taught for several years, one school being her home school, Johnsfield. During that year or two she became a good friend of Mr. and Mrs. Mike Eichinger. Their home was next to the school; their lush vegetable garden was separated from the schoolyard by a fence. Before there was a well with a pump in the schoolyard, drinking water for the pupils was obtained by students taking the water pail over to Eichinger's, via a path through the garden. This arrangement made it necessary for the teacher to ensure the pupils' good behavior. Apparently Ella was a good supervisor and found favor in the eyes of the Eichingers because they named their third child Ella in her honor.

While Ella was teaching, her sisters had moved away; Minnie married and moved to Elgin, Illinois. Talka went to the University of Michigan to study nursing, and Emma soon followed Talka and studied nursing at Harper Hospital in Detroit. Her brothers were, one by one, leaving the old home. After three or four years of teaching, Ella joined her sister in Elgin where she worked for a few years with her brother-in-law, Lou Gabler, at the Elgin Watch Factory. Then she decided to become a nurse, so studied at the Sherman Hospital in Elgin. After a few years she took the position of Resident Nurse for the Moody Bible Institute in Chicago. While in that position she not only gave nursing attention to sick students but also taught courses in first aid and communicable diseases. Since many students at Moody were preparing to become missionaries in all parts of the world, the courses Aunt Ella taught were an important part of their education. After she retired from this position, she worked as an industrial nurse for a plant near Elgin. While working in Elgin she made her home with the Gablers. Throughout these years Talka, who was wheelchair-bound, also lived with Minnie and Louis Gabler. It was while there in August 1959, that her sister Emma died in Detroit. A little over a year after that, Ella married George Flutur, the man who had been Emma's husband for thirty-eight years.

Ella had never had the responsibility of maintaining a home. The Flutur's home on Monte Vista Avenue in Detroit was large and beautifully kept. Ella felt it was too much for her, so she and George, after two or three years, sold the home and moved to an apartment in Redford, near Detroit. George felt a responsibility for helping to oversee the affairs of the Central Gospel Hall so they continued to live in Redford; he had retired from his work at the Ford Motor Co.

Ella had done much traveling before her marriage and had a lively interest in visiting foreign places. She now convinced George that he, too, should travel, and soon the two of them made several trips via trains and planes. George's eyesight deteriorated, so he had to give up driving a car. While still unmarried and living in Elgin, Ella had taken driving lessons. She had flunked her first test and repeated the course. She flunked the second test. So she relinquished the idea that she would be the one and only female driver of the Original Ten. She had to endure much teasing from her friends and relatives, but she took it all in good spirit. But when George gave up driving it meant the two of them had to rely on relatives and friends for getting around. It usually was George's son Duane or his wife Lorraine who transported them.

After a few years of apartment living in Redford, it was decided the more practical and comfortable place for them would be in one of the apartments on the grounds of Rest Haven in Grand Rapids, Michigan. This is a retirement home with facilities for nursing care if the need arises. It was originated and owned by the Pell family and still is utilized exclusively by members of Gospel Halls in Michigan and also other states. Duane and Lorraine helped them move and saw to it that their living arrangements were comfortable. Here George and Ella enjoyed fellowship with old friends as well as new ones, and could continue to live as they had always done with fellow Christians throughout their early life. When George's health continued to decline, they relinquished their apartment living and moved into the infirmary wing of the main building. Here there was twenty-four-hour nursing care available. Ella had found she was incapable of meeting the demands of his care by herself, and welcomed the attention supplied. She continued to maintain her status as a registered nurse in the state of Illinois. Her explanation was, "I want George to always have an R.N. nearby"; she was meticulous about signing her name with the R.N. attached to it. After George died on May 4, 1979, Ella continued to live at Rest Haven for four more years until she died on July 28, 1983 at the age of ninety. She had lived longer than did any other of the Original Ten. She and George had lived nineteen years as husband and wife.

Ella was a loyal friend and kept up a correspondence with many, many folks. She had a quiet, droll sense of humor. Several of her friends in Standish have given me letters written by her throughout the years. As a child I do not remember much about Ella as a young woman. My memories are of a gentle and kind woman who always spoke softly and seemed to stay in the background of any group or conversation. She did some beautiful tatting as the delicate and dainty doilies and handkerchief edging in all of our homes can prove.

In 1980 I made plans to drive my new car to San Augustine, Texas, to witness the marriage of Wyatt's older son, Jan, to Terri Roper. My sister Jean was to ride with me. When we told Aunt Ella of our plans, the longing in her eyes spoke for her. With some reservations about the fortitude of an eighty-seven-year-old being able to stand the rigors, we asked if she would like to go with us. No hesitation!

It was the middle of May and the countryside was beautiful. We made four or five overnight stops along the way. Ella helped Jean and me watch the road signs. She didn't miss a thing!

Wyatt's family and the rest of us relatives and several family friends stayed together in the same beautiful motel in the little town of San Augustine. We had some wonderful visits, and again, Aunt Ella didn't miss a thing. The bride and groom were (and are) professors at John Brown University in Arkansas, so several of their colleagues were also present. Aunt Ella was in her element—nothing shy about her there!

During the lull in the wedding functions several of us were entertaining ourselves with some sight-seeing. As we walked the streets of the lovely little town we made a stop at a little church. Aunt Ella prevailed upon Cheryl to sing some hymns for us as her sister Luise played the piano. Cheryl and Luise are Wyatt's daughters. Cheryl is a talented, trained singer. Luise teaches piano in her home town of Lititz, Pennsylvania. We enjoyed our private little concert but it was Aunt Ella who enjoyed it most of all.

After the wedding, and after the reception at the church, we were having a supper on the lawn of the bride's parents. Someone had heard Aunt Ella, at some previous time, present a humorous skit. When asked, she got up in front of about thirty people and recited that story of the Dutch couple who got along well because the wife was a loving slave to her demanding husband. Ella used Dutch accents, and bobbed up and down mocking the obeisance of the wife to perfection. She was a howling success! One would never guess she was eighty-seven years old!

On our trip back to Michigan we did some sight-seeing along the way. One could see that she was getting tired, but there was never one word of complaint of discomfort or weariness. She was one grand lady.

She lived three more years after this trip. She became quite thin. Whenever we visited her, a frequent remark was, "I don't have an ache or a pain. My heavenly Father is so good to me!"

Ella left her stamp on the world. Her individual uniqueness endeared her to us all.

"Weeping Lena"

Contributed by Ruth Wubbena Tulloch, Daughter of John Wubbena

Delivered by Tante [Aunt] Ella Flutur at Jan Wubbena's wedding on May 17, 1980. Ella was eighty-seven at the time.

A well-soaked large hanky was in play all the time, mopping her eyes amid choking and sobbing:

"I've had five husbands, all died. But Hans, he was the best. My, he was so GOOT. So kind to me. In the morning ven it vas cold, I vould say 'Hans, you stay in bed nice and warm' und I vould go out and shake up the stove, and put on the coffee. Und fry the bacon and make the pancakes, und ven all vas ready, I vould call him to come, (choking) und he vould come right avay! He was so *goot* that vay. And ven he vas done I vould clear up the table, nice and neat, and sweep up the floor. And in the vinter ven the snow vas high, I vould get my coat nice and warm, and tie on my scarf, all around the ears and under the chin, so cold out, and get the mittens, and dear Hans, he vould help me pull them on!! So kind. Then I vould put a rocker by the vindow so he could see me, and out I vould go, into the snow vid the shovel. And back and forth, back in forth, in front of the vindow, and Hans, he vould *vave at me*! (Fresh burst of tears)

In the summer time, ven it vas hot, I vould go out to the two trees by the house, one here and one here. I vould tie up the hammock, nice and tight so it vouldn't slip. Tie here, and tie here. Then Hans could be safe in it. The grass vas high, so I got the mower machine to push. Und I vould push it back and forth, back and forth, und ven I was by the hammock, Hans vould *smile at me*!! He vas *so* kind.

Und ven I vas done, he vould look at me und say, "You are so pretty; your face is so RED.""

(collapses in weeping)

Recollections of Aunt Ella
by Lorraine Flutur

Dad Flutur married Ella in October 1960. They were married in our house in front of the fireplace. Duane was best man. Margaret Gabler (Pickett) was

Maid of Honor. Just the immediate family and Ingrams attended. John Govan (the preacher) married them. The reception was held in Devon Gables, Bloomfield Hills.

This was a new experience for us. Our children called Ella "Grandma Ella" and we called her "Aunt Ella." She was the best thing that could have happened in Dad Flutur's life. They lived together for twenty years. She loved Dad dearly and they had a happy life together. They would sit together and hold hands and even when they went walking together they would hold hands. Aunt Ella loved to travel, and even though Dad didn't have that same love for traveling they traveled quite a bit. They traveled to see Aunt Minnie in Elgin, Uncle Fred in Federal Way, Washington, and we all remember a special trip she planned for the entire family to see Washington, D.C.—Virginia and Gus and family and our whole family. We drove in two cars. She and Dad financed the whole trip. We stayed at Uncle Bill's and Aunt Maude's while in Washington. Uncle Bill was our tour guide and what a great guide he was. We saw the White House, Pentagon Building, Washington and Lincoln Memorials, the Mint, the Senate dining room (where we had lunch), Arlington Cemetery (Kennedy Memorial), etc. Had a busy three days there. Don't know how Uncle Bill and Aunt Maude put up with us but we all slept there. We also saw Annapolis and we visited Wyatt and Ricky and family in Delaware. On the way home we stopped and saw Gettysburg. In Washington we also visited the wax museum and had our picture taken around the wax form of President Johnson.

Aunt Ella loved eating out and celebrating every occasion so there were always special things being done. Either she would take us out or have us over to their apartment.

They lived on Monte Vista for several years, and finally after several break-ins they moved to an apartment in Redford. Aunt Ella was a saver and we had quite a time moving a six-room house into a small two-bedroom apartment. It was like putting three pounds of tomatoes in a two pound bag.

After several years in the apartment, because Dad no longer could drive and his memory had faded, Ella decided to move to Rest Haven Home in Grand Rapids. She was their number one press agent! She loved it there and was such a big help. Everyone loved her also. Even today we'll meet nurses there that remember her and how special she was. She was always taking someone out to eat as she loved to be on the go. She often visited Margaret Pickett in Tennessee when Dad could no longer go. She also visited Uncle Fred several times. Dad passed away in May 1979 at eighty-seven years of age. Aunt Ella remained at the home till she died July 28, 1983 at the age of ninety, passing away very quickly, although she had been failing badly that last year. Interment was in Grand Lawn Cemetery, Detroit, Michigan.

She was always an interesting part of our lives. She had traveled so much in her lifetime that she had many interesting stories to relate. It was quite an experience for her to become a mother and a mother-in-law and grandmother at sixty-seven years of age. I can remember that on our nineteenth wedding anniversary in 1965 Aunt Ella and Dad moved into our house for a week and kept an eye on, and cooked for, our three sons who at that time were 17-15-13. That was quite an undertaking but they all got along well.

When our children were married she was so proud to be part of the wedding. We often mention how fortunate our children have been to have both sets of their grandparents at their weddings and also to see most of their children born. Aunt Ella was particularly fond of Virginia's Kelly as she was the only grandchild born after she married Dad.

We can truthfully say that we enjoyed having her a part of our lives and we are so thankful for her care for Dad over all the years.

WILLIAM LOUIS WUBBENA
(1894–1967)

Reflections on a Good Man by His Son
by William L. Wubbena, Jr.

William Louis Wubbena, Sr., was born January 5, 1894 in Standish, Michigan on the old "homestead" and died February 7, 1967 in Lanham, Maryland, of a heart attack. In that short span of years he managed to carve out at least three careers, raise a family, and gather hundreds of friends.

My first memories of Dad were his size and his passion. He was big—six feet—and raw-boned. I recall large hands and big wrists and arm muscles and I longed to grow to similar size. His passion in all things was palpable: he never made a half-hearted move or statement.

Our family circle seemed to center at the supper table. It was there that we'd chat and learn. Conversations ranged from family to school, politics to history and beyond. Religion, for example, was a likely topic. Dad would tell of his early days, the grinding poverty and privation, and the miraculous family unity and surrounding love that made it bearable.

His boyhood held deprivation but joy also; his brothers and sisters all participated in his development. His discussions of hand-me-down clothes, scant food, and no frills were never bitter. His descriptions were matter-of-fact, with the underlying message that family unity and combined effort could conquer any adversity. As a farm boy he did the normal chores and progressed in school until the eighth grade, when he went to work. This stoppage of his education scarred him, but he made his way despite it. And one of the proudest events of his life was finishing high school at age fifty-eight (while a patient at a Veteran's Hospital in Martinsburg, West Virginia, for his second bout with tuberculosis).

Because money was scarce, all the Wubbenas had to contribute however they could. I believe Dad's first paying job was in the lumber camps as a swamp angel—the one who went before the wagons and teams, clearing branches and brush out of their way. I don't believe he ever became a full-fledged lumberjack like Uncle John or Uncle Charles, but he may have, at least for a while. Life in the lumber camps continued the annealing process of the farm. The work was hard, the men were tough, and he was further strengthened.

Dad's first real career was on the railroad, first as a telegraph operator, then station agent, and finally as traveling auditor. I believe that Uncle Harry got him the job and perhaps helped to train him as a telegrapher. Dad also mentioned attending Ferris Institute for a short time to learn telegraphy and several other subjects. His elder brothers and sisters sacrificed to make it possible.

There is some evidence that Dad had the requisite allocation of wild oats and was fairly proficient at sowing them. His older brothers watched carefully and helped keep him on track. Uncle Harry also introduced Dad to Masonry, which was ever a moral guidepost to him. He loved Harry and forever held a special fondness for the Masons and railroading. He eventually became a member of the Shrine and enjoyed the fellowship as well as the good work pursued by Shriners. He was sad and disappointed that I never joined the Masons, but never pressed me or mentioned it except obliquely.

At about this time in his life, World War I called him to the Army. Uncle Fred and Aunt Talke also served. I think Aunt Talke caught the illness that eventually invalided her while serving as an Army Nurse. Because of his telegraphy experience, Dad was in the Signal Corps. He told many war stories, but never gory ones. His remarks of events were always human interest stories of the fatigue, fright, hunger, and comradeship . . . things I found unchanged later in Vietnam. One example: the mess sergeant in charge of the serving line for a meal shouting, "Give them all the bread they want!" while holding up one finger to make clear that the ration was a single slice. I also remember his description of bully beef, hard tack, and salmon ("goldfish"). He never again would eat salmon.

His knowledge of German was a valuable asset to his unit and of course to him personally. He regretted never being allowed to visit the family origins while on occupation duty, but made up for it years later—in the mid-1950s—by making a trip to Neermoor to see his Aunt Lukke.

Returning to the railroad after the war, Dad remained associated with the

Army in a reserve status. He would consider the Army his second career and supported a strong national defense the rest of his life. I remember his listening to (and translating) Hitler's speeches and voicing his grave concerns as war clouds gathered in the 1930s. Because of his intense thirst for news plus political and economic information, our family was better informed than most about history and current events. I wish we had tapes of supper conversations, even those that found me being scolded for frequent infractions.

Eventually, Dad met the most remarkable woman of his life, courted and married her on July 7, 1922. This wonderful person, Maude Zuleme Martin, was born on February 16, 1902 in Gulliver, Michigan. Like Dad, she had a difficult childhood and foreshortened education, and was working as a housekeeper when they met. For Dad she was the perfect companion and confidant, a splendid homemaker and manager. For us, her children, she was a model of a devoted, understanding, and helpful Mother. When times were difficult, she was strong; when they were better, she remained humble, while grateful. Mom did many things wonderfully well—including baking (I still crave her cinnamon rolls)—and managed a fiercely tight budget. She had more courage than anyone else and was undaunted by any challenge. Mom's great common sense and understanding were the glue for our family, especially when Dad was on the road so much. Anyway, Dad's life truly blossomed when he married dear Maude.

After a few years in Marquette, Michigan, we moved to Hankinson, North Dakota. I'm sure the move was due to the Depression, and we moved again to Aurora, Colorado. Dad had been working on the railroad when he went to Army reserve summer duty at Fort Riley, Kansas. An automobile wreck landed him in the hospital where X-rays for broken ribs also revealed tuberculosis. He was sent to Fitzsimmons General (Army) Hospital for treatment, and we joined him in Aurora. These events are sketchy for me, but I do remember that times were indeed tough. Dad spent many, many months in the hospital, but was permitted home visits. When he was released, he got a temporary night job with the post office in downtown Denver sorting mail. To avoid being laid off, he would practice at home, pitching flash cards into an arrangement of pigeon holes he fashioned out of boxes. He was determined to sort more mail than anyone else. He hated that job, but it helped us survive.

As a young boy in Aurora, I became aware of Dad's absolute insistence on discipline, responsibility, reputation, and respect for property. (As tenants, we always had to leave things better than when we found them.) He repeated often that it takes years to establish a good reputation but only a day to destroy it. Dad expected everyone's best effort in any activity and would not tolerate less. "Push your work; don't let your work push you!" was another favorite maxim. And he could shower love on you in many different ways. Once, sister Dawn was very sick with a mastoid and was away in a Denver hospital for a long time. It was late in the year, and Dad decided we'd just keep Christmas on hold until she came home. We had our Christmas in February. And somehow he started us on music. Eileen learned trombone and Dawn cornet. Later I borrowed Dawn's horn to learn.

I also recall that we always had a garden. It was much more than economy; Dad was driven back to the soil. He loved gardening and yard work and was ambitious and meticulous. Because he was away so much, we youngsters had much of the tending as chores. I hated it, but he was unyielding—it was part of our education. One of my responsibilities was to keep dandelions out of the yard, dug out by the roots. If he came home to find a blossom, my backside was reminded to be more attentive and thorough.

As World War II approached, it became clear to Dad that we would be in it. His overtures to re-enter the Army were rebuffed because of his tuberculosis history. But somehow he was offered a job as a civilian in the Army Headquarters in Washington, D.C. Again, my memories may be out of sequence, but I believe that Dad came to Washington alone to work in the Railroad Retirement Board in a temporary status. We stayed in Aurora. Dad left the post office because he feared a health breakdown from working nights. He had also found other railroad work in Colorado. Possibly he sought other jobs while in Washington and made contact with a Colonel Tillman, whom he had known at Camp McCoy, Wisconsin, while on reserve duty. Colonel Tillman was in the Finance Corps and offered Dad a job involving Army payments to railroads for various shipments. He described it as "checking freight rates" and I suppose it was an auditor-type position to ensure the Army was not cheated.

To travel to Washington, Mom and Dad bought an ancient Model A Ford which only Mom would drive. After his automobile accident at Fort Riley, Dad never attempted to drive again (but he sure "helped" others). They drove to Washington, D.C. in that Ford in the winter of 1938–39, and it must have been a real adventure. Mom's widowed sister, Leona, stayed with us in Aurora. When an apartment was found in Washington, Aunt Leona put us on the bus, with sister Eileen in charge, and we three kids rejoined Mom and Dad a few days later. I suffered from motion sickness and had a miserable trip, but Eileen did a great job.

Events came in a rush after that. Dad's third (government) career progressed steadily, with his eventual move to the newly formed Transportation Corps, which he adored and never left. We moved to suburban Maryland and never left. Mom began working also in government as a clerk in the

Labor Department. Things became brighter financially, especially when we children finished school. Eileen and Dawn were married and I went to West Point.

But the effects of poverty were long-lived. Dad was a fierce Democrat and very leftist politically. He once proposed that if we draft young men to serve and perhaps die, we should also confiscate wealth. In later years, he mellowed. Never voted Republican, but he became at least a moderate, if not conservative, Democrat.

After he could afford it, he bought tailored clothes and had a pair of shoes hand-tailored—as if to erase the hand-me-downs of childhood. I took those shoes to the cobbler once, later on, and forgot them on the bus. Telling Dad was one of the most difficult things I ever had to do. He was, of course, crushed and remarked that it was vain for him to presume to have those shoes—that God didn't mean for him to have them. Then he wryly smiled and said that someone else had *his* hand-me-downs. Whether from earlier privation or not, Dad always tended to buy the largest size box, the biggest portion, the wholesale quantity. If one or two was good, a dozen was better. He was lavish in his generosity, when able, and would buy inordinate amounts of candy, or strawberries, or whatever the 'giftee' particularly liked.

Then there was another major setback. After an arduous nation-wide trip for the Army in 1949–50, Dad again came down with tuberculosis and spent about a year in the Veteran's Hospital in Martinsburg, West Virginia. Those were tough days, and Mom had to have major surgery soon after.

They both recovered enough to come to my graduation. Dad was so proud. He had always wanted me to go to West Point and feared he might have soured me on the idea by being so fiercely in favor of it. When I decided, in prep school, that my future was the Army, he was very happy. Also on graduation day I married Marie Joan Schroer, my high school sweetheart. Mom and Dad loved her as their own and also liked her parents, Emma and Philip. Dad especially doted on Marie and could not do enough for her, to the point of saturation. He remarked to me, each time we were together, that we both were extremely lucky to have wives like Mom and Marie. He wanted to please her and always sought to do extra things. When I was ordered to return to West Point, Dad and I drove up to get the house ready. Marie (with eleven-month-old Philip) had to make a sudden trip to Tucson, Arizona to visit her parents. Her father was in a VA hospital after suffering a heart attack while on a trip through the West.

Without Marie, I really needed Dad's help. He did many extra things so that Marie could just enter and be instantly operational. He craved her praise and would ask if this or that completed task was to her liking. Once, on a subsequent visit, while staining an unfinished chest in anticipation of Jon's birth, he set the color tone as he would have preferred, ignoring her instructions. When he asked if the chest was OK, she replied, "Well, if you didn't want to do it my way, why ask me now if it is OK?" He was chastened and always related the incident to show how Marie had a mind of her own. He never again departed from her preferences.

The Army often sent us far from home, but Mom and Dad would visit whenever possible—even traveling to Germany. Marie suffered several miscarriages, but William Philip finally arrived August 30, 1959 in Rio de Janeiro, Brazil, where I was sent to learn Portuguese. Later on, back in Cornwall, New York, while expecting our second child, Marie threatened to again miscarry. Mom came to take over and put Marie in bed for three months until the danger had passed. Jon Kevin was born on October 15, 1961. Without Mother's total, devoted help, it would not have happened.

Mom and Dad soon truly began to enjoy life and their kids and their grandchildren. Dad was an avid walker; it was his favorite exercise. He hiked with me in the earlier years, and later, hand-in-hand with young Mike Hendricks, Dawn and Burt's son. The sight of those two walking would melt you. Later he would walk with our son, Philip, for huge distances. It was a lot for a two-year-old, but Philip loved it. He once tried to interrupt Dad's yard work to take a walk toward some band music from a nearby school. Dad pretended to ignore him, so Philip took Dad's hands off the lawnmower and pointed in the direction to take. Dad could not ignore that! He also pulled Philip on the sled for at least two or three miles one winter day. He loved to play with Philip and Jon. Jon especially enjoyed "roughhouse" and would seek out Dad for the "special flip" (skin the cat). Dad would also hold him aloft by one arm or ankle and pretend to drop him—only to catch him at the last instant. Dad was also a fierce tickler.

Soon came their time to retire and enjoy the golden years. Dad was presented with a large panel at his retirement ceremony. It recounts his career(s) and is signed by all his co-workers. One portion is a special tribute which says:

"Raconteur and FRIEND
(The Biggest Smile on Earth)
Our Wubbena known as "Bill"
Gallant to the ladies
Friend to All
Wise in Council
Rich in knowledge
Wealthy in self-respect

Secure in his esteem by all
Missed by all of us"

Marie and I have kept that panel prominently displayed.

After retirement Mom and Dad bought a cozy home in Lanham, Maryland and had a ball. Dad had a huge yard, lots of trees and shrubs and a large garden. He was so happy! As mentioned earlier, they visited us in New York (I was then an instructor of Portuguese at West Point), and he did yard work there, too. While in Brazil I had a Masonic/Shrine ring designed and made for him. He treasured it greatly, but lost it while raking and burning leaves on one visit. He was disappointed and increasingly saddened as he searched and searched to no avail. And he said again, as he had for the shoes, that God did not intend for him to have that ring. But on his next visit the following spring he found it in the ashes beneath the trash can we used for burning. His joy was matched by ours.

Dad was always busy. He had a well-developed capacity to repair things, especially with glue. On one visit to us, our son Philip presented Dad with a broken toy. Dad went to work with "Mr. Glue" as Philip looked on — admiringly. The toy was soon as good as new. The next day, when Dad woke up, the hallway was lined with toys to be repaired! He fixed them all, and revelled in the "compliment." Despite a mild heart attack in Lanham, he thrived.

He became very active in community affairs and would canvass the neighborhood for petitions or support for a sheriff or local politician. He was a natural and, had he been so inclined, could have held office. And Dad helped others constantly. Lanham became a way station for friends or people in need. His early years taught him that circumstances did not truly reflect basic value. I had many friends that owe a lot to his hospitality and guidance. Mom and Dad extended themselves to others often and did what they could whether with advice, or solace, and frequently with money.

The years rushed by and Dad's time ran out. During a snow storm on February 7, 1967, he was impatient to get the snow off the driveway. He put the grading blade on his home tractor and began to clear the snow. Then his heart failed. His funeral was on a day after a huge snowfall. Despite the bad road conditions many, many friends, relatives and neighbors came. The family was astounded by the number of cars in the procession — a tribute to the many lives he had touched.

His death was a cruel, crushing blow to Mom. She lingered, in successive stages of failing health, until April 29, 1980. But her life was a shadow after Dad left.

I have appended some earlier notes I authored reflecting on Dad and the Wubbena Original Ten, plus a letter from Uncle Harry to Uncle John about

Dad's wild oats. The letter pictures a little of the relationship between the siblings: the younger ones viewed the older ones as parents, and the older ones tried to fulfill that role, as all the while each one of the ten felt the ties between them.

That family had all winners—solid, principled citizens that made this a better world. Dad was a solid, principled citizen who loved his family and his country. I am proud to share his name.

Wubbena Family Recollections
by William L. Wubbena, Jr.

My early days are increasingly hazy, but I do have distinct memories of certain events and situations: the Wubbenas loved music, fun, visits, gardening, and travel.

The youngest of the Original Ten was William L., our Dad. Actually, according to the family Bible at Uncle John's, his name was a string of German—Wilhelm, Ludwig, Karl, Friedrich, etc. Dad loved to sing and was a gifted parlor entertainer, playing the guitar or "chording" on the piano while singing humorous and catchy songs. His magic tricks and ventriloquism were fun also, and he did perform for our class at school. Even after he showed me how to palm or hide those little paper wads between his fingers, it still seemed that he was really moving them magically from one hat to another on the floor. Also, his leaning stick trick still seemed real even after he showed me how he held it with thread. He could make fun out of very little, from peculiar accents to pretended powers (like 'sniffing' his way home after convincing sister Dawn they were lost or commanding the sun to hide and then reappear among the clouds).

He loved to walk—anywhere—but a hike in the woods was great sport. A day spent hiking and then cooking over a campfire was a special treat for him. Of course Mom did not enjoy a kitchen full of sooty pots—they were hard to clean. Oh yes, any baseball game was a magnet; he loved that sport and even taught Mom how to keep score from radio accounts and relate world series games for him when he'd get home from his traveling job. And, his days as a telegrapher came in handy when listening to "remote" games because he could decipher the relayed code faster than the announcer.

The bond between the Original Ten was inspirational. Looking back, they must have been the closest family ever. It seemed to me that visits were constant. In our Colorado days, Aunt Minnie, Uncle Louis, Aunt Talke, Aunt Ella and Muriel, Margaret and Louis, Jr. came (I don't know how Mom found places for them to sleep or how she prepared meals in that small bun-

galow). Aunt Talke was the oldest sister and revered by Dad. She was confined to a wheelchair and unable to participate in all excursions but enjoyed
the outings. I remember we once washed her face with snow in the mountains. I also recall her fear of those dizzying mountain roads, having a lock
grip on the strap with both hands. She steadfastly looked inward whenever
Dad called her attention to something far below; she would cheerfully
exclaim, "Yes, yes, Billy, I see!" but was afraid to turn her head. One time,
in the mountains, the group went walking to seek arrowheads or petrified
wood and I stayed with Aunt Talke in the car (I suffered a lot from motion
sickness). The conversation went well—I guess I was five years old—but
ended with our becoming "man and wife." The ceremony was quite solemn:
"I'm your Indian, you're my squaw. Now we're married, haw, haw, haw."
Dad, upon learning of the event (I was so proud), gave me a stern lecture on
my responsibilities with this serious step. Anyway, from that day on until she
died, Talke always referred to me as her husband and sent special cards and
greetings from time to time.

The Elgin clan visited us in Washington, too, and we also became well
acquainted with Aunt Emma, Uncle George, and Duane and Virginia. Likewise with those in Standish. As I say, the visits were fairly constant and
always welcome.

Wubbenas could tease, too. Laughter was food. One game at the farm
was to "weigh sheep," wherein all candidates were seated in a circle and covered with a blanket. As they "baa-ed," people outside would pick up the candidates randomly and declare them too heavy or too light, except the
intended victim, who was raised, declared just right and put back down—
but in a pan of water thrust under the blanket at the last second.

Dad often remarked that the railroad educated him, the Army taught him
discipline, and the Masons kept him out of trouble. He loved all three institutions. But his biggest love was his family. His recounting of the early days
of grinding poverty was never bitter but full of love for his brothers and sisters, especially Talke and John, who sacrificed so much for the rest. John did
not marry until age thirty-seven because he supported the younger siblings,
and Talke never married. The rest of the older ones supported also—everyone did what they could, but John and Talke, the eldest son and eldest daughter, took the lead.

It was a marvellous treat to listen to the Original Ten and learn of the
early days, the lumber camps (where Uncle Charles never kept inventory of
the trees he felled, merely added one or two more than anyone else and—
when challenged at the end of the season because the supervisors could not
find those trees—retorted "For God's sake don't lose those trees, I worked
like hell cutting 'em"), or Uncle Henry describing how they erected telephone

(telegraph) poles. Henry was fun to listen to—very witty and droll. His wife, Aunt Martha, held sufficient love to fill the entire world and expressed it through sumptuous meals and treats. Their family, to me, seemed the intellectuals. Lois the nurse, Florence also, Bernice the teacher (knew Latin!) and Raymond, master of all crafts. Uncle John and Aunt Laura had a family as solid as their roots, which I was privileged to witness firsthand in Standish, spending summers on the farm. From Wyatt to Shirley there was a powerful link of love reflecting the Original Ten. One of my proudest moments was to act as witness at Shirley's wedding to Jeannette. Her sister, Carol, was the other witness.

Those summers were educational for a skinny, teenage city boy. The work was hard, but there was fun, too, and it was a great opportunity to hear Uncle John relate stories of the early days:

- Dad could shingle roofs. Once, while shingling the barn, he saw his brothers and sisters engaged in horseplay down below. Fearful that they might be caught and punished for playing rather than working, Dad wished to protect them and sang a nonsense song whose impromptu lyric was "I will whistle when he comes." Great idea, but very impractical, since grandfather heard it also—so Dad got spanked.

- One time my father caught his hand in a pulley (holding onto a rope too long) and was badly hurt. Uncle John hitched up the buggy and drove him to town for treatment. He didn't know how to comfort Dad so told him, "Sing, Billy, Sing!" He did, but was left-handed from then on.

- Dad noticed one day that Wyatt was fearful of the geese because they nipped him. (Wyatt could only have been four years old.) All day he prompted Wyatt to hiss like the geese, asking, "Wyatt, what do the geese say?" Wyatt would respond with a loud, prolonged "SSShhh." At supper Dad waited until Wyatt had a mouthful of food and popped the question. The response sprayed the room. One more example of Wubbena fun—like weighing sheep.

- Dad loved blueberries—and so did the rest. Uncle John, in his seventies, would go to the woods early in the morning and return at noon, sweaty and sore, with a large pail filled to the brim with blueberries.

On visits to Standish, Dad insisted on buying huge amounts of smoked whitefish to take to the farm because "John loves it so." Of course, the greatest craving was my Dad's.

Uncle John could tease, too. At one time his bull was kept mostly in the enclosure surrounded by one strand of wire—an electric fence. I was perhaps thirteen and scared to death of that bull. One of my tasks was to go out to the distant pasture and bring the cows and bull from their grazing for evening milking. The cows would be milked and the bull would be placed in his enclosure. Those were terrible times for me, certain that the bull would gore and trample me at any instant. As the days went by my confidence grew—it was Uncle John's way of helping me grow. Once the bull walked through the wire when the current was off. Uncle John asked me to get the bull back inside and then re-tie the wire together. I did, but had a very hard time tying the wire because my hands kept jerking. I looked up and saw Uncle John convulsed in glee. He had the current on! It was only three volts and no danger, but it must have been fun to watch.

I only got to "see" Uncle Harry at his funeral, and I did not meet Uncle Fred until late in his life. Uncle Fred was a delight who stepped forward after Dad died, writing: "I am the only uncle you have, and we must keep in touch." After Aunt Mildred died, he later wrote to us overseas. He was past eighty years of age, but found romance. His report: "I suggested that we get married, but she said, 'Oh, Fred, who would have us?' But I persisted and committed matrimony." He would close every letter inviting us to visit, saying "The latch string is out and the dog tied up." We were able to talk on the phone once in a while, and I always regret not knowing him earlier.

One touching incident involved Aunt Ella, who later married Uncle George after Aunt Emma died. Aunt Ella came to visit Brazil with a large group just after our Philip was born. Philip had a rough start and was not too fond of this world or the people in it. Aunt Ella was able to separate from her group for one evening, and we took her to supper. Anyway, upon seeing her, Philip reached out to go to her. She took him in her arms, cooing and nuzzling, and he responded. One other example of the palpable, infectious love of that wonderful family.

Until he died, Dad loved gardening and was quite good at it. Of course, he was intolerant of anything less than perfection. We did not share that passion and felt that one weed was not an infestation, but his garden (and yard) reflected neatness, great care and effort, great variety and innovation and amazing results. His gardening, I understand now, was a return to the soil and the farm, a statement that hard work and constant effort would bring desired results, just as they did for his brothers and sisters.

Letter from Harry to John Regarding Bill
(Duluth, South Shore and Atlantic Stationery)

Ewen, Michigan   10/26/14

Dear Bro. John

Well I suppose you have Bill with you now. The little rascal would not work here. He had the best position here. It was a night job but paid $62.50 per month and he got fooling with his guitar and girls until someone turned him in to headquarters. I did not know about it till yesterday. Fred told me. I am so sorry because if he had wanted to make good he could have done it but he is too full of foolishness. He used to have a bunch of boys hang around in the office. It really is a shame.

It's his own fault he is not in a nice, warm office. This winter as he was told by both Fred and I—to leave the girls alone and get down to business—as he had a fine place to study and would not take advantage of it. Fred feels real mad at him and I don't think Fred will help him again.

Fred no doubt will write you boys about him too.

How are you all getting along and are you farming the crops now. We had a nice snowstorm here last night. There is still some snow on the ground tonight. I have two cords of hardwood to split up and put in the shed in the morning. How is Laura and the children. Lenore is fine. We went to Sault Saint Marie yesterday to buy some winter clothes. Len got a coat. Well, John, give my love to all and write soon. Your loving brother, Harry.

Additional Memories of the *William L. Wubbena, Sr.* Family
by *Eileen Wubbena Catt, Daughter of William L. Wubbena, Sr.*

My earliest memory of my father is when I was four years old. It was my mother's birthday and my dad took me with him to a very expensive grocery store so we could get my mother a present. We bought fresh asparagus and strawberries. It was in February so they must have been expensive. I have no idea what else he bought but do remember that we took the package home and hid it in the back entryway. My mother was thrilled when he presented them, and I was so proud to have been part of the whole plan.

My dad and mom were very strict with us and really worked on the concepts of honesty, industry, and goals. They didn't call them that but, in thinking back, every bit of our behavior was guided by these tenets.

My father was constantly studying and trying to learn all he could. He was especially interested in history and I don't think there is an historical sign in Pennsylvania, Maryland, or Virginia that we didn't stop to read. Weemo (i.e., Bill, Jr.), Dawn, and I were bored stiff but now realize the value of those stops.

Dad was gone much of the time in our early years. He was a traveling auditor for the railroad. Mother was wonderful. We read lots of poetry. Money was scarce and we had a lot of "Depression Dishes." I still fix some of them. I also remember her saying "I'm proud of patches." Truly she hated them as much as we did. When Dad would get home for the weekend, we did lots of singing and played lots of games. Wonderful times!

My dad always said he was a self-made man and he was! He didn't go to high school but that did not deter him. He studied to better himself and was a telegrapher for the railroad. Then he studied accounting and became an auditor. He stayed in the Army Reserve and eventually became a first lieutenant. Quite a feat, since he had no formal education beyond eighth grade.

When the Depression brought the merger of the Duluth, South Shore and Atlantic Railroad with the Soo Line Railroad, we moved from Marquette, Michigan, to Hankinson, North Dakota. Dad was gone much of the time but we did lots of fun things with Mom. In time (one and one-half years) the Soo Line cut forces and Dad lost his job. He called on his resources and soon was called to active duty with the Army as a Finance Officer at Fort Riley, Kansas. The Post Commander was General Jonathan M. (Skinny) Wainwright.

We stayed in Hankinson until he could find housing for us. However, while at Fort Riley, on a trip back from the city bank with a payroll, Dad was in an automobile accident. He had some broken ribs and when the x-rays were read, the doctor found that he had tuberculosis. He was sent to Fitzsimmons General (Army) Hospital in Denver, Colorado, for treatment. As a reserve officer he was not entitled to receive any pay while a patient. Fortunately, he did have some health insurance which helped.

Times were really lean! We moved to Colorado and found a house in Aurora, which was about a mile from the hospital. We had very little but everyone else was in the same boat. Dad could get an afternoon pass and he would walk home, usually once a week.

He was released from the hospital after about two years. He went to work as a relief man for the Denver and Rio Grande Railroad. Again he was gone a lot.

Finally he wrote a Civil Service exam for the Post Office and passed it. He was hired by the Denver Post Office. He worked nights. He hated the hours, he hated the job, he hated everything about it, but to quote him, "It puts flour in the flour bin."

He stayed in that job until he found a position with the Railroad Retirement Board in Washington, D.C. Again he left and we stayed. He was put on furlough after a few months and came home. Finally he was called back to work.

This time Mother went to Washington, D.C. with him, leaving the three children with Mother's sister, Leona. We stayed with her until school was out and through the summer. In early September 1940 they sent for us. We boarded a bus in Denver and went to Chicago where Aunt Min and Uncle Lou met us. We rested for a day or so and then boarded a bus for Washington. What a long ride! We finally got to D.C. and Dad and Mom met us. Tears, laughs and giggles were the order of the day.

Washington, in those days, was wonderful. It was safe and so rich in educational opportunities. The schools were very good and because our father was a civil service employee, we could go to school in the District of Columbia. Much time was spent in the museums and art galleries as well as the historical places around Washington D.C., Virginia, and Maryland. We three were active in all phases of school, and were also very much involved in extra-curricular activities and lots of music. We were in band, orchestra, and choirs (both school and church) and our parents were always behind us and at our performances.

At home there was always lots of music, too. We lived in an apartment our first year in D.C. The manager of the apartment house lived on the floor below, right under our apartment. She told my mother that her family planned its dinner hour right after ours so they could listen to us sing as we were doing the dishes. We learned to sing parts and had quite a group going. Much fun!

There was always lots to do. All-City Band, All-City Choir, etc. I was in the Redskin's Band as well as the American Security Bank Orchestra. No matter what was involved it was a family activity.

After high school, I went to the University of Michigan School of Nursing, Dawn went to the University of Michigan School of Business Administration, and Weemo went to the U.S. Military Academy.

By now things were easing for our parents. They were able to do some of the things that had been impossible in earlier years. While Weemo and Marie were stationed in Germany and Dawn and Burt were in the Netherlands, our parents were able to visit them. While there they visited relatives of the Wubbena clan in Neermoor, Germany.

As grandchildren were born they were able to visit and greet each one. That was very nice for all of us. In their later years they were pretty well able to afford to do the things they wanted to do. On one visit to Chicago when Keith was stationed at the Office of Naval Research branch office, Dad and Mom came to visit us. Dad went to the local butcher shop and bought fourteen New York strip steaks—some for dinner and some for the freezer. He was always very generous.

When he was curing from tuberculosis (for the second time) in the VA Hospital in Martinsburg, West Virginia, a doctor named Hollingsworth was reading his x-rays. This doctor was a patient there, but was also acting part-time as a physician. As fate (divine intervention?) would have it, I had been a scrub nurse in an operating room at the University of Michigan Hospital where I had worked with this same Dr. Hollingsworth. Because the name was so unusual Dr. Hollingsworth asked Dad if he was related to me. When he learned that Dad was my father he took an added interest in Dad's case.

The medical board's recommendation was for surgery (thoracoplasty). It was a terrible time for Dad, but he was resigned to undergoing the operation. However, upon returning to the hospital from presurgery leave, new x-rays, etc. were taken. When Dr. Hollingsworth reviewed them, he noticed that Dad's condition was very much improved and that he would not need surgery!

The life of our family was not easy but it was always interesting. Our parents always operated on the theory "Do the Best You Can—always." That was the rule and I believe we all tried to abide by it (then and now).

Our heritage is something special. Our hope is that we can pass this same feeling on to our children and grandchildren.

Part Six

SOME
THOUGHTS
IN
RETROSPECT

SOME THOUGHTS
IN RETROSPECT

by Dawn W. Hendricks,
Daughter of William Wubbena

And so we come to the end of our story about Jan and Catharina and what happened to them and their ten children.

Perhaps it is fitting that the first writing in our book is by Catherine Wubbena, the eldest daughter of the eldest of the ten children, while these last thoughts are by me, the youngest daughter of the youngest. Catharina and her four daughters were strong women and her six sons all married strong women. One can't understand how all ten children got through their times of struggle and reached middle-class stability unless one understands this. That isn't to mean that the men weren't strong. They were. The point is that the women were, too.

This is a book that by all odds should not have happened. Some of us started thinking about the project in the 1970s, and did considerable talking about it through the 1980s. The underlying reason that nothing was done at that time was a belief that it would be impossible to gather sufficient material to make it worthwhile. Finally, in the 1990s we started, several years after the last of Jan's children had died. To our surprise we found that the problem was not to find sufficient material. Instead, it was to decide what we had to cut in order to keep the book within manageable size.

Where we have cut we apologize. We realize the effort the individual contributors made but after thinking long and hard we reluctantly concluded that we had to do some melding and some cutting in order to make the size of the book manageable.

Our objective when we started was to record what happened, so that our children and children's children and the generations beyond would know something about their roots. From our point of view we more or less felt that we already knew all we wanted to know. How wrong we were! We didn't realize how fascinating it would become for us, the participants, to learn more about our origins.

The story is a classic example of how America became what it is. Jan, a poor German seaman with the rating of steersman, born out of wedlock but carrying his father's name, married Catharina, a girl ten years his junior. They made their home in Neermoor, Germany, which is in Friesland near the Dutch border. His mother lived with them. They worked hard, were God-fearing, had children, and always dreamed of emigrating to the United States in order to improve their lot. They especially wanted to do this in order to give their children a better future and, in addition, avoid compulsory service of their sons in the German army.

By the time four children had arrived, Jan's mother had died. At this point they decided to act on their dream. In 1886 they sold their home and other belongings, and sailed for America on the steamship *Trave*. They landed in New York at Castle Garden, because Ellis Island was not yet in existence.

They had intended to go to Iowa where Jan had friends (relatives?), but were convinced by a (glib?) sales agent to buy land just outside Standish, Michigan. When they arrived there they found their land to be poor and covered with stumps. Life was very hard but they survived through faith in God, hard work, and the friendship of their neighbors.

As the years passed the family increased in size. Nineteen days after the tenth child arrived Catharina died of childbed fever at the age of thirty-nine. Though Jan did not remarry, he held the family together. Twelve-year-old Talka, the eldest daughter and fourth child, left school to assume the role of homemaker.

Thirteen years later, when Jan was sixty-two, he died. The five youngest children ranged from thirteen to eighteen at that point. John and Talka, the oldest son and oldest daughter, were thirty-three and just short of twenty-six years old, respectively. They again postponed their own already-postponed careers in order to act as parents to these younger children as they finished growing up.

All ten of the children reached adulthood. Their lives were not easy, but all made solid advancement from where they started. Each one achieved an established, middle-class position in his or her community. None was ever on relief, even during the Great Depression. All were self-supporting for their entire adult lives. None ever saw the inside of a penal institution as an inmate. Nine married, and the marriages turned out well. All lasted until death. Seven of these unions produced offspring. As far as we know none of their issue were ever on relief or incarcerated in a penal institution.

Though spread geographically from Washington, D.C. to the state of

Washington, the ten remained unusually close during their entire lives. Throughout their lives they corresponded and visited with each other. In later years they kept in touch by circulating a round robin letter, which they also called "the chain letter." It consisted of a perpetually circulating nine-part letter, passed in turn from the youngest (William) to the oldest (John), who then passed it to William from whence it again would start up the "age ladder." Each brother or sister, upon receipt of the letter would absorb the news from his or her nine siblings, add a few pages of comments at the end of the letter, and take out and discard those pages at the front that had been written by the next youngest sibling to whom the letter was next to be sent. Thus each sibling received in turn an entirely new nine-part letter telling of news from the rest of the brothers and sisters and their families. This cycle was completed about once each quarter. As the members of The Original Ten died, their spouses were substituted.*

They had differences about religion, with some cleaving to their Gospel Hall upbringing with great dedication while others adopted alternate religious affiliations or practices. There was even bitterness felt by some regarding what was intrepreted to be the holier-than-thou attitude of certain of their siblings.

There were differences as to politics, since some were conservative while others tended to be quite liberal. Some were pro-management in view while others tended to be pro-labor. They didn't hide those differences from each other. In fact, they debated them in their correspondence.

In spite of distances and differences they all stayed close, loved one another dearly, and gave each other moral support. I remember in the depths of the Depression when my father William was in Fitzsimmons General (Army) Hospital recovering from tuberculosis. He had no income, since the regulations provided no pay for reserve officers in his situation, and no prospect of a disability pension. (In those peacetime days of the 1930s, if a reserve officer of the U.S. Army who was on active duty became incapable of passing the physical, he was discharged without a pension, even if his disability was incurred while on active duty!) He had a wife and three young children, one of whom was in another hospital recovering from a mastoid operation. He had no job, and almost no assets.

William's nine siblings learned of his circumstances. Though times were

---

Ed. Note: This tradition continues in a modified form even up to the present day. Though The Original Ten and their spouses are all gone, the letter still circulates among one descendant of each of the seven of The Original Ten who had children.

hard for all of them, nine checks were sent to Bill (one from each of his siblings) "to help tide him over." The needs of our home were bordering on desperate, but all nine checks were returned by Bill, uncashed with a statement of, "Thanks, but we'll make it." Bill always remembered with emotion this expression of love and support on the part of his brothers and sisters.

When I was in my teens I once made a somewhat disparaging remark to my Dad about either Aunt Talka or Uncle John. I don't remember which, and don't remember what the remark was. But I do remember his reaction. He paused, and then calmly said that he could stand most things, but he simply could not stand any derogation of his oldest brother or oldest sister in view of all that they had done for him and the rest of the Standish family. He asked me to never forget that and I never did.

What enabled them to overcome their disadvantages and rise up to stations in life that represented true accomplishment from where they started? Why were there no cases of failure, or inability to take care of themselves and their loved ones? How did it happen that none of them, and none of their children, ever got into serious trouble with the law? How could it be that all ten remained close for their entire lives when in most families of that size at least some schisms tend to develop? I don't know, but would like to suggest some factors that were involved.

Jan was born of a union that was not solemnized by marriage. A few years earlier that same couple had had a child that had been given the name Jan. When that child died and Jan was born he then was given the same name. We know that Jan's father stood up in church at the point of christening and acknowledged that he was the father. We don't know why the couple never married, but it is obvious that their relationship was not that of a passing fancy. Probably there is a fascinating story here. We will never know.

But some things are clear. Jan and Catharina valued their marriage and cared about their family. Jan in his sorrow and poverty cared enough even to keep the large family together after Catharina died—a daunting task that would make the strongest of men quail. And he did this even when others in the community desired to adopt the youngest ones.

In order for Jan and Catharina, and later Jan alone, to feel this way, each must have been raised in a home where strong values and high standards were held and imprinted on their children. It could not be otherwise. Let's look at some of the other values that they held, practiced, and passed on to their children.

It is clear that Jan and Catharina cared about their community and believed in paying their dues. We know that when they arrived in Standish their neighbors were very helpful to them, and we know that that assistance continued through the years. But over the years it was a two-way street, with Jan's household giving more than it got. By his standards it was unthinkable not to support the community and lend a hand to neighbors who needed help.

Catherine Wubbena tells how after Jan died the older boys played a joke on Talka by falsely telling her that someone on a neighboring farm had died. Talka's instant reaction was to go to that farm with a loaf of bread. The boys may have done that as a joke, but what fascinates me is that her instant reaction was to go to help the neighbor. She must have learned that first from her mother and then from her father.

Catharina and Jan found solace and support in their faith and their church. Though they were associated with the German Reformed Church in Neermoor, they changed to the Lutheran church when they came to Standish, principally because there was no congregation of their church in the vicinity. Lutheranism was, of course, a denomination with a strong German heritage. After Catharina died Jan joined Gospel Hall, bringing the children who were still at home into the congregation with him. It was here that the motherless family found spiritual refuge and moral support. This is especially interesting, because Gospel Hall in origin is an offshoot from the Plymouth Brethren, which group is English in origin.

It sounds strange at first that he chose a church of English origins over one of German, but I'm sure to Jan it was quite logical. Gospel Hall is where he found people who worshipped and gave support to each other in a manner with which he was comfortable. To him the fact that the church wasn't German in origin wasn't relevant. In the same way that he had insisted that English was to be spoken by his family—all ten learned that language so well that in adulthood they spoke without an accent—he saw no sufficiently compelling reason in the worship of his God to cling to Old World church associations.

Lastly, we know that Jan insisted on standards of hard work and discipline for his children. He did it by setting an example and then insisting that the work standards be observed. He did not tolerate slackness by the children when it came to doing their assigned tasks.

So the picture we have is of two parents, and later a single parent, setting and living by these values and standards: family unity; hard work and discipline; duty to the community and one's neighbors who are in need; and a deep relationship with one's God. I submit that these values are pretty much the same values that were related in the stories written about the ten children. In other words, the standards he set were the standards that his children adopted for their lives.

Jan left little of material value when he died. But Jan and Catharina gave us something far more valuable. By virtue of the standards and values they espoused and lived, they left a heritage that affected their children and children's children to help them make a contribution and improve their lot. It is in this context that Jan and Catharina's lives must be judged to be outstandingly successful. May each of us in subsequent generations do as well!

APPENDICES

INTRODUCTION
TO APPENDICES

by Dawn W. Hendricks

Wubbena is an unusual family name. (See further discussion at end of this section.) Most Americans that carry it seem to have but sparse knowledge of their origins in Europe, except that their ancestors came from Northern Germany. We have never met a Wubbena in the United States who said that his or her forebears came from anywhere else, although the name is Friesian and there are also people who bear that name in Northeastern Holland (Dutch Friesland).

In the course of preparing this book we have received considerable information regarding Jan's and Catharina's origins in Ostfriesland, as well as knowledge about other Wubbena families now living in the United States.

It seemed to make sense that this information be recorded. Accordingly, set forth hereinafter are the following:

Appendix A. Article by my husband and co-editor, Burton B. Hendricks dated January 12, 1995, revised through August 27, 1995, titled, "Notes on the Different Wubbena Families in the United States," identifying what is known by us about the various American Wubbena groups as of this writing.

Appendix B. A series of six letters from Günter O. Fassbender, pastor of the Evangelical Reformed church of Tergast, Germany, to (at first) Catherine Wubbena and (then) me. Through his kindness we have been able to understand many things about the background of Jan and Catharina. It seems best to record these letters. Those with Jan's blood in their veins who choose to study them will learn much about their heritage.

Appendix C. Family tree of Mensen Harm Wübbena with whom the Jan Wübbena branch has a common ancestry through the *daughters* of Pastor Johannes Wübbena who served the Tergast Reformed congregation from 1711 to 1734. This family tree was prepared in segments by members of the individual branches of Harm's descendants. With minor exceptions it has not been updated since the early 1970s. Merle Wubbena of Sibley, Iowa (phone (712) 754-3642) has been a most valuable contact to us from this branch.

Appendix D. A "family tree" in German that we think should be pre-served, at the least as a matter of historical curiosity, and at the most as a future resource for studying more about the family's origins, should any member of a future generation become interested in doing so. Fred Wubbena gave it to Bob Wubbena, telling him it was "Hitler's search of family records to determine if Jan's family was 'pure German'." We make no judgment of the accuracy of the document, and aren't even sure how it came to the United States.

Fred's daughter Margaret believes that it may have been given to Fred by a nurse named Margrit Wübbena who worked for a few years in the Washington D.C. area before returning to Emden in Ostfriesland. Fred told Bob in a 1974 letter that they had not been in touch with Margrit for several years and surmised that she may have "committed matrimony." (Typical Fred humor.)

Appendix E. Chart for the Jungjohann family that is the equivalent to the Wubbena chart in Appendix D (i.e., prepared by the Nazi regime). It was supplied to us by Jan Jungjohann of Reiherstr. 8, 26802 Moormerland, Germany on October 31, 1995. He is Engelke's grandson and thus Catharina would be his great (half) aunt.

More on the Wubbena Family Name

We don't know how few persons with the family name of Wubbena there are, but here are some interesting facts:

1. Of Jan and Catharina's 198 living descendants, only nineteen living descendants carry the family name of Wubbena. This small percent of total descendants happened in this way:

(a) Only John, Henry, Fred and William had sons who survived to adulthood (six), and

(b) None of those six sons had more than two sons.

This is not unusual. A principle of genealogy is that all family names tend to die out over several generations. As the number of descendants of a person expands, the proportion of them that bear his family name tends to decrease. A genealogist once told me that the average time for the family name of any person to disappear from the roster of his descendants is about five to seven generations.

2. The Harm Wubbena family tree that we have was created (updated?) in the late sixties to early seventies. At that point there were 425 living descendants of Harm of which only sixty-eight bore the Wubbena name. That proportion is probably smaller yet by now.

3. Günter O. Fassbender, pastor of the Reformed chuch of Tergast where Jan's ancestors had worshipped for centuries, said that he no longer has any Wubbenas in his Tergast congregation or in the other nearby congregation he serves, although he said the name does still exist in Ostfriesland.

4. One of the "commercial genealogy houses" recently published a book on the Wubbena families. That book's material regarding the Wubbenas was disappointingly minimal, most of the content being general information on how to search for ancestors. But the book listed a register of 103 known Wubbena families in the western world, based (they said) on a search of an impressive listing of data bases which they enumerated, and from this they estimated that there were 301 Wubbenas in the United States, 13 in the Netherlands, and none in the rest of the Western world, for a total of 314. We found in their listing only about one-fifth of the American Wubbenas we either know, or specifically know of. We do not intend to be critical of their starting attempt. Though we believe it to be inaccurate, it is at least a start. However, that 314 number is illustrative of the fact that the Wubbena name is not carried by many people.

Though we don't know how to make an accurate estimate, we would find it to be believable that there are 2,000 or fewer persons in the world now carrying that name.

APPENDIX A

Notes on the Different Wubbena
Families in the United States

The overall purposes of this writing are: (1) to record what is known as to who the various Wubbena families are and where they came from and (2) to try to set down a record of those anecdotal reports of "non-relative" Wubbenas of which we are aware, and (3) to try to fit them into a pattern. Until the latter is done there can never be a clear picture of just how many different families there are.

We need a word to describe the various lines or families. It only adds confusion to call each of them overall a family, or a line, because each of those words can be used in so many different ways. Accordingly in these notes each separate group that at this point is independent—in that it can't be connected *closely* with any other Wubbena group in the United States—is, for effectiveness in identification, called a Tribe. The word may not be elegant, but should serve to help us keep them better defined.

As far as I know to this point there are three Tribes, though there may be more, and probably are. These three are:

I. The Jan and Catharina descendants.

II. The descendants of Mensen Harm Wubbena, born in Tergast in the 1700s, and Nelka (Nellie) Simons. This is the Tribe of the many-paged family tree given Lois Wubbena Dick by Merle John Wubbena [Sibley, Iowa (712) 754-3642]. (See Appendix C, pp. 649–669.) As far as I know this appears to be the largest of the three Tribes by a wide margin.

Mensen and Nelka had four sons and one daughter, apparently all born in the first half of the nineteenth century. They and their sons all emigrated to the Midwest. [See Sheets IX, X, XI, and XII.]

I recently talked to Merle and he told me that the family tree had been worked on by him for his branch of his Tribe and by others for the other branches. He said that their knowledge about Tergast is because someone quite a few years ago made contact and learned about their origins there. I'm not clear if he said that the person or persons that did this went over there but I believe that he said that they did.

Merle also told me that there are other Wubbenas that he and his wife called on in Illinois who are neither of Tribe #1 or #2. This is interesting, because the town was Forreston, and he said that they were of no relation to him. Yet that is the town where a member of another branch of his Tribe married a local girl many years ago. Merle observed to me that the immigrants from Ostfriesland tended to cluster around each other.

By letter of January 17, 1995 Gunter O. Fassbender, Pastor of the Evangelical Reformed church of Tergast told us that he had established the relationship between Tribe #1 and Tribe #2 as follows:

1. The Pastor of the Tergast church from 1711–1734 was Johannes Wübbena.

2. The Jan and Catharina Tribe (Tribe #1) is descended from his *daughter* Helena Christina, born May 3, 1723 of his (second marriage) to Sarah Catharina van Gilst, while Tribe #2 is descended from his *daughter* Geeske, born January 6, 1704 of his (first) marriage to Francina Margarita Schoedircks.

III. The third Tribe, descended from Hinrich Harms Wübbena, Sr. and Janje Janssen Klashen. This is the Tribe that contains: (1), the Charles Wubbena of Waterloo, Iowa [phone (319) 232-4815] that our Charles Wubbena discovered; (2), the Dennis Wubbena that Bill Wubbena met while they were both in the service assigned to the Pentagon; and (3), the Robert Wubbena of Washington state [4547 Highline Dr SE, Olympia, Washington 98501; (360) 491-3843] who struck up a friendship with Fred Wubbena in his old age. These three are all brothers.

Robert is very active in professional circles in his field of water purification. He travels a lot, and has been to Ostfriesland trying to locate the roots of their family. Apparently they are descended from Wübbenas that come from the area up around Emden and north of there. (Pastor Fassbender in one of his letters mentioned that there was "even a Wübbena family in the Krummhorn, which is the area north of Emden.") Robert mentioned to me the hamlets of Eilesum, Pewsum, and Jennelt as being places where his ancestors came from, especially the first and third. That is about 40 km northwest of the Tergast-Neermoor area, just northwest of Emden.

He has phoned Wubbenas from wherever he traveled and has talked to Kurt Wubbena in Washington and sent him some information.

| |

The following summarizes what Robert told me about his relatives:

Robert (born September 10, 1942) and Joan Wubbena, 4547 Highline Drive, Olympia, Washington.

His children: Tyler, Robin and Wende.

His brothers and sisters: James, Bristow, Iowa; Janice (Waterman), Waterloo, Iowa; Roger, Stanton, Iowa; Charles, Waterloo, Iowa; and Dennis, Springfield, Missouri.

His parents: Reiner Oltman Wubbena (deceased) and Louise Wubbena, Bristow, Iowa.

His father's brother and sisters: Henry and Helen Wubbena, Allison, Iowa; Carl and Jenny (Wubbena) Krull, Allison, Iowa: Henry and Helen (Wubbena) Fry, Allison, Iowa; and John and Henrietta (Wubbena) Jungling, Dumont, Iowa.

His grandparents: Hinrich Harms Wubbena, Jr. (Allison, Iowa area) born March 29 and baptized April 22, 1877.

His grandfather's brothers: Jan Hinderks (Coulter, Iowa, area) born January 1 and baptised January 17, 1875; Harm Hinrich (Allison, Iowa, area) born January 30 and baptised March 2, 1873; Michael (Allison, Iowa, area) born September 2, 1880 and baptised October 7, 1883; Harmke (Parkersburg, Iowa, area) born August 24 and baptised October 7, 1883; Rolph Hinrichs (Allison, Iowa, area) born October 13 and baptised November 6, 1887.

His grandfather and his grandfather's brothers were all born in Ostfriesland. The above dates came from the church records Geburts and Taufbuch Der Parochie Jennelt, just north of Emden Germany.

Hinrich Harms, Jr. and Rolph Hinrichs came to the United States first, as teenagers to escape the draft, and then later the rest of the sons and their parents (Hinrich Harms, Sr., and Janje Janssen Klaashen) came. They all settled in the general area of Allison, Iowa, where most of the descendants still live.

Hinrich Harms, Sr. was born in Pewsum on May 3 and baptised on May 10, 1846. He married Janje Janssen Klaashen. Bob thinks he had a sister named Feeke born June 15, 1853.

They think, but aren't sure, that Hinrich, Sr.'s, father was Hinderk Harms Wübbena born September 2, 1821 in the Eilsum area.

APPENDIX B

*Six Letters from
Günter O. Fassbender, Pastor
of the Evangelical Reformed
Church of Tergast, Germany*

Herr, ich habe lieb die Stätte deines Hauses
und den Ort, da deine Ehre wohnet. (Psalm 26, 8)

Evangelisch-reformierte Gemeinde Tergast

— Der Kirchenrat —

Evangelisch-reformierte Gemeinde Tergast · Pastor-Busch-Straße 7 · 2956 Tergast

Miss
Catherine Wübbena
4406 S. Melita Road
Standish, Michigan 48658
U.S.A.

2956 Moormerland-Tergast, den July 19, 1993
Pastor-Busch-Straße 7
Telefon (04924) 2029

Dear Miss Wübbena,

I am deeply sorry to tell you that there is no remark about the wedding of **Jan Janssen Wübbena** and **Catharina Jungjohann** in the early seventies of the last century here at Tergast. In 1871 a *Jan Janssen Wübbena* appears in the wedding record, but he was born in 1837. An other **Jan Janssen (Wübbena) Reuvezaad** was born in Tergast on April 10, 1845 and baptised on April 20. He was the illegitimate son of **Taalke Janssen Reuvezaad**, widow of *Harm Klaasen Linnemann*, and **Jannes Freeks Wübbena**, who "accepted this child to be his son by holding it at the baptism". An other son of the two above with the same name was born on October 27, baptised on November 8, 1840 and died on March 6, 1844.

Jannes Freeks Wübbena was born on September 13, 1812 and baptised on September 20. His parents are **Freek Jannes Wübbena** (born as *Frerik Jannes* on January 7, 1774) and **Martje Heeren Ulferts** (born on January 3, 1780) who were married May 18, 1806 at Tergast.

The parents of **Frerik Jannes Wübbena, Jannes Alberts** and **Feetje Dirks**, were married on April 23, 1769 at Tergast. Nothing more is to be found in our records on this branch of the family.
The parents of **Martje Heeren Ulferts, Heere Ulfers Eyelts** (born on September 12, 1756 at Tergast) and **Antje Aarens** (born on August 9, 1754), were married on April 30, 1779 at Tergast.

The parents of **Heere Ulfers Eyelts** are **Ajelt Heeren** and **Helena Christina Wübbena** (born May 3, 1723) were married on May 13, 1744 at Tergast.
The parents of **Antje Aarens** are **Arend Coops Leijden** and **Marje Jurjens van Kiensborg** were married on December 9, 1753.

The parents of **Helena Christina Wübbena** are **Johannes Wübbena**, pastor at Tergast from 1711-1734, and **Sara Catharina van Gilst**.

More is not to bee found in our records. Unfortunately the paper of our church records is of such a quality that it is not possible to take any xerographic of them. So I hope you are content with my excerpts.

To get an answer to your question about the marriage of **Jan Janssen Wübbena** and **Catharina Jungjohann** I would suggest that you contact

> **Pastor i.R.**
> **Jan Ringena**
> **Gartenstraße 11**
> **49828 Neuenhaus**
> **Germany**

He has micro-copies of all church-records and should be able to help you. There are too many parishes in this area and it would take to long - and also a too great amount of postage - to write to each single pastor.

If there might appear other questions concerning the people mentioned above please feel free to get in contact with me again. For today I am hoping this letter could be of any help to you

very sincerely

      Yours *Günter O. Faßbender, P.*

          Günter O. Faßbender, Pastor

Herr, ich habe lieb die Stätte deines Hauses
und den Ort, da deine Ehre wohnet. (Psalm 26, 8)

Evangelisch-reformierte Gemeinde Tergast

— Der Kirchenrat —

Evangelisch-reformierte Gemeinde Tergast · Pastor-Busch-Straße 7 · 2956 Tergast

Mrs.
Dawn Wübbena Hendricks
56 Brownstone Drive
Hershey PA 17033
USA

Pastor Günter O. Faßbender

2956 Moormerland-Tergast, den 7. 11. 1994
Pastor-Busch-Straße 7
Telefon (04924) 2029

Dear Mrs. Hendricks,

thank you very much for your kind letter from Sept. 22, 1994 that waited for me when I came back from a longer journey to North Africa, Tunesia and the Sahara dessert last week. So please excuse the short delay and be sure that I answer as quick as my time allows.

Now, of course I will try to help you to find out more about the Wübbena-family and answer the five questions you mentioned in your letter. But the difficulties begin already with the first question: Where were Jan an Catherina married? So I have to do some research in the parishes around Tergast, hoping that my colleagues will support my efforts. Once I found the place of the marriage it will be no great difficulty to get the names of brothers and sisters and the rest of the family-history as far as it is mentioned in the church-registers.

Much more easier is it for me to answer your last two questions: as I am pastor of the two small parishes of Tergast and Gandersum for almost twelve years, I happen to know all my parish-member very well. But I am sorry to tell you that there is no Wübbena-family amongst them. But may be that I find one or more of de descendants during my search.

But to do all this I must ask you for one thing: time. I will do the research work in the next weeks; but as the different places where I can have a look into the records etc. are a bit spread out in the country of Ostfriesland it will take some time to visit all of them. But I want to assure you that I will write my results as quick as possible.

So for today there is at first not much more to say then thank you for your generous check and to assure you once again that I will do my very best to help you.

Very sincerely Yours

Günter O. Faßbender, Pastor

Herr, ich habe lieb die Stätte deines Hauses
und den Ort, da deine Ehre wohnet. (Psalm 26, 8)

Evangelisch-reformierte Gemeinde Tergast

— Der Kirchenrat —

Evangelisch-reformierte Gemeinde Tergast · Pastor-Busch-Straße 7 · 2956 Tergast

Pastor Günter O. Faßbender

Mrs.
Dawn Wübbena Hendricks
56 Brownstone Drive
Hershey PA 17033
USA

2956 Moormerland-Tergast, den
Pastor-Busch-Straße 7
Telefon (04924) 2029

December 22, 1994

Dear Mrs. Hendricks,

it took some time until I have the opportunity to answer your letter, but I hope it was worth waiting. After a lot of research work I am happy to be able to answer most of your questions. In your kind letter dated on September 22, you mentioned that you would like to know 5 things:

1. Where an when were Jan and Catherina married? They were married at Neermoor on December 7, 1873. Catharinas father came in the early fifties of the last century from Unna to Neermoor. Unna is a town in the Ruhr-area, one of Germanys industrial centers. He took over the job of a railroad worker, when the railroad from the port of Emden to the Ruhr-area was build. Finally he worked as a level crossing attendant. That meant he lived with his family in an well build house somewhere outside the village of Neermoor besides the railroad track; there was a huge garden to feed the family and some cows, pigs, chicken and other farm animals. So socially he was a respected member of the upper middle class in these days.

He had three children: Engelke who became a tailor, Gesine who remained unmarried and works at the salvation army in Berlin, and Catharina. Engelke Jungjohann married Lükke Büscher at Neermoor and they had ten children that were spread over the country, but one of them, Jan, is still living in his mothers house at Neermoor. He still remembers that in the early time after world war II the family received several support-packages from a Wübbena-family in the States, but unfortunately the contact got lost. He still has an old family-biblebook, in which his grandmother (a sister-in-law of Catherina) wrote some notice about the family history. So, as far as I could find out,

Mr. Jan Jungjohann
Reiherstraße 8
26 802 Neermoor
Germany

is the last living member in our area of the Jungjohann-family. Unfortunately he does not speak English, so he ask me to give you his warmest greetings. If there are any further questions referring to this branch of your family, please don't hesitate to write again; I will try to get in contact with Mr. Jungjohann.

On the other hand: these is the first information I got from Neermoor. I must admit, I am not quite sure about the relationship between the persons here mentioned. I will talk to Mr. Jungjohann early next year to find out more. So please consider this information as a not proved one.

Diakoniekasse Tergast: Raiffeisenbank Oldersum 13022201 (BLZ 28069755)
Kirchenkasse: Kreis- und Stadtsparkasse Leer 504407 (BLZ 28550000)

2. Who were the half-brothers and -sisters of Jan? And 3. Which of Jan's brothers and sisters emigrated to the United States and where did they go? As I told already Miss Catherine Wübbena Jan was the illegitimate son of Taalke Janssen Reuvezaad and Jannes Freerks Wübbena. Taalke was married to Harm Klaasen Linnemann, but as far as I could find out the marriage remained childless. In 1840 on October 27, the first son of Taalke Janssen Reuvezaad an Jannes Freerks Wübbena was born and baptized on November 8; his name was **Jan Janssen** and the pastor first wrote „Wübbena" as last name, marked it out an wrote „Reuvezaad" over it. He died on March 6, 1844, I suppose from tuberculosis (there is a hard to be read notice like „hot sickness" in the record).

Then on April 10, 1845 **Jan Janssen** (the second) was born and once again the pastor had some difficulties with the last name which he wrote like this: *Reuvezaad*
(Wübbena). And as far as our parish is concerned, these are the only children of Taalke and Jannes. I could not find out when and where the died and where they were buried, but I suppose they found their last rest at Neermoor.

In addition to what I wrote to Miss Wübbena in July 1993 let me please tell you something more about the Wübbena family here in Tergast and you will find an answer to your other question about the Wübbenas in America:

Before I do this I would like to tell you what I found out about **Taalke Janssen Reuvezaad**. She was born February 2, 1805 and baptized on February 20. Her sister *Elisabeth* was born December 2, 1807, her brother *Wilke* on April 2, 1811. **Jan Hinrichs Reuvezaad** was her father, he is mentioned to be the master of the weavers at Tergast. He was born about 1762 at Midwolde in the Netherlands. At his wedding with **Eltje Wilken** at February 11, 1798 he is mentioned to be a widower, but unfortunately it is not said to whom and where he was married before. He died on December 24, 1846 at Tergast.
Eltje Wilken, his second wife, was born on August 19, 1769 at Tergast; her date of death is unknown, but it must have been before 1846. She had seven brothers and sisters, born between 1754 and 1772. Her parents were **Wilke Poppen**, who was born in March 1732 and died on September 15, 1810 at Tergast, and **Brechtje Harms**, who died somewhen in autumn on the 29th 1795 (the name of the month is not be read). Wilke Poppens parents were **Poppe Remmers** and **Elysabeth Wilken**, they married about 1727.
Brechtje Harms first husband (marriage on February 2, 1749) was **Wilke Tammen**, born on December 24, 1724 and died on April 9, 1752. They had two children, Jantje (* 1749) and Harm (* 1751). Brechtje Harms came from Großefehn; her parents were **Harm Everts** and **Greetje Geerds**.

But now to the Wübbena branch of the family: **Jannes Freerks Wübbena** was born on September 13, 1812. His parents were **Freerk Janssen Wübbena** (born January 7, 1774) and **Martje Heeren Ulferts** (born January 3, 1780), who married on April 12, 1806. Freerk died on October 25, 1838 - Martje on January 2, 1838, both in Tergast.
Jannes Alberts Wübbena and **Feetje Dirks**, the parents of Freerk Janssen, were married on April 23, 1769. Feetje died on January 4, 1785. Nothing more is to be found in the records, but I strongly suppose that Jannes Alberts Wübbena was one distant relative to the other Wübbenas mentioned below.
Martje Heeren had one twin-sister *Saarke*, at least on other sister *Helena Christina* (* 1783) and three brothers *Eilt* (*1781) and *Arend Seiden* (*1784), *Jannes* (*1788). The parents **Heere Ulferts Eilts** (born September 12, 1756) and **Antje Aaren(d)s** (born August 9, 1754) married on April 30, 1779. Heere died on January 19, 1798 - Antje on October 31, 1824
Before I turn to the Wübbenas again the Aaren(d)s branch is quickly told: **Arend Coops Sejden** and **Marje Jurjens van Kiensborg** were the parents of Antje. They married on September 9, 1753. From Marje there is nothing further known. Arend was born on October 11, 1698 and died on February 5, 1782 at Tergast. His parents were **Zeyde Coops** and **Antje Arends**, who married on October 15,

1689. And here we have reached the end - or I should better say the beginning of our church records; the first notice is from 1661.

Heere Ulfert Eilts is the son of **Ayelt Heeren** and **Helena Christina Wübbena**, who married on Mai 13, 1744 at Tergast. Ayelt was born on October 23, 1708 and died on January 23, 1785. His parents were **Heere Wirtjes Ulferts** (born on March 29, 1671) and **Hindrickjin Hindricks** (born about 1684) ; they married on April 4, 1708. Heere is the son of **Ulfert Ayelts** and **Schwantje Harms**, who married on August 16, 1667 - and Hindrickjin is the daughter of **Hindrick Dircks** and **Grietje Janssen**, who married on January 17, 1684. And here once again the church record gives us no more answer.

Helena Christina Wübbena was one of the children of **Pastor Johannes Wübbena** (born on February 19, 1671 at Leer, died in November 1734 at Tergast) and **Sarah Catharina van Gilst**. She was born end of April 1723, baptized on May 3 and died on April 26, 1791 at Tergast. Before her father became pastor at Tergast he was in the parish of Simonswolde. Probably there he married Francina *Margareta Schoedircks*, who died between 1714 and 1722. From this first marriage came the children *Etta* (*1702), *Geeske* (*1704), *Susanna Margareta* (*1708), *Garlacus* (*1710), *Justus Mauritz* (*1712) and *Hindrina Bonno* (*1714). Some of them appear again in the church records of Oldersum, our neighbor parish, and I think that here we have the connection to the Jannes Alberts Wübbena mentioned above.

The name „Wübbena" is spread all over Ostfriesland even in these early days. There is a Wübbena family in the Krummhörn, which is the area north of Emden. They are located at Pewsum and Rysum in the 18th century. There is an other clan of Wübbenas in the Rheiderland, on the other side of the river Ems. And there seams to be an old Wübbena clan near Papenburg in the south of Ostfriesland at Mittling Mark, who has some relations to most of the other Wübbenas in Ostfriesland. As you might know the ending „-ena" gives in the old friesian language a hint to a free and wealthy family of clan chiefs. So it appears to be possible that a Wibbe or Wibben settled down in a stone build house at Mitling Mark in the 13th or 14th century and named himself and his family „Wübbena" and so became the forefather of all Wübbenas following.

And now you might understand that off course some of the descendants emigrated to the States during the last century from all the places I mentioned above. But to find out the grade of relationship is very difficult unless you can name one of the Ostfriesian forefathers.

4. <u>Does any person of the Wübbena family in Tergast have any contact with any of the descendants?</u> The inhabitantship of our parish has changed completely during the last century. So there is no descendant of this family living in Tergast.

5. <u>Are there any living descendants of Jan?</u> Yes, the only Mr. Jungjohann in our surrounding:

Mr. Jan Jungjohann
Reiherstraße 8
26 802 Neermoor
Germany

So I hope once again that I did not take too much of your patience waiting for these first results of my research work. After Christmas and New Year I will get in contact with Mr. Jungjohann to get some more information; he told me at the telephone that he will use the family meeting at the holidays to talk to other members of his family and we will see, what now perhaps is still buried in the dark of the remembrance. So I will write once again soon next month.

Perhaps if you find the time to answer you could tell me of which of the notices in the church record you would like to have a more detailed copy. As I wrote already to Miss Wübbena the old paper got very dark during the centuries and it is not possible to get a readable xerographic. But I could do a copy by hand I you like.

Now at the end of my letter for today let me wish you and your family a blessed and peaceful Christmas and a utmost happy New Year 1995.

Very sincerely Yours

Günter O. Faßbender, Pastor

Herr, ich habe lieb die Stätte deines Hauses
und den Ort, da deine Ehre wohnet. (Psalm 26, 8)

Evangelisch-reformierte Gemeinde Tergast

— Der Kirchenrat —

Evangelisch-reformierte Gemeinde Tergast · Pastor-Busch-Straße 7 · 2956 Tergast

Pastor Günter O. Faßbender

Mrs.
Dawn Wübbena Hendricks
56 Brownstone Drive
Hershey PA 17033
USA

2956 Moormerland-Tergast, den
Pastor-Busch-Straße 7
Telefon (04924) 2029

Tuesday, 17. January 1995

Dear Mrs. Hendricks,

first of all let me say thank you once again for your generosity to accept my little efforts to help you. It was a great pleasure for me to read that you could find out a bit more about the history of your family. And now here is the second part of my humble attempts to bring some light in the dark lines of the past. As I had not yet the opportunity to talk to the Jungjohann family at Neermoor I can only try to answer a part of your questions, but let me assure you that as soon as I have talk to them I will send you the now still missing results of this research.

Questions about Jannes Freerks Wübbena and his relationship with Taalke Janssen Reuvezaad

I am sorry to say that I could not find out anything about **Harm Klaasen Linnemann**. Neither in the wedding record nor in the register of the born and baptized of the parish of Tergast his name could be found. The pages of our register for the dead are in such a bad shape that I am not able to make any reliable statements.

And I am not very sure at all that he lived with his wife Taalke at Tergast. I suppose that he perhaps was a weaver or a tradesman or an inland sailor (I found this expression in the dictionary and hope you understand what I mean) more likely than a farmer or farmworker and dwelt in an other village. This has something to do with his last name which is very unusual in our area, even the fact that he has one: Linnemann. The farmers and other people had - as you see in the line of your family - mostly the names of their fathers and grandfathers as their last name. A name such as Reuvezaad or Linnemann gives hints more into the direction of an urban civil life than to the countryside. If he or his family came from Leer or Emden of course he would have taken his wife home and lived together with her there. After he passed away his widow returned to Tergast as there were no children who had to be raised until they could take over the heritage of their father. Taalke probably lived again in the household of her father and taking over other work in the farms and houses at Tergast.

The name „Linnemann" may be also a hint to Harm Klaasens or his father's profession, as „linen" or „cloth" is a part of it. People who produce linen or cloth may get in contact with sailors, of course they have connections to weavers such as Jan Hinrichs Reuvezaad was at Tergast. So as I said he might have come to Tergast in one of this professions and became to know Taalke and finally they got married.

An other possibility is that he came as a colonist to the new developed morass areas northwest of Tergast or that he settled there as a sailor on the canals and rivers in this part of the country. In these days the colonization of large moor-areas came to a first summit. The Prussian government started a program to develop agriculture in these deserted landscapes and bring them under plow. So people from all over the country, most of them from the poor areas of Oldenburg and the Netherlands, immigrated to Ostfriesland and made use of the advantages the government offered to them. As there were only a few uncertain roads through the morass the main traffic used the canals that drained these areas. So not only colonist started a new life there but also inland sailors. And more than the farmers they found their prosperity in the new villages.

So, I am sorry to say, these hypothesizes and fantasies is all I can tell you about Harm Klasen Linnemann. Nothing about his place and date of birth nor of his date and place of death is known here.

The Wübbena people at Tergast are mostly characterized as being „Warfslüden". That means they leased a farm and lived from it. Normally the farm was owned by a relative, sometimes a very close relative, and the contribution to be paid was a kind of lifelong pension instead of paying a big sum of money as part of a heritage. But of course there was also a „normal" leasing as we know it from our days. So Jannes Freerks and his father, Freerk Janssen, lived and worked as farmers on a farm that was not their own. Which of our farm places it was I can not tell. The owners changed since then of course, but for centuries the number farm places and their location remained the same. So perhaps on one of the photographs of Tergast in the old days I enclose there might be shown this very place.

To the social questions about the relationship between Jannes and Taalke I also con only tell you me opinion or hypothesizes. There is no other mark or notice in our records that point to an other wedding. He seams to have remained a bachelor, only Taalke and their two sons show the other side of his life. Perhaps she came to his or his fathers farm to milk the cows, may be that she did some work in the household, may also be - and from the durance of this relation I personally think of it more probably - that she left the house of her father and lived together with Jannes as unmarried man and wife. I presume that there were no big differences in their social level. Both as I would say were members of the middle class with a certain personal history or fate that brought them a bit aside from „normal" society. But this are terms of our days. To me it seams that the society of such a village like Tergast was quite tolerant, so they had nothing to fear neither from church nor from their families and there were only little disadvantages.

In these times two other children were born out of wedlock to other woman; both of them didn't say anything about the fathers, so as it was usual the pastor turned the register around and wrote the birth of this two children on the bottom of the page. May be that there was a painful conversation between the pastor, members of the church council and the mothers before the children were baptized. But normally that was all - for our standards today it is more than enough. People here at Tergast even still today have their own laws and moral opinion. One of the pastors in the 18th century wrote one or two remarks an the moral life in his parish and then draw a line under it and said that it won't change anything in the thinking of the people here. There is no hint for a public censure of the two mothers and also not for Taalke or Jannes. So since these days I would not say that the moral of the inhabitants of Tergast is worst or better then in other places - it is as it is and people get along with it - as Jannes and Taalke got along with it in their days. And in such a situation I think for Jannes and Taalke it was not necessary to legalize such a relation. As far as I know they did not marry.

The connection to other Wübbenas

Indeed there is a connection between your branch of the Wübbena family and Mensen Harm Wübbena:

Pastor Johannes Wübbena I mentioned in my last letter was married to **Sara Catharina van Gilst**. During his time being pastor at Simonswolde Geeske was born as second daughter and baptized on January 6, 1704. She married before 1733 **Albert Freerks** at Tergast. They had at least six children: Freerk * 1733, Johannes * 1734, Hester * 1740, Gerlacus * 1743, and Klara * 1746. But of interest for you is that on January 29, 1737 their daughter **Francina Margaretha** was baptized at Tergast.

As Fr. Marg. Alberts on May 9, 1757 she married **Meint Harms**, the son of **Harmen Berends** and **Aafke Meints**, born in December 1730. As far as I could find out they had at least eight children born at Tergast: Harm born January 27, 1760, Albert born April 9, 1763, Jannes born July 9, 1766, Frerich born November 19, 1769, Gerlacus born March 11, 1772, Aafke born September 30, 1776 who died before 1778, Aafke born August 14, 1778 and Gerdina, born April 14, 1782. Meint died January 23, 1792, Francina died on March 8, 1822.

Just to tell what happened to the others here the results of a quick look through our church records:
Albert Meints Wübbena - the second son - is first married to **Grietje Eernts**, who died October 18, 1805. Three children could I find in our records: Tetje * 1795, Ernst * 1795 and Ernst * 1799; but one, Meint Alberts Wübbena, I could not find in the birth register. June 28, 1807 Albert marries Taatje Janssen, daughter of Jan Kornelius and Geerdje Roolfs from Simonswolde. He dies on April 10, 1826.
And on February 11, **Meint Alberts Wübbena** marries **Foelke Freeriks**, daughter of Freerik Harms and Hilke Heyen from Bagband.
Jannes Meints Wübbena - the third son - marries on May 4, 1792 **Taalke Claaßen**, daughter of Claas Egberts and Engel Edzards from Petkum. They had six children: Klaas Egberts * 1793, Engel * 1798, Frantzina * 1796, Meint Harm * 1800, Esdert Klaaßen * 1802, Engel * 1805. Jannes Meints Wübbena dies on January 7, 1837 at Tergast.

Harm (Meint) Wübbena marries Elzebeen Hinderks before 1787, because on October 25, 1787 a son is born whose name is not readable as the page broke away in our record. But he must have died as a child. Also his mother Elzebeen Hinderks must have died before 1798, because about 1798 **Mensen Harm Wübbena** must be born, who is said to be the oldest son of Harm Meint Wübbena and Aafke Mensen, when he marries Neelke Simons Meinders on April 1830, oldest daughter of Simon Meindert an Taalke Müller from Jarssum. I enclose a as I hope good and readable copy of our records with the birth register of the children from Mensen Harm Wübbena and Neelke Simons Meinders. The other pages are not to bee copied because they are covered with a special chemical paper to protect them, but which makes copy just black.

So you see, the connection between this Mensen Harm Wübbena and Jannes Freerks Wübbena is that they are descendants from Pastor Johannes Wübbena and his second wife Sara Catharina van Gilst.

And now to your question about brothers and sisters of Jannes Freerks Wübbena, children of Freerk Jannes Wübbena and Martje Heeren:

The parents got married on April 12, 1806. The first son, **Heere Aielts**, is born on May 27, 1807. He marries as Heere Freerks Wübbena at the neighbor-village of Oldersum Geeske Engelkes Poppen, daughter of Engelke Poppen Harms and Geeske Geerds Kuur, on April 20, 1836. He marries his second wife, Hanna Friedrichs Schweerkes, daughter of Friedrich Schweerkes and Louise Schmidt, born 1806 at Gandersum, widow of Berend Geerds Post, on April 12, 1850. He dies on March 30, 1854, his second wife Hanna on September 16, 1861.
Jannes Alberts is born on January 16, 1809. On April 10, 1839 he marries as Jan Alberts (in the meantime an other Jannes Alberts Wübbena, son of Alberts Janssen Wübbena and Geeske Janssen occurred in the records) Anette Hinrichs Tuitjer, who died on February 28, 1881. Her husband Jan passed away already on June 19, 1861.
Then, as you already know, on September 13, 1812, **Jannes** is born.
He is followed by **Eilt Heeren**, who is born on April 13, 1816 and he died on January 7, 1827.

The Wübbena Name

The meaning of *Wibbe* is not be found out. To understand this, let me tell you something about the very early history of the Friesian people:

They were a western German tribe, living at the north Dutch and northwestern German coast (between Brügge and Bremen in our days). Only a few of them took part in the great German tribal migration in the second and first century before Christ. They maintained their territory also in the next centuries, preserved their culture, religion and language. In some way they isolated themselves from influences from the south, where Germany was dominated by the romans and later from the franks. Only at 785 the Friesian chiefs surrendered to King Charles the great, but they understood to keep their own identity. The „free Friesians" were only under the control of the king himself, no earls or barons ruled over them like it was usual in other parts of the German country. But this was more or less a government written on some paper, but very seldom really carried out. And also the nature was on their side: large impenetrable forests and big dangerous morasses gave shelter in the south, the unpredictable stream of the river Weser in the west made it quite an adventure to come to this country. And in the north there was the sea and the mudflats where only the sailors from this area could find a way through.

So the Friesians were left alone, they lived in their „splendid isolation". And this meant mainly the old Friesian language and tribal organization in a semi-democratic federation. Until the middle ages the Friesian language was spoken, but it was driven back more and more as the influences from the Dutch areas raised. This area was called „lower Germany" and the language spoken there was „low-German" or „Plattdeutsch". The Friesian language survived in some paroles like the motto of the Friesian counts: „Eala frya Fresena" - „always a free Friesian country". And of course it survived in the old names like Fokko, Onno, Uke, Habbe, Okko, and *Wibbe*. But the meaning got lost during the time. And in our days the Friesian language is more a academic problem for people interested in the old history, but only a few professors speak it.

And as you may quickly understand it is a small step from *Wibbe* to *Wübbe*. People in all times spoke - and as I must admit: speak - very careless. And in the low German language „i" and „ü" are very close and you must listen very carefully to tell the difference. And also we Protestant pastors and other university graduates have to be blamed in this case. In the 15th and 16th century we Protestants used the Latin language, the language of the educated and studied people, only during the education at the university and when we where together with people of our social level. Out in the country, especially out in the Friesian country, among slow thinking and less speaking farmers and workers, they had to speak low German or Dutch - languages that were considered to be simple and simple minded. But when they wrote in the church records, alone in their studies, they latinised what they wrote. So an „i" or „ii" became „y". And later, in the 18th and 19th century again the Protestant pastors „re-germanized" the Latin words and names. So for a long time many ways of writing the name *Wibbe / Wübbe / Wybbe / Wibben / Wiibbe / Wübbe / Wibbena / Wybbena / Wübbena / Wybbena* existed parallel.

About the ending „ena" I told you already. In the old Friesian language it is something like a noble title. In German the noble tile is „von" or in Low-German „van" - like the red baron Manfred von Richthofen. Not so in Friesian, here it is „ena", and once again I am unfortunately not able to tell you the meaning of it.

And people with the privileged of an „ena"-ending in their names had the right to live in a stone build house. The „stone build house", where your forefather Wibbe might have lived at Mitling Mark, is a special expression of the Friesian history. I don't know whether you ever have been here in Ostfriesland. For a long time all houses here were build of wood, as we had big forests of oaks and beechwoods. There are only a few natural stones in our ground - remainings of the Ice Age. The soil is normally dried out seeground: heavy, moistured and like clay. During the history the Friesian chiefs became wealthier and wealthier by the trade with England and Scandinavia. So they could import natural stones from further areas to build more resistant houses as the times got harder. When Ostfriesland was christianized in the 10th century the monks brought with them the knowledge of making bricks out of clay. But the chiefs feared that their privilege of living in stone build houses was dismantled. So they allowed only churches and cloisters to be build of the new bricks - and their own residences. But during the struggle about the leadership in the late 14th and early 15th century the way of building houses of bricks became more and more democratic and the chiefs finally lost their privilege. But the expression remained; in Ostfriesland a „stone house" still means the residence of a former chief, of a person with an „ena"-ending in his name. Some of the old chief residences can still be found. Several of them were torn down and replaced by newer houses. And the knowledge of others is only handed down by oral tradition in the villages. As far as I know the stone build house of the Wübbena-family in Mitling Mark is only history, a hypothesis that explains most of the questions of the history of the Wübbena origin in our area. May be that there is still a rumor in Mitling-Mark about the place where the old house was, may be that in old maps of this area such a place is marked, but once again unfortunately I am unable to tell. As a small contribution I add a copy of a map and I marked the two places of interest: Midling/Mitling and Oldersumer gast/Tergast.

So far for today. As I come deeper and deeper into the history of your family I find more and more questions that might be of further interest. But before my letters reach the volume of little books I think it is better to stop at this point. And I also come to my wits end with my humble English I learned at school; even when I try to explain certain connections in the history to you I feel a great lack of vocabulary and the dictionary is of no great help. But anyway, please feel free to ask for more information and I will try to do my best. Give my warmest regards to all members of the Wübbena family and I am

very sincerely Yours

Günther O. Fassbender, P.

P. S.: Just this morning I made a date to see the Jungjohann family on Tuesday, January 24. I'll write as quick as possible.

G. F.

Herr, ich habe lieb die Stätte deines Hauses
und den Ort, da deine Ehre wohnet. (Psalm 26, 8)

Evangelisch reformierte Gemeinde
Tergast
— Der Kirchenrat —

Evangelisch-reformierte Gemeinde Tergast · Pastor-Busch-Straße 7 · 2956 Tergast

Pastor Günter O. Faßbender

Mrs.
Dawn Wübbena Hendricks
56 Brownstone Drive
Hershey PA 17033
USA

2956 Moormerland-Tergast, den
Pastor-Busch-Straße 7
Telefon (04924) 2029

Tuesday, 24. January 1995

Dear Mrs. Hendricks,

I hope my letter from January 17 has reached you in the meantime. As I told you I had a date to see Mr. Jan Jungjohann today and we had a very interesting conversation. Before I come to the details let me tell you that he sends his warmest regards to you and that he is glad to be of any help to you. His son Jan, who is working as a engineer at the Mercedes factory at Stuttgart, is also very interested in family history. In his summer vacation 1995 he is planing to trace the Jungjohann line at Hessen. As he also speaks English, his father asked me to tell you, please don't hesitate to get in contact with him at Neermoor for further and more personnel information.

Now to the results of my visit: Jan Anthaus Hinderikus Jungjohann, born August 16, 1932 at Neermoor Kolonie, is married since November 14, 1956 to Gesine Freese, born November 24, 1934 also at Neermoor Kolonie. They have two children: Jan Anthaus Hinderikus, born June 27, 1958 (the Mercedes engineer), and Karin Gudrun, born August 13, 1962.

Jan is the son of Jan Anthäus Hinderikus Jungjohann, born May 24, 1899 at Neermoor, and Gesche Eilers, who was born on January 25, 1899 at Hatshausen. They married on August 11, 1921 at Neermoor; Jan died March 26, 1984 and Gesche on May 23, 1979.

Jan (again) is son of Engelke Jungjohann, born April 30, 1863 at Neermoor, and Lükke Buisker, born December 11, 1868 at Neermoor. They married on February 25, 1893 at Neermoor and died on June 13, 1927 (Engelke) and November 20, 1958 (Lükke). The parents of Lükke are Jan Harms Buisker, born August 1837 at Neermoor, and Antje Janssen Pull, born June 6, 1838 at Neermoor; they were married at Neermoor on April 6, 1859; Jan died June 1, 1915 and Antje November 5, 1921.

The parents of Engelke are Karl Jungjohann, born February 25, 1824 at Uslar at Hessen (near Frankfurt), and Hindertje Buss, born November 6, 1833. They were married at Veenhusen on April 20, 1861. Karl died October 7, 1898 and Hindertje on September 13, 1898, both at Neermoor.

But now it becomes a bit complicated: it is firmly known that Karl was married twice. With his first wife he had one daughter, Gesine, whose date of birth is unknown. She left Ostfriesland, remained unmarried and worked at the Salvation Army at Berlin, where she died October 20, 1925. And there was a sister, Catherina, but nobody still living now knows anything about her. Only Grandma Lükke told something about a sister-in-law, that went away. Now I made an other date for Tuesday next week with my colleague at Neermoor and we will both look through the records of her parish to find something more about this period of the Jungjohann family history.

Diakoniekasse Tergast: Raiffeisenbank Oldersum 13022201 (BLZ 28069755)
Kirchenkasse: Kreis- und Stadtsparkasse Leer 504407 (BLZ 28550000)

1

So I am deeply sorry being not able to give you any more proved information and to put you off from week to week. But I thought, these results you should know immediately. And I hope next week I can tell you better news. By the way, Mr. Jungjohann showed me a letter he received from the States from an organization that did not seem to be very confident to him. They say to work on a world book of the Jungjohann family and they give promises that - as we who do family research really can judge - hardly can be kept. But as there is an address over in the States perhaps you can find out more about the seriousness of this organization. I enclose the letter. Until my next letter I am

very sincerely Yours

Herr, ich habe lieb die Stätte deines Hauses
und den Ort, da deine Ehre wohnet. (Psalm 26, 8)

Evangelisch-reformierte Gemeinde Tergast

— Der Kirchenrat —

Evangelisch-reformierte Gemeinde Tergast · Pastor-Busch-Straße 7 · 2956 Tergast

Pastor Günter O. Faßbender

Mrs.
Dawn Wübbena Hendricks
56 Brownstone Drive
Hershey PA 17033
USA

2956 Moormerland-Tergast, den
Pastor-Busch-Straße 7
Telefon (04924) 2029

Tuesday, 31. January 1995

Dear Mrs. Hendricks,

now here I am back again with the newest results of my research at Neermoor. And things become more understandable. First of all, I copied the wedding remark Of Jan and Catharina from the church records at Neermoor; it reads in German like this:

> *No. 13 - Reuzaad, genannt Wübbena, Jan Janssen, unverehelichter Steuermann zu Neermoor - geboren den 10. April 1845 zu Tergast - Sohn des Webergesellen Jannes Freerks Wübbena und dessen Braut Taalke Janssen Reuzaad -*
> *17. Dezember 1873 zu Neermoor getraut mit -*
> *Jungjohann, Catharina Caroline Louise, unverehelichte Dienstmagd zu Leer - geboren den 31. März 1855 zu Neermoor - Tochter des Eisenbahnwärters Carl Friedrich Jungjohann und dessen Ehefrau Catharina Elisabeth Wilhelmine, geb. Klemme*

and in English:

> *No. 13 - Reuzaad, called Wübbena, Jan Janssen, single helmsman / first mate at Neermoor - born April 10, 1845 at Tergast - son of weavers journeyman Jannes Freerks Wübbena and his bride Taalke Janssen Reuzaad -*
> *on December 17, 1873 married to -*
> *Jungjohann, Catharina Caroline Louise, single maid / servant at Leer - born March, 31, 1855 at Neermoor - daughter of gatekeeper Carl Friedrich Jungjohann and his wife Catharina Elisabeth Wilhelmie, born Klemme*

And now to the difficulties with Catharina's brothers and sisters I mentioned in my letter last week: It is quite simple, as her father, Carl Friedrich Jungjohann was married twice. It seams that he arrived here at Neermoor married to Catharina Elisabeth Wilhelmine Klemme. Perhaps their daughter Gesine (died 1925 at Berlin and worked at the salvation army) was born before they settled down at Neermoor, because I cold not find any trace of her in the church records. Carl and Catharina had at least three children (or four, if my assumption according to Gesine is right): Catharina Caroline Louise, born March, 31, 1855; Heinrich Friedrich Ludwig Gottlob, born June 26, 1857; Carl Friedrich, born March 10, 1860. And on April 21, 1861 Catharina Elisabeth Wilhelmine dies at Neermoor.

You wonder? Right, there was a mistake. Carl did not marry Hindertje Buß the day before his first wife Catharina died, but one year later, April 21, 1862 - and not 1861. And in his second wedlock there were three sons born: Engelke, April 30, 1863; Carl Friedrich Theodor, February 14, 1865; Gerhard Hinricus, April 28, 1867. And from the descendants of Engelke I told you in my last letter. I cold not find out what happened to the other half-brothers of Catharina, Carl and Hinricus. Perhaps the research of the Jungjohann son from Neermoor will bring out more about it this summer.

So much again for today. If there are further questions, please don't hesitate to ask. And let my assure you, if one or more of your family want's to visit the home of his or her forefathers or to proof one ore the other information, let me know; everybody of your family is heartily welcome in our home and we will give any support needed. And for now I remain

very sincerely Yours

Günther O. Fassbender, P.

APPENDIX C

*The Family Tree of the
Mensen Harm Wubbena Family*

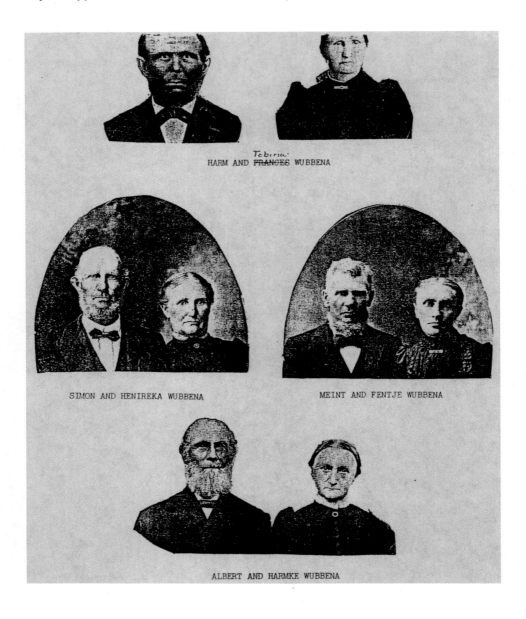

HARM AND FRANCES WUBBENA

SIMON AND HENIREKA WUBBENA

MEINT AND FENTJE WUBBENA

ALBERT AND HARMKE WUBBENA

THE "WUBBENA" FAMILY TREE

I. <u>Mensen Harm Wubbena</u>   Born _____, 17____ in Tergast, Germany
                          Died _____: ____
    Married Nelke (Nellie) Simons _____: ____
      (5 Children: Harm, Taleah, Simon, Albert, Meint)

    11. (1) Harm H_____ Wubbena   B. February, 26, 1831
                             D. October 11, 1898
        M. Tobina DeVries   March   1858
        (Children: John, Mense, Leah, Nellie, Francis, Simon,
                Henry, Albert, Ralph)

       111. (1) John H. Wubbena   B. June 5, 1860
                          D. Nov. 8, 1941
         M. Dena Henning   March 9, 1887
          (7 Children: Martha, Herman, Everett, Agnes, Ben,
                Joseph, Arthur) *Daughter - Bena Died in Infancy*
      iV (1) Martha Mertie Wubbena (adopted) B. Sept. 11, 1885
                                      D. Jan. 2, 1961
         M. Henry Arends   April 11, 1905
          (5 children: George, Luella, Maybelle,
                Clara, Arthur)
        V, (1) George William Arends   B. Nov. 26, 1906
                               D. Nov. 26, 1906
        V. (2) Luella Marie Arends   B. July 22, 1908
          M. George Frank Kampmeyer   Feb. 21, 1928
          (2 Children: Robert, Richard)
          V1 (1) Robert Ray Kampmeyer   B. Sept. 26, 1929
                             D. May 10, 1934
            (2) Richard Lee Kampmeyer   B. April 8, 1938
              M. Judith Ann Besser   Jan. 8, 1966
        V. (3) Maybelle Viola Arends   B. May 11, 1910
          M. Edwin John Crane   Sept. 9, 1930
          (2 Children: James, Judy)
          V1. (1) James Henry Crane   B. March 27, 1931
              M. Cecila Augustine   Jan. 6, 1957
            (3 Children: Ann, Mary, Edwin)
            V11. (1) Ann Marie Crane   B. Nov. 23, 1957
                (2) Mary Ann Crane   B. Dec. 2, 1959
                (3) Edwin Lewis Crane B. April 28, 1962
            (2) Judy May Crane   B. _____
             M. Steve Gulla   Dec. 16, 1956
            V11. (1) Juli Marie Gulla   B. April 15, 1965
        V. (4) Clara Isabelle Arends   B. Aug. 29, 1912
          M. John Ernest Groen   April 11, 1930
          (3 Children: Earl Dean, Mertie Jane, Jerry Lee)
          V1. (1) Earl Dean Groen   B. March 29, 1931
              M. Shirley Lumby   April 10, 1955
            (2 children: Kenneth, Carrie)
            V11. (1) Kenneth Groen   B. Jan. 14, 1956
                (2) Carrie Groen   B. Nv. 4, 1957
          V1. (2) Mertie Jane Groen   B. Oct. 21, 1935
             M. Horace Edward Holder   April 12, 1952
            (5 Children: Michael, Michell, Lorri,
                Horace, Cynthia)
            V11. (1) Michael Holder   B. Nov. 14, 1953
                (2) Michell Holder   B. Dec. 24, 1955
                (3) Lorri Holder   B. Mar. 9, 1957
                (4) Horace Holder   B. Mar. 25, 1958
                (5) Cynthia Holder   B. Sept. 21, 1959

3

--2--

```
   V1. (3) Jerry Lee Groen                B. Dec. 17, 1945
       M. Rudi Smith                          June 8, 1966
          (2 Children: Jamie, John)
          V11. (1) Jamie Groen             B. Sept. 25, 1968
               (2) John Groen             B. Dec. 31, 1969
 V. (5) Arthur Raymond Arends             B. July 31, 1916
     M. Mertie Louise Dungan                 Jan. 12, 1935
        (2 Children: Louise, Karen)
        VI. (1) Louise Arlene Arends       B. July 22, 1936
             M. Arthur Ayola                  Oct. 21, 1964
             (2) Karen Rae Arends          B. Aug. 22, 1942
             M. Robert Allen Ransdell         Aug. 31, 1958
            (3 Children: Darald, Randy, Cindy)
            V11. (1) Darald Ransdell       B. Sept. 21, 1960
                 (2) Randy Ransdell        B. Feb. 10, 1962
                 (3) Cindy Ransdell        B. Dec. 29, 1963
         Arthur Raymond Arends
         Married Beulah Brashers              June 30, 1961
1V. (2) Herman _____ Wubbena            B. May 23, 18___
                                           D. Dec. 12, 1931
      M. (1) Sophie Overbeck                          19___
             (1 Child: Louise)
         V. Louise _____ Wubbena        B. _____ 19___
            M. Urban Harken                        _____ 19___
              (Children:
```

```
      M. (2) Minnie Hickman                   Jan. 12, 1916
             (1 Child: Blanche)
         V. Blanche _____ Wubbena       B. April 9, 1917
            M. Marvin Lamfers                 Mar. 2, 1960
1V. (3) Everett J. Wubbena                 B. Oct. 1, 1892
                                           D. March 1, 1960
      M. Maggie Loerts                         Jan. 26, 1916
         (2 Children: John, Marjorie
         V. (1) John _____ Wubbena      B. March 16, 1917
                                           D. July 5, 1917
            (2) Marjorie _____ Wubbena  B. Aug. 19, 1924
            M. Kenneth M. Winkel              Aug. 23, 1946
              (5 Children)
              VI. (1) Dale G. Winkel       B. Je. 6, 1947
                  Married Linda Schmidt       Apr. 4, 1970
                      V11. (1) Angela Beth B. Je. 13, 1971
                                           D Je. 13, 1971

              V1. (2) Donna R. Winkel      B. April 14, 1949

              V1. (3) Delbert R. Winkel    B. July 19, 1954

              V1. (4) Delores K. Winkel    B. July 19, 1954

              V1. (5) David K. Winkel      B. June 8, 1957
```

(712) - 724 6331

==3==

```
1V. (4) Agnes Marie Wubbena            B. Aug. 30, 1898
         M. Robert M. Hickman           Dec. 21, 1915

1V. (5) Ben Manuel Wubbena             B. June 19, 1901  D 13/13
         M. Lena Rose                   March 14, 1922  D 7/
         (2 Children)
    ---V. (1) Merle John Wubbena        B. Oct. 12, 1922
             M. Evelyn Frey             Feb. 13, 1943
             (2 Children)
             VI. (1) Diane Rae Wubbena  B. May 4, 1946
                 (2) Dean ____ Wubbena  B. June 15, 1948
                     M. Bonnie Whiters  Oct. 12, 1968
                     VII. (1) Scott Eric Wubbna B. April 21, 1970
       V. (2) Cleo Thelma Wubbena       B. March 8, 1924
             M. Merton Oliver Winkel    Feb. 7, 1945
             VI. Rosann Winkel          B. Dec. 7, 1947

1V. (6) Joseph Jonathan Wubbena        B. June 19, 1901
         M. Josephine Ann Miller        Feb. 18, 1925
         (3 Children: Lois, Dorothy, Norma
         V. (1) Lois Jean Wubbena       B. April 4, 1929
                M. Stanley Duane Johnson  Dec. 29, 1954
                (4 Children)
                VI. (1) Randall Duane Johnson B. Dec. 11, 1955
                    (2) Melanie Sue Johnson   B. Jan. 14, 1957
                    (3) Robin Kay Johnson     B. Oct. 10, 1962
                    (4) Jamie Joel Johnson    B. Apr. 9, 1966
         V. (2) Dorothy Joy Wubbena     B. Apr. 28, 1933
                M. Daniel Wilbert Swain   Dec. 27, 1958
                (3 Children)
                VI. (1) Elizabeth Ann Swain  B. Jan. 4, 1960
                    (2) Amy Carolyn Swain    B. Sept. 28, 1961
                    (3) William Joseph Swain B. Aug. 1, 1964
1V          V. (3) Norma Jane Wubbena    B. Aug. 28, 1940
1V. (7) Arthur Calvin Wubbena          B. Nov. 14, 1908
         M. Margaret Rhodes
         V. (1) Child Calvin John        B. Nov. 13, 1932
                                          D. Sept. 16, 1952
         M. Jean Elizabeth Howe          Feb. 14, 1919
         V. (1) Child: Jon Fletcher Wubbena  B. May 2, 1943
                VI. Married Carol Ann Dochterman
                    VII. Child: James Fletcher Wubbena B. June 12, 1970
         M. Permilla Marie Edwards       June 28, 1925
         V. (2 Children)
                VI. (1) Molly Wubbena    B. Sept. 21, 1945
                    (2) Arthur Dean Wubbena (Dan)  B. Feb. 28, 1952
111. (2) Mense H. Wubbena              { B. Feb. 28, 1862
         M. Leah Wubbena Sept. 6, 1888  { D. Dec. 21, 1933
         ( 2 Children
         1V. (1) Harm Wubbena           B. July 6, 1895
                                         D. April 5, 1896
             (2) Herman Edwin Wubbena    B. Feb. 23, 1897
                                         D. Aug. 31, 1957
             M. Sadie Ruter              June 3, 1924
             (2) Children:
             V. 1-Leona Irene Mildred Wubbena B. Aug. 5, 1925
                M. Carl Fry                    Oct. 20, 1951
                (2 Children
                VI. 1-Lorraine Elizabeth Fry B. Sept. 17, 1956
                    2-Linda Elaine Fry        B. Nov. 18, 1958
```

.5

--4--

```
          V. 2-Rosanna Ruth R. Wubbena        B. Sept. 18, 1927
                M. Robert Dietmeier                Aug. 3, 1952
                (3 Children: Eric, Shawn, Juliana)
                   V1. (1) Eric Lane Dietmeier  B. June 7, 1954
                       (2) Shawn Lee Dietmeier  B. May 10, 1956
                       (3) Juliana Kay Dietmeier B. Jan. 13, 1961
111.(3) Leah Wubbena (Died at sea)
111.(4) Nellie Wubbena                         B. Nov. 16, 1865
                                               D. May 8, 1954
        M. (1) Martin Hassebrook               Jan. 8, 1900
               (1 son died in infancy)
               (2 Adopted children - Roy, Irene)
            1V. (1) Roy Hassebrook             B
                                               D



            1V. (2) Irene Hassebrook
                    M. Charles Poter




        M. (2) David Aswegan                       1932


111. (5) Frances Wubbena                       B. April 10, 1867
                                               D. July 23, 1897

111. (6) Simon H. Wubbena                      B. Nov. 10, 1868
                                               D. Oct. 29, 1961
       M. Hattie DeWeert                         Mar. 31, 1903
           (4 Children: Harvey, Alethea, Esther, Maurice)
       1V.  (1) Harvey Ollie Wubbena           B. Feb. 8, 1904
                M. Edna Herbert                    April 17, 1937
           (2) Alethea June Wubbena            B. Nov. 8, 1906
                                               D. Jan. 30, 1971
           (3) Esther Carrie Wubbena           B. Feb. 10, 1910
                M. Edward Lingbeck                 Feb. 22, 1930
                (3 Children: Elmer, Roger, Betty)
                V. (1) Elmer Edward Lingbeck    B. June 22, 1930
                       M. Patricia May Cain         July 29, 1951
                       (3 Children: Kenneth, Donna, Diane)
                      V1. (1) Kenneth Dale Lindbeck  B. July 12, 1959
                          (2) Donna Kay Lindbeck     B. July 3, 1966
                          (3) Diane Kelly Lingbeck   B. Feb. 27, 1968
                       (2) Roger Dale Lingbeck       B. Oct. 27, 1931
                                                     D. July 29, 1941
                      (3) Betty Jane Lingbeck        B. Aug. 7, 1933
                          M. Robert Raley                July 12, 1953
                          (No Children)
           (4) - - - -Maurice Max Wubbena       B. May 15, 1914
                M. Lucille Marie Hake               Aug. 23, 1937
                (4 Children: Rodney, Farida, Randall, Sharyle)
```

6

--5--

```
V. (1) Rodney Maurice Wubbena          B. March 31,1938
   (2) Farida Lou Wubbena              B. Sept. 11,1942
       M. Ronald Toepfer               B.
       (1 Child)
       VI. (1) Jeffry Allen Toepfer      B. Nov. 30, 1966
   (3) Randall Lee Wubbena             B. Oct. 23, 1946
   (4) Sharyle Kay Wubbena             B. June 14, 1951
       M. Steven Wollny (1)               Aug.    1968
       VI. (1) Douglas Stephen Wollny B. Nov. 3, 1968
       M. (2) Raymond Richardson         Oct. 25, 1970
```

```
111. (7) Henry H. Wubbena                 B. Oct. 28, 1870
                                          D. April 29, 1964
         M. Wilhelmina Ratmeier           Mar. 4, 1898
         (7 Children: Arthur, Edna, Florence, Lillian, Dorothy,
                 Marvin, Ellen)
     IV. (1) Arthur Harm Wubbena          B. May 23, 1900
             M. Ivah Link                 Jan. 24, 1923
             V. (1) Donald Arthur Wubbena B. Sept. 18, 1924
                    M. Florence Boals     Feb. 14, 1954
                    (2 Children: David - Joyce)
                    VI. (1) David Allen Wubbena  B. Nov. 15, 1954
                        (2) Joyce Ann            B. Feb. 26, 1957
                (2) Clyde William Wubbena        B. Nov. 26, 1929
                                                 D. March 31, 1940
         (2) Edna Elizabeth Wubbena       B. Sept. 4, 1902
             M. William Martin            June 11, 1927
             (4 Children - Marlene, Carol, Wayne, Eugene)
             V. (1) Marlene Audrey Martin B. Aug. 16, 1933
                    M. Bernard Baker       May 10, 1952
                    (6 Children: Monica, Randall, Joseph,
                     Terry, Jonathan, Carole)
                    VI. (1) Monica Anne Baker  B. Nov. 27, 1952
                            M. Kevin GEne Lucas  Oct. 31, 1970
                            1 Child: Melissa)
                            VII.(1) Melissa Sue Lucas B. Mar. 23, 1971
                        (2) Randall Alan Baker   B. June 26, 1954
                        (3) Joseph Peter Baker   B. Aug. 12, 1955
                                                 D. Nov. 15, 1955
                        (4) Terry Joseph Baker   B. Aug. 16, 1957
                        (5) Jonathan David Baker B. Nov. 4, 1958
                        (6) Carole Elizabeth Baker B. Dec. 16, 1959
                (2) Carol Fern Martin       B. May 2, 1936
                    M. Charles Deppee         Oct. 16, 1954
                    (4 Children: Barbara, William, David,
                     Carol)
                    VI. (1) Barbara Diane Deppee B. Oct. 5, 1956
                        (2) William Francis Deppee B. July 10, 1958
                        (3) David Charles Deppee B. July 31, 1960
                        (4) Carol Ruth Deppee    B. Jan. 15, 1964
                (3) Wayne Lee Martin        B. June 10, 1938
                    M. Jane Meredith Luethke      July 17, 1971

                (4) Eugene Glenn Martin     B. Dec. 7, 1939
                    M. (1) Linda Downs             196
                    VI. (1) Daniel Eugene Martin B. June 24, 1963
                        (2) Dennis ____ Martin   B. May -- 1964
                    M. (2) Jean                   196
                        (3) 1 Child:Timothy Martin B. Apr.  1968
```

7

--6--

IV. (3) Florence Luella Wubbena   B. Jan. 1, 1905
  (4) Lillian Adele Wubbena   B. Jan. 13, 1907
    M. Howard Johnson   July 17, 1943
    (2 Children: Jarol, Ronald)
  V. (1) Jarol Paul Johnson   B. May 27, 1946
    M. Anita Robinson   Aug. 18, 1968

    (2) Ronald Mark Johnson   B. March 5, 1951

  (5) Dorothy Evelyn Wubbena   B. May 8, 1910
    M. Donald Bradford   Oct. 11, 1934
  (6) Marvin Benjamin Wubbena   B. Sept. 30, 1914
                         D. July 9, 1915
  (7) Ellen Leona Wubbena   B. ~~July 9, 1915~~ Dec. 31 1916
                         D. Aug. 12, 1931

III. (8) Albert H. Wubbena   B. June 12, 1873
                   D. Feb. 16, 1948
  M. (1) Elizabeth (Libby) Brugman   April 4, 1900
  M. (2) Anni Hinricks   June 22, 1937
  (7 Children: Boy, Ray, Lillian, Girl, Alyce,
         Lester, Florence)
IV. (1) Boy - Born April 19, 1902   D. April 19, 1902
  (2) Ray Harm Wubbena   B. May 16, 1903
                   D. Aug. 16, 1963
    M. Letitia Coster   May 9, 1959
  (3) Lillian Tena Wubbena   B. Oct. 1, 1908
    M. Roy Sirl VanNingen   June 1, 1933
    (3 Children: Norman, Lionel, Jerome)
  V. (1) Norman Lee VanNingen   B. May 2, 1934
    M. Arleen Avis Lee   Sept. 6, 1953
    (4 Children: Gregory, Rodney, Cynthia,
             Pamela)
    VI. (1) Gregory Lee VanNingen   B. May 2, 1955
      (2) Rodney Allen VanNingen   B. Aug. 8, 1956
      (3) Cynthia Rae VanNingen   B. Apr. 8, 1959
      (4) Pamela Sue VanNingen   B. Feb. 11, 1961
    (2) Lionel DeVere VanNingen   B. Aug. 15, 1935
    M. Maryln Fae Tschetter   July 24, 1959
    (3 Children: Dylan, Cheryle, Carla)
    VI. (1) Dylan LaVerne VanNingen   B. March 31, 1960
      (2) Cheryle Lynna VanNingen   B. May 25, 1962
      (3) Carla Jean VanNingen   B. May 18, 1964
    (3) Jerome Cortney VanNingen   B. July 25, 1936
    M. Peggy Ann Sims   Sept. 4, 1956
    (2 Children: Lori, Bryan)
    VI. (1) Lori Ann VanNingen   B. June 10, 1959
      (2) Bryan Jerome VanNingen   B. March 31, 1963
IV. (4) Baby Girl   B. June 4, 1910   -D. June 4, 1910
  (5) Alyce Tobina Wubbena   B. March 28, 1911
    M. Elvin Carl Hamen   Aug. 26, 1936
    (2 Children: Kenneth, Gene)
  V. (1) Kenneth Ray Hamen   B. Dec. 29, 1937
    M. Judy Ann Hale   Apr. 24, 1959
    (2 Children: Kelly, Craig)
    VI. (1) Kelly Marie Hamen   B. March 30, 1968
      (2) Craig Allen Hamen   B. Nov. 21, 1970
    (2) Gene Curtis Hamen,   B. March 22, 1940
    M. Gayle Glenice Jenson   Dec. 13, 1959

δ

--7--

```
                    (3 Children, Todd, Troy, Stacey)
            VI. (1) Todd Curtis Hamen              B. Sept. 1, 1961
                (2) Troy Chris Hamen               B. Dec. 6, 1965
                (3) Stacey LeAnn (Adopted at 7 weeks)
    IV. (6) Lester Arend Wubbena                   B. Oct. 7, 1913
            M. Geraldine Mae Sprang                   Sept. 9, 1941
            (2 Children: Carol, Judy)
        V. (1) Carol Jean Wubbena                  B. Nov. 19, 1942
               M. Jack Raile Carter                   April 15, 1962
               (3 Children: Jack, Linda, Barbara)
            VI. (1) Jack Arlin Carter              B. Sept. 7, 1963
                (2) Linda Jean Carter              B. Nov. 16, 1964
                (3) Barbara Kay Carter             B. Jan. 5, 1967
            (2) Judy Kay Wubbena                   B. Sept. 27, 1945
                M. Clifford Albert Poppen             June 5, 1966
                (2 Children: Tim, _____
                VI. (1) Tim Allen Poppen           B. May 19, 1968
                    (2) _____ Poppen           B. Sept. 1971
    IV. (7) Florence Alena Wubbena                 B. Oct. 26, 1915
            M. Clarence Dallas VanNingen              Sept. 7, 1938
            (2 Children: Stephen, Patrice
        V. (1) Stephen Clarence VanNingen          B. July 17, 1942
               M. Sydnie Junice Salthouse             Jan. 2, 1965
               (1 Child: Shawn)
            VI. (1) Shawn Michele VanNingen        B. Aug. 21, 1969
            (2) Patrice Danielle VanNingen         B. Nov. 19, 1947
                M. Walter Wayne Curtis                Nov. 21, 1967

III. (9) Ralph H. Wubbena                          B. April 3, 1877
                                                   D. March 17, 1954
         M. Anna Wichman                              Feb. 15, 1905
         (1 Child: Ralph)
    IV. (1) Ralph Jr. Wubbena                      B. May 22, 1909
            M. Minnie Meyer                           Sept. 28, 1935
            (2 Children: Irvin, Ethel)
        V. (1) Irvin Stanley Wubbena               B. Dec. 17, 1936
               M. Doris Garber                        Nov. 24, 1960
               (1 Child: Trudy)
            VI. (1) Trudy Lynn Wubbena             B. May 8, 1964
            (2) Ethel Delores Wubbena              B. Aug. 17, 1939
                M. Ronald Timm                        June 24, 1961
                (2 Children: David, Scott)
            VI. (1) David William Timm             B. March 27, 1962
                (2) Scott Anthony Timm             B. April 9, 1970
```

- - - - - - - - - - - -

THE ONLY 7 GENERATION WUBBENA FROM II HARM H. WUBBENA

```
I   Mensen Harm Wubbena
 II  Harm H. Wubbena
  III John H. Wubbena
     IV Ben Manuel Wubbena
       V Merle John Wubbena
        VI Dean Wubbena
          VII Scott Eric Wubbena
```

THE FAMILIES OF MIENT WUBBENA
Born in Tergast Ostfriesland - November 23, 1842 - Died April 12, 1912
And Fantje Dessens Harms - Born June 26, 1855, Died Feb. 26, 1914
Youngest Son of Mensen and Nelka Wubbena

Mense, Nelka and Harm died in infancy.
   Three grew to adulthood: Manuel, Harm and Nellie
MANUEL - Born August 8, 1883
      Married Reka Fruhling - April 22, 1911
      (Fannie, Mabel, Lillian, Erma, Andrew
   1. Fannie Marie - Born May 30, 1912, Married Carl Ruthe Nov. 28, 1931
      (2 Children)
         a. Robert Carl, Born June 4, 1932 - Died October 18, 1954
            Married Marcella Zumdahl - December 10, 1949
               (2 Children) Judith Kay - Born May 20, 1950
                           Jacquilyn Faye - Born January 26, 1953
         b. Vernon Roger - Born Sept. 16, 1935
            Married Sharon Schwarze - October 22, 1960
               1 Child: Adopted-Joel Robert -(April 1, 1970 Born)

   2. Mabel Martha - Born March 8, 1917   - Died m_____
      Married Forbes DeVries - Feb. 10, 1937
      (3 Children: Norman, Miriam, Ronald
         a. Norman David - Born July 16, 1940
            Married Marilyn Overchain Aug. 30, 1960
               (4 Children: Wendell David - Born June 10, 1963
                           Delbert David - Born Jan. 7, 1966
                           Shelden David, Born April 4, 1967
                           Eric David Born March 6, 1971
         b. Miriam Joyce - Born Nov. 1, 1949 - Not Married
         c. Ronald Steven, Born July 13, 1956 - Died Young

   3. Florence Dorothy - Born April 15, 1918
      Married Relman DeVries - December 5, 1939
      (3 Children: Sandra Kay, Myrna Fay, Darlene May)
         a. Sandra Kay - Born April 15, 1940- Married Gillingham(Carroll)
            (3 Children)   June 23, 1962
            David Alan - Born Aug. 16, 1963
            Teresa Kay - Born November 7, 1964
            Nancy Lyn - Born July 13, 1968
         b. Myrna Fay - Born March 14, 1947
            Married Carl Gassmund   1964
            (3 Children: Bradley James - Born June 26, 1965
                        Cheryl Fay, Jan. 3, 1967
                        Connie Alice - Born Oct. 14, 1970
         c. Darlene Kay - Not Married

   4. Lillian Elsie Born Sept. 13, 1921
      Married John (Jack) Kerkhoff - No Children (Dec. 29, 1943

   5. Irma Mae - Born June 3, 1926 - Married Dean Sanders April 18, 1947
      (3 Children: David Dean - Born Dec. 3, 1923 June 6 - 1950
                  Ruth Ann- Born Feb. 10, 1957
                  May Lynn - Born May 15, 1961
   6. Andrew Born April 6, 1914 - Died April 18, 1917

                  HARM M WUBBENA FAMILY
HARM - Born Feb. 12, 1886
   Married Sadie Meyer - March 20, 1913 - Sadie Died Aug. 24, 1970
      (4 Children: Arthur, Esther, Lucille, Irene)
   1. Arthur - Born Oct. 9, 1914 - Married Ruth DeWall June 3, 1938
      (3 Children- Allen Dennis, Delmer Verlye, Marcia Lynn
         a. Allen Dennis Q-Born Dec. 9, 1938
            Married Marian Heck October 3, 1964
               Children: Denise Lorene - Born Dec. 17, 1966
                        Jr' ny Allen - Born Dec. 5, 1969

```
          Delmar Verlye - Born March 21, 1942
          Married Constance Kaneman - August 1, 1964
             a. Child: (Adopted Joel Robert - Born July 31, 1965
     c. Marcia Lynn - Born April 17, 1945
        Married Jack Willard - September 5, 1964
          Children  1. Bambi Lynn - Born July 28, 1966
                    2. Nickalas Dwayne - Born November 20, 1967
                    3. Rebecca Suzanne  Born August 18, 1970
  2. Esther -- Born December 15, 1916
        Married  Glenn McGraw - June 2, 1945
           1 Child: Kathy (adopted) Born Feb. 7, 1951
  3. Lucille -- Born March 24, 1923 - Married Howard Dittmar June 9, 1957
           1 Child: Ann Marie -- Born October 13, 1958
  4. Irene Lois - Born June 2, 1929 -Married Victor LaBelle-June 26, 1959
           1 Child: Lori Irene - Born Nov. 10, 1964
NELLIE - Born January 12, 1896
     Married Evert Sneek - December 30, 1933 - Died  May 2, 1939
     Married Cornelious Meyer - June 29, 1940 - Died April 4, 1959
        (2 Children:  Clarence Sneek  - Shirley Sneek)

     1. Clarence - Born November 14, 1934
        Married Shelby Benoy - January 24, 1955
           Children:  a.  Sheila Kay - Born July 9, 1955
                      b.  Mark David - Born Oct. 16, 1957
                      c.  Dawn Denise - Born July 13, 1959
                      d.  Matthew Scott - Born  July 12, 1961
                      e.  Wendy-Jo  Born N v. 13, 1964

     2. Shirley Esther - Born July- 5, 1936
        Married  Alfred Person  - Nov. 25, 1961
           Children:  a.  Tamara Sue - Born June 26, 1962
                      b.  Roxanna Marie - Born April 1, 1964
                      c.  Jennifer Renee - Born June 14, 1965
                      d.  Eric Emil -- Born January 29, 1967
                        == - - - - - - ==
IMON WUBBENA     Born Feb.   1836    Died May 19, 1913
Married Henericka DeVries
     Children: John S. Mense S. Harm S. Henry S. Leah(Mrs. Henry
     Wilhelms, Nellie(Mrs. Christ Wilhelms, Toby(Mrs. Geo. Denekas,
     Frances (Mrs. Earnest Meyer)
  JOHN S. Born June 6, 1875    - Died March 10, 1924
           Married Martha Poppen
           Child: Zelma  Born April 30, 1901 - Not Married
                              Resides in Chicago
  MENSE S.      Born November 13, 1878 - Died  March 18, 1955
           Married Emma Moring - Died Oct. 5, 1937
        Children: Mabel, Ada Minnie, Alta May
        1. Mabel Born Oct. 27, 1904
              Married Christ Drake     Jan. 18, 1928
              (3 Children: Delores, Marlene, Eleanor
                a. Delores - Born June 14, 1931
                   Married Dale Edwards - Nov. 24, 1951
                      Children:  Pamela Sue -B. Sept. 19,1953
                                 Andrew Dale, B. NAv. 5, 1956
                b. Marlene - Born Aug. 9, 1936
                   Married Kenneth Palmer    Sept. 14, 1957
                   Children: Bonnie Kay B. June 27, 1958
                             Beverley Jean B. Feb. 21, 1960
                c. Eleanor - Born June 18, 1939
                   Married Rev. Merle Nelson
```

2. Ada Minnie Wubbena - Born May 19, 1908 -Died Dec. 6, 1946
   Married Frederick Neisemeier Feb. 18, 1931
   (Children: Doris, Richard, Gary)
   a. Doris Marie - Born October 9, 1931
      Married Vernon Linker - March 25, 1950
      1.a Verna Marie - Born March 15, 1951
         Married Randell Woessner - May 31, 1970
      2a.Vicki M. Born June 1-53,3a.Frederick.Born Jan.3/62
   2. Richard Lee - Born November 6, 1933
      Married Judith Ann Johnson Aug. 16, 1959
         Children: Amy Elaine Born June 13, 1965
                    Eric Richard Born July 4, 1966
                    Alex Jacob Born Sept. 4, 1969
                    Jason Wesley Born Nov. 18, 1970
   3. Gary Frederick - Born July 3, 1942
      Married Linda Lou Duncan Oct. 22, 1966
         Children: Frederick Gary -B. Aug. 8, 1967
                    Cathy Lynn - Born May 24, 1970

3. Alta May -- Born July 1, 1916
   Married Merrill Runte July 7, 1936
   (Children: Marlys Kay, Roger Lee)
   a. Marlys Kay Born Aug. 24, 1937
      Married Max Edler - Dec. 1, 1957
         Children: Randy Max Born Sept. 2, 1958
                   Bryan Rex - Born Feb. 17, 1960
                   Robert Lee - Born Aug. 14, 1961
                   Kay Suzanne - Born Oct. 12, 1962
                   Renna Marlys - Born April 22, 1964

      Roger Lee - Born Jan. 1, 1939
      Married Sue Ellen Paul - Aug. 20, 1957
         Children: Lori Jean - Born Aug. 7, 1958
                   Stephen Roger - Born Oct. 31, 1959
                   Gerald Lee - Born Oct. 5, 1961
                   Linda Sue - Born Jan. 18, 1965

HARM S. Died As a Little Boy,

HENRY S. Born September 24, 1882   Died Jan. 10, 1965
   Married Nettie Moring 1905
   (Children: Clarence, Elva, Lucille, Dorothy)
   1. Clarence - Born Sept. 16, 1907
      Married Vera Edler   1937
         Child: Courtney - Born April 11, 1949 - Not Married

   2. Elva -- Born Septmeber 25, 1910
      Married John A. DeWall 1933
         Children: Donald, Eldon, Leola, Verlo, Anita
         a. Donald Born Sept. 6, 1935
            Married Marian Brown - 1953
               Children: Born - Louanne - April 29, 1954
                          Joanne - March 17, 1959
                          Susanne - Jan. 27, 1961
                          Deanne - Feb. 8, 1962
                          Darrell - Jan. 28, 1963
         b. Eldon - Born June 30, 1937
            Married Elsie Bochman 1959
               Children: Evelyn - Born Aug. 4, 1964
                          (Evan - Born July 1, 1966
                          (Everett Born July 1, 1966
                          Everlse Born July 19, 1969

    c. Leola - Born November 26, 1938
        Married Kenneth Jurgens - 1959
           Children: Harlan - Born May 30, 1961
                  Valeria - Born Aug. 30, 1964
    d. Verlo - Born June 22, 1941
        Married Ardath Flack   -   1965
           Children: Steven: Born Sept. 29, 1966
                  Jeffrey Born Dec. 2, 1969

    e. Anita - Born January 17, 1947
        Married Robert DeVries   1966
           Children: Renee   - Born Nov. 17, 1966
                  Rosalie - Born April 21, 1969
                  Robert - Born Feb. 14, 1971

3. Lucille - Born July 2, 1919
   Married Leonard DeWall   1939
      Child: Larry - Born - May 31, 1941
          Married Mary Ellen Gulley 1962
             Children: Celina Born May 25, 1963
                  Rhett - Born June 6, 1965

4. Dorothy - Born November 16, 1923
   Married Alvin Jenner - 1941
      Child: Jerry Born March 27, 1948 -Died Oct. 7, 1968
              - - - - - - =

LEAH WUBBENA   Born -   1874   - Died May 17, 1968
Married Henry O. Wilhelms
  1. Child: Oliver H. - Born Oct. 21, 1895 - Died May 19, 1964
        Married Matilda Denekas
        (a) Child: LeRoy Wilhelms - Born Aug. 3, 1918
           Married Marjorie Fairbairn
          1a. Children: Lyle Wilhelms - Born Feb. 10,
             Married Darlene Smith
                Children: Lana Wilhelms B. March 17, 1963
                      Doreen Wilhelms B. Aug. 3, 1964
        (b) Gale Wilhelms - Born July 3, 1947
           Married Linda Craid Born May 12, 1947
             Children: Jodi O Born Sept. 14, 1968
                    Died Sept. 14, 1968
                DeAnn Wilhelms Born Sept. 27, 1969
        (c) Sharon Wilhelms Born November 23, 1950
           Married James Balles
             Child: Susan K. Balles Born April 30, 1970

        (d) Darrell Wilhelms Born August 21, 1954

        (e) Miriam Wilhelms Born Dec. 12, 1922
           Married Delbert (Bud) Harnish
           Children: 1a. Nancy Harnish Born Oct. 1, 1946
                Married Daryld Gahm
                  Children: Michael Gahm B. May 14, 1966
                      Steven Gahm B. May 11, 1969
             2a. Gerry Harnish B. January 7, 1949
        (f) June Wilhelms Born Jan. 19, 1926
           Married Hobart Gaar
           Children: Cathy Jo Born May 1, 1956
               David   Born June 21, 1962

(g)Paul Wilhelms Born Feb. 3, 1927
    Married Marie Hargasser
    ChildreN:
    <u>1a</u>. Ingrid - Born Aug. 27, 1947
        Married Donald Heilman
            Children: Darin - Born Dec. 28, 1966
                      Stacy - Born Sept. 12, 1969
    <u>2a</u>. Shirley Wilhelms - Born Oct. 1S, 1949
        Married Richard Leeman
            Child: Angela Leeman - Born Aug. 8, 1970

    3a. Deborah Wilhelms - Born July 1, 1953
    4a. Steven Wilhelms - Born March 17, 1954 -Died Mar. 17-54
    5a. Gary Wilhelms - Born October 1, 1955
    6a. Sandy Wilhelms - Born Feb. 21, 1962
    7a. Laurie Wilhelms - Born May 3, 1965
    8a. Tammy Wilhelms - Born Sept. 21, 1967
    9a. Jeffrey Wilhelms - Born July 22, 1969
Russell Wilhelms - Born Nov. 17, 1929
Dorothy Wilhelms - Born Feb. 14, 1931 - Died Nov. 14, 1931

Carolyn Wilhelms -Born June 5, 1933
    Married S. James Amodeo
        Children: Karen Amodeo - Born Feb. 8, 1954
                  Jaime - Born Sept. 4, 1955
                  Gino - Born N A. 13, 1959
                  Dan - Born - Nov. 5, 1965
                  Paul - Born Nov. 5, 1965
                  Amy - Born May 15, 1968
Wayne Wilhelms - Born March 6, 1937
    Married Donna Hubbard
        Children: Scott - Born June 5, 1957
                  Christy - Born Feb. 19, 1959
                  Derrick - Born April 23, 1965
                  JeoDeen - Born May 5, 1971

SAMUEL - Second Son of Leah Wubbena and Henry O Wilhelms
    Born Aug. 17, 1897 -- Married Luella E. Otto
        Children:
        1. Marsden - Born Feb. 10, 1922
            Married Lavon Leerhoff
                ChildreN: Stephanie Wilhelms - Born Nov. 17, 1949
                          Kathleen Wilhelms - Born Jan. 20, 1951
                          Kevin - Born July 1S, 1952
                          Tracy- - Born Aug. 30, 1956
                          Lyndon - Born Dec. 25, 1961

        2. Verla Wilhelms - Born June 3, 1924
            Married Bruce Kelley
                Children:
                a. David Kelley - Born Apri 11, 1945
                    Married Gail Whitehead
                        Children: Leah Ann - Born April 18, 1969
                                  Jacqualin Kelley Born Jan. 7, 1971
                b. Max Kelley - Born Oct. 7, 1946
                    Married G il Reed
                c. Jeffrey Kelley Born May 6, 1948
                d. Bradford Kelley - Born March 23, 1952
                e. Kurtis Kelley - Born March 23, 1952
                f. Jana Kelley - Born Dec. 27, 1953

3. Betty J. Wilhelms - Born April 23, 1927
   Married Ray Pruitt
      Children: Rhonda - Born January 25, 1952
                Brian - Born November 9, 1954
                Gregory - Born October 18, 1956
                Rodney - Born August 15, 1959

4. Kenneth Wilhelms - Born April 21, 1932
   Married Lorraine Olthoff
      Children: Debra Jo - Born July 29, 1956
                Douglas - Born Septmeber 20, 1958

MINNIE WILHELMS -- Eldest daughter of Leah Wubbena and Henry Wilhelms
Married A. L. Hershberger
   Children:
      a. Roger Hershberger - Born Nov. 3, 1925
         Married Gloria Retrum
            Children: Michael -- Born Nov. 28, 1962
                      Thomas - Born May 12, 1965
      b. Don Hershberger - Born Aug. 26, 1927
         Married Patricia Smith
            Children: Christy - Born Dec. 29, 1951
                      Peter - Born Dec. 6, 1953
                      Robin - Born June 20, 1955
                      David - Born Oct. 2, 1959
                      Andrew - Born Dec. 7, 1963

      c. Phyllis Hershberger - Born March 15, 1933
         Married Donald Schoonhoven
            Children: Cindy - Born April 26, 1954
                      Jill Schoonhoven - Born May 5, 1957
                      Timothy - Born April 13, 1959
                      Daniel - Born Nov. 19, 1962

RACHEL WILHELMS - youngest daughter of Leah Wubbena & Henry Wilhelms
         Born January 31 1902 - Died Oct.   1936
         - -- -- ----- -- - -

NELLIE WUBBENA WILHELMS - Born March 8, 1869 -- Died Jan. 31, 1936
Married Christ O. Wilhelms
   Children:
      a. Oltman C. Wilhelms - Born December 25, 1892 Died Dec. 5, 1964
         Married Emma Louise Gitz
            Children:
            1. Earl John - Born Aug. 21, 1915
               Married Ruth Schell
                  Children: Jean Louise - Born July 28, 1947
                            Married Lawrence Wilson Moore
                               Roger Earl -- Born Dec. 6, 1951
            2. Harold Reynold Wilhelms O Born Sept. 16, 1926
               Married Joyce Zier
                  Child: Emily Kay - Born June 8, 1963

      b. Simon C. Wilhelms - Born June 28, 1894
         Married Alta M. Heeren
         Child: Evelyn DeLoris - Born March 3, 1918
         Married William McCully
            Children: 1.Craig Wm. - Born Oct. 7, 1942
                      2.Sherrie Ann-- Born Aug. 7, 1945
                        Married Robert Grob
                           Children:Randall Scott-Born Sept. 27, 1965
                                    Gary Wayne - Born Dec. 3, 1970
                      3. Janice Ellen -- Born Oct. 12, 1954

Third Son of Nellie Wubbena and Christ O. Wilhelms
~·c.   Christ T. Wilhelms - Born Dec. 6, 1899
        Married Lillian L. Woessner
        Children:
            1. DeLores Jean - Born April 26, 1927
                Married J. Harlan Meiners
                    Children: Steven J. - Born Jan. 7, 1955
                              Jeffrey W. - Born Aug. 15, 1958
                              Micheal H. - Born April 18, 1962

            2. Omar C. Whihelms - Born May 18, 1932
                Married   Janice Rae Craddock
                    Children:
                        Robin Rae - Born April 22, 1957
                        Candac e Jane - Born June 22, 1961

TOBY Wubbena - Married George Denekas - No Children Both Deceased

FRANCIS WUBBENA: Born March 20, 1872   Died Aug. 1951
    Married Ernest Meyer
        Children: John - December 5, 1900-Died Feb. 10, 1967
                   Married Gretchen Schoohnoven
                        Child: Rogene - Born April 6, 1925
                        Married Eldon LaBudde
                            Child: David - Born Feb. 13, 1956

            Sam - Born   1902 - Died 1953
                Married Ruth Martin
                    No Children
                    Both Deceased

FOURTH CHILD OF MENSEN HARM WUBBENA
AND NELKE SIMONS WUBBENA

GRANDPARENTS: Albert M. Wubbena, Born - December 9, 1837 at Tergast,
Ostfriesland. Married Harmke Saathoff, Born March 23, 1840 at Forreston,
Illinois on February 6, 1867.

CHILDREN BORN

1.	Leah	Oct. 6, 1867	7.	Ventje (Fanny)	Aug. 13, 1876
2.	Harm	Nov. 19, 1868	8.	Nelke (Nellie)	Mar. 16, 1878
3.	Mense A.	April 1, 1870	9.	(Twin Albert died at 4 months)	
4.	Simon A.	Oct. 3, 1871	10.	Albert A.	August 13, 1879
5.	Maria	May 5, 1873	11.	Harmke (Emma)	March 20, 1882
6.	Mient A.	Oct. 2, 1874	12.	Frederich (Fred)	July 19, 1884

GENERATION III
LEAH: Born October 6, 1867 - Died - November 15, 1944
     Talea Married Mense H. Wubbena   Died - December 21, 1933
     Children: Harm - Herman E.

a. Harm - Born July 6, 1895 - Died April 5, 1896

b. Herman E. - Born February 23, 1897 - Died August 31, 1957
   Married Sadie Ruter - June 3, 1924
   (2 Children: (1) Leona (2) Rosanna

      (1) Leona M. Born August 5, 1925
          Married Carl Frey, October 20, 1951
                    Children: Lorraine E. Born Sept. 17, 195_
                              Linda Elaine, Born Nov. 18, 1958

      (2) Rosanna R. Born Sept. 18, 1927
          Married Robert Dietmeier - August 3, 1952
                    Children: Eric L. Born June 7, 1954
                              Sharon L. Born May 10, 1956
                              Julianna, Born Jan. 13, 1961
                              Died September 7, 1932
HARM A. Born November 19, 1868 - - xxxxxxxxxxxxxxxxxxxxxxxxx
     Married Myrtle Ewing - No Children

MENSE A. Born April 1, 1870 - Died December 11/ 1945
     Married Minnie Meyer March 12, 1907 She died Oct. 21, 1970
     Children: Emily, Hermanus, Albert

a. Emily Esther - Born June 24, 1908 - Not Married

b. Hermanus C. - Born May 17, 1911

c. Albert William - Born August 26, 1913
   Married Ruth Heeren
   (3 Children: (1) Faith - Born Sept. 19, 1948
                (2) David - Born Sept. 5, 1952
                (3) Lloyd Alan - Born February 2, 1957

SIMON A. Born - October 3, 1871 - Died December 30, 1938
     Married Minnie Heeren - November 25, 1896 She died June 29, 1948
     (7n Children: Emma, Lydia, Samuel, Harry, Amelia, Paul, Alvin)
a. Emma: Born April 9, 1898
         Married - John Schroeder October 3, 1922 - Died November 1, 1960
         (4 Children: Simon, David, Janet, Kathleen

-2-

1. Simon - Born August 22, 1924
    Married Lena LaBudde   1949
       (2 Children)
          Louise A. Born January 8, 1950
          Married Ronald Meyer - August 28, 1970

          Judith K. Born January 12, 1954

2. David - Born January 25, 1927
    Married Lucille Zier - March 17, 1956
       No Children

3. Janet - Born February 16, 1929
    Married John Leadingham - December 1, 1956
       (2 Children)
          John - Born June 12, 1958
          Ann - Born January 9, 1968

4. Kathleen - Born September 20, 1934
    Married Michael Atherton   1959
       (4 Children)
          Cynthia Ann - Born September 24, 1959
          Mark Anthony - Born April 28, 1961
          Pamela - Born April 10, 1963
          Kim - Born May 21, 1965

b. Lydia - Born December 7, 1900
    Married Christian Ludwig - February 27, 1924
       (4 Children: Donald, Robert, Marlene, Stanley
       (1) Donald - Born December 2 1924 (2)
           Married Betty Bocker
              (4 Children:
                 Gregory - Born April 4, 1948
                 Married Shirley Hinders August 14, 1971

                 Beverley -- Born June 25, 1950

                 Gary - Born September 18, 1951

                 Hohn - Born February 14, 1961
       (2) Robert - Born December 23, 1926 - Died August 13, 1939

       (3) Marlene - Born November 11, 1934
           Married Richard Tedrow - Died December 30, 1967
              (3 Children)
                 Debra - Born October 31, 1957 - Died May 10, 1960
                 Leslie - Born October 7, 1962
                 Christopher - Born May 30, 1964
           Married Jerry Lau September 13, 1969
       (4) Stanley - Born September 12, 1942
           Married Karen Johnson - August 27, 1965
              (3 Children)
                 Gretechen -- Born January 6, 1966 - Died July 19, 1966
                 Matthew - Born May 30, 1967
                 Joel - Born November 17, 1969

-3-

c. Samuel A. Born   May 25, 1902   -   Died May 21, 1970
        Married Martha Swalve -FEBRUARY 16, 1928 (Died May 16, 1970
        (3 Children: Phillip, Lorraine, Leonard)
            (1) Phillip - Born December 3, 1929
                    Married Betty Jo Gale   February 1, 1953
                        (4 Children)
                            Christine - Born October 16, 1954
                            Rodney   - Born May 25, 1957
                            Audrey   - Born September 15, 1959
                            Keith   - -Born January 19, 1961
            (2) Lorraine - Born February 2, 1933
                    Married Eugene Butler - August 29, 1957
                        (2 Children)
                            Elizabeth - Born May 30, 1967
                            Suzanne - Born Sept. 12, 1968

            (3) Leonard -- Born August 20, 1934
                    Married Jean Miller - October 16, 1965
                        (3 Children)
                            Angela, Born January 31, 1967
                            Anita, Born August 16, 1969
                            Kevin, Born January 26, 1971

d. Harry - Born June 17, 1904
        Married Edith Folkerts - March 1, 1927
            (3 Children: Richard, James, Stephen
        (1) Richard - Born - - March 27, 1931
                Married Janice Brattrud - March 3, 1951
                    (4 Children)
                        Rachel Lynn, Born July 24, 1952
                        Brian, Born Oct. 29, 1954
                        Curtis, Born Nov. 9, 1957
                        Bradley, Born July 15, 1961

        (2) James - Born July 20, 1934
                Married Jean Messinger - September 27, 1958
                    (2 Children:)
                        Jacqueline, Born Sept. 15, 1960
                        Jolene,   Born December 4, 1963
        (3) Stephen - Born October 20, 1939
                    Not Married

e. Amelia - Born April 21, 1906 - Died December 5, 1945
                    Not Married
f. Paul - Born July 28, 1910
        Married Emma Arjes   June 6, 1936
                    (3 Children: Paul II, Gerald, Jon
        1. Paul II Born January 25, 1937
                Married: Sarah Cunningham - June 17, 1961
                    (3 Children)
                        Vicki Lynn - Born Sept. 13, 1962
                        Deborah   - Born November 15, 1964
                        Paul III   - Born November 22, 1966
        2. Gerald - Born April 9, 1938
                Married Martha Caluski - December 29, 1962
                    (2 Children)
                        Laura Ann -- Born November 25, 1963
                        Kimberley   Born September 28, 1968

--4--

3. Jon - Born July 15, 1939
        Married Frankie Sumner - January 27, 1961
            (3 Children)
                    Joseph - Born August 23, 1961
                    Charles - Born April 23, 1963
                    Sandra - Born   (Adopted)

g. Alvin -- Born January 16, 1912
        Married Bertha Ratmeyer - February 15, 1935
            (4 Children: Roger, Eleanor, Larry, Sharon)

    (1) Roger - Born October 16, 1935 - Died November 18, 1953

    (2) Eleanor - Born November 19, 1936
            Married David Snapp - June 7, 1957
                (2 Children)
                        Jeffrey - Born October 27, 1963
                        Jody - Born August 2, 1966

    (3) Larry - Born March 27, 1941
            Married - Myrna Andeburg - July 15, 1966
                    No Children

    (4) Sharon - Born February 15, 1954 *1954*
            Married Gary Koch July 12, 1968
                    No Children

NELKA (NELLIE) Born March 16, 1877 - Died April 18, 1966
    Married Klaus Meyer - January 4, 1905 - Died June 6, 1913
        (3 Children: Herman, Alfred, Lenora)
a. Herman Born April 23, 1907
        Married Helen Sinish - September 13, 1939
            (5 Children: Lenora, Stanley, William, Ruth, Paul)
    1. Lenora - Born July 22, 1940
            Married Gerald D. Wool   June 10, 1960
                (2 Children)
                        Lisa
                        Bryan
    2. Stanley -- Born June 22, 1942 - Not Married

    3 William - Born August 2, 1945
            Married Martha Snyder - June 17, 1967
    4. Ruth Born July 17, 1948
            Married Christian Koher, Jr. June 27, 1970

    5. Paul - Born February 23, 1954

b. Alfred - Born June 6, 1910
        Married - Helen Lubbers - Sept. 6, 1939
            (4 Children: Richard, Larry, Ronald, Janice)
    1. Richard - Born Sept. 1, 1940
            Married Judy Trei - Sept. 24, 1960
                (2 Children)
                        David - Born August 22, 1961
                        Susan - Born August 13, 1963

    2. Larry - Born January 31, 1943
            Married - Susan Adams - February 10, 1968
    3. Ronald - Born June 29, 1948
            Married Louise Schroeder - August 28, 1970

    4. Janice - Born January 20, 1952

--5--

 c. Lenora Meyer - Born December 13, 1912

MARIA - Born May 5, 1873 = Died June 5, 1952
 Married John Heeren   1918-   Died April 12, 1959
     No Children

MEINT A. Born Oct. 2, 1874   - Died April 5, 1894
     Not Married

VENTJE (Fanny) Born August 13, 1876 - Died August 14, 1919
 Married Henry Bokker
  (2 Children - Albert - Clarence)
    a. Albert Born December 15, 1910 - Died July 26, 1911
    b. Clarence Born   1913   - Died   1919

Rev. Albert WUBBENA - Born August 13, 1879   Died April 6, 1941
 Married Matilda DeFeyter   -   Died Nov. 20, 1955
     No Children

HARMKE (Emma) Born March 20, 1882 - Died Sept. 18, 1968
 Married Henry Bokker   Feb. 7, 1921   Died Jan. 20, 1949
     No Children

FREDERICK (Fred) Born July 19, 1884   - Died Oct. 19, 1956
  Married Gertie DeVries Nov. 26, 1919   Died Nov. 17, 1953
  (2 Children: Martha - Robert)
   a. Martha Born June 25, 1921
     Married Walter Martin   September 6, 1958
     (2 Children)
       Skyler Born May 29, 1961
       Steven Born Sept. 22, 1963

   b. Robert Born August 28, 1925
     Married Dorothy Artman   Sept. 27, 1956
     (3 Children)

       1. Darald - Born Sept. 7, 1947
        Married Cindy Swalve - January 12, 1970

       2. Wayne - Born December 12, 1949

       3. Darlene - Born March 29, 1953

APPENDIX D

*Wübbena Family Tree Records
Prepared in Germany During
the Nazi Regime*

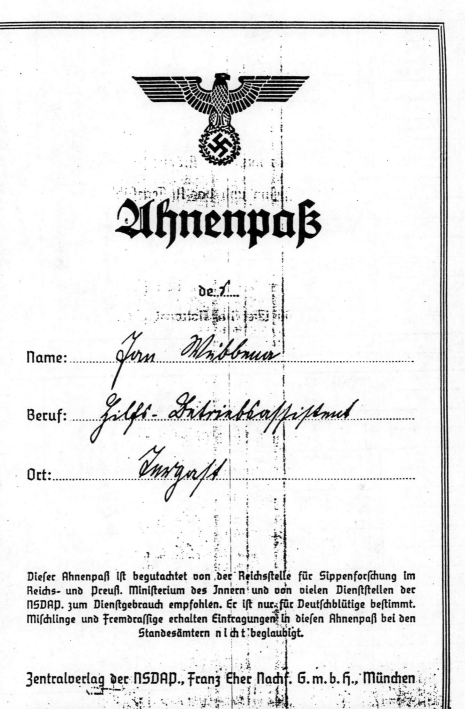

Ahnenpaß

des

Name: *Jörn Wübbena*

Beruf: *Hilfs-Betriebsassistent*

Ort: *Inzgast*

Dieser Ahnenpaß ist begutachtet von der Reichsstelle für Sippenforschung im Reichs- und Preuß. Ministerium des Innern und von vielen Dienststellen der NSDAP. zum Dienstgebrauch empfohlen. Er ist nur für Deutschblütige bestimmt. Mischlinge und Fremdrassige erhalten Eintragungen in diesen Ahnenpaß bei den Standesämtern n i ch t beglaubigt.

Zentralverlag der NSDAP., Franz Eher Nachf. G. m. b. H., München

Ahnen-tafel

12

(Vater von 6)

Familienname: Dozen.

Vornamen: Hinrich Oltjes

geboren am 16. Aug 1833 in Brinkum

als Sohn des (24) Oltjes Janssen Dozen

und der (25) Fronke Hinrichs

Bekenntnis: ev. luth. Tauftag: 29. Aug 1833

Beurk. b. Standesamt: .... Geb.-Reg.-Nr. ....

b. Pfarramt: Holtland Tauf-Reg.-Nr. 8

gestorben am .... in ....

beurk. b. Standesamt — Pfarramt .... Reg.-Nr. ....

Die Richtigkeit des Eintrages wird auf Grund vorgelegter Urkunden beglaubigt. — Worte hinzugefügt. Standesbeamter Kirchenbuchführer. Siegel

Für nebenstehenden Eintrag ist Beglaubigung nicht erforderlich.

12/13

Die Eheschließung des Hinrich Oltjes Dozen

Beruf: .... Bekenntnis: ev. luth.

und der Gesche Garrels Dozen

geborene Ostendorf Bekenntnis: ev. luth.

erfolgte am 28. Juli 1860 in Nortmoor

beurk. b. Standesamt — <u>Pfarramt</u> Nortmoor Reg.-Nr. 14

Die Richtigkeit des Eintrages wird auf Grund vorgelegter Urkunden beglaubigt. — Worte hinzugefügt. Standesbeamter Kirchenbuchführer. Siegel

13

(Mutter von 6)

Geburtsname: Ostendorf

Vornamen: Gesche Garrels

geboren am 10. Febr. 1834 in Nortmoor

als Tochter des (26) Garrelt Oltjes Ostendorf

und der (27) Anna Casjens Gerdes

Bekenntnis: ev. luth. Tauftag: 15. Febr. 1834

Beurk. b. Standesamt: .... Geb.-Reg.-Nr. ....

b. Pfarramt: Nortmoor Tauf-Reg.-Nr. ....

gestorben am .... in ....

beurk. b. Standesamt — Pfarramt Reg.-Nr. ....

Die Richtigkeit des Eintrages wird auf Grund vorgelegter Urkunden beglaubigt. — Worte hinzugefügt. — gestrichen. Standesbeamter Kirchenbuchführer.

Für nebenstehenden Eintrag ist Beglaubigung nicht erforderlich.

14

(Vater von 7)

Familienname: Schoon

Vornamen: Volkert

geboren am 23. Febr. 1828 in Lammertsfehn

als Sohn des (28) Harm Volkerts Schoon

und der (29) Hicke Gerdes

Bekenntnis: ev. luth. Tauftag: 25. Febr. 1828

Beurk. b. Standesamt: .... Geb.-Reg.-Nr. ....

b. Pfarramt: Filsum Tauf-Reg.-Nr. 6

gestorben am .... in ....

beurk. b. Standesamt — Pfarramt .... Reg.-Nr. ....

Die Richtigkeit des Eintrages wird auf Grund vorgelegter Urkunden beglaubigt. — Worte hinzugefügt.

Für nebenstehenden Eintrag ist Beglaubigung nicht erforderlich.

14/15

Die Eheschließung des Volkert Schoon

Beruf: Arbeiter Bekenntnis: ev. luth.

und der Trientje Schoon

geborene Meyer Bekenntnis: ev. luth.

erfolgte am 20. Dez. 1852 in Filsum

beurk. b. Standesamt — <u>Pfarramt</u> Filsum Reg.-Nr. 6

Die Richtigkeit des Eintrages wird auf Grund vorgelegter Urkunden beglaubigt. — Worte gestr. — Worte hinzugef.

15

(Mutter von 7)

Geburtsname: Meyer

Vornamen: Trientje

geboren am 13. März 1832 in Lammertsfehn

als Tochter des (30) Meint Marcus Meyer

und der (31) Fronke Jakobs Bohlen

Bekenntnis: ev. luth. Tauftag: 16. März 1832

Beurk. b. Standesamt: .... Geb.-Reg.-Nr. ....

b. Pfarramt: Filsum Tauf-Reg.-Nr. 2

gestorben am .... in ....

beurk. b. Standesamt Pfarramt Reg.-Nr. ....

Die Richtigkeit des Eintrages wird auf Grund vorgelegter Urkunden beglaubigt. — Worte hinzugefügt. Siegel

Für nebenstehenden Eintrag ist Beglaubigung nicht erforderlich.

4 Urgroßeltern mütterlich 15

13

10

(Vater von 5)
Familienname: _Branowski_
Dornamen: _Herbert_
geboren am _25. Aug. 1819_ in _Mammmütt_
als Sohn des (20) _Jürgen Gerauld Branowski_
und der (21) _Emilija Henrike Schneider_
Bekenntnis: _ev. ref._ Tauftag: _29. Aug. 1819_
Beurk. b. Standesamt: _____ Geb.-Reg.-Nr.
b. Pfarramt: _Mammmütt_ Tauf-Reg.-Nr.

gestorben am _____ in _____
beurk. b. Standesamt — Pfarramt:

10/11

Die Eheschließung des _Heinrich Siegmund Branowski_
Beruf: _____ Bekenntnis: _ev. ref._
und der _Veronika Hartmann_ Bekenntnis: _ev. ref._
geborene _____
erfolgte am _12. Okt. 1853_ in _Zimmerwald_
beurk. b. Standesamt — Pfarramt: _Zimmerwald_ Reg.-Nr. _10_

11

(Mutter von 5)
Geburtsname: _Hartmann_
Dornamen: _Veronika_
geboren am _06. Aug. 1825_ in _Zimmerwald_
als Tochter des (22) _Verena Kaufmann Hartmann_
und der (23) _Evelyn Grieß Grieß_
Bekenntnis: _ev. ref._ Tauftag: _1. Jan. 1826_
Beurk. b. Standesamt: _____ Geb.-Reg.-Nr.
b. Pfarramt: _Zimmerwald_ Tauf-Reg.-Nr. _31_

gestorben am _____ in _____
beurk. b. Standesamt — Pfarramt:

väterlich

Urgroßeltern

8

(Vater von 4)
Familienname: _Winkelmann_
Dornamen: _Konrad Alberto_
geboren am _13. Okt. 1812_ in _Forzych_
als Sohn des (16) _Gerard Hanns Winkelmann_
und der (17) _Marija Hannau Alberto_
Bekenntnis: _ev. ref._ Tauftag: _20. Okt. 1812_
Beurk. b. Standesamt: _Forzych_ Geb.-Reg.-Nr.
b. Pfarramt: _Forzych_ Tauf-Reg.-Nr.

gestorben am _1. März 1863_ in _Forzych_
beurk. b. Standesamt — Pfarramt: _Forzych_

8/9

Die Eheschließung des _____
Beruf: _____ Bekenntnis: _____
und der _____ Bekenntnis: _____
geborene _____
erfolgte am _____ in _____
beurk. b. Standesamt — Pfarramt: _____

9

(Mutter von 4)
Geburtsname: _Alberto_
Dornamen: _Hannesika Grieß_
geboren am _24. Aug. 1813_ in _Konrad Herb_
als Tochter des (18) _Ignaz Gerrylud Bönisch_
und der (19) _Anelija Zinke_
Bekenntnis: _ev. ref._ Tauftag: _26. Aug. 1813_
Beurk. b. Standesamt: _____ Geb.-Reg.-Nr.
b. Pfarramt: _Matthenpin_ Tauf-Reg.-Nr. _368/30_

gestorben am _11. Jan. 1895_ in _Forzych_
beurk. b. Standesamt — Pfarramt: _Forzych_

Großeltern mütterlich

(Vater von 3)

Familienname: ....
Vornamen: ....
geboren am .... als Sohn des (12) ....
und der (13) ....
Bekenntnis: ....
Beur. b. Standesamt: ....
b. Pfarramt: ....
gestorben am ....
beurk. b. Standesamt — Pfarramt ....

Die Eheschließung des ....
Beruf: ....
und der ....
geborene ....
erfolgte am .... in ....
beurk. b. Standesamt — Pfarramt ....

(Mutter von 3)

Geburtsname: ....
Vornamen: ....
geboren am .... als Tochter des (14) ....
und der (15) ....
Bekenntnis: ....
Beur. b. Standesamt: ....
b. Pfarramt: ....
gestorben am ....
beurk. b. Standesamt — Pfarramt ....

Großeltern väterlich

(Vater von 2)

Familienname: ....
Vornamen: ....
geboren am .... als Sohn des (8) ....
und der (9) ....
Bekenntnis: ....
Beur. b. Standesamt: ....
b. Pfarramt: ....
gestorben am ....
beurk. b. Standesamt — Pfarramt ....

Die Eheschließung des ....
Beruf: ....
und der ....
geborene ....
erfolgte am .... in ....
beurk. b. Standesamt — Pfarramt ....

(Mutter von 2)

Geburtsname: ....
Vornamen: ....
geboren am .... als Tochter des (10) ....
und der (11) ....
Bekenntnis: ....
Beur. b. Standesamt: ....
b. Pfarramt: ....
gestorben am ....
beurk. b. Standesamt — Pfarramt ....

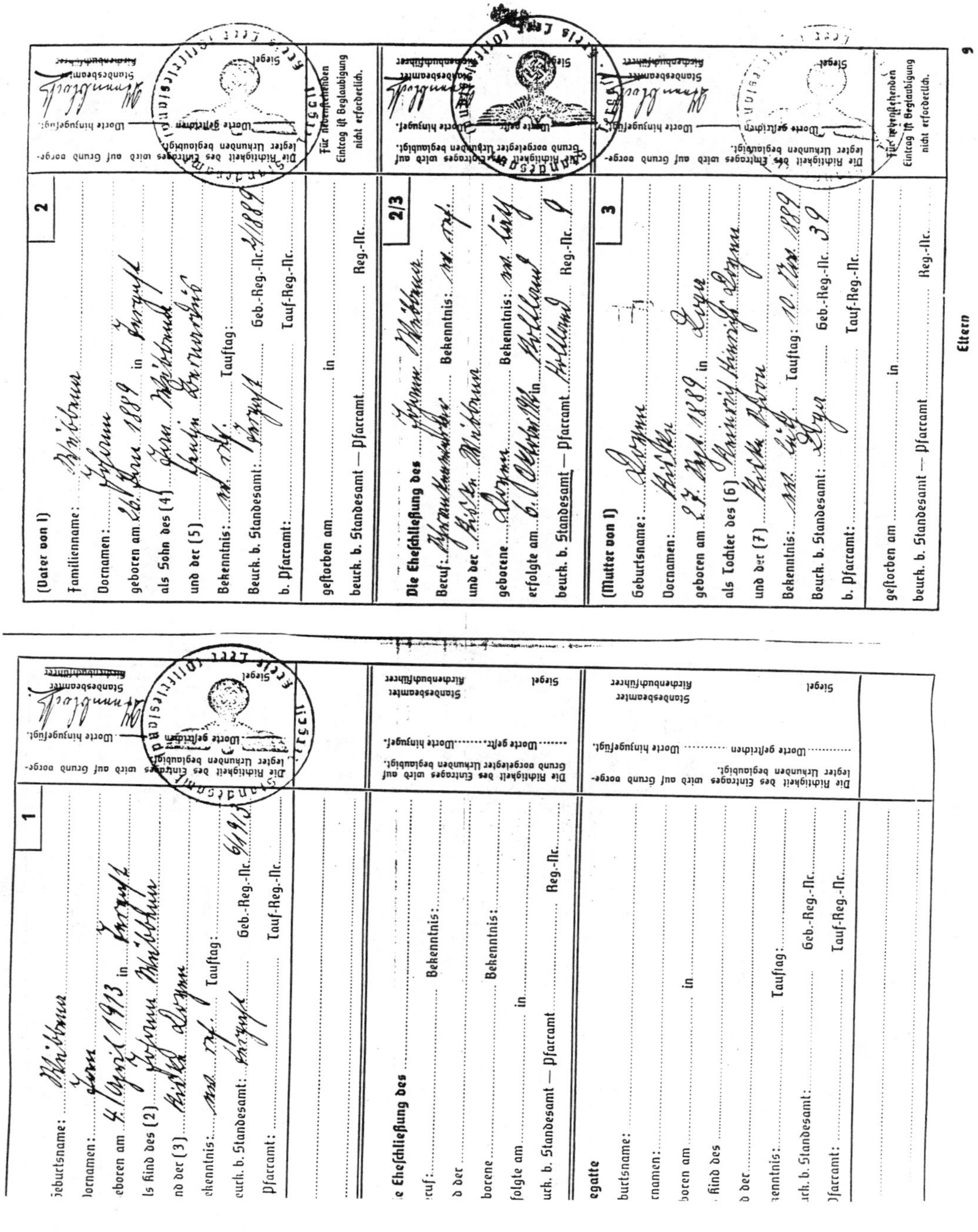

(Vater von 1) — 2
Familienname: [illegible]
Vornamen: [illegible]
geboren am 26. Juni 1889 in [illegible]
als Sohn des (4) [illegible]
und der (5) [illegible]
Bekenntnis: ev. ref. Tauftag:
Beurk. b. Standesamt: [illegible] Geb.-Reg.-Nr. 2/1889
b. Pfarramt: Tauf-Reg.-Nr.
gestorben am ... in ...
beurk. b. Standesamt — Pfarramt ... Reg.-Nr.
Die Richtigkeit des Eintrages wird auf Grund vorgelegter Urkunden beglaubigt. ... Worte gestrichen ... Worte hinzugefügt. Siegel Standesbeamter Kirchenbuchführer
Für nebenstehenden Eintrag ist Beglaubigung nicht erforderlich.

2/3
Die Eheschließung des [illegible]
Beruf: [illegible] Bekenntnis: ev. ref.
und der [illegible] Bekenntnis: ev. luth.
geborene [illegible]
erfolgte am 6. Oktober 1911 in [illegible]
beurk. b. Standesamt — Pfarramt [illegible] Reg.-Nr. 9
Die Richtigkeit des Eintrages wird auf Grund vorgelegter Urkunden beglaubigt. ... Worte gestr. ... Worte hinzugef. Siegel Standesbeamter Kirchenbuchführer

(Mutter von 1) — 3
Geburtsname: [illegible]
Vornamen: [illegible]
geboren am 27. Sept. 1889 in [illegible]
als Tochter des (6) [illegible]
und der (7) [illegible]
Bekenntnis: ev. luth. Tauftag: 10. Nov. 1889
Beurk. b. Standesamt: [illegible] Geb.-Reg.-Nr. 39
b. Pfarramt: Tauf-Reg.-Nr.
gestorben am ... in ...
beurk. b. Standesamt — Pfarramt ... Reg.-Nr.
Die Richtigkeit des Eintrages wird auf Grund vorgelegter Urkunden beglaubigt. ... Worte gestrichen ... Worte hinzugefügt. Siegel Standesbeamter Kirchenbuchführer
Für nebenstehenden Eintrag ist Beglaubigung nicht erforderlich.

Eltern

1
Geburtsname: [illegible]
Vornamen: [illegible]
geboren am 4. April 1913 in [illegible]
als Kind des (2) [illegible]
und der (3) [illegible]
Bekenntnis: ev. ref. Tauftag:
Beurk. b. Standesamt: [illegible] Geb.-Reg.-Nr. 6/1913
b. Pfarramt: Tauf-Reg.-Nr.
Die Richtigkeit des Eintrages wird auf Grund vorgelegter Urkunden beglaubigt. ... Worte gestrichen ... Worte hinzugefügt. Siegel Standesbeamter Kirchenbuchführer

Die Eheschließung des ...
Beruf: ... Bekenntnis:
und der ... Bekenntnis:
geborene ...
erfolgte am ... in ...
beurk. b. Standesamt — Pfarramt ... Reg.-Nr.
Die Richtigkeit des Eintrages wird auf Grund vorgelegter Urkunden beglaubigt. ... Worte gestr. ... Worte hinzugef. Siegel Standesbeamter Kirchenbuchführer

Ehegatte
Geburtsname:
Vornamen:
geboren am ... in
als Kind des
und der
Bekenntnis: Tauftag:
Beurk. b. Standesamt: Geb.-Reg.-Nr.
b. Pfarramt: Tauf-Reg.-Nr.
Die Richtigkeit des Eintrages wird auf Grund vorgelegter Urkunden beglaubigt. ... Worte gestrichen ... Worte hinzugefügt. Siegel Standesbeamter Kirchenbuchführer

APPENDIX E

*Jungjohann Family Tree Records
Prepared in Germany During
the Nazi Regime*

═ Ahnen

8 Urgroßvater
Jungjohann Karl

Stand: _Bahnwärter_
* am _25.2. 1824_
~ am _29.2. 1824_
in _Uslar_
Bekenntnis: _ev. luth._
† am _7.10. 1898_
□ am _____
in _Neermoor_

9 Urgroßmutter
Buss, Hinderke

* am _6.11. 1833_
~ am _10.11. 1833_
in _Veenhusen_
Bekenntnis: _refm._
† am _13.9. 1898_
□ am _____
in _Neermoor_

∞ am 24.4.1861 in Veenhusen

10 Urgroßvater
Büürker,
Jan Harm

Stand: _Kolonist_
* am _31.8. 1837_
~ am _4.9. 1837_
in _Neermoor_
Bekenntnis: _refm._
† am _1.6. 1915_
□ am _____
in _Neermoor_

11 Urgroßmutter
Puil,
Antje Janßen

* am _11.6. 1838_
~ am _17.6. 1838_
in _Neermoor_
Bekenntnis: _____
† am _5.11. 1911_
□ am _____
in _Neermoor_

∞ am 6.4.1859 in Neermoor

4 Großvater (Vaters Vater)
Jngalk Jungjohann
Stand: _Schneidermeister_
* am _30.4.1863_ in _Neermoor_
~ am _10.5.1863_ in _Neermoor_
Bekenntnis: _refm._
† am _13.6.1927_ in _Neermoor_
□ am _____ in _____

5 Großmutter (Vaters Mutter)
Lübke Jungjohann geb. Büürker
Schneiderin
* am _11.11.1868_ in _Neermoor Kol._
~ am _20.12.1868_ in _Neermoor_
Bekenntnis: _alt refm._
† am _24.11.1958_ in _Neermoor_
□ am _____ in _____

∞ am 1.5. in Neermoor

Zeichenerklärung
* = geboren
~ = getauft
∞ = verheiratet.

2 Vater: Jan Anthaus Hinderikus Jungjohann
Stand: _Reichsbahn Lokomotiv-Heizer_   Bekenntnis: _evangl. ref._
* am _24.5.1899_   ☨ am _23.3.1984_   in _Neermoor_
Geschwister: _Kind, ihr Name, Karl, Hinderk, Karl, Hinrich_

∞ am
in _Neer_
Kirchspi

Ehre nicht nur Vater u. Mutter, sondern ehre auch deine Ahnen!
Reichserziehungsmin. Rust.

1 Ahnenträger: _Jan Anthaus Hinderikus Ju_
* am _16.8.1933_ am _____ in _Neermoor_
Meine Geschwister: _Lüpke, Gesines, Jngel, Gerd_
geb. 26.1.1922   19.8.13   4.2.25   24.10.27
_† 27.10.3_

Nationalverlag "Westfalia" Inh. Har

Tafel =–

12 Urgroßvater	**13 Urgroßmutter**	**14 Urgroßvater**	**15 Urgroßmutter**
Eilers, Jan Eggen	Buhr, Maseka	Hilkens, Okke Beereds	Buss, Arend...
Stand: Kolonist		Stand:	
* am 2.12.1821	* am 31.10.1829	* am 7.9.1833	* am 22.12.1843
~ cm	~ am 2.11.1829	~ am 9.9.1833	~ am 31.12.1843
in Strackholt	in Vosburg	in Waringerfehnpolder (chan.)	in Yorgab
Bekenntnis: evg. luth.	Bekenntnis: evg. luth.	Bekenntnis: ref.	Bekenntnis:
+ am 10.1.1892	+ am 14.2.1898	+ am 2.3.1909	+ am 16.6.1886
□ am	□ am	□ am	□ am
in Firrel	in Firrel	in Waringerfehnpolder	in Waringerfehnpolder

6 Großvater (Mutters Vater)	**7 Großmutter (Mutters Mutter)**
Eggen, Jasper Eilers, Kolonist	Hilkens, Geeske Okkes
Stand:	
* am 9.2.1862 in Firrel	* am 29.8.1865 in Holzhausen
~ am 5.10.1862 in Firrel	~ am 16.2.1865 in Holzhausen
Bekenntnis: evang. luth.	Bekenntnis: evang. luth.
+ am in	+ am in
□ am in	□ am in

3
Mutter: Geeske Jungjohann geborne Eilers
Bekenntnis: evangel. ref.
* am 15.1.1899   ┼ am 13.5.1471   in Holzhausen
Geschwister:

Zeichen-
erklärung

+ = gestorben
X = gefallen
□ = begraben

Die Richtigkeit der Eintragungen wird auf Grund vorgelegter Urkunden bescheinigt:

— Worte hinzugefügt, — Worte gestrichen.

Neermoor, den 5. Mai 1938.

(Siegel)

Standesbeamter — Kirchbuchführer

August Rumpf · Dortmund i/W.

Kol. Reihe st. 8   Bekenntnis: evang. ref.

INDEX

Page references in italics indicate the presence of illustrations; references followed by "*n*" refer to footnotes.

An asterisk (*) following a page range indicates that there are seven or more intermittent mentions of a topic rather than a single continuous discussion of it.

Books and periodicals are entered directly under their titles. Titles of hymns, songs, Scripture passages, and verse are grouped together under "Hymns," "Songs," "Bible quotations," and "Poems" respectively.

Abbreviations: "b." (born); "d." (died); "fl." (flourished); "W." (Wubbena).